O'BRIEN'S

COLLECTING
TOY TRAINS

Identification and Value Guide

Edition No. 5

Edited by Elizabeth A. Stephan

Published by

**krause
publications**

700 E. State Street • Iola, WI 54990-0001
Telephone: 715/445-2214

Please call or write for our free catalog.
Our toll-free number to place an order or obtain a free catalog is 800-258-0929
or please use our regular business telephone 715-445-2214
for editorial comment and further information.

ISBN: 0-87341-769-0

Printed in the United States of America

Contents

4

Editor's Note

It's the end of the world as we know it . . .

This phrase keeps going through my mind as we get closer to the end of the twentieth century. It may be the end of one era, but it is the beginning of another. Richard O'Brien, longtime author of several collectibles books including *Collecting Toys* and *Collecting Toy Cars & Trucks*, has retired and Krause Publications have taken over his toy-related titles.

I have the pleasure to pick up the editorial torch and continue these respected toys and collectibles books. Though price guides are not a new venture for me, the subject is. I have been working on various price guides and collectibles books for over five years, but my knowledge of trains is limited. I would like to thank all the contributors to this book—Richard MacNary on Marx, Walter Smith on postwar Lionel, Dennis Leon Clad on modern-era Lionel, and John Gibson on Tootsietoy. My thanks also goes out to the other experts, collectors and friends who lent me a hand—Allan W. Miller, Don Gulbrandsen and Colin Bruce. They offered advice, answered my questions and clarified many of the mysteries surrounding the world of trains. Larry Peterson of New London, Wisconsin, lent me the trains pictured on the cover. Ross Hubbard, Krause Publications' photographer, set up (and played with) the trains, and Kevin Sauter designed the cover. Cheryl Hayburn, Bonnie Tetzlaff and Shelly Johnson of book production paginated the book you hold in your hands.

Pricing consultants are always needed for a book like this, if you feel you could contribute something to the next edition, let me know. E-mail or write me at the address below. Comments, questions and suggestions are always welcome.

Elizabeth A. Stephan, Editor
700 East State St.
Iola, WI 54990
stephane@krause.com

A Note on Pricing and Gauge

You will notice the pricing grades change from chapter to chapter. Most vintage trains were played with and finding them in C10 (Mint in Box) condition is almost impossible, therefore, many chapters are listed with the condition grade of C5, C7 and C9. These are equal to Good, Very Good and Near Mint. In categories where the items can still be found Mint in Box (Tootsietoys) or where there is no market for the item out of the box, i.e., modern-era Lionel, C10 is the highest grade.

Prices listed are buyer prices. The price listed is the price you would pay when buying the item from a dealer, not the price a dealer would pay you for the item. Remember—a dealer needs to make a profit.

Gauge

Gauge is the measurement between the inside of the rails.
2-7/8" = 2-7/8"
Standard = 2-1/8"
No. 1 = 1-3/4"
No. 2 = 2"
O = 1-1/4"
S = 7/8"
HO = 5/8"

What's On the Cover?

Front Cover

Top row, left to right: American Flyer No. 332AC engine with tender, $390; Lionel Hoagie Train

Middle: Marx No. 666 locomotive, $50; No. 234 tender, $40

Bottom: Lionel No. 2033 engine, $350

Back Cover

Top: American Flyer No. 930 caboose, $28

Middle: American Flyer No. 940 hopper, $22

Bottom: American Flyer HO Boxcars. Top row, left to right: No. 33012 Santa Fe, $180; No. 33522 B$M, $60; No. 33513 B&O, $75. Bottom row, left to right: No. 33002 NYC, $45; No. 33512 NH, $36; No. 514 SBD Silver Meteor; D&RGW "Cookie Box," $30

American Flyer

American Flyer began in 1900 when William Hafner of Chicago, Illinois went into business as a toy manufacturer. When wind-up trains were added to the line-up, William Coleman was brought in as a financial partner. By 1910, trains were the firm's strongest line, and the company's name was changed to American Flyer.

Hafner left in 1914, with Coleman remaining. In 1937, A.C. Gilbert, best known at the time for his Erector sets, began to negotiate a take over of American Flyer and by 1938 the deal was consummated. The base of operations then began to slowly shift from Chicago to New Haven, Connecticut where Gilbert began to redesign the trains. HO-scale were introduced in Gilbert's first catalog, and in 1939, he began 3:16-scale which were more highly detailed and realistic-looking than anything in the previous history of toy trains. By 1941, the entire line was 3:16-scale, which, despite its heightened realism, still ran on three-rail tracks.

After the end of World War II, Gilbert dropped its previous line and introduced accurately-scaled trains that moved on a two-rail system. By 1950, all of Gilbert's innovations had pushed American Flyer into sixth position among all toy makers in terms of sales. However, a thorn in the firm's side was the new two-rail S-Gauge trains, which never really took off.

A.C. Gilbert died in 1961, and Jack Wrather, owner of the television series *The Lone Ranger* and *Lassie*, took over. Wrather cut back drastically, but even though sales rose thirty percent in 1965, borrowed capital and production costs offset the increase. In 1966, Lionel purchased American Flyer.

	C5	C7	C9
Boxcar, O ga., beige and blue, w/brass trim	25	43	85
Bubbling Watertower	13	23	45
Caboose, O ga., red and black, w/brass trim, eight wheel	36	60	120
Catalog, 1925	40	60	80
Catalog, 1926	35	53	70
Catalog, 1927	35	53	70
Catalog, 1928	35	53	70
Catalog, 1929	35	53	70
Catalog, 1930	26	39	52
Catalog, 1931	30	45	60
Catalog, 1932	48	72	96
Catalog, 1933	25	38	50
Catalog, 1934	27	41	55
Catalog, 1935	35	52	70
Catalog, 1936	20	30	40
Catalog, 1937	17	26	35
Catalog, 1938	48	72	95
Catalog, 1939	20	30	40
Catalog, 1940	20	30	40
Catalog, 1941	18	27	36
Catalog, 1942	23	34	45
Catalog, 1944	23	34	45
Catalog, 1945	23	34	45
Catalog, 1946, D1451, thirty-two pages	63	95	125
Catalog, 1947, D1473, thirty-two pages	23	34	45
Catalog, 1948, D1507, thirty-two pages	27	41	54
Catalog, 1949, D1536, forty pages	20	30	40
Catalog, 1950, D1604, fifty-six pages	27	41	55
Catalog, 1951, D1640, forty-eight pages	13	19	25
Catalog, 1952, D1677, forty-eight pages	17	26	35
Catalog, 1953, D1715, fifty-two pages	10	15	20
Catalog, 1954, D1760, forty-eight pages	10	15	20
Catalog, 1955, D1801, forty-four pages	9	13	18
Catalog, 1956, D1866, fifty-two pages	10	15	20
Catalog, 1957, D2006, forty-two pages	9	14	19
Catalog, 1958, D2047, forty-eight pages	13	19	25
Catalog, 1959, D2115, twenty-four pages	18	27	35
Catalog, 1960, D2230, twenty pages	13	19	25
Catalog, 1961, D2239, thirty-six pages	7	11	14
Catalog, 1962, D2278, thirty-six pages	7	11	14
Catalog, 1963, X-863-3, thirty-two pages	6	10	13
Catalog, 1964, X-264-6, forty pages	6	9	12
Catalog, 1965, X165-12RV, twenty pages	7	11	14
Catalog, 1966, X466-1, twenty-four pages	2	3	4

Page 36 from an American Flyer catalog points out the high points of their wind-up trains. Courtesy 1940s American Flyer Catalog.

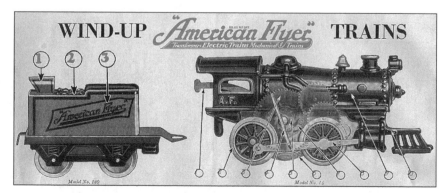

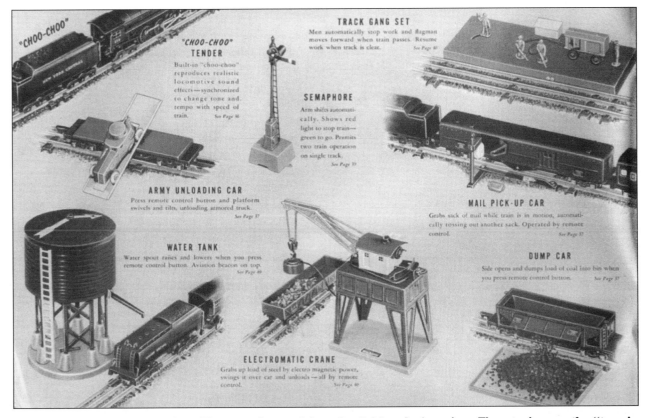

Page 3 from the 1941 American Flyer catalog explains why 3:16-scale American Flyer trains are the "tops in realism."

	C5	C7	C9
Cattle, four black, four brown, for cattle corral	10	15	20
Center Coaches, O ga., Union Pacific	45	75	150
Central Station, plastic, w/sound...	48	80	160
Circus Train Set, complete	1080	1800	3600
Coach, O ga., lithographed, yellow and blue, marked "Empire Express"	18	30	60
Coach Car, Standard ga., lithographed, blue and yellow, w/brass trim, marked "West Point"	135	225	450
Coach Car, O ga., yellow and two-tone green	36	60	120
Coach Car, O ga., red and yellow..	36	60	120
Coach Car, O ga., blue w/orange roof...	36	60	120
Coach Car, O ga., green and yellow, marked "Chicago"	42	70	140

	C5	C7	C9
Coach Car, O ga., lithographed, black and two-tone green, marked "Illini"	32	40	80
Crossover, O ga., 45 degrees	3	5	10
Crossover, O ga., 90 degrees	2	3	8
Engine, O ga., 4-4-4 and tender, orange, gray, and black, w/nickel trim, marked "Hiawatha"..............................	150	250	500
Gondola, O ga., green, w/brass trim, 3000 series......................	18	30	60
Hiawatha Set, O ga., tinplate, lithographed, electric, includes engine, tender, three cars, marked "Hiawatha"..................	150	250	500
Hiawatha Set, O ga., includes engine, tender and three cars, marked "Hiawatha"..................	300	500	1000
Hiawatha Set, O ga., tinplate, lithographed, wind-up, includes engine, tender, three cars, marked "Hiawatha"..................	210	350	700

	C5	C7	C9
Locomotive, O ga., 0-4-0, black, w/328 tender	66	110	220
Locomotive, O ga., yellow and brown, Union Pacific, marked "City of Denver"	90	150	300
Locomotive, Franklin, w/two cars.	120	200	400
Locomotive, O ga., 0-4-0, wind-up, black, w/red tender	45	75	150
Locomotive, O ga., 0-4-0, black, w/tender	60	100	200
Locomotive, O ga., 2-4-2, black, brass trim, w/tender	66	110	220
Locomotive, O ga., 2-4-2, black and white, w/copper trim, w/121 Tender	72	120	240
Locomotive, O ga., 2-6-4, black and white, w/copper and brass trim, w/tender	120	200	400
Locomotive, Franklin, w/three cars	150	250	500
Locomotive, O ga., 0-4-0, gray and yellow, w/copper trim, w/tender	60	100	200
Lumber Car, O ga., yellow	13	23	45
Lumber Car, O ga., black, w/nickel trim	13	23	45
Mail Car, Standard ga., lithographed, blue and yellow lithographed, w/brass trim, marked "Limited"	60	100	200
Observation Car, Standard ga., red w/dark red roof, marked "Pleasant View"	68	113	225
Observation Car, Standard ga., lithographed, black, orange and maroon, w/brass trim, marked "Yorktown"	135	225	450
Observation Car, Standard ga., lithographed, orange and green, w/brass trim, marked "Yorktown"	135	225	450
Observation Car, Standard ga., lithographed, brown and black, "Valley Forge"	135	225	450
Observation Car, O ga., Union Pacific	45	75	150
Observation Car, Standard ga., lithographed, red, w/brass trim, Eagle	54	90	180

	C5	C7	C9
Observation Car, O ga., lithographed, black, two-tone green, marked "Illini"	32	40	80
Observation Car, Standard ga., Pleasant Valley	60	100	200
Observation Car, O ga., yellow and two-tone green, eight-wheel	42	70	140
Observation Car, O ga., red and yellow, eight wheel	42	70	140
Observation Car, O ga., yellow, maroon and gray, w/brass trim, marked "Hiawatha"	45	75	150
Observation Car, Standard ga., lithographed, blue and yellow, w/brass trim, marked "Annapolis"	120	200	400
Observation Car, Standard ga., lithographed, green, orange and black, w/brass trim, marked "America"	105	175	350
Passenger Car, Standard ga., marked "Pleasant View"	68	113	225
Passenger Car, Standard ga., orange and maroon, w/black lithographed, brass trim, marked "Bunker Hill"	60	100	200
Passenger Coaches, O ga., maroon, yellow and gray, marked "Hiawatha," set of three	135	225	450
Post Office Car, O ga., lithographed, red, blue and yellow w/dark red roof lithographed, marked "Nationwide Lines Railway," made for JC Penney Wells Fargo & Co., Overland Flyer boxcar body	60	100	200
Pullman, Standard ga., lithographed, red, w/brass trim, marked "Eagle"	54	90	180
Pullman, Standard ga., lithographed, brown and black, w/brass and nickel trim, marked "Washington Limited"	135	225	450
Station, Mystic talking w/button	150	225	300
Streamline Engine, O ga., 0-4-4-0, orange, silver, w/attached car	66	110	220
Switches, manual	15	23	30

	C5	C7	C9
Switches, electric autom...............	50	75	100
Tank Car, O ga., yellow and black, w/nickel trim............................	12	20	40
Track, HO ga., curved or straight..	20	30	50
Track, Race Car, three lane controllers, one connecting track, set of 44	12	20	40
1 Locomotive, O ga., wind-up........	30	50	100
1 Transformer, 25 watt	10	15	20
1 Transformer, 35 watt	13	19	25
2 Locomotive, cast iron, wind-up..	42	70	140
1-1/2 Transformer, 45 watt...........	15	23	30
1-1/2B Transformer, 50 watt	20	30	40
2 Transformer, 75 watt	25	38	50
1-1/2 Transformer, 50 watt...........	20	30	40
3 Locomotive, O ga., wind-up........	27	45	90
4 Locomotive, 0-4-0, wind-up........	36	60	120
4A Locomotive, O ga., wind-up..................................	42	70	140
8B Transformer	28	42	55
8B Transformer, 100 watt, w/bulb covers..................................	35	53	70
8B Transformer, 100 watt, without bulb covers............................	30	45	60
8B Transformer, w/uncoupler, track, manual and buttons	35	53	70
9 Locomotive, 0-4-0, wind-up........	36	60	120
10 Locomotive, 0-4-0, cast iron, wind-up..................................	33	55	110
10 Locomotive, 1925, electric........	72	120	240
11 Locomotive, 0-4-0, wind-up..................................	54	90	180
12 Locomotive, O ga., cast iron..............................	30	50	100
12 Smoke Cartridges	—	—	4
13 Locomotive and Tender, 0-4-0, wind-up, black, orange and green	45	75	150
14 Locomotive, 0-4-0, wind-up..................................	27	45	90

No. 15, Locomotive, O gauge, wind-up, $70

	C5	C7	C9
15 Locomotive, O ga., wind-up..................................	21	35	70
16 Locomotive, O ga., 0-4-0, electric.....................................	33	55	110
18B Transformer........................	60	90	120
19B Transformer, 300 watt w/volt and amp..................................	50	75	100
28 Locomotive, 0-4-0, wind-up..................................	25	42	84
29 Locomotive, O ga., cast iron, first electric, wind-up	45	75	150
34 Locomotive, 0-4-0, wind-up..................................	42	70	140
36 Observation Car, Standard ga. ...	21	35	70
40 Locomotive, 0-4-0, wind-up..................................	42	70	140
92 Switch Tower..........................	40	60	80
96 Station, O ga., c. 1931...............	20	30	40
104 Kenilworth Station..................	12	18	25
105 Pullman	18	30	60
119 Hiawatha Locomotive, O ga., tin-plate, wind-up, w/tender	36	60	120
119 Hiawatha Locomotive, O ga., tin-plate, electric	54	90	180
119 Hiawatha Locomotive, O ga., w/tender..................................	210	350	700
119 Tender, O ga.	18	30	60
120 Tender, O ga.	24	40	80
121 Tender, O ga., black and white, marked "No. 121"	18	30	60
152 Locomotive, O ga., wind-up ...	27	45	90
228 Log Car, O ga.	13	21	42

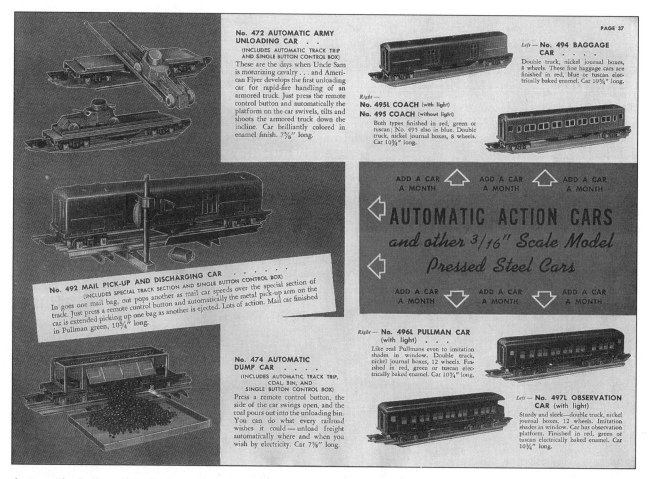

Automatic Action Cars included Nos. 472, 494, 492, 474, and 496L. Courtesy 1941 American Flyer Catalog, $115

	C5	C7	C9
229 Boxcar, O ga.	13	21	42
230 Dump Car, O ga.	13	21	42
231 Tank Car, O ga.	13	21	42
234 Engine, HO ga., diesel, Chesapeake & Ohio	72	120	240
323 Coach, O ga.	36	60	100
328 Tender, O ga.	18	30	60
356 Tender, O ga., Comet	24	40	80
384 Tender, Standard ga.	54	90	180
401 Locomotive, O ga., 2-4-2	53	88	175
401 Locomotive, 2-4-4, Pennsylvania	21	35	70
403 Locomotive, O ga., 2-4-4	39	65	130
404 Pullman, O ga.	18	30	60
405 Observation Car, O ga.	18	30	60
406 Log Car, O ga.	11	18	35

	C5	C7	C9
407 Sand Car, O ga.	13	21	42
408 Boxcar, O ga.	14	23	45
409 Dump Car, O ga.	20	33	65
410 Locomotive, O ga.	33	55	110
410 Tank Car, O ga.	17	28	55
411 Caboose, O ga.	12	20	40
412 Milk Car, O ga.	29	48	95
415 Floodlight Car, O ga.	27	45	90
416 Wrecker Car, O ga.	59	98	195
419 Locomotive, O ga., streamliner	81	135	270
420 Locomotive, O ga., American Flyer Lines	72	120	240
420 Locomotive, O ga., die-cast, w/tender	60	100	200
421 Tender, O ga.	21	35	70

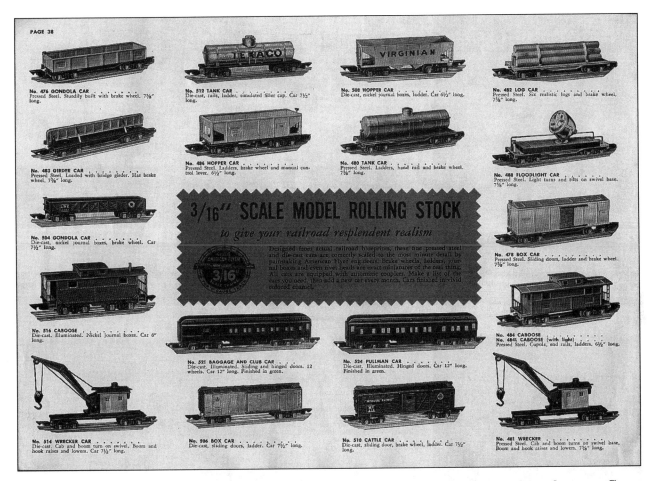

Rolling stock available in 1941 included gondolas, tank cars, hoppers, floodlight cars and wrecker cars. Courtesy 1941 American Flyer Catalog.

	C5	C7	C9
422 Locomotive, O ga., 2-4-2	75	125	250
423 Locomotive, O ga.	54	90	180
424 Locomotive, O ga., 2-4-4	36	60	120
425 Locomotive, O ga., 2-6-4	63	105	210
427 Locomotive, O ga., 2-6-4	120	200	400
429 Locomotive, O ga., 0-6-0	125	208	415
431 Locomotive, O ga., 0-6-0	250	420	840
432 Locomotive, O ga., 4-4-2	180	300	600
434 Locomotive, O ga., 4-4-2	210	350	700
436 Locomotive, O ga., 4-6-2	330	550	1100
437 Locomotive, O ga., 2-4-2	168	280	560
446 Locomotive, HO ga., 4-6-4	51	85	170
449 Locomotive, O ga., 2-6-4	500	840	1680
472 Unloading Car, O ga., Army, w/Tootsietoy army tank as load	35	58	115

	C5	C7	C9
474 Dump Car, O ga., automatic ...	60	100	200
476 Gondola, O ga.	14	24	48
478 Boxcar, O ga.	11	19	37
480 Tank Car, O ga., yellow, Shell	16	26	52
481 Wrecker Car, O ga.	24	40	80
482 Lumber Car, O ga.	20	33	65
483 Girder Car, O ga.	15	25	50
484 Caboose, O ga.	10	17	33
486 Hopper, O ga.	23	39	78
488 Floodlight Car	30	50	100
490 Whistle Car, O ga., red	23	38	75
492 Mail Pickup Car, O ga.	18	30	60
494 Baggage Car, O ga.	17	29	58
495 Coach Car, O ga., red, two pieces	20	34	68

No. 484, Caboose, O gauge, $33

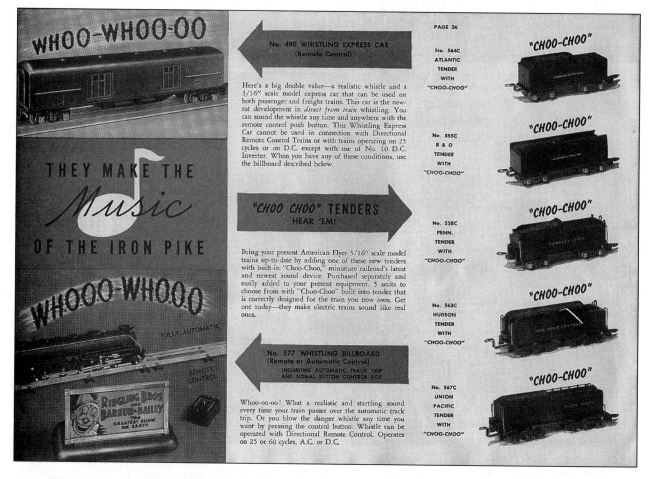

A few of the Choo-Choo cars featured in the 1941 American Flyer catalog: Nos. 490, 564C, 553C, 558C, 563C and the 567C.

	C5	C7	C9
496 Pullman, O ga.	53	88	175
497 Observation Car, O ga.	29	48	95
500 Pullman, O ga., lithographed..	33	55	110
500 Tank Car, HO ga.	11	18	35
501 Hopper, HO ga.	11	18	35
504 Gondola, O ga.	60	100	200
504 Tender, O ga., Choo-choo and smoke unit	15	25	50
506 Caboose, HO ga.	11	18	35
508 Hopper, O ga.	39	65	130
510 Cattle Car, O ga.	23	38	75
512 Cattle Car, O ga.	23	38	75
512 Tank Car, O ga.	23	38	75
513 Observation Car, O ga.	8	13	25
514 Wrecker Car, O ga.	34	90	180
515 Automobile Car, O ga.	9	15	30

	C5	C7	C9
515 Coach Car, O ga., tin-plate, lithographed, yellow, red, black and orange, early	8	13	25
516 Caboose, O ga., illuminated....	25	43	85
518 Baggage Car, O ga.	15	25	50
519 Pullman, O ga.	15	25	50
521 Baggage-Club Car, O ga.	63	105	210
524 Pullman, O ga.	180	300	600
531 Locomotive, O ga., 4-6-4	270	450	900
534 Locomotive, O ga., 4-8-4	980	1400	2800
545 Locomotive, O ga., 4-4-2	30	50	100
553 Locomotive, steam	33	55	110
553 Tender, O ga.	23	38	75
555C Tender, O ga.	18	30	60
555 Tender, black	12	20	40
556 Locomotive, royal blue	34	56	112

The 534 O-gauge American Flyer as shown in the 1941 catalog.

No. 1093, Locomotive, O gauge, Many of American Flyer's locomotives featured track reverse (Nos. 1346 or 3115) and remote control reverse (No. 4000). Courtesy 1904s American Flyer catalog.

	C5	C7	C9
558C Tender, O ga., w/chugger	20	33	66
558 Tender, O ga., without chugger	15	25	50
559 Locomotive, O ga., 4-6-2	105	175	350
561 Locomotive, steam	63	105	210
563C Locomotive, w/tender	45	75	150
564 Locomotive, O ga., 4-6-4	750	1250	2500
564C Tender	15	25	50
565 Locomotive	45	75	150
568 Locomotive, O ga., 4-8-4	900	1500	3000
570 Locomotive, O ga., 4-6-4	90	150	300
572 Locomotive, O ga., 4-8-4	119	198	395
574B Locomotive, O ga., 0-8-0	600	1000	2000
574 Locomotive, O ga., 0-8-0, switcher	420	700	1400

	C5	C7	C9
575B Locomotive, O ga., 0-8-0	360	600	1200
597 Passenger and Freight Station	21	35	70
616 Locomotive, O ga., wind-up	45	75	150
617 Locomotive, O ga., 2-4-2	30	50	100
622 Locomotive, O ga.	24	40	80
641 Locomotive, O ga., 2-4-2	210	350	700
816 Locomotive, wind-up, three cars	180	300	600
830 Locomotive, wind-up, two cars	84	140	280
832 Locomotive, wind-up, three cars	84	140	280
960T Locomotive, O ga., two cars	105	175	350
961T Locomotive, O ga., 0-4-0, three cars	84	140	280

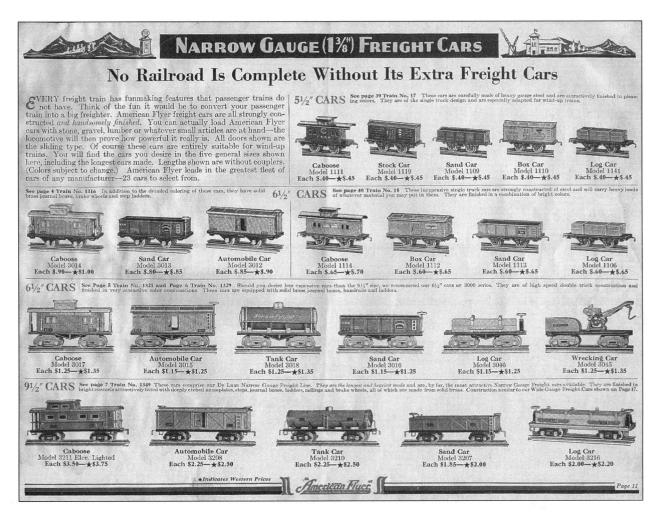

This American Flyer catalog from the 1940s the twenty-three different freight cars available that year.

	C5	C7	C9
964T Locomotive, O ga., three cars	120	200	400
970T Hiawatha Set, O ga., includes locomotive tender, two coaches and observation car	200	335	670
1025 Railway Express Mail Car, O ga.	18	30	60
1026 Passenger Car, O ga.	7	13	25
1045 Transformer, 25 watt	10	15	20
1093 Locomotive, O ga.	132	220	440
1094 Locomotive, O ga.	210	350	700
1096 Box Cab Locomotive, O ga., 0-4-0, w/square headlight, rubber stamped	43	73	145
1097 Engine, O ga., 0-4-0, lithographed, orange, green and red, w/nickel trim	43	73	145

	C5	C7	C9
1102 Coach, O ga.	21	35	70
1103 Locomotive, O ga.	195	325	650
1103 Passenger Car	18	30	60
1104 Baggage, O ga.	18	30	60
1105 Baggage Car, marked "American Express"	36	60	120
1105 Canadian National Railways Dominion Flyer, O ga., lithographed, red and black, w/nickel trim	18	30	60
1106 Coach, O ga., lithographed, brown and black, marked "Dominion Flyer"	24	40	80
1106 Lumber Car, 1930, black	11	18	35
1106 Parlor Car, O ga., lithographed, yellow, black and green	18	30	60

	C5	C7	C9
1106 Parlor Car, lithographed, green w/black roof, four wheels	18	30	60
1107 Coach Car, O ga., lithographed	11	18	35
1108 Baggage Car, O ga., lithographed	14	23	45
1109 Sand Car, O ga., lithographed, red	14	18	35
1110 Boxcar, O ga.	15	25	50
1111 Caboose, O ga.	15	25	50
1112 Boxcar, 1925, lithographed, red	18	30	60
1112 Boxcar, 1930, lithographed, yellow	21	35	70
1113 Gondola, 1925, lithographed, green	11	18	35
1114 Caboose, O ga., lithographed, red, green and white, w/brass trim	15	25	50
1115 Automobile Boxcar, O ga., later	24	40	80
1115 Boxcar, O ga.	18	30	60
1116 Gondola, O ga.	15	25	50
1116 Sand Car, O ga.	36	60	120
1117 Caboose, O ga.	21	35	70
1118 Tank Car, O ga., lithographed, gray-white and black	27	45	90
1119 Stock Car, O ga.	24	40	80
1120 Caboose, O ga.	15	25	50
1120 Passenger Car, O ga.	15	25	50
1121 Locomotive, O ga., w/whistle and tender	18	30	60
1122 Bluestreak Passenger Car, O ga.	15	25	50
1123 Passenger Car, O ga., Tuscan	12	20	40
1123 Passenger Car, O ga.	12	20	40
1124 Pullman, O ga.	36	60	120
1127 Caboose, O ga.	9	15	30
1128 Tank Car, O ga.	9	15	30
1141 Log Car, O ga.	24	40	80
1146 Log Car, O ga.	24	40	80

	C5	C7	C9
1147 Observation Car, O ga.	31	52	104
1157 Observation Car, O ga.	31	52	104
1200 Baggage Car, O ga., lithographed, four wheel	18	30	60
1200 Baggage Car, O ga., lithographed, eight wheel	18	30	60
1201 Locomotive, O ga.	27	45	90
1201 Passenger Car, lithographed, red w/black roof	18	30	60
1202 Baggage Car, Express	19	33	66
1202 Baggage Car, O ga., Electric Service	23	39	78
1203 Coach Car, O ga., lithographed, eight wheel, early	20	33	65
1203 Passenger Car, lithographed, blue w/black roof	20	33	65
1204 Baggage Car, O ga.	30	60	120
1205 Baggage Car, O ga.	18	30	60
1205 Mail Car, O ga.	18	30	60
1206 Coach Car, O ga.	23	38	75
1206 Passenger Car	23	38	75
1206 Pullman, O ga.	23	38	75
1207 Observation Car, 1926	24	40	80
1208 Locomotive, O ga.	48	80	160
1209 Observation Car, O ga.	36	60	120
1211 Passenger Coach, O ga.	18	30	60
1212 Observation Car, O ga.	60	100	200
1213 Pullman, O ga.	36	60	120
1214 Baggage, O ga.	36	60	120
1217 Locomotive, 0-4-0, electric	36	60	120
1218 Engine, 0-4-0, black, lettering on side, w/nickel and brass trim	36	60	120
1218 Locomotive, O ga., red, black and yellow	36	60	120
1218 Locomotive, O ga., 0-4-0, black, red and yellow, electric	42	70	140
1219 Coach Car, O ga.	11	18	36
1223 Coach Car, O ga.	11	18	36
1225 Locomotive, O ga., 1919, 0-4-0, cast iron	60	100	200
1257 Observation Car, O ga.	72	120	240

	C5	C7	C9
1270 Locomotive, O ga.	60	100	200
1286 Pullman, O ga.	27	45	90
1287 Observation Car, Chicago	27	45	90
1290 Transformer	20	30	40
1306 Passenger Car	15	25	50
1322RT Locomotive, O ga., four cars	330	550	1100
1620 Pullman, O ga.	30	50	100
1621 Pullman, O ga.	40	68	135
1622 Observation Car, O ga.	40	68	135
1681 Locomotive, O ga., 2-6-4	150	250	500
1683 Locomotive, O ga.	420	700	1400
1684 Locomotive, O ga.	360	600	1200
1686 Locomotive, O ga.	66	110	220
1687 Locomotive, O ga., 2-4-2	210	350	700
1688 Locomotive, 2-4-2	84	140	280
1710 Locomotive, O ga.	42	70	140
1730RW Streamliner, 1935, Union Pacific, 51" long	126	210	420
1736 Freight Set, O ga., B&O	144	240	480
1835TW Tender	42	70	140
2005 Triangle Light	30	45	60
2010 Double Arc Lamp Post, 12-1/2" high	21	35	70
2020 Electric Loco, O ga., 4-4-4	120	200	400
2020 Water Tank, O ga.	30	50	100
2029 Whistle Unit, remote control	18	30	60
2043 Semaphore	112	168	225
2210 Lamp, Standard ga., double arm	18	30	60
3000 Baggage, O ga., lithographed, black and two-tone green	30	50	100
3001 Pullman, O ga., Illini	30	50	100
3004 Caboose, O ga., illuminated	36	60	120
3005 Observation Car, O ga., Illini	18	30	60
3006 Flat Car	6	10	20

	C5	C7	C9
3007 Sand Car, O ga.	150	250	500
3008 Boxcar, O ga., lithographed, black and yellow	15	25	50
3009 Dump Car, O ga., decaled set	3	5	10
3010 Tank Car, O ga., gray w/black nickel trim	30	50	100
3011 Locomotive	54	90	180
3012 Auto Car	30	50	100
3012 Boxcar, O ga., rubber stamped, decaled set	9	15	30
3012 Locomotive, O ga., 0-4-0, lithographed, headlight in cab, electric	54	90	180
3013 Gondola, O ga., decaled set	15	25	50
3013 Locomotive, O ga.	240	400	800
3014 Caboose, O ga., decaled set	15	25	50
3014 Locomotive, O ga.	330	550	1100
3015 Auto Car, O ga.	15	25	50
3015 Boxcar, O ga.	12	20	40
3015 Locomotive	84	140	280
3016 Sand Car, O ga.	15	25	50
3017 Caboose, O ga., eight wheel	8	13	25
3018 Tank Car, O ga., eight wheel	48	80	160
3018 Tank Car, O ga., yellow and black, w/copper trim	19	33	66
3019 Dump Car, O ga., eight wheel	11	18	36
3019 Dump Car, O ga.	11	18	36
3019 Electric Loco, O ga., dark green, black frame and maroon windows, rubber stamped, headlight	120	200	400
3020 Engine, O ga., 4-4-4, maroon and black, w/nickel trim	150	250	500
3020 Engine, O ga., 4-4-4, black and yellow, w/nickel trim	120	200	400
3025 Crane Car, O ga.	29	48	95
3045 Wrecker Car, O ga.	42	70	140
3046 Lumber Car, O ga., eight wheel	12	20	40
3080 Mail Car, O ga.	24	40	80
3081 Pullman, O ga., Illini	24	40	80
3085 Observation Car, O ga., Columbia	24	40	80

	C5	C7	C9
3100 Locomotive, O ga., 0-4-0 red, black, gold, w/brass trim and plates	36	60	120
3102 Locomotive, 1926, lithographed	30	50	100
3102 Tanker, O ga.	12	20	40
3103 Locomotive, O ga.	132	225	450
3105 Locomotive, blue	85	140	240
3107 Engine, O ga., 0-4-0	17	78	155
3107RC Locomotive, O ga.	150	250	500
3107 Lumber Car, O ga.	9	15	30
3109 Engine, O ga., 0-4-0, green, brown, w/brass trim	80	100	200
3110 Locomotive, O ga., 0-4-0, w/headlight	75	125	250
3111 Gondola, O ga.	12	20	40
3112 Boxcar, O ga., lithographed	27	45	90

	C5	C7	C9
3112 Engine and Baggage Car, baggage car marked "United States Mail Railway Post Office"	75	125	250
3112 Hopper	13	23	45
3113 Locomotive, O ga.	66	110	220
3113 Locomotive, O ga., 0-4-0, two-tone blue w/two-tone blue coaches marked "Nationwide Lines" made for J.C. Penney Co., extremely rare; set complete in original boxes	3000	5000	10000
3113 Locomotive, O ga., 0-4-0, two-tone blue w/two-tone blue coaches marked, American Flyer Bluebird, American Flyer Lines lettering	300	500	1000
3115 Engine, O ga., 0-4-0, peacock blue, w/brass trim	36	60	120

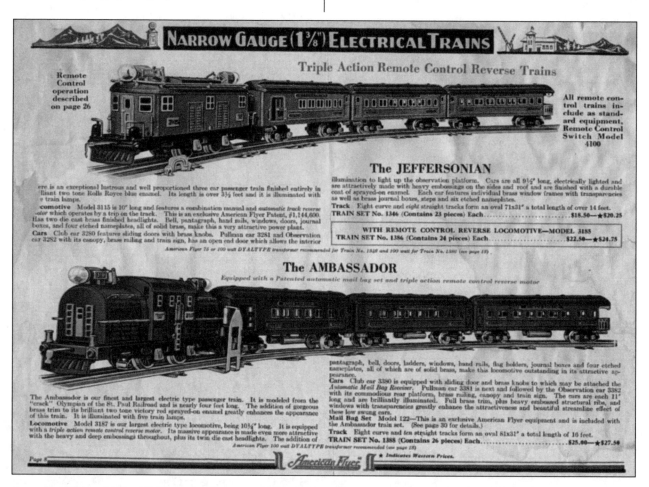

American Flyer's No. 3115 engine is part of The Jeffersonian train set. The Ambassador set was lead by the No. 3187 locomotive.

	C5	C7	C9
3116 Engine, O ga., 0-4-0, turquoise and black, w/brass trim..............................	120	200	400
3117 Engine, O ga., 0-4-0, red w/brass trim	90	150	300
3140 Club Car, O ga......................	42	70	140
3141 Coach Car, O ga., red, black and gold, w/brass trim	27	45	90
3141 Pullman, O ga., red and black, w/brass trim...................	27	45	90
3142 Observation Car, O ga., red, black and gold, w/brass trim.....	27	45	90
3150 Baggage Car	26	43	85
3151 Passenger Car	16	27	54
3152 Observation Car, O ga., two-tone orange, w/brass trim..........	30	50	100
3152 Passenger Car	36	60	120
3161 Passenger Car	44	73	145
3162 Observation Car, O ga., turquoise, blue and gray, w/brass trim	18	30	60
3171 Pullman, O ga., beige and green, w/brass trim	11	19	38
3172 Observation Car, O ga., beige and green, w/brass trim ...	11	19	38
3176 Pullman, O ga........................	15	25	50
3177 Observation Car, O ga.	18	30	60
3178 Coach, O ga.	120	200	400
3180 Club Car, O ga., beige and green, w/brass trim, marked "Potomac".................................	23	38	75
3180 Club Car, O ga., two-tone red, green, w/brass trim	15	25	50
3181 Pullman, O ga., beige and green, w/brass trim, marked "Potomac".................................	23	38	75
3182 Locomotive, O ga., 0-4-0..............	120	200	400
3182 Obseration, O ga., beige and green, w/brass trim, marked "Potomac".................................	23	38	75
3184 Locomotive, O ga., 0-4-0..............	150	250	500
3185 Locomotive, turquoise/teal blue	135	225	450

	C5	C7	C9
3186 Locomotive, O ga.	240	400	800
3187 Locomotive, O ga.	180	300	600
3188 Locomotive, 0-4-0	150	250	500
3189 Tender, 1933, tin....................	45	75	150
3190 Locomotive, O ga., 0-4-0, remote control reverse..............	30	50	100
3191 Locomotive, O ga., 2-4-2...	96	160	320
3192 Locomotive, 1937	24	40	80
3192 Tender, O ga.	33	55	110
3195 Locomotive, cast iron	39	65	130
3197 Locomotive, O ga., 0-4-0...	150	250	500
3198 Locomotive, O ga., cast iron.	54	90	180
3201 Caboose, O ga......................	15	25	50
3206 Flat Car, orange, w/lumber ...	27	45	90
3207 Gondola, O ga......................	11	18	35
3208 Boxcar, 1938, orange and blue	33	55	110
3210 Tank Car, 1938, silver and green..	27	45	90
3211 Caboose, O ga......................	23	38	75
3212 Milk Car, 1938.....................	24	40	80
3213 Floodlight Car, O ga.	45	75	150
3216 Log Car, 1937	19	32	63
3219 Dump Car, 1938...................	24	40	80
3280 Club Car, turquoise/teal blue	54	90	180
3281 Pullman, O ga., green and two-tone red, marked "Jeffersonian"	36	60	120
3281 Pullman, turquoise/teal blue .	54	90	180
3282 Observation Car, O ga., green and two-tone red, w/ brass trim, marked "Golden State"..	108	180	360
3282 Observation Car, turquoise/teal blue	54	90	180
3302 Locomotive, O ga., 2-4-2...	150	250	500
3304 Locomotive, O ga., 2-4-2...	90	150	300

	C5	C7	C9
3307 Locomotive, O ga., bell in cab......	60	100	200
3308 Locomotive, O ga., 2-4-2......	90	150	300
3309 Locomotive, O ga., 2-4-2......	120	200	400
3310 Locomotive, O ga., 2-4-2......	60	100	200
3313 Locomotive, O ga., 2-4-2......	120	200	400
3315 Locomotive, O ga.	210	350	700
3316 Locomotive, O ga., 2-4-2......	18	30	60
3316 Tender, O ga.	11	18	36
3323 Locomotive, O ga., 2-4-2......	150	250	500

	C5	C7	C9
3324 Locomotive, O ga., 2-4-2......	150	250	500
3326 Locomotive, O ga., 2-4-2......	40	67	135
3380 Baggage Car, O ga., red w/dark red roof and brass window inserts and decals, eight wheel, lighted......	36	60	120
3381 Coach Car, O ga., red w/dark red roof and brass window insert and decal, eight wheel, lighted	36	60	120
3382 Observation Car, O ga., red w/dark red roof and brass window insert and decal, eight wheel, lighted......	36	60	120
3541 Pullman, O ga.	42	70	140
3542 Observation Car, O ga.	42	70	140

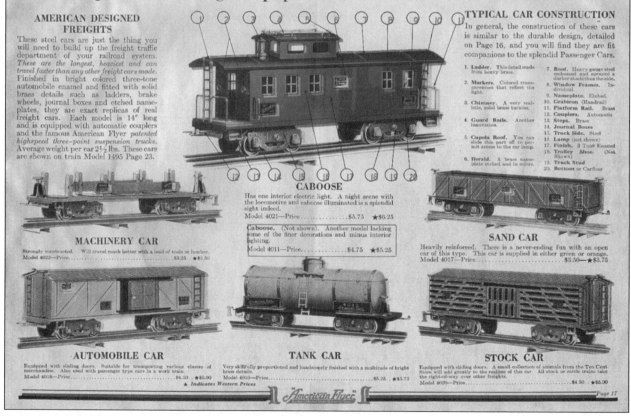

With twenty points of superiority, American Flyer's freight cars were the perfect companion to the other cars available in the 1940s. Courtesy 1940s American Flyer catalog.

	C5	C7	C9
3579 Pullman, O ga.	24	40	80
3750 Coach, O ga.	30	50	100
3751 Coach, O ga.	30	50	100
3752 Observation Car, O ga.	45	75	150
4000 Locomotive, Standard ga., maroon	60	100	200
4002 Locomotive, O ga., 2-6-4, black and white, w/copper trim, w/tender	30	50	100
4005 Stock Car, Standard ga.	60	100	200
4006 Hopper Car, Standard ga.	145	243	485
4007 Sand Car, Standard ga.	180	300	600
4008 Boxcar, Standard ga.	108	180	360
4010 Tank Car, Standard ga., yellow	128	213	425
4010 Tank Car, Standard ga., blue	420	700	1400
4011 Caboose, Standard ga.	93	155	310
4012 Lumber, Standard ga., blue and black, w/brass trim	37	63	125
4017 Gondola, Standard ga., green	63	105	210
4018 Boxcar, Standard ga., beige and blue	90	150	300
4019 Engine, Standard ga., 0-4-0, maroon and black, w/brass trim	135	225	450
4020 Cattle Car, Standard ga., green and blue	75	125	250
4020 Cattle Car, Standard ga., two-tone blue	77	128	255
4021 Caboose, Standard ga., two-tone red w/brass trim	51	85	170
4022 Lumber Car, Standard ga., orange and turquoise, w/brass trim	54	90	180
4023 Lumber Car, Standard ga., w/load	66	110	220
4039 Locomotive, Standard ga., 0-4-0, brown and black, w/brass trim	195	325	650
4040 Baggage Car, Standard ga., maroon	33	55	110

	C5	C7	C9
4040 Mail Car, Standard ga., lithographed, green, orange and black, marked "United States Mail Railway Post Office"	54	70	140
4040 Mail Car, Standard ga., lithographed, red	36	60	120
4041 Pullman, Standard ga., maroon	33	55	110
4042 Crossing Gate, Standard ga., automatic	30	45	60
4042 Observation Car, Standard ga., maroon	33	55	110
4080 Baggage Car, Standard ga.	45	75	150
4081 Washington Car, Standard ga.	45	75	150
4082 Valley Forge Car, Standard ga.	45	75	150
4090 Baggabe and Mail Car, Standard ga.	120	200	400
4091 Pullman, Standard ga., Annapolis	120	200	400
4092 Observation Car, Standard ga., West Point	120	200	400
4122 Mail Car, two-tone blue	60	100	200
4141 Passenger Car, Standard ga., Bunker Hill	180	300	600
4142 Observation Car, Standard ga., Yorktown	180	300	600
4151 Pullman, Standard ga., Pleasant View	78	130	260
4152 Observation Car, Standard ga., Pleasant View	78	130	260
4220 Bridge	270	450	900
4250 Club Car, Standard ga., lithographed, turquoise and red, w/brass trim, marked "Lone Scout"	67	113	225
4251 Pullman, Standard ga., lithographed, turquoise, red, w/brass, marked "Lone Scout"	67	113	225
4252 Observation Car, Standard ga., turquoise and red, w/brass trim, marked "Lone Scout"	67	113	225
4321 Locomotive, O ga., 0-6-0, black and white, w/nickel trim, w/tender	67	113	225

	C5	C7	C9
4331 Observation Car, Standard ga., red, w/brass doors	75	125	250
4331 Pullman, Standard ga., two-tone red, w/brass inserts and brass windows...........................	75	125	250
4331 Pullman Car, Standard ga., red	75	125	250
4332 Observation Car, Standard ga., red, w/brass doors	68	113	225
4332 Observation Car, Standard ga., two-tone red, w/brass inserts and brass windows	135	225	450
4332 Passenger Car, Standard ga., red	75	125	250
4340 Club Car, Standard ga., beige, green, w/brass plates and brass windows, marked "Pocohontas"	135	225	450

No. 4340, Club car, standard gauge, two-tone red with brass trim, $400

	C5	C7	C9
4340 Club Car, Standard ga., two-tone red w/brass trim, marked "Hamiltonian"...........................	120	200	400
4341 Pullman, Standard ga., beige, green, w/brass plates and brass windows...................................	120	200	400
4341 Pullman, Standard ga., two-tone red, w/brass trim, marked "Hamiltonian"...........................	120	200	400
4341 Pullman, Standard ga., beige and green, w/brass trim, marked "Pocohontas".............................	120	200	400
4342 Observation Car, Standard ga., beige and green, w/brass plates and brass windows, marked "Pocohontas"	90	150	300

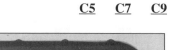

No. 4342, Observation car, standard gauge, beige and green, with brass plates and brass windows, $300

	C5	C7	C9
4342 Observation Car, Standard ga., two-tone red, w/brass trim, marked "Hamiltonian"	90	150	300
4343 Observation Car, Standard ga., beige and green, w/brass trim, marked "Pocohontas"	105	175	350

No. 4343, Observation car, standard gauge, beige and green, with brass trim, $350

	C5	C7	C9
4350 Club Car, Standard ga., blue green w/red roof........................	90	150	300
4351 Club Car, Standard ga., blue green w/red roof........................	90	150	300
4352 Club Car, Standard ga., blue green w/red roof........................	90	150	300
4380 Baggage Car, Standard ga., beige and green, w/brass trim, marked "Hancock"....................	120	200	400
4380 Pullman, Standard ga., blue, w/brass trim, marked "Flying Colonel-Madison".....................	120	200	400
4381 Pullman, Standard ga., blue, brass trim, marked "Flying Colonel-Adams"	120	200	400
4381 Pullman, Standard ga., green and beige, brass trim, marked "Hancock".................................	120	200	400

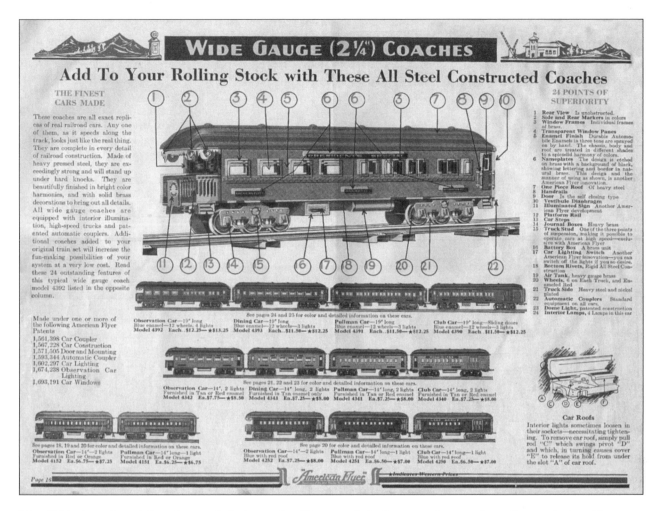

No. 4341, American Flyer boasted their steel rolling stock had twenty-four points of superiority. Courtesy 1940s American Flyer catalog.

	C5	C7	C9
4382 Observation Car, Standard ga., blue, w/brass trim, marked "Flying Colonel-Hancock"	120	200	400
4382 Observation Car, Standard ga., beige and green, w/brass trim, marked "Hancock"	120	200	400
4390 Club Car, Standard ga., two-tone blue, West Point	180	300	600
4391 Pullman Car, Standard ga., two-tone blue, Annapolis	180	300	600
4392 Observation Car, Standard ga., two-tone blue, Army-Navy	180	300	600
4393 Dining Car, Standard ga., two-tone blue, marked "President's Special-Academy"	180	300	600
4403 Locomotive, O ga.	45	75	150

	C5	C7	C9
4603 Locomotive, O ga., 2-4-4	90	150	300
4615 Locomotive, O ga., 2-4-2	210	350	700
4629 Locomotive, O ga.	90	150	300
4633 Locomotive	210	350	700
4635 Locomotive, Standard ga., red w/brass trim, Shasta	160	285	570
4637 Engine, Standard ga., 0-4-0, Auto Bell, green and beige, w/brass trim	360	600	1200
4637 Locomotive, Standard ga., green, Shasta	195	325	650
4642 Boxcar, Standard ga., red and black	120	200	400
4643 Engine, Standard ga., 0-4-0, green and black, w/brass trim	90	150	300

A few of the Choo-Choo cars featured in the 1941 American Flyer catalog: Nos. 490, 564C, 553C, 558C, 563C and the 567C.

	C5	C7	C9
4644 Engine, Standard ga., 0-4-0, red and gray, w/brass trim	83	138	275
4644 Loco, Standard ga., red and gray, Shasta	165	275	550
4644RC Locomotive, Standard ga.	135	225	450
4644 Observation Car, Standard ga., lithographed, Eagle	66	110	220

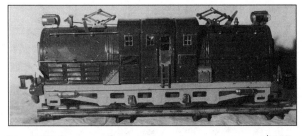

No. 4637 Locomotive, standard gauge, green, $650

	C5	C7	C9
4644 Pullman, Standard ga., lithographed, Eagle	66	110	220
4653 Engine, Standard ga., 0-4-0, orange and black, w/brass trim	120	200	400
4654 Locomotive, Standard ga.	135	225	450
4660 Locomotive	150	250	500
4667 Engine, Standard ga., 0-4-0, red and black, w/brass trim	120	200	400

	C5	C7	C9
4670 Consist Loco, w/4671 tender	300	500	1000
4670 Locomotive, Standard ga., 2-4-2, black w/green stripe and brass trim, w/tender	600	1000	2000
4670 Locomotive, Standard ga., 4-4-2, black w/green stripe and brass and nickel trim, w/tender	360	600	1200
4671 Locomotive, cast iron	210	350	700

No. 4670 Locomotive, standard gauge, 4-4-2, black with green stripe and brass and nickel trim, with tender, $1,200

	C5	C7	C9
4675 Locomotive, Standard ga., 4-4-2	480	800	1600
4677 Locomotive, Standard ga.	255	425	850
4677 Locomotive, O ga.	180	300	600
4678 Engine, Standard ga., 0-4-0, red and gray, w/brass trim	300	500	1000

	C5	C7	C9
4680 Locomotive, Standard ga.	225	375	750
4680 Locomotive, Standard ga., Golden State	450	750	1500
4680 Locomotive, Standard ga., 2-4-4	750	1250	2500
4680 Locomotive, 1933, w/4671 coal tender	420	600	1200
4681 Locomotive, Standard ga., 4-4-2	450	750	1500
4683 Locomotive	300	500	1000
4684 Locomotive	300	500	1000
4685 Locomotive, Standard ga.	180	300	600

	C5	C7	C9
4686 Engine, Standard ga., 4-4-4, black red and two-tone blue, w/brass trim, marked "The Ace"	360	600	1200
4687 Engine, Standard ga., 4-4-4, blue and black, w/brass trim	750	1250	2500
4687 Locomotive, Standard ga., lithographed, blue, marked "President's Special"	690	1150	2300
4689 Engine, Standard ga., 4-4-4, peacock blue and black, w/brass and nickel trim, marked "The Commander"	150	2500	5000
4692 Locomotive, Tri-valve steam	300	500	1000

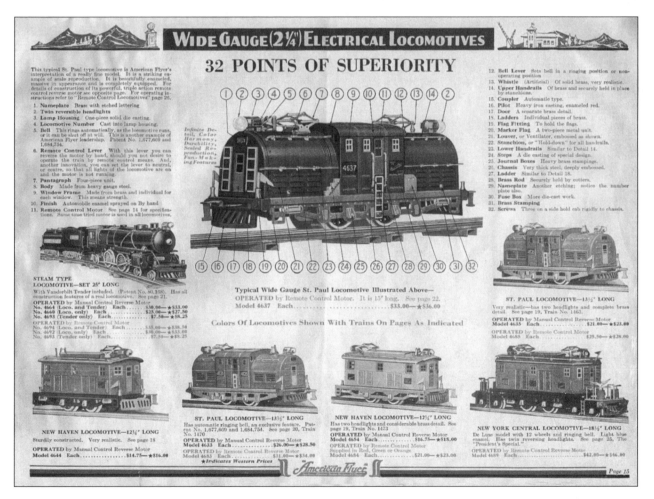

A page from a 1940s American Flyer catalog illustrates the thirty-two points of superiority of their engines. Here the No. 4637 engine is used a an example.

No. 4671 Locomotive, cast iron, $700

No. 4687, Locomotive, standard gauge, litho-graphed, blue, $2,300

No. 4694, Locomotive, standard gauge, beige, green, w/brass plates and windows, $900

No. 9900, Locomotive, O gauge, Burlington Zephyr, $175

	C5	C7	C9
4693 Locomotive, Standard ga., 4-4-2, blue w/brass and copper trim..............................	420	700	1400
4693 Locomotive, Standard ga., 4-4-2, black w/green stripe, brass and nickel trim, w/tender..........	360	600	1200
4693 Tender..................................	120	200	400
4694 Locomotive, Standard ga.	540	900	1800
4694 Locomotive, Standard ga., beige, green, w/brass plates and windows....................................	270	450	900
4695 Locomotive, Standard ga.	330	550	1100

	C5	C7	C9
4696 Locomotive, Standard ga., 2-4-2	840	1400	2800
4890 Pullman, O ga.	24	40	80
5130 Observation Car, O ga.	27	45	90
5160 Caboose, Union Pacific	15	25	50
5640 Hudson, O ga., 4-6-4, w/tender....................................	210	350	700
9217 Street Lamp, green metal...	9	15	30
9900 Locomotive, O ga., cast aluminum, electric, Burlington Zephyr	158	263	525
9900 Locomotive, O ga., wind-up, Burlington Zephyr....................	53	88	175

	C5	C7	C9
9900 Locomotive, O ga., tinplate, electric, Burlington Zephyr.......	83	138	275
9911 Baggage Car, O ga................	90	150	300
9912 Observation Car, O ga.	90	150	300
9913 Pullman, O ga.	90	150	300
9914 Locomotive, O ga.	360	600	1200
9915 Locomotive, O ga.	240	400	800
19220 Auto Rama T Intersections, for HO-scale items...................	5	10	15

	C5	C7	C9
22006 Transformer, twenty-five watt...	30	45	60
25671 Track Trip	1	2	4
26672 Track Trip	1	2	4
26782 Trestle Set	14	23	45
31004 Switcher Loco, HO ga., 0-6-0	75	125	250

American Flyer HO

Although commonly referred to as American Flyer HO, this pseudonym was only one title given to this line of HO originating in 1938 and coming to an abrupt end in 1963.

The original cataloged line of 1938 was dubbed the Gilbert Tru-Model Trains, heavy die-cast models offered in both ready-to-run and kit form. The introductory HO steam locomotive was the New York Central style Alco J3a, and this popular 4-6-4 loco endured to the end of production. The Tru-Model Trains line was quite limited, offering only a refrigerator car, flat car, tank car, gondola, caboose, passenger car and combine, along with the Hudson. Interestingly, the early HO line had a similar appearance to pieces offered by American Flyer in O gauge, and the line in later years was a reflection of what Gilbert was offering in their more popular S-gauge line. From the beginning, the Flyer HO line was called the tinplate HO, and rightly so, considering the more prototypical appearance of the competition. A popular 0-6-0 steam switcher introduced in 1949, and the Hudson, included the famous American Flyer smoke and choo-choo sound found in Gilbert's bigger trains. In later years the smoke and choo-choo was eliminated from some locomotives to help reduce costs when the HO line was faltering.

After World War II the die-cast HO line was offered in a plastic body with die-cast frame, except for the flat car, 0-6-0 switcher, and Hudson which remained die-cast. Interestingly, neither a boxcar nor a hopper car (the backbone of the real American railroads) was offered by Gilbert in HO until 1955—seventeen years after the line's introduction. After an early 1950s lull in production for re-tooling, Gilbert sought the help of Gordon Varney to produce new HO products to be introduced in 1955. With much fanfare Gilbert introduced its new revitalized line, known as Gilbert HO, which was primarily (but not all) Varney rolling stock having a Gilbert number and packaged in Gilbert's new state-of-the-art HO window box. This new line also included a Varney-produced EMD F-3 A-B diesel set.

Gilbert began to add to the line with its beautiful Northern Pacific passenger set, including cars made by Gilbert and the F-3 diesels by Varney. The line was further enriched through the mid-to-late-1950s with attractive diesels including an Alco DL-600 and a die-cast industrial switcher, improved Hudson locomotives, and expanded rolling stock. By 1957, Gilbert had taken over production, eliminating Varney-produced items. Also in 1957 Gilbert switched from a three-digit to a five-digit piece identification system for both the HO- and S-gauge lines. Some of the five-digit pieces tend to be scarcer than the three-digit counterparts as the five-digit version production runs at times were short-lived.

In continuing the saga of this peculiar line of HO trains, it must be noted that Mantua-Tyco was contracted in 1959 to produce the HO version of the FY&P old-time passenger set (also sold in an S-gauge version) to commemorate Gilbert's Fifty Years of Progress. Oddly, this train was a 100 percent Mantua-Tyco model, except for the American Flyer HO box sticker, but may be the most sought after and best representation of American Flyer's HO line. This fiftieth anniversary year introduced the new pseudonym American Flyer HO, as the Gilbert name was now being reserved for chemistry and auto racing sets.

Although the popularity of HO (and trains in general) grew in the 1950s, Gilbert was shortsighted on what the consumer wanted. Most Gilbert rolling stock hosted such tinplate characteristics as molded-in brake wheels and roof walks, coarse and heavy detailing on the car body, and with a move to producing items on dies from the Far East, very cheap toy-like cars and diesels which ran poorly. Even the Hudson and 0-6-0 switcher eventually lost their classic Flyer appearance. These were the infamous Pikemaster HO years, a name A.C. Gilbert would never be proud of.

All model train manufacturers suffered in the early 1960s due to heavy competition with slot car racing and numerous other modern inventions. But the American Flyer HO line, now being referred to as Miniature American Flyer, was especially in trouble as it attempted to offer toy-like action cars and accessories to compete. Children, and especially adults, were not interested since the majority of HO producers were pushing scale and prototypical realism. However, Tru-Scale Models was contracted to produce three Maintenance-of-Way (MOW) cars for Gilbert in 1959, and these were somewhat successful due to their prototypical appearance. These MOW cars require their original Gilbert packaging to distinguish them from common Tru-Scale production.

A few last minute efforts were made to revitalize the HO line for 1963 by introducing some higher quality HO products, such as the Missouri Pacific passenger set which included a Varney diesel, but the inevitable was about to take place and the line was dropped in 1963.

American Flyer HO by any name is highly sought after by collectors. It is somewhat difficult to find and prices for certain pieces can far outweigh the S gage counterparts. Often a mirror image of the S- and/or O-gauge American Flyer lines, this is one HO line that does not fit the typical HO mold.

The price list does not contain every variation; therefore, only the most popular or common variations are listed. It is important to note that prices do vary across the continental United States.

Contributor: Rick Tonet, rtonet@netscape.net. Tonet has been collecting and researching American Flyer HO for fifteen years and possesses a nearly complete collection. He has had articles about American Flyer HO published in *Classic Toy Trains* magazine, with Keith Willis in *Railroad Model Craftsman*, The Train Collectors Quarterly, and several articles in *The Collector*, the official quarterly of the American Flyer Collector's Club. Tonet's collection is featured in a hardback book titled *Gilbert American Flyer HO 1938-1963* by Gary Klein.

Notes
*Due to a problem with the die-cast weight affixed to the underside of Pikemaster Gondolas which caused them to bow or break in half from stress (even when new), whole or only slightly bowed Gondolas bring premium prices. Listed prices are for broken, re-glued, or bowed Gondolas.

PM = Pikemaster Production. Pikemaster pieces do closely resemble Marx HO.

Kleer-Pak boxes are very desirable and do place considerable added value on pieces listed. Even common Gilbert cardboard boxes will add value to a piece. **S/CC** = Smoke and Choo Choo sound included.

Note: Gilbert's individual HO accessories including signals, buildings, track, transformers, etc number around 200 pieces. Only the more popular accessories have been listed. The accessory number does not commonly appear on the piece.

Examples of Gilbert packaging over the years. Photo by Lloyd Shick.

	C6	C8	C10
119 Flat Car, IC, w/three wheel sets, die-cast, gray, no number, couplers connected	25	45	75
123 Refrigerator Car, PFE, encircled SP, orange and brown	22	45	65
123 Refrigerator Car, PFE, encircled SP, all orange	100	140	180
124 Refrigerator Car, MDT, white and brown	8	15	25
125 Tank Car, Shell, plastic w/die-cast frame, silver......................	10	35	45
126 Tank Car, Sinclair, plastic w/die-cast frame, black.............	15	40	50

	C6	C8	C10
127 Gondola, T&P, embossed "A.C. Gilbert Co.," gray	12	28	40
127 Gondola, T&P, embossed "A.C. Gilbert Co.," green..........	15	25	32
128 Gondola, LNE, embossed "A.C. Gilbert Co.," gray	30	55	100
129 Flat Car, NYNH&H, w/transformer, die-cast, black...	20	35	50
131 Caboose, RDG, center cupola, illuminated, red	12	20	35
133 Baggage Car, NH, "American Flyer Style," green	40	70	110
135 Coach, NH, "American Flyer Style," green.............................	25	65	100

No. 126 Sinclair Tank car, $50. Photo by Lloyd Shick.

No. 135 NH Coach, $100. Photo by Lloyd Shick.

	C6	C8	C10
155 Switcher, PRR, B6sb 0-6-0 slantback steam, S/CC	65	110	160
216 Flat Car, IC, die-cast, gray, w/three wheel sets, no number, couplers connected to body, couplers connected to body, car also available in kit form	25	45	75
252 Block Sign, black	—	50	100
253 Roadside Diner, yellow w/sign and antenna	—	45	95
257 Talking Station, 1950	—	150	300
258 Passenger Station, metal, white/green/red	—	70	100
259 Whistling Station, similar to 258, w/whistle	—	150	200

No. 259 Whistling station, $200. Also pictured is a Plasticville station with "Gilbert HO" stamped on the underside. Photo by Lloyd Shick.

	C6	C8	C10
420 Locomotive, Lack., F-3 A-unit GMD powered diesel, silver	45	75	90
421 Locomotive, B&O, F-3 A-unit GMD powered diesel, blue and gray	50	75	100
422 Locomotive, B&O, F-3 A-unit GMD dummy diesel, blue and ray	80	150	175
423 Locomotive, NP, F-3 A-unit GMD powered diesel, green	85	120	140
424 Locomotive, NP, F-3 A-unit GMD dummy diesel, green	60	100	125

Left to right: No. 425 Lackawanna Locomotive, $200; No. 420 Lackawanna Locomotive, $90. Photo by Lloyd Shick.

	C6	C8	C10
425 Locomotive, Lack., F-3 B-unit GMD dummy diesel, no number, silver	100	150	200
426 Locomotive, B&O, F-3 B-unit GMD dummy diesel, blue and gray	100	150	200
427 Locomotive, NP, F-3 B-unit GMD dummy diesel, green	100	150	200
430 DL-600 Demonstrator, Alco, powered, maroon and gray	50	70	100
433 Switcher, PRR, B6sb 0-6-0 slantback steam, S/CC	50	75	100

Back to front: No. 443 NYC Locomotive, $125; No. 433 PRR Switcher, $100. Photo by Lloyd Shick.

	C6	C8	C10
443 Locomotive, NYC, J3a Hudson 4-6-4, whitewall drive wheels, S/CC	60	90	125
446 Locomotive, NYC, J3a Hudson 4-6-4, whitewall drive wheels, w/whistle, S/CC	70	100	150
500 Tank Car, Gulf, Varney version, silver, single dome	7	12	18
500 Tank Car, Gulf, Gilbert version, silver, single dome	12	20	32
501 Hopper, CB&Q, Varney version, brown, panel sides, w/Coal Load	4	8	12

	C6	C8	C10
501 Hopper, CB&Q, Gilbert version, Brown, Smooth Sides, w/Coal Load	8	15	20
502 Stock Car, MKT, Varney version, yellow/brown	5	8	12
502 Stock Car, MKT, Gilbert version, yellow/brown	7	12	20
503 Flat Car, NYNH&H, black, w/transformer load	22	32	45
504 Refrigerator Car, PFE, encircled SP, orange, one herald	12	24	36
504 Refrigerator Car, PFE/UP, SP/UP Heralds, orange, two herald	22	45	70
505 Hopper, N&W, black, ink-stamped "Gilbert HO," early model	5	12	20
506 Caboose, RDG, red, w/center cupola,	10	18	28
506 Caboose, PRR, red, w/center cupola,	8	12	20
510 Hopper, covered, Monon, Varney version, gray, w/panel side	4	8	12
510 Hopper, covered, Monon, Gilbert version, gray, w/smooth side	10	22	30
511 Tank Car, Gulf, silver, w/three domes	22	35	48
512 Boxcar, NH, orange	10	15	20
513 Boxcar, B&O, blue and orange	18	30	55

	C6	C8	C10
514 Boxcar, SBD, "Silver Meteor," brown	15	30	45
516 Caboose, NYC, brown, lighted, w/center cupola	22	32	45

No. 516 NYC Caboose, $45; No. 33616 C&O Caboose, $80. Photo by Lloyd Shick.

	C6	C8	C10
516 Caboose, RDG, red, lighted, center cupola	22	32	45
517 Tank Car, Mobilgas, Varney version, red	3	10	15
517 Tank Car, Mobilgas, Gilbert version, red	7	17	27
518 Tank Car, Koppers, Varney version, black	10	18	30
518 Tank Car, Koppers, Gilbert version, black	20	30	45
520 Refrigerator Car, CNW, "Northwestern," green and yellow	25	35	50
521 Refrigerator Car, NP, orange w/silver roof and ends	60	75	110
521 Refrigerator Car, NP, orange w/brown roof and ends	12	25	30
522 Boxcar, B&M, blue and black	15	25	45
523 Boxcar, D&RGW, "Cookie Box," white	18	22	30

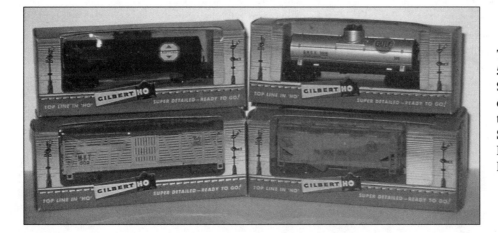

Top row, left to right: No. 518 Koppers Tank car, $30; No. 500 Gulf Tank car, $18. Bottom row, left to right: No. 502 MKT Stock car, $12; No. 510 Monon Hopper, $30. Photo by Lloyd Shick.

	C6	C8	C10
524 Refrigerator Car, Morrell, orange and brown	15	28	40
525 Hopper Car, B&O, Varney version, black, panel sides, w/load	6	12	20
525 Hopper Car, B&O, Gilbert version, black, smooth sides, no load	10	18	28
526 Refrigerator Car, GB&W, "Green Bay Route," gray and red	22	35	55
540 Combine Car, NP, green, lighted	25	35	50
541 Coach Car, NP, green, lighted	28	38	53
542 Vista Dome, NP, green, lighted	30	40	55
543 Observation Car, NP, green, lighted	28	38	53
700 Girder Bridge, silver or red, "Lackawanna"	—	10	30
711 Flasher Signal	—	15	40
L1001 Locomotive, NP, F-3 A-unit pikemaster, powered diesel, green	125	150	200
C1002 Combine Car, NP, pikemaster, non-lighted, green	100	150	200
L1002 Locomotive, C&O, F-3 A-unit pikemaster, dummy diesel, blue	110	130	170
C1003 Vista Dome, NP, pikemaster, non-lighted, green	100	150	200
C1004 Observation Car, NP, pikemaster, non-lighted, green	100	150	200
C1006 Hopper, C&O, covered, pikemaster, yellow and white	90	150	200
C1007 Hopper, T&P, some are covered, pikemaster, green and white	90	150	200
2764 Baggage Car, NH, AF, couplers on trucks, car also available in kit form, cataloged as item 121	28	48	85
2764 Baggage Car, NH, AF, couplers on body, car also available in kit form, cataloged as item 215	30	50	95

	C6	C8	C10
L3003 Locomotive, SF, F-3 A-unit pikemaster, powered diesel, red	25	40	55
C3008 Caboose, SF, bay window, pikemaster, red	8	15	25
5318 Locomotive, NYC, J3a Hudson 4-6-4 steam, A-C Spur Drive, headlight, remote control, Bakelite wheels w/brass rims, cataloged as item 112, also available in kit form as HO-112	60	100	130

No. 5318 NYC Locomotive, $150. Photo by Lloyd Shick.

	C6	C8	C10
5318 Locomotive, NYC, J3a Hudson 4-6-4 steam, D-C Worm Drive, smoke-in-soiler, no headlight, whitewall drive wheels, cataloged as item 151	125	170	200
5318 Locomotive, NYC, J3a Hudson 4-6-4 steam, D-C worm drive, headlight, piston smoke unit in tender, whitewall drive wheels, cataloged as item 151	75	125	170

No. 5318 NYC Locomotive, $150. Photo by Lloyd Shick.

	C6	C8	C10
5318 Locomotive, NYC, J3a Hudson, D-C worm drive, headlight, bellows smoke unit in tender, whitewall drive wheels, cataloged as item 151, 1947-49	75	125	170
5318 Locomotive, NYC, J3a Hudson 4-6-4 steam, D-C worm drive, w/headlight, piston smoke unit in tender, no cab number, whitewall drive wheels, cataloged as item 151, 1947-48	80	130	175
5318 Locomotive, NYC, J3a Hudson 4-6-4 steam, A-C Spur Drive, w/headlight, remote control, die-cast drive wheels, cataloged as item 112, also available in kit form HO-112....	80	150	200
5318 Locomotive, NYC, J3a Hudson 4-6-4 steam, A-C Spur Drive, w/headlight, remote control, Bakelite wheels w/brass rims, cataloged as item 200, also available in kit form as HO-1	60	100	130
5318 Locomotive, NYC, J3a Hudson 4-6-4 steam, A-C spur drive, no headlight, Bakelite wheels, single red window strut, cataloged 200, also available in kit form as HO-1 ...	75	120	150
5318 Locomotive, NYC, J3a Hudson 4-6-4 steam, D-C Worm Drive, w/headlight, smoke unit in tender, whitewall drive wheels, cataloged as item 151	75	125	170
5802 Tank Car, gasoline, Texaco, die-cast, silver, couplers on trucks, car also available in kit form	15	30	50
5802 Tank Car, gasoline, Texaco, die-cast, silver, couplers on body, car also available in kit form	10	22	45
8302 Coach Car, NH, AF, die-cast, couplers on trucks, car also available in kit form, cataloged 122, also available in kit form ..	25	40	80

	C6	C8	C10
8302 Coach Car, NH, AF, die-cast, couplers on body, car also available in kit form, cataloged 122, also available in kit form...	25	40	80
15503 Gondola, LNE, die-cast, black or gray, couplers on body, cataloged as item 205, car also available in kit form	10	25	45
15503 Gondola, LNE, die-cast, black, couplers on trucks, cataloged as item 117, car also available in kit form	10	22	45
24712 Tank Car, gasoline, Sinclair, die-cast, black, couplers on body, cataloged as item 204, car also available in kit form	10	22	45
24712 Tank Car, gasoline, Sinclair, die-cast, black, couplers on trucks, cataloged as item 116, car also available in kit form	15	30	50
31004 Switcher, PRR, B6sb 0-6-0 slantback S/CC	40	65	85
31005 Locomotive, NYC, J3a Hudson 4-6-4 steam S/CC	55	80	110
31007 Locomotive, B&O, F-3 A-unit GMD powered diesel, blue and gray	95	140	180
31008 Locomotive, B&O, F-3 B-unit GMD dummy diesel, blue and gray	200	300	400
31009 Locomotive, B&O, F-3 A-unit GMD dummy diesel, blue and gray	90	140	160
31010 Locomotive, NP, F-3 A-unit GMD powered diesel, green	100	150	170
31011 Locomotive, NP, F-3 B-unit GMD dummy diesel, green	100	125	150
31012 Locomotive, NP, F-3 A-unit GMD dummy diesel, green	100	125	150
31013 Locomotive, Industrial, transfer diesel, black, w/counterweight	80	125	160

	C6	C8	C10
31014 Locomotive, SP, F-3 A-unit GMD powered diesel, orange	110	160	200
31017 Locomotive, C&O, Alco DL-600, 600 on number boards, blue and yellow	115	170	210

Left to right: No. No. 31017 C&O Locomotive, $210; No. 430 Alco DL-600 Demonstrator, $100. Photo by Lloyd Shick.

	C6	C8	C10
31019 Switcher, B&O, B6sb 0-6-0 slantback S/CC	95	155	210
31021 Locomotive, Industrial, transfer diesel, blue, no counterweight	30	45	60

Left to right: No. 31021 Industrial Locomotive, $60; No. 31013 Industrial Locomotive, $160. Photo by Lloyd Shick.

	C6	C8	C10
31022 Locomotive, C&O, Alco DL-600 w/ringing bell (see 31017), blue	70	140	180
31025 Locomotive, C&O, F-3 A-unit pikemaster powered diesel, blue plastic	25	50	75
31025 Locomotive, C&O, F-3 A-unit pikemaster, blue	100	150	200
31031 Locomotive, B&O, B6sb 0-6-0 slantback, no S/CC	45	70	90
31032 Locomotive, NP, F-3 A-unit pikemaster powered diesel	50	70	95
31036 Locomotive, Erie, B6sb 0-6-0 slantback switcher, no S/CC	40	65	80
31037 Locomotive, M&StL, F-3 A-unit pikemaster, w/o headlight, red/white	95	145	175
31037 Locomotive, M&StL, F-3 A-unit pikemaster powered diesel, red and white	70	90	120
31038 Locomotive, M&StL, F-3 A-unit pikemaster dummy diesel, red and white	100	120	140
31039 Locomotive, MP, F-3 A-unit GMD powered diesel, sliver and blue	150	225	300
31045 Locomotive, WAB, J3a Hudson 4-6-4 steam S/CC	70	110	165

Pikemaster-era diesel engines made in the Far East. Left to right: No. 31025 C&O Locomotive, $75; No. 31037 M&STL Locomotive, $120; No. 31010 NP Locomotive, $170; No. L3003 SF Locomotive, $55; No. L1002 Locomotive, $$170. Photo by Lloyd Shick.

Early Varney product. Left to right: No. 31039 MP Locomotive, $300; No. 31014 SP Locomotive, $200; No. 423 NP Locomotive, $140; No. 421 B&O Locomotive, $100. Photo by Lloyd Shick.

Back row, left to right: No 33120 T&P Gondola, $130; No. 147313 PRR Gondola, $50; No. No. 128 LNE Gondola. Front row, left to right: No. 33317 NH Gondola, $150; No. 33120 Gondola, $130. Photo by Lloyd Shick.

	C6	C8	C10
31088 Locomotive, FY&P, Franklin 4-4-0 Old Time (Tyco), green and red	150	250	325
32404 Caboose, NYC, die-cast, red, couplers on trucks, cataloged as item 120, car also available in kit form, w/center cupola, 1939	12	28	58
32404 Caboose, NYC, die-cast, brown, couplers on body, cataloged as item 207, car also available in kit form, w/center cupola, 1938	18	32	65
32404 Caboose, NYC, die-cast, red, couplers on body, cataloged as item 127, car also available in kit form, w/center cupola, 1939	12	26	55
33002 Boxcar, NYC, w/large NYC oval sticker, green and white	27	35	45
33004 Stock Car, NP, "Pig Palace," red w/silver roof	100	150	200
33006 Stock Car, GN, hay-jector eliminated, red	80	110	150
33009 Stock Car, WAB, hay-jector eliminated, blue	80	110	150
33010 Stock Car, UP, hay-jector eliminated, yellow	90	140	190

Left to right: No. 33010 UP Stock car, $190; No. 33819 NYC Cattle car, $70. Photo by Lloyd Shick.

	C6	C8	C10
33012 Boxcar, SF, large Santa Fe cross, red and white	80	140	180
33115 Ballast Car, MW, by TruScale, gray, Kleer-Pak or cardboard Gilbert box required	40	80	110
33119 Gondola, Monon, pikemaster, white and red*	45	90	110
33120 Gondola, T&P, pikemaster, green and white*	60	100	130
33121 Gondola, NH, "Trap Rock," pikemaster, tan and yellow*	80	150	200
33122 Gondola, N&W, pikemaster, black*	50	95	125
33211 Hopper, C&EI, no load, gray	10	20	30
33212 Hopper, SF, w/gray stone load, red	20	32	45
33214 Hopper, SF, covered, red and white	10	22	35
33215 Hopper, Peabody, no load, tan (tan color varies)	15	22	42
33217 Hopper, NYC, covered, green/white	10	20	30
33219 Hopper, B&O, no load, black	60	75	115
33220 Hopper, CB&Q, w/covered, red and white	160	260	375
33312 Tank Car, Karo, "Karo Syrup," white/red	150	250	350
33313 Tank Car, Hooker, chemical, orange/black	75	110	140
33314 Tank Car, Cities, "Cities Service," green	350	425	500
33315 Tank Car, SOHIO, "Sohio," black	375	450	550
33316 Gondola, Bethlehem Steel, w/rail load, gray and red	45	85	125

Left to right: No. 126 Sinclair Tank car, $50; No. 33312 Karo tank car, $350; No. 33500 Gulf Tank car, 35. Photo by Lloyd Shick.

	C6	C8	C10
33316 Gondola, Bethlehem Steel, PM version, w/rail load, gray and red	80	125	155
33317 Gondola, NH, pikemaster, black and orange*	70	130	150
33403 Refrigerator Car, BAR, large BAR sticker, red	70	100	150

Back row, left to right: BAR 33403 Refrigerator car, $150; No. 33520 CNW Refrigerator car, $150. Front row: No. 521 Refrigerator car, $110. Photo by Lloyd Shick.

	C6	C8	C10
33500 Tank Car, Gulf, single dome, silver	12	25	35
33501 Hopper Car, CB&Q, smooth side, brown, w/coal load	18	28	40

Left to right: No. MKT 33502 MKT Stock car, $95; No. 33004 NP Stock car, $200. Photo by Lloyd Shick.

	C6	C8	C10
33502 Stock Car, MKT, yellow and brown.................................	55	75	95
33503 Flat Car, NYNH&H, w/transformer Load, black	50	75	125
33505 Gondola, N&W, black and white..	10	22	32
33506 Caboose, PRR, red, w/center cupola	5	12	20
33507 Gondola, D&H, brown, w/canister load	30	60	75
33507 Gondola, D&H, pikemaster version, brown..........................	100	200	300
33508 Gondola, C&O, black and yellow, w/pipe load	20	35	55
33509 Flat Car, WM, brown, w/RISS trailer load	42	55	80
33510 Hopper, Monon, covered, gray and red.............................	80	130	170
33511 Tank Car, Gulf, three domes, silver	12	25	35
33512 Boxcar, NH, orange	12	24	36
33513 Boxcar, B&O, blue and orange...	30	50	75
33514 Boxcar, SBD, "Silver Meteor," brown	20	45	65
33515 Caboose, C&O, lighted, yellow, w/center cupola	45	75	120
33516 Caboose, NYC, lighted, brown, w/center cupola.............	12	22	35

Left to right: No. 33510 Monon Hopper, $170; No. 33219 B&O Hopper, $115; No. 33220 CB&G Hopper, $375. Photo by Lloyd Shick.

Back row, left to right: No. 33531 SP Coach car, $160; No. 33722 MP Coach car, $220. Front row: No. 33541 NP Coach car, $65. Photo by Lloyd Shick.

Back row, left to right: No. 33539 RI Flat car, $100; No. 33537 Track Cleaning car, $65. Front row: No. 33503 NYNH&H Flat car, $125. Photo by Lloyd Shick.

	C6	C8	C10
33517 Tank Car, Mobil, "Mobilgas," red	12	18	25
33518 Tank Car, Koppers, chemical, black	60	100	150
33519 Caboos, B&O, red, w/center cupola	10	22	35
33520 Refrigerator Car, CNW, green and yellow	75	120	150
33521 Refrigerator Car, NP, orange and brown	18	27	42
33522 Boxcar, B&M, blue and black	25	40	60
33523 Boxcar, D&RGW, "Cookie Box," white and red	20	30	45
33524 Refrigerator Car, Morrel Ref, Morrel, Orange and silver.	25	35	65
33525 Hopper Car, B&O, no load, smooth side, black	45	90	120
33526 Refrigerator Car, GB&W, "Green Bay Route," gray and red	30	42	55
33527 Flat Car, NH, w/lumber load and stakes, black	20	32	45
33530 Combine Car, SP, lighted, silver/orange	60	120	160

	C6	C8	C10
33531 Coach Car, SP, lighted, silver and orange	60	120	160
33536 Flat Car, PRR, w/ten stakes, brown	60	95	135
33537 Track Cleaning Car, D&H, w/D&H Canister, black	22	40	65
33538 Flat Car, USAF, w/two nike rockets, dark green	55	110	135
33538 Flat Car, US Air Force, w/two Nike rockets, dark green	60	155	155
33539 Flat Car, RI, w/two railcar trucks, gray and black	38	65	100
33540 Combine Car, NP, lighted, green	25	35	50
33541 Coach Car, NP, lighted, green	35	50	65
33542 Vista Dome, NP, lighted, green	30	45	60
33543 Observation Car, NP, lighted, green	32	45	62
33544 Flat Car, CP, red, w/Christmas tree load	100	175	225
33545 Flat Car, National, w/Borden's Milk Tank, black and white	20	40	80

TruScale Models. Top: No. 33548 Crane, $200; Bottom, left to right: No. 33115 Ballast car, $110; No. 33549 Crane tender, $100. Photo by Lloyd Shick.

	C6	C8	C10
33546 Flat Car, IC, w/jet engine case, black	25	50	90
33548 Crane, MW, X74 Brownhoist, by TruScale, red cab, Kleer-Pak or cardboard Gilbert	90	150	200
33549 Crane Tender, MW, by TruScale, typically 642, gray, Kleer-Pak or cardboard	40	70	100
33555 Flat Car, IC, w/containers, lumber, pipes, brown	45	70	90
33557 Flat Car, WM, w/Riss trailer van, brown	42	55	80
33558 Flat Car, IC, w/load, similar to 33555, brown	25	40	50

	C6	C8	C10
33615 Caboose, NYC, brown, w/center cupola	15	20	30
33616 Caboose, C&O, lighted, yellow, w/center cupola	33	55	80
33618 Caboose, Erie, bay window, pikemaster, red	8	15	25
33620 Caboose, WAB, bay window, pikemaster, blue	22	35	50

Left to right: No. 33620 Wabash Caboose, $50; No. 5318 NYC Caboose, $160. Photo by Lloyd Shick.

Back row, left to right: No. 33623 MT&SL Caboose, $52; No. C3008 SF Caboose, $25; No. 33625 NYC Caboose, $160; No. 33627 PRR Caboose, $65; No. 33618 Erie Caboose, $25. Front row, left to right: Two versions of C&O No. 33621 Caboose, $32, each; No. 33620 Wabash Caboose, $50. Photo by Lloyd Shick.

	C6	C8	C10
33621 Caboose, C&O, bay window, pikemaster, yellow	12	20	32
33623 Caboose, M&StL, bay window, pikemaster, red	25	42	52
33625 Caboose, NYC, bay window, pikemaster, red	90	125	160
33626 Caboose, work, Erie, no tie-jector, see 33820	85	120	150

Left to right: No, 33626 Eries Work Caboose, $150; No. 33820 AF Work Caboose, $35. Photo by Lloyd Shick.

	C6	C8	C10
33627 Caboose, PRR, bay window, pikemaster, red	32	45	65
33720 Coach, FY&P, Old Time, by Mantua-Tyco, yellow	95	150	210
33721 Combine Car, MP, lighted, silver and blue	75	125	150
33722 Coach Car, MP, lighted (sold separately only), silver and blue	120	180	200
33723 Vista Dome, MP, lighted, silver and blue	75	125	150
33724 Observation Car, MP, lighted, silver/blue	75	125	150
33804 Boxcar, TNT, exploding "Boxcar," black/yellow	40	55	90
33806 Boxcar, MINE, Mine Carrying/Exploding "Boxcar," yellow	30	45	70

	C6	C8	C10
33812 Rocket Launcher Car, USAF, w/Rocket, yellow/blue	25	40	80
33818 Cattle Car, GN, ejects hay bale, red	20	45	65
33819 Cattle Car, NYC, ejects hay bale, green	25	50	70
33820 Caboose, work, AF, Tie Car, ejects tie, orange and gray	10	20	35
33835 Hopper Car, C&O, dumps coal load, black	18	28	48
35105 Motorized Vehicle, Inspection, w/two figures, green	400	600	800
35210 Radar Tower, made for Ideal by Gilbert	—	15	40
35212 Crossing Gate, made for Ideal by Gilbert	—	10	35
35213 Oil Storage Depot	—	40	75
35759 Drum Loadiing Conveyor, "Oil Depot"	—	50	100
35780 Coal Loader, "Elm City Coal Gravel & Sand Co."	—	50	70
35785 Automatic Coal Unloader, w/35785 hopper car	—	50	90
35785 Hopper Car, C&O, dumps coal load, black	18	28	48
35790 Piggyback Unloader, w/Riss van trailer	—	80	140
35901 Refrigerator Car, PFE, die-cast, orange, couplers on body, cataloged as item 201, car also available in kit form	20	40	60
35901 Refrigerator Car, PFE, die-cast, orange, couplers on trucks, cataloged as item 113, car also available kit form	20	40	60

The 50th anniversary set made by Tyco for Gilbert in 1959, includes, left to right: No. 33720 FY&P Coach, $10, each; No. 31088 Locomotive, $325. Photo by Lloyd Shick.

Left to right: No. 35785 C&O Hopper car, $48; No. 35759 Drum Loading conveyor, $100. Photo by Lloyd Shick.

	C6	C8	C10
49611 Refrigerator Car, MDT, die-cast, white/brown, couplers on trucks, cataloged as item 114, car also available in kit form	20	40	60
49611 Refrigerator Car, MDT, die-cast, white/brown, couplers on body, cataloged as item 202, car also available in kit form	20	40	60

	C6	C8	C10
147313 Gondola, PRR, die-cast, brown, couplers on body, cataloged as item 118, car also available in kit form	12	28	50
147313 Gondola, PRR, die-cast, brown, couplers on body, cataloged as item 206, car also available in kit form	12	28	50
352414 Automatic Crossing Watchman	—	20	45

American Flyer S Gauge

S-gauge Definitions and Notes

Gauge of Track: 7/8-inch or 0.875-inch (space between rails)
Scale: 1:64
2-4-2, 0-6-0 refers to the articulation of the wheels on a steam engine.

Grading

C4: Good. All complete and original, well used with scratches and perhaps small dents, perhaps dirty, but not broken.

C6: Very good. Relatively clean, few scratches, no dents or rust, complete and original.

C8: Excellent. Extremely clean, minute scratches, no discoloration, no dents or rust. All complete and original.

C10: Mint in Box (MIB). Appears as it did when it was manufactured. Original carton, inserts, and instructions must come with it. Add 30-35% over Excellent value for MIB price.

Abbreviations

L/C: Link Coupler
K/C: Knuckle Coupler
P/M: Pike Master
Reefer: Refrigerator Box Car
Coach: Pullman or Passenger
Combine: Baggage/Club Car

	C5	C7	C9
1B Transformer, 1956, 50 watt	5	8	10
2/2B Transformer, 1947-1952, 75 watt	8	11	15
4B Transformer, 1949-1956, 75/100/110 watt	8	11	15
5/5A/5B Transformer, 1946, 50 watt	6	9	12
6/6A Transformer, 1946, 75 watt ..	6	9	12
7B Transformer, 1946, 75 watt	6	9	12
8B Transformer, 1946-1952, 100 watt	17	26	35
9B Transformer, 1946, 150 watt ...	25	38	50
12B Transformer, 1946-1952, 250 watt	68	102	135
15B Transformer, 1953-1956, 110 watt	28	42	55
16B Transformer, 1953, 190 watt .	25	38	50

	C5	C7	C9
16B Transformer, 1954-1956, 175 watt..	38	56	75
17B Transformer, 190 watt............	38	56	75
18B Transformer, 1953, 190 watt, dual controls..............................	50	75	100
19B Transformer, 1952-1955, 300 watt, dual controls	50	75	100
20 Coach Car, 1959-1960, Fy & PRR, yellow, K/C	40	60	80
21/21A Imitation Grass, 1949-1956, grass, half-pound, full bag...	—	—	23
22 Scenery Gravel, 1949-1956, 22 ounces, full bag	—	—	15
23 Artifical Coal, 1949-1956, half pound, full bag	—	—	19
24 Multicolor Wire, 1949-1956, 25-feet	—	—	18

American Flyer offered several different transformers in their 1953 catalog, including the No. 19B, No. 16B, No. 15B, No. 4B and the No. 13 Circuit breaker. Each ranged in power from 110 to 300 watts.

	C5	C7	C9
25 Smoke Fluid Cartridges, 1947-1956, twelve in box	—	—	32
26 Service Kit, 1952-1956	—	—	18
27 Track Cleaning Fluid, 1952-1956, 8 ounces	—	—	8
28/28A Track Ballast, 1950-1953, 8 ounces	—	—	18
29/29A Imitation Snow, 1950-55, 4 ounces	—	—	75
30 Baggage, 1959-1960, FY & PRR, yellow, K/C	45	75	150
30/30A Highway Sign Set, 1949-1952, three yellow, five white	80	120	160
30B Transformer, 1953-1955, 300 watt, dual control	75	112	150
31/31A A Railroad Signs, white, set of eight	24	80	160
32 City Street Set, 1949-1950, eight pieces	54	90	180
32A Park Set, 1951, twelve pieces	45	75	150
33 Passenger & Train Figure Set, 1951-1952, eight figures	45	75	150
34 Railway Figure Set, 1953, twenty-five pieces	82	163	325
35 Brakeman w/Lantern, three brakemen	38	63	125

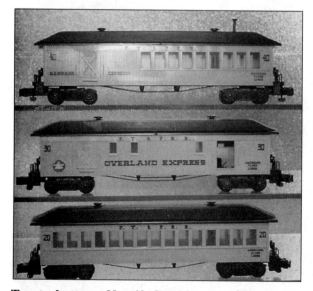

Top to bottom: No. 40 Combine car, $90; No. 20 Coach car, $80; No. 30 Baggage car, $150

	C5	C7	C9
40 Combine Car, 1959-1960, FY & PRR, yellow, K/C	27	45	90
40 Smoke Set, 1953-55	5	7	9
50 Combine Car, 1960-61, K/C	45	75	150
50 District School, 1953-54, illuminated	68	102	135
55 Box Car, 1960-61, Gold Belt Line, K/C, P/M	18	30	60
65 Flat Car, 1960-61, F.Y & P.R.R., cannon load, K/C	54	90	180
88 Steam Locomotive, 1959, FY88&P Franklin 4-4-0, K/C	54	90	180
89 Steam Locomotive, 1960-61, FY89&PRR, Washington 4-4-0, K/C	68	113	225
160 Station Platform, 1953, non-illuminated	150	225	300
161 Bungalow, 1953, illuminated	150	225	300
162 Factory, "Mysto-Magic Company"	67	112	225
163 Flyerville Station, 1953	88	132	175
164 Barn, 1953, illuminated	150	225	300
165 Grain Elevator, 1953, illuminated	130	195	260
166 Church, 1953, illuminated	200	300	400
167 Town Hall, 1953, illuminated	96	160	320
168 Hotel, 1953, illuminated	200	300	400
234 GP-7, 1961-62, Chesapeake & Ohio, K/C	250	375	500
247 Tunnel, 1946-48, 11"	15	22	30
248 Tunnel, 1946-48, 14"	18	26	35
249 Tunnel, 1947-56, 11-1/2"	8	12	17
270 News & Frank Stand, 1952-53	93	140	185
271 Whistle Stop Set, 1952-53, includes Newsstand, Frank Stand, Waiting Stand	102	153	205
272 Glendale Station, illuminated	105	158	210
273 Suburban Station, 1952-53, illuminated	58	87	115
274 Harbor Junction Freight Station, 1952-53, illuminated	95	143	190
275 Eureka Diner, 1952-53, illuminated	110	165	220

	C5	C7	C9
282 Steam Locomotive, 1952-53, C&NW, Pacific, 4-6-2, L/C, K/C	23	38	75
283 Steam Locomotive, 1954-57, C&NW, Pacific, 4-6-2, K/C	27	45	90
285 Steam Locomotive, 1952, C&NW, Pacific, 4-6-2, L/C	24	40	80
287 Steam Locomotive, C&NW, Pacific	19	31	62
289 Steam Locomotive, 1956, C&NW, Pacific, 4-6-2, K/C	75	125	250
290 Steam Locomotive, 1949-1951, Reading, Pacific, 4-6-2, L/C	35	58	115
293 Steam Locomotive, 1953-1958, NYNH & Hartford, Pacific, 4-6-2, K/C	54	90	180

	C5	C7	C9
295 Steam Locomotive, 1951, A.F., Pacific, 4-6-2, L/C	90	150	300
296 Steam Locomotive, 1955, New Haven, Pacific, 4-6-2, K/C	75	125	250
299 Steam Locomotive, 1954, Reading AFL, Atlantic, 4-4-2, L/C	60	100	200
300 Steam Locomotive, 1946-1947, Reading, Atlantic, 4-4-2, L/C	20	33	65
300AC Steam Locomotive, 1949-1951, Reading, Atlantic, 4-4-2, L/C	20	33	65
301 Steam Locomotive, 1946-1953, Reading, Atlantic, 4-4-2, L/C	20	33	65
302 Steam Locomotive, 1948-1952-1953, Reading, Atlantic, 4-4-2, L/C	23	38	75

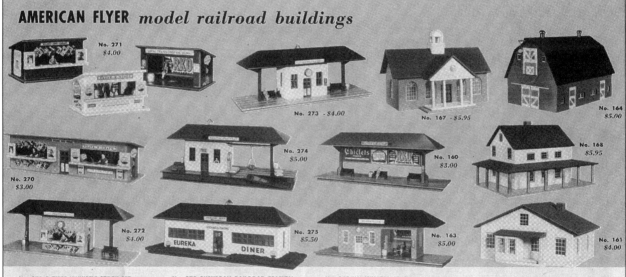

American Flyer model railroad buildings from a 1953 catalog. Top row, left to right: No. 271, No. 273, No. 167, No. 164; Second row, left to right: No. 270, No. 274, No. 160, No. 168; Bottom row, left to right: No. 272, No. 275, No. 163, No. 161

	C5	C7	C9
302AC Steam Locomotive, 1950-1951, Reading, Atlantic, 4-4-2, L/C	23	38	75
303 Steam Locomotive, 1954-1957, Reading, Atlantic, 4-4-2, K/C	23	38	75
307 Steam Locomotive, 1954-1955, Reading, Atlantic, 4-4-2, K/C	20	33	65
308 Steam Locomotive, 1956, Reading, Atlantic, 4-4-2, K/C...	22	36	72
310 Steam Locomotive, 1946, P.R.R., K-5, 4-6-2, L/C, "Pennsylvania" tender	33	55	110
310 Steam Locomotive, 1947, A.F.L. PRR K-5, 4-6-2, L/C	40	68	135
312 Steam Locomotive, 1946-1948, 1952, P.R.R., K-5, 4-6-2, L/C	57	95	190

	C5	C7	C9
312AC Steam Locomotive, 1949-1951, PRR, K-5, 4-6-2, L/C......	55	93	185
313 Steam Locomotive, 1955-1957, PRR, K-5, 4-6-2, K/C	105	175	350
314AW Steam Locomotive, 1949-1950, PRR, K-5, 4-6-2, L/C......	113	188	375
315 Steam Locomotive, 1952, PRR, K-5, 4-6-2, L/C	54	90	180
316 Steam Locomotive, 1953-1954, PRR, K-5, 4-6-2, K/C	78	130	260
320 Steam Locomotive, 1946-1947, New York Central, Hudson, 4-6-4, L/C	60	100	200
321 Steam Locomotive, 1946-1947, New York Central, Hudson, 4-6-4, L/C Tender with, "New York Central System"	75	125	250

Remote-control locomotives featured in the 1953 American Flyer catalog. Top to bottom: No. 293 Steam Locomotive, 4-6-2, $180; No. 343 Stream Locomotive, 0-8-0, $340; No. 316 Steam Locomotive, 4-6-2, $260; No. 326 Steam Locomotive, 4-6-4, No. 336 Steam Locomotive, 4-8-4, $420

Top to bottom: No. 312 Steam Locomotive, $190; No. 322 Steam Locomotive, $170; K335 Steam Locomotive, $465

	C5	C7	C9
322 Steam Locomotive, 1946-1948, New York Central, Hudson, 4-6-4, L/C Tender with, "New York Central System," in oval	51	85	170
322 Steam Locomotive, 1947, New York Central, Hudson, 4-6-4, L/C, "American Flyer Lines" on tender	45	75	150
322AC Steam Locomotive, 1949-1951, New York Central, Hudson, 4-6-4, L/C	39	65	130
324AC Steam Locomotive, 1950, New York Central, Hudson, 4-6-4, L/C	39	65	130
325AC Steam Locomotive, 1951, New York Central, Hudson, 4-6-4, L/C	40	68	135
K325 Steam Locomotive, 1952, New York Central, Hudson, 4-6-4, K/C	68	113	225
326 Steam Locomotive, 1953-1957, New York Central, Hudson, 4-6-4, K/C	78	130	260
332 Steam Locomotive, 1946-1949, Union Pacific, Northern 4-8-4, L/C Tender lettered, "Union Pacific," rare	285	475	950
332 Steam Locomotive, 1946-1949, Union Pacific, Northern, 4-8-4, L/C. "Union Pacific" on shield on tender	117	195	390

	C5	C7	C9
332DC Steam Locomotive, 1950, Union Pacific, Northern, 4-8-4, L/C	180	300	600
332AC Steam Locomotive, 1950-1951, Union Pacific, Northern, 4-8-4, L/C	117	195	390
334DC Steam Locomotive, 1950, Union Pacific, Northern, 4-8-4, L/C	120	200	400
K335 Steam Locomotive, 1952, Union Pacific, Northern, K/C	140	238	465
336 Steam Locomotive, 1953-1957, Union Pacific, Northern, 4-8-4, K/C	126	210	420
342 Steam Locomotive, 1946, nickel plate, switcher, 0-8-0, L/C, tender marked "Nickel Plate Road," rare	450	750	1500
342 Steam Locomotive, 1947-1948, 1952, nickel plate, switcher, 0-8-0, L/C, tender reads "A.F.L. & Nickel Plate Road"	130	218	435
342DC Steam Locomotive, 1948-1950, nickel plate, switcher, 0-8-0, L/C	134	223	445
342AC Steam Locomotive, 1949-1951, nickel plate, switcher, 0-8-0, L/C	129	215	430
343 Steam Locomotive, 1953-1958, nickel plate, switcher, 0-8-0, K/C	102	170	340

	C5	C7	C9
346 Steam Locomotive, 1955, nickel plate, switcher, 0-8-0, K/C............................	192	320	640
350 Steam Locomotive, 1948-1950, B&O, Royal Blue, Pacific, 4-6-2, L/C	40	68	135
353 Steam Locomotive, 1950-1951, American Flyer Circus, Pacific, 4-6-2, L/C	132	220	440
354 Steam Locomotive, 1954, Silver Bullet, Pacific, 4-6-2, K/C............................	120	200	400
355 Switcher, 1957, C&NW, K/C.	48	80	160
356 Steam Locomotive, 1953, Silver Bullet, Pacific, 4-6-2, L/C, chrome	90	150	300
360-361 Alco A&B, 1950-1952, Santa Fe, silver and chrome, L/C, priced as set	90	150	300
360-364 Alco A&B, 1951-1952, Santa Fe, silver finish, L/C, priced as set	85	143	285
370 GP-7, G.M.-A.F. Road Switcher, 1950-1953, Coupler Bar, K/C, L/C.....................	55	93	185
371 GP-7, G.M.-A.F. Road Switcher, 1954, K/C	45	75	150
372 GP-7, 1955-1957, Union Pacific, road switcher, K/C, marked "Built by Gilbert" on side............................	83	138	275

	C5	C7	C9
372 GP-7, 1955-1957, Union Pacific, road switcher, K/C, marked "Made by American Flyer" on side........................	75	125	250
375 GP-7, 1953, GM, A.F., road switcher, K/C, rare	180	300	600
374-375 GP-7, 1955, Texas & Pacific, road switcher, K/C, priced as set..............................	132	220	440
377-78 GP-7, 1956-1957, Texas & Pacific, road switcher, K/C, priced as set..............................	147	245	490
405 Alco A, 1952, Silver Streak, L/C	75	125	250
460 A.F. Bulb Assortment, boxed set of fifty-four	40	60	80
466 Alco A, 1953-1955, Silver Comet, K/C	68	112	225
472 Alco A, 1956, Santa Fe, K/C ..	87	145	290
470-471-473 Alco A-B-A, 1953-1957, Santa Fe, K/C, priced as set	147	245	490
474-475 Alco A-A, 1953-1955, Silver Rocket, K/C	117	195	390
477-478 Alco A-B, 1953-1954, Silver Flash, K/C.....................	150	250	500
479 Alco A, 1955, Silver Flash, K/C...	83	138	275
480 Alco B, 1955, Silver Flash, K/C...	240	400	800

Top to bottom: No. 370 GP-7, $185; No. 355 Baldwin Switcher, $160; No. 21206-21206-1 F-9 Santa Fe, $385

	C5	C7	C9
481 Alco A, 1956, Silver Flash, K/C	90	150	300
484-485-486 Alco A-B-A, 1956-1957, Santa Fe, K/C, priced as set	255	428	855
490-492 Alco A, A, 1956-1957, Northern Pacific, K/C, priced as set	162	270	540
490-491-493 Alco A-B-A, 1956-1957, Northern Pacific, K/C, priced as set, rare	420	700	1400
494-495 Alco A.A., 1956, New Haven, K/C, priced as set	204	340	680
497 Alco A, 1957, New Haven, w/Pantographs, K/C	153	255	510
500 Combine Car, 1952, AFL, chrome finish, L/C	60	100	200

	C5	C7	C9
500 Combine Car, 1952, AFL, silver finish, L/C	105	175	350
501 Coach Car, 1952, AFL, silver finish, L/C	105	175	350
502 Vista Dome, 1952, AFL, chrome finish, L/C	114	190	380
502 Vista Dome, 1952, AFL, silver finish, L/C	135	225	450
503 Observation Car, 1952, AFL, silver finish, L/C	135	225	450
520 Knuckle Coupler Kit, 1954-1956	8	11	15
561 Diesel Billboard Santa Fe Alcos, 1955-1956	16	27	54
566 Whistling Billboard, Santa Fe Alco or Steam Engine picture on billboard	24	36	48

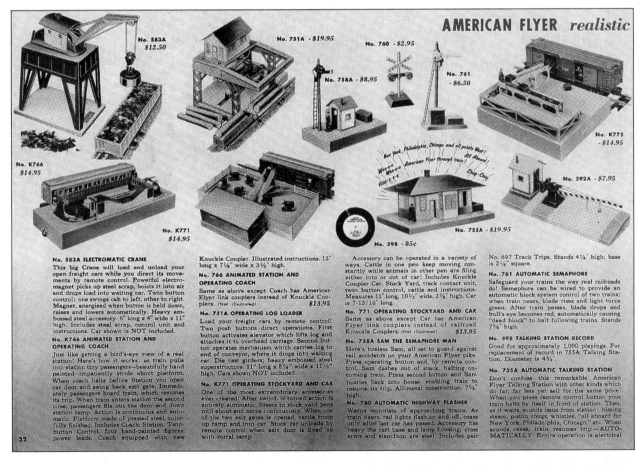

Accessories available from American Flyer. Top row, left to right: No. 583A, No. 751A, No. 758A, No. 760, No. 761, No. K775; Bottom row, left to right: No. K771, No. 598, No. 754A, No. 592A. Courtesy 1953 American Flyer Catalog.

	C5	C7	C9
568 Whistling Billboard, 1956	33	48	65
571 Truss Girder Bridge, 1955-1956	15	22	30
577 Whistling Billboard, 1946-1950, "Ringling Bros. & Barnum & Bailey"	37	56	75
577NL Whistling Billboard, 1950, "Ringling Bros. & Barnum & Bailey"	37	56	75
578 Station Figure Set, w/box	96	160	320
579 Single Street Lamp, 1946-1949	6	11	21
580 Double Street Lamp, 1946-1949	21	35	70
581 Girder Bridge, 1946-1956, marked "Lackawanna" or "American Flyer"	28	42	56

	C5	C7	C9
582 Automatic Blinker Signal, 1946-1948	30	45	60
583 Electro Magnetic Crane, 1946-1949, single button control	62	103	205
583A Electro Magnetic Crane, 1950-1953, double button control	75	125	250
584 Bell Danger Signal, 1946-1947..	75	112	150
585 Tool Shed, 1946-1952	55	83	110
586F Wayside Station, 1946-1956	55	83	110
587 Block Signal, 1946-1947	30	45	60
588 Semaphore Signal, 1946-1948	175	263	350
589 Passenger & Freight Station, 1946-1956, illuminated	37	56	75

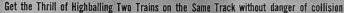

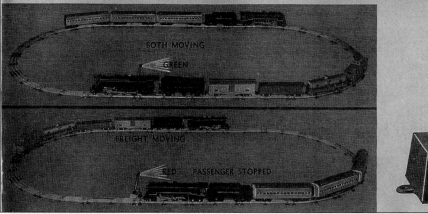

American Flyer's 1941 catalog advised train enthusiasts to make 'safety first' the watchword of their train lay-out. The No. 587 Block Signal and the No. 588 Semaphore Signal would help them reach their safety goal.

	C5	C7	C9
590 Control Tower, 1955-1956, illuminated, manufactured by Bachman for A.C. Gilbert.........	80	120	160
591 Crossing Gate, 1946-1948, single arm	50	75	100
592 Crossing Gate, double arm	50	75	100
592A Crossing Gate, 1951-1953, double arm	35	52	70
593 Signal Tower, 1946-1954, illuminated	60	90	120
594 Animated Track Gang Set, 1946-1947, rare........................	900	1350	1800
596 Water Tank, 1946-1956..........	42	63	85
598 Talking Station Record, 1946-1956, replacement.....................	32	48	65
599 Talking Station Record, 1956, replacement.............................	32	48	65
600 Crossing Gate, 1954-1956, w/Bell.......................................	37	56	75
605 Flat Car, 1953, AFL, w/log load, L/C	11	18	35
606 Crane Car, 1953, AFL, L/C....	14	23	45
607 Work Caboose, 1953, AFL, L/C..	15	25	50
609 Flat Car, 1953, AFL, w/girder load, L/C	15	25	50
612 Freight & Passenger Station, 1946-1954, w/crane, illuminated...............................	80	120	160
613 Box Car, 1953, Great Northern, brown, L/C, K/C.......	15	25	50
620 Gondola, 1953, Southern, black, L/C	8	13	25
622 Box Car, 1953, GAEX, L/C ...	12	20	40
623 Reefer, 1953, Illinois Central, orange, L/C	9	15	30
625G Tank Car, 1952-1953, Gulf, silver, L/C	7	12	23
627 Flat Car, 1947-1950, C&NW, w/girder load, L/C....................	21	35	70
627 Flat Car, 1950, AFL, w/girder load, L/C	20	33	65
628 Flat Car, 1946-1953, C&NW, w/log load, L/C, K/C	10	16	32

	C5	C7	C9
629 Stock Car, 1943-1953, Missouri Pacific, red, L/C.........	8	14	28
630 Caboose, 1946-1953, AFL, red, L/C, K/C..............................	6	10	20
630 Caboose, 1946-1953, Reading, red, L/C, K/C	5	8	15
631 Gondola, 1946-1953, Texas & Pacific, L/C	4	6	12
632 Hopper, 1946-1949, Virginian, L/C......................	25	43	85
632 Hopper, 1946-1953, Lehigh-New England, gray, L/C	8	13	26
633 Box Car, 1948-1953, B&O, three color variations on sides: white, red, brown, L/C	6	10	20
633 Reefer, 1948-1953, B&O, two color variations: red or brown, L/C	8	13	25
634 Floodlight, 1946-1949, 1953, C&NW, AFL, L/C, K/C	13	22	43
635 Crane Car, 1946-1949, C&NWRY, L/C	15	25	50
635 Crane Car, 1946-1949, C&NWRY, L/C	15	25	50
636 Flat Car, 1948-1953, depressed center, w/spool load, L/C	13	22	43
637 Box Car, 1949-1953, MKT, yellow, L/C	10	17	34
638 Caboose, 1949-1953, AFL, AF, red, L/C, K/C	4	6	12
639 Box Car, 1949-1952, A.F., brown or yellow, L/C...............	12	20	40
639 Reefer, 1951-1952, A.F., yellow, L/C	12	20	40
640 Hopper, 1949-1953, A.F., gray, L/C	5	8	15
640 Hopper, 1953, Wabash, black, L/C	15	25	50
641 Gondola, 1949-1951, A.F., red or green, L/C	5	8	16
641 Gondola, 1953, Frisco, brown, L/C	8	13	25
642 Box Car, 1950-1952, A.F., brown or red, L/C....................	8	13	25

	C5	C7	C9
642 Box Car, 1953, seaboard, light brown, L/C	7	12	24
642 Reefer, 1952, A.F., brown or red, L/C	8	14	28
643 Flat Car, 1950-1953, A.F. Circus, w/circus load, L/C	67	112	225
644 Crane Car, 1950-1953, Industrial Brown hoist A.F., L/C	35	58	115
645 Work Caboose, 1950-1951, A.F., L/C	16	26	52
645A Work Caboose, 1951-1953, AFL, L/C	17	28	55
646 Floodlight, 1950-1953, Erie, depressed center, L/C	17	28	55
647 Reefer, 1952-1953, Northern Pacific, orange side, L/C	18	30	60
648 Track Cleaning Car, 1952-1954, A.F., depressed center, L/C, K/C	14	23	45
649 Coach Car Circus, 1950-1952, yellow, L/C	54	90	180
650 Coach Car, 1946-1952, New Haven, green or red, L/C	17	28	55
651 Baggage, 1946-1952, New Haven, green or red, L/C	19	32	63
651 Baggage, 1953, AFL, green or red, L/C	25	43	85
652 Pullman, 1946-1953, green or red, L/C	31	53	109
653 Combine Car, 1946-1953, green or red, L/C	45	75	150
654 Observation Car Car, 1946-1952, green or red, L/C	54	90	180
655 Coach Car, 1953, Silver Bullet, silver or chrome, L/C	25	43	85
655 Coach Car, 1953, AFL, green or red, L/C	23	38	75
660 Combine Car, 1950-1952, AFL, aluminum or chrome, L/C	18	30	60
661 Coach Car, 1950-1952, AFL, aluminum or chrome	20	34	68
662 Vista-Dome, 1950-1952, AFL, aluminum or chrome, L/C	21	35	70

	C5	C7	C9
663 Observation Car Car, 1950-1952, AFL, aluminum or chrome, L/C	19	32	64
668 Manual Switch, left, non-illuminated	8	12	16
669 Manual Switch, right, non-illuminated	8	12	16
690 Track Terminal, 1946-1956	—	—	1
691 Track Pins, 1946-1948, twelve per pack	—	—	1
692 Fiber Track Pin, 1946-1948, four per pack	—	—	1
693 Track Lock, twenty-six per pack	—	1	2
694 Automatic Coupler Truck Unit, 1946-1953	8	11	15
700 Straight Track	—	—	1
701 Straight Track, half section	—	—	1
702 Curve Track	—	—	1
703 Curve Track, half section	—	—	1
704 Manual Uncoupler	1	2	2
705 Remote Uncoupler, 1946-1947	2	2	3
706 Remote Uncoupler, 1948-1956	4	6	8
707 Track Terminal	—	—	1
708 Diesel Whistle Control	3	5	6
709 Lockout Eliminator, 1950-1956	3	4	5
710 Steam Whistle Control	10	15	20
711 Mail Pick-ups, used w/718-719 mail cars	5	8	10
713 Mail Hook, 1953-1955, includes track terminal	5	8	10
714 Log Unloading Car, 1951-1954, A.F., w/log load, L/C	23	38	75
715 Auto Unloading Car, 1946-1954, AFL, w/car load, L/C, K/C	30	50	100
716 Operating Hopper, 1946-1951, AFL, L/C	20	33	65
717 Log Unloading Car, 1946-1952, AFL, w/log load, L/C	23	38	75

	C5	C7	C9
718 Mail Pickup, 1946-1954, AFL/New Haven, red or green, L/C	25	43	85
719 Coal Dump Car, 1950-1954, CB&Q, maroon, L/C	30	50	100
720/720A Remote Control Switches, left and right, w/controls, pair	20	30	40
722/722A Manual Control Switches, left and right, pair	12	18	25
726 Rubber Road Bed, black or gray, straight	1	2	2
727 Rubber Road Bed, black or gray, curve	1	2	2
728 Rerailer, 1956	7	11	15
730 Bumper, 1946, green	7	11	15
730 Bumper, 1946, red	50	75	100
731 Pike Planning Kit, 1952-1956	15	23	30

	C5	C7	C9
732 Operating Baggage Car, 1950-1954, AFL, green or red, L/C, K/C	27	45	90
734 Operating Box Car, 1950-1954, AF, brown/red, L/C	25	43	85
735 Animated Coach Car, 1952-1954, AFL-New Haven, red, L/C, K/C	24	40	80
736 Operating Cattle Car, 1950-1954, Missouri Pacific, L/C	15	25	50
740 Hand Car, 1952-1954, AFL	29	48	95
742 Hand Car, 1955-1956, AFL, reversing mechanism	40	68	135
748 Overhead Footbridge, 1951-1952, gray and silver	35	52	70
749 Street Lamp Set, 1950-1952, plastic, set of three	17	26	35
750 Trestle Bridge, black, silver and metallic blue	42	63	85

Various types of track available from the 1953 American Flyer catalog. Today, pieces of track runs in the $1-$2 range.

	C5	C7	C9
751/751A Log Loader, 1946-1950	60	100	200
752 Seaboard Coaler, 1946-1950 ..	102	170	340
752A Seaboard Coaler, 1951-1952	108	180	360
753 Trestle Bridge with Beacon, 1952	72	120	240
754 Double Trestle Bridge, 1950-1952	118	117	235
755 Talking Station, 1948-1958, illuminated	72	120	240
758 Sam the Semaphore Man, 1949-1950	33	55	110
758A Sam the Semaphore Man, 1950-1956	35	58	115
759 Bell Danger Signal, 1953-1956	35	52	70
760 Automatic Highway Flasher, 1949-1956	23	35	45
761 Semaphore, 1949-1956, two track trips	22	36	72
762 Billboard, 1949-1950, two-in-one whistle, two-button control	30	50	100
763 Mountain Set, 1949-1950, three pieces	160	240	320
764 Express Office, 1950-1951, illuminated	105	158	210
766 Animated Station, 1952-1954, w/four plastic passengers and 735 Pullman	105	158	210

	C5	C7	C9
K766 Animated Station, 1953-1955	105	158	210
767 Roadside Diner, Branford Diner, 1950-1954, illuminated ..	50	75	100
768 Oil Supply Depot, 1950-1953, Gulf	58	87	115
768 Oil Supply Depot, 1950-1953, Shell	45	68	90
769/769A Revolving Aircraft Beacon, 1951-1956	28	42	55
770 Baggage Loading Platform, 1950-1952	85	128	170
771 Operating Stockyard Set, 1950-1954, includes eight black and white rubber cattle w/brush bases, 736 Cattle Car	58	87	115
K771 Operating Stockyard Set, 1950-1954, includes eight black and white rubber cattle w/brush bases, 976 Cattle Car w/knuckle couplers	65	98	130
772 Water Tower, 1950-1956, plain tank	50	75	100
772 Water Tower, 1950-1956, checkerboard design on tank	60	90	120
773 Oil Derrick, 1950-1952, gray tower w/red base, Colber	83	125	165
773 Oil Derrick, 1950-1952, gray tower w/gray base or red tower w/red base	125	188	250

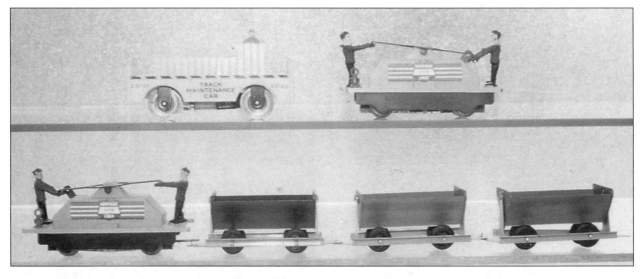

Top row, left to right: No. 23743 Track Maintenance car, $90; No. 740 Hand car, $95; Bottom row, right to left: No. 740 Hand car and three Tipple cars

New accessories in 1953 included the No. 740 Hand car, No. 741 Hand car and shed, No. 759 Bell Danger Beacon, No. 772 Automatic Water Tower, No. 769A and the No. 774 Floodlight Tower. Courtesy 1953 American Flyer Catalog.

	C5	C7	C9
774 Floodlight Tower, 1951-1956, illuminated	75	112	150
775/K775 Baggage Loading Platform, 1953-1956	63	95	125
778 Street Lamp Set, 1953-1956, plain, mailbox and firebox, set of three	100	150	200
779 Oil Drum Loader, 1955-1956, w/eight oil barrels	80	120	160
780 Railroad Trestle Set, 1953-1956, plastic, twenty-four pieces	10	15	20
781 Railroad Abutment Set, 1953	30	45	60
782 Railroad Abutment Set, 1953	30	45	60
783 Hi-Trestle Sections, 1954-1956	21	32	42
784 Railroad Hump Set, 1955, rare	150	250	500

	C5	C7	C9
785 Operating Coal Loader, 1955-1956	100	150	200
787 Log Loader, 1955-1956	125	188	250
788 Suburban Station, 1956, illuminated	37	56	75
789 Station and Baggage-Smasher, 1956, illuminated	138	207	275
792 Railroad Terminal, 1954-1956	130	195	260
793 Union Station, 1955-1956, illuminated	55	82	110
794 Union Station, illuminated, includes firebox, mailbox and lampposts	75	112	150
795 Union Station and Terminal, 1954	163	245	325
799 Automatic Talking Station, 1954-1956	75	112	150

railroad accessories

No. 593 $5.95 · No. 566 $6.95 · No. 581 - $1.95 · No. 586F $3.95 · No. 778 - $3.00 · No. 750 $4.00 · No. 50 $2.95 · No. 596 $5.95 · No. 589 - $6.95 · No. 612 - $7.95 · No. 767 $5.00 · No. 768 - $3.95

—no flashlight batteries required. Measures 6" x 12" x 8".

No. K775 BAGGAGE LOADING PLATFORM AND CAR
Here's a thrilling accessory that's all set to handle your rush rail shipments with ease—and all at the touch of a button. Die cast Packing Boxes are placed on loading ramp. Each time control button is pressed, a box is fed singly to trainman who lowers chute extension and sends the miniature crate into the Knuckle Coupler Box Car. Beautifully finished in realistic colors. Measures 7" long x 8½" wide x 3¾" high.

No. 775 BAGGAGE LOADING PLATFORM AND CAR *(Not illustrated)*
Same as above except that Car has American Flyer link couplers instead of new Knuckle type. *$13.95*

No. 592A CROSSING GATE
A necessity for all highway crossings on your model pike! Completely automatic in action. When train approaches gate lowers and red light goes on. After last car passes gate rises and light is extinguished. Includes No. 697 Track Trip. Measures 8⅞" long x 2⅞" wide.

No. 593 SIGNAL TOWER
The nerve center of every train yard: the busy two-story Signal Tower where trains are routed on the maze of track that services big cities. Your American Flyer layout should have at least one of these authentically-scaled accessories. Has interior lighting, colorful enamel finish. Measures 7⅝" high x 5½" square.

No. 596 OPERATING WATER TANK
Set up this realistic accessory in your yards for colorful railroad action. Press remote control button and spout lowers over tender; release button and spout snaps back to vertical position. Aircraft warning light and direction arrows on roof. Supports are simulated concrete piling. 6" x 6½" x 11".

No. 581 GIRDER BRIDGE
Heavy die-cast bridge patterned after real railroad type. Slips under any straight track section. Can be used singly or in multiple. Measures 10" x 1¾" x 4⅝".

No. 566 WHISTLING BILLBOARD
Just the ticket for your non-whistling locomotives. Sound true-to-life long blasts and short toots by remote control. Mechanism concealed in housing. 4" x 7½" x 4".

No. 589 PASSENGER AND FREIGHT STATION
Modeled after the combination stations seen in rural areas and way stops. Baggage door slides open and shut; waiting room door swings on hinges. Realistic windows finished in bright trim. Station fully illuminated. Measures 12" long x 8" wide x 6" high.

No. 586F WAYSIDE STATION
Just like the stations seen along suburban and commuter rail lines. Brightly finished in red, green and yellow. Heavy steel base; die cast supporting girders. Wealth of detail throughout. Twin bulbs cascade light from underside of roof. Includes redcap and baggage operator with truck. 12" long x 3¾" wide x 5" high.

No. 778 STREET LAMP SET
Dress up your model pike with these realistic street lamps. One has mail box, another a fire alarm box. Create striking night scenes; just the thing for roads, boulevards, parkways, etc. Set of three. 5½" high.

No. 612 FREIGHT AND PASSENGER STATION
With the freight crane included with this station you can unload Gondola and Box Car right at railside! Boom raises and lowers; cab makes full swing. Station is illuminated. 19" x 8" x 5¼".

No. 50 DISTRICT SCHOOL
No rural scene is complete without an old fashioned little red schoolhouse. And here it is, with its familiar recess bell and multi-paned windows. Measures 6⅞" long x 5¼" wide x 5" high.

No. 750 TRESTLE BRIDGE
Heavy, rolled-steel bridge designed to span rivers and gorges on your model railroad. Bridge Tender's house is illuminated inside. 17¾" x 8¼" x 4¼".

No. 767 ROADSIDE DINER
No busy rail center is complete unless it has at least one of these familiar "bean wagons" where off-duty trainmen can gather. This colorful yellow and red accessory is fully illuminated and has inset windows and hinged doors. TV antenna adds up-to-date touch! 12" long x 3¼" wide x 5¼" high.

No. 768 OIL SUPPLY DEPOT
An oil storage center suitable for your big rail terminals. Two scale model tanks, complete with feed lines and hose, mount on heavy metal base. Pump house also made of metal. Tanks have authentic GULF markings. Measures 12" x 4½" x 3".

33

Realistic accessories from American Flyer in 1953. Top row, left to right: No. 593, No. 566, No. 581, No. 586F, No. 778, No. 750, No. 50; Bottom row: No. 596; No. 589; No. 612; No. 767; No. 768. Courtesy 1953 American Flyer Catalog.

	C5	C7	C9
801 Hopper, 1956-1957, B&O, black, K/C	14	23	45
802 Reefer, 1956-1957, Illinois Central, orange, K/C	8	13	25
803 Box Car, 1956, Santa Fe, K/C	10	16	32
804 Gondola, 1956-1957, Norfolk & Western, black, K/C	5	9	17
805 Gondola, 1956-1957, Pennsylvania, K/C	6	10	20
806 Caboose, 1956, AFL, red, K/C, P/M	4	7	14
807 Box Car, 1957, Rio Grande, white, K/C	12	20	40
900 Combine Car, 1956, Northern Pacific, green, L/C, K/C	120	200	400
901 Coach Car, 1956, Northern Pacific, green, L/C, K/C	75	125	250
902 Vista Dome, 1956, Northern Pacific, green, L/C, K/C	75	125	250
903 Observation Car Car, 1956, Northern Pacific, green, L/C, K/C	120	200	400
904 Caboose, 1956, AFL, red, K/C	5	9	18
905 Flat Car, 1954, AFL, log load, K/C	11	19	38
906 Crane Car, 1954, AFL, K/C	14	23	45
907 Work Caboose, 1954, AFL, K/C	7	11	22
909 Flat Car, 1954, AFL, w/girder load, K/C	12	20	40

	C5	C7	C9
910 Tank Car, 1954, Gilbert Chemical, green, K/C	105	175	350
911 Gondola, 1955-1957, C&O, black, K/C, w/pipe load	11	16	36
912 Tank Car, 1955-1956, Koppers, black, K/C	23	38	75

No. 912, Tank car, $75

	C5	C7	C9
913 Box Car, 1953-1958, Great Northern, K/C	13	22	44
914 Log Unloading Car, 1953-1957, AFL, w/log load, K/C	25	43	85
915 Auto Unloading Car, 1953-1957, AFL, w/car load, K/C	27	45	90
916 Gondola, 1955-1957, D&H, K/C, w/cannister load	11	18	35
918 Mail Pick-Up, 1953-1956, AFL/New Haven, red, K/C	33	55	110
919 Coal Dump Car, 1953-1957, CB&Q, K/C	30	50	100
920 Gondola, 1953-1957, Southern, black, K/C	8	14	28

Remote control action cars from 1953. Top row, left to right: No. 914 Log Unloading car, $90; No. 918 Mail Pick-up car, $110. Middle row, left to right: No. 919 Coal Dump car, $100; No. 915 Auto Unloading car, $85. Bottom row: No. 732 Operating Baggage car, $90; Operating Boxcar, $110-150. Courtesy 1953 American Flyer Catalog.

	C5	C7	C9
921 Hopper, 1953-1957, CB&Q, w/coal load, K/C	9	15	30
922 Box Car, 1953-1956, GAEX, green, K/C	10	17	33
923 Reefer, 1954-1955, Illinois Central, orange, K/C	8	14	27
924 Hopper, 1953-1957, Jersey Central, w/coal load, gray, K/C	8	13	25
925 Tank Car, 1953-1956, Gulf, silver, K/C	8	13	26
926 Tank Car, 1955-1956, Gulf, silver, K/C	17	28	55
928 Flat Car, 1954, New Haven, w/log load, K/C	9	15	30
928 Flat Car, 1956-1957, C&NNRY, w/log load, K/C	11	18	35

	C5	C7	C9
928 Flat Car, 1956-1957, New Haven, w/lumber load, K/C	11	19	37
929 Stock Car, 1952-1956, Missouri Pacific, red, K/C	9	15	30
930 Caboose, 1952, AF, red, L/C	8	14	28
930 Caboose, 1953-1957, AFL, red/brown, K/C	9	15	30
931 Gondola, 1952-1955, Texas & Pacific, green, K/C	5	9	18
933 Box Car, 1953-1954, Baltimore & Ohio, white sides, K/C	14	23	45
934 Caboose, 1955, AFL, red, K/C	21	35	70
934 Floodlight, 1953-1954, C&NW, K/C	20	33	65

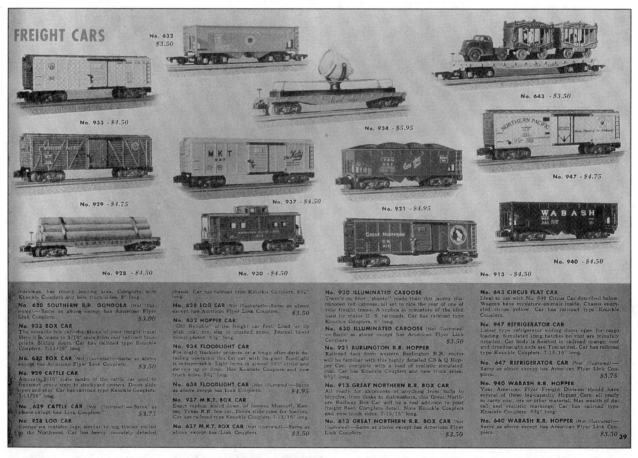

Freight cars from 1953. Top row, left to right: No. 933 Boxcar, $45; No. 632 Hopper, $60-$85; No. 934 Floodlight, $65; No. 643 Flatcar, $225. Middle row, left to right: No. 929 Stock car, $30; No. 937 Boxcar, $35; No. 921 Hopper, $30; No. 947 Reefer, $46. Bottom row: No. 928 Flatcar, $35-$50; No. 930 Caboose, $30; No. 913 Boxcar, $44; No. 940 Hopper, $15. Courtesy 1953 American Flyer Catalog.

	C5	C7	C9
934 Floodlight, 1954-1955, Southern Pacific, K/C	20	33	65
935 Caboose, 1957, AFL, Bay Window, brown, K/C	36	60	120
936 Flat Car, 1953-1954, Pennsylvania, depressed center, spool load, K/C	54	70	140

No. 936 Flat car, $75

	C5	C7	C9
936 Flat Car, 1953-1954, Erie, depressed center, spool load, K/C	23	38	75
937 Box Car, 1953-1955, MKT, yellow, K/C	11	18	35
938 Caboose, 1954-1955, AFL, red, K/C	5	8	15
940 Hopper, 1953-1957, Wabash, black, K/C	7	11	22
941 Gondola, 1953-1957, Frisco, K/C	5	8	15
942 Box Car, 1954, Seaboard, K/C	12	18	35
944 Crane Car, 1952-1957, Industrial Brownhoist, AF, K/C	17	29	58
945 Work Caboose, 1953-1957, AFL, K/C	11	19	38

Freight cars from 1953. First row, top to bottom: No. 946 Floodlight car $54; No. 948; No. 936 Flat car, $75; No. 941 Gondola, $15. Middle row, top to bottom: No. 924 Hopper, $25; No. 944 Crane car, $58; No. 925 Tank car, $26. Third row, top to bottom: No. 922 Boxcar, $33; No. 945 Work Caboose, $38; No. 931, Gondola, $18; No. 920 Gondola, $28. Courtesy 1953 American Flyer Catalog.

	C5	C7	C9
946 Floodlight, 1953-1954, Erie, depressed center, K/C	16	27	54

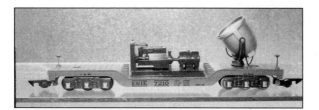

No. 946 Floodlight, $54

	C5	C7	C9
947 Reefer, 1953-1958, Northern Pacific, orange, K/C	14	23	46
951 Baggage, 1953-1956, AFL/Railway Express Agency, green or red, K/C	24	40	80
952 Pullman, 1953-1956, Pikes Peak, green or red, K/C	78	130	260

Top to bottom: No. 952 Pullman, $260; No. 953 Combine car, $175; No. 954 Observation car, $260

	C5	C7	C9
953 Combine Car, 1953-1956, Niagara Falls, green or red, K/C	53	88	175
954 Observation Car, 1953-1956, Grand Canyon, green or red, K/C	54	70	140
955 Coach Car, 1954, AFL, green or red, K/C	39	65	130
955 Coach Car, 1954, Silver Bullet, K/C	21	35	70
956 Flat Car, 1956-1957, Monon, w/piggyback van load, K/C	38	63	125
957 Operating Box Car, 1957, Erie, K/C w/aluminum barrels	29	48	95

	C5	C7	C9
958 Tank Car, 1957, Mobilgas, red, K/C	22	36	72
960 Combine Car, 1953-1957, New Haven, orange stripe	35	58	115
960 Combine Car, 1953-1957, Silver Rocket, green stripe	36	60	120
960 Combine Car, 1953-1957, Silver Flash, brown stripe	47	78	155
960 Combine Car, 1953-1957, AFL, "Columbus," chrome or silver, K/C, without color stripe	30	50	100
960 Combine Car, 1953-1957, Silver Comet, blue stripe	30	50	100
960 Combine Car, 1953-1957, Santa Fe, red stripe	36	60	120
961 Coach Car, 1953-1957, AFL, "Jefferson," chrome or silver, K/C, without color stripe	30	50	100
961 Coach Car, 1953-1957, orange stripe	53	88	175
961 Coach Car, 1953-1957, Red stripe	42	70	140
961 Coach Car, 1953-1957, brown stripe	47	78	155
961 Coach Car, 1953-1957, green stripe	39	65	130
962 Vista-Dome, 1953-1957, red stripe, "Hamilton"	45	75	150
962 Vista-Dome, 1953-1957, green stripe, "Hamilton"	33	55	110
962 Vista-Dome, 1953-1957, blue stripe, "Hamilton"	30	50	100
962 Vista-Dome, 1953-1957, Orange stripe, "Hamilton"	38	63	125
962 Vista-Dome, 1953-1957, chrome or silver, K/C, without color stripe, "Hamilton"	30	50	100
962 Vista-Dome, 1953-1957, brown stripe, "Hamilton"	50	83	165
963 Observation Car, 1953-1957, chrome or silver, K/C, without color stripe, "Washington"	30	50	100
963 Observation Car, 1953-1957, orange stripe, "Washington"	35	58	115
963 Observation Car, 1953-1957, red stripe, "Washington"	42	70	140

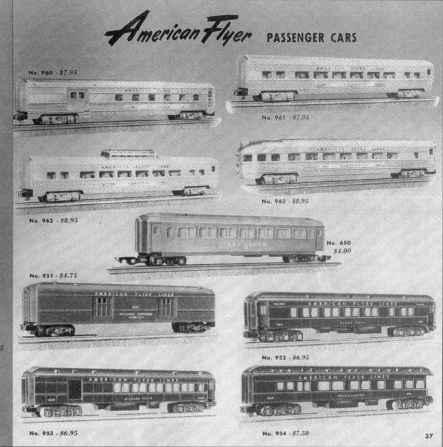

No. 960 BAGGAGE AND CLUB CAR
A real beauty—aluminum finish body and heavy metal chassis features modern, up-to-date styling. Made to resemble the gleaming stainless steel baggage and club cars used by the New York Central, the New York, New Haven & Hartford and other real-life roads. Passengers are silhouetted in windows, interior lighting. Equipped with railroad type Knuckle Couplers. 12½" long.

No. 961 STREAMLINED COACH
Big wide picture windows where your passengers (they're silhouetted inside!) can relax and enjoy the scenery. Bright aluminum finish body, on heavy chassis, resembles stainless steel de luxe coaches. Streamlined sides and top are corrugated. Illuminated inside. Die cast trucks beautifully detailed. Has railroad type Knuckle Couplers. 12½" long.

No. 962 VISTA DOME PULLMAN CAR
Intricately detailed model of the car which has created a sensation on real-life railroads. Observation dome on roof enables passengers to view entire train and countryside. Body has bright aluminum finish with streamlined corrugated sides and top. Heavy chassis; die cast trucks. Silhouetted passengers. Full illumination. 12½" long.

No. 963 STREAMLINED OBSERVATION
Here's the finest, most luxurious lounge car ever made! Built to accurate 3/16" scale, it has the full sweep and length of real observations. "Boat-tail" end gracefully rounded; windows are extra size. Red warning light on rear is illuminated. Fully lighted inside. Silhouetted passengers. Die cast trucks minutely detailed. Has railroad type Knuckle Couplers. 12½" long.

No. 951 BAGGAGE CAR
Patterned after the famous Railway Express Agency cars. Roof detail includes ventilators; chassis rides on double sintered iron trucks. Red or green finish. Equipped with railroad type Knuckle Couplers. 10¾" long.

No. 651 BAGGAGE CAR—Same as above except has Link Couplers. Red or green finish. (Not illustrated) $3.75

No. 952 ILLUMINATED PULLMAN
A real masterpiece of scale modeling! Detail even includes imitation shades in inset windows! Lounge windows are opaque, as on real cars. Fully lighted inside. Accurate 3/16" scale throughout. Double sintered iron trucks. Choice of either red or green finish. 12" long.

No. 652 ILLUMINATED PULLMAN—Same as above except has Link Couplers. Red or green finish. (Not illustrated) $5.95

No. 953 BAGGAGE AND CLUB CAR
Companion car to No. 952 and 954 Observation. Baggage door slides open to receive cargo; door at passenger end is hinged for opening and closing. Has railroad type Knuckle Couplers. Red or green finish. 12" long.

No. 954 OBSERVATION CAR
Railing is brightly finished; steps, double inset windows, hinged open-and-close doors, imitation window shades and other detail make this illuminated car a real buy. Sintered iron trucks. Has railroad type Knuckle Couplers. Red or green finish. 12" long.

American Flyer PASSENGER CARS

No. 960 - $7.95
No. 961 - $7.95
No. 962 - $8.95
No. 963 - $8.95
No. 650 $4.00
No. 951 - $4.75
No. 952 - $6.95
No. 953 - $6.95
No. 954 - $7.50

Passenger cars circa 1953. Top: No. 960 Combine car, $100-150; No. 961 Coach, $100-175; No. 962 Vista-Dome Pullman car, $100-165. Middle: No. 650 Baggage car, $55. Bottom: No. 951 Baggage car, $80; No. 952 Pullman car, $200; No. 953 Combine car, $175; No. 954 Observation car, $140. Courtesy 1953 American Flyer Catalog.

	C5	C7	C9
963 Observation Car, 1953-1957, blue stripe, "Washington"	30	50	100
963 Observation Car, 1953-1957, brown stripe, "Washington"	47	78	155
963 Observation Car, 1953-1957, green stripe, "Washington"	30	50	100
969 Rocket Launcher, 1957-1958, K/C	21	35	70
970 Walking Brakeman Car, 1956-1957, seaboard, K/C	24	40	80
971 Lumber Unloading Car, 1956-1957, Southern Pacific, w/lumber load, K/C	39	65	130
973 Operating Milk Car, 1956, Gilbert, white, K/C, w/plastic cans	54	88	175

No. 973 Operating Milk car, $175

	C5	C7	C9
974 Operating Box Car, 1953-1954, AFL, K/C	33	55	110
974 Operating Box Car, 1955, Erie, K/C	45	75	150
975 Animated Coach Car, 1955, red, K/C	33	55	110
976 Operating Cattle Car, 1953-1960, MP	27	45	90

	C5	C7	C9
977 Caboose, 1955-1958, AFL, brown, K/C, w/moving brakeman	18	30	60

No. 977 Caboose, $60

	C5	C7	C9
978 Observation Car Action Car, 1956-1958, Grand Canyon, K/C	121	219	438
979 Caboose, 1957, bay window, brown, K/C, w/moving brakeman	28	46	92
980 Box Car, 1956-1957, B&O, blue, K/C	37	61	122
981 Box Car, 1956, Central of Georgia, black, K/C	34	58	115
982 Box Car, 1956-1957, State of Maine, red, white and blue, K/C	39	65	130
983 Box Car, 1956, Missouri Pacific, blue-gray, K/C	44	73	145
984 Box Car, 1956-1957, New Haven, orange, K/C	30	50	100
985 Box Car, 1957, Boston & Maine, blue, K/C	40	68	135
988 Reefer, 1956-1957, ART, orange, K/C	31	53	105
989 Reefer, 1956-1958, C&NW, K/C	75	125	250
994 Stock Car, 1957, Union Pacific, yellow, K/C	54	85	170
C2001 Box Car, 1962, Post, white, K/C	53	88	175
C2001 Box Car, 1962, Post, white, P/M	25	43	85
L2001 Steam Locomotive, 1963, Casey Jones, 4-4-0	15	25	50
L2002 Steam Locomotive, 1963, Erie, 4-4-0	90	150	300
L2002 Steam Locomotive, 1963, Burlington Route, 4-4-0	114	190	380

	C5	C7	C9
L2004 F-9, Rio Grande, 1962, K/C	98	163	325
C2009 Gondola, 1962-1964, Texas & Pacific, light green, P/M	5	8	16
21004 Steam Locomotive, 1957, P.R.R., switcher, 0-6-0, K/C	99	165	330

No. 21004 Steam Locomotive, $330

	C5	C7	C9
21005 Steam Locomotive, 1958, P.R.R., switcher, 0-6-0, K/C	108	180	360
21084 Steam Locomotive, 1957, C&NW, Pacific, 4-6-2, K/C	54	90	180
21085 Steam Locomotive, 1962-1963, 1965, C&NW or CMSP&P Pacific, 4-6-2, K/C, P/M	28	46	92
21089 Steam Locomotive, 1960-1961, FY&PRR, Washington, 4-4-0, K/C	150	250	500
21095 Steam Locomotive, 1958, New Haven, Pacific, 4-6-2, K/C, rare	375	625	1250
21099 Steam Locomotive, 1958, New Haven, Pacific, 4-6-2, K/C	90	150	300
21100 Steam Locomotive, 1957, Reading, Atlantic, 4-4-2, K/C	12	20	40
21105 Steam Locomotive, 1957-1960, Reading, Atlantic, 4-4-2, K/C	12	20	40
21106 Steam Locomotive, 1959, Reading, Atlantic, 4-4-2, K/C	36	60	120
21107 Steam Locomotive, 1964-1966, PRR, Atlantic, 4-4-2, K/C	15	25	50
21107 Steam Locomotive, 1965, Burlington, Atlantic, 4-4-2, K/C	15	25	50
21115 Steam Locomotive, 1958, PRR, K-5, 4-6-2, K/C	285	475	950
21129 Steam Locomotive, 1958, New York Central, Hudson, 4-6-4, K/C	240	400	800

	C5	C7	C9
21130 Steam Locomotive, 1959-1960, 1962-1963, New York Central, Hudson, K/C	90	150	300
21139 Steam Locomotive, 1958, Union Pacific, Northern, 4-8-4, K/C	285	475	950
21140 Steam Locomotive, 1959-1960, Union Pacific, Northern, 4-8-4, K/C	503	838	1675
21145 Steam Locomotive, 1958, "Nickel Plate Road," switcher, 0-8-0, K/C	218	363	725
21155 Steam Locomotive, 1958, docksider switcher, 0-6-0, K/C.	105	175	350
21156 Steam Locomotive, 1959, docksider switcher, 0-6-0, K/C.	90	150	300
21158 Steam Locomotive, 1960, docksider switcher, 0-6-0, K/C.	54	70	140
21160 Steam Locomotive, 1960, Reading, Atlantic, 4-4-2, K/C	11	18	35
21161 Steam Locomotive, 1960, Reading, Atlantic, 4-4-2, K/C	11	18	35
21161 Steam Locomotive, 1960, Reading, Atlantic, 4-4-2, K/C, "Prestone Car Care Express"	105	175	350
21165 Steam Locomotive, 1961-1965, Erie, Casey Jones, 4-4-0, K/C	8	13	26
21166 Steam Locomotive, 1963-1964, Burlington, Casey Jones, 4-4-0, P/M	8	13	26
21168 Steam Locomotive, 1961-1963, Southern, Casey Jones, 4-4-0, P/M	27	45	90
21205-21205-1 F-9, Boston & Maine, 1961, K/C, priced as set	115	193	385
21206-21206-1 F-9, Santa Fe, 1962, K/C, priced as set	115	193	385
21207-21207-1 F-9, Great Northern, 1963-1964, K/C, priced as set	115	193	385
21210 F-9, Burlington, 1961, K/C	80	133	265
21215, 21215-1 F-9, Union Pacifc, 1961-1962, K/C, priced as set	90	150	300
21551 Alco A, 1958, Northern Pacific, K/C	120	200	400

	C5	C7	C9
21561 Alco A, 1958, New Haven, K/C	114	190	380
21573 G.E. Electric, 1958-1959, New Haven, w/Pantographs, K/C	165	275	550
21720 Alco B, 1958, Santa Fe, K/C, rare	270	450	900
21801 Switcher, 1958, C&NW, K/C	45	75	150
21801-1 Switcher, 1958, C&NW, K/C, Dummy Unit	45	75	150
21808 Switcher, 1958, C&NW, K/C	54	90	180
21813 Switcher, 1958, M&SL, K/C	165	275	550
21831 GP-7, 1958, AFL, K/C	150	250	500
21831 GP-7, Texas & Pacific, 1958, K/C	165	275	550
21902, 21902-1, 21902-2 Alco A-B-A, 1958, Santa Fe, K/C, priced as set	300	500	1000
21910, 21910-1, 21910-2 Alco A-B-A, 1957-1958, Santa Fe, K/C, priced as set	210	350	700
21918, 21918-1 Switcher, 1958, seaboard, K/C, priced as set	270	450	900
21920, 21920-1 Alco A-A, 1958, Missouri Pacific, K/C, double motor in 21920, priced as set, rare	300	500	1000
21920, 21920-1 Alco A-A, 1963-1964, Missouri Pacific, K/C, single motor in 21920, priced as set	255	425	850
21922, 21922-1 Alco A-A, 1959-1960, Missouri Pacific, K/C, priced as set	195	325	650
21925/21925-1 Alco A-A, 1959-1960, Union Pacific, K/C, rare	270	450	900
21927 Alco A, 1960-1962, Santa Fe, K/C	83	138	275
22020 Transformer, 1957-1964, 50 watt	4	6	8
22030 Transformer, 1957-1964, 100 watt	8	12	16
22035 Transformer, 1957-1964, 175 watt	38	52	75

	C5	C7	C9
22040 Transformer, 1957-1958, 110 watt	11	16	22
22050 Transformer, 1957-1958, 175 watt	35	52	70
22060 Transformer, 1957-1958, 175 watt, dual controls	40	60	80
22080 Transformer, 1957-1958, 300 watt, dual controls	45	67	90
22090 Transformer, 1959-1964, 350 watt, dual controls	75	112	150
23021 Imitation Grass, 1957-1960, half pound	—	—	30
23022 Scenery Gravel, 1956-1960, 22 ounces	—	—	30
23023 Artificial Coal, 1957-1960, half pound	—	—	30
23024 Multicolor Wire, 1957-1964, 25 feet	—	—	30
23025 Smoke Fluid Cartridges, 1957-1960, box of twelve	—	—	15
23026 Service Kit, 1957-1964	15	22	30
23027 Track Cleaning Fluid, 1957-1959, 8 ounces	—	—	9
23032 Railroad Equipment Kit, 1960	90	150	300
23249 Tunnel, 1957-1964, 11-1/2"	11	18	35
23561 Billboard Horn	18	30	60
23568 Whistling Billboard, 1957-1964	18	30	60
23571 Truss Girder Bridge, 1957-1964	24	40	80
23581 Girder Bridge, 1957-1964, marked "American Flyer"	10	15	20
23586 Wayside Station, 1956-1959	35	52	70
23589 Passenger and Freight Station, 1957-1959, illuminated	40	60	80
23590 Control Tower, 1957-1959, illuminated	45	68	90
23596 Water Tank, 1957-1958	50	75	100
23598 Talking Station Record, 1957-1959	30	45	60
23599 Talking Station Record, 1957	35	52	70

	C5	C7	C9
23600 Crossing Gate with Bell, 1957-1962	30	45	60
23743 Track Maintenance Car	27	45	90
23750 Trestle Bridge	42	63	85
23758 Sam the Semaphore Man, 1957	33	55	110
23759 Bell Danger Signal, 1957-1960	18	30	60
23760 Automatic Highway Flasher, 1957-1960	24	40	80
23761 Semaphore, 1957-1964, two track trips	34	51	68
23769 Revolving Aircraft Beacon, 1957-1964	55	83	110
23771 Operating Stockyard Set, 1957-1961	54	70	140
23772 Water Tower, 1957-1964, checkerboard design on tank	39	65	130
23772 Water Tower, 1957-1964, plain tank	20	33	65
23774 Floodlight Tower, 1957-1964, illuminated	18	30	60
23778 Streetlamp Set, 1957-1964	12	20	40
23779 Oil Drum Loader, 1958-1961, eight oil barrels	29	48	95
23780 Gabe the Lamplighter, 1958-1959	285	475	950
23785 Operating Coal Loader, 1957-1960	63	105	210
23786 Talking Station, 1957-1959	100	150	200
23787 Log Loader, 1957-1960	36	60	120
23788 Suburban Station, 1958, illuminated	25	38	50
23789 Station and Baggage-Smasher, 1958-1959, illuminated	175	263	350
23791 Cow-On-Track, 1957-1959	24	40	80
23796 Sawmill, 1957-1964	63	105	210
23830 Piggyback Unloader, 1959-1960	33	55	110
24003 Box Car, 1958, Santa Fe, K/C	19	31	62
24016 Box Car, 1961, MKT, all yellow w/brown top, K/C, rare	270	450	900

	C5	C7	C9
24019 Box Car, 1958, Seaboard, K/C	12	20	40
24023 Box Car, 1958-1959, B&O, dark blue, K/C	53	88	175
24026 Box Car, 1957-1958, Central of Georgia, black, K/C.	48	80	160
24029 Box Car, 1958-1960, State of Maine, red, white and blue, K/C	48	80	160
24030 Box Car, 1960, MKT, yellow, P/M	12	20	40
24033 Box Car, 1958, Missouri Pacific, K/C	40	68	135
24036 Box Car, 1958-1960, New Haven, orange, K/C	24	40	80
24039 Box Car, 1959, Rio Grande, white, K/C	20	33	65
24043 Box Car, 1958-1960, Boston & Maine, blue, K/C	38	63	125
24047 Box Car, 1959, Great Northern, red, K/C	70	118	235
24048 Box Car, 1959-1962, M.St.L., red, K/C	44	73	145
24052 Box Car, 1961, UFGE Bananas, yellow, P/M	5	9	18
24054 Box Car, 1962-1966, Santa Fe, P/M	21	35	70
24056 Box Car, 1961, Boston & Maine, blue, P/M	40	68	135
24057 Box Car, 1962, Mounds, white or ivory, P/M	9	15	30
24058 Box Car, 1963-1964, Post, white or ivory, K/C, P/M	8	14	27
24059 Box Car, 1963, Boston & Maine, blue, P/M	45	75	150
24060 Box Car, 1963-1964, M.St.L., P/M	33	55	110
24065 Box Car, 1960-1964, New York Central, green, K/C, P/M.	23	38	75
24066 Box Car, 1960, Louisville & Nashville, blue, K/C	56	93	185
24067 Box Car, 1960, Keystone Camera, orange, K/C, rare	600	1000	2000
24068 Box Car, 1961, Planters Peanuts, white, P/M, rare	960	1600	3200

	C5	C7	C9
24076 Stock Car, 1958-1966, Union Pacific, yellow, K/C, P/M	30	50	100
24077 Stock Car, 1959-1962, Northern Pacific, red, K/C, P/M	68	113	225
24103 Gondola, 1958, 1963-1964, N&W, black, K/C	6	10	20
24106 Gondola, 1960, Pennsylvania, K/C	5	8	16
24109 Gondola, 1958-1960, C&O, black, K/C, w/pipe load	30	50	100
24109 Gondola, 1958-1960, C&O, black, K/C, Brown, w/pipe load	13	21	42
24110 Gondola, 1960, Pennsylvania, K/C	6	11	21
24113 Gondola, 1958-1959, D&H, brown, K/C, Container load	33	55	110
24116 Gondola, 1958-1960, Southern, black, K/C	18	30	60
24120 Gondola, 1960, Texas & Pacific, green, P/M	30	50	100
24124 Gondola, 1963-1964, Boston & Maine, blue, P/M	9	15	30
24125 Gondola, 1960-1965, Bethlehem Steel, gray, K/C, P/M	8	13	25
24126 Gondola, 1961, Frisco, P/M	27	45	90
24127 Gondola, 1961, 1963-1966, Monon, gray, K/C, P/M	8	14	28
24130 Gondola, 1960, Pennsylvania, P/M	8	14	28
24203 Hopper, 1958, 1963-1964, B&O, black, K/C, P/M	24	40	80
24206 Hopper, 1958, CB&Q, w/coal load, brown, K/C	29	48	95
24209 Hopper, 1958-1960, Jersey Central, gray, w/hatch covers, K/C	29	48	95
24213 Hopper, 1958-1960, Wabash, black, K/C	11	19	38
24216 Hopper, 1958-1960, Union Pacific, K/C	26	44	88
24219 Hopper, 1958-1959, Western Maryland, K/C	48	80	160
24221 Hopper, 1959-1960, C&EI, gray, K/C	44	73	145

	C5	C7	C9
24222 Hopper, 1963-1964, Domino Sugar, yellow, w/hatch covers, K/C, P/M, rare	90	150	300
24225 Hopper, 1960-1966, Santa Fe, red, w/gravel load, P/M	14	24	48
24230 Hopper, 1961-1964, Peabody, K/C, P/M	23	39	78
24309 Tank Car, 1958, Gulf, silver, K/C	6	10	20
24310 Tank Car, 1958-1960, Gulf, silver, K/C	10	16	32
24313 Tank Car, 1957-1960, Gulf, silver, K/C	15	25	50
24316 Tank Car, 1958-1961, 1965-1966, Mobilgas, red, K/C, P/M	20	34	67
24319 Tank Car, 1958, Pennsylvania Salt, K/C, rare	135	225	450
24320 Tank Car, 1960, Deep Rock, black, P/M	114	190	380
24321 Tank Car, 1959, Deep Rock, black, K/C	27	45	90
24322 Tank Car, 1959, Gulf, silver, K/C	27	45	90
24323 Tank Car, 1959-1960, Bakers, white w/gray ends, K/C	150	250	500
24323 Tank Car, 1959-1960, Bakers, white w/white ends, K/C, rare	378	630	1260
24324 Tank Car, 1959-1960, Hooker, orange, K/C	38	63	125
24325 Tank Car, 1960, Gulf, silver, K/C	17	28	55
24328 Tank Car, 1962-1966, Shell, yellow, P/M	6	10	20
24329 Tank Car, 1961, 1963-1966, Hooker, orange, P/M	15	25	50
24330 Tank Car, 1961-1962, Baker's Chocolate, white, P/M.	45	75	150
24403 Reefer, 1958, Illinois Central, orange, K/C	9	15	30
24409 Reefer, 1958, Northern Pacific, orange sides, K/C	360	600	1200
24413 Reefer, 1958-1960, ART, orange sides, K/C	36	60	120

	C5	C7	C9
24416 Reefer, 1958-1959, C&NW, dark green, K/C, rare ..	510	850	1700
24419 Reefer, 1958-1959, Canadian National, gray, K/C ...	75	125	250
24420 Reefer, 1958, Simmons, orange, K/C, rare	360	600	1200
24422 Box Car, 1966, Great Northern, light green, P/M	60	100	200
24422 Reefer, 1965-1966, Great Northern, light green, P/M	18	30	60
24425 Reefer, 1960, Bar, red, K/C	180	300	600
24426 Reefer, 1960-1961, Rath Packing, orange sides, K/C	150	250	500
24516 Flat Car, 1958-1959, New Haven, w/lumber load, K/C	8	13	25
24519 Flat Car, 1958, Pennsylvania, depressed center, W.E. spool load, K/C, rare	188	313	625
24529 Floodlight, 1958, Erie, depressed center, K/C	12	20	40
24533 Track Cleaning Car, 1957-1966, AFL, depressed center, K/C, P/M	12	20	40
24536 Flat Car, 1958, Monon, w/trailer load, K/C	18	30	60
24537 Flat Car, 1957, New Haven, w/pipe load, K/C	24	40	80
24539 Flat Car, 1958-1959, 1963-1964, New Haven, w/pipe load, K/C, P/M	36	60	120
24540 Flat Car, 1960, New Haven, w/pipe load, K/C	36	60	120
24543 Crane Car, 1958, Industrial Brownhoist, AFL, K/C	27	45	90
24546 Work Caboose, 1958-1964, AF, K/C	18	30	60
24547 Floodlight, 1958, Erie, K/C	225	375	750
24549 Floodlight, 1958-1966, Erie, R/C, P/M	14	23	45
24550 Flat Car, 1959-1964, Monon, w/trailer load, K/C	33	55	110
24553 Flat Car, 1958-1960, Rocket Transport, K/C	28	48	95
24556 Flat Car, 1959, Rock Island, wheel transport, K/C	26	44	88

	C5	C7	C9
24557 Flat Car, 1959-1960, U.S. Navy, w/Jeep load, K/C............	48	80	160
24558 Flat Car, 1959-1960, Canadian Pacific, w/Christmas tree load, K/C...........................	83	138	275
24559 Flat Car, 1959, New Haven, no load, K/C...........................	9	15	30
24561 Crane Car, 1959-1966, Industrial Brownhoist, AFL, K/C, P/M.................................	14	23	45
24562 Flat Car, 1960, N.Y. Central, no load, K/C................	17	28	55
24564 Flat Car, 1960, New Haven, w/pipe load, P/M......................	17	28	55
24566 Flat Car, 1961-1966, New Haven, auto transport, P/M.......	25	43	85
24569 Crane Car, 1961-1966, Industrial Brownhoist, AFL, P/M..	9	15	30
24572 Flat Car, 1961, U.S. Navy, w/Jeep load, P/M	60	100	200
24574 Flat Car, 1960-1961, U.S. Air Force, w/fuel container load, K/C..................................	45	75	150
24575 Flat Car, 1960-1966, National, w/milk container load, P/M	21	35	70
24577 Flat Car, 1960-1961, 1963-1964, Illinois Central, w/jet engine container load, K/C, P/M	48	80	160
24578 Flat Car, 1962-1963, New Haven, w/Corvette load, P/M ...	54	90	180
24579 Flat Car, 1960-1961, Illinois Central, w/multiload, K/C, P/M.................................	68	113	229
24603 Caboose, 1958-1959, AFL, red, K/C	3	5	9
24610 Caboose, 1960, AFL, red, K/C...................................	4	6	12
24619 Caboose, 1958, Bay window, AFL, brown, K/C.......	23	38	75
24626 Caboose, 1958, AFL, yellow, K/C..............................	5	8	15
24627 Caboose, 1959-1960, AFL, red, K/C	3	5	10

	C5	C7	C9
24630 Caboose, 1960, AFL, red, K/C....................................	3	5	10
24631 Caboose, 1959-1961, AFL, yellow, K/C, P/M	15	25	50
24632 Caboose, 1959, AFL, yellow, K/C	24	40	80
24633 Caboose, 1959-1962, bay window, AFL, silver, P/M	27	45	90
24634 Caboose, 1963-1966, bay window, AFL, red, P/M	25	43	85
24636 Caboose, 1960-1966, AFL, yellow, P/M, rare......................	120	200	400
24636 Caboose, 1960-1966, AFL, red, P/M..................................	2	3	6
24638 Caboose, 1962, bay Window, AFL, silver, P/M	45	75	150
24773 Combine Car, 1957-1958, 1960-1962, silver, K/C, red stripe, "Columbus"....................	36	60	120
24776 Combine Car, 1959, silver, K/C, orange stripe, "Columbus"..............................	36	60	120
24793 Coach Car, 1957-1958, 1960-1962, silver, K/C, red stripe, "Jefferson"	36	60	120
24813 Vista-Dome, 1957-1958, 1960-1962, silver, red stripe, "Hamilton"	45	75	150
24816 Vista-Dome, 1959, silver, K/C, orange stripe, "Hamilton"	45	75	150
24833 Observation Car, 1957-1958, 1960-1962, silver, K/C, red stripe, "Washington"...........	30	50	100
24836 Observation Car, 1959, silver, K/C, orange stripe, "Washington"...........................	30	50	100
24837 Combine Car, 1959-1960, Union Pacific, yellow and gray, K/C, rare.................................	75	125	250
24838 Coach Car, 1959-1960, Union Pacific, yellow and gray, K/C, rare.................................	75	125	250
24839 Vista-Dome, 1959-1960, Union Pacific, yellow and gray, K/C, rare.................................	83	138	275
24840 Observation Car, 1959-1960, Union Pacific, yellow and gray, K/C, rare..................	75	125	250

	C5	C7	C9
24843 Combine Car, 1958, Northern Pacific, green, K/C	45	75	150
24846 Coach Car, 1958, Northern Pacific, green, K/C..................	45	75	150
24849 Vista-Dome, 1958, Northern Pacific, green, K/C	48	80	160
24853 Observation Car, 1958, Northern Pacific, green, K/C	75	125	250
24856 Combine Car, P/M..............	90	150	300
24856 Combine Car, 1958 & 1964, Missouri Pacific, silver and blue, K/C, rare...................	105	175	350
24859 Coach Car, P/M	90	150	300
24859 Coach Car, 1958, 1963-1964, Missouri Pacific, silver and blue, K/C, rare...................	105	175	350
24863 Vista-Dome, P/M................	78	130	260
24863 Vista-Dome, 1958, 1963-1964, Missouri Pacific, silver and blue, K/C, rare...................	90	150	300
24866 Observation Car, P/M........	75	125	250
24866 Observation Car, 1958, 1963-1964, Missouri Pacific, silver and blue, K/C, rare.........	90	150	300
24867 Combine Car, 1958, AFL, silver, K/C.................................	45	75	150
24868 Observation Car, 1958, AFL, silver, K/C	45	75	150
24869 Coach Car, 1958, AFL, silver, K/C.................................	45	75	150
25003 Log Unloading Car, 1958-1960, AFL, log, K/C	60	100	200
25016 Lumber Unloading Car, 1958-1960, Southern Pacific, w/lumber load, K/C	45	75	150
25019 Operating Milk Car, 1957-1960, Gilbert, white, K/C, w/plastic cans..........................	65	108	215
25025 Coal Dump Car, 1958-1960, CB&Q, K/C	53	88	175
25042 Operating Box Car, 1958, Erie, brown, K/C, w/aluminum barrels	60	100	200
25045 Rocket Launcher, 1958-1960, vertical launch, K/C........	25	43	85

	C5	C7	C9
25046 Rocket Launcher, 1960, 45 degrees angle launch, K/C........	29	48	95
25049 Walking Brakeman Car, 1958-1960, Rio Grande, white, K/C..	90	150	300
25052 Caboose, 1960, bay window, AFL, silver, K/C, rare, "Moving Brakeman"	44	73	145
25056 Detonator Car, 1959, USMC, yellow, K/C..................	90	150	300
25056 Rocket Launcher, 1959, USMC, yellow, K/C.................	90	150	300
25057 Exploding Box Car, 1960, T.N.T..	60	100	200
25058 Lumber Unloading Car, 1961-1964, Southern Pacific, w/lumber load, P/M	36	60	120
25059 Rocket Launcher, 1961-1964, U.S.A.F., forty-five degrees angle launch, P/M	29	48	95
25060 Coal Dump Car, 1961-1964, CB&Q, maroon, K/C	45	75	150
25061 Exploding Box Car, 1961, TNT...	60	100	200
25062 Exploding Box Car, 1962-1964, mine carrier, P/M	235	393	785
25071 Tie-Jector Car, 1961-1964, AF, tie load, P/M.......................	11	18	35
25081 Box Car, 1961-1964, NYC, w/hayjector, light green, P/M....	11	19	38
25082 Box Car, 1961-1964, New Haven, w/hayjector, orange, P/M...	18	30	60
25515 Flat Car, 1960-1963, USAF, w/rocket sled load, P/M	57	95	190
26101 Scenic Panel Curve, 1965 ...	10	15	20
26121 Scenic Panel Straight, 1965	15	23	30
26122 Scenic Panel Straight, 1965	13	19	25
26141 Scenic Panel Right/Left Switch, 1965	10	15	20
26151 Scenic Panel Crossover, 1965...................................	8	12	15
26300 Straight Track P/M	15	25	30
26301 Straight Track P/M	15	25	30
26302 Straight Track, w/uncoupler	1	2	2

	C5	C7	C9
26310 Curve Track, P/M	15	22	30
26320/321 Remote Control Switches, left and right w/controls P/M, Pair	13	19	25
26322 Crossing, 90 degrees, P/M	2	2	3
26323/324 Manual Switches, P/M, pair	5	8	10
26601 Fiber Road BG, straight	—	—	1
26602 Fiber Road BG, curved	—	—	1
26700 Straight Track	—	—	1
26710 Straight Track	—	—	1
26720 Curve Track	—	—	1
26726 Rubber Road	—	—	1
26727 Rubber Road, half curve	—	—	1

	C5	C7	C9
26730 Curve Track, half section	—	—	1
26744 Manual Switches, pair	8	11	15
26745 90 Degrees Crossing	2	2	3
26746 Rubber Roadbed, 1957-1964, black or gray, straight	—	1	2
26747 Rubber Roadbed, 1957-1964, black or gray, curved	—	1	2
26749 Bumper, 1957-1960, green	4	6	8
26751 Pike Planning Kit, 1957-1959	8	11	15
26760 Remote Control Switches, left and right, w/controls, pair	15	22	30
26770 Manuel Switches, pair	11	16	23
5300T 740 Handcar, w/three tipple cars: blue, green and red	130	195	260

Buddy "L"

Buddy "L" toys were first manufactured by the Moline Pressed Steel Company, Moline, Illinois, in 1921, and were named after the son of the owner, Fred Lundahl. Lundahl started the company eight years earlier, manufacturing auto and truck parts. Toys were originally made as special items for his son, Buddy, but when his playmates began to clamor for similar toys of their own and their fathers began asking Lundahl senior to make duplicate toys for their sons, Lundahl went into the toy business.

Buddy "L" toys were large, typically twenty-one to twenty-four or more inches long for trucks and fire engines. Construction was of heavy steel strong enough to support a man's weight. These were made until the early 1930s, when the line was modified and lighter-weight materials were employed.

Fred Lundahl lost control of the company in 1930, he passed away later that year. The company has since changed names several times, being known as the Buddy "L" Corp., Buddy "L" Toy Co. and has, in recent years, dropped the quotes around the L. Continuing to make toys till the present day, the company even put out a few wooden toys during World War II, when its main plant made nothing but war-related items.

Buddy "L" trains were first manufactured in 1921 and ended production in 1931.

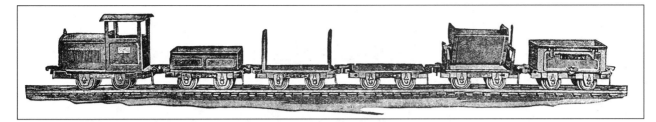

Buddy "L" Industrial Train No. 50 A-G, Complete sets, $1,500

Buddy "L" Industrial Train

	C5	C7	C9
Handcar, No. 2 ga., 1929-1931, orange, rare	2000	3000	4000
50 A-G Complete sets, No. 2 ga., 1929-1931, various	750	1125	1500
51 Locomotive, No. 2 ga., 1929-1931, decals BL 12, BL 14, or BL 16, dark green	287	430	575
52 Stake Car, No. 2 ga., 1929-1931, flatcar, red	70	105	140
53 Rock Car, No. 2 ga., 1929-1931, red	70	105	140
54 Gondola, No. 2 ga., 1929-1931, red	70	105	140
55 Ballast Car, No. 2 ga., 1929-1931, side dump, red	130	195	260
56 Rocker Dump Car, No. 2 ga., 1929-1931, red	130	195	260
70 Straight Track, No. 2 ga., 1929-1931, dark green, 24", price per section	15	22	30
71 Curved Track, No. 2 ga., 1929-1931, dark green, per section	10	15	20
72R Switch, No. 2 ga., 1929-1931, dark green	45	68	90
73L Switch, No. 2 ga., 1929-1931, dark green	45	68	90
74 Turn-Out Curve, No. 2 ga., 1929-1931, dark green	7	11	15
75 Ninety Degrees Crossing, No. 2 ga., 1929-1931, dark green	25	38	50
76 Sixty Degrees Crossing, No. 2 ga., 1929-1931, dark green	50	75	100
77 Loose Latch Plate, No. 2 ga., 1929-1931, dark green	3	5	6
78 1/4 Straight Track, 6", No. 2 ga., 1929-1931, Dark green	15	22	30

	C5	C7	C9
79 1/2 Straight Track 12", No. 2 ga., 1929-1931, dark green	15	22	30
80 Three Stall Roundhouse and Turntable, No. 2 ga., 1929-1931, dark green	1250	1875	2500
81 One Stall Roundhouse and Turntable, No. 2 ga., 1929-1931, dark green	1000	1500	2000

Buddy "L" Outdoor Railroad

	C5	C7	C9
Supporting Piers, 3-1/4" ga., black	125	188	250
Trestle Sections, 3-1/4" ga., black	250	375	500
1000 Locomotive and Tender, 3-1/4" ga., 1921-1931, decal reads 963, black	1100	1650	2200
1001 Caboose, 3-1/4" ga., 1921-1931, decal 3017, red	750	1125	1500
1002 Boxcar, 3-1/4" ga., 1921-1931, red	500	750	1000

Buddy "L" Outdoor Railroad. Left to right: No. 1002 Boxcar, closed top, $1,000; No. 1003 Tank car, $1,500

Buddy "L" Outdoor Railroad. Left to right: No. 1002 Boxcar, open top, $1000; No. 1006, $1,000

Buddy "L" Outdoor Railroad. Top and middle: No. 1000 Locomotive and Tender, $1000; Bottom: No. 1004 Stock car, $750

	C5	C7	C9
1003 Tankcar, 3-1/4" ga., 1921-1931, dark red, yellow and silver	750	1125	1500
1004 Stock Car, 3-1/4" ga., 1921-1931, red	375	562	750

Buddy "L" Outdoor Railroad. Left to right: No. 1004 Stock car, $750; No. 1001 Caboose, $1,500

	C5	C7	C9
1005 Gondola, 3-1/4" ga., 1921-1931, coal car, black	500	750	1000
1006 Flatcar, 3-1/4" ga., 1926-1931, black	450	675	900
1007 Hopper, 3-1/4" ga., 1928-1931, bottom dump, black	750	1125	1500
1008 Ballast Car, 3-1/4" ga., 1928-1931, side dump, black, 23"	700	1050	1400
1009 Construction Car, 3-1/4" ga., 1930-1931, single truck, dark green, 11"	1700	2550	3400
1020 Locomotive Wrecking Crane, 3-1/4" ga., 1927-1930, black, red	2000	3000	4000
1021 Locomotive Dredge, 3-1/4" ga., 1927-1930, black and red	2000	3000	4000

Buddy "L" Outdoor Railroad. No. 1020, Locomotive wrecking crane, $4,000

Buddy "L" Outdoor Railroad. Top to bottom: No. 1022 Locomotive pile driver, $5,200; No. 1023 Locomotive shovel, $4,200

	C5	C7	C9
1022 Locomotive Pile Driver, 3-1/4" ga., 1927-1930, black and red	2600	3900	5200
1023 Locomotive Shovel, 3-1/4" ga., 1928-1930, black and red	2200	3300	4400
1200 Straight Track, 3-1/4" ga., 4' long	27	41	55
1201 Curved Track, 3-1/4" ga., 4' long, 26' dia.	17	26	35
1202 Right-hand Switch, 3-1/4" ga., 7'	375	563	750
1203 Left-hand Switch, 3-1/4" ga., 7'	375	563	750

Carlisle and Finch

As, at an earlier date, Ives had opened the frontier in the area of toy manufacturing, so Carlisle and Finch helped pioneer the production of electric trains. Although the Novelty Electric Company based in Philadelphia had been the first to market electric trains in the 1880s, Carlisle and Finch was the first to make it a viable commercial venture. Based in Cincinnati, Ohio, Carlisle and Finch produced primarily marine navigational and electrical equipment but decided in 1896 to embark on a venture in toy trains. At that time, electrical items were the cutting edge of technology, and the time seemed ripe to exploit the electrical novelty market.

Their debut on the market in 1896 was in the form of a three-rail, direct current trolley. The following year, it became two-rail; the line was off and running. Their chosen gauge was two inch, and from then on stayed the same, although the line continued to be expanded and changed virtually annually through nineteen years of production.

The first ten years of the twentieth century were good to Carlisle and Finch, but by the beginning of the second decade, their grip on the market was beginning to slip. Other domestic companies such as Ives, Lionel, Voltamp, Knapp, Howard, and the fledgling Edmunds-Metzel, who later became American Flyer, as well as foreign companies such as Bing, Marklin, and Carette, were beginning to cut sizable pieces out of the market pie. Consequently sales began to dwindle seriously by 1911. In 1915, the company began to devote full attention of their facilities to production for the war effort, and toy train production ground to a halt.

Carlisle and Finch never resumed production of toy trains, although they considered the thought briefly around 1932. At that point, some prototype pieces were made, but the project never went any further.

Throughout their production history, Carlisle and Finch never displayed their name on their trains or equipment. All items must be identified solely by road names, numbers and characteristics. Once you know what to look for, however, it is fairly easy to ascertain the identity of a Carlisle and Finch piece.

There is a certain charm to the early, crude tin-plate trains for which, like old wines, it takes time to acquire a taste. Old trains take patience and special care to operate, and perform none of the maneuvers that later cars and equipment can, but they represent an historical perspective which made all of the later production possible. In collecting items in the two-inch gauge category, it is always interesting to come across variations which are unusual or different from those on your shelf. Since in the early days trains were toys made to play with, concern was given to quality and endurance more than to consistency in appearance. Some factory workers applied paint and colors a little differently than other; consequently, painted lines and numbers appear on some items and not on other contemporary pieces. Some items were put together to fill out a set or an outfit needed at a certain time, so one car may be assembled differently than another. Transition pieces occur when a catalog change was made, and the old body appears on new trucks with new couplers, or when a new motor was placed in an engine from the previous year, or vice-versa. As toys, it was more important to use up existing materials and keep production costs down, than to exactly match the catalog production in the first part of a new year. So don't be surprised to find mixed characteristics on some items when major changes are catalogued.

Trucks

There were two types of trucks basically used on Carlisle and Finch cars.

• **Wooden.** These were usually a green, flat block of wood roughly 2-1/2-inches long by 1-3/4-inches wide by 3/8-inches thick. They generally had four cast-iron wheels held to them by nails used as axles. The wheels were 1-1/4-inches in diameter. This truck assembly was in turn nailed to a wooden bolster roughly 1-1/4-inches by 1-1/8-inches by 3/4-inches high which was attached by a screw or nut and bolt to the wooden floor (or in some case, metal) of the car. These existed on the small passenger and freight cars from 1899 until 1908.

• **Metal.** These trucks were stamped brass on steel, an open type of truck which were bolted to the bottom of the cars. The wheels were stamped out of brass and had a small inner hub of insulating material which kept them from shorting out the axles of the trucks. These were used on the large freight and passenger cars from 1904 until 1915, and on the small passenger and freight cars from 1909-1915.

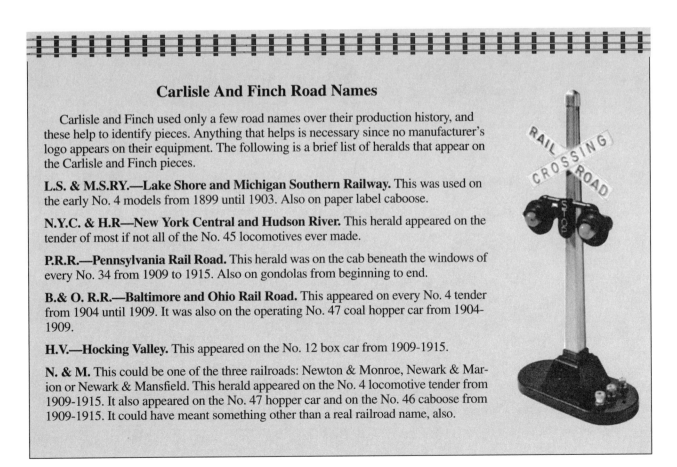

Carlisle And Finch Road Names

Carlisle and Finch used only a few road names over their production history, and these help to identify pieces. Anything that helps is necessary since no manufacturer's logo appears on their equipment. The following is a brief list of heralds that appear on the Carlisle and Finch pieces.

L.S. & M.S.RY.—Lake Shore and Michigan Southern Railway. This was used on the early No. 4 models from 1899 until 1903. Also on paper label caboose.

N.Y.C. & H.R—New York Central and Hudson River. This herald appeared on the tender of most if not all of the No. 45 locomotives ever made.

P.R.R.—Pennsylvania Rail Road. This herald was on the cab beneath the windows of every No. 34 from 1909 to 1915. Also on gondolas from beginning to end.

B.& O. R.R.—Baltimore and Ohio Rail Road. This appeared on every No. 4 tender from 1904 until 1909. It was also on the operating No. 47 coal hopper car from 1904-1909.

H.V.—Hocking Valley. This appeared on the No. 12 box car from 1909-1915.

N. & M. This could be one of the three railroads: Newton & Monroe, Newark & Marion or Newark & Mansfield. This herald appeared on the No. 4 locomotive tender from 1909-1915. It also appeared on the No. 47 hopper car and on the No. 46 caboose from 1909-1915. It could have meant something other than a real railroad name, also.

Couplers

There were two basic couplers used in Carlisle and Finch production in their history, plus a third type used on trolley cars and trailers.

• **Link and pin.** This was used from 1897 until 1903. Two small, flat U-shaped plates with holes in the cars were aligned parallel to each other at the ends of the cars, and a pin fit through the holes and held them together. It was a good system, but like the later Lionel latch couplers, your hands had to be nimble to get between the cars.

• **Bumper type.** Most common. Used from 1903 until 1915. They were simply a flat strip of metal mounted across each end of a car frame, and bellied out toward the next car. A U-shaped pin was placed over the two bumpers to hold the cars together. The simplicity of this system made it extremely serviceable.

• **Trolley and trail car connections.** Often a trolley would have a screw-in piece or rod bent at a ninety-degree angle over which a screw-eye on the frame of the trail car would be placed to hold them together. This also was simplicity itself.

Mining Equipment

First in Carlisle and Finch locomotive equipment, the mining locomotive and cars endured through the entire run of production history. Available in various sets and combinations, the mining locomotive had a charm that kept its popularity alive. The motor was the same three-pole reversible used in the No. 4 and No. 20, and the reverse lever protruded up through the body shell. Always four wheels in O-B-O arrangement.

Accessories

	C7	C9
5 Ornamental Bridge, 1897-1898, sides made of lacquered brass and held together by two wooden ends and two wooden cross-ties; 12" l., 7" w., 4-3/4" h.	40	75
5 Ornamental Bridge, 1899-1915, sides made of cast iron, w/wooden ends and cross-ties; 12" l., 7" w., 4-3/4" h.	35	70
6 90 Degree Crossing, 1899-1915, for figure-eight layouts; made for use w/strip steel track; all electrical connections were finished w/crossing	4	5
9 Passenger Station, 1897-1907, tin body covered w/a paper label w/red brick design; total of five windows and two doors on both front and back w/three square and one round window at each end; marked "Buffalo" on front and back; top of middle window reads "Ticket Office"; black clerestory-type roof; wood base; 10" l., 6" h.	95	175
9 Passenger Station, 1909-1915, tin covered w/paper label w/red brick design; wood base; dormer on roof front and back; some versions had two semaphores while others had only one; black clerestory type roof; arched windows at each end; front and back have five arched windows and two doors w/transoms; top panes of middle window marked "Ticket Office." Still brick facing on paper label; 12" l., 7-1/2" w., 7" h.	95	175
10 Switch, 1898-1900, Y-type; made for strip steel track	15	20
10 Switch, 1901-1915, suitable for use w/strip steel track; 10-R is right, 10-L is left	15	20
14 Rail Connector, 1899-1904, U-shaped piece of metal w/two screws each to attach to one end of abutting tracks	1	2
14 Rail Connector, 1905-1915, wooden block w/slats cut lined w/brass for track to be set; 1-1/2" x 1"	1	2
54 Elevating Posts, 1905-1908, used to mount elevated railway track	10	15

	C7	C9
55 Loading Platform, 1904, wooden base; made to sit along track; has same motorized derrick on platform as No. 53 Derrick car; 12" l., 5" w., 2-3/4" h.	150	250
56 Large Bridge, 1904-1915, furnished w/track; built similar to No. 5, w/wooden cross-ties and ends holding two cast-iron sides together; made of cast-iron, painted orange; 23" l.	90	150
57 Suspension Bridge, 1904-1915, furnished w/track; consists of four cast-iron pieces bolted together and joined side to side by wooden ties and ends; painted either red, yellow or orange; 36" l.	250	475
58 Switches, 1904-1905, 58-L and 58-R; made for strip steel track to go w/the No. 45 locomotive; large radius switches	15	25
85 Track Bumper, 1904-1915, made primarily of wood for strip steel track; used to prevent trains derailing at end of siding	15	30
93 T-Rail Track Sections, early examples were made of brass w/wood cross ties and steel pins in ends to join track 24" long; later examples were made of tin w/wood ties and end pins of steel; U: straight section, W: curved section, X: short straight section, Y: short curved section for No. 94-R switch, Z: short curved section for No. 94-L switch; per section	—	2
94 Switches, 1905-1915, 94RT: right switch for T-rail; 94LT: left switch for T-rail.	15	25
96 Freight Depot with Loading Derrick, 1905-1908, wooden base w/cast-iron columns supporting tin roof; derrick w/hand windlass on wooden pivot platform; 29" l., 14" w., 11-1/2" h.	150	250
97 Passenger Station, 1905-1908, cast-iron w/sheet metal roof; painted and embossed "Railroad Depot"; wooden floor; made to go between two tracks; 36" l., 14" w., 12" h.	200	400
103 Caternary Poles, 1905-1907, used for construction of caternary trolley railway; cast-iron poles w/brass clips at ends of arms for wires; came both as single and double poles	10	15

	C7	C9

Freight Cars

The No. 11 gondola (1899-1915) was made to go with the No. 4 locomotive, and later with the No. 20 and No. 34. The No. 11 always had two four-wheel trucks and P.R.R. livery.

	C7	C9
11 Gondola, 1899-1902, car about an inch deep, and made from tin covered w/a red or blue paper label marked "131 PRR 131" on each side; wooden trucks w/cast-iron wheels; link-and-pin couplers; 10" l., 3" w., 2-1/2" h.	85	155
11 Gondola, 1903-1908, some versions still w/paper label, others may be embossed "131 PRR 131" on sides; body made of tin and painted blue; bumper couplers; wooden trucks w/cast-iron wheels; 10" l., 3" w., 2-1/2" h.	60	95
11 Gondola, 1909-1915, generally the same as previous versions; some blue, others are red; sides embossed "131 PRR 131"; metal trucks w/stamped brass wheels; 10" l., 3" w., 2-1/2" h.	55	85

The No. 12 boxcar (1899-1915) always has two four-wheel trucks. Each sides features one sliding door. It was made to go with the No. 4 locomotive and later the No. 20 and No. 34 locomotives.

	C7	C9
12 Boxcar, 1899-1902, body made of tin covered entirely w/paper label; labels on ends reads "1141," side labels read "1141 C.B. & Q.R.R."; doors labeled "1141 C.B. & Q.R.R. Fast Freight"; roof made of tin painted black; link-and-pin couplers; wood trucks w/cast-iron wheels; 10" l., 3" w., 4-3/4" h.	100	225

No. 12 Boxcar, c. 1901, $225; above is the underside of No. 47 Coal hopper, 1899-1902, $225

	C7	C9

No. 12 Boxcar, special made for Prince Majestic Flour

	C7	C9
12 Boxcar, 1903-1908, generally same as previous versions; yellow label completely covers tin body; black tin roof; bumper couplers; 10" l., 3" w., 4-3/4" h.	95	185
12 Boxcar, 1909-1915, tin body painted orange; sides embossed "HV," doors embossed "26"; tin roof painted black; bumper couplers; metal trucks w/stamped brass wheels; 10" l., 3" w., 4-3/4" h.	90	135

The No. 46 caboose (1903-1915) featured two four-wheel trucks and was made to go with the No. 4 engine. In addition to the No. 4, it was used with the No. 45, No. 20 and later the No. 34 locomotives.

	C7	C9
46 Caboose, 1903-1908, tin body covered w/red paper label simulating wood; three punched-out windows on each side outlined w/sash detail on paper label (some versions have windows printed on paper labels, metal sides are not punched out); marked "L.S. & M.S.RY" above windows "8681" and below; doors on each end punched out w/frame detailed on paper label; tin roof, floor, cupola and cupola roof are painted black; cupola has two windows on each side and two windows on each end; black tin vestibule ends and steps are at each end of car; grab rails from floor to ceiling; wooden trucks w/cast-iron wheels; bumper couplers; 10" l., 3" w., 5-1/2" h.	150	250

	C7	C9

46 Caboose, 1909-1915, tin body painted red w/black painted roof, vestibule ends, steps, and cupola roof all painted black; cupola painted red; body w/three windows per side and one door at each end; cupola has two windows on each side and two at each end; body windows have embossed reinforcement sashes; sides of body embossed "N & M"; metal trucks w/brass stamped wheels; no grab rails; some early versions have the paper label sides and metal trucks; 10" l., 3" w., 5-1/2" h. 100   180

The No. 47 coal car (1904-1915) is an operating hopper featuring doors on the bottom of the car. Always made with two four-wheel trucks, the No. 47 can be paired with the No. 4, No. 20 and No. 34 locomotives.

47 Coal Car, 1904-1905, wooden frame and trucks, cast-iron wheels; tin body painted orange w/"B & O" painted on side; trap doors in bottom operated by windlass on side of car; bumper couplers; 10" l., 3" w., 4" h................. 125   200

47 Coal Car, 1906-1908, operating hopper; same body as previous version, but w/metal floor replacing wood; trucks are still wood and livery is still "B & O"; bumper coupler; 10" l., 3" w., 4" h. 100   175

47 Coal Car, 1909-1915, body, frame, trap doors all tin; operating hopper, but now windlass is replaced by lever on lower side of ca; sides embossed "N & M"; brass-stamped wheels on metal trucks; 10" l., 3" w., 4" h............ 100   150

48 Cattle Car, 1904-1915, The No. 48 cattle car (1904-1915) was made to go with the No. 4, No. 20 and No. 34 locomotives and always featured two four-wheel trucks.

48 Cattle Car, 1904-1908, wooden floor and trucks, cast-iron wheels; body constructed of strips of sheet tin soldered together; doors also made of separate strips set into outside guides that allow them slide; body painted yellow and sometimes maroon; tin roof painted black; bumper coupler; 10" l., 3" w., 4-3/4" h. 85   135

48 Cattle Car, 1909-1915, body is stamped tin and less complicated on this version; tin floor and body are painted yellow w/black roof; metal trucks w/stamped brass wheels and bumper couplers; sliding door on outside track; some early bodies still appear on the late trucks; 10" l., 3" w., 4-3/4" h... 80   135

The No. 49 oil car (1904-1916) was made for the No. 4, No. 20 and No. 34 locomotives and always featured two four-wheel trucks.

49 Oil Car, 1904-1908, tin frame, wood trucks and tin oil tank; this is essentially a tank fitted onto a No. 50 flat car by means of saddles at each end; brake wheels appear at each end of car; handrails on each side of tank; short rounded dome; whole car usually painted yellow; 10" l., 3" w., 4-3/4" h... 90   150

49 Oil Car, 1909-1915, not catalogued in 1911, but probably available; same tank and flat car as used in previous years, tin frame, tank, saddles and brake wheels; metal trucks, brass stamped wheels and bumper couplers; 10" l., 3" w., 4-3/4" h. 85   140

The No. 50 flat car (1904-1915) features a stamped tin body and was made for the No. 4, No. 20 and No. 34 locomotives. It also serves as the base of the No. 49 oil car. The car is always an unusual shade of yellow and features brake wheels at both ends. During its production, the length of the car varied by as much as 3/4".

50 Flat Car, 1904-1908, wooden trucks w/cast-iron wheels; skirted sides embossed "171"; bumper couplers; 10" l., 3" w., 2" h................................ 45   75

50 Flat Car, 1909-1915, skirted sides embossed "171"; metal trucks w/stamped brass wheels; bumper couplers 40   65

53 Derrick Car, 1904-1907, wooden frame and wooden trucks w/four cast-iron wheels; derrick frame is cast-iron w/electrical motor mounted on swiveling wooden platform mounted to car frame; small metal hook mounted to end of cable; derrick motor ran off of power supplied by track rails; 10-1/2" l., 3" w., 9-1/2" h... 300   500

	C7	**C9**

90 Gondola, 1905-1915, made to go
w/No. 34 locomotive; painted tin body
w/two four-wheel stamped-metal
trucks and stamped-brass wheels;
sides embossed "N.Y.C. & H.R.";
brake wheel at each end; bumper
couplers; 13-1/2" l., 4" w., 3" h. 200 400

91 Boxcar, 1905-1915, made for No. 45
locomotive; painted tin body w/two
four-wheel stamped-metal trucks and
stamped-brass wheels; sides embossed
"N.Y.C. & H.R."; sliding door
w/outside track; tin roof painted black;
brake wheel at each end; bumper
couplers; 13-1/2" l., 4" w., 5-1/4" h. 250 450

92 Caboose, 1905-1915, made for No. 45
locomotive; two stamped-metal four-
wheel trucks w/brass wheels; body
painted tin w/six windows on each
side; roof and cupola roof are tin
painted black; cupola has two
windows on all four sides; black
platform ends and handrails; bumper
couplers; 13-1/2" l., 4" w., 6-3/4" h. 300 500

Mining Cars

3 Ore Car, 1897-1908, cast-iron body
mounted on a wood slab frame, w/four
cast-iron wheels one-inch in diameter
nailed into wood; earliest examples
were link and pin, later examples had
bumper-type coupler; body has a bar
from end to end in middle w/holes to
screw it to frame 25 45

Left to right: No. 3 Dump car; No. 2 motor, c. 1899

3 Dump Car, 1904-1908, same wooden
frame as ore car, but coal bunker is
now rounded at bottom and ends are
mounted to stanchions; lever at one
end permits the hopper to tipple; 2-
1/2" l., 2-1/4" w., 3-1/2" h. 40 75

	C7	**C9**

3 Dump Car, 1909-1915, same as
previous years, but not on metal frame
like the ore car; saddle beneath hopper
holds it in place when not being
tippled; 2-1/2" l., 2-1/4" w.,
3-1/2" h... 40 75

Left to right: No. 3 Dump car; No. 2 motor, c. 1899

3 Ore Car, 1909-1915, cast-iron body
mounted on tin frame which covers
the wheels and has axle holes; the
wheels are now made out of stamped
brass 30 50

4 Inclined Plane Railway, 1897, modeled
after inclines where coal was mined on
a hillside or where cities had high
hills. two cars side by side, one in
ascent while other in descent; motor
reversed when one car reached top of
incline, iron cars w/brass wheels could
each carry one pound of weight,
reversing switch allows cars to change
direction or stop at any time; wood
base; tin house covered w/a brick-like
paper label and windows sat on the top
of the platform; incline: 28" l., and 14-
1/4" h.; house: 6" x 5" x 4" w/3-3/4"
h. chimney.. 350 600

Mining Equipment

3 Mining Locomotive, 1897-1898, O-B-
O; brass body w/yellow paper label;
wooden frame w/1" diameter cast-iron
wheels nailed into frame; pulley
system from armature shaft to
flywheel to drive wheel powers
locomotive; link and pin coupler
system to couple to cars; marked
"Electric Railway"; 7" l., 3-1/4" w.,
4" h... 230 325

	C7	C9

3 Mining Locomotive, 1899-1902, O-B-O; seven-spoke wheels, same as No. 4; motor-driven wheels w/open gear system; brass body, covered w/paper label; link and pin coupler system; flat brass drive rods couple wheels; marked "Electric Coal Mining Locomotive"; 7" l., 3-1/4" w., 4" h...... 175 250

3 Mining Locomotive, 1903, O-B-O; stamped tin body painted yellow; spoke drive wheels w/brass coupling rods; bumper couplers mounted to cross ties nailed to wooden frame; sides embossed "Mining Locomotive"; 7" l., 3-1/4" w., 4" h..... 150 200

3 Mining Locomotive, 1904-1906, O-B-O; stamped tin body painted yellow or maroon; twelve-spoke drive wheels w/brass coupling rods; bumper couplers mounted to cross ties nailed to wooden frame; sides embossed "Mining Locomotive"; 7" l., 3-1/4" w., 4" h................. 150 225

3 Mining Locomotive, 1907-1908, O-B-O; nickel-plated body painted yellow or maroon; twelve-spoke drive wheels w/brass coupling rods; bumper couplers mounted to cross ties nailed to wooden frame; sides embossed "Mining Locomotive"; 7" l., 3-1/4" w., 4" h................. 200 300

3 Mining Locomotive, 1909-1911, O-B-O; stamped tin body painted yellow or maroon; twelve-spoke drive wheels w/brass coupling rods; bumper couplers mounted to cross ties nailed to wooden frame; sides embossed "Mining Locomotive"; 7" l., 3-1/4" w., 4" h................. 150 225

3 Mining Locomotive, 1912-1915, O-B-O; smaller motor, bumper couplers mounted to cross ties nailed to wooden frame; green tin hump-backed body giving it a turtle appearance; body comes down over frame instead of sitting on top of it; twelve-spoke wheels, brass coupling rods; reverse lever changes internally somewhat; embossed "Mining Locomotive"; 7-1/2" l., 3-1/2" w., 4" h........................ 175 250

Passenger Cars

The No. 13 passenger car was made from 1899 to 1915 to accompany the No. 4 and the No. 45 locomotive until cars were developed specifically this engine. The No. 13 shared the same body stamping with the No. 2 trolley in the early years, but stayed the same when the No. 2 changed.

13 Coach, 1899-1902, No. 2 body, wood floor, cast-iron 1" diameter wheels nailed into wood bolsters, making two four-wheel trucks; body; roof made three pieces of brass soldered together; seven windows punched out per side, above yellow paper labeled marked "Electric Railway"; single door at each end; steps and platform ends made of brass; roof w/clerestory strip; link and pin couplers; 12" l., 3-1/2" w., 5" h..................... 213 425

The No. 13-B baggage car (1900-1915) was made to go with the No. 13 coach in its various applications. Developed a year after the coach, the No. 13-B also went with the No. 20 locomotive.

13-B Baggage Car, 1900-1902, tin body covered w/paper label marked "Baggage Express"; label depicts door and two windows outlined in red at each end; sliding door in the middle of each side; tin roof painted black w/clerestory strip; black steps and platform ends; two wooden trucks w/four cast-iron 1" diameter wheels; link-and-pin couplers; 12" l., 3-1/2" w., 5" h. 150 250

13 Coach, 1903-1906, generally the same as previous edition, but roof is now one-piece of stamped brass; body, platform ends and steps all made of brass; roof has clerestory strip; seven windows per side and single door on each end; sides embossed "Electric Railway"; bumper-type couplers; 12" l., 3-1/2" w., 5" h................................ 200 400

13-B Baggage Car, 1903-1908, tin body covered w/paper label marked "Baggage Express"; label depicts door

	C7	C9

and two windows outlined in red at each end; sliding door in the middle of each side; tin roof painted black w/clerestory strip; black steps and platform ends; two wooden trucks w/four cast-iron 1" diameter wheels; bumper couplers; 12" l., 3-1/2" w., 5" h. 125   225

13 Coach, 1907-1908, generally the same as previous version, but now w/nickel-plated body, roof, platform ends and steps; wooden trucks w/cast-iron wheels; wooden floor; w/bumper couplers; 12" l., 3-1/2" w., 5" h. 375   750

13-B Baggage Car, 1909-1915, car painted orange w/black roof, ends and steps; sides embossed "Electric Railway" and doors embossed "26"; wooden floor w/metal trucks and stamped brass wheels; sliding door same previous model's; bumper couplers; 12" l., 3-1/2" w., 5" h. 100   200

13 Coach, 1909-1915, generally body style as previous versions, except the windows have embossed reinforcing around sashes; tin body is painted orange; roof, platform ends and steps are tin painted black; trucks are now metal, wheels are stamped brass; bumper coupler; 12" l., 3-1/2" w., 5" h. 170   340

51 Baggage Car, 1904-1910, made to go w/No. 45 locomotive; body made of tin and painted orange w/sliding door on each side; side embossed "Baggage Express"; roof w/clerestory strip; steps and platform ends all painted black; doors marked "111"; two four-wheel brass trucks; brass wheels; bumper couplers; 19" l., 3-3/4" w., 6" h. 150   250

52 Passenger Coach, 1904-1910, made for No. 45 locomotive; polished brass body; tin roof painted black w/clerestory strip; platform ends and steps painted black; brass trucks and wheels, two four-wheel trucks per car; while some cars have smooth sides, some may be embossed "Electric Railway"; others may have paper label marked "Electric Railway"; bumper couplers; 19" l., 3-3/4" w., 6" h. 225   325

59 Baggage Car, 1909-1915, designed to be used w/the No. 34 locomotive (though in 1911 the large No. 51 and No. 52 cars were dropped, and the No. 59 was catalogued w/the No. 45); the

	C7	C9

No. 34 kept same form throughout its whole run; tin body was either painted orange or red and embossed "Baggage Express"; tin roof painted black w/clerestory strip; platform ends and steps painted black; metal four-wheel trucks w/stamped brass wheels; bumper couplers; 15-1/2" l., 3-1/2" w., 6" h. 150   225

60 Passenger Coach, 1909-1915, made to go w/No. 34 locomotive (catalogued w/No. 45 after No. 51 and No. 52 were dropped in 1911); brass car body had nine windows on each side and one door per end; windows w/embossed sashes; tin roof painted black w/clerestory; platform ends and steps painted black; metal three-wheel trucks w/brass wheels; bumper couplers; 15-1/2" l., 3-1/2" w., 15-1/2" h. 200   300

87 Pullman Coach, 1905-1906, made for No. 45 locomotive; Carlisle and Finch's only six-wheel-truck car; made w/seats and vestibules; each side had five arched windows between single porthole windows at each end; polished brass body and roof clerestory strip; bumper couplers; 18" l., 3-1/2" w., 5" w............. 300   500

Steam Locomotive

4 Locomotive, 1899-1902, metal body, cab windows not punched out of the metal; paper label on cab shows two square cab window outlines on each side, "683" is marked in a rectangle beneath the windows, arched windows depicted on the label on the front of the cab; back two-thirds of the boiler covered w/paper label showing four boiler bands that continue down over the side catwalk boards; wooden headlight mounted on boiler top; front of the boiler is wooden; tin stack, wooden bell, and a tin sand dome with a rounded wooden top; four seven-spoke drive wheels w/square-ended brass sheet coupling rods in 1899 and round piston drive rods; 1900-1902 models had thicker coupling rods w/rounded ends tender w/black paper label marked w/number "683" on rear and "L.S. & M.S.RY." on each side in yellow-gold lettering; wood floor w/two four-wheel wooden trucks w/cast iron wheels; link and pin coupler 600   1000

	C7	C9

4 1899-1915, Always an 0-4-0 steamer, the No. 4 locomotive was the first of the four steamers that Carlisle and Finch made from 1899 to 1915. Although it went through eight or nine changes throughout its history, it remained basically the same. It always had a 3-pole reversible motor mounted on a wooden frame that drives one set of wheels with a large spur gear off the armature. Crude but charming, these engines were essentially modeled from the American Standard locomotive of the time, but with a straighter boiler, and a Vauclain-like compound boiler. The reverse lever was always mounted beneath the cab. Although the No. 4 went through external changes, the motor and wood frame remained virtually the same. For the early and middle years, the binder bands were embossed into the body of the locomotive. Toward the end of production, these bands were separate pieces, and, for a short time grab rails were also added. The No. 4 was offered by itself, as a freight and as part of a passenger set. Locomotive and tender 19" l., 4" w., 5-1/2" h.

4 Locomotive, 1903, cab and rear two-thirds of boiler is nickel-plated tin; embossed boiler bonds, copper bell, nickel-plated dome and cast-iron dummy headlight (some have wooden bell and headlight); seven-spoke wheels; front of boiler wooden; bumper-type coupler; punched-out windows in cab; embossed "171"under windows; paper label on tender reads "L.S. & M.S.RY" on the sides and "683" on back 500   800

4 Locomotive, 1904-1907, similar to 1903 version, but cab and rear two-third of boiler are nickel-plated tin while the front is black; front of boiler is still wooden; w/twelve-spoke cast iron wheels; tender w/trucks and wood floor, sides are now painted; "B & O" livery appears on the sides.................. 325   650

4 Locomotive, 1907-1908, basically the same as previous versions, but cab is tin painted black; boiler is nickel painted black; front of boiler is wooden; nickel sand dome, copper bell, tin stock and cast-iron oil-type headlight; porthole-type arched side windows and forward facing windows on cab; embossed "171" beneath windows; some headlights have "171" in yellow painted on sides; bumper-type coupler; tender remained the same, marked "B & O" in orange........ 325   650

4 Locomotive, 1909-1910, boiler has slightly higher profile, w/grab rails added to sides; two boiler bands now added; first ones are nickel cab and part of boiler w/number "131" embossed beneath cab windows, later examples are tin painted black w/"131" embossed and painted gold; cab windows on later examples are painted gold around the arch frames; side rods same as previous years; bumper coupler; detail on top of engine still same, but boiler front now metal; square gold strip on cab roof and catwalk, some versions don't have grab rails; black tender embossed w/"N&M" on sides, some have orange-painted lettering; wood floor w/metal trucks and stamped brass wheels 325   650

4 Locomotive, 1911-1915, last model issued; whole engine now black painted tin w/orange square outlined on roof; "131" painted orange beneath square cab windows; shorter sand dome and cab roof; side rods flat w/rounded ends go into piston cylinder; all metal tender w/metal trucks and brass wheels, marked "N&M" on sides 450   900

20 Locomotive, 1904-1905, shorter boiler w/nickel-plated sand dome, bell, black tin stack and cast-iron oil-type headlight; some have seven-spoke wheels, rest have twelve-spoke wheels; wooden boiler front (same as No. 4); pilot mounted on wooden cross-tie is black-painted tin and bent forward at a 90-degree angle; bunker in back is black tin w/bumper coupler; motor comes back into cab through wooden floor; bumper couplers front and rear; 10" l., 4" w., 5-1/2" h. 350   550

20 Locomotive, 1904-1915, An 0-4-0 switch engine made for yard work and short hauling, the No. 20 locomotive was made from 1904 to 1915. The tank-type locomotive has a coal bunker behind cab and a reverse unit inside coal bunker. The No. 20 locomotive features the same motor as used in No. 4. This engine went through few changes during its history and always had wooden frame and a three-pole reversible motor. Also used the same side rods as the No. 4. The cab remained the same as the No. 4 with forward facing porthole windows.

	C7	C9

20 Locomotive, 1906-1907, most familiar version; boiler front and cab are both black; cab embossed and painted "171"; nickel-plated sand dome, bell; black tin stack and oil-type cast-iron headlight; twelve-spoke cast-iron wheels; wooden frame and cab floor; arched cab windows; bumper couplers on front and rear; front pilot is L-shaped tin piece mounted to wooden cross-tie nailed to wooden frame; wooden boiler front 325   500

20 Suburban Locomotive, 1908, some version have nickel cab and some are painted black; basically same model as previous year w/one pilot on the rear of the coal bunker and one mounted to a cross tie on the front of the engine frame; pilots are the same as on the No. 4; headlight on some unpainted, on others black w/"171" marked on sides; nickel dome, bell and tin stack. 13" l., 4" w., 5-1/2" h. 400   600

20 Suburban Locomotive, 1909-1910, generally the same as the 1908 model of No. 20, but pilot on front is now attached to a piece of tin instead of a wooden tie; nickel cabs w/embossed "131" beneath arched cab windows; nickel dome, brass bell and black brass stack painted black; black boiler front w/oil-type headlight; round brass piston rods all the way into cylinder; 13" l, 4" w., 5-1/2" h. 350   550

20 Suburban Locomotive, 1911-1915, Same general locomotive as 1909 No. 20, but cab is now black w/orange square outlined on roof, shorter cab w/square windows; "131" is embossed and painted orange beneath windows w/orange strip above and below lettering; flat brass piston rods all the way into cylinder; block boiler; black short dome, brass bell and brass stack painted black; black electric-type headlight; two boiler bands added on to boiler separately; pilot w/bumper couplers at both ends; 13" l., 4" w., 5-1/2" h. 750   1250

	C7	C9

A 4-4-2 Atlantic-type steamer (1908-1915), it is powered by same basic motor as No. 4 and No. 20. Originally made to pull same cars as No. 4, but passenger cars were made the following years for the No. 34. Larger than No. 4, smaller than No. 45, the No. 34 was one of the nicest locomotives made at that time by any company, and it ran its tenure with only cosmetic changes. It had the reversing motor with the lever under the cab.

34 Locomotive, 1908-1909, nickel cab w/"P.R.R." embossed beneath square windows; cab has rounded roof and rectangular forward facing windows; nickel-plated boiler w/black front, four embossed boiler bands; two nickel domes, nickel bell, brass stack painted black and cup-type round electric type headlight; four brass-stamped wheels on front truck, two on back; four cast iron drivers; flat brass connecting and cylinder rods; copper grab rails and steam piping on sides of boiler; nine-spoke front pilot; all metal tender with "131" stamped on sides; two metal trucks w/four stamped wheels apiece; engine and tender: 23" l., 4-3/4" w., 6-1/2" h. 1500   2000

34 Locomotive, 1910-1911, generally the same as 1909 version; painted black w/a gold square outlined on the cab roof, and "P.R.R." embossed on sides and painted gold; catwalk on sides of boiler has gold strip; copper bell, black domes and stock; oil-type cast-iron headlight; three separate boiler bands; copper piping on boiler sides and no grab rails on boiler; tender same as before, marked "131" in orange centered between two orange stripes; 23" l., 4-3/4" w., 6-1/2" h. 1500   2000

34 Locomotive, 1912-1915, generally the same as previous versions, but the lettering on engine and numbering on tender is orange; orange square outlined on roof of cab; shorter domes than previous year; round electric-type headlight; all metal tender; metal trucks and brass stamped wheels; 23" l., 4-3/4" w., 6-1/2" h. 1500   2000

C7   C9

The 4-4-2 No. 45 locomotive was an innovative model for the time, and the authentically-scaled Atlantic engine was on of the nicest made by any manufacturer. Attentive to detail, and undoubtedly a joy to the train enthusiast fortunate enough to own one. All in all, Carlisle and Finch's nicest piece of equipment.

45 Locomotive, 1902, engine w/brass piping and handrails; cab and boiler front are black and center of boiler is nickel-plated; lettering on engine is orange; sixteen-spoke drive wheels, stamped brass pilot and trailing truck wheels; seven pole armature, flat coupling and drive rods; trailing wheels covered by metal trucks; arched cab windows and rounded roof w/no ventilator; marked "82" beneath cab windows; headlight on the front of boiler top; black stack, copper bell, nickeled domes and steam whistle; crosshead guides U-shaped around driving rod; metal tender w/link and pin coupler; two four-wheel metal trucks w/stamped brass wheels; marked "N.Y.C. & H.R." in orange; coffin-type tender; engine and tender: 27-1/2" l., 6-1/4" h.............................. 2000   2500

45 Locomotive, 1903-1908, generally the same as earlier versions, bumper coupler now employed; black painted cab has round roof without ventilator; marked "82"below rectangular windows; boiler front painted black w/nickel-plated middle; oil-type headlight mounted on top of boiler; black painted brass stack and copper bell; two nickel domes and nickel steam whistle; copper boiler bands separate, copper piping and handrails; single crosshead guide; tender has higher sides and is longer than before; sides marked in orange "N.Y.C. & H.R."; grab rails at the front and rear of tender; brass trucks w/four brass stamped wheels each; motor became a three-pole armature type and a roof ventilator was added to the top of the cab; open trailing truck; tender has bumper coupler; 27 1/2" l., 6 1/4" h. ... 1800   2350

45 Locomotive, 1909-1913, generally same as previous version, w/black cast-iron domes instead of nickel-plated; tender same as before; range trim, orange square outlined on cab roof; 27 1/2" l., 4 3/4" w., 7" h. 1800   2350

C7   C9

45 Locomotive, 1914, same as 1913 version, w/shorter domes pinned to the boiler; piping and handrails are still brass w/copper boiler bands; cab is black w/orange square outlined on roof; lettering and lines on cab sides is orange; marked "82" beneath cab windows; tender marked "N.Y.C. & H.R." w/same outline as previous example; round electric-type headlight; 27 1/2" l., 4 3/4" w., 7" h.. 1800   2350

45 Locomotive, 1915, same as 1914 version in outline and appearance, except the entire locomotive is painted black; orange lettering beneath the cab windows reads "3238", some may still be marked "82"; tender has bumper coupler. 27-1/2" l., 4-3/4" w., 7" h...... 1900   2400

Trolleys

The No. 1 trolley was Carlisle and Finch's debut into toy train-making in 1896. It was first made as a three-rail trolley, then changed to a two-rail for the next version. Its single motor was inside the body, mounted on a wooden floor. The four cast-iron wheels were driven by a pulley mounted on the armature shaft w/a rubber or flexible metal band. This trolley was generally 7" long and 2-5/8" wide. Trail Cars, unmotorized, were available from 1897 until 1907.

1 Trolley, 1896, made to run on three-rail direct current track; four cast-iron wheels mounted to wooden floor; block tin ends and roof w/clerestory; tin body covered w/yellow paper label made to look like double doors and four windows on each side; marked w/logo "Electric Railway"; single motor w/two-pole armature................. 500   800

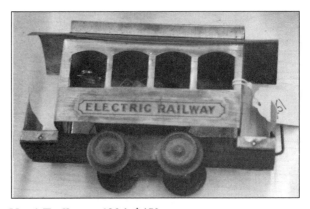

No. 1 Trolley, c. 1904, $450

	C7	C9

1 Trolley, 1897, now made to run on two-rail track; two-pole armature motor, wooden floor; painted black tin ends and roof w/clerestory strip; tin body covered w/yellow paper label made to look like two windows and two doors on each end and four windows on each side; marked w/logo "Electric Railway" below windows....................450　650

1 Trolley, 1897, now made to run on two-rail track; two-pole armature motor, wooden floor; black painted tin ends and roof w/clerestory; tin body w/four windows punched out on each side; body covered w/yellow paper label made to look like two doors and two windows on each end; marked w/logo "Electric Railway" below side windows..400　600

1 Trolley, 1897, catalogued version; now made to run on two-rail track; two-pole armature motor, wooden floor; polished brass body w/one door and two windows punched on each end, and four windows punched on each side; roof was either painted tin or polished brass w/clerestory; platform ends were polished brass; small paper label on each side w/logo "Electric Railway"...375　525

1 Trolley, 1898-1903, polished brass body w/one door and two windows punched on each end, and four windows punched on each side; roof was either painted tin or polished brass w/clerestory; platform ends were polished brass; small paper label on each side w/logo "Electric Railway"...325　475

1 Trolley, 1904-1906, polished brass body w/door and two windows punched out on each end, four windows punched out on each side; black painted tin roof w/clerestory strip and platform ends; logo "Electric Railway" embossed on each side.........300　450

1R Trolley, 1899-1906, same as No. 1 except that there is a three-pole armature and a reversing lever at the end of the trolley body.........................325　450

Designed to give customers the option of a larger street-car type trolley, this was an eight-wheel version made in 1897 and continued through production to the end of the Carlisle and Finch line. It was originally a medium-sized, double motor trolley and eventually became a large interurban type.

2 Trolley, 1897-1902, body, platform ends and clerestory roof of polished brass; plain sides w/seven windows punched out on each side w/centered yellow paper label; two windows and one door punched out on each end; this floor did not have a floor, so the two motors suspended from inside the body of the trolley on two cross braces running between the sides and rest on a small wooden platform to which the cast-iron wheels were also mounted and a band drove a single wheel from a pulley mounted on the armature shaft; w/logo "Electric Railway"; 12" l., 3-1/2" w., 5" h. ....　800　1200

2 Interurban, 1903, double truck, but only one three pole motor mounted beneath wooden floor, driving one pair of wheels by a gear; reversing switch mounted at end of body on platform; brass body and ends w/black painted tin roof, some polished brass w/clerestory strip, stamped brass wheels; ten arched windows on each side w/one door and two windows at each end; w/yellow paper label marked "Interurban Railway"; 19" l., 4" w., 6" h. ....　900　1300

2 Interurban, 1904-1906, double truck, w/single three-pole motor mounted beneath wooden floor; brass body w/black painted tin roof w/clerestory strip and end; wheels stamped brass; reverse lever at end of body on platform; sides have ten arched windows w/one and two windows at then end of car; embossed lettering read "Electric Railway"; 19" l., 4" w., 6" h. ....　800　1200

2 Interurban, 1907-1908, double truck w/one truck motor driven by gear; polished nickel-plated tin body w/nickel-plated tin roof w/clerestory strip and platform ends; sides have ten arched windows w/one and two windows at then end of car; embossed lettering read "Electric Railway"; 19" l., 4" w., 6" h. ....　900　1400

	C7	**C9**

2 Interurban, 1909-1915, redesigned body, brass; trucks also redesigned, black painted tin platform ends and roof w/clerestory strip; five large arched windows on each side w/two windows and one door on each end; reversing lever at end of body, double truck w/one truck gear driven by three-pole motor; embossed "Electric Railway" above arched windows; 19" l., 4" w., 6" h........ 800 1200

2-S Trolley, 1897-1898, same as the No. 2 of those years, but the motors were designed to be run on house current using an electric light as resistance between power source and track, as opposed to the regular No. 2 made to be run on wet batteries; made essentially to be used as continuously running store display 900 1200

18 Trolley, 1904-1915, there were inside seats along the windows and the motor was mounted beneath the wooden floor, where it drove one pair of wheels; brass truss-type truck system and four wheels which were stamped brass; motor was a three-pole reversible type; reverse lever is at the end of the car on the platform like an engineer's throttle; each side had four arched windows and one door and two windows at each end; embossed "Electric Railway" above arched windows. Trolley was made to meet the demand for an outfit larger than the No. 1, but smaller than the interurban. Some of these were fitted with trolley poles to run on a caternary system.

18 Trolley, 1904-1906, brass body w/brass platform ends and painted tin roof w/clerestory strip; black painted steps at platform ends; three-pole reversible motor w/lever on platform; four arched windows; embossed "Electric Railway" beneath arched windows; 13-1/3" l., 3-1/2" w., 6" h... 900 1300

18 Trolley, 1907-1908, body made of nickel-plated brass or nickel-plated tin w/nickel-plated platform ends; black painted tin roof w/clerestory strips; four arched windows on each side; nickel-plated steps at each end of platform w/three-pole motor w/lever on platform; embossed "Electric Railway" below windows; 13-1/2" l., 3-1/2" w., 6" h.. 950 1350

18 Trolley, 1909-1915, brass body and ends, black painted tin roof w/clerestory strip; three-pole motor beneath floor

w/lever on platform; four arched windows on each side w/black painted steps at each end of platform; embossed "Electric Railway" below arched windows; 13-1/2" l., 3-1/2" w., 6" h. 900 1300

19 Trolley, 1904-1912, same general construction as No. 18 w/open or summer pattern; the backs of the seats on this model were movable so that they could be turned to face in the direction of travel; motor is beneath the floor w/reverse lever was at the end of the platform like the; body was made of painted tin, while the roof and platform ends were made of polished brass; motor had brass gears; truck assembly was a brass truss-type screwed into the wooden floor of the trolley; sides were painted yellow; partial wall w/two windows at each end to separate the interior from the platform; came mounted w/a trolley allowing it to be run on a caternary system; 13-1/2" l., 3-1/2" w., 6" h. 1000 1450

This trolley was made to be a little larger than the No. 1 outfit. The motor originally came up into the body like the No. 1, but around 1909 the design was changed and the body was mounted beneath the floor of the trolley. The No. 42 always had a three-pole reversing motor, and the lever was on the end platform. The floor on these was always made of wood, with body attached by small nails. Trail cars were available for the No. 43 from 1902 until they disappeared from the catalog in 1911.

42 Trolley, 1902, Brass body, tin platform ends, steps and roof w/clerestory strip black painted; motor mounted through wooden floor, four cast-iron wheels mounted on a brass truss-type frame; one axle driven by spur gear system; one door at each end and five arched windows per side; yellow paper label reads "Electric Railway"; 8" l., 3" w., 5" h. 475 650

42 Trolley, 1903, brass body, tin steps, platform ends and roof w/clerestory strip black painted; brass truss-type frame w/four-stamped brass wheels; motor comes through floor up into body of trolley; one door at each end and five windows per side; paper label reads "Electric Railway"; 8" l., 3" w., 5" h. 450 600

	C7	C9

42 Trolley, 1904-1906, brass body, tin platform ends, steps and roof w/clerestory painted black; brass truss-type frame and stamped brass wheels; motor protrudes through floor into body cavity; five arched windows on each side and on door on each end; legend "Electric Railway" embossed in the side; 8" l., 3" w., 5" h................. 375 550

42 Trolley, 1907-1908, nickel-plated brass or tin body; tin platform ends, steps and roof w/clerestory strip painted black; brass truss-type frame; four stamped brass wheels; motor protrudes through wooden floor up into body cavity; large brass spur gear drive; headlight shroud; five windows on each side and one door on each end; sides embossed "Electric Railway" below five windows; 8" l., 3" w., 5" h. 500 700

42 Trolley, 1909-1915, tin platform ends, steps and roof w/clerestory strip painted black; brass body; motor beneath floor w/brass wheels and stamped tin frame of somewhat higher profile than older truss-type of brass; smaller motor and small gear on armature shaft drives brass gear on axle; light mounted inside the body; four arched windows on each side and one door on each end; embossed logo "Electric Railway" on side 400 550

	C7	C9

99 Trolley, 1905-1907, brass body w/brass platform ends and painted tin roof w/clerestory strip; black painted steps at platform ends; three-pole reversible motor w/lever on platform; trolley pole mounted on top to enable it to run on a caternary system; four arched windows; embossed "Electric Railway" beneath arched windows; 13-1/3" l., 3-1/2" w., 6" h. 1000 1500

100 Trolley, 1905-1906, same general construction as No. 18 w/open or summer pattern; the backs of the seats on this model were movable so that they could be turned to face in the direction of travel; motor is beneath the floor w/reverse lever was at the end of the platform like the; body was made of painted tin, while the roof and platform ends were made of polished brass; motor had brass gears; trolley pole mounted on top to enable it to run on a caternary system; truck assembly was a brass truss-type screwed into the wooden floor of the trolley; sides were painted yellow; partial wall w/two windows at each end to separate the interior from the platform; came mounted w/a trolley allowing it to be run on a caternary system; 13-1/2" l., 3-1/2" w., 6" h. 1100 1600

Carlisle and Finch Outfits

98   1905-1908, Elevated railway. #42 trolley, ten #54 elevating posts

99   1905-1907, Trolley railway. #18 trolley, twelve #3 caternary posts w/wire

100   1905-1906, #19 summer trolley, twelve #103 caternary posts w/wire

101   1905-1906, Trolley railway. #18 trolley, ten #103 double caternary posts, sixteen #103 single caternary posts, wire

102   1905-1906, #19 summer trolley, ten #103 double caternary posts, sixteen #103 single caternary posts, wire

104   1905-1906, #4 locomotive tender, #13-B, #13, #13, #10 switches, #57 bridge

104   1907, #4 locomotive, tender, #11, #12, #46, #47, #48, #49, #10 switches, #56 bridge

104   1908-1915, #4 locomotive, tender, #13-B, #13, #13, #10 switches, #57 bridge

105   1905-1915, #4 locomotive, tender, #13-B, #13, #13, #10 switches, #57 bridge

106   1905-1907, two #4 locomotives, tenders, #13-B, #13, #13, #11, #12, #46, #20 locomotive, #57 bridge, #97 station, #10 switches

107   1905-1909, #4 locomotive, tender #11, #12, #48, #49, #46, #57 bridge, #96 freight depot, #10 switches

108   1905-1906, #45 locomotive, tender, #51, #52, #52, #97 station, #58 switches

108   1907-1908, #45 locomotive, tender, #51, #52, #52, #97 station, #10 switches

Dorfan

Dorfan produced trains for only ten years, from 1924-1933, but during that time was one of the Big Four of American Train making, along with Ives, Lionel and American Flyer.

Julius and Milton Forcheimer, worked at the German firm of Jos. Krau & Co. until 1923 in the production and sales departments, respectively. Also working at Fandor was John C. Koerber, who had previously designed many of Bing's trains. Koerber eventually moved to Fandor to fulfill the same function. In 1923, after considerable planning, the three men moved to the United States and founded Dorfan.

Dorfan was the first train manufacturer to produce mechanical die-cast engines. By 1925, the company brought out its first electric model, the Electric Constructive Locomotive. This was marked "51," but was sold as numbers 255 and 260, the latter a more deluxe version with a headlight and brass handrails. These engines represented another innovation by Dorfan, as they were the first practical construction set in the field. Other companies reaction to the die-casting was similar to the original reaction to Fulton's steamboat, but as Julius Forcheimer once recalled, "[T]welve years later they were all using it."

However, despite the company's originality and the quality of its product, the stock market crash of 1929 and the Depression were fatal to the company.

Collectors should note that the alloy used by Dorfan was a mix of copper and zinc, and while it was a wise choice at the time, the impurities in the alloy caused the metal to expand; therefore, many Dorfan trains have cracked castings. Reproduction castings are available, and because of their relative rarity replacing a deteriorating casting with a reproduction does not do much harm the value.

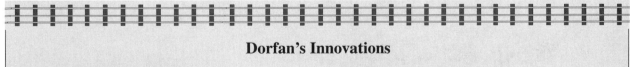

Dorfan's Innovations

- Die-cast locomotive bodies
- Easily assembled locomotive construction sets
- Upright lamp post
- Switchboard or "Panel Board"
- Lacquered lithographed cars
- Sets to build both locomotive and motor from same parts
- Double-track O-gauge working hopper car
- Inserted window frames in passenger cars (inserted from outside of car)
- One-unit removable drive wheels and axles
- First automatic circuit breaker

- Die-cast trucks
- Die-cast car wheels
- Ball-bearing locomotive
- O-gauge derrick car
- Die-cast steam-outline electric locomotive
- Remote-controlled train-stop signals
- Directional remote control for locomotives
- Steam-type locomotives with separate polished metal domes and stacks
- Model position-light signals
- Model signal bridge
- Remote control uncoupler

	C5	C7	C9
Arch Lamp	30	50	100
Atlanta Pullman, red	20	33	65
Champion, 100-watt transformer	6	10	20
Coach, maroon and yellow, w/brass trim, also done in red and yellow, "Boston"	54	90	180
Coach, peacock, blue, "Boston"	48	80	160
Coach, green, w/brass window inserts, "Chicago"	50	83	165
Coach, red w/brass trim, "Seattle"	21	36	72
Coach, red and yellow, "Seattle"	21	36	72
Coach, green w/brass windows, "Washington"	48	80	160
Engine, 0-4-0, orange and green, w/brass trim	210	350	700

	C5	C7	C9
Gondola, lithographed, orange and black	38	63	125
Gondola, lithographed, yellow	43	72	145
Locomotive, 0-4-0, wind-up, black	66	112	225
Locomotive, steam, maroon and yellow, w/brass and nickel trim, w/tender	108	180	360
Locomotive, 0-4-0, steam, red and yellow, w/brass trim, w/tender	108	180	360
Locomotive, 0-4-0, wind-up, black and red, w/four-wheel tender	105	175	350
Locomotive, Union Pacific, wind-up, w/two cars	72	120	240
Lumber Car, eight wheel	108	180	360
Observation Car, peacock blue, w/people and lights	48	80	160

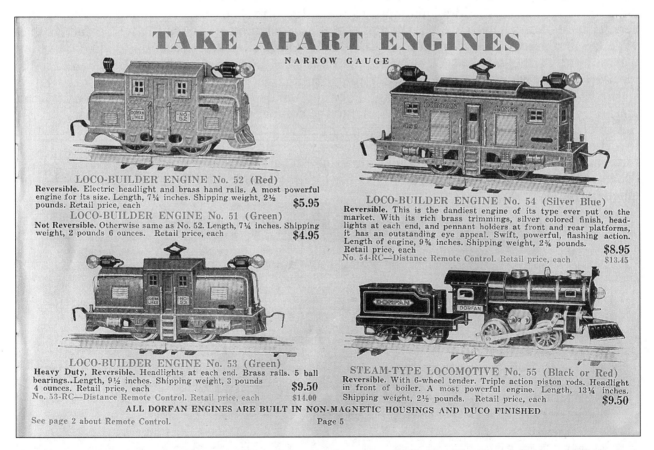

Dorfan Take Apart Engines: Top row, left to right: No. 52, green, $150; No. 54, silver and blue, $420. Bottom row, left to right: No. 53, green, $360; No. 55, black or red, $350. Courtesy 1930 Dorfan catalog.

	C5	C7	C9
Observation Car, peacock blue, red and black............................	22	36	72
Observation Car, red and yellow...	48	80	160
Observation Car, red, w/brass trim, w/people in windows	54	90	180
Observation Car, green, w/brass windows...................................	48	80	160
Observation Car, maroon and yellow, w/brass trim, also done in red and yellow, "Boston"	54	90	180
Pullman, peacock blue, red and black..	21	36	72
Pullman, red, "Boston"	54	90	180
Pullman, red, "Seattle"	21	36	72
Pullman, "Chicago".....................	180	300	600
Pullman, lithographed, yellow and red	21	36	72
Pullman, "Washington"................	72	120	240

	C5	C7	C9
Steam Loco, 0-4-0, wind-up, black, maroon and Yellow, w/brass trim, w/tender..............	66	112	225
Super Dorfan Set, includes engine, lumber car, two cars, and caboose..............................	900	1500	3000
Tank Car, lithographed, robin's-egg blue and maroon, w/brass trim..	144	240	480
Tank Car, robin's-egg blue	144	240	480
Tank Car, lithographed, reddish-brown, Indian Refining Co., early...	36	60	120
Tender, six wheel, crackle black and yellow	36	60	120
Transformer, 50 watt....................	5	9	18
Trestle Bridge	30	50	100
Tunnel, lithographed, w/cows, horse and wagon, car, house, trees and mountains...................	24	48	80

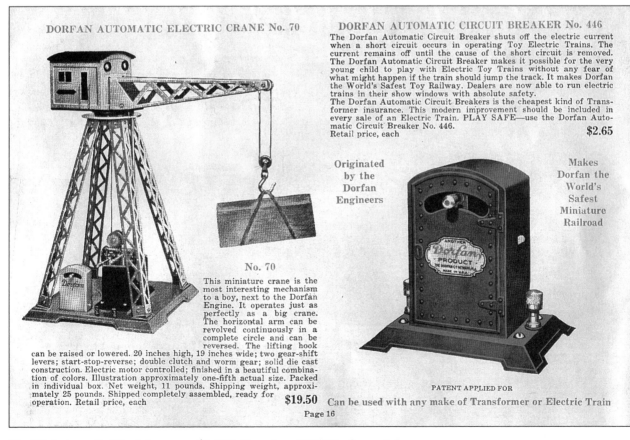

DORFAN AUTOMATIC ELECTRIC CRANE No. 70

No. 70

This miniature crane is the most interesting mechanism to a boy, next to the Dorfan Engine. It operates just as perfectly as a big crane. The horizontal arm can be revolved continuously in a complete circle and can be reversed. The lifting hook can be raised or lowered. 20 inches high, 19 inches wide; two gear-shift levers; start-stop-reverse; double clutch and worm gear; solid die cast construction. Electric motor controlled; finished in a beautiful combination of colors. Illustration approximately one-fifth actual size. Packed in individual box. Net weight, 11 pounds. Shipping weight, approximately 25 pounds. Shipped completely assembled, ready for operation. Retail price, each   **$19.50**

DORFAN AUTOMATIC CIRCUIT BREAKER No. 446

The Dorfan Automatic Circuit Breaker shuts off the electric current when a short circuit occurs in operating Toy Electric Trains. The current remains off until the cause of the short circuit is removed. The Dorfan Automatic Circuit Breaker makes it possible for the very young child to play with Electric Toy Trains without any fear of what might happen if the train should jump the track. It makes Dorfan the World's Safest Toy Railway. Dealers are now able to run electric trains in their show windows with absolute safety.

The Dorfan Automatic Circuit Breakers is the cheapest kind of Transformer insurance. This modern improvement should be included in every sale of an Electric Train. PLAY SAFE—use the Dorfan Automatic Circuit Breaker No. 446.

Retail price, each   **$2.65**

Originated by the Dorfan Engineers

Makes Dorfan the World's Safest Miniature Railroad

PATENT APPLIED FOR

Can be used with any make of Transformer or Electric Train

Page 16

No. 70 Automatic Electric crane, $1,200. Courtesy 1930 Dorfan catalog.

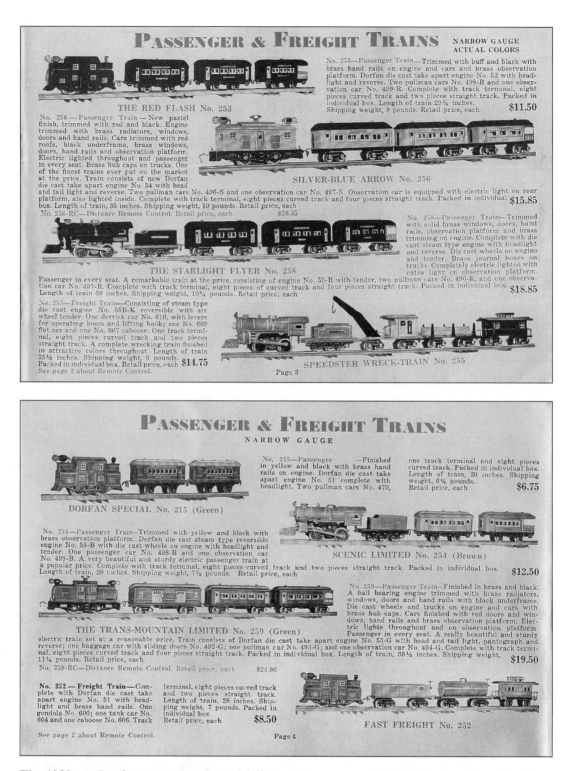

PASSENGER & FREIGHT TRAINS NARROW GAUGE ACTUAL COLORS

THE RED FLASH No. 253

No. 253—Passenger Train—Trimmed with buff and black with brass hand rails on engine and cars and brass observation platform. Dorfan die cast take apart engine No. 52 with headlight and reverse. Two pullman cars No. 498-R and one observation car No. 499-R. Complete with track terminal, eight pieces curved track and two pieces straight track. Packed in individual box. Length of train 29¾ inches. Shipping weight, 8 pounds. Retail price, each   **$11.50**

No. 256—Passenger Train—New pastel finish, trimmed with red and black. Engine trimmed with brass radiators, windows, doors and hand rails. Cars trimmed with red roofs, black underframe, brass windows, doors, hand rails and observation platform. Electric lighted throughout and passenger in every seat. Brass hub caps on trucks. One of the finest trains ever put on the market at the price. Train consists of new Dorfan die cast take apart engine No. 54 with head and tail light and reverse. Two pullman cars No. 496-S and one observation car No. 497-S. Observation car is equipped with electric light on rear platform, also lighted inside. Complete with track terminal, eight pieces curved track and four pieces straight track. Packed in individual box. Length of train, 35 inches. Shipping weight, 10 pounds. Retail price, each   **$15.85**
No. 256-RC—Distance Remote Control. Retail price, each $20.35

SILVER-BLUE ARROW No. 256

THE STARLIGHT FLYER No. 258

Passenger in every seat. A remarkable train at the price, consisting of engine No. 55-R with tender, two pullman cars No. 496-R, and one observation car No. 497-R. Complete with track terminal, eight pieces of curved track and four pieces straight track. Packed in individual box. Length of train 39 inches. Shipping weight, 10¼ pounds. Retail price, each

No. 258—Passenger Train—Trimmed with solid brass windows, doors, hand rails, observation platform and brass trimming on engine. Complete with die cast steam type engine with headlight and reverse. Die cast wheels on engine and tender. Brass journal boxes on trucks. Completely electric lighted with extra light on observation platform.   **$18.85**

No. 255—Freight Train—Consisting of steam type die cast engine No. 55B-K reversible with six wheel tender. One derrick car No. 610, with levers for operating boom and lifting hook; one No. 609 flat car and one No. 607 caboose. One track terminal, eight pieces curved track and two pieces straight track. A complete wrecking train finished in attractive colors throughout. Length of train 35½ inches. Shipping weight, 9 pounds. Packed in individual box. Retail price, each **$14.75**
See page 2 about Remote Control.

SPEEDSTER WRECK-TRAIN No. 255

Page 3

PASSENGER & FREIGHT TRAINS
NARROW GAUGE

DORFAN SPECIAL No. 215 (Green)

No. 215—Passenger   —Finished in yellow and black with brass hand rails on engine. Dorfan die cast take apart engine No. 51 complete with headlight. Two pullman cars No. 470,

one track terminal and eight pieces curved track. Packed in individual box. Length of train, 20 inches. Shipping weight, 6¼ pounds. Retail price, each   **$6.75**

No. 254—Passenger Train—Trimmed with yellow and black with brass observation platform. Dorfan die cast steam type reversible engine No. 55-B with die cast wheels on engine with headlight and tender. One passenger car No. 498-B and one observation car No. 499-B. A very beautiful and sturdy electric passenger train at a popular price. Complete with track terminal, eight pieces curved track and two pieces straight track. Packed in individual box. Length of train, 28 inches. Shipping weight, 7½ pounds. Retail price, each   **$12.50**

SCENIC LIMITED No. 254 (Brown)

THE TRANS-MOUNTAIN LIMITED No. 259 (Green)

electric train set at a reasonable price. Train consists of Dorfan die cast take apart engine No. 53-G with head and tail light, pantograph and reverse; one baggage car with sliding doors No. 492-G; one pullman car No. 493-G; and one observation car No. 494-G. Complete with track terminal, eight pieces curved track and four pieces straight track. Packed in individual box. Length of train, 38½ inches. Shipping weight, 11¼ pounds. Retail price, each
No. 259-RC—Distance Remote Control. Retail price, each $24.00

No. 259—Passenger Train—Finished in brass and black. A ball bearing engine trimmed with brass radiators, windows, doors and hand rails with black underframe. Die cast wheels and trucks on engine and cars with brass hub caps. Cars finished with red doors and windows, hand rails and brass observation platform. Electric lights throughout and on observation platform. Passenger in every seat. A really beautiful and sturdy   **$19.50**

No. 252 — Freight Train—Complete with Dorfan die cast take apart engine No. 51 with headlight and brass hand rails. One gondola No. 600; one tank car No. 604 and one caboose No. 606. Track terminal, eight pieces curved track and two pieces straight track. Length of train, 28 inches. Shipping weight, 7 pounds. Packed in individual box. Retail price, each   **$8.50**

FAST FREIGHT No. 252

See page 2 about Remote Control.

Page 4

The 1930 catalog features a number of different passenger and freight trains offered by Dorfan.

ACCESSORIES

Stations

STATION No. 424
Small metal station, 5 by 7½ inches. Shipping weight, 10 oz. Retail price, each **$1.00**

STATION No. 426
Three-story building, resembling brick. Electrically lighted. Covered platform; clock dial; arcade. Height, 9½ inches, with 12½ inches base. Shipping weight, 3 pounds, 4 ounces. Retail price, each **$4.85**

(See also Page 14.)

Bridges

BRIDGE No. 410
Narrow Gauge—Strongly built, duco finish. Length, 30½ inches. Height, 5½ inches. Width, 5¼ inches. Shipping weight, 2½ pounds. Retail price, each **$3.25**

BRIDGE No. 413
Wide Gauge—Length, 42 inches. Height, 8½ inches. Width, 7½ inches. Shipping weight, 6 pounds. Retail price, each **$5.50**

BRIDGE No. 411
Narrow Gauge—Similar to No. 410, but with an additional section of bridge. Length, 40½ inches. Height, 5½ inches. Width, 5¼ inches. Shipping weight, 4 pounds. Retail price, each **$5.50**

BRIDGE No. 414
Wide Gauge—Same as No. 411. Length, 56 inches. Height, 8½ inches. Width, 7½ inches. For wide gauge trains. Shipping weight, 9 pounds. Retail price, each **$8.95**

BRIDGE No. 412
Narrow Gauge—Illuminated double span. The four posts are lighted. Length, 40½ inches. Height, 5½ inches. Shipping weight, 4¼ pounds. Retail price, each **$8.95**

(See also Page 14.)

Tunnels

DORFAN TUNNEL No. 3
For small mecha cal trains. Leng 7½ inches. Heig 5 inches. Width, inches. Shippi weight, 11 ounc Retail price, each **$.**

No. 310

TUNNEL No. 31
Made of durable com sition in one piece. E bossed and decorated colors. Length, inches. Width, 8 inch Height, 8 inches. Retail price, each **$1.**

TUNNEL No. 32
Same as No. 319, larger. Length, 1 inches. Width, 7 inch Height, 8¼ inch **$2.**

No. 319

Shipping weight, 4 pounds. Retail price, each

TUNNEL No. 322
Same as No. 321, but larger. Length, 12¼ inch Width, 8½ inches. Height, 11¾ inches. Shippi weight, 4½ pounds. Retail price, each **$3.**

TUNNEL No. 323
Same as No. 321, but much larger. Length, 14 inches. Width, 10 inches. Height, 12 inches. Shippi weight, 5½ pounds. Retail price, each **$5.**

Dorfan's 1930 catalog illustrates the wide array of accessories available, including the No. 410 Bridge ($170). Courtesy 1930 Dorfan catalog.

	C5	C7	C9
5 Caboose, lithographed, brown, yellow, green and black	36	60	120
51 Engine, 0-4-0, green and yellow	36	60	120
52 Engine, green	45	75	150
53 Engine, 0-4-0, peacock blue and yellow, w/brass trim	108	180	360
53 Engine, 0-4-0, green and maroon	108	180	360
53 Engine, 0-4-0, red	108	180	360
54 Engine, 0-4-0, green	108	180	360
54 Engine, 0-4-0, silver and blue	126	210	420
54 Engine, 0-4-0, silver and gray, w/brass trim	108	180	360
55 Engine, 0-4-0, black or red	105	175	350
70 Automatic Electric Crane	360	600	1200
L.R.C.X. 84 Tank Car, lithographed , red and black	36	60	120

	C5	C7	C9
160 Tender	21	35	70
410 Bridge	54	85	170
421 Electric Crossing Gate	60	100	200
492 Baggage Car, green and maroon, w/brass trim	36	60	120
493 Coach, green and maroon, w/brass trim, "Seattle"	30	50	100
493 Coach, peacock blue, "Seattle"	32	54	108
494 Observation Car, green and maroon, w/brass trim	27	45	90
496 Passenger, red or silver-blue	36	60	100
497 Observation Car, red or silver-blue	51	85	170
498 Passenger, red or brown	36	60	100
499 Observation Car, red or brown	36	60	100
600 Gondola, narrow gauge	20	32	65
601 Boxcar, narrow gauge	10	17	35

A wide variety of track, switches and crossovers were available from Dorfan, as shown in the 1930 catalog.

Dorfan accessories. Courtesy 1930 Dorfan catalog.

Top row, left to right: No. 492 baggage car, $120; No. 493 coach, $100; No. 494 observation car, $90. Bottom row, left to right: No. 496 passenger car, $100; No. 497 observation car, $170; No. 498 passenger car, $100; No. 499 observation car, $100. Courtesy 1930 Dorfan catalog.

	C5	C7	C9		C5	C7	C9
604 Tank Car, narrow gauge	10	17	35	772 Coach, yellow and red, w/brass and nickel trim, "Washington"	162	270	540
605 Hopper, narrow gauge	13	21	42				
606 Caboose	13	21	42	773 Observation Car, orange and black, w/people in windows	67	112	225
607 Caboose, narrow gauge	27	45	90				
609 Lumber Car, narrow gauge.....	20	33	65	773 Observation Car, crackle green, black and red, w/nickel and brass trim	162	270	540
610 Derrick, narrow gauge	33	55	110				
770 Baggage Car, green, black and red, w/nickel trim.....................	162	270	540	789 Coach, maroon and yellow, "Mountain Brook"	162	270	540
771 Coach, orange and black, w/people in windows	162	270	540	789 Coach, orange and Green........	62	270	540
771 Passenger Car, green, black and red, w/nickel trim, "San Francisco"	216	360	720	789 Coach, green and light brown, "Mountain Brook"	87	145	290
772 Coach, blue and yellow	162	270	540	789 Coach, black and red, "Mountain Brook"	144	240	480
772 Coach, crackle brown and green	162	270	540	790 Coach, maroon and yellow, "Pleasant View"	75	125	250
				800 Gondola..................................	33	55	110

	C5	C7	C9
801 Boxcar	40	67	135
804 Tank Car	60	100	200
805 Hopper	54	90	180
806 Caboose	33	55	110
809 Lumber Car	33	55	110
1201 Car, lithographed gray	108	180	360
3919 Engine, 0-4-0, orange	324	540	1080
3920 Engine, 0-4-0, red	324	540	1080
3930 Locomotive, 4-4-4, electric	540	900	1800
3931 Locomotive, 4-4-4, black, electric	540	900	1800
3931 Locomotive, 4-4-4, green, electric	540	900	1800
5402 Coach, red, black and yellow, "Washington"	21	36	72

	C5	C7	C9
11201 Hopper, gray	16	27	72
14048 Gondola, lithographed, yellow, w/nickel trim	9	15	30
21499 Boxcar, lithographed, black, red, green, brown, w/brass, "Santa Fe"	180	300	600
126432 Boxcar, green and black	33	55	110
S182999 Boxcar, lithographed, yellow and black	18	30	60
234561 Gondola, orange and black	180	300	600
293325 Tank Car, robin's-egg blue, red, black and white	180	300	600
486751 Caboose, brown, green, red, yellow and black	180	300	600
517953 Boxcar, orange and brown	16	27	54

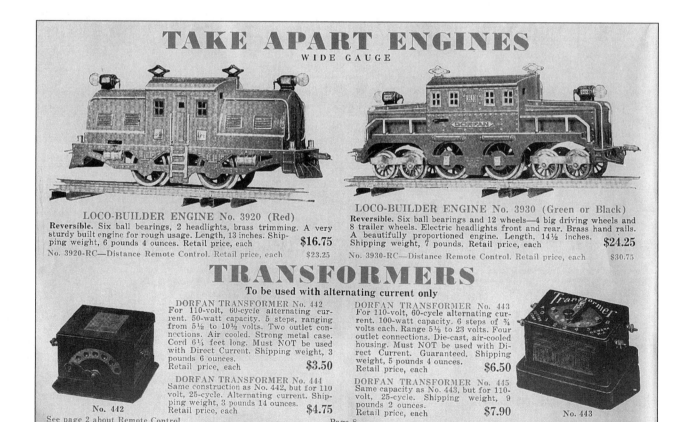

Top row, left to right: No. 3920 Engine, $1,080; No. 3930 Engine, $1,800. Courtesy 1930 Dorfan catalog.

Elektoy

L ittle is known about Elektoy, the trade name of a series of detailed stamped-metal trains. Started by J.K. Osborn Mfg. Co. of Harrison, New Jersey, the length of time they were in production has been cited by some as 1911-1913 and by others as 1910 to 1917. It is difficult for to say whether production was halted due to mismanagement, poor distribution or the lack of materials, either way, production was never restored following World War I. The duration, although short, was apparently prolific, as a surprising amount of Elektoy continues to surface. In addition to quantity, quite a variety remains.

Elektoy trains like those made by Ives and Marklin were not sold through national department stores; instead, Elektoy sold their trains through small hardware stores and electric supply outlets.

Elektoy trains were cursed by a poor coupling system. Some believe this may have hastened the lines demise. Osborn's solution to the already patented hook-slot couplers and Ives automatic couplers was a flat piece of metal attached to one end of the car. Bent upward, this metal piece fit into a slot in the back of the next car. Poorly designed and subject to structural fatigue, these couplers often broke. Going to a new coupler style would have required extensive retooling and substantial financial outlay. This may have been an insurmountable hurdle for the still-fledgling company.

Many interesting pieces have survived the intervening years, to turn up and delight us today as they undoubtedly delighted our grandfathers over eighty years ago.

All Elektoy is Gauge #1, which is 1-7/8-inch from outside rail to outside rail.

	C7	C9

901 Trolley, 1912-1913, four wheel, single non-reversing motor with brass spur gearing, brass trucks; steel body painted in four colors; separate roof w/clerestory strip; 8" l., 36-1/2" h., 36-3/4" w. 250 400

902 Trolley, 1912-1913, eight wheel, double truck, nickel-plated body, trucks and wheels; six double windows per side; body came painted in four colors; separate roof w/clerestory strip; 9" l., 2-3/4" w., 4-1/2" h. 300 500

903 Locomotive, 1912, 0-4-0; switcher-type w/coal bunker, no tender; six pole reversible motor; black cab and boiler, nickel dome, stack, cylinders, rods, crossheads, and wheels; nickel-plated operating headlight; eight-spoke drive wheels; step-type cow-catcher pilot; two arched-cab windows per side; reverse unit in coal bunker; "976" stamped on cab sides 250 400

903 Locomotive, 1913, 0-4-0; freight loco w/tender; gunmetal finish and enameled colors w/nickel trim; eight-spoke drive wheels; reversible motor; eight-wheel tender w/nickel trucks, black or gray body w/coal load; tender lettered for Pennsylvania Lines. Length: 17-1/2" l., 3-1/2" w., 4-3/4" h. 250 400

No. 903, Locomotive, 1913, $400

No. 903, Tender, 1913

	C7	C9

904 Locomotive, 1911-1913, 0-4-0; S-2 style nickel-plated center cab, electric; w/door and two windows per side; same motor as 903; operating headlight and bell on one hood, headlight and pantograph on other; maroon, gray or black hood; eight-spoke drive wheels w/coupling rods; "No 9" on one hood; each side marked "PRR"; 11" l., 4" w., 4-3/4" h. 1050 2100

905 Locomotive, 1911-1913, 0-4-0; passenger-type; brass boiler, nickel cab, running gear, wheels, cylinders and operating headlight; same motor as 903; two-arched windows on cab; eight-spoke drive wheels w/coupling rods; handrail on each side of boiler; tender has polished brass sides, black floor, nickel trucks and wheels; marked "Pennsylvania Lines"; 18" l., 3-1/2" w., Height: 4-3/4" h 750 1500

906 Dump Car, 1911-1913, four-wheel; frame w/saddles holding bucket at either end; finished in two colors, metal parts nickel-plated; 5" l., 2-1/2" w., 3-3/8" w 150 300

No. 906, Dump car, 1911-1913, $300

907 Coal Car, 1911-1913, eight-wheel; hopper w/bottom trap door controlled by side handle; nickel-plated trucks, black body and frame; marked for Erie, or C.R.R. of New Jersey; 9-3/4" l., 2-3/4" w., 3-3/8" w 75 100

908 Lumber Car, 1911-1913, eight wheel; black body with ten removable stakes to make flat car; nickel-plated trucks and wheels; 9-3/4" l., 2-3/4" w., 2-3/8" h 65 85

	C7	C9

909 Gravel Car, 1911-1913, eight wheel; finished in three colors w/nickel trucks and wheels; marked "Pennsylvania Lines"; 9-3/4" l., 2-3/4" w., 2-3/4" h. ... 70 90

910 Live Stock Car, 1911-1913, eight wheel; red or yellow, with brown roof; slotted sides have soldered diagonal and sliding door; brakewheel at each end; nickel-plated trucks and wheels; 9-3/4" l., 2-3/4" w., 4-3/4" h. 90 110

No. 910, Live Stock car, 1911-1913, $110

911 Boxcar, 1911-1913, eight wheel; red or yellow, w/lithographed sliding door on each side; brakewheel at each end; nickel-plated trucks and wheels; marked "Fast Freight" w/"New York Central" in logo or "Merchant's Dispatch Transportation Company" w/"Refrigeration" and "Dairy Products Express"; 9-3/4" l., 2-3/4" w., 4-3/4" h. 90 110

No. 911, Boxcar, 1911-1913, $110

	C7	C9

912 Caboose, 1911-1913, eight wheel; simulated-wood lithograph w/painted roof and cupola; two windows on each side and three on cupola; handrail at each end; nickel-plated trucks and wheels; marked "Pennsylvania Lines"; 9-3/4 l., 2-3/4" w., 5-1/4" h. 95 120

913 Passenger Coach, 1911-1913, eight wheel; simulated-wood lithograph, red or Tuscan body, w/brown roof; eight windows per side; marked "Pennsylvania Limited" above windows, "2518" below; w/clerestory strip on roof; nickel-plated wheels and trucks; 10" l., 2-3/4" w., 4-1/2" h. 90 110

914 Combination Baggage and Smoker Car, 1911-1913, eight wheel; simulated-wood lithograph, red or Tuscan body, w/brown roof; eight windows per side, sliding door on each side; marked "Pennsylvania Limited" above windows, "2518" below; w/clerestory strip on roof; nickel-plated wheels and trucks; 10" l., 2-3/4" w., 4-1/2" h. 90 110

915 Pullman Car, 1911-1913, eight wheel; simulated-wood lithograph, red or Tuscan body, w/brown roof; nine windows per side w/two-colored celluloid inside; marked "Pullman" above windows, "electra" below; w/clerestory strip on roof; nickel-plated wheels and trucks; 10" l., 2-3/4" w., 4-1/2" h. 90 110

916 Track, 1911-1913, curved and straight; steel w/fiber insulators; straight track: 12" l. curved track: 30" or 36" dia. .... — 1

917 Switches, 1911-1913, left and right; self-locking operating lever and represents signal 3 5

918-45 45 degree crossing, 1911-1913, ... 2 3

918-90 90 degree crossing, 1911-1913, ... 2 3

	C7	C9

919 Track Bumper, 1911-1913, steel w/sprung bumpers on bar; works on straight or curved track 5 8

920 Controller, 1911-1913, speed regulator with seven available positions; 3-1/4" square 2 3

921 Locomotive, 1913, 0-4-0; S-2 center cab, electric, non-reversible, double spur-geared motor; gray body, copper roof, nickel-plated running gear; two windows and one door per side; whistle on one hood, pantograph on other; no headlight or coupling rods; nickel-plated stamped disk wheels; spoked pilot at front, L-shaped step-type pilot and coupler at rear; marked "P.R.R." on one hood, "328" or "237" on other; 9-1/2" l., 3-3/4" w., 4-1/2" h. 300 500

934 Loco, 1913, 0-4-0; S-2 type center cab electric, reversible motor, double spur-geared motor; gray body, copper roof, nickel-plated running gear; two windows and one door per side; whistle on one hood, pantograph on other; operating headlight or coupling rods; nickel-plated stamped disk wheels; spoked pilot at front, L-shaped step-type pilot and coupler at rear; marked "P.R.R." on one hood, "328" or "237" on other; 9-1/2" l., 3-3/4" w., 4-1/2" h. 300 500

935 Loco, 1913, 0-4-0; S-2 type center cab electric, reversible motor, double spur-geared motor; elaborate finish, copper roof, nickel-plated running gear; two windows and one door per side; whistle on one hood, pantograph on other; operating headlight or coupling rods;

	C7	C9

large drive wheels and coupling rods; spoked pilot at front, L-shaped step-type pilot; marked "P.R.R." on one hood, "328" or "237" on other; 9-1/2" l., 3-3/4" w., 4-1/2" h. 300 500

No. 935, Locomotive, 1913, $500

937 Special Small Passenger Car, 1913, made to go with the 921, 934, and 935 engines; painted, with lithographed detail; nickel-plated wheels and trucks; 8" l, 3-1/2" w., 3-3/4" h. 70 90

938 Oil Car, 1913, eight wheel; red body w/black frame; grab rail on either side of tank; nickel-plated wheels and trucks; 9-3/4" l., 2-3/4" w., 4" h. 80 100

No. 938, Oil car, 1913, $100

Elektoy Outfits

922	1913 921, (3) 906, 920
923	1913 921, 908, (2) 909, 920
924	1913 934, (3) 937, 920
925	1913 934, 911, 910, 909, 912
926	1913, 903, 909, 911, 908, 912, 920
927	1913 903, (4) 907, 920

928	1913 903, (2) 911, 910, 912, 920
929	1913 904, (2) 913, 914, 920
930	1913 904, (2) 915, 914, 920
931:	1913 905, (2) 913, 914, 920
932:	1913 905, (2) 915, 914, 920
933:	1913 905, (2) 913, (3) 915, 920

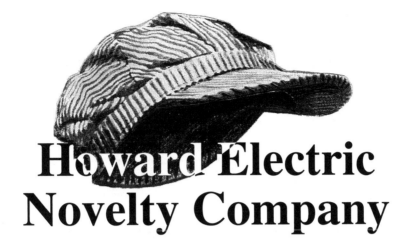

Howard Electric Novelty Company

The history of the Howard Electric Novelty Company, named after its location on Howard Street in New York City, is somewhat obscure. Train production began in 1904, and a variety of items were cataloged over the next few years, until Howard Electric got out of the train business in 1909. This astounding brevity, however, is surpassed by Elektoy, whose reign in No. 1 gauge seems to have been from 1911 to 1913. Of the two-inch gauge competitors, however, Howard seems most similar to Carlisle and Finch production. For a time they were even producing some equipment with their own coupler and a bumper-type coupler, as well, to accommodate rail fans with Carlisle and Finch equipment who wished to add Howard, or vice versa.

Howard was another example of crude early production with an alluring charm. Nowadays LGB and similar equipment has come to capture the hearts of many rail fans, and while with today's technology it is easy to mass produce large plastic equipment with lots of detail built into the dies, in the early part of the century production was a much more painstaking and laborious undertaking. Simplicity with style and grace marks the production of the early toy train pioneers, and although they seem primitive compared to today, they opened up the road of opportunity with their innovations and made today's production possible.

	C7	C9

1 Trolley, 1904-1909, tin body and platform ends painted yellow or red; door at each end; punched windows on each side; two-pole motor under floor, brass spur gears; stamped-metal trucks w/embossed rivet detail; black tin roof w/clerestory strip, block steps; body can be removed, leaving flat car w/steps; stamped brass wheels; sides marked "Electric R.R."; trail car was available; 7-1/2" l., 4-1/2" h. 400 600

2 Trolley, 1904-1909, three-pole motor w/reversing lever; tin ends, steps and body painted three colors; six windows per side; black tin roof w/clerestory strip; one door at each end; nickel-plated truck w/embossed rivet detail; four brass wheels; marked "459" and "Electric Traction Line" beneath widows; trail car was available; 12" l., 5-1/2" h. 400 600

3 Express Car, 1904-1909, three-pole reversible motor beneath floor w/lever; painted-tin gondola body; nickel-plated truck w/embossed rivet detail; "Express" logo painted on sides; 9" l., 3-3/8"w 275 400

4 Trolley, 1904-1909, painted tin body fits over top of express car to form trolley; three-pole reversing motor w/lever beneath floor; six windows on each side; nickel-plated truck w/embossed rivet detail; express car 9" l, 3-3/8" w; trolley 12" l., 5-1/2" h. 450 650

5 Mining Locomotive, 1904-1909, O-B-O; three-pole reversible motor in boiler; steeple cab w/two windows on either side and two at each end; grab rails and steps up back of body, dummy headlight at front; reverse lever; L-shaped pilots at each end; four brass open-drive w/brass coupling rods; 12" l., 3-1/4" w., 5" h. 650 900

6 Locomotive, 1904-1905, 4-2-0; wooden frame w/motor beneath; black tin body, nickel boiler bands; boiler extends back into cab; large steam dome w/two arched windows on either cab side; black coal bunker; round electric-type headlight beyond boiler front; sheet metal L-shaped pilot; solid brass drive wheels, stamped brass pilot wheels; round side rods; cataloged in B & O livery as No. 890; 10" l., Height: 4-1/2" h. 450 650

6 Locomotive, 1906-1909, 4-2-0; three-pole reversing-type motor w/reduction gearing; metal frame w/high-profile cab w/two arched windows on either side; nickel-plated boiler bands; Russian-iron boiler w/self adjusting and regulating bushes; black body and nickel-plated coal bunker; 10" l., 4-1/2" h. 450 650

7 Locomotive, 1904-1905, 0-4-0; two-pole switch engine inside boiler w/reverse lever; black tin body w/nickel-plated trim; cab w/two arched windows on either side; wooden frame; dummy headlight mounted on front of metal boiler; boiler extends back into cab; L-shaped tin pilot; brass wheels; black coal bunker, round cylinder rods flat brass coupling rods; cataloged in N.Y.C. & H.R. livery as no. 3584. 12" l., 4-1/2" w., 6" h. 400 600

8 Locomotive, 1904-1909, 4-4-0; three-pole reversible motor in boiler; black body; cabs w/two arched cab on either side; nickel-plated trim and brass driving wheels; nickel-plated boiler bands, brass rivets and nickel-plated piping; bell; flat coupling rods; cylinder rods w/separate round rod into piston; marked "1897" beneath windows; modeled after the Empire State Express of 1893; 21" l., 6"h. ... 500 700

10 Locomotive, 1906-1908, 4-4-0; three-pole reversible motor; larger than #8; Russian-iron boiler; brass cab and trimmings; two arched windows on either side of cab; electric headlight; two four-wheel swivel trucks w/brass wheels; brass stack, domes are brass and flat coupling rods, round piston rods; tender has tool box and water tank; marked "N.Y.C. & H.R." 600 850

	C7	C9
10 Locomotive, 1908-1909, 4-4-0; three-pole reversible motor; larger than #8; Russian-iron boiler; brass cab and trimmings; two arched windows on either side of cab; reversible headlight; two four-wheel swivel trucks w/brass wheels; brass stack, domes are brass and flat coupling rods, round piston rods; tender has tool box and water tank; marked "N.Y.C. & H.R."	700	900
20 Flat Car, 1904-1909, painted tin body w/brake wheel at either end; two nickel-plated trucks, each w/four brass wheels; marked "97"; 10" l., 2" h.	75	95
21 Gondola, 1904-1909, painted tin body w/brake wheel at either end; two nickel-plated trucks, each w/four brass wheels; N.Y.C. & H.R. livery, no. 1157; 10" l., 3-1/3" h.	75	95
22 Passenger Coach, 1904-1909, painted tin body; black tin roof w/clerestory strip; six windows on either side, one door at either end; wooden floor w/painted metal steps and end railings; two nickel-plated trucks, each w/four brass wheels; painted lettering; cataloged in D.L. & W. livery; 12" l., 3-3/8" w., 5-1/4" h.	150	275
23 Baggage Car, 1904-1909, painted metal body and metal roof w/clerestory; two nickel-plated trucks, each w/four brass wheels; sliding doors marked "Baggage," sides marked "N.Y.C. & H.R."; 12" l., 3-3/8" w., 5-1/4" h.	125	250
24 Boxcar, 1904-1909, painted tin body w/brake wheel at either end of car; two nickel plated trucks, each w/four brass wheels; marked "N.Y.C. & H.R." and "8907," sliding doors marked "N.Y. Central & H.R. Fast Freight"; 10" l., 3-1/4" w., 4-3/4" h.	100	185
25 Caboose, 1901-1909, red or yellow painted tin body; black roof and cupola w/two windows on either side and two windows at each end; painted steps and ends w/one door at each end; two nickel-plated trucks, each w/four brass wheels; marked "N.Y.C. & H.R.R." under windows; 10-1/2" l.; 3-3/4" w., 5-1/2" h.	175	250
26 Dump Car, 1904-1909, painted metal bucket and frame w/spring-release catch to tipple bucket; nickel-plated trucks, each w/four brass wheels	75	95
27 Oil Car, 1904-1909, ruby-red painted metal body and frame w/nickel-plated bands; hand rail on each side and brake wheel at each end; 12" l.	110	185
28 Pullman Baggage, 1905-1909, made for 1904-1909 4-4-0 locomotive; painted tin body w/brake wheel at each end and a sliding door on either side; two nickel-plated, Babbit-metal trucks w/oil boxes and springs, each w/four brass wheels; marked "Pennsylvania," "Baggage," "U.S. Mail," "Fast Mail," "Express," "Railway Office" and "PPR"; 16" l., 3-1/4" w., 5-1/4" h.	175	275
29 Pullman Chair Car, 1905-1909, made for 1904-1909 4-4-0 locomotive; painted tin body w/hand railings, steps and one sliding door at either end; nine windows on either side; black-painted roof w/clerestory; seats turn to face either direction; two Babbitt-metal trucks, each w/4 brass wheels each; 16" l., 3-1/4" w., 5-1/4" h.	175	275
30 Pullman Palace Car, 1905-1909, made for 1904-1909 4-4-0 locomotive; painted tin body w/four windows and a door on either side; no steps; roof with clerestory; marked "Pennsylvania Limited" above window and "Adair" below; 16" l., 3-1/4" w., 5-1/4" h.	195	285
50 Track Bumper, 1904-1909, wood and metal w/spring bumper; used to prevent derailing on track sidings	20	35
51 90-degree Crossing, 1904-1909, w/electrical connections	10	18
52 Switch, 1904-1909, Y-type	10	20

	C7	C9
52-R Switch, 1904-1909, right hand	10	20
53-L Switch, 1904-1909, left hand	10	20
55 Station, 1904-1909, w/two automatic semaphores on one pole, run by electromagnets; came w/special track		

	C7	C9
section; wood base w/paper-covered tin body depicting bricks; two windows front and back; roof with chimney; sign reads "Station"	125	210
56 Rail Connector, 1904-1909, U-shaped piece of metal w/two screws to hold two track ends together	—	1

Howard Electric Outfits

101 1904-19091, 55
102 1904-19094, 55
103 1904-19093, (3) 26
104 1904-19096, 20, 24, 25
105 1904-19096, 23, (2) 22
106 1904-19057, 21, 24, 25, 26, 27
107 1904-19057, 21, 24, 25, 26, 27, 51, (2) 52R, (2) 52L

107 1906-19098, 21, 24, 25, 26, 27, 51, (2) 52R, (2) 52L
108 1904-19098, (2) 22, 23, (1) 52R, 52L
109 1904-19098, (2) 22, 23, 20, 24, 25, 26, 27, 52L, 52R
110 1904-19098, 28, 29, 30, 52, 52L, 52R
111 1906-190910, 28, 29, 30, 52, 52L, 52R

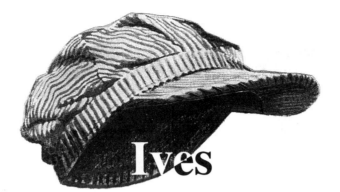

The grandfather of America's toy industry was certainly Ives. Beginning in 1868, in a plant in Bridgeport, Connecticut, Ives manufactured sixty years worth of such quality toys that they were backed by an unconditional guaranty. Most early Ives toys showed no mark of identification, but many patent dates and key words appearing on pieces can tip off the canny collector as to the manufacturer. Many old toys and floor trains as well as clockwork powerboats and track trains exist today. This chapter will concern itself with Ives production from around 1903 until 1932, when it was being phased out. Most items made after 1903 have the Ives name or particular identifying characteristics appearing on them.

The Ives factory suffered a massive fire in 1900, and when they were back in production in 1902, they began running the trains on track and O-gauge was born. Ives production evolved over time from clockwork motors to electric motors, though the clockwork line was never dropped from production. Ives was the first company to establish O-gauge as a standard, and in 1904 embarked on the production of No. 1-gauge, which was popular in Europe. With the exception of Elektoy, Ives was the only American company to produce No. 1-gauge commercially. In the sixteen year tenure of this venture, some of the finest examples of craftsmanship to ever come from the Ives shops were produced. For example, the No. 3239 and No. 3240 center cab electrics in cast iron.

Ives goes Electric

In 1910, Ives joined the bandwagon in production of electric track trains. By this time, companies like Carlisle and Finch, Voltamp, Knapp, Howard, Lionel and American Miniature Railway were already in the electric market. But electricity was not yet a common household commodity across the country, and clockwork trains were still the only self-propelled models which could be used in many places. So Ives clockwork production still held forth strongly in both O-gauge and No. 1 gauge. Lack of electricity and slow, laborious shipping kept most Ives concentrated on the East coast.

Many early clockwork cabs and boilers saw double duty as electric engines. Steam numbers were prefixed with the number 11, so a clockwork engine like the grand old 25 became an electric 1125.

In 1920, Ives phased out No. 1 gauge and began production of standard or wide gauge in its place. Some of the remaining stock of No. 1-gauge equipment was fitted for standard gauge. Ives went on to develop quite an interesting variety of new equipment over the next ten years.

With smooth-running motors on a patented reverse unit superior to their competitors, Ives rode a well-deserved wave of popularity with their electric trains until they stumbled upon rocky ground in 1928. They reorganized under a bankruptcy, and Lionel and American Flyer jointly took over control of the foundering company. Soon thereafter, American Flyer relinquished their interest to Lionel, who moved the factory to Irvington, New Jersey where they continued the Ives name into 1932. In 1933, they manufactured some trains with a Lionel-Ives marking, then phased the line out completely, ending sadly a glorious reign in the field of American toy making.

Condition

Today, due to vintage and usage, most Ives is found at best in Good (C6) to Excellent (C8) condition, with some appearing to be like new. Few are able to meet the classic definition of Mint (C10), which technically means new in the box and only test run. Much of the best condition equipment has been handed down through generations from the original owner, and, when sold, tend to go privately, rather than on the open market. Prices here are taken from the market, and are not attempting to establish a subjective collector value. Such things are difficult to gauge, as value is internal to the collector. Prices are often difficult to average, because some pieces turn up so infrequently that they cannot be comparably priced. The scarcity of much Ives leads to the scarcity of Ives collectors and somewhat helps keep some of the prices lower than prices of comparable pieces made by other manufacturers.

Many of us are in the toy train hobby out of a sheer love of the trains and accessories, as well as the freeze-frame moment of history contained in any individual piece. However, a growing number of people are coming into the hobby out of a love for the money they see inherent in it. Hopefully this book will reach out to more of the former than the latter.

Special Cars

There were some oddities made during World War I which surface from time to time. Among these are some No. 129, No. 130, and No. 131 cars which were green without any wood litho, and which just had their numbers and identifying words rubber stamped on them. Apparently, there are also some herald cars which were made this way. Four heralds are known to be done in this fashion, and there are probably more. This is probably also the origin of the red-orange enameled stock cars with the rubber stamped lettering.

Another special car was made up in 1926. It consisted of a No. 129 Saratoga passenger car, bent behind the last set of windows so that the door on each side became rear observation deck doors. A brass observation platform railing was then added, and the car essentially became a No. 132 observation car. This was in the Green Mountain Express set.

A special Standard-gauge car was made for the Harmony Creamery Co. of Pittsburgh. It consisted of a No. 196 flat car with two special milk vats and was marked "Harmony Creamery."

In 1928, the "Interstate Limited" came with a No. 3254 locomotive, two No. 137 parlor cars, and a No. 138 observation. They were a variation between the No. 133 and No. 135 parlor cars, and the No. 134 and No. 136 observation cars, with elements of each.

Also in 1928, Ives catalogued two sets of O-gauge painted gray with mottled black spattering as though they had come through the Mojave Desert. The sets were No. 474 and No. 476.

General notes

- Engine numbers 00 through 32 are clockwork (wind-up), as are numbers 66 and 176. Also No. 1 gauge locomotive numbers 40 and 41.
- Set prices often tend to run somewhat less than the sum of the prices of the integral parts of the set, with notable exceptions such as the National Limited, Chief, and Black Diamond. Also especially the copper-plated "Prosperity Special" which commands in the vicinity of $10,000.
- Standard and wide gauge are the same. It is 2-1/4-inch between outside rails.
- No. 1 gauge is 1-7/8-inch between outside rails.
- O-gauge is 1-1/2-inch between outside rails.
- Ungauged entries are generally O-gauge. No. 1 gauge and standard gauge (W) are generally marked as such.
- Although very few items are actually to be considered as Mint (C10), those that are should certainly have the original boxes.
- Reproductions of some pieces, notably the No. 3245, the No. 1694, the No. 89 water tower, and the No. 121 and No. 122 stations have been made.
- Uncataloged specials were made over the years for various companies and department stores. FAO Schwarz had No. 3239 locomotives stamped out with their initials. John Wannamaker had No. 3241, No. 3242, and No. 3243 locomotives stamped with their logo as well as passenger cars to go with them. They also made passenger cars in O-gauge and sold them with some of the No. 3250 series locomotives. The Pony Express set was a special for an unidentifiable store. There was also a run of standard gauge flat cars with milk vats for the Harmony Creamery in Pittsburgh. There are other specials, including Southern Pacific Lines, but these are a few of the most common examples.

- Heralds are the road names of rail lines which Ives put on some of their box cars during their years of production. Some heralds are scarcer than others, so prices tend to vary, generally to un-agreed upon parameters. A ball park range on them is from $40 to $175. This values is, of course, dependent upon condition, and desire to possess a particular-item. The available heralds are as follows:
- No. 125 cars: Union Pacific, M.K. & T., Corn Belt Route, Salt Lake Route, Frisco Lines, Wabash, Cotton Belt Route, Star Union Line.
- No. 64, 564: Baltimore & Ohio, Atlantic Coast Line, Chicago & Northwestern, Rock Island, Santa Fe, Canadian Pacific, Illinois Central, Northern Pacific, Pennsylvania, Lehigh Valley, Star Union, N.Y.C., Burlington Route, Erie, and N.Y., N.H. & H.
- Tenders were always tin, except some die-cast from 1929 on.
- Engines are always priced with tenders.
- Prices also take into consideration that item is complete; wheels, roof, couplers, trim, pieces, etc. Deletions affect price accordingly.
- Dating by trucks and couplers:
- Inboard trucks:1904-1909
- T-Trucks: 1910-1917
- Marklin trucks: 1912-1917
- TYPE D trucks:
- Flat side: 1918
- Detailed, no journal slots 1919-1924
- Same, journal slots 1925-1928
- Slots with journals 1929-1930
- Flat loop couplers-1901-1909
- Hook slot couplers-1904-1930
- Automatic couplers-1912-1930

	C7	C9
Train Set, cast-iron, big six locomotive w/tender and two gondolas	1875	2500
0 Locomotive, 1903-1905, O ga., 2-2-0; tin body, embossed boiler bands, black and red litho; four-wheel painted tender w/cast-iron wheels; arched windows on each side	225	450
0 Locomotive, 1906, O ga., 2-2-0; tin body, embossed boiler bands; blue and white or green and white lithograph, some red and white; F.E. No. 1 tender, four-wheels, two windows per cab side w/number beneath	200	400
0 Locomotive, 1907-1909, O ga., 2-2-0; cast-iron body, wheel arrangement reverse bicycle type, w/drivers in front; lithographed plates under cab windows "IVES No. 0," rectangular cab window; separate tin boiler bands; dummy headlight; F.E. No. 1 tender w/tin wheels.	175	350
0 Locomotive, 1910-1912, O ga., 2-2-0; cast-iron body w/lithographed number boards beneath cab windows; large drive wheels behind smaller tin wheels; dummy headlight, two separate boiler bands; F.E. No. 1 tender.	150	300
0 Locomotive, 1913-1915, O ga., 2-2-0; black cast-iron body, separate boiler bands, dummy headlight; same wheel arrangement as previous year, same general engine; number stamped beneath rectangular window; No. 1 tender	125	250
00 Locomotive, 1930, O ga., 0-4-0; black or red cast-iron boiler, no boiler band; two rectangular windows per cab side marked "IVES No. 00" beneath; tin wheels; dummy headlight in boiler front; No. 9 tender	145	290
1 Tender, 1903-1905, O ga., hand painted; four cast-iron wheels, tin body	100	200
1 Locomotive, 1906, O ga., 2-2-0; painted and lithographed tin in blue and white or green and white; embossed boiler bands; two rectangular windows on both sides of cab w/number beneath; F.E. No. 1 tender w/tin wheels	200	400

	C7	C9
1 Tender, 1906-1909, O ga., F.E. No. 1, four tin wheels, tin body, red lithograph	75	150
1 Locomotive, 1907-1909, O ga., 2-2-0; black painted cast-iron w/two separate boiler bands, dummy headlight; drive wheels in front w/two small tin wheels trail behind; lithographed plates below rectangular cab window read "IVES No. 1"; four-wheel F.E. No. 1 tender	175	350
1 Locomotive, 1910-1912, O ga., 2-2-0; drive wheels behind small tin wheels, two separate boiler bands; rectangular cab window w/lithograph number board beneath; dummy headlight; four-wheel F.E. No. 1 tender	150	300

No. 1, Locomotive with tender, 1910-1912, $300

	C7	C9
1 Tender, 1910-1913, O ga., tin body lithographed "F.E. No. 1," four tin wheels	55	110
1 Tender, 1914, O ga., tin body lithographed "IVES No. 1," four tin wheels	50	100
1 Locomotive, 1926-1928, O ga., 0-4-0; cataloged in black w/one separate tin boiler band, tin wheels, no side rods; rectangular cab window stamped "IVES No. No. 11" beneath; four-wheel No. 11 tender in NYC & HR livery; dummy headlight in boiler front...	125	250

No. 1, Locomotive with tender, 1926-1928, $250

	C7	C9
1 Locomotive, 1929, O ga., 0-4-0, same basic design as previous year, but now cataloged w/handbrake.	135	270
2 Locomotive, 1906, O ga., 2-2-0; painted tin body, embossed boiler bands; two rectangular cab windows on either side w/number painted beneath; F.E. No. 1 tender w/tin wheels	200	400
2 Locomotive, 1907-1909, O ga., 2-2-0; black painted cast-iron w/two separate boiler bands, dummy headlight; drive wheels are in front of tin trailing wheels; rectangular cab window on both side, plates below lithographed "IVES No. 2," F.E. No. 1 tender	175	350
2 Locomotive, 1910-1912, O ga., 2-2-0, black cast-iron boiler w/two separate boiler bands, dummy headlight; drive wheels behind small tin wheels now; rectangular window on both sides of cab, plates below lithographed "IVES No. 2"; F.E. No. 1 tender	150	300
2 Locomotive, 1913-1915, O ga., 2-2-0; black cast-iron boiler, same general engine as previous year, stamped number now; Ives No. 1 tender	135	270
3 Locomotive, 1903-1905, O ga., 2-2-0; painted tin body, lithographed roof, embossed boiler bands; same as No. 0, w/stronger spring; one arched cab window per side, stack is only detail on boiler top; painted tender w/cast-iron wheels	225	450
3 Locomotive, 1906, O ga., 2-2-0; painted and lithographed tin in blue and white or green and white; embossed boiler bands; two rectangular windows per cab side w/number painted beneath; F.E. No. 1 tender w/tin wheels	200	400
3 Locomotive, 1907-1909, O ga., 2-2-0; reverse bicycle wheel pattern w/large drive wheels in front; black cast-iron body w/two separate boiler bands, dummy headlight; lithographed plate below rectangular cab window reads "Ives No. 3"; F.E. No. 1 tender	175	350

	C7	C9
3 Locomotive, 1910-1911, O ga., 2-2-0; black cast-iron body w/dummy headlight, two separate boiler bands; drive wheels now behind small tin wheels; rectangular cab window per side, lithographed "IVES No. 3" on plate below; F.E. No. 1 tender	150	300
3 Locomotive, 1912, O ga., 0-4-0; black boiler, two separate boiler bands, dummy headlight; four cast-iron wheels w/drive rods; rectangular cab window lithographed "IVES No. 3" on plate below; F.E. No. 1 tender w/tin wheels	125	250
4 Locomotive, 1910-1912, O ga., 2-2-0; black cast-iron boiler w/two separate boiler bands, drive wheels behind small tin wheels; dummy headlight; w/rectangular cab window lithographed "IVES No. 4" on plate below; F.E. No. 1 tender	125	250
4 Locomotive, 1912, O ga., 0-4-0; black cast-iron boiler w/two separate boiler bands, dummy headlight; four cast-iron wheels w/drive rods; rectangular cab window lithographed "IVES No. 4" on plate below; F.E. No. 1 tender w/tin wheels	115	230
5 Locomotive, 1913-1916, O ga., 0-4-0; black cast-iron body, separate boiler bands; cast-iron wheels, dummy headlight on top of boiler; single rectangular cab window stamped "IVES No. 5" below; No. 1 tender	110	220
5 Locomotive, 1917-1922, O ga., 0-4-0; black cast-iron body, tin wheels, two separate boiler bands, dummy headlight in center of boiler front; two rectangular windows on both sides of cab stamped "IVES No. 5" below; No. 11 tender	85	170

No. 5, Locomotive with tender, 1913-1916, $220

	C7	C9

6 Locomotive, 1913-1916, O ga., 0-4-0; black cast-iron body, cast-iron wheels w/straight side rods, dummy headlight on top of boiler; singular rectangular cab window stamped "IVES No. 6" below; Ives No. 1 tender 85   170

No. 6, Locomotive with tender, 1913-1916, $170

6 Locomotive, 1917-1925, O ga., 0-4-0; black cast-iron body w/cast-iron wheels w/straight drive rods; dummy headlight in center of boiler front; two rectangular windows on both sides of cab stamped "IVES No. 6" below; No. 11 tender 85   170

6 Locomotive, 1926-1928, O ga., 0-4-0; black cast-iron body w/die-cast wheels w/straight drive rods; dummy headlight in boiler front center; two rectangular cab windows on both sides stamped "IVES No. 6"; NYC & HR No. 11 tender 85   170

No. 6, Locomotive with tender, 1926-1928, $170

6 Locomotive, 1929, O ga., 0-4-0; black boiler, die-cast wheels w/straight drive rods, dummy headlight in boiler front; same engine as previous year, but now a handbrake has been added; two rectangular cab windows per side stamped "IVES No. 6" below; No. 12 tender 85   170

9 Tender, 1930, O ga., same basic body and frame as No. 11 without rivet or spring detail; plain, flat surface; four tin wheels; often no stamping of legend on tender 50   100

10 Locomotive, 1930, O ga., 0-4-0; came w/Pequot set; black cast-iron body, tin wheels, without drivers; rectangular cab window marked "IVES No. 10" below; No. 11 tender 175   350

10 Locomotive, 1931-1932, 0-B-0; tin body, center cab electric style locomotive, often in peacock blue or cadet blue; St. Paul-type of engine, headlights at both ends, pantograph and bell or whistle on top of motor hoods; two windows and one door on either side and one door per end; same as 10-E w/automatic reverse 140   285

11 Locomotive, 1904-1905, 2-2-0; black cast-iron body w/tapered boiler, integral boiler bands, and dummy headlight on front top of boiler; rectangular cab window w/red area beneath; L.V.E. No. 11 tender 175   350

11 Tender, 1904-1913, O ga., LVE No. 11 tin body, four tin wheels, red lithograph 58   115

11 Locomotive, 1906-1907, O ga., 0-4-0; black cast-iron body w/four separate boiler bands, gold trim, red area below rectangular cab window; four cast-iron wheels. Dummy headlight on top of boiler. Boiler tapers towards the front like those on American Standard locomotives; LVE No. 11 tender 165   330

11 Locomotive, 1908-1909, O ga., 0-4-0, black cast-iron boiler w/three separate bands; straight boiler w/dummy headlight on top; red area below cab; L.V.E. No. 11 tender 160   320

No. 11, Locomotive with tender, 1906-1907, $330

	C7	C9

11 Locomotive, 1910-1913, O ga., 0-4-0, black boiler and cab, lithographed plates beneath arched cab windows say "IVES No. 11"; cast-iron wheels, three separate boiler bands; L.V.E. No. 11 tender; dummy headlight on boiler top.. 155   310

11 Locomotive, 1914-1916, O ga., 0-4-0, black cast-iron boiler, two boiler bands, cast-iron wheels; two square windows per cab side, w/"IVES No. 11" stamped beneath them; dummy headlight on boiler top. Ives No. 11 tender. 138   275

No. 11, Locomotive with tender, 1914-1916, $275

11 Tender, 1914-1930, O ga., tin body w/four tin wheels, marked "NYC & HR," Ives No. 11. 48   95

12 Tender, 1928-1930, O ga., Tin body, four tin wheels; same basic tender as No. 11, but w/coal load........................ 45   90

17 Locomotive, 1904-1905, O ga., 2-2-0, black cast-iron boiler tapers towards front; dummy headlight on boiler top, four separate boiler bands; rectangular cab window w/red area beneath; L.V.E. No. 11 tender, handbrake in cab.. 228   455

17 Locomotive, 1906-1907, O ga., 0-4-0, same body casting as No. 11, but has a handbrake located inside cab; black body, four separate boiler bands; gold trim, red area beneath cab rectangular window. cast-iron wheels, dummy headlight; boiler tapers towards front; L.V.E. No. 11 tender............................ 218   435

17 Locomotive, 1908-1909, O ga., 0-4-0, black straight cast-iron body, w/three separate bands; dummy headlight on top; same as No. 11 of the period; L.V.E. No. 11 tender; handbrake......... 205   410

	C7	C9

No. 17, Locomotive with tender, 1908-1909, $410

No. 17, Locomotive, the engine on the right has red trim, 1910-1913, $380

No. 17, Locomotive with tender, 1914-1916, $360

17 Locomotive, 1910-1913, O ga., 0-4-0, same as No. 11; black boiler cab, arched cab windows w/"IVES No. 17" beneath; cast-iron wheels, straight side rods, three separate boiler bands; dummy headlight on boiler top. L.V.E. No. 11 tender; handbrake in cab 190   380

17 Locomotive, 1914-1916, O ga., 0-4-0, same as No. 11 of the same period; black cast-iron body, two square windows per side, w/"IVES No. 17", stamped beneath; dummy headlight on boiler top; "IVES No. 11" tender, cast-iron wheels w/straight side rods; handbrake in cab 180   360

C7   C9

No. 17, Locomotive with tender, 1917-1925, $360

17 Locomotive, 1917-1925, O ga., 0-4-0, black boiler and cab w/dummy headlight in boiler center front, separate boiler band; handbrake in cab; NYC & HR No. 17 tender; straight side rods; single cab window w/"IVES No. 17" stamped beneath..................................... 180   360

17 Tender, 1917-1927, four-wheels of tin, tin body, stamped lettering says "IVES No. 17" or "NYC & HR"; comes w/coal load 45   90

17 Locomotive, 1926-1927, O ga., 0-4-0, black cast-iron body w/one boiler band; die-cast wheels w/straight side rods, one arched cab window w/"IVES No. 17" stamped beneath; headlight back on top of boiler now; NYC & HR No. 17 tender; handbrake.................................... 175   350

17 Locomotive, 1928-1929, O ga., 0-4-0, black cast-iron body w/one boiler band; die-cast wheels w/straight side rods, one arched cab window w/"IVES No. 17" stamped beneath; headlight back on top of boiler now; NYC & HR No. 12 tender w/coal load; handbrake.......... 175   350

19 Locomotive, 1917-1925, O ga., 0-4-0, black cast-iron boiler and cab w/handbrake, two arched windows and "IVES No. 19" beneath; cast-iron wheels w/straight drive rods, single separate boiler band; dummy headlight centered in boiler front; NYC & HR No. 17 tender............................... 225   450

19 Locomotive, 1926-1927, O ga., 0-4-0, black cast-iron body w/one boiler band, dummy headlight on top of boiler; one boiler band separate; two arched cab windows marked "IVES No. 19" beneath; die-cast wheels w/straight drive rods; No. 17 NYC & HR tender............................... 200   400

19 Locomotive, 1928-1929, O ga., 0-4-0, black cast-iron body w/one boiler band, dummy headlight on top of boiler; one boiler band separate; two arched cab windows marked "IVES No. 19" beneath; die-cast wheels w/straight drive rods; No. 12 tender....................... 200   400

20 Locomotive, 1908-1909, O ga., 0-4-0, cast-iron body w/separate boiler bands; red area beneath two cab windows; dummy headlight on top of boiler; cast-iron wheels w/straight drive rods; reverse lever, brake speed governor; four-wheel No. 25 tender..................... 220   440

20 Locomotive, 1910-1914, O ga., 0-4-0, straight boiler, cast-iron body w/grab rails on boiler sides. Dummy headlight on top of boiler, two rectangular cab windows w/lithographed plate marked beneath "IVES No. 20"; speed governor, reverse and brake; cast-iron wheels w/straight drive rods; eight wheel.. 195   390

No. 20, Locomotive with tender, 1908-1909, $440

No. 20, Locomotive with tender, 1910-1914, $390

No. 20, Locomotive with tender, 1915-1916, $390

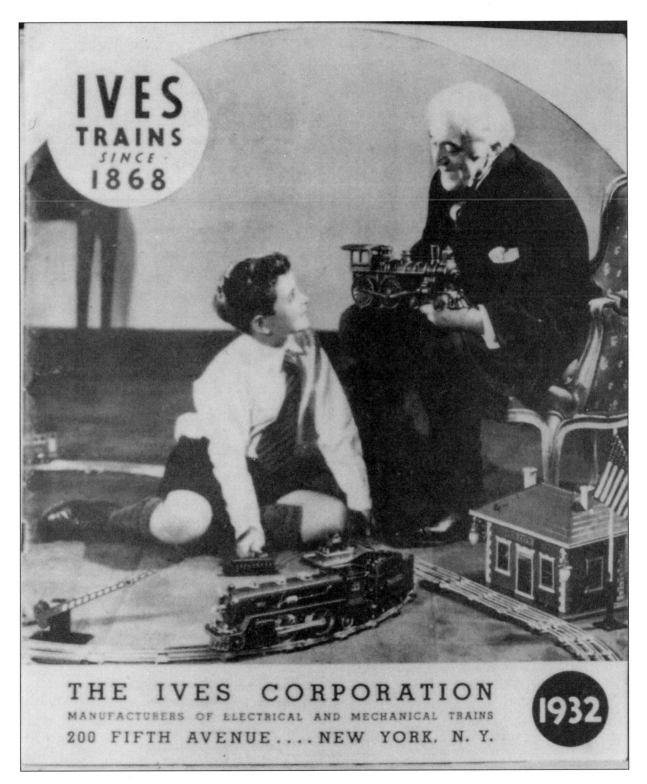

1932 Ives Catalog

Ives boxed White owl set with catalog and direction book, c. 1927

	C7	C9
20 Locomotive, 1915-1916, O ga., 0-4-0, straight boiler, cast-iron body w/grab rails on boiler sides. Dummy headlight on top of boiler, two rectangular cab windows w/lithographed plate stamped beneath "IVES No. 20"; speed governor, reverse and brake; cast-iron wheels w/straight drive rods; eight wheel; No. 25 tender	195	390
20 Livestock Car, 1928-1929, Standard ga., American Flyer body on two four-wheel Ives trucks; sliding doors, brass plates; green body, red roof or orange body, red roof	190	380
20 Gondola, 1928-1929, Standard ga., American Flyer body on two four-wheel Ives trucks	158	315
20 Caboose, 1928-1929, Standard ga., American Flyer body on two four-wheel Ives trucks; red body, mirror roof; brass trim and plates	140	280

	C7	C9
20 Gondola, 1928-1929, Standard ga., black American Flyer body mounted on two four-wheel Ives trucks; brass plates and trim	135	270
20 Boxcar, 1928-1929, Standard ga., American Flyer body on two four-wheel Ives trucks; brass plates, sliding doors; yellow body w/blue roof or green body w/red roof	190	380
25 Locomotive, 1903, O ga., 4-4-0; black cast-iron body w/four cast boiler bands, dummy headlight on top of boiler, boiler tapers towards front; cast-iron wheels; three square windows on both sides of cab w/red area painted beneath; reverse and hand brake; hand-painted tin tender w/four cast-iron wheels	325	650

	C7	C9

25 Locomotive, 1904, O ga., 4-4-0; black cast-iron body w/six separate boiler band; dummy headlight on boiler top; three square cab windows on both sides of cab w/red area painted beneath; tin pony wheels; reverse brake; L.V.E. No. 11 tender w/tin wheels 300 600

25 Locomotive, 1905, O ga., 4-4-0; black cast-iron tapering boiler w/six separate boiler bands, dummy headlight on top of boiler; three square cab windows on both sides w/gold frame and, gold stripes beneath; tin pony wheels; handbrake and reverse; L.V.E. No. 11 tender w/red square outline on roof..... 295 590

25 Locomotive, 1906-1907, O ga., 4-4-2; black body, boiler tapers toward front, w/four separate boiler bands, dummy headlight on top of boiler; three square windows on both sides of cab w/gold frames and stripes, gold outline on roof; tin pony wheels; handbrake and reverse; four-wheel L.V.E. No. 25 tender, no side rods 275 550

25 Tender, 1906-1909, O ga., four tin wheels; black tin body w/red lithographed spring detail and side boards; L.V.E. No. 25 black lettering on red background 150 300

25 Locomotive, 1908-1909, O ga., 4-4-2; same general characteristics and casting as previous year; three square cab windows w/gold frames and two gold stripes beneath; gold square outline on cab roof; handbrake and reverse; L.V.E. No. 25 tender, no side rods 263 525

25 Locomotive, 1910, O ga., 4-4-2; black cast-iron body, w/straight boiler, three separate boiler bands separate, stanchions for grab rails are cast into body; dummy headlight on top of boiler; two rectangular windows on both sides of cab, lithographed plate below reads "IVES No. 25"; handbrake and reverse; tin pony wheels; eight wheel No. 25 tender; angled side rods 238 475

25 Tender, 1910-1912, O ga., eight tin wheel, black body marked "Limited Vestibule Express" in white framed in gold, blue painted interior 150 300

25 Locomotive, 1911-1914, O ga., 4-4-2; black cast-iron boiler, w/3 separate boiler bands, dummy headlight on top front of boiler, grab rails on connected by cotter pins; two rectangular windows on both sides of cab w/plate below lithographed "IVES No. 25"; red and gold trim; tin wheels on pony truck, cast-iron drivers w/angled side rods; handbrake and reverse; L.V.E. tender... 388 775

25 Tender, 1913-1914, O ga., eight wheel, black tin body marked "Limited Vestibule Express" in white framed in gold 150 300

25 Locomotive, 1915-1916, O ga., 0-4-0; body casting and general detail same as previous model, some have tin pony or spoked cast-iron wheels; handbrake and reverse; latter version of tender, either marked "IVES No. 25" or "No. 25"... 225 450

25 Tender, 1915-1920, O ga., eight wheel, black tin body, sides marked "IVES No. 25" in white, back marked "No. 25" in white 145 295

25 Tender, 1928-1930, O ga., die-cast body w/coal load, two four-wheel trucks w/die-cast wheels; tool boxes cast into tender sides 150 300

Top to bottom: No. 141 Parlor car, $160; No. 25 Tender, c. 1930, $300

	C7	C9

30 Locomotive, 1921-1927, O ga., 0-4-0 clockwork; w/electric center cab; green or red tin body on cast frame like 3250 series; cast-iron wheels until 1924, die-cast after 1925 .... 200 400

30 Locomotive, 1928, O ga., 0-B-0, clockwork w/electric box cab w/headlight and whistle; same body as 3258; stamped tin frame, tin lithographed body 200 400

31 Locomotive, 1921-1925, 0-4-0, clockwork; same general unit as No. 30, but cataloged w/brake; same body as 3250 series w/handrails; cast-iron wheels until 1924, die-cast after 1925; red or green cast-iron frame, tin body . 200 400

32 Locomotive, 1921-1927, O ga., 0-4-0, clockwork; electric center cab; same body as the 3253 loco w/handrails. one door stamped "32 N.Y.C. & H.R." the other "The IVES Railway Lines"; cast-iron frame w/tin body; cast-iron wheels until 1924, die-cast from 1925-1927 .... 225 450

40 Locomotive, 1904-1909, 1 ga., 4-4-0, clockwork; black cast-iron body, straight boiler w/four separate boiler bands, grab rails; nickel-plated steam dome, sand dome, bell w/front dummy headlight on top of boiler; nickel-plated side rails w/separate piston rods; two rectangular cab windows on either side w/"No 40" on lithographed plate below; handbrake and reverse levers in cab; cast-iron drivers, tin pilot wheels; eight wheel tender marked "T.C.L.E. No. 40".................. 1100 2200

40 Tender, 1904-1911, eight wheel, tin body w/rivet detail, grab rail behind body of tender; step on both sides of body; marked "T.C.L.E." inside rectangular red and gold stripes; red stripes on T-type four-wheel trucks..... 250 500

40 Locomotive, 1908-1909, 1 ga., 4-4-0, clockwork; Same as previous year without red and gold square outlines appear on cab roof. 1100 2200

	C7	C9

40 Locomotive, 1910-1911, 1 ga., 4-4-0, clockwork; black cast-iron body w/dummy headlight on top of boiler front; three separate boiler bands, grab rails on each side of boiler; two rectangular cab windows above lithograph plate marked "IVES No. 40"; tin pony wheels, cast-iron drivers w/nickel-plated side rods w/attached piston rods; sand dome, stack and headlight part of casting, nickel bell separate; handbrake and reverse levers in cab; tender same as before 900 1800

40 Locomotive, 1912-1915, 1 ga., 4-4-0, black cast-iron body w/steam dome, sand dome, stack and dummy headlight cast together; separate brass bell; two rectangular windows on either side of cab stamped "No. 40" below; grab rails on boiler sides; cast-iron pony wheels and drive wheels w/nickel-plated drive rods w/U-shaped cross head guides; gold and red square outline on cab roof; four boiler bands painted between boiler rivets; pilot has supporting rods to boiler; reverse and handbrake levers inside cab; eight-wheel tender stamped "No. 40" 900 1800

40 Tender, 1912-1920, 1 ga., eight wheel tin body and frame; rivet detail on body, tool boxes at inside front of each side w/opening lids; rivet detail on trucks, steps on both sides of frame; sides marked "No. 40" inside two white/silver rectangles; used w/late No. 40 and No. 1129 .... 225 450

41 Locomotive, 1908-1911, 1 ga., 0-4-0, clockwork; body casting similar to 1910 No. 40; dummy headlight, stack and steam dome part of casting w/separate brass bell; three separate boiler bands attached to body w/stanchions; cab has two windows on both sides marked "IVES No. 41" below in white on red lithographed plate; cast-iron drive wheels w/straight nickel-plated side rods; No. 40 TCLE tender w/hook coupler on front pilot 1000 2000

50 Baggage Car, 1901-1905, O ga., four cast-iron wheels, hand-painted red, green or blue body and roof, clerestory w/white painted side 175 350

	C7	C9

50 Baggage Car, 1906-1907, O ga., red, white or yellow body lithographed to simulate wood; four tin wheels, steps, vestibules; unpunched door on each side, one marked "Limited Vestibule Express Baggage Car," the other "United States Mail Exp. Service"; black roof w/clerestory frame w/red lithographed spring detail; vestibules separate 195 390

50 Baggage Car, 1908-1909, O ga., four wheel; red lithographed frame has spring detail and striped steps; white/silver body; sides marked "Limited Vestibule Express," "United States Mail Baggage Car" and "Express Service No. 50"; three doors on both sides and one on each end; black roof w/clerestory; vestibules part of body.. 150 300

50 Baggage Car, 1910-1913, O ga., four tin wheels; lithographed yellow tin body w/open frame, black roof and clerestory; sides marked "Pennsylvania Lines"; punched center door marked "Baggage No. 50" and "Express Mail"; two doors lithographed on other side; wood sheathing on sides................................ 83 165

	C7	C9

50 Baggage Car, 1914, four tin wheels, lithographed tin body and frame; same general car as previous year, but now marked "The Ives Railway Lines"...... 75 150

50 Baggage Car, 1915-1930, four tin wheels; red, yellow, green and tan tin body lithographed to resemble steel, tin frame; marked "The Ives Railway Lines" below roof line and "Baggage No. 50" and "U.S. Express Mail" on each side; open center doors and two lithographed doors w/open windows on side; black frame w/spring detail over wheels, black roof w/small clerestory strip. Because so many of these cars were made, the molds were rendered useless. 25 50

51 Passenger Car, 1901-1905, O ga., four cast-iron wheels, hand-painted tin body w/six windows on each side and vestibules at each end; roof w/clerestory strip w/white accents; red, blue or green body w/horizontal white or cream stripe beneath windows 175 350

51 Passenger Car, 1906-1907, O ga., four tin wheels, red lithographed spring detail on frame w/vestibule at each end; lithographed body marked "Mohawk," "Hiawatha" or "Iroquois" and "Limited Vestibule Express" below roof line; roof w/clerestory strip 195 390

Ives No. 262 is the motor for Struct-Iron Sets.

	C7	C9

51 Passenger Car, 1908-1909, four tin wheels, tin lithographed white body w/red detail, w/black frame w/red lithographed detail; body marked "Limited Vestibule Express" below roof line; six windows marked "Brooklyn" below windows on lithographed plate; vestibules part of car 170 260

51 Passenger Car, 1910-1913, O ga., four tin wheels, tin body lithographed to resemble wood grain sheathing; black, green or gray frame w/holes over axle area; body marked "Pennsylvania Lines" below roof line; seven windows marked "Newark" below; doors replaced vestibules at end of car; roof w/clerestory strip........................ 95 190

51 Passenger Car, 1914, O ga., four tin wheels, tin body, roof w/clerestory strip; same car as previous year's but w/"The Ives Railway Lines" lettered below roof line..................................... 75 150

51 Passenger Car, 1915-1930, O ga., four tin wheels, tin body lithographed to simulate steel; simple frame w/spring detail over axles; came in variety of colors: red, green, orange, yellow and tan; seven windows and two doors on each side; body marked "IVES Railway Lines" below roof line and "51 Chair Car 51" below windows...... 25 50

52 Passenger Car, 1908-1910, O ga., four tin wheels, tin body lithographed to simulate wood; four windows w/transoms and two doors on each side; marked "Limited Vestibule Express" below roof line and "Buffalo" below windows; roof w/clerestory strip; same body used for No. 801 trolley in 1910; cataloged as "Drawing Room Car" 125 250

52 Passenger Car, 1911-1913, O ga., four tin wheels, tin body lithographed to simulate wood siding; green, gray or black frame w/holes above axles; five windows and two doors on each side; body marked "Pennsylvania Lines" below roof line and "Washington" below windows; roof w/clerestory strip.. 100 200

52 Passenger Car, 1914, O ga., four tin wheels, tin body lithographed to simulate wood siding; green, gray or black frame w/holes above axles; five windows and two doors on each side; body marked "Pennsylvania Lines" below roof line and "The Ives Railway Lines" above windows; roof w/clerestory strip................................. 95 190

52 Passenger Car, 1915-1930, O ga., four tin wheels, tin body lithographed to simulate steel; five windows and two doors on each side; marked "The Ives Railway Lines" below roof line and "52 Parlor Car 52" below windows; roof w/clerestory strip 45 90

53 Freight Car, 1910-1914, O ga., four tin wheels, white body, frame w/holes over axle; open doorway on both sides; marked "Pennsylvania Lines" on one side of doorway and "PA.R.R. Co." and "No. 53" on the other.......... 90 180

53 Freight Car, 1915-1930, O ga., Same as previous frame w/spring-detail frame 68 135

54 Gravel Car, 1903-1904, O ga., four cast-iron wheels, hand-painted tin body.. 100 200

54 Gravel Car, 1905-1909, O ga., four tin wheels, tin body lithographed to simulate wood; red lithographed spring detail on frame 95 190

54 Gravel Car, 1910-1914, O ga., four tin wheels, tin lithographed body on frame w/holes over axle; body marked "No. 54" 55 110

54 Gravel Car, 1915-1930, O ga., four tin wheels, tin body lithographed simulated wood; later frame w/spring detail; body marked lithographed "No. 54".. 40 80

55 Stock Car, 1910-1914, O ga., four tin wheels, yellow tin body lithographed to simulate wood; frame w/holes above axle; marked "Livestock Transportation" below roof line; no doors, just doorway on each side 50 100

	C7	C9

55 Stock Car, 1915-1930, O ga., four tin wheels, tin body lithographed to simulate wood; later frame w/spring detail. marked "Livestock Transportation" above doorway **40 80**

56 Caboose, 1910-1914, O ga., four tin wheels, white or red tin body lithographed to simulate wood; single open door on each side, w/window on each side of door; small cupola on roof; frame w/holes over axles; marked "Pennsylvania Lines" above door.. **113 225**

56 Caboose, 1915-1930, O ga., four tin wheels, tin body lithographed to simulate wood; frame w/spring detail; open door; marked "Pennsylvania Lines" over door and "Caboose No. 56" on both sides **100 200**

57 Lumber Car, 1910-1914, O ga., four tin wheels, tin frame w/hole over axles; painted tin body, w/lumber load **40 80**

57 Lumber Car, 1915-1930, O ga., four tin wheels, later frame w/spring detail; painted tin body w/lumber load.......... **30 60**

60 Baggage Car, 1905-1909, O ga., four tin wheels; tin body lithographed to simulate wood; tin roof w/clerestory strip; sliding lithographed door; sides marked "United States Mail Exp. Service," "Limited Vestibule Express Baggage Car" and "No. 60" **325 650**

60 Baggage Car, 1910-1913, O ga., eight wheels, red, blue, white, rose or yellow tin body lithographed to simulate wood; sliding lithographed door; truss rods on frame w/single support in middle; tin roof w/separate clerestory strip; flat truss rods in 1910 and 1911, later rounded; marked "Limited Vestibule Express" below roof line, "Express Service Baggage" to left of door and "United States Mail" to right **135 270**

60 Baggage Car, 1914-1915, O ga., same as previous year, marked "The Ives Railway Lines" below roof line........... **120 240**

60 Baggage Car, 1915-1920, O ga., eight wheels, tin roof w/clerestory strip, green or red tin body lithographed to simulate steel sides w/rivet detail; lithographed in single-sliding door single in middle of side; truss rods on each side of frame; marked "The Ives Railway Lines" below roof level and "Express Service Baggage" to left of door and "U.S. Mail" to right of door . **75 150**

60 Baggage Car, 1921-1923, O ga., eight wheels, tin roof and body. same as previous year, without truss rods on the frame **70 140**

60 Baggage Car, 1924-1930, O ga., eight wheel, tin roof w/clerestory strip; red, red-brown or blue-green lithographed without rivet detail and gold trim and brass journals; same general car as before, w/truss rods **110 220**

61 Passenger Car, 1905-1909, O ga., four tin wheels; yellow, red, blue, buff and white bodies; tin body lithographed to simulate wood; vestibules part of body; body marked "Limited Vestibule Express" below roof line, "Express" below eight windows **345 690**

61 Passenger Car, 1910-1913, O ga., eight wheel, white, blue, yellow, red or rose tin lithographed to simulate wood; truss rod on each side of frame and door at each end of side where vestibules were previously; tin roof w/separate clerestory strip, body marked "Limited Vestibule Express" below roof line and "Yale" below eight windows. .... **155 ♦ 310**

61 Passenger Car, 1914-1915, O ga., same as previous year without markings above windows.................... **150 300**

61 Chair Car, 1916-1920, O ga., eight wheel; green, red, or olive tin body lithographed to simulate steel w/rivet detail; truss rods on frame; door at each end of side; one-piece roof w/clerestory strip; body marked "The Ives Railway Lines" above windows and "61 Chair Car 61" below eight windows **75 150**

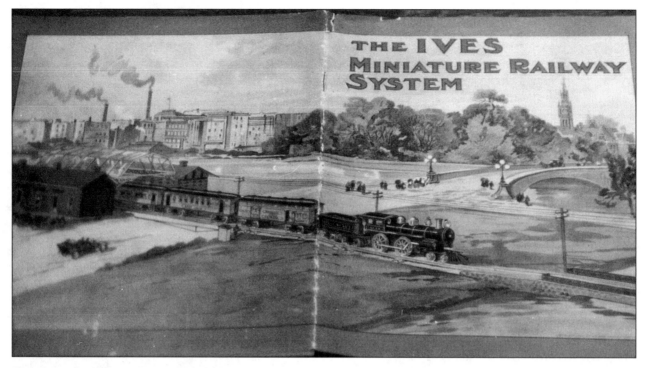

Front and back cover for a 1906 Ives catalog.

	C7	C9

No. 61, Chair car, 1921-1923, $135

61 Chair Car, 1921-1923, O ga., same car as previous year; green or red body lithographed to simulate steel; without truss rods on frame 68   135

61 Chair Car, 1924-1930, O ga., same car as previous year; eight wheel; red, red-brown or blue-green body lithographed to simulate steel without rivet detail; frame w/truss rods 68   135

62 Parlor Car, 1905-1909, O ga., four-wheel, yellow, red, blue, buff and white tin body lithographed to simulate wood; tin one piece roof; three windows and two doors per side; "Limited Vestibule Express" below roof line and "Princess" below windows 395   790

62 Parlor Car, 1910-1913, O ga., eight wheels; red, white, blue, yellow or rose tin body lithographed to simulate wood; truss rods on frame; tin roof w/separate clerestory strip; five windows and two doors per side; marked "Limited Vestibule Express" below roof line and "Harvard" below windows 180   360

62 Parlor Car, 1914-1915, O ga., same as previous year, w/"The Ives Railway Lines" above windows 150   300

	C7	C9
62 Parlor Car, 1916-1920, O ga., eight wheel; tin lithographed steel w/rivet detail; frame w/truss rods; one-piece tin roof w/clerestory strip; five windows and two doors on each side; marked "The Ives Railway Lines" below roof line and "Parlor Car" below the windows	75	150
62 Parlor Car, 1921-1923, O ga., same car as previous year but without truss rods on frame; eight wheel; one-piece tin roof w/clerestory strip	68	135
62 Parlor Car, 1924-1930, O ga., same car without rivet detail; eight wheel; red-brown, red, emerald green or blue-green; one-piece roof w/clerestory strip; five windows, two doors on each side; marked "The Ives Railway Lines" above windows and "62 Parlor Car 62"	68	135
63 Gravel Car, 1904-1907, O ga., four-wheel; tin body painted w/vertical stripes w/cast-iron wheels	70	140
63 Gravel Car, 1908-1909, O ga., four-wheel; tin lithographed body simulates wood w/tin wheels	50	100
63 Gravel Car, 1910-1911, O ga., eight wheel; dark green lithographed body w/incomplete lithographed on each end. Flat truss rods on frame	48	95
63 Gravel Car, 1912, O ga., eight wheel; dark green body w/complete lithographed at ends, flat truss rods on frame	35	70
63 Gravel Car, 1913-1914, O ga., eight wheel; kelly green body, same as previous year, w/half-round truss rods	35	70
63 Gravel Car, 1915-1916, O ga., eight wheel; gray lithographed w/pinkish tones; w/rounded truss rods; marked "63" on sides	30	60
63 Gravel Car, 1917-1920, O ga., eight wheel; gray lithographed tin body without pinkish coloration; rounded truss rods	25	50
63 Gravel Car, 1921-1923, O ga., eight wheel; gray lithographed body, no truss rods on frame	25	50

	C7	C9
63 Gravel Car, 1924-1929, O ga., eight wheel; gray lithographed body, rounded truss rods on frame, journal slots on trucks	25	50
63 Gravel Car, 1930, O ga., eight wheel; gray lithographed body, rounded truss rods on frame, brass journals on trucks...................................	25	90
64 Merchandise Car, 1908-1909, O ga., four-wheel; painted frame and roof, single sliding door; body marked "Fast Freight Line" to left of door and "General Merchandise Car" to right ...	95	190
64 Merchandise Car, 1910-1912, O ga., eight wheel; lithographed tin body simulates wood; tin roof, white w/lithographed blue and red stripes; T-trucks and flat truss rods on frame; single sliding door in middle of side; body marked "General Mdse. Car No. 64," "Union Line" w/star logo to left of door and "Merchandise Car No. 64 Pennsylvania Line" to right of door....	90	180

64 Merchandise Car, 1910-1930, O ga., There are many variations of this car, and different years and different lithograph ink provided a rich palette of colors in each given herald. Because the heralds are listed at the end of the chapter, only the major changes in the car will be listed here; Union Star lines was the first, others weren't cataloged until 1913. All were produced between 1913 and 1930.

	C7	C9
64 Merchandise Car, 1913-1917, O ga., eight wheel, tin body lithographed to simulate wood; frame w/rounded truss rods; painted tin roof, T-trucks; all heralds available..................................	100	200
64 Merchandise Car, 1918, O ga., eight wheel; same car, new trucks w/no detail, type D w/flat sides; all heralds available	100	225

No. 63, Gravel car, 1921-1923, $50

	C7	C9

64 Merchandise Car, 1919-1920, O ga., eight wheel; same car, type-D trucks w/rivet detail, no journal slots 150 250

64 Merchandise Car, 1921-1923, O ga., eight wheel; same car, without truss rods on side frames 100 200

64 Merchandise Car, 1924, O ga., eight wheel; same car, w/side frame truss rods 90 180

64 Merchandise Car, 1925-1928, O ga., eight wheel; same general cars, type-D trucks w/journal slots........................... 100 200

64 Merchandise Car, 1929-1930, O ga., same general car, red roof, type-D trucks w/brass journals 100 200

65 Stock Car, 1908-1909, O ga., four-wheel; body lithographed w/rivet detail; roof striped w/brake wheel at one end; horizontal slots punched out; striped lithographed door below "Livestock Transportation" 63 125

65 Livestock Car, 1910-1912, O ga., eight wheel; white or gray-white body lithographed to simulating wood; dark green frame w/flat truss rods; striped lithographed roof w/catwalk, punched out sides; single sliding door on each side below "Livestock Transportation" 55 110

65 Livestock Car, 1913-1917, O ga., eight wheel; painted orange body w/single sliding door on each side; painted roof w/catwalk; T-trucks; sides marked "Livestock," "Transportation" and "The Ives R.R."; c. 1916-1917 car changed to yellow lithographed body w/lithographed door; some doors have slots punched in them 38 75

65 Livestock Car, 1918, O ga., eight wheel; lithographed body in orange-yellow to simulate wood detail; type-D trucks without detail; gray painted roof w/catwalk; sides marked "Livestock," "Transportation" and "The Ives R.R." 25 50

	C7	C9

65 Livestock Car, 1919-1920, O ga., same as previous year, eight wheel, type-D trucks w/detail........................ 25 50

65 Livestock Car, 1921-1923, O ga., same as previous year, eight wheel, without truss rods on side frames........ 23 45

No. 65, Livestock car, 1921-1923, $45

65 Livestock Car, 1924, O ga., same as previous years, w/truss rods................ 23 45

65 Livestock Car, 1925-1928, O ga., same as previous years, eight wheel, type-D trucks w/journal slots.............. 23 45

65 Livestock Car, 1929-1930, O ga., same as previous years, w/brass journals on trucks; some lithography is now more orange then orange-yellow; roof is now painted red 23 45

No. 65, Livestock car with red roof, 1929-1930, $45

66 Tank Car, 1910-1912, O ga., eight wheel; flat truss rods on frame; painted dome and tank body mounted right onto frame, w/stripes, rivet detail and "Tank Line" painted on sides; T-trucks; red or green body 75 150

	C7	C9

66 Tank Car, 1913-1915, O ga., eight wheel; frame w/round truss rods; T-trucks; black tank body on saddles w/gold band painted around each end of tank; no lettering on sides, and "TL No. 66" stamped on each end; short dome 48 95

66 Tank Car, 1916-1917, O ga., eight wheel; T-trucks; gray painted body on saddles mounted to frame; black dome; sides are lettered "66 Standard Oil 66," "Air Brake," "Made In The Ives Shops" and "Cap'y 100000 Gals"; ends stamped "66" 30 60

66 Tank Car, 1918, O ga., Type-D flat truck; same characteristics as previous year, changed "Cap'y 100000 Gals" to read "Cap'y 10,000 Gals" 23 45

66 Tank Car, 1919-1920, O ga., eight wheel, same as previous year, without type D-2 trucks 23 45

66 Tank Car, 1921-1923, O ga., eight wheel. same as before, without truss rods on frame sides 20 60

No. 66, Tank car, 1921-1923, $60

66 Tank Car, 1924, O ga., eight wheel, same, without truss rods on frame 23 45

66 Tank Car, 1925-1928, O ga., eight wheel; orange body, black dome. body mounted to frame by saddles; sides marked "66 Standard Oil 66," "Air Brake," "Made In The Ives Shops" and "Cap'y 10,000 Gals"; ends marked "66"; type D-3 trucks w/journal slots.............................. 23 45

	C7	C9

66 Tank Car, 1929-1930, O ga., eight wheel; same car as before previous years; w/type D-4 trucks w/brass journals.. 150 300

67 Caboose, 1910-1912, O ga., eight wheel; white body lithographed to simulate wood sheathing; some main roofs are lithographed w/stripes, some are painted; single lithographed sliding door on each side; sides marked "Pennsylvania Lines," "Caboose No. 67"; window to right of door marked "No. 67" below; flat truss rods on frame............................ 105 210

No. 67, Caboose, 1910-1912, $210

67 Caboose, 1913-1917, O ga., eight wheel; lithographed body w/single sliding door on each side; gray painted tin roof w/red cupola and red roof; body is red or brown-red; white lettering below roof line reads "The Ives Railway Lines"; window to left of door marked "Caboose 67" below; window to right of door marked "Caboose 67"; ends of car marked "The Ives Miniature Railway System" and "PARR/67"; rounded truss rods on frame 43 85

67 Caboose, 1918, O ga., eight wheel; same as previous years w/type D-1 trucks; marked "The Ives Railway Line" below right window 38 75

67 Caboose, 1919-1920, O ga., eight wheel; same as before w/type D-2 trucks.. 38 75

	C7	C9
67 Caboose, 1921-1923, O ga., eight wheel; same as before, no truss rods on frame sides	38	75
67 Caboose, 1924, O ga., eight wheel; same as before, w/truss rods back on frame	38	75
67 Caboose, 1925-1928, O ga., eight wheel; same car as previous years, w/type D-3 trucks without journals	38	75
67 Caboose, 1929-1930, O ga., eight wheel; same basic car as previous years, but more of a red-orange cast to lithography and yellow lettering; green cupola roof; trucks w/brass journals	38	75
68 Reefer, 1910-1912, O ga., eight wheel; lithographed white body; lithographed roof w/catwalk; lithographed and sliding doors; T-trucks; flat truss; sides marked "Merchants Dispatch Transportation Company," "Refrigerator No. 68," "Refrigerator No. 68 Dairy Line Express"	155	310
68 Reefer, 1913-1917, O ga., eight wheel; same car as previous; white body w/painted roof; truss rods on frame are rounded; no brake wheel on roof	143	285
68 Reefer, 1918, O ga., eight wheel; same as previous year, but flat side type D-1 trucks	138	275
68 Reefer, 1919-1924, O ga., eight wheel; same as previous year, type D-2 trucks	138	275
68 Reefer, 1925-1928, O ga., eight wheel; Same as previous year; w/type D-3 trucks	138	275
68 Observation Car, 1925-1930, O ga., eight wheel; emerald green and blue-green body tin lithographed to simulate steel; tin roof w/clerestory strip; brass observation platform; one door and five windows on both sides; brass journals; sides marked "The Ives Railway Lines"	60	100

	C7	C9
68 Reefer, 1929-1930, O ga., eight wheel; same as previous years, w/red roof and trucks w/brass journals	138	275
69 Lumber Car, 1910-1912, O ga., eight wheel; black painted body w/six red stakes, lumber load held on by three chains over the top; flat truss rods on side frame; T-trucks	65	130
69 Lumber Car, 1913-1917, O ga., eight wheel; black painted body, six red stakes, rounded truss rods; lumber load held on by three chains; T-trucks	50	100
69 Lumber Car, 1918, O ga., eight wheel; black painted body, red stakes; lumber load held on by chains; type D-1 flat trucks; rounded truss rods	45	90
69 Lumber Car, 1919-1920, O ga., eight wheel; painted body; lumber load held on by chains; type D-2 trucks; rounded truss rods	45	90
69 Lumber Car, 1921-1923, O ga., eight wheel; red-brown painted body and stakes; lumber load held on by three chains; type D-2 trucks; frame without truss rods	45	90
69 Lumber Car, 1924, O ga., eight wheel; red-brown body and stakes; lumber load held on by three chain;, type D-2 trucks; frame has truss rods	45	90
69 Lumber Car, 1925-1928, eight wheel; maroon or tan painted body and stakes; lumber load held on by three chains; type D-3 trucks	45	90
69 Lumber Car, 1929-1930, O ga., eight wheel; green painted body and stakes; some have short lumber load, others have regular both held on by three chains; type D-4 trucks w/brass journals	45	90
70 Baggage Car, 1904-1909, 1 ga., eight wheel; wheat and yellow tin body lithographed to simulate wood sheathing; tin wheels, black trucks w/red striping; black tin roof w/white clerestory strip; two doors and two mail windows on each side. sides marked "Twentieth Century Limited Express," "U.S. mail" and "Baggage And Express"	325	650

	C7	C9

70 Baggage Car, 1910-1915, 1 ga., eight wheel; white, yellow or brown body lithographed to simulate wood; tin wheels, tin roof w/clerestory strip; center doors on both sides and end, window next to each side door; sides marked "Twentieth Century Limited Express" or "New York Central Lines," "Baggage Express No. 70," "New York and Chicago," "United States Mail"; steps beneath each side end door; still cataloged in 1916.......... 250   500

70 Baggage Car, 1923-1925, O ga., eight wheel; red lithographed body simulates steel; tin roof w/clerestory strip; sliding door in center and small door at each end of side; sides marked "The Ives Railway Lines," "Express Baggage Service," "60" and "U.S. Mail"...................................... 30   60

70 Caboose, 1929-1930, O ga., eight wheel; tin roof w/red cupola roof 1929, green in 1930; catalog shows No. 67 in cut for 1929, but 1930 the car was made w/a red Lionel body 270   540

No. 70, Caboose, 1929-1930, $540

71 Combination Car, 1904-1909, 1 ga., eight wheel; yellow or wheat tin lithographed to simulate wood; tin roof, black w/white painted clerestory strip; black trucks w/red striping; door at each end of side w/six windows between them; sides marked "Twentieth Century Limited Express," "Saint Louis," "Baggage," and "No. 71"...................................... 375   750

71 Combination Car, 1910-1915, 1 ga., eight wheel; yellow or brown tin body lithographed to simulate wood; tin roof w/clerestory strip; two doors and three double windows on each side; white, marked "Twentieth Century Limited Express," "Baggage," "New York," "Chicago" and "Buffet Car" ... 300   600

71 Combination Car, 1916-1920, 1 ga., eight wheel; brown tin body lithographed to simulate steel; tin roof w/clerestory strip separate; two doors per side, three double windows and one small window; marked "The Ives Railway Lines," "Baggage," "No. 71," "New York and Chicago" 300   600

71 Chair Car, 1923-1925, O ga., eight wheel; red lithographed body simulates steel without rivet detail; tin roof w/clerestory strip; eight windows; marked "The Ives Railway Lines," "71" "Chair Car" and "71" 30   60

72 Parlor Car, 1904-1909, 1 ga., eight wheel; tin body lithographed to simulate wood; tin black roof w/white clerestory sides; black trucks w/red striping; door at each end of side w/four double windows between them; sides marked "Twentieth Century Limited Express," "No 72" and "San Francisco"............................ 488   975

72 Parlor Car, 1910-1915, 1 ga., eight wheel; white, yellow or brown tin body lithographed to simulate wood; tin roof w/clerestory strip; four double windows, three small windows, and door at each end of side, steps below door; sides marked "Twentieth Century Limited Express"; "No. 72," "Chicago," "No. 72" 488   975

72 Parlor Car, 1916-1920, 1 ga., eight wheel; brown tin body lithographed to simulate steeple; tin roof w/clerestory strip separate; four windows, three small windows and two doors w/steps below on each side; sides marked "The Ives Railway Lines," "No. 72" and "Washington" 425   850

	C7	C9

72 Drawing Room Car, 1923-1925, O ga., eight wheel; red tin body lithographed to simulate steel without rivet detail; tin roof w/clerestory strip; five windows, two doors per side; marked "72," "Drawing room Car" and "72," "The Ives Railway Lines" ... 45 90

72 Accessory, 1928-1930, Standard ga., Pole wagon for circus set 45 90

73 Observation Car, 1916-1920, 1 ga., eight wheel; brown tin lithographed to simulate steel; tin roof w/separate clerestory strip; four double windows, three small windows, and one door on each side; sides marked "The Ives Railway Lines," "No. 73," "Observation" and "No. 73" 300 600

73 Observation Car, 1923-1925, O ga., eight wheel; red tin body lithographed to simulate steel without rivet detail; tin roof w/clerestory; five windows and one door per side; brass platform at rear; sides marked "Observation" and "73," "The Ives Railway Lines" ... 45 90

73 Pole Wagon, 1928-1930, Standard ga., for circus set 45 90

	C7	C9

74 Animal Set, 1928-1930, Standard ga., for circus set 95 190

75 Car Runways, 1928-1930, Standard ga., for circus set 25 50

80 Telegraph Poles, 1906-1930, early examples attached right to track ties, later ones stood on their own stands ... 7 14

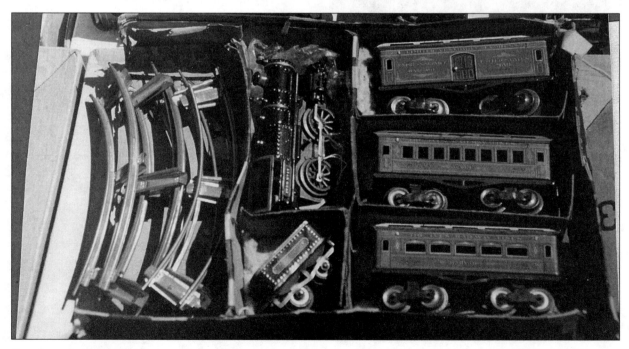

Telegraph Poles, 1906-1930, $14

Ives boxed set, c. 1913

	C7	C9
87 Flag Pole, 1923-1930	50	100
88 Lamp Bracket, 1923-1930, to attach to stations to illuminate them..................	10	20
89 Water Tower, 1923-1929, orange body, black frame and ladder; movable spout on counterweight; side marked "The Ives Railway Lines".......	50	100

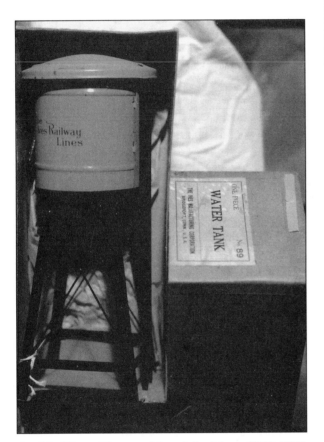

No. 89, Water Tower with original box, 1923-1929, $100

	C7	C9
89 Water Tower, 1930, larger model, yellow tank w/decal mounted on Lionel base; brass plate on base marked "The Ives Railway Lines"; later reproduction has rectangular border around this lettering..................	175	350
90 Drop Bridge, 1129-1930, O ga., w/trip lever, for mechanical track	135	270
90 Bridge, 1912-1922, two simulated stone approaches w/culvert formed under juncture; meant for mechanical trains	45	90

	C7	C9
90-3 Bridge, 1912-1922, O ga., two simulated stone approaches w/culvert formed under juncture; meant for electrical trains	0	0
91-3 Bridge, 1912-1922, O ga., two approach ramps w/double viaduct center; stonework design; for electrical trains	45	90
91 Bridge, 1912-1922, O ga., two approach ramps w/double viaduct center; stonework design; for mechanical trains	45	90
91 Bridge, 1923-1930, O ga., two approach ramps w/double viaduct center; earthen design; for mechanical trains; 21" long.................................	45	90
91-3 Bridge, 1923-1930, O ga., two approach ramps w/double viaduct center; earthen design; for electrical trains; 21" long.................................	45	90
92 Bridge, 1912-1922, O ga., two approach ramps w/double viaduct center; stonework; for mechanical trains; 42" long.................................	60	120
92-3 Bridge, 1912-1922, O ga., two approach ramps w/double viaduct center; stonework; for electrical trains; 42" long...	60	120
92 Bridge, 1923-1930, O ga., w/semaphore signal; two approach ramps w/double viaduct center, and railings on sides; for mechanical trains; earthen design	50	100
92-3 Bridge, 1923-1930, w/semaphore signal; two approach ramps w/double viaduct center, and railings on sides; for electrical trains; earthen design	50	100
95 Bridge, 1929-1930, Standard ga., two approach ramps w/center span w/girders	50	100
96 Bridge, 1929-1930, Standard ga., two approach ramps w/two center spans w/girders	65	130
97 Swing Drawbridge, 1906-1912, O ga., two stonework approaches w/revolving center span; lattice-type griders on trestles; for mechanical track; 31" l..	175	130

	C7	C9
97 Bridge, 1929-1930, Standard ga., two approach ramps w/three center spans w/girders	65	130
98 Bridge, 1906-1907, O ga., two approach ramps, stonework, double viaduct center; lattice-type girders on trestle; for mechanical trains; 31" l......	65	130
98 Bridge, 1908-1912, O ga., two approach ramps, stonework sides, double stonework viaduct; flat stamped girders on trestle; plain-sided center base, straight corner braces; for mechanical track. 31" l.	45	90
98 Bridge, 1911-1920, two approach ramps of stone or earthen design; one single viaduct center span of stonework design; flat stamped trestle sections; for mechanical 1 ga. track; 42" l.	50	100
98-3 Bridge, 1911-1922, O ga., two approach ramps of stone or earthen design; one single viaduct center span of stonework design; flat stamped trestle sections; for electrical O ga. track; 42" l.	45	90
98 Bridge, 1913-1922, O ga., two approach ramps of stone or earthen design; one single viaduct center span of stonework design; flat stamped trestle sections; for mechanical track	45	90
98 Bridge, 1923-1930, O ga., two approaches of earthwork design w/square stones along track, center span of flat steel trestles set upon stonework base; for mechanical track; 31" l.	45	90
98-3 Bridge, 1923-1930, O ga., two approaches of earthwork design w/square stones along track, center span of flat steel trestles set upon stonework base; for electrical track; 31" l.	45	90
99 Bridge, 1906-1907, O ga., two approach ramps, stonework, double viaduct center; w/two center spans; lattice-type girders on trestle; for mechanical trains; 41" l.	75	150
99 Bridge, 1908-1912, O ga., same as contemporary No. 98 but w/two center spans; 41" l.	65	130
99-1-3 Bridge, 1911-1920, 1 ga., two approach ramps of stone or earthen design; two viaduct center span of stonework design; flat stamped trestle sections; for mechanical 1 ga. track; 56" l.	75	150
99-1 Bridge, 1911-1920, 1 ga., same as contemporary No. 98, but w/two center spans. 56" l.	75	150
99-3 Bridge, 1911-1922, O ga., two approach ramps of stone or earthen design; two viaduct center span of stonework design; flat stamped trestle sections; for electrical O ga. track; 41 " l.	50	100
99 Bridge, 1913-1922, O ga., two approach ramps of stone or earthen design; two viaduct center span of stonework design; flat stamped trestle sections; for mechanical track, 41" l.	60	120
99-2-3 Bridge, 1923-1928, Standard ga., two approach spans, two center spans.....................................	350	700
99-3 Bridge, 1926-1928, O ga., same as No. 98 of these years; 41-1/4" l.	50	100
100 Bridge, 1906-1917, O ga., two approach sections forming a single viaduct between the center juncture; painted groundwork; for mechanical track; 21" l.	35	70
100-1 Bridge, 1906-1917, 1 ga., two approach sections w/painted scenery on sides, forming a culvert between the two halves; for mechanical track; 28" l.	40	80
100-3 Bridge, 1910-1917, O ga., two approach sections forming a single viaduct between the center juncture; painted groundwork; for electrical track; 21" l.	40	80
100-1-3 Bridge, 1910-1917, 1 ga., two approach sections w/painted scenery on sides, forming a culvert between the two halves; for electrical track; 28" l.	40	80

	C7	C9
100 Accessory Set, 1930-1932, includes clock, telegraph poles, crossing gate, crossing signal, single and double semaphore; ten pieces	55	110
101-1 Bridge, 1906-1920, 1 ga., two approaches, one center span w/two viaducts, railings on both sides of track; for mechanical track; 42" l.	55	110
101 Bridge, 1906-1922, O ga., bridge; two approaches, one center span w/two viaducts, railings on both sides of track; for mechanical trains; 31" l. ...	50	100
101-1-3 Bridge, 1910-1920, 1 ga., two approach ramps, center section w/two viaducts, railings on each side of track; for electrical track; 42" l.	55	110
101-3 Bridge, 1910-1922, O ga., two approach ramps, center section w/two viaducts, railings on both sides of track; for electrical track; 31" l.	50	100
101-2-3 Bridge, 1921-1922, Standard ga., two approach ramps, center section w/two viaducts, railing on each side of track; for electrical track	55	110
102 Tunnel, 1928, papier-máché, 18" l. ...	15	30
103 Tunnel, 1910-1927, papier-máché, 6" l.	12	25
103 Tunnel, 1928-1930, papier-máché, 8" l.	12	25
104 Tunnel, 1906-1927, papier-máché, 8 1/2" l.	25	50
104 Tunnel, 1928-1930, papier-máché, 10" long.	25	50
105 Tunnel, 1906-1912, papier-máché, 11" long.	12	25
105-E Tunnel, 1913-1919, papier-máché, 11" long	12	25
105 Tunnel, 1913-1922, 1924-1927, papier-máché, 14" long......................	12	25
105 Tunnel, 1928, papier-máché, 12" long..	12	25
106 Tunnel, 1906-1912, papier-máché, 14" long.	15	30

	C7	C9
106-E Tunnel, 1910-1912, papier-máché, 16" long.....................................	15	30
106 Tunnel, 1913-1928, papier-máché, 16" long.....................................	15	30
106 Tunnel, 1929-1930, papier-máché, 19" long.....................................	15	30
107 Semaphore, 1905-1917, O ga., w/check; arm on post, w/a signal and brake attachment at the base to stop mechanical train	30	60
107-S Semaphore, 1907-1930, single arm w/wire attached to signal to operate manually..	10	20
107-D Semaphore, 1907-1930, double arm w/wires to operate signals manually..	14	28
107 Tunnel, 1929-1930, papier-máché, 23" long...................................	18	35
108 Semaphore, 1908-1917, 1 ga., w/check; arm on post w/a signal and brake attachment at the base to stop mechanical train	25	50
109 Double Semaphore Tower, 1906-1922, two signals mounted on upright base, early examples had ladder going up to platform, later ones deleted this feature	35	70
110 Track Bumper, 1906-1928, for sidings, to keep trains from derailing; early examples were just a post w/two pieces of track angled up from road surface and attached to either side of the post; later ones were a more elaborate system w/a sprung bumper for the train touch against	12	25
110-1 Track Bumper, 1917, for sidings, to keep trains from derailing; early examples were just a post w/two pieces of track angled up from road surface and attached to either side of the post; later ones were a more elaborate system w/a sprung bumper for the train touch against, for 1 ga. mechanical track	20	40
110 Birdge Span, 1931-1932, Standard ga., Lionel No. 110	30	60

	C7	C9

111 Track Elevating Post, 1904-1907, made for O ga. mechanical track for elevated railways; see set section at end of chapter 20   40

111 Crossing Sign, 1912-1928 10   20

111 Crossing Sign, 1929, Lionel No. 0-68 10   20

112 Track Plates, 1906-1932, O ga., for connecting track together at ends beneath ties 1   1

112-1 Track Plates, 1912-1920, 1 ga., for connecting track together.................... 1   1

113 Passenger Station, 1906-1911, red body lithographed w/cast-iron door frames and window frames; lithographed roof w/shingles and base w/tiles; sign above; marked "Ticket Office" on one side of window and "Telegraph Office" on the other 163   325

113 Passenger Station, 1912-1928, painted base and roof w/red brick lithographed body; w/people in windows; front and back are identical on some models w/two doors and three windows; others have one door and two windows; tin chimney on roof   88   175

113-3 Passenger Station, 1924-1928, Same as 113, w/No. 88 lamp brackets to illuminate it externally; most stations w/factory illumination have a distinctly yellow cast to the lithographed brickwork; tin chimney ..   88   175

114 Passenger Station, 1906-1911, lithographed roof w/simulated shingles, lithographed base simulating tiles; lithographed yellow body w/red cast-iron door on window frames; some examples have lithographed plate on base w/Ives name on it, others marked "Passenger Station," "Ticket Office" and "Telegraph Office" on plates on body; cast-iron chimney on roof... 95   190

	C7	C9

114 Passenger Station, 1912-1916, lithographed roof w/simulated shingles and w/lithographed base simulated tiles; body lithographed w/clerk in window on front and back, ladies in one end window and gentlemen in other; two doors on front and back of station; tin chimney on roof.. 73   145

114 Passenger Station, 1917-1922, Same as previous year, w/painted, not lithographed, roof and base; tin chimney... 65   130

114 Passenger Station, 1923-1928, Same as previous years, roof has stamped shingle pattern; station body is shorter than previous years; tin chimney 65   130

115 Freight Station, 1906-1911, lithographed block base w/ramp and platform, small yellow lithographed station set on platform; sliding door w/lithographed plate on one side and lettered "Freight," the other side lettered "Station"; body lithographed to simulate wood, roof lithographed to simulate shingles; cast-iron chimney on roof.. 145   290

115 Freight Station, 1912-1916, lithographed block base w/ramp and platform; yellow lithographed body w/open door on front and back; clerk lithographed in window w/handcart carrying Ives packages; scale w/blue shadow lithographed on front and back of building; brown and green door and window trim; tin roof w/tin chimney; clerk visible in end windows   700   1400

No. 115, Freight Station, 1912-1916, $1,400

	C7	C9

115 Freight Station, 1917-1922, Early examples have yellow lithographed bodies w/painted roof and flat base; painted base and roof; most are the new white lithographed body, but w/same appearance as the last version ... **70   130**

115 Freight station, 1923-1928, generally the same as previous years, but w/corrugated tin roof and tin chimney; roof has vertical embossed ridges between the gutter and the roof ledge; may not have been made for all five years, but examples w/this roof seem to have an orange shadow beneath the scales, as opposed to the standard blue shadow on other models of the same station.. **70   130**

No. 115, Freight Station; station on right has brown roof and example on right has green roof., 1917-1922, $130

No. 115, Freight Station, 1923-1928, $130

	C7	C9

116 Passenger Station, 1906-1911, roof w/simulated shingles, lithographed base simulates tiles; body is lithographed yellowish brick w/cast-iron doors and windows; roof has bay gable front and back marked "Grand Central Station" U-shaped bay on front and back of station w/window on each side of U; marked "Ticket Office" above one window and "Telegraph Office" above other; two cast-iron chimneys on roof.................. **500 1000**

116 Passenger Station, 1912-1916, lithographed roof w/single pattern, bay gable front and back marked "Grand Central Station"; roof w/one, two or three cast-iron chimneys; lithographed base simulates tiles; lithographed body now w/rectangular bay in center w/windows on each side, window in center w/clerk sitting at desk; doors are now part of station body, and have lithographed stained glass pattern **175   350**

116 Passenger Station, 1917-1928, lithographed body is as previous year; roof and base are now painted; bay gable at front and rear is marked "Union Station"; first examples in 1917 had a variety of combinations of old and new parts **175   350**

116-3 Passenger Station, 1926-1928, same as the contemporary No. 116 station, w/two or four No. 88 lamp brackets mounted to the exterior for illumination **160   320**

117 Passenger Station, 1906-1911, covered; two base pieces w/lithographed tile pattern; roof supported by eight posts; train passed through between bases; lithographed sign on roof reads "Suburban Station"; one bench between center two posts on each base **550 1100**

117 Passenger Station, 1912-1922, covered; two base pieces, each w/four posts supporting painted tin roof; train passes through between bases; one bench on each base.............................. **450   900**

	C7	C9

117 Passenger Station, 1923-1928, covered; two base pieces, each w/three posts supporting painted tin roof; two benches per base; train passes between bases.. 450 900

118 Platform Station, 1905, covered, small lithographed base w/one post supporting lithographed roof; two lithographed plates read "Suburban" and "Station".. 125 250

118 Platform Station, 1906-1912, covered; small lithographed base w/one post supporting lithographed roof; single lithographed plate reads "Suburban Station" on single lithographed plate 95 190

119 Platform Station, 1905, covered; lithographed tile floor w/two posts supporting lithographed shingle roof; two lithographed plates read "Suburban" and "Station".................... 125 250

119 Platform Station, 1906-1912, covered; lithographed tile floor w/two posts supporting lithographed shingle roof; one lithographed plate reads "Suburban Station".............................. 100 200

119 Platform Station, 1913-1914, covered; painted floor w/two posts supporting painted roof w/no lettering 75 150

120 Platform Station, 1905, covered; lithographed tile base w/candy-stripe railing on three sides w/four wooden posts supporting lithographed shingled roof; two lithographed read "Suburban" and "Station"; came w/the plates lettered "Passenger" and "Station" 135 270

No. 120, Platform Station, 1905, $270

	C7	C9

120 Platform Station, 1906-1911, covered; lithographed tile base w/painted railing on one side and both ends; four posts supporting lithographed shingle roof; lithographed sign reads "Suburban Station" 125 250

120 Platform Station, 1912-1916, covered; painted base w/painted railing on one side and both ends; four posts supporting painted roof w/no lettering; some of these still had lithographed roof w/lithographed sign reading "Suburban Station" 110 220

121 Platform Station, 1906-1909, covered; two lithographed bases simulating tilework, one bench apiece, four posts apiece supporting roof made of metal ribs w/thirty-two pieces of stained glass among them; lattice border around bottom of roof.............. 600 1200

121 Platform Station, 1910-1916, covered; two lithographed covered; bases simulating tilework, two benches on each base; three posts on each base supporting roof w/metal ribs and eight separate pieces of glass; lattice border around bottom of roof ... 200 400

121 Platform Station, 1917-1927, covered; two painted bases w/three supporting posts and two benches on each; metal ribbed roof w/eight pieces of glass; no lattice border 160 320

121 Caboose, 1929, O ga., eight wheel; red American Flyer body No. 3211 w/Ives trucks w/brass journals; four side windows w/brass inserts and brass end railings................................ 100 200

No. 121, Caboose with American Flyer body, 1929, $200

	C7	C9

No. 121, Caboose with Lionel body, 1930, $170

121 Caboose, 1930, O ga., eight wheel; Lionel No. 817; red body w/short green cupola roof and trucks w/brass journals; brass end railings and window inserts; w/brass plates marked "121" and "Ives Lines" 85 170

122 Passenger Station, 1906-1916, combination of the No. 116 passenger station of these years and the No. 121 glass dome of the same period; glass dome was attached to a special shortened roof on one side of the station, and had one supporting base for the other side; see descriptions of No. 116 and No. 121 .... 200 300

122 Passenger Station, 1917-1923, combination of No. 116 and No. 121 of the same years; glass dome is supported on one side by posts coming up from a specially widened base on the No. 116 station, and by a normal No. 121 base on the other side; see contemporary No. 116 and No. 121 for further description............................... 200 300

122 Tank Car, 1929-1930, O ga., eight wheel; orange Lionel No. 815 body, Ives journals w/brass trucks; brass domes, hand rail and ladders; brake wheel at both ends 90 180

123 Double Station, 1906-1923, combination of two No. 116 stations w/a No. 121 glass dome. For more see No. 122, No. 116, and No. 121 for description 200 300

123 Lumber Car, 1910-1912, O ga., eight wheel; black flat truss rod frame w/eight red painted stakes; lumber load held on by four chains; 9" l.......... 70 140

	C7	C9

123 Lumber Car, 1913-1917, O ga., eight wheel; black body, red stake; lumber load held on w/four chains; round truss rods on frame; 9" l..................... 55 110

123 Lumber Car, 1918-1924, O ga., eight wheel; tan or brown painted body and stakes, lumber load held on by four chains; round truss rods; 9" l.............. 55 110

123 Lumber Car, 1925-1928, O ga., eight wheel; tan, brown-red or maroon body and stakes; lumber load held on by four chains; round truss rods; 9" l....... 50 100

123 Lumber Car, 1929-1930, O ga., eight wheel; green body and stakes; lumber load held on by four chains; rounded truss rods; trucks w/brass journals; 9" l. 50 100

124 Reefer, 1912-1917, O ga., eight wheel; uncataloged, but first ones came w/lithographed roof w/stripes and catwalk; white body lithographed to simulate wood; sliding door in center of each side; side marked "Merchants Dispatch Transportation Company" and "Refrigerator No. 124 Dairy Express Line"; rounded truss rods w/two posts 100 200

124 Reefer, 1918-1924, O ga., eight wheel; uncataloged, but first ones came w/lithographed roof w/stripes and catwalk; white body lithographed to simulate wood; sliding door in center of each side; w/type D-1 trucks in 1918, D-2 in the other years to 1924; door lithographed "Refrigerator No. 124" on sides; the second "e" is often misspelled as an "f" 95 190

124 Reefer, 1925-1928, O ga., eight wheel; uncataloged, but first ones came w/lithographed roof w/stripes and catwalk; white body lithographed to simulate wood; sliding door in center of each side; w/type D-3 trucks; door lithographed "Refrigerator No. 124" on sides; the second "e" is often misspelled as an "f" 95 190

	C7	C9

124 Reefer, 1929-1930, O ga., eight wheel; uncataloged, but first ones came w/lithographed roof w/stripes and catwalk; white body lithographed to simulate wood; sliding door in center of each side; w/type D-4 trucks w/brass journals; door lithographed "Refrigerator No. 124" on sides; the second "e" is often misspelled as an "f" 95 190

125 Merchandise Car, 1905-1909, O ga., eight wheel; yellow body lithographed to simulate wood; red lithographed roof w/horizontal stripes; inboard trucks; single sliding lithographed door marked "Fast Freight Line" to left and "General Merchandise Car" to right.. 338 675

125 Merchandise Car, 1910-1912, O ga., eight wheel; white body lithographed to simulate wood sheathing w/vertical stripes; w/catwalk; T-trucks, flat truss rods on sides of frame; single sliding door on each side, door marked "General Mcdse. Car No. 125"; sides marked "Union Line" and "Merchandise Car No. 125 Pennsylvania Lines" 155 310

125 Merchandise Car, 1913-1917, O ga., eight wheel; same description as before but w/gray painted roof; some w/Marklin-type trucks 138 275

125 Merchandise Car, 1915-1930, O ga., eight wheel; in 1915, the catalog states beneath the Union Star cut, that "No. 125 shows a Star Union Car. Under this number comes a large assortment of freights w/the heralds of different roads." Please refer to the general notes section of this chapter for more detail 250 500

125 Merchandise Car, 1918, O ga., eight wheel; same description as before but w/gray painted roof; some w/type D-1 trucks 138 275

125 Merchandise Car, 1919-1924, O ga., eight wheel; same description as before but w/gray painted roof; w/type D-2 trucks 125 250

125 Merchandise Car, 1925-1928, O ga., eight wheel; same description as before but w/gray painted roof; w/type D-3 trucks.. 125 250

125 Merchandise Car, 1929-1930, O ga., eight wheel; same description as before but w/red painted roof; w/type D-4 trucks w/brass journals 118 235

126 Caboose, 1904-1905, O ga., four-wheel; gray lithographed body, black and red roof; sliding lithographed door; sides marked "Fast Freight," "No. 126," "Caboose" 135 270

126 Caboose, 1906-1909, four-wheel; buff-colored lithographed body, black and red lithographed roof; same general characteristics as previous years 125 250

127 Stock Car, 1904-1909, O ga., eight wheel; gray lithographed body simulating wood, black and red horizontal striped lithographed roof; inboard trucks; sliding door on each side; marked "Livestock Transportation" 145 290

127 Stock Car, 1910-1912, O ga., eight wheel; gray body lithographed to simulate wood; frame w/flat truss rods; lithographed cross braces on diagonal on car sides; w/catwalk and lithographed roof w/vertical stripes; sliding lithographed door, marked "Livestock Transportation".................. 95 190

127 Stock Car, 1913-1917, O ga., eight wheel; yellow lithographed body w/gray painted roof; Marklin truck style; lithographed sliding door, w/"Livestock" on diagonal to left, and "Transportation" on diagonal to right; side marked "The Ives RR" 50 100

127 Stock Car, 1918, O ga., eight wheel; yellow lithographed body w/gray painted roof; w/type D-1 trucks; lithographed sliding door, w/"Livestock" on diagonal to left, and "Transportation" on diagonal to right; side marked "The Ives RR" 45 90

	C7	C9

127 Stock Car, 1919-1924, O ga., eight wheel; yellow lithographed body w/gray painted roof; w/type D-2 trucks; lithographed sliding door, w/"Livestock" on diagonal to left, and "Transportation" on diagonal to right; side marked "The Ives RR" 45 90

127 Stock Car, 1925-1928, O ga., eight wheel. yellow lithographed body w/gray painted roof; w/type D-3 trucks; lithographed sliding door, w/"Livestock" on diagonal to left, and "Transportation" on diagonal to right; side marked "The Ives RR" 45 90

127 Stock Car, 1929-1930, O ga., eight wheel. same lithographed pattern as previous models, but more of a yellow-orange; 1930 has some very orange examples; red roof; brass trucks have journals 45 90

128 Gravel Car, 1905-1909, O ga., eight wheel; gray body lithographed to simulate wood; inboard trucks............ 125 250

128 Gravel Car, 1910-1911, O ga., eight wheel; dark green body w/white lithographed striping, incomplete on each side; dark green frame w/flat truss rods, T-trucks; marked "New York Central" 60 120

128 Gravel Car, 1912, eight wheel; dark green w/lithographed striping; w/frame has rounded truss rods; two support posts; marked "New York Central".. 55 110

128 Gravel Car, 1913-1915, O ga., eight wheel; lighter green lithographed body w/same general pattern as previous models; Marklin trucks; two support posts in body...................................... 50 100

128 Gravel Car, 1916-1917, O ga., eight wheel; gray lithographed body w/reddish brown lithographed detail; two support posts across inside of body 50 100

128 Gravel Car, 1918, O ga., eight wheel; gray lithographed body w/reddish-brown lithographed detail; rounded truss rods, type D-1 trucks; two support posts inside body 50 100

128 Gravel Car, 1919-1924, O ga., eight wheel; gray lithographed body w/reddish-brown lithographed detail; rounded truss rods, type D-2 trucks; two support posts inside body............. 50 100

128 Gravel Car, 1925-1928, O ga., eight wheel. gray lithographed body w/reddish-brown lithographed detail; rounded truss rods, type D-3 trucks; two support posts inside body............. 50 100

128 Gravel Car, 1929, O ga., eight wheels; gray lithographed body w/reddish-brown lithographed detail; rounded truss rods, brass journals on the type D-4 trucks; two support posts inside body 50 100

128 Gravel Car, 1930, O ga., eight wheel; gray lithographed body w/reddish-brown lithographed detail; frame w/rounded truss rods; brass journals on type D-4 trucks; some bodies have a lithographed that is almost white, and many examples are not punched for the two support rods across the inside of the body.............................. 50 100

129 Parlor Car, 1904-1909, O ga., eight wheel; yellow body lithograph to simulate wood (also cataloged in red); lithograph roof, some w/stripes, some have a black roof w/lithographed clerestory; inboard trucks; two doors and five windows on each side; sides marked "Limited Vestibule Express" and "Philadelphia" 300 600

129 Drawing Room Car, 1910-1912, O ga., eight wheel; green body lithographed to simulate wood; dark green frame w/flat truss rods, T-trucks; gray roof w/green or red clerestory strip separate; door at each end of side and four double windows; marked "Limited Vestibule Express," "Saratoga" and "129".......................... 70 140

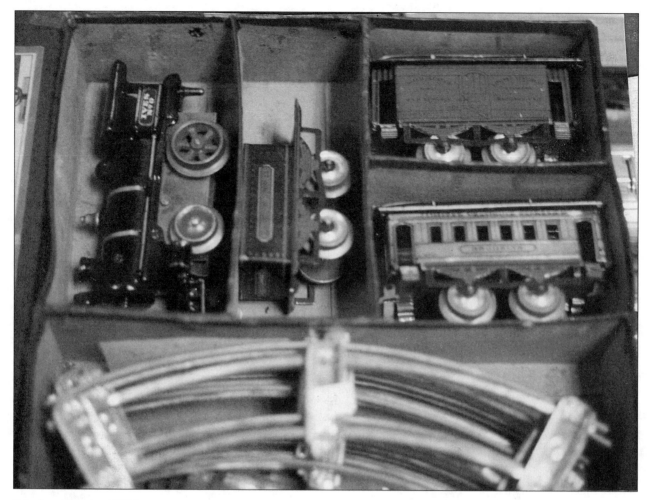

Ives boxed set, c. 1910

	C7	C9
129 Drawing Room Car, 1913-1917, O ga., eight wheel; green body lithographed to simulate wood; rounded truss rods on the side frame; Marklin trucks; gray roof w/green or red clerestory strip separate; door at each end of side and four double windows; marked "Limited Vestibule Express," "Saratoga" and "129"	70	140
129 Drawing Room Car, 1918-1924, O ga., eight wheel; green body lithographed to simulate steel; gray roof is one-piece w/clerestory strip, although some used up the existing supply of two-piece roofs; type D-2 trucks; four double windows and door at each end; marked "The Ives Railway Lines," "129" and "Saratoga"	70	140
129 Drawing Room Car, 1925-1926, O ga., eight wheel; green body lithographed to simulate steel; gray roof is one-piece w/clerestory strip, although some used up the existing supply of two-piece roofs; w/type D-3 trucks; four double windows and door at each end; marked "The Ives Railway Lines," "129" and "Saratoga." Saratoga car was used in 1926 in the "Green Mountain Express" set as an observation car by bending it behind the last set of windows and adding a brass observation railing. Also cataloged in orange in 1926	70	140

	C7	C9
129 Drawing Room Car, 1927-1929, O ga., eight wheel; orange body lithographed to simulate steel without rivet detail; orange one-piece roof w/clerestory strip; type D-3 or D-4 trucks; four double windows on both sides w/a door at each end of side; marked "The Ives Railway Lines," "Saratoga" and "129"	63	125
129 Drawing Room Car, 1930, O ga., eight wheel; orange body lithographed to simulate steel without rivet detail; orange one-piece roof w/clerestory strip; type D-3 D-4 trucks w/brass journals; four double windows on both sides w/a door at each end of side; marked "The Ives Railway Lines," "Saratoga" and "129"	63	125
130 Combination Car, 1904-1909, O ga., eight wheel; yellow lithograph body; black lithographed roof w/red stripes and painted and lithographed clerestory (some roofs are just painted); inboard trucks; baggage door at one end of side, passenger door w/steps at other end of side and six windows between them; sides marked "Limited Vestibule Express," "Buffet," "Baggage" and "New York"	150	300
130 Combination Car, 1910-1912, O ga., eight wheel; green body lithographed simulate wood; gray roof gray w/red or green clerestory strip; T-truck and flat truss rods on side frames; baggage door at one end of side, passenger door w/steps at other end of side and three double windows between them; side marked "Limited Vestibule Express," "130," "Buffet" and "130"	70	140
130 Combination Car, 1913-1917, O ga., eight wheel; green body lithographed simulate wood; gray roof gray w/red or green clerestory strip; Marklin trucks and rounded truss rods on side frames; baggage door at one end of side, passenger door w/steps at other end of side and three double windows between them; side marked "Limited Vestibule Express," "130," "Buffet" and "130"	70	140
130 Combination Car, 1918-1924, O ga., eight wheel; green body lithographed to simulate steel w/rivet detail; one-piece roof w/clerestory strip, all painted gray (some used up existing supply of two-piece roofs early on); baggage door at one end of windows, passenger door at other end above three double windows; type D-2 trucks; sides marked "The Ives Railway Lines," "No. 130," "Buffet," and "130"	72	145
130 Combination Car, 1925-1926, O ga., eight wheel; green body lithographed to simulate steel w/rivet detail; one-piece roof w/clerestory strip, all painted gray (some used up existing supply of two-piece roofs early on); baggage door at one end of windows, passenger door at other end above three double windows; type D-3 trucks; sides marked "The Ives Railway Lines," "No. 130," "Buffet," and "130"; also cataloged in orange in 1926.....................................	70	140
130 Combination Car, 1927-1929, O ga., eight wheel; orange steel lithographed body without rivet detail; brass journals on type D-3 or D-4 trucks; baggage door at one end of windows, passenger door at other end above three double windows; sides marked "The Ives Railway Lines," "130," "Buffet"	60	120
131 Baggage Car, 1904-1909, O ga., eight wheel; yellow body lithographed to simulate wood; black and red striped roof w/painted or lithographed clerestory strip; inboard trucks; two baggage doors per side, mail window to left of first one; sides marked "U.S. Mail," "Baggage Car," "Chicago," "Limited Vestibule Express"	250	500
131 Baggage Car, 1910-1912, O ga., eight wheel; green body lithographed to simulate wood; dark green frame T-trucks and flat truss rods; gray roof w/separate red or green clerestory; passenger door at each side end w/two sliding baggage doors between them; sides marked "Limited Vestibule Express," "No. 131" and "Baggage Express"	98	195

	C7	C9

131 Baggage Car, 1913-1917, O ga., eight wheel; green body lithographed to simulate wood; dark green frame Markiln trucks and rounded truss rods; gray roof w/separate red or green clerestory; passenger door at each side end w/two sliding baggage doors between them; sides marked "Limited Vestibule Express," "No. 131" and "Baggage Express" 85   170

131 Baggage Car, 1924-1926, O ga., eight wheel; green body lithographed body to simulate steel; gray one-piece roof w/clerestory strip; type D-2 trucks on 1924 car, D-3 on 1925-1926 car; passenger door at end and baggage door; sides marked "The Ives Railway Lines," "No. 131," "Baggage Express" and "U.S. Mail"; also cataloged in orange in 1926 32   65

131 Baggage Car, 1927-1929, O ga., eight wheel; orange steel body lithographed without rivet detail; type D-3 or D-4 trucks; one passenger door at each end, two baggage doors in middle; marked "Ives Railway Lines," "No. 131," "Baggage Express" and "U.S. Mail" 30   55

131 Baggage Car, 1930, O ga., eight wheel; orange steel body lithographed without rivet detail; type D-4 trucks w/brass journals; one passenger door at each end, two baggage doors in middle; sides marked "Ives Railway Lines," "No. 131," "Baggage Express" and "U.S. Mail" 30   55

132 Observation Car, 1926-1929, O ga., eight wheel; one version was made from the 129 Saratoga car in 1926. Also cataloged w/orange lithographed body version; D-3 trucks; one-piece roof w/clerestory strip w/brass observation platform railing, four double windows and one door lithographed on each side; sides marked "The Ives Railway Lines," "No. 132," "Observation" 32   65

132 Observation Car, 1930, O ga., eight wheel; orange lithographed body version; D-4 trucks w/brass journals; one-piece roof w/clerestory strip and brass observation platform railing; four double windows and one door lithographed on each side; sides marked "The Ives Railway Lines," "No. 132," "Observation" 32   65

133 Parlor Car, 1928-1930, O ga., eight wheel; Painted body and roof w/brass window inserts, brass plates and D-3 trucks; sides marked "133 Parlor Car 133"; cataloged in various colors, but generally came in either orange or red; Same body as 135 w/less trim; not cataloged w/lights but some cars had them 53   105

134 Observation Car, 1928-1930, O ga., eight wheel; orange or red painted body and roof w/brass window inserts, observation platform, brass plates and D-3 trucks; sides marked "134 Observation 134"; same car as 136, but less trim; not cataloged w/lights, but some cars had them 53   105

135 Parlor Car, 1926-1930, O ga., eight wheel; painted body and roof; interior lights; brass window inserts and brass plates; brass journals on type D-four trucks; four celluloid windows; sides marked "Pullman," "Parlor Car"; 1926 — tan body; 1927 — blue body; 1928 — orange body; 1929 — red body w/black roof and brass vestibules; 1930 — orange body w/black roof, red body w/black roof, or blue body w/red roof 88   175

136 Observation Car, 1926-1930, O ga., eight wheel; painted body and roof; interior and platform lights; four celluloid windows w/brass window inserts and observation railing; brass journals on D-4 trucks; brass plates; sides marked "Pullman," "136 Observation 136"; 1926 — tan body; 1927 — blue body; 1928 — orange body; 1929 — red body, black roof, brass vestibules; 1930 — orange body w/black roof, or red body w/black roof, or blue body w/red roof 88   175

IVES   141

	C7	C9

137 Parlor Car, 1928, O ga., eight wheel; black painted roof w/red body; another version of the 135 car; D-3 trucks; brass window inserts, celluloid windows; without lights or journals; brass plates read "137 Parlor Car 137"   45   90

138 Observation Car, 1928, O ga., eight wheel; black painted roof w/red body; another version of the 136 car; brass window inserts w/celluloid windows; no lights or brass journals; D-3 trucks; brass observation platform; brass plate marked "138 Observation 138" 45   90

140 Automatic Crossing Gates, 1906-1920, O ga., lithographed or painted base w/lithographed building and crossing gate tripped by oncoming train; for mechanical trains; 20-1/2" l. 35   70

140-3 Automatic Crossing Gates, 1910-1920, O ga., lithographed or painted base w/lithographed building and crossing gate tripped by oncoming train; for electrical trains; 20-1/2" l. 35   70

141 Parlor Car, 1926-1930, O ga., eight wheel; longer than the No. 135, painted gray, orange or black body and roof; brass journals; five double windows w/brass window inserts and two doors on each side; some have vestibules, and brass plate; w/lights; "Pullman," "Parlor Car," "141" and "Made In The Ives Shops".................. 80   160

No. 141, Two Parlor cars, part of Greyhound Set, 1926-1930, $160

No. 142, Observation car, part of Greyhound Set, 1926-1930, $160

142 Observation Car, 1926-1930, O ga., eight wheel; body generally painted gray orange or black, painted roof; longer than the No. 136; brass journals; five double windows w/brass window; lights; observation platform and vestibules; marked "Pullman," "Observation," "142" and "Made In The Ives Shops" 80   160

145 Turntable, 1910-1930, O ga., four track outside, w/inside table rotated by clockwork mechanism; brake and signal on turning table portion; painted base and table; for mechanical trains .. 50   100

146 Turntable, 1906-1919, O ga., automatic; four truck outside; inside table rotated by clockwork mechanism; brake and signal on turning table portion; painted base and table; mechanical trains...................... 75   150

170 Buffet Car, 1924-1925, Standard ga., eight wheel; painted green w/mustard-colored window trim (1925) or tan w/red window trim (1924) body; painted roof w/clerestory strip; sliding door and four double windows; marked "The Ives Railway Lines," "170" and "Buffet" below; same lettering w/larger format and mustard colored window trim in 1925 32   65

171 Buffet Car, 1924, Standard ga., eight wheel; green body w/red trim; sides marked "The Ives Railway Line," "171" and "Buffet"; cataloged version... 32   65

	C7	C9

171 Parlor Car, 1924-1925, Standard ga., eight wheel; painted green w/mustard-colored window trim (1925) or tan w/red window trim (1924); five large windows; sides marked "The Ives Railway Lines," "171" "Parlor Car"; 1925 model had larger format lettering 32   65

172 Parlor Car, 1924, Standard ga., eight wheel; green body w/red trim; marked "The Ives Railway Lines" above windows and "172," "Parlor Car" and "172" below; cataloged version 32   65

172-3 Parlor Car, 1924, Standard ga., eight wheel; green body w/red trim; w/interior lighting; marked "The Ives Railway Lines" above windows and "172," "Parlor Car" and "172" below; cataloged version 32   65

172 Observation Car, 1924-1925, Standard ga., eight wheel; painted green w/mustard-colored trim (1925) or tan w/red window trim (1924); marked "The Ives Railway Lines" "172" above windows and "Observation" below; same lettering in 1925 w/larger format 32   65

173 Observation Car, 1924, Standard ga., eight wheel; green body w/red trim; "The Ives Railway Lines" above windows and "173," "Observation" and "173" below window; cataloged version 32   65

176 Locomotive, 1930, O ga., 0-4-0; black cast-iron body w/clockwork engine and hand brake; marked "Ives No. 176" beneath cab windows; 1930 version of the No. 17 locomotive; w/No. 17 tender w/decal 110   220

180 Club Car, 1925-1928, Standard ga., twelve wheel; red, orange, or green body w/painted roof and separate clerestory strip; brass journals on trucks; passenger door at one end of side and baggage door at other; four windows; brass plate over windows marked "Pullman," brass plate below reads "Club Car"; marked "180" each door on small plate; also came rubber stamped 70   140

181 Buffet Car, 1912-1920, 1 ga., eight wheel; green body w/painted roof and separate clerestory; round truss rods, steps at both ends; passenger door at left end of each side, baggage door at right; seven windows; marked "The Ives Railway Lines" above windows, and "Buffet" below; marked "No. 181" to left of baggage door 250   500

181 Parlor Car, 1925-1928, Standard ga., twelve wheel; red, orange, or green body w/painted roof w/separate clerestory strip; brass journals; passenger doors at each end of side and six windows; sides marked "Made In the Ives Shops" and "181" near doors and "Pullman" above windows and "Parlor Car" below 70   140

182 Parlor Car, 1912-1920, 1 ga., eight wheel; green body w/painted roof w/separate clerestory strip; round truss rods; steps at each end; passenger door at each side end and 6 large windows; marked "The Ives Railway Lines" above windows and "Parlor Car" below and "No. 182" near each door 250   500

182 Observation Car, 1925-1928, Standard ga., twelve wheel; Red, orange, or green body w/painted roof w/separate clerestory strip; brass journals; six windows; marked "Pullman" on brass plate above windows and "Observation" below and "Made In The Ives Shops" and "182" on smaller plates 70   140

183 Observation Car, 1912-1920, 1 ga., eight wheel; green body w/separate clerestory strip on painted roof; round truss rods; steps at each end; passenger door at front and eight various windows along side; stamped "The Ives Railway Lines" stamped above windows and "Observation" below; also stamped "No. 183" at each end 250   500

	C7	C9

184 Buffet Car, 1921-1925, Standard ga., eight wheel; pained body generally red or green w/painted roof; passenger door w/steps at one end of side, baggage door at other and four windows; stamped lettering reads "The Ives Railway Lines" above windows and "184," "Buffet" and "184" below 70   140

184 Club Car, 1926-1930, Standard ga., eight wheel; painted body brown, green, red, orange or cadet blue; passenger door w/steps at one end of side, baggage door at other and four windows; painted roof; brass plates over windows marked "Pullman," plates below windows read "184," "Club Car," and "Made In The Ives Shops" 83   165

Top to bottom: No. 3235-R Locomotive, Club car, 1924-1929, $195; No. 184 Club car, $165, 1926-1930, $165

184-3 Club Car, 1926-1930, Standard ga., eight wheel; painted body brown, green, red, orange or cadet blue; passenger door w/steps at one end of side, baggage door at other and four windows; interior illumination; painted roof; brass plates over windows marked "Pullman," plates below windows read "184," "Club Car," and "Made In The Ives Shops" 83   165

185 Parlor Car, 1921-1925, Standard ga., eight wheel; body generally painted red or green; painted roof; passenger door w/steps at each end of side and five large windows; rubber-stamped lettering reads "The Ives Railway Lines" above windows and "185," "Parlor Car" and "185" below 118   235

185-3 Parlor Car, 1926-1930, Standard ga., eight wheel; body painted brown, red, green, orange, or cadet blue; painted roof; passenger door w/steps at each end of side and five large; interior illumination; w/brass plates over windows reads "Pullman," and "Made In The Ives Shops" and "Parlor Car" and "185" on lower plate........... 118   235

185 Parlor Car, 1926-1930, Sandard ga., eight wheel; body painted brown, red, green, orange, or cadet blue; painted roof; passenger door w/steps at each end of side and five large windows; w/brass plates over windows reads "Pullman," and "Made In The Ives Shops" and "Parlor Car" and "185" on lower plate.. 118   235

186 Observation Car, 1922-1925, Standard ga., eight wheel; painted body painted green or red; painted roof; passenger door w/steps at front of side, steps on observation platform at sides; five large windows; "The Ives Railway Lines" rubber stamped above windows and "186," "Observation" and "186" below 118   235

Top to bottom: No. 184 Club car, 1926-1930, $165; No. 186 Observation car, 1922-1925, $235

	C7	C9

186-3 Observation Car, 1926-1930, Standard ga., eight wheel; body painted brown, red, green, orange, or cadet blue; painted roof; passenger door w/steps at front of side, steps at side of observation platform; interior illumination; five large windows, brass plate above windows read "Pullman" and "186," "Observation" and "Made In The Ives Shops" below.   100   200

186 Observation Car, 1926-1930, Standard ga., eight wheel; body painted brown, red, green, orange, or cadet blue; painted roof; passenger door w/steps at front of side, steps at side of observation platform; five large windows, brass plate above windows read "Pullman" and "186," "Observation" and "Made In The Ives Shops" below......................................   100   200

	C7	C9

187 Buffet Car, 1921-1928, Standard ga., eight wheel; body painted orange, red, green, gray, or cadet blue; painted roof w/separate clerestory; passenger door at end of side, w/steps, and baggage door at other end; four large windows; stamped "The Ives Railway Lines" above windows and "187;" "Buffet" and "187" below; cataloged as 187-1 in 1921   83   165

187-3 Buffet Car, 1923, eight wheel; body painted orange, red, green, gray, or cadet blue; painted roof w/separate clerestory; passenger door at end of side, w/steps, and baggage door at other end; interior illumination (after this year, interior lights were standard on this series); four large windows; stamped "The Ives Railway Lines" above windows and "187;" "Buffet" and "187" below; cataloged as 187-1 in 1921   118   235

Back row, left to right: No. 189 Observation car, 1921-1928, $160; No. 188 Parlor car, 1921-1928, $180; No. 187, Buffet car, c. 1921-1928, $16. ; Middle: Several Ives accessories, including a water tower, freight station and passenger station; front: No. 3242 Locomotive, $450

	C7	C9

188 Parlor Car, 1921-1928, Standard ga., eight wheel; body painted orange, red, green, gray, or cadet blue; painted roof w/separate clerestory; passenger door w/steps at each end of side; six large windows; "The Ives Railway Lines" above windows and "188," "Parlor Car" and "188" below; cataloged as 188-1 in 1921 .... 90 180

188-3 Parlor Car, 1923, Standard ga., eight wheel; body painted orange, red, green, gray, or cadet blue; painted roof w/separate clerestory; passenger door w/steps at each end of side; interior illumination (after this year, interior lights were standard on this series); six large windows; "The Ives Railway Lines" above windows and "188," "Parlor Car" and "188" below; cataloged as 188-1 in 1921 .... 70 140

189 Observation Car, 1921-1928, Standard ga., eight wheel; body painted orange, red, green, gray, or cadet blue; painted roof w/separate clerestory; passenger door w/steps at front of side, steps at sides of observation platform six large windows; stamped "The Ives Railway Lines" above six large windows and "188," "Observation" and "188" below window; cataloged as 189-1 in 1921 .... 80 160

189-3 Observation Car, 1923, Standard ga., eight wheel; body painted orange, red, green, gray, or cadet blue; painted roof w/separate clerestory; passenger door w/steps at front of side, steps at sides of observation platform; interior illumination (after this year, interior lights were standard on this series); six large windows; stamped "The Ives Railway Lines" above six large windows and "188," "Observation" and "188" below window; cataloged as 189-1 in 1921 .... 70 140

190 Tank Car, 1921-1923, Standard ga., eight wheel; same body and frame assembly as the 1 ga. tank car; gray body w/black dome w/vent pipe; frame girdles tank body w/air tank below; marked "190" and "Texas Oil" 95 190

190 Tank Car, 1923-1928, Standard ga., eight wheel; orange body of tank now attached to standard car frame by saddle-type supports; w/black dome and vent pipe; grab rails and brake wheel; marked "190" and "Texas Oil" 95 190

190 Tank Car, 1929-1930, Standard ga., eight wheel; collage of parts from Ives, Lionel, and Flyer — Lionel No. 215 tank car w/brass domes, American Flyer frame and Ives trucks; No. 190 car from original 1930 set which used 1921 body and frame, 1930 trucks and as a 1 ga. tank; brass plates read "Ives" and "190" 100 200

191 Coke Car, 1921-1930, Standard ga., eight wheel; at first, the same as the 1 ga. Coke car, but numbered 191; brown or greenish body made up of several pieces soldered together on standard frame; stayed virtually the same throughout its history; marked "Penna R.R." and "191" on sides........ 70 140

192 Merchandise Car, 1921-1928, Standard ga., eight wheel; painted body and roof w/single sliding door on each side; brake wheel and ladders; marked to left of door "Ventilator and Refrigerator" and "S.F.R.D." w/the Santa Fe logo to right of door 95 190

192-C Circus Car, 1928, No. 192 painted yellow w/red roof; marked for the "The Ives Railway Circus" 500 1000

20-192 Merchandise Car, 1929, Standard ga., green or yellow American Flyer body on Ives trucks; sliding door on each end; brass plates on Ives trucks; brass plates marked "The Ives Railway Lines" and "20-192" 300 600

192 Merchandise Car, 1930, Standard ga., eight wheel; Lionel No. 214 w/Ives trucks; body painted yellow w/painted roof; double sliding doors; brass plates read "Ives" and "192"...... 95 190

	C7	C9

193 Livestock Car, 1921-1928, Standard ga., eight wheel; same general car as the 1 ga. model from 1920; car made up of basic frame and ends w/separate soldered pieces constructing the body; body generally painted brown, gray or orange; painted roof; sliding door on each side; marked "The Ives Railway Lines," "193" and "Livestock" 138 275

193-C Circus Car, 1928, Standard ga., eight wheel. same general car as the 1 ga. model from 1920; car made up of basic frame and ends w/separate soldered pieces constructing the body; body painted yellow w/red roof; marked for the "The Ives Railway Circus" 500 1000

20-193 Livestock Car, 1929, Standard ga., eight wheel; American flyer body and roof painted green w/Ives trucks; single sliding door w/step on both sides at each end; brass plates read "The Ives Railway Lines" and "20-193" 95 190

20-193-C Circus Car, 1929, Standard ga., eight wheel; eight wheel; American flyer body painted yellow and red roof; single sliding door w/step on both sides at each end; marked for "The Ives Railway Circus" 500 1000

20-193 Livestock Car, 1930, eight wheel; Lionel No. 213 body painted orange w/red roof; Ives trucks; brass plates read "Ives" and "193" 95 190

194 Coal Car, 1921-1930, Standard ga., eight wheel; body painted gray, black, or maroon w/black ribs; brake wheel; steps at each end; rubber stamped "Penna Coal & Coke Co." w/a P.R.R. logo in keystone 125 250

195 Caboose, 1921-1927, Standard ga., eight wheel; same as 1 ga. model converted to Standard ga. trucks; red body and cupola w/black roof on both; smoke chimney and support on roof; brake wheel on one platform; coal box beneath body; five windows; "The Ives Railway Lines" above windows and "Caboose" and "195" below window level 138 265

195 Caboose, 1928, Standard ga., eight wheel; red body and cupola and black roof on both; two windows; stamped "The Ives Railway Lines" above windows and "195" and "Caboose" below 125 250

20-195 Caboose, 1928-1929, Standard ga., eight wheel; American Flyer body on Ives trucks; red body w/red roof and red or green cupola roof; six windows w/brass window inserts and plates that read "The Ives Railway Lines" centered between windows and "Made In The Ives Shops" and "20-195" below windows.......................... 100 200

195 Caboose, 1930, Standard ga., eight wheel; Lionel 217 caboose body on Ives trucks; short cupola w/green roof; two windows w/brass inserts, brass plates "195," "Ives," and "195" below window level; brass end railings; red body, red roof 100 200

196 Flat Car, 1922, Standard ga., eight wheel; special version w/milk vats marked for the "Harmony Creamery" company 400 800

196 Flat Car, 1922-1930, Standard ga., eight wheel; body painted in green, maroon, and orange; originally had a standard frame, low sides were added in 1924. sides stamped "196," "The Ives Railway Lines" and "196".......... 65 130

196-C Circus Car, 1928-1929, Standard ga., eight wheel; body painted in green, maroon, and orange; originally had a standard frame, low sides were added in 1924; body painted yellow and marked for "The Ives Railway Circus" 400 800

197 Lumber Car, 1928-1929, Standard ga., eight wheel; standard frame w/eight stakes holding wires to secure load; body painted green, orange or brown; marked "197," "The Ives Railway Lines" and "197" 125 250

197 Lumber Car, 1930, Standard ga., eight wheel; Lionel No. 211 car w/stakes and Ives trucks; body and stakes painted green 125 250

	C7	C9
20-198 Gravel Car, 1929, Standard ga., eight wheel; American Flyer body w/Ives trucks; black body, brass ladders; w/brake wheel; brass plates marked "The Ives Railway Lines" and "20-198"	110	220
198 Gravel Car, 1930, Standard ga., eight wheel; Lionel No. 212 body w/Ives trucks; body painted black; brass brake wheels; brass plates marked "Ives" and "No. 198"	110	220
199 Derrick Car, 1929-1930, Standard ga., eight wheel; Lionel No. 219 body on Ives trucks; body painted peacock blue w/black frame w/brass handrail on sides of cab; sides stamped "199," brass plates on rear of car read "The Ives Railway Lines" and "Ives"	370	700
200 Power House, 1910-1914, lithographed roof and building, w/round painted or square lithographed smokestack; houses batteries	450	900
200 Freight Station, 1923-1928, small lithographed station w/freight punched out in open doorway; roof embossed w/shingle pattern; green or brown painted roof and base; became No. 220 in 1929	55	110
201 Power House, 1910-1914, lithographed roof and building w/round painted or square lithographed smokestack; made to house transformer and connections for alternating current	450	900
201 Passenger Station, 1923-1928, small lithographed station w/embossed base and roof painted brown or green; goes w/No. 200 freight station	55	110
201-3 Passenger Station, 1923-1928, small lithographed station w/embossed base and roof painted brown or green; goes w/No. 200 freight station; w/No. 88 lamp brackets for illumination	55	110
202 Power House, 1910-1914, lithographed roof and building, w/round painted or square lithographed smokestack; made to house transformer and connections for direct current	450	900

	C7	C9
203 Transformer	10	20
203 Power House, 1912-1914, lithographed roof and building, round painted or square lithographed smokestack; made to house two transformers and connections	850	1700
204 Transformer	10	20
205 Transformer	10	20
206 Transformer	10	20
208 Transformer	10	20
211 Transformer	10	20
212 Transformer	10	20
215 Crossing Gate, 1923-1930, O ga., lithographed base simulating earth; two fences w/pole gate between them; manually operated	22	45
216 Crossing Gate, 1923-1927, Standard ga., lithographed base simulating earth; two fences w/pole gate between them; manually operated	35	70
220 Freight Station, 1929-1930, lithographed building w/freight punched out in open doorway; red painted roof, green or brown painted base; formerly No. 200	55	110
221 Passenger Station, 1929-1930, lithographed building w/embossed red roof and embossed base painted brown or green; companion piece to No. 220 freight station	55	110
225 Passenger Station, 1929-1930, Lionel No. 127 station; white body, red or orange roof w/ green base; brass plate above door reads "Ives R.R."	150	300
226 Passenger Station, 1929-1930, Lionel No. 126; crackle red finish on station w/green roof and base; brass plate over center window marked "Ives R.R. Lines"	160	320
228 Station, 1929-1930, similar to odd No. 117 w/solid base; green base and red roof w/six roof supports; four benches rest on base	85	170

Left to right: two No. 551 Chair cars and a No. 221 Passenger Station, 1929-1930, $110

	C7	C9
230 Passenger Station, 1929-1930, Lionel No. 122 station w/special paint for Ives; embossed brickwork body painted yellow w/gray windows, door, and corner trim; red windows and doors open inward; brass plate over doorway reads "Waiting Room" and brass plate on roof front reads "The Ives Railway Lines".............................	200	400
230-3XX Station Set, 1929-1930, No. 230-X and two of No. 228	350	700
230-3 Passenger station, 1929-1930, Lionel No. 122 station w/special paint for Ives; embossed brickwork body painted yellow w/gray windows, door, and corner trim; red windows and doors open inward; interior and exterior illumination; brass plate over doorway reads "Waiting Room" and brass plate on roof front reads "The Ives Railway Lines"............................	200	400
230-3X Station Set, 1929-1930, No. 230-X and No. 228	285	570

	C7	C9
241 Club Car, 1928-1929, Standard ga., twelve wheel; American Flyer body, Ives trucks; body painted Black, green, or orange; Sliding baggage doors; illuminated; fourteen windows; brass plate above window read "The Ives Railway Lines," brass plates below window read "Made In The Ives Shops," "Club Car" and "241"....	400	800
242 Parlor Car, 1928-1929, Standard ga., twelve wheel; American Flyer body on Ives trucks; black, green or orange body; passenger door at each end of side; illuminated eight windows; brass plate reads "The Ives Railway Lines" above window and "Made In The Ives Shops," "Parlor Car" and "242"..........	300	600

No. 242, Parlor car, 1928-1929, $600

	C7	C9

243 Observation Car, 1928-1929, Standard ga., twelve wheel; American Flyer body on Ives trucks; body painted black, green, or orange painted body; illuminated; windows; w/brass platform railing; brass plates above windows reads "The Ives Railway Lines"; brass plate below window reads "Made In The Ives Shops," "Observation" and "243".................... 300   600

246 Dining Car, 1930, Standard ga., twelve wheel; Lionel body on Ives trucks; body painted orange, black, blue or yellow; roof w/separate clerestory; air tanks beneath car; opening passenger door at each end of side; illuminated; five double windows; decal above windows read "The Ives Railway Lines" and "Dining Car," "Made In the Ives Shops Dining Car" and "Ives No. 246"...................... 450   900

247 Club Car, 1930, Standard ga., twelve wheel; Lionel body on Ives trucks; body painted orange, black, blue and yellow; painted roof w/separate clerestory strip; air tanks beneath car; opening passenger door at each end of side w/sliding baggage door; three double windows; illuminated; decal over door reads "The Ives Railway Lines" and "Made In The Ives Shops," "Ives No. 247" and "Club Car" 200   400

248 Pullman Car, 1930, Standard ga., twelve wheel; Lionel body on Ives trucks; body painted body orange, black, blue, or yellow; illuminated; painted roof w/separate clerestory; air tanks beneath body; opening passenger doors at each end of side; five double windows; decal above windows reads "The Ives Railway Lines," and "Made In The Ives Shops," "Ives No. 248", and "Pullman" below the windows 400   800

249 Observation Car, 1930, Standard ga., twelve wheel; Lionel body on Ives trucks; body painted orange, black, blue and yellow; painted roof w/separate clerestory; Air tanks beneath body; illuminated; passenger door at front and brass observation railing at rear; five double windows; decal above windows reads "The Ives Railway Lines," and below window level "Made In The Ives Shops," "Observation" and "Ives No. 249" below windows 400   800

250 Village House, 1929-1930, lithographed building w/painted base; Lionel No. 184 bungalow, Ives name on bottom 95   190

251 Dutch Colonial House, 1929-1930, painted body and roof w/lithographed brick chimney, Ives name on bottom.. 100   200

252 Village House, 1929-1930, Lionel No. 191 Villa; crackle red finish on house w/green roof; Ives name on bottom 100   200

253 Power House, 1929-1930, Lionel No. 435 Power station; white house, green or brown base w/red roof; Ives name on bottom 150   300

254 Power House, 1929, Lionel No. 436 station, Ives name on bottom; larger than No. 253 160   320

255 Signal Tower, 1929-1930, Lionel No. 438 signal tower painted red-orange w/green roof; switch on back of station.. 150   300

257 Locomotive, 1931, O ga., 2-4-0; Lionel No. 257, w/No. 257T four-wheel tender; black paint locomotive w/orange and brass trim; No reverse unit; nickel journals on tender; brass plates reads "Ives Lines" and "Ives No. 257".. 200   400

No. 257, Locomotive with tender, 1931, $400

	C7	C9
258 Locomotive, 1931-1932, O ga., 2-4-0 w/No. 1663 Tender; black painted locomotive w/orange and copper trim, hand reverse unit w/brass plate that reads "Ives Lines" and "Ives No. 258"; eight- wheel black tender w/brass journals	230	460
300 Semaphore, 1922-1930, manual operation, single arm; track leads illuminate box behind signal arm	40	80
301 Semaphore, 1922-1930, Mechanical operation, double arm; track leads illuminate boxes behind signal arms	45	90
302 Platform Signal, 1923-1928, two semaphore posts on raised platform w/ladder; manual operation, electric lights in boxes behind signal arms; same general appearance as No. 109	50	100
306 Electric Street Lamp, 1923-1932, double gooseneck arms, cast-iron or die-cast base	38	75
307 Electric Street Lamp, 1923-1931, double gooseneck arms, cast-iron or die-cast base	100	200
308 Electric Street Lamp, 1928-1930, single columnar lamp, die-cast	35	70
310 Platform Signal, 1923-1926, two semaphore arms on platform w/ladder; manual operation; same as No. 302 without lights; new version of old No. 109	30	60
330 Semaphore, 1924-1930, automatic, black, single arm w/ladder; electrically operated signal and lights; brass mast and Lionel signal arm in 1930	45	90
331 Target Signal, 1924-1930, electrically operated; two colored cellophane pieces behind round target face w/white painted metal face and green base w/white post; maroon base and brass face in 1930	50	100
332 Bell Signal, 1924-1930, automatic; green base, white post w/bell in center of diamond shaped sign lettered "Railroad Crossing. Look Out For engine"; bell operated electrically; 1930 had maroon base w/brass diamond	35	70

	C7	C9
332 Baggage Car, 1931-1932, Standard ga., eight wheel; Lionel car; body painted peacock blue w/orange doors w/painted roof; illuminated; four windows, two baggage doors on each side; "The Ives Railway Lines" decal below roof line marked "332," "Railway Mail" and "332" stamped below window level	75	150
333 Banjo Signal, 1924-1930, mechanism enclosed in white case w/front cellophane insert for light, green base, white post and body, bell on rear of signal; marked "Railroad Crossing Look Out For Engine" and "Danger Stop Look And Listen"; activated by train and operated electrically; 1930 maroon base, body, brass face	40	80
334 Crossing Gate, 1928-1930, automatic; lithographed base simulates earth and roadway; fence on one side, signal shanty on other side w/crossing gate operated by oncoming train	95	190
338 Bridge Approach Telltale, 1924-1930, cast base, white post and arm w/hanging chains	50	100
339 Track Bumper, 1928-1930, Standard ga., Lionel bumper w/red light on top	12	25
339-0 Track Bumper, 1928-1930, O ga., Lionel bumper w/red light on top	12	25
339 Pullman Car, 1931-1932, Standard ga., eight wheel; Lionel car; peacock blue body w/orange trim; illuminated; six double windows w/two passenger doors per side, steps beneath doors; "The Ives Railway Lines" on decal below roof; stamped "339," "Pullman" and "339" below window	85	170
340-0 Spring Bumper, 1929-1930, O ga., sheet-steel w/spring cross bar; Lionel	10	20
340 Spring Bumper, 1929-1930, Standard ga., sheet-steel w/spring cross bar; Lionel	10	20

	C7	C9

341 Observation Car, 1931-1932, Standard ga., eight wheel. Lionel car. peacock blue body w/orange w/brass platform railing; illuminated; six double windows; "The Ives Railway Lines" on decal above windows and "341," "Observation" and "341" stamped below windows 85 170

550 Baggage Car, 1913-1915, O ga., four-wheel; painted one piece roof, lithographed body simulating wood detail Red, rose or white body; passenger door at each end of side, leaf springs on frame; marked "The Ives Railway Lines" center door and "Baggage No. 550" to left of door, and "Express Mail" to right 58 115

550 Baggage Car, 1916-1926, O ga., four-wheel; green lithographed body simulates steel, painted roof; flat springs on frame; passenger door at each end of side, open doorway in center; marked "The Ives Railway Lines" above door, "Express Service Baggage 550" to left and "U.S. Mail 550" to right; sometimes 60 series cars were used for these 58 115

550 Baggage Car, 1927-1930, O ga., four-wheel; lithographed green steel body, flat spring frame; white body, red roof in 1927 for White Owl set, blue and buff body w/blue roof in 1930 for Blue Vagabond set, green and buff body w/blue roof in 1930 for Pequot set, also red body w/blue roof in 1930; open doorway in center of car, passenger door at each end of side; marked "The Ives Railway Lines" above doorway; "Express Service Baggage 550" to left of center door and "U.S. Mail 550" to the right. 58 115

551 Chair Car, 1913-1915, O ga., four-wheel; red, white or rose body lithographed to simulate wood sheathing; painted one-piece roof; leaf springs on frame; eight square windows and door at the end of each side "The Ives Railway Lines" lettered above eight square windows; marked "No. 61," "Yale" and "No. 61" below windows 55 110

551 Chair Car, 1916-1926, O ga., four-wheel; green body lithographed to simulate steel; painted one-piece roof; flat springs on frame; eight windows and passenger door at the end of each side; "The Ives Railway Lines" above 8 windows, "551", "Chair Car", and "551" below window level; 60 series cars were sometimes used 55 110

551 Chair Car, 1927-1930, O ga., four-wheel; green body lithographed to simulate steel; white w/red roof in 1927 for White Owl set, blue and buff w/blue roof in 1930 for Blue Vagabond, green and buff in 1930 for Pequot, also came w/red body and blue roof in 1930; painted one-piece roof. eight windows and passenger doors at the end of each side; marked "The Ives Railway Lines" above windows and "551," "Chair Car," and "551" below window 55 110

No. 551, Chair car, 1916-1926, $110

No. 550, Baggage car, 1927-1930, $115

	C7	C9

552 Parlor Car, 1913-1915, O ga., four-wheel; red, white, or rose body lithographed to simulate wood; one-piece painted roof; leaf springs on frame; five wide windows and passenger door at the end of each side; marked "The Ives Railway Lines" windows, and "No. 62," "Harvard," and "No. 62" below windows.............. 55 110

552 Parlor Car, 1916-1926, O ga., four-wheel; one-piece painted roof. green body lithographed to simulate steel; flat springs on frame; five wide windows and passenger door at the end of each side; marked "The Ives Railway Lines" above windows, and "552," "Parlor Car," and "552" below 55 110

552 Parlor Car, 1927-1930, O ga., four-wheel; green body lithographed to simulate steel; white w/red roof in 1927 for White Owl set, blue and buff w/blue roof in 1930 for Blue Vagabond set, green and buff in 1930 for Pequot set, also red body w/blue roof in 1930; painted one-piece roof; flat springs on frame; five wide windows and passenger door at the end of each side; marked "The Ives Railway Lines" above windows and "552," "Parlor Car" and "552" below 55 110

558 Observation Car, 1927-1930, O ga., four-wheel; green body lithographed to simulate steel; painted one-piece roof; white in 1927 for White Owl set, blue and buff in 1930 for Blue Vagabond set, also red w/blue roof in 1930; flat springs on frame; five wide windows and passenger door at the front of each side; brass observation railing; marked "The Ives Railway Lines" above windows and "558," "Observation" and "558".................... 55 110

562 Caboose, 1930, O ga., four-wheel; red Lionel No. 807 body w/brass window inserts and green cupola roof; flat springs on trucks............................ 68 135

563 Gravel Car, 1913-1930, O ga., four-wheel; gray or green body lithographed to simulate steel.............. 35 70

	C7	C9

564 Merchandise Car, 1913-1930, O ga., four-wheel; this series utilized the No. 64 box car series detailed in the 60 series section and in general notes 125 250

565 Livestock Car, 1913-1930, O ga., four-wheel; red orange body lithographed to simulate wood (some examples had yellow body similar to No. 65 stock car); painted one-piece roof w/catwalk; some versions had sliding door; early examples marked w/"Livestock Transportation"............. 45 90

566 Tank Car, 1913-1929, O ga., four-wheel. painted body frame; follows evolution of No. 66 tank car see this car's description for more detail; ends marked "566"; sides read "Standard Oil"....................................... 45 90

566 Tank Car, 1930, O ga., Lionel No. 804 tank car w/brass domes; orange body; brass handrail and ladders; brass plates read "Ives" and "No. 566"........ 60 120

567 Caboose, 1913-1930, O ga., four-wheel; lithographed body w/painted roof and cupola; see caboose No. 67 for details 45 90

569 Lumber Car, 1913-1930, O ga., four-wheel; body and stakes painted tan, maroon, brown, green or black; two chain supports hold carries lumber load; supported load........................... 40 80

600 Electric Arc light, 1915-1922, single arm street light w/various shapes and lamp...................................... 30 60

601 Electric Arc light, 1915-1922, double arm street light w/various shapes and lamps................................... 40 80

610 Pullman Car, 1931-1932, O ga., eight wheel; Lionel car; green body and roof; Air tanks beneath car; Lionel latch couplers; eight windows and passenger doors at each end of side; decal above windows reads "The Ives Lines," marked "610," "Pullman" and "610" below windows........................ 70 140

	C7	C9

612 Observation Car, 1931-1932, O ga., eight wheel; Lionel car; green body and roof; Lionel latch couplers; air tanks beneath car; observation platform of brass on rear; eight windows and passenger doors at the front of each side; decal above windows reads "The Ives Lines"; marked "612," "Observation" and "612" below windows **70 140**

800 Trolley, 1910-1913, O ga., four-wheel; mechanical works w/trolley pole on roof; tin wheels and hinged pilots; four windows and passenger door at each end of side; marked "Local and Suburban Service" above windows and "Trolley" below; 6-1/2" l. **800 1600**

801 Trolley, 1910-1913, O ga., four-wheel; mechanical works w/spring pole on roof; lithographed body; tin wheels; four windows and two doors on each side; marked "Limited Vestibule Express" above windows "Buffalo" below; can also be marked "Pennsylvania Lines" "Newark" and "Washington"; 5" l. **600 1200**

805 Trolley Car Trailer, 1913-1915, O ga., four-wheel; lithographed body w/cast pilot; roof w/separate clerestory; no trolley pole; cast-iron spoke wheels; five windows and one open and one blocked passenger door each on side; unpowered...................... **175 350**

809 Streetcar, 1913-1915, O ga., four-wheel; lithographed body w/cast pilot; roof w/separate clerestory; no trolley pole; cast-iron spoke wheels; five windows and one open and one blocked passenger door each on side; marked "Suburban" below windows and "Ives No. 809" on side; 7-3/4" l.... **500 1000**

810 Trolley, 1910-1912, O ga., four-wheel; same general configuration as No. 809; roof w/separate clerestory; ten caternary poles; trolley pole on roof collected current for motor; tin wheels; sides lithographed "Suburban" and "Ives No. 810" on side; 7-1/2" l. **500 1000**

	C7	C9

1100 Locomotive, 1910-1912, O ga., 2-2-0; cast black body; dummy headlight, two tin boiler bands, painted stack and bell; tin front wheels; cast drivers; no drive rods w/F.E. No. 1 tender; brass plates below rectangular window reads "Ives No. 1100" **155 310**

1100 Locomotive, 1913-1914, O ga., 0-4-0; similar to 1912 version w/slightly different casting to accommodate front drive wheels; dummy headlight, two tin boiler bands, painted stack and bell; seven spoke wheels; w/L.V.E. No. 11 tender; lithographed plate beneath cab roof reads "Ives No. 1100"... **140 280**

1100 Locomotive, 1915-1916, O ga., 0-4-0; cast-iron black body; straight boiler w/dummy headlight on boiler top; two tin boiler bands; rectangular cab window; drive rods; seven or twelve spoke cast-iron wheels; stamped "Ives No. 1100" stamped below window; w/tender marked "Ives No. 11" **125 250**

1100 Locomotive, 1917-1922, O ga., 0-4-0; cast-iron black body; one tin boiler band and dummy headlight in boiler front; cast-iron wheels; rectangular cab window; drive rods; w/No. 11 tender; At some point during production (probably around 1920) 1100s were made from 1116 castings w/operating headlight in boiler front, probably around **95 190**

1116 Locomotive, 1917-1922, O ga., 0-4-0; same casting as No. 1100, but w/operating headlight in boiler front center; straight drive rods, No. 11 tender; see 1100 for more details **150 300**

No. 1100, Locomotive with tender, 1917-1922, $190

No. 1117, Locomotive with tender, 1910-1914, $300

1117 Locomotive, 1910-1914, O ga., 0-4-0; black cast-iron boiler, cast-iron wheels w/angled drive rods; body extension over armature end in 1910; two tin boiler bands and dummy headlight on top of boiler; two cab windows; w/L.V.E. No. 11 tender; lithographed plates beneath windows read "Ives No. 1117" 150   300

1117 Locomotive, 1915-1916, O ga., 0-4-0; same boiler casting; cast-iron body and wheels w/angled drive rods; two tin boiler bands; w/Ives No. 11 tender; w/rubber stamped "Ives No. 1117" beneath windows 140   280

1118 Locomotive, 1910-1914, O ga., 0-4-0; same boiler No. 1117, w/operative headlight on boiler top; body covers armature in 1910 version; two tin boiler bands; cast-iron body and wheels w/angled drive rods; two cab windows; lithographed plate below windows reads "Ives No. 1118"; w/Ives No. 11 tender.......................... 150   300

1118 Locomotive, 1915-1916, O ga., 0-4-0; same as previous version but w/rubber stamped lettering beneath cab windows instead of lithographed plate 140   280

No. 1118, Locomotive with tender, 1917-1925, $220

1118 Locomotive, 1917-1925, O ga., 0-4-0; larger w/higher body casting; cast-iron body, cast-iron wheels w/straight drive rods; headlight in center of boiler; one casting has extra sheeting below cab w/large rivet detail; w/Ives No. 17 tender; two rectangular windows; stamped "Ives No. 1118" below window 110   220

1120 Locomotive, 1916, 0-4-0; same as No. 1118; cast-iron body and wheels w/drive rods; generally stamped "Ives No. 1120" below windows, although at least one version has lithograph plates; see 1118 for more details......... 388   775

1120 Locomotive, 1928, O ga., 4-4-0; cast-iron body w/arched cab windows; die-cast wheels w/straight drive rods; separate grab rails and braces from boiler to pilot; w/No. 25 tender w/coal load; marked "Ives NYC & HR"; boiler stamped "Ives No. 1120" below windows 475   950

1122 Locomotive, 1929-1930, O ga., 4-4-2; die-cast body, headlight in boiler center and bell on boiler front; brass handrails, copper tubing and die-cast drive rods; die-cast wheels; drivers w/nickel tires; No. 25 die-cast tender; brass plate below cab windows reads "The Ives Railway Lines" and brass plate below boiler front reads "Made In The Ives Shops"; tender marked "The Ives Railway Lines" on brass plate..................................... 300   600

No. 1120, Locomotive with tender, 1928, $950

No. 1122, Locomotive with tender, 1929-1930, $600

	C7	C9

1125 Locomotive, 1910-1913, O ga., 4-4-0; tin pony wheels; cast-iron spoked drivers w/angled rods; operating headlight on boiler top; separate handrails; two cab windows; plates below windows lithographed "Ives No. 1125"; w/eight-wheel tender w/sides lithographed "Limited Vestibule Express" 250   500

1125 Locomotive, 1914-1917, O ga., 4-4-2; cast-iron spoked pony wheels and drivers w/angled drive rods; separate grab rails, operating headlight on top of boiler; Marklin trucks; plates beneath cab windows lithographed "Ives No. 25"; w/eight-wheel No. 25 tender marked "NYC & HR" or "Ives No. 25" on sides................................... 250   500

1125 Locomotive, 1930, O ga., 0-4-0; chunky-looking cast-iron body w/one separate boiler band; brass bell on boiler, operational headlight operates on boiler front; black or blue body; gold decal beneath cab windows read "Ives RR Lines"; "1125" cast on cab sides; w/No. 17 tender w/round Ives decal on sides and coal load 225   450

1129 Locomotive, 1915-1920, 1 ga., 2-4-2; black cast-iron body, pony and drive wheels; three-piece drive rods; two separate boiler bands and nickel bell; two arched cab windows; marked "Ives No. 1129" below windows; w/No. 40 tender 850   1700

1132-R Locomotive, Standard ga., same as above engines w/automatic reverse.. 950   1900

1132 Locomotive, 1921-1926, Standard ga., 0-4-0; black, tan, or white cast-iron body w/two boiler bands; cast-iron drive wheels w/three piece rods; nickel bell and grab rails; cast-iron or die-cast wheels; headlight in center of boiler front; two cab windows; marked "Ives 1132" below windows, w/tin No. 40 tender 500   1000

1132 Locomotive, 1928, Standard ga., 4-4-0; uncataloged model; cast-iron body, similar to 1927 No. 1134 but without engineer figure inside; headlight on top of boiler w/separate grab rails; die-cast wheels and four-piece drive rods; w/die-cast No. 40 tender.................................... 950   1900

1134-R Locomotive, Standard ga., same as above engines w/automatic reverse   1100   2200

1134 Locomotive, 1927, Standard ga., 4-4-0; President Washington model; olive cast-iron body w/headlight on top of boiler; die-cast wheels w/four-piece drive rods; engineer in cab w/tin No. 40 tender..................................... 1050   2100

1134 Locomotive, 1928-1930, Standard ga., 4-4-2; die-cast body and wheels, w/die-cast No. 40 tender; headlight on boiler top or in center front; separate handrails, brass bell; brass plates marked "Made In The Ives Shops" on front of engine; also marked "The Ives Railway Lines" below cab windows and on the side of tender 1100   2200

No. 1134, Locomotive with tender, 1928-1930, $2,200

1501 Locomotive, 1931-1932, O ga., 0-4-0; mechanized red tin body, die-cast wheels without drive rod; speed governed; w/bell activated during running; hand brake; no marks on engine; sides of tender marked "1502 Ives R.R. Lines 1502" on yellow simulated letterboard.......................... 125   250

1504 Pullman Car, 1931-1932, O ga., four-wheel; one-piece red lithographed tin body w/blue roof and yellow trim; tin wheels; five double windows; sides marked "1504 Pullman 1504" below windows 45   90

	C7	C9
1506 Locomotive, 1931-1932, mechanical; larger than No. 1502; tin body painted black w/die-cast wheels and straight drive rods; bell and handbrake; black No. 1507 tender w/red lithographed rectangle marked "1507 Ives R.R. Lines 1507"	125	250
1512 Gondola, 1931-1932, O ga., four-wheel; blue tin body	40	80
1513 Cattle Car, 1931-1932, O ga., four-wheel; green lithographed body w/sliding doors	40	80
1514 Boxcar, 1931-1932, O ga., four-wheel; yellow tin body w/blue roof and sliding doors; "Erie" logo on sides	40	80
1515 Tank Car, 1931-1932, O ga., four-wheel; silver body w/brass and copper trim; "Sunoco" logo on sides	40	80
1517 Caboose, 1931-1932, O ga., four-wheel; red lithographed tin body w/red-brown roof; "NYC" logo on sides	40	80
1550 Switch, 1931-1932, O ga., left and right; for clockwork trains	8	16
1555 Crossing, 1931-1932, O ga., 90 degrees for clockwork trains	6	12
1558 AccessoryBumper, 1931-1932, O ga., for clockwork track	10	20
1559 Crossing gate, 1931-1932, O ga., w/striped lithographed arm	10	20
1560 Station, 1931-1932, O ga., lithographed body and roof; housed either transformer or whistle	40	80
1561 Tunnel., 1931-1932, O ga., papier-mâché; 8" l.	10	20
1562 WaterTtower, 1931-1932, green and maroon, w/hinged spout	25	50
1563 Telegraph Pole, 1931-1932	3	6
1564 Bridge, 1931-1932, O ga., same as No. 91, for clockwork track	30	60
1565 Semaphore, 1931-1932, Same as No. 107-S; single arm	10	20
1566 Semaphore, 1931-1932, same as No. 107-D; double arm	10	20

	C7	C9
1567 Crossing Sign, 1931-1932, same as No. 111	4	8
1568 Clock, 1931-1932, tin base; lithographed face w/movable hands; diamond shaped	4	8
1569 Accessory Set, 1932, four telegraph poles, one clock, one crossing sign and one semaphore; w/box; seven pieces	40	80
1570 Gift Set, 1932, includes No. 1572, No. 1514, No. 1515 and No. 1517; w/box	175	350
1571 Telegraph Post, 1932, red and white	3	6
1572 Semaphore, 1932	6	12
1573 Warning signal, 1932, square post; diamond-shaped sign	6	12
1574 Clock, 1932, square post; diamond-shaped face w/movable hands	4	8
1575 Crossing Gate, 1932, lithographed gate, painted base. Manual.	8	16
1651 Locomotive, 1932, O ga., 0-4-0; electric-type box cab; lithographed steel in either red w/maroon roof or yellow w/blue roof; die-cast wheels; brass trim and journals; marked "Ives R.R. Lines" below roof line; also marked "1651" beneath windows	150	300
1661 Locomotive, 1932, O ga., 2-4-0; black tin body w/red trim; die-cast wheels; some versions have drive rods and a hand reverse unit; copper and brass trim; No. 1661 tender marked "Ives R.R. Lines"	100	200

No. 1661, Locomotive with tender, 1932, $200

	C7	C9
1663 Locomotive, 1931-1932, O ga., 2-4-2; Lionel engine w/Ives plates; die-cast body and wheels; nickel-plated drive rods; die-cast eight-wheel tender No. 1663; both painted black cast-iron	213	525

	C7	C9

1677 Gondola, 1931-1932, O ga., eight wheel; blue body lithographed to simulates steel; brass journals; ovals on each side read "Ives R.R. Lines" and "1677" 31   62

1678 Cattle Car, 1931-1932, O ga., eight wheel; green body lithographed to simulate wood w/sliding door and brass journals 31   62

1679 Boxcar, 1931-1932, O ga., eight wheel; yellow lithographed sides and blue roof; brass journals; marked "Ives R.R. Lines" and "1679" on sides 31   62

1680 Tank Car, 1931-1932, O ga., eight wheel; painted silver body w/brass and copper trim; brass journals; marked "Ives Tank Lines," "Fuel Oil" and "1680" on sides 31   62

1682 Caboose, 1931-1932, O ga., eight wheel; red lithographed body w/red-brown roof; brass journals; sides marked "Ives R.R. Lines" in oval and "1682" in rectangle 31   62

1690 Pullman, 1931-1932, O ga., eight wheel; red lithographed body w/maroon roof and cream trim or yellow body w/blue roof and orange trim; brass handrails and journals; six double windows and door at each end of side; "1690," "Ives R.R. Lines" and "1690" beneath windows 35   70

1691 Observation Car, 1931-1932, O ga., eight wheel; red lithographed body w/maroon roof and cream trim or yellow body w/blue roof and orange trim; brass handrails, journals and railing; w/door at front of each end and windows on both sides; marked "Ives R.R. Lines" and "1691" below windows 35   70

1694 Locomotive, 1932, O ga., 4-4-4; New Haven-style electric box cab; puff painted sides w/maroon roof and brass trim; headlights at each end; die-cast wheels w/nickel-plated drive rods; punched ventilators on sides; brass plates read "1694" "Ives Lines" and "1694" 500   1000

1695 Pullman Car, 1932, O ga., twelve wheel; buff painted body w/maroon roof; copper journals. 6 double windows; decals below windows read "1695," "The Ives Lines" and "1695" 175   350

1696 Baggage Car, 1932, O ga., twelve wheel; buff painted body w/maroon roof; copper journals; baggage and mail doors on each side, w/three windows near each. "1696," "The Ives Lines" and "1696" decals on each side 175   350

1697 Observation Car, 1932, O ga., twelve wheel; buff body w/maroon roof; brass observation platform and copper journals; passenger door at front and six double windows on each side; decal below windows read "1697," "The Ives Lines," and "1697" 175   350

1707 Gondola, 1932, O ga., eight wheel; body lithographed body to simulate wood w/cross braces; brass journals; "Ives" logo in oval on side 45   90

1708 Cattle Car, 1932, O ga., eight wheel; green body lithographed to simulates boards w/spaces between them; ovals on sides lithographed "1708" and "Ives" 135   270

1709 Boxcar, 1932, O ga., eight wheel; lithographed blue body w/painted roof; yellow sliding doors and brass journals; ovals on sides read "170" and "Ives" 45   90

1712 Caboose, 1932, O ga., eight wheel; red lithographed body w/maroon roof; brass journals; ovals on sides read "1712" and "Ives" 45   90

1760 Locomotive, 1931, Standard ga., 2-4-0; black Lionel No. 384 w/Ives plate on front marked "Made In The Ives Shops"; also marked "Ives 1760" beneath cab windows; w/No. 1760 tender w/copper journals 263   525

	C7	C9

1764 Locomotive, 1932, Standard ga., 4-4-4; New Haven-style electric box cab; terra-cotta and maroon; die-cast wheels w/nickel tires and nickel drive rods; brass railings and headlights at each end; brass plates read "1764" 1500 3000

1766 Pullman Car, 1932, Standard ga., twelve wheel; terra-cotta and maroon; illuminated; copper journals; door at each end of side w/steps and handrails; seven double windows; brass plates below windows read "1766," "Ives Lines" and "1766" 500 1000

1767 Baggage Car, 1932, Standard ga., twelve wheel; terra-cotta and maroon, baggage door and mail door on each side; illuminated; copper journals; brass plates read "1767," "Ives Lines" and "1767" 500 1000

1768 Observation Car, 1932, Standard ga., twelve wheel; terra-cotta and maroon; door at front and seven double windows on each side; brass platform railings; copper journals; brass plates read "1768," "Observation," and "1768" 500 1000

1770 Locomotive, 1932, Standard ga., 2-4-4; black Lionel No. 390 w/Ives plates marked "Made In The Ives Shops" in front and "Ives 1770" beneath car windows; No. 1770 tender w/copper journals 350 700

1771 Lumber Car, 1931-1932, Standard ga., eight wheel; black Lionel No. 511, nickel stakes, copper or nickel journals; single wood piece simulated load; stamped "Ives No. 1771" on bottom.. 50 100

	C7	C9

1772 Gondola, 1931-1932, Standard ga., eight wheel; peacock Lionel No. 512, Copper or nickel journals; brass plates read "Ives" and "No. 1772" 50 100

1773 Cattle Car, 1931-1932, Standard ga., eight wheel; green Lionel No. 513, orange roof, nickel or copper journals; brass plates read "Ives" and "No. 1773" 175 350

1774 Boxcar, 1931-1932, Standard ga., eight wheel; yellow No. 514 w/orange roof; nickel or copper journals; brass plates read "Ives" and "No. 1774" 280 560

1775 Tank Car, 1931-1932, Standard ga., eight wheel; white Lionel No. 515 w/brass ladders and trim; nickel or copper journals; brass plates read "Ives" and "No. 1775" 375 750

1776 Coal Car, 1931-1932, Standard ga., eight wheel; red Lionel No. 516, nickel or copper journals; brass plates read "Ives" and "No. 1776" 250 500

1777 Caboose, 1931-1932, Standard ga., eight wheel; green Lionel No. 517 w/brass platforms and windows inserts; nickel or copper journals; brass plates read "Ives" and "No. 1777"... 68 135

1778 Reefer, 1931-1932, Standard ga., white Lionel No. 514R w/peacock roof, nickel or copper journals; two doors per side, brass plates read "Ives" and "No. 1778" 500 1000

1779 Derrick, 1931-1932, Standard ga., eight wheel; green Lionel No. 219; nickel or copper journals; brass plates marked "Ives" and "No. 1779" 325 650

No. 1810, Locomotive, $190, and two No. 1811 Pullman cars, $80 each

	C7	C9
1810 Locomotive, 1931-1932, O ga., 0-4-0; electric-style box cab; green body, red roof w/yellow trim; brass pantograph and dummy headlight; sides marked "Ives R.R. Lines" above windows and ventilators and "1810" near each end	95	190
1811 Pullman Car, 1931-1932, O ga., four-wheel; green body, red roof w/yellow trim; door at each end of sides; marked "Ives R.R. Lines" above four double windows and "1811," "Pullman," "1811" below	40	80
1812 Observation Car, 1931-1932, O ga., four-wheel; green body, red roof w/yellow trim; door at front, observation platform at rear; marked "Ives R.R. Lines" above five double windows; "1812," "Observation" and "1812" below	40	80
1813 Baggage Car, 1931-1932, O ga., four-wheel; green body, red roof w/yellow trim; marked "Ives R.R. Lines" between two doors and "1813," "Baggage," and "1813" at lower level of car	40	80
1815 Locomotive, 1931-1932, O ga., 0-4-0; lack tin body w/red trim; die-cast wheels and nickel drive rods; dummy headlight; no reverse; w/black No. 1815 tender marked "Ives R.R. Lines"	95	190

No. 1815, Locomotive with tender, 1931-1932, $190

	C7	C9
1851 Crossing, 1931-1932, O ga., 90 degrees	4	8
1853 Crossing, 1931-1932, O ga., 45 degrees	4	8
1854 Crossing, 1931-1932, Standard ga., 45 degrees	4	8
1855 Bumper, 1931-1932, O ga., sprung bar type	10	20

	C7	C9
1856 Bumper, 1931-1932, Standard ga., sprung bar type	10	20
1857 Bumper, 1931-1932, O ga., sprung bar type w/illumination	10	20
1858 Bumper, 1931-1932, Standard ga., sprung bar type w/illumination	10	20
1859 Tunnel, 1931-1932, O ga., papier-mâché, 11" l.	15	30
1860 Tunnel, 1931-1932, O ga., papier-mâché, 16" l.	15	30
1861 Tunnel, 1931-1932, Standard ga., papier-mâché, 19" l.	15	30
1862 Tunnel, 1931-1932, Standard ga., papier-mâché, 23" l.	15	30
1863 Bridge Approach Signal, 1931-1932, O ga., die-cast base; painted round post w/arm and chairs; formerly Ives No. 338	45	90
1864 Semaphore, 1931-1932, Standard ga., single blade, cast base, manual operation; formerly Ives No. 300	45	90
1865 Semaphore, 1931-1932, Standard ga., double blade, cast base, manual operation; formerly Ives No. 301	45	90
1866 Flag Pole, 1931-1932, American flag; raised and lowered on string	40	80
1867 Signal Tower, 1931-1932, Lionel No. 438 tower w/switches on back "Ives" plates	150	300
1868 Villa, 1931-1932, O ga., Lionel No. 191, red and green, illuminated; "Ives" stamped on bottom	75	150
1869 Colonial House, 1931-1932, O ga., white Lionel No. 189, illuminated; "Ives" stamped on bottom	80	160
1870 Cottage, 1931-1932, O ga., tan and green Lionel No. 184, illuminated; w/"Ives" stamped on bottom	75	150
1871 Suburban Station, 1931-1932, red and green Lionel No. 126; two windows and door; dormer on roof; marked "Ives Town" above window	125	250

	C7	C9
1872 Station, 1931-1932, ivory and red Lionel No. 127 w/green and yellow windows, marked "Ives Town" plate above middle doors	100	200
1873 City Station, 1931-1932, terra-cotta Lionel No. 122 w/green roof, yellow trim and swinging doors; plate above center window reads "Ives Town"	150	300
1874 City Station, 1931-1932, same as 1873 but w/exterior illumination	150	300
1875 Freight Shed, 1931-1932, terra-cotta roof, maroon base and green piers; Lionel No. 155 w/illumination	180	360
1876 Power House, 1931-1932, buff, terra-cotta and green Lionel No. 435 three windows on front door on each end; w/smokestack; "Ives" stamped on bottom	145	290
1877 Circuit Breaker, 1931-1932, same as Lionel No. 81 but illuminated	30	60
1878 Crossing Gate, 1931-1932, O ga., automatically operated, lithographed arm, illuminated Lionel No. 077	30	60
1879 Crossing gate., 1931-1932, Standard ga., automatic operation, lithographed arm, illuminated; Lionel No. 77	30	60
1880 Warning Signal, 1931-1932, Standard ga., white Lionel No. 79, illuminated; brass sign face	65	130
1881 Signal Traffic Light, 1931-1932, blinking type; Lionel No. 83; yellow w/red base	60	120
1882 Lamp Post, 1931-1932, electric, boulevard type; green upright die-cast base w/signal bulb	45	90
1883 Bell Signal, 1931-1932, Standard ga., automatic; green base, brass diamond warning sign and bells on back	60	120
1884 Bell Signal, 1931-1932, O ga., automatic; green base, brass diamond warning sign and bells on back	60	120
1885 Target Signal, 1931-1932, Standard ga., automatic; cast base; same as No. 331	65	130

	C7	C9
1886 Target Signal, 1931-1932, O ga., automatic; green base, brass diamond warning sign and bells on back	65	130
1887-1891 Transformers, 1931-1932	10	20
1893 D.C. Reducer, 1931-1932, for houses w/direct current to run transformers	10	20
1894 Rheostat, 1931-1932, used to control train speeds	10	20
1895 Switches, 1931-1932, O ga., manual, illuminated	15	30
1896 Switches, 1931-1932, Standard ga., manual, illuminated	15	30
1897 Switches, 1931-1932, O ga., electrically operated, illuminated	20	40
1898 Switches, 1931-1932, Standard ga., electrically operated, illuminated	20	40
1899 Crossing, 1931-1932, Standard ga., 90 degrees	8	16
1901 Panel Board, 1932, red; controls six separate trains or accessories by means of knife switches; Lionel No. 439	75	150
1902 Floodlight Tower, 1932, two lights on steel tower; green and terra-cotta; Lionel No. 92	75	150
1903 Semaphore, 1932, Standard ga., single blade, automatic; Lionel 80	75	150
1904 Semaphore, 1932, O ga., single blade, automatic; Same as 1903	75	150
1905 Lamp Post, 1932, gooseneck-style, double arm; same as No. 307	50	100
1906 Freight Station Set, boxed, 1932, includes two land trucks, a dump truck and a baggage truck; Lionel No. 163	75	150
1907 Train Control, 1932, O ga., automatic, stops and starts train; Lionel No. 078	75	150
1908 Train Control, 1932, Standard ga., automatic, stops and starts train; same as No. 1907	75	150
1926 Light Bulb, 1931-1932, 6 volt, round	—	1

	C7	C9
1927 Light Bulb, 1931-1932, 12 volt, round..	—	1
1928 Light Bulb, 1931-1932, 18 volt, round..	—	1
1939 Light Bulb, 1931-1932, 12 volt, pear shaped	—	1
1940 Light Bulb, 1931-1932, 18 volt, pear shaped	—	1
3200 Locomotive, 1910, O ga., 0-4-0; cast-iron S-1 type electric body; painted gold pantograph and dummy headlight on each hood; no air tanks; steps beneath door in cab center; tin wheels held on w/nuts; separate pilots; raised lettering beneath windows reads "Ives" and "3200"...............................	400	800

	C7	C9
3200 Locomotive, 1911, O ga., 0-4-0. cast-iron S-1 type electric center cab. green or black body; gold painted pantograph and dummy headlight on each hood; separate pilots; cast-iron six-spoke wheels; center door flanked by two windows; steps below; air tanks; raised lettering reads "Ives" and "3200" below windows........................	250	500
3200 Locomotive, 1912-1913, O ga., 0-4-0; cast-iron S-1 type center cab electric; maroon or black body w/separate pilots; gold painted pantograph and dummy headlight on each hood; cast-iron ten-spoke wheels; centered door on side w/steps below; air tanks; stamped "The Ives Railway Lines" below left window and "Motor 3200" beneath right window	150	300

Ives boxed set, c. 1907

	C7	C9

3200 Locomotive, 1914, O ga., 0-4-0; cast-iron S-2 type center cab electric; black painted body w/separate pilots; gold painted pantograph and dummy headlight on each hood; centered ten-spoke wheels; centered door w/steps below and air tanks; stamped "The Ives Railway Lines" beneath left window and "Motor 3200" beneath right window.. 150   300

3200 Locomotive, 1915-1916, O ga., 0-4-0; S-1 type cast-iron center cab electric; black body w/integral pilots; painted gold pantograph and dummy headlight on each hood; ten-poke wheels; center door w/steps; marked "The Ives Railway Lines" beneath left window and "Motor 3200" beneath right window.. 150   300

3216 Locomotive, 1917, O ga., 0-4-0; cast-iron S-1 type center cab electric, larger than 3200, shorter and smaller than 3218; squared hoods, dummy headlight on one, operating headlight on the other; cast-iron ten-spoke wheels; silver painted pantograph on each hood; center door w/steps below; stamped "The Ives Railway Lines" beneath left window and "Motor 3216" beneath right window................ 175   350

3217 Locomotive, 1911, O ga., 0-4-0; cast-iron S-1 type center cab electric, larger than 3216; maroon or red body; dummy headlight and pantograph on painted gold hood; separate pilots; one door and two windows on side; six-spoke wheels; raised lettering reads "Ives 3217" on sides........................... 275   550

3217 Locomotive, 1912-1913, O ga., 0-4-0; cast-iron type S-1 center cab electric; maroon or red body; gold dummy headlight and pantograph on each hood; separate pilots; ten-spoke wheels; one door and two windows on cab side; raised lettering reads "Ives" and "3217".. 250   500

3217 Locomotive, 1914, O ga., 0-4-0; cast-iron S-1 type center cab electric; black body; dummy headlight and pantograph at each end, painted silver or gold; separate pilots; cast-iron ten-spoke wheels; door and two windows on cab side, stamped lettering reads "The Ives Railway Lines" on left and "Motor 3217" to right 150   300

3217 Locomotive, 1915-1916, O ga., 0-4-0; cast-iron S-1 type center cab electric; black body; dummy headlight and pantograph on each hood; cast-iron ten-spoke wheels; pilots cast integrally to body; center door flanked by two windows on cab side center, stamped "The Ives Railway Lines" stamped beneath left window and "Motor 3217" beneath right window .. 150   300

3218 Locomotive, 1911, O ga., 0-4-0; cast-iron electric S-1 type center cab; maroon or red body; gold painted pantograph on each hood w/operational headlight on one and dummy on other; cast-iron six-spoke windows; separate pilots; centered door flanked by window; raised lettering reads "Ives" and "3218" 500   1000

3218 Locomotive, 1912-1913, O ga., 0-4-0; cast-iron electric S-type center cab; maroon or red body; gold pantograph on each hood w/operating headlight on one and dummy on other; separate pilots; cast-iron ten-spoke wheels; door and window on side; raised lettering reads "Ives" and "3218"... 450   900

3218 Locomotive, 1914, O ga., 0-4-0; cast-iron electric S-1 type center cab electric; black body; silver painted pantographs; w/both dummy and operating headlight; separate pilots; ten cast-iron wheels; center door flanked by two windows; stamped "The Ives Railway Lines" to left of door and "Motor 3218" to right 200   400

	C7	C9

3218 Locomotive, 1915-1917, O ga., 0-4-0; cast-iron electric S-1 type center cab; gray or black body; silver pantographs; dummy headlight on one hood, operating one on the other; pilots cast integrally to body; window above each door; stamped "The Ives Railway Lines" to left of door and "Motor 3218" to right 200   400

3220 Locomotive, 1916, O ga., 0-4-0; cast-iron electric S-1 type center cab; black body; silver pantographs, one dummy and one operating headlight; pilots separate from body; window above door; stamped "The Ives Railway Lines" to left of door and "Motor 3220" 375   750

3235 Locomotive, 1924, Standard ga., 0-4-0; electric box cab; green or brown tin body w/cast-iron frame and wheels; hand reverse; operating headlight, brass pantographs and brass bell; three windows per side, door on each end; marked "The Ives Railway Lines" beneath left window and "3235 N.Y.C. & H.R." beneath right window   98   195

3235-R Locomotive, 1924-1929, Standard ga., 0-4-0; electric box cab; green tin body w/stamped steel frame; automatic reverse; operating headlight, brass pantographs and brass bell; die-cast wheels w/nickel tires; three windows per side, door at each end; brass plates read "The Ives Railway Lines" and "Motor 3235" beneath windows   98   195

3235 Locomotive, 1925-1927, Standard ga., 0-4-0; electric box cab; green or brown tin body, w/cast-iron frame; hand reverse; die-cast wheels w/nickel tires; operating headlight, brass pantographs and brass bell; three windows per side and door at each end; brass plate marked "The Ives Railway Lines" beneath left window and "Motor 3235" beneath right window   98   195

	C7	C9

3235 Locomotive, 1928-1929, Standard ga., 0-4-0; electric box cab; green tin body w/stamped steel frame; operating headlight, brass pantographs and brass bell; die-cast wheels w/nickel tires; three windows per side, door at each end; brass plates read "The Ives Railway Lines" and "Motor 3235" beneath windows................................   98   195

3236 Locomotive, 1925-1927, Standard ga., 0-4-0; electric box cab; tan or red tin body w/cast-iron frame; die-cast wheels w/nickel tires; operating headlight, brass pantographs and bell; hand reverse; three windows per side, door at each end; brass plates read "The Ives Railway Lines" and "Motor 3236"   263   525

No. 3236, Locomotive, 1925-1927, $525

3236-R Locomotive, 1925-1930, 0-4-0; electric box cab; black, blue or red body tin body similar to Lionel No. 8; stamped steel frame w/brass journals and trim; automatic reverse; operating headlight; brass rail around roof on brass stanchions; rectangular brass plates read "Ives," "Made By The Ives Corp.," and "3236"   263   525

3236 Locomotive, 1928, Standard ga., 0-4-0; electric box cab; tan or red tin body w/stamped steel frame; die-cast wheels w/nickel tires; operating headlight, brass pantographs and bell; brass journals; three windows per side door at each end. Brass plates w/"The Ives Railway Lines" and "Motor 3236"   263   525

	C7	C9

3236 Locomotive, 1929-1930, Standard ga., 0-4-0; electric box cab; black, blue or red body tin body similar to Lionel No. 8; stamped steel frame w/brass journals and trim; hand reverse; operating headlight; brass rail around roof on brass stanchions; rectangular brass plates read "Ives," "Made By The Ives Corp.," and "3236".. 263 525

3237-R Locomotive, 1926-1930, Standard ga., 0-4-0; St. Paul-type electric center cab; green or black steel body, stamped-steel frame w/separate pilots; two operating headlights, brass pantograph, bell and whistle; die-cast wheels w/nickel tires; automatic reverse; brass journals and springs on frame; brass window inserts; grab rails; brass plates read "The Ives Railway Lines" and "Motor 3237"...... 325 650

3237 Locomotive, 1926-1930, Standard ga., 0-4-0; St. Paul-type electric center cab; green or black steel body, stamped-steel frame w/separate pilots; two operating headlights, brass pantograph, bell and whistle; die-cast wheels w/nickel tires; hand reverse; brass journals and springs on frame; brass window inserts; grab rails; brass plates read "The Ives Railway Lines" and "Motor 3237"................................ 325 650

3238 Locomotive, 1910-1912, O ga., 2-4-2; cast-iron electric S-1 type center cab; black body w/operating headlight on each hood; gold painted bell and whistle; manual reverse; tin pilot wheels w/ten-spoke drive wheels; raised lettering reads "New York Central Lines" to left of door and "3238 NYC & HR" to right.................. 308 615

3238 Locomotive, 1913-1917, 1 ga., 2-4-2; cast-iron electric S-1 type center cab; black body some w/gray roof; two operating headlights; cast pantographs; spoked pilot and drive wheels; manual reverse; no bell or whistle; stamped "The Ives Railway Lines" to left of cab door and "Motor 3238" to right...................................... 250 500

No. 3239, Locomotive, 1913-1916, $1,200

3239 Locomotive, 1913-1916, 1 ga., 0-4-4-0; cast-iron electric S-1 type center cab; black body w/one operating headlight and one dummy; silver pantograph on each hood; axle journals on side frames do not line up w/axles; one truck has motor; manual reverse; marked "The Ives Railway Lines" beneath window to left of door and "Motor 3239" beneath right 600 1200

3239 Locomotive, 1917-1920, 1 ga., 0-4-4-0; cast-iron electric S-3 type center cab; gray, black or olive body w/one operating and one dummy headlight; nickel pantograph, whistle and bell; axle journals now line up w/axles; one power truck; manual reverse; stamped "The Ives Railway Lines" beneath window and "Motor 3239" beneath right window............... 575 1150

No. 3239, Locomotive, 1917-1920, $1,150

C7   C9   C7   C9

No. 3240, Locomotive, 1912-1916, $1,800

3240 Locomotive, 1912-1916, 1 ga.,
0-4-4-0; cast-iron electric S-1 type
center cab; black body w/two
operating headlights, nickel
pantographs, bell and whistle; separate
grab rails; chains between trucks and
between end railings; axle journals on
side frames do not line up w/axles; one
power truck; manual reverse; stamped
"The Ives Railway Lines" beneath
window and "Motor 3240" beneath
right window... 900   1800

3240 Locomotive, 1917-1920, 1 ga.,
0-4-4-0; cast-iron electric S-3 type
center cab; black or gray body w/two
operating headlights; nickel
pantographs, bell and whistle; one
truck has motor; axle journals line up
w/axle; manual reverse; stamped "The
Ives Railway Lines" stamped beneath
window and "Motor 3240" beneath
right window... 600   1200

3240 Locomotive, 1921, 0-4-4-0; cast-
iron electric S-3 type center cab; black
or gray body w/two operating
headlights; nickel pantographs, bell
and whistle; one truck has motor; axle
journals line up w/axle; frames were
altered to accommodate use on
standard gauge track; manual reverse;
stamped "The Ives Railway Lines"
stamped beneath window and "Motor
3240" beneath right window............... 1000 2000

3241-R Locomotive, 1921-1925, 0-4-0;
red or green tin body, cast-iron frame,
sometimes w/third rail pickup hoes
like No. 3242; no handrails; type-S
electric center cab; operating
headlight, brass pantographs and brass
bell; cast-iron wheels through 1924,
die-cast w/nickel tires in 1925;
automatic reverse; stamped "The Ives
Railway Lines" beneath window and
"3241 N.Y.C. & H.R." beneath right
window... 150   300

3241 Locomotive, 1921-1925, Standard
ga., 0-4-0; red or green tin body, cast-
iron frame, sometimes w/third rail
pickup hoes like No. 3242; no
handrails; type-S electric center cab;
operating headlight, brass pantographs
and brass bell; cast-iron wheels
through 1924, die-cast w/nickel tires
in 1925; hand reverse; stamped "The
Ives Railway Lines" beneath window
and "3241 N.Y.C. & H.R." beneath
right window... 150   300

No. 3240, Locomotive, 1917-1920, $1,200

No. 3241, Locomotive, 1921-1925, $300

	C7	C9

3242 Locomotive, 1921-1924, Standard ga., 0-4-0; S-type electric center cab; red or green body; cast-iron frame w/outside rail pick-up shoes; two operating headlights and brass pantographs; cast-iron wheels; hand rails on sides and ends; stamped "The Ives Railway Lines" below window and "3242 N.Y.C. & H.R." beneath right window... 225   450

3242 Locomotive, 1921-1930, Standard ga., 0-4-0; S-type electric center cab; tan, red, orange, green, black, or cadet blue body; cast-iron frame in 1925 and 1926 and stamped steel w/brass journals and springs after that; die-cast wheels w/nickel tires; two operating headlights, brass pantographs; handrails; automatic reverse; brass plates read "The Ives Railway Lines," "New York Central Lines" and "3242"... 225   450

3242 Locomotive, 1925-1930, Standard ga., 0-4-0; S-type electric center cab; tan, red, orange, green, black, or cadet blue body; cast-iron frame in 1925 and 1926 and stamped steel w/brass journals and springs after that; die-cast wheels w/nickel tires; two operating headlights, brass pantographs; handrails; hand reverse; brass plates read "The Ives Railway Lines," "New York Central Lines" and "3242" 225   450

3243 Locomotive, 1921-1924, Standard ga., 4-4-4; type-S electric center cab; green or orange tin body w/cast-iron frame; two operating headlights; handrails on sides and ends; brass pantographs, bell and whistle; cast iron wheels; stamped "The Ives Railway Lines" to left window and "3243 N.Y.C. & H.R." below right window 450   900

No. 3243, Locomotive, 1921-1924, $900

3243-R Locomotive, 1921-1928, Standard ga., 4-4-4; S-type electric center cab; black or cadet blue steel body w/stamped steel frame; grab rails on sides and ends; brass journals and trim; two operating headlights; brass pantographs, bell and whistle; die-cast wheels w/nickel tires; automatic reverse; brass plates read "The Ives Railway Lines," "New York Central Lines" and "3243"............................. 550   1100

3243 Locomotive, 1925-1927, Standard ga., 4-4-4; type-S electric center cab; red, green or orange tin body w/cast-iron frame; two operating headlights; handrails on sides and ends; brass pantographs, bell and whistle; die-cast wheels w/nickel tires; brass plates read "3243," "The Ives Railway Lines," "New York Central Lines" and "3243"... 500   1000

3243 Locomotive, 1928, Standard ga., 4-4-4; S-type electric center cab; black or cadet blue steel body w/stamped steel frame; grab rails on sides and ends; brass journals and trim; two operating headlights; brass pantographs, bell and whistle; die-cast wheels w/nickel tires; hand reverse; brass plates read "The Ives Railway Lines," "New York Central Lines" and "3243" 500   1000

3245 Locomotive, 1928, Standard ga., 4-4-4; electric center cab; No. 3237 black body on black stamped-steel frame w/brass journals and springs; brass ventilator on hoods, brass window inserts and doors; two operating headlights; brass bell and pantograph; die-cast wheels w/nickel tires; brass plates read "The Ives Railway Lines" and "Motor 3245" 1000   2000

3245-R Locomotive, 1928-1930, Standard ga., 4-4-4; enter electric cab; longer steel hoods, same cab as before; black body w/orange stamped-steel frame; die-cast wheels w/nickel tires; brass ventilators, window inserts and doors; handrails on hoods, ends and by doors on sides; larger, working nickel pantographs, bell, whistle, and headlight shrouds; automatic reverse; brass plates reads "Motor 3245" and "The Ives Railway Lines".................. 1000   2000

	C7	C9

3245 Locomotive, 1929-1930, Standard ga., 4-4-4; enter electric cab; longer steel hoods, same cab as before; black body w/orange stamped-steel frame; die-cast wheels w/nickel tires; brass ventilators, window inserts and doors; handrails on hoods, ends and by doors on sides; larger, working nickel pantographs, bell, whistle, and headlight shrouds; hand reverse; brass plates reads "Motor 3245" and "The Ives Railway Lines".............................. 1000 2000

3250 Locomotive, 1918-1924, O ga., 0-4-0; electric center cab; generally green, brown or red stamped-metal body on cast-iron frame; cast-iron spoked wheels; bell and whistle on top, operating headlight late in production; no handrails; stamped "The Ives Railway Lines" to left of cab door and "Motor 3250" or "3250 N.Y.C. & H.R." to right of cab door ... 108 215

3250 Locomotive, 1925, O ga., 0-4-0; electric center cab; generally green, brown or red stamped-metal body on cast-iron frame; cast-iron spoked wheels; bell and whistle on top, operating headlight; no handrails; die-cast wheels; stamped "The Ives Railway Lines" to left of cab door and "Motor 3250" or "3250 N.Y.C. & H.R." to right of cab door 108 215

No. 3250, Locomotive, 1918-1924, $215

No. 3251, Locomotive, 1918-1924, $215

3251 Locomotive, 1918-1924, O ga., 0-4-0; center electric cab; green, red or brown body and frame the same as No. 3250 w/handrails on hoods; operating headlight and bell; cast-iron wheels; stamped "The Ives Railway Lines" and "Motor 3251" or "3251 N.Y.C. & H.R." on either side of doorway.. 108 215

3251 Locomotive, 1925-1927, O ga., 0-4-0; center electric cab; green, red or brown tin body w/cast-iron frame; operating headlight; brass bell, brass plate to left of door; die-cast wheels w/nickel tires; marked "The Ives Railway Lines" and "Motor 3251" to right of door 108 215

3252 Locomotive, 1918-1924, O ga., 0-4-0; center electric cab; brown, red, burgundy, or green body and frame the same as No. 3251; operating headlight; brass bell and handrails; cast-iron wheels; stamped "The Ives Railway Lines" to left of cab door and either "Motor 3252" or "3252 N.Y.C. & H.R." to right of cab door 108 215

3252 Locomotive, 1925-1927, O ga., 0-4-0. center electric cab; red, green, orange, or brown body, same general characteristics as before except w/die-cast wheels w/or without nickel tires; brass plates to the left of cab door read "The Ives Railway Lines"; plate to the right reads "Motor 3252" 138 275

C7   C9

C7   C9

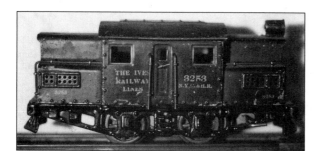

No. 3253, Locomotive, 1918-1924, $350

No. 3255-R, Locomotive, 1925-1930, $220

No. 3255, Locomotive, 1928-1930, $250

3253 Locomotive, 1918-1924, O ga., 0-4-0; center electric cab; red or green stamped steel body w/cast-iron frame; larger than No. 3252; one operating headlight; handrails and nickel or brass bell; cast-iron wheels; hand reverse; stamped "The Ives Railway Lines" to left of cab door and either "Motor 3253" or "3253 N.Y.C. & H.R." to right of cab door 175   350

3253 Locomotive, 1925-1927, O ga., 0-4-0; center electric cab; green, orange or light brown stamped-steel body w/cast-iron frame; operating headlight and brass bell; die-cast wheels w/or without nickel tires; hand reverse; brass plate to the left of cab door reads "The Ives Railway Lines" and plate to the right of door reads "Motor 3253" 188   375

3254 Locomotive, 1925-1927, O ga., 0-4-0; center electric cab stamped-metal body and cast-iron frame; die-cast wheels w/nickel tires; hand reverse; brass plates read "Motor 3255" to the right of cab door 70   140

3255-R Locomotive, 1925-1930, O ga., 0-4-0; center electric cab stamped-metal body; orange w/black frame, black w/red frame or blue w/red stamped-metal frame; brass journals; two operating headlights; grab rails and brass whistle; automatic reverse; brass plates read "Motor 3255" to the right of cab door 110   220

3255 Locomotive, 1928-1930, O ga., 0-4-0; center electric cab stamped-metal body; orange w/black frame, black w/red frame or blue w/red stamped-metal frame; brass journals; two operating headlights; grab rails and brass whistle; reverse lever in different position; brass plates read "Motor 3255" to the right of cab door   125   250

3257-R Locomotive, 1926-1930, O ga., 0-4-0; sheet metal St. Paul-type locomotive on stamped steel frame w/journals; gray, orange or black body; two operating headlights; brass bell and whistle w/hand rails; die-cast wheels w/nickel tires; cast iron or die cast pilots; automatic reverse; brass plates to the left of cab door read "The Ives Railway Lines" and brass plate to the right of cab door reads "Motor 3257" 450   900

C7   C9

No. 3257-R, Locomotive, 1926-1930, $900

3257 Locomotive, 1926-1930, O ga.,
0-4-0; sheet metal St. Paul-type
locomotive on stamped steel frame
w/journals; gray, orange or black body;
two operating headlights; brass bell and
whistle w/hand rails; die-cast wheels
w/nickel tires; cast iron or die-cast
pilots; hand reverse; brass plates to the
left of cab door read "The Ives Railway
Lines" and brass plate to the right of
cab door reads "Motor 3257" 313   625

3258 Locomotive, 1926-1930, O ga.,
0-4-0; New Haven-type body;
lithographed yellow body w/green
roof or green body w/red roof;
stamped-steel frame; operating
headlight w/brass whistle; die-cast
wheels w/nickel tires; two windows
per side w/door on each end;
lithographed plate marked "Made In
The Ives Shops" and "3258" 100   200

3259 Locomotive, 1927, O ga., 0-4-0;
New Haven-type body; lithographed
yellow body w/green roof or green
body w/red roof (w/white body and red
roof for the White Owl set); stamped-
steel frame; operating headlight
w/brass whistle and journals; die-cast
wheels w/nickel tires; two windows per
side w/door on each end; lithographed
plate marked "Made In The Ives
Shops" and "3258" 225   450

C7   C9

No. 3260, Locomotive, 1928-1929, $240

3260 Locomotive, 1928-1929, O ga.,
0-4-0; stamped-steel New Haven body
w/inserted ventilator and plate pieces;
blue green, black or cadet blue Lionel
No. 248 body; die-cast or stamped
steel frame; operating headlight, brass
whistle and pantograph on top; brass
doors and journals; die-cast wheels
w/nickel tires; two plates on side read
"Made In The Ives Shops"; plate
inserts stamped "Ives" and "3260" 120   240

3261 Locomotive, 1929-1930, O ga.,
0-4-0; stamped-steel New Haven body
w/inserted ventilator and plate pieces;
black Lionel No. 248 body; die-cast or
stamped steel orange or red frame;
operating headlight, brass whistle and
pantograph on top; brass doors and
journals; die-cast wheels w/nickel
tires; hand reverse; two plates on side
read "Made In The Ives Shops"; plate
inserts stamped "Ives" and "3261" 120   240

7345 Merchandise Car, 1915-1920, 1 ga.,
eight wheel; yellow tin body w/blue
roof w/catwalk; brake wheel; sliding
door on each side; marked
"Ventilator" and "Refrigerator" to left
of door and "S.F.R.D. 7345" w/Santa
Fe logo to right of door 150   300

	C7	C9
7446 Livestock Car, 1915-1920, 1 ga., eight wheel; brown body made up of tin strips soldered together on a stock frame; brown roof w/catwalk; sliding doors also made of soldered pieces; brake wheel on one end; marked "Livestock" and "7446" below roof line and "P.R.R." and "Air Brake" on frame sides	125	250
7546 Caboose, 1915-1920, 1 ga., eight wheel; red tin body and cupola w/brown roof; black smokestack, ladders and window trim; tool boxes beneath frame; five windows on each side; marked "The Ives Railway Lines" above windows and "Made In The Ives Shops," "Caboose" and "7546" windows	160	320

	C7	C9
7648 Hopper Car, 1915-1920, 1 ga., eight wheel; black or gray w/black ribs; brake wheels and steps; marked "Penna coal & Coke Co" w/"P.R.R." logo on sides	130	260
7849 Tank Car, 1915-1920, 1 ga., eight wheel; dark gray tank w/mounted trucks; catwalk frame soldered to sides of tank; Air tank below main tank; single dome w/air vent; marked "Texas Oil," w/"Air Brake" and "7849" also on sides	165	330
7950 Coke Car, 1915-1920, 1 ga., eight wheel; brown car made up of many soldered together; w/pieces of tin mounted to standard frame; brake wheel at one end; marked "Air Brake," "P.R.R." and "7950" on frame sides	165	330

Ives Set List

Note: Given sets are in order of locomotive, tender (t) (if locomotive is a steam type), followed by car numbers. And when two sets in the same year are identical, amount of track varied.

Note: The difference between No. 0, 1, 2, and 3 was spring strength. All engines are priced with tender. "Litho" stands for lithograph; "T" is for tender; "loco" stands for locomotive.

1904

0E	Tin locomotive, T, passenger car, (6) 111 posts.
2E	Tin locomotive, T, vestibule passenger car, (8)111 posts.
3E	Tin locomotive, T, baggage, (2) vestibule passenger cars, (10) 111 posts.
11E	Iron locomotive, T, Baggage, vestibule passenger car, (8) 111 posts.
00	Tin locomotive, 1T, passenger car.
10	Tin locomotive, 1T, vestibule passenger car.
2	3 tin locomotive, 1T, baggage car, vestibule passenger car
3	3 tin locomotive, 1T, (2) vestibule passenger car passenger car
11	11, 11T, 50, 51
12	11, 11T, 50, 51, 51
13	17, 11T, 50, 51, 51
14	17, 11T, 50, 51, 51
15	17, 11T, 60, 61
16	17, 11T, 60, 61, 62, (2) flat cars

17	17, 11T, 60, 61, 62
20R	25, 11T, 130
21R	25, 11T, 130, 129
22R	25, 11T, 130, 129
23R	25, 11T, 131, 129
24R	25, 11T, 130, 131, 129
30R	25, 11T, 127, 127, 126
42	40, 40T, 71
43	40, 40T, 71, 72
44	40, 40T, 70, 71, 72

1905

OE	Tin locomotive, T, passenger car (6) 111 posts
2E	Tin locomotive, T, baggage car, vestibule passenger car, (8) 111 posts
3E	Tin locomotive, T, baggage car, (2) vestibule passenger car, (10) 111 posts
11E	Iron locomotive, T, baggage car, vestibule passenger car, (8) 111 posts
0	0 tin locomotive, 1T, passenger car
1	1 tin locomotive, 1T, vestibule passenger car
2	2 tin locomotive, 1T, vestibule passenger car
3	3 tin locomotive, 1T, baggage car, (2) vestibule
11	11, L.U.E., 11T, 50, 51
12	11, 11T, 50, 51, 51
13	17, 11T, 50, 51, 51
14	17, 11T, 50, 51, 51
15	17, 11T, 60, 61, 62

16	17, 11T, 60, 61, 62 (2) flat cars
17	17, 11T, 60, 61, 62
20R	25, 11T, 130
21R	25, 11T, 130, 129
22R	25, 11T, 130, 129
23R	25, 11T, 130, 129
24R	25, 11T, 130, 129, 131
30R	25, 11T, 127, 125, 126
42	40, 40T, 71
43	40, 40T, 71
44	40, 40T, 70, 71, 72

1906

OE	O tin locomotive, 1T, passenger car, (6) 111 posts
2E	2 tin locomotive, 1T, vestibule passenger car, (8) 111 posts
3E	3 tin locomotive, 1T, baggage car, (2) vestibule passenger cars, (10) 111 posts
11E	11 iron locomotive, 11T, baggage car, vestibule passenger car, (8) 111 posts
0	O, 1T, passenger car
1	1, 1T, vestibule passenger car
2	2, 1T, baggage car, vestibule passenger car
3	3, 1T, baggage car, (2) vestibule passenger car
11	11, 11T, 50, 51
12	11, 11T, 50, 51, 51
13	17, 11T, 50, 51, 51
14	17, 11T, 50, 51, 51
15	17, 11T, 60, 61, 62
16	17, 11T, 60, 61, 62
17	17, 11T, 60, 61, 62
20R	25, 25T, 130
21R	25, 25T, 130, 129
22R	25, 25T, 130, 129
23R	25, 25T, 131, 129
24R	25, 25T, 130, 131, 129
30R	25, 25T, 127, 125, 126
42	40, 40T, 71
43	40, 40T, 71, 72
44	40, 40T, 70, 71, 72

1907

0	0, 1T, passenger car
1	1, 1T, vestibule passenger car
2	2, 1T, baggage car, vestibule passenger car
3	3, 1T, baggage car, vestibule passenger car, drawing room car
4	3, 1T, baggage car, vestibule passenger car, drawing room car
11	11, 11T, 50, 51
12	11, 11T, 50, 51, 51
13	17, 11T, 50, 51, 51
14	17, 11T, 50, 51, 51
15	17, 11T, 60, 61, 62
16	20, 25T, 60, 61, 62
17	20, 25T, 60, 61, 62

20R	25, 25T, 130
21R	25, 25T, 130, 129
22R	25, 25T, 130, 129
23R	25, 25T, 131, 129
24R	25, 25T, 130, 131, 129
30R	25, 25T, 127, 125, 126
42	40, 40T, 71
43	40, 40T, 71, 72
44	40, 40T, 70, 71, 72
45	41, 40T, 71
46	41, 40T, 71, 72
47	41, 40T, 70, 71, 72

1908

0	0, 1T, 51
1	1, 1T, 51
2	2, 1T, 50, 51
3	3, 1T, 50, 51, 52
4	3, 1T, 50, 51
11	11, 11T, 60, 61
12	11, 11T, 60, 61, 62
13	17, 11T, 50, 51, 52
14	17, 11T, 50, 51, 52
15	17, 11T, 60, 61, 62
16	20, 25T, 60, 61, 62
17	20, 25T, 60, 61, 62
20R	25, 25T, 130
21R	25, 25T, 130, 129
22R	25, 25T, 130, 129
23R	25, 25T, 131, 129
24R	25, 25T, 130, 131, 129
30R	25, 25T, 127, 125, 126
42	40, 40T, 71
43	40, 40T, 71, 72
44	40, 40T, 70, 71, 72
45	41, 40T, 71
46	41, 40T, 71, 72
47	41, 40T, 70, 71, 72

1909

0	0, 1T, 51
1	1, 1T, 51
2	2, 1T, 50, 51
3	3, 1T, 50, 51, 52
4	3, 1T, 50, 51
11	11, 11T, 60, 61
12	11, 11T, 60, 61, 62
13	17, 11T, 50, 51, 52
14	17, 11T, 50, 51, 52
15	17, 11T, 60, 61, 62
16	20, 25T, 60, 61, 62
17	20, 25T, 60, 61, 62
20R	25, 25T, 130
21R	25, 25T, 130, 129
22R	25, 25T, 130, 129
23R	25, 25T, 131, 129
24R	25, 25T, 130, 131, 129
30R	25, 25T, 127, 125, 126

42	40, 40T, 71
43	40, 40T, 71, 72
44	40, 40T, 70, 71, 72
45	41, 40T, 71
46	41, 40T, 71, 72
47	41, 40T, 70, 71, 72

1910

0	0, 1T, 51
1	1, 1T, 51
2	2, 1T, 50, 51
3	3, 1T, 50, 51, 52
4	4, 1T, 50, 51
5	2, 1T, 56, 57
6	2, 1T, 53, 55, 56
7	4, 1T, 54, 54, 54, 56
8	17, 11T, 69, 67
9	17, 11T, 64, 64, 67
10	17, 11T, 68, 64, 65, 67
11	17, 11T, 60, 61
12	17, 11T, 60, 61, 62
13	17, 11T, 60, 61, 62
14	17, 11T, 60, 61, 62
15	17, 11T, 60, 61, 62
16	20, 25T, 60, 61, 62
17	20, 25T, 60, 61, 62
19R	25, 25T, 128, 128, 67
20R	25, 25T, 130
21R	25, 25T, 130, 129
22R	25, 25T, 130, 129
23R	25, 25T, 131, 129
24R	25, 25T, 131, 130, 129
30R	25, 25T, 123, 125, 67
42	40, 40T, 71
43	40, 40T, 71, 72
44	40, 40T, 70, 71, 72
45	41, 40T, 77, 75
46	41, 40T, 76, 76, 75
47	41, 41T, 74, 73, 77, 75
1105	1100, 11T, 50, 51, 52
1114	1117, 11T, 60, 61
1115	1118, 11T, 60, 61, 62
1126	1125, 25T, 129, 130, 131
1127	3238, 129, 130, 131

1911

0	0, 1T, 51
1	1, 1T, 51
2	2, 1T, 50, 51
3	3, 1T, 50, 51, 52
4	4, 1T, 50, 51 49
5	2, 1T, 57, 56
6	4, 1T, 53, 55, 56
7	4, 1T, 54, 54, 54, 56
8	17, 11T, 69, 67
9	17, 11T, 63, 63, 67
10	17, 11T, 68, 65, 64, 67
11	17, 11T, 60, 61

12	17, 11T, 60, 61
13	17, 11T, 60, 61, 62
14	17, 11T, 60, 61, 62
15	17, 11T, 60, 61, 62
16	20, 25T, 60, 61, 62
17	20, 25T, 60, 61, 62
19R	25, 25T, 128, 128, 67
20R	25, 25T, 130
21R	25, 25T, 130, 129
22R	25, 25T, 130, 129
24R	25, 25T, 131, 130, 129
30R	25, 25T, 123, 125, 67
1105	1100, 1T, 50, 51, 52
1105X	3200, 50, 51, 52
1114	1117, 11T, 60, 61
1114X	3217, 60, 61
1115	1118, 11T, 60, 61, 62
1115X	3218, 60, 61, 62
1126	1125, 25T, 129, 130, 131
1127	3238, 129, 130, 131

1912

0	0, 1T, 51
1	1, 1T, 51
2	2, 1T, 50, 51
3	3, 1T, 50, 51, 52
4	4, 1T, 50, 51
5	2, 1T, 57, 56
6	4, 1T, 53, 55, 56
7	4, 1T, 54, 54, 54, 56
8	17, 11T, 69, 67
9	17, 11T, 63, 63, 67
10	17, 11T, 68, 65, 64, 67
11	17, 11T, 60, 61
12	17, 11T, 60, 61, 62
13	17, 11T, 60, 61, 62
14	17, 11T, 60, 61, 62
15	17, 11T, 60, 61, 62
16	20, 25T, 60, 61, 62
17	20, 25T, 60, 61, 62
19R	25, 25T, 128, 128, 67
20R	25, 25T, 130
21R	25, 25T, 130, 129
22R	25, 25T, 130, 129
23R	25, 25T, 131, 129
24R	25, 25T, 131, 130, 129
30R	25, 25T, 123, 125, 67
49	40, 40R, 181, 182, 183
1102S	1100, 11T, 50, 51
1105	1100, 11T, 60, 61
1105X	3200, 60, 61
1114	1117, 11T, 130, 129
1114X	3217, 130, 129
1115	1118, 11T, 129, 130, 131
1115X	3218, 129, 130, 131
1127	3238, 70, 71, 72
1140	3240, 181, 182, 183

1913

0	5, 1T, 51
1	5, 1T, 52
2	5, 1T, 50, 51
3	5, 1T, 50, 51, 52
4	6, 1T, 50, 52
5	5, 1T, 57, 56
6	6, 1T, 53, 55, 56
7	6, 1T, 54, 54, 54, 56
8	17, 11T, 69 67
9	17, 11T, 63, 63, 67
10	17, 11T, 68, 65, 64, 67
11	17, 11T, 60, 61
12	17, 11T, 60, 61, 62
13	17, 11T, 60, 61, 62
14	17, 11T, 60, 61, 62
15	20, 25T, 131, 129, 130
16	25, 25T, 131, 129, 130
19	20, 25T, 128, 125, 67
30	25, 25T, 124, 123, 67
1102	1100, 1T, 50, 51
1102X	3200, 50, 51
1102F	1100, 1T, 57, 56
1105	1117, 11T, 550, 551, 552
1105X	3217, 550, 551, 552
1105F	1117, 11T, 554, 556, 557
1114	1118, 11T, 60, 61, 62
1114X	3218, 11T, 60, 61, 62
1114F	11 18, 11T, 63, 64, 67
1115	1125, 25T, 129, 130, 131
1115X	3238, 129, 130, 131
1115F	1125, 25T, 125, 127, 67
1130	3239, 70, 71, 72
1140	3240, 181, 182, 183

1914

0	2, 1T, 51
1	5, 1T, 52
2	5, 1T, 51, 52
3	6, 1T, 50, 51, 52
4	11, 11T, 550, 551
5	5, 1T, 57, 56
6	6, 1T, 53, 55, 56
7	11, 11T, 553, 557
8	17, 11T, 60, 67
9	17, 11T, 67, 63, 67
10	17, 11T, 68, 65, 64, 67
11	17, 11T, 60, 61
12	17, 11T, 60, 61, 62
13	17, 11T, 60, 61, 62
14	17, 11T, 60, 61, 62
15	20, 25T, 131, 129, 130
16	25, 25T, 131, 129, 130
19	20, 25T, 125, 128, 67
30	25, 25T, 124, 123, 67
47	40, 40T, 73, 77, 75
49	40, 40T, 71, 72, 72
1102	1100, 1T, 50, 51

1102	X3200, 50, 51
1102F	1100, 1T, 57, 56
1105	1117, 11T, 550, 551, 552
1105X	3217, 550, 551, 552
1105F	1117, 11T, 554, 556, 557
1114	1118, 11T, 60, 61, 62
1114X	3218, 60, 61, 62
1114F	1118, 11T, 63, 64, 67
1115	1125, 25T, 129, 130, 131
1115X	3238, 129, 130, 131
1115F	1125, 25T, 125, 127, 67
1130	3239, 71, 72, 72
1140	3240, 181, 182, 183

1915

3	6, 1T, 50, 51, 52
4	11, 11T, 550, 551
5	5, 1T, 57, 56
6	6, 1T, 53, 55, 56
7	11, 11T, 563, 567
8	17, 17T, 69, 67
9	17, 17T, 63, 63, 67
10	17, 17T, 64, 65, 68, 67
11	17, 17T, 60, 61
12	17, 17T, 60, 61, 62
13	17, 17T, 60, 61, 62
14	17, 17T, 60, 61, 62
19	20, 25T, 128, 125, 67
30	25, 25T, 123, 124, 67
1102	1100, 11T, 50, 51
1102X	3200, 50, 51
1105	1117, 11T, 550, 551, 552
1105X	3217, 550, 551, 552
1114	11 18, 17T, 60, 61, 62
1114X	3218, 60, 61, 62
1115	1125, 25T, 130, 131, 129
1115X	3238, 130, 131, 129
1130	1129, 40T, 71, 72, 72
1130X	3239, 71, 72, 72
1140	1129, 181, 182, 183
1140X	3240, 181, 182, 183

1916

0	2, 11T, 52
2	5, 11T, 50, 51
3	6, 11T, 50, 51, 52
4	11, 11T, 550, 551
5	5, 11T, 50, 51
6	6, 11T, 53, 55, 56
7	11, 11T, 563, 567
8	17, 17T, 69, 67
9	17, 17T, 63, 63, 67
10	17, 17T, 64, 65, 68, 67
11	17, 17T, 60, 61
12	17, 17T, 60, 61, 62
13	17, 17T, 60, 61, 62
14	17, 17T, 60, 61, 62
15	20, 25T, 131, 130, 129

16	25, 25T, 131, 130, 129
19	20, 25T, 128, 125, 67
30	25, 25T, 123, 124, 67
47	40, 40T, 7345, 7950, 7546
49	40, 40T, 71, 72, 73
1102	1100, 11T, 50, 51
1102X	3200, 50, 51
1105	1117, 11T, 550, 551
1105X	3217, 550, 551
1112	1120, 17T, 60, 62
1112X	3220, 60, 62
1114	11 18, 17T, 60, 61, 62
1114X	3218, 17T, 60, 61, 62
1115	1125, 25T, 131, 130, 129
1115X	3238, 131, 130, 129
1130	1129, 40T, 71, 72, 73
1130X	3239, 71, 72, 73
1140	1129, 40T, 181, 182, 183
1140X	3240, 181, 182, 183

1917

1	5, 11T, 52
2	5, 11T, 50, 51
3	6, 11T, 50, 51, 52
4	17, 11T, 551
5	5, 11T, 57, 56
6	6, 11T, 55, 53, 56
7	17, 11T, 563, 567
8	17, 11T, 564, 569, 567
9	19, 17T, 69, 67
10	19, 17T, 64, 63, 67
11	17, 11T, 550, 551
12	17, 11T, 550, 551, 552
13	19, 17T, 62
14	19, 17T, 60, 61
15	19, 17T, 60, 61, 62
16	25, 25T, 130
17	25, 25T, 130, 129
18	25, 25T, 130, 131, 129
19	25, 25T, 128, 67
30	25, 25T, 125, 123, 67
1102	1100, 11T, 551
1105	1116, 11T, 550, 552
1105X	3216, 550, 552
1112	1116, 11T, 550, 551, 552
1112X	3216, 550, 551, 552
1113	11 18, 17T, 61
1114	11 18, 17T, 60, 61
1114X	3218, 60, 61
1115	11 18, 17T, 60, 61, 62
1115X	3218, 60, 61, 62
1126	1125, 25T, 130
1127	1125, 25T, 130, 129
1128	1125, 25T, 130, 129, 129
1128X	3238, 130, 129, 129
1130X	3239, 71, 72
1131X	3239, 71, 72, 73
1140	1129, 40T, 181, 183

1141	1129, 40T, 181, 182, 183
1145	3240, 181, 182, 183
1150	1129, 40T, 7345, 7546
1151	1129, 40T, 7849, 7648, 7546
1152	1129, 40T, 7648, 7446, 7345, 7546

1918

1	5, 11T, 52
2	5, 11T, 50, 52
3	6, 11T, 50, 51, 52
4	5, 11T, 50, 51
5	5, 11T, 54, 56
8	17, 11T, 564, 563, 567
10	19, 17T, 64, 63, 67
11	17, 11T, 550, 551
12	17, 11T, 550, 551, 552
14	19, 17T, 60, 61
15	19, 17T, 60, 61, 62
20	6, 11T, 50, 51, 52
400	1100, 11T, 550, 551
401	1116, 11T, 550, 551, 552
402	11 18, 17T, 60, 61
403	11 18, 25T, 130, 129, 129
500	3250, 550, 551
501	3251, 550, 551, 552
502	3252, 60, 61
503	3253, 60, 61, 62
504	3253, 130, 129, 129
1130X	3239, 71, 72
1131X	3239, 71, 72, 73
1140X	1129, 40T, 181, 183
1141X	1129, 40T, 181, 182, 183

1919

1	5, 11T, 52
2	5, 11T, 50, 52
3	6, 11T, 50, 51, 52
4	5, 11T, 50, 51
5	5, 11T, 54, 56
8	17, 11T, 564, 563, 567
10	19, 17T, 64, 63, 67
11	17, 11T, 550, 551
12	17, 11T, 550, 551, 552
14	19, 17T, 60, 61
15	19, 17T, 60, 61, 62
20	6, 11T, 50, 51, 52
400	1100, 11T, 550, 551
401	1116, 11T, 550, 551, 552
402	1118, 17T, 60, 61
403	11 18, 25T, 130, 129, 129
500	3250, 500, 551
501	3251, 550, 551, 552
502	3252, 60, 61
503	3253, 60, 61, 62
504	3253, 130, 129, 129
1130X	3239, 71, 72
1131X	3239, 71, 72, 73
1140X	1129, 40T, 181, 183
1141X	1129, 40T, 181, 182, 183

1920

1	5, 11T, 52
2	5, 11T, 50, 51
3	6, 11T, 50, 51, 52
4	5, 11T, 50, 51
11	17, 11T, 550, 551
12	17, 11T, 550, 551, 552
14	19, 17T, 60, 61
15	19, 17T, 60, 61, 62
400	1100, 11T, 550, 551
401	1116, 11T, 550, 551, 552
402	11 18, 17T, 60, 61
403	11 18, 25T, 130, 129, 129
500	3250, 550, 551
501	3251, 550, 551, 552
502	3252, 60, 61
504	3253, 30, 129, 129
1130X	3239, 71, 72
1131X	3239, 71, 72, 73
1145	3240, 181, 182, 183
1151	1129, 40T, 7849, 7648, 7546

1921

1	5, 11T, 52
2	5, 11T, 50, 51
3	6, 11T, 50, 51, 52
4	5, 11T, 50, 51
5	5, 11T, 57, 56
6	6, 11T, 53, 55, 56
8	17, 11T, 564, 569, 567
10	19, 17T, 64, 63, 67
11	17, 11T, 550, 551
12	17, 11T, 550, 551, 552
14	19, 17T, 60, 61
15	19, 17T, 60, 61, 62
20	6, 11T, 50, 51, 52
21	21, 550, 551
22	31, 60, 61, 62
23	32, 130, 129, 129
40	01100, 11T, 550, 551
401	1116, 11T, 550, 551, 552
402	11 18, 17T, 60, 61, 62
500	3250, 550, 551
501	3251, 550, 551, 552
502	3252, 60, 61, 62
503	3253, 130, 129
504	3253, 130, 129, 129
700	3241, 184, 185
701	3241, 184, 185, 185
702	3242, 187, 189
703	3242, 187, 188, 189
704	3243, 187-1, 188-1, 189-1
705	1132, 40T, 184, 185, 185
710	1132, 40T, 191, 195, 192

1922

1	5, 11T, 52
2	5, 11T, 51, 52

3	6, 11T, 50, 51, 52
4	5, 11T, 51, 52
5	55, 11T, 54, 56
6	6, 11T, 53, 55, 56
8	17, 11T, 564, 569, 567
10	19, 17T, 64, 63, 67
11	17, 11T, 550, 551
12	17, 11T, 550, 551, 552
14	19, 17T, 60, 61
15	19, 17T, 60, 61, 62
20	6, 11T, 50, 51, 52
21	30, 550, 551
22	31, 60, 61, 62
23	32, 130, 129, 129
400	1100, 11T, 550, 551
401	1116, 11T, 550, 551, 552
402	11 18, 17T, 60, 61, 62
500	3250, 550, 551
501	3251, 550, 551, 552
502	3252, 60, 61, 62
503	3253, 130, 129
504	3253, 130, 129, 129
505	3250, 50, 51
506	3250, 53, 56
510	3251, 563, 564, 567
511	3252, 66, 64, 67
515	3253, 127, 67
516	3253, 127, 128, 67
700	3241, 184, 186
701	3241, 184, 185, 186
702	3242, 187, 189
703	3242, 187, 188, 189
705	1132, 40T, 184, 185, 186
710	1132, 40T, 191, 192, 195
711	3241, 196, 191
712	3241, 196, 192, 191, 195
713	3242, 196, 196, 191, 192, 193, 195

1923

1	1, 11T, 52
2	1, 11T, 50, 51
3	6, 11T, 50, 51
4	6, 11T, 50, 51, 52
8	17, 11T, 564, 569, 567
10	19, 17T, 64, 63, 67
11	17, 11T, 550, 551
12	17, 11T, 550, 551, 552
14	19, 17T, 70, 72
15	19, 17T, 70, 72, 72
20	6, 11T, 50, 51
21	30, 550, 551
22	31, 70, 72, 72
23	32, 130, 129, 129
400	1118, 17T, 550, 551
401	1118, 17T, 550, 551, 552
402	1118, 17T, 70, 72, 72
500	3250, 550, 551
501	3251, 550, 551, 552

502	3252, 70, 72, 72
503	3253, 130, 129
504	3253, 130, 129, 129
505	3250, 50, 51
506	3250, 54, 56
510	3251, 563, 564, 567
511	3252, 66, 64, 67
515	3253, 125, 67
516	3253, 127, 128, 67
610	3251, 550, 552, 201, 203, 107-S
611	3252, 70, 72, 72, 201, 215, 103, 107, (6) 86
612	3253, 130, 124, 129, 600, 310, 103, 111, 114, (6) 86
620	1, 11T, 50, 51, 52, 215, 107-S, 201, 103
700	3241, 184, 186
701	3241, 184, 185, 186
702	3242, 187, 189
703	3242, 187-188, 189
704	3243, 187-3, 188-3, 189-3
711	3241, 196, 195
712	3241, 196, 192, 191, 195
713	3242, 196, 196, 191, 192, 193, 195

1924

1	1, 11T, 52
2	1, 11T, 50, 51
3	6, 11T, 50, 51, 52
4	1, 11T, 50, 51
8	17, 11T, 564, 469, 567
10	19, 17T, 64, 63, 67
11	17, 11T, 550, 551
12	17, 11T, 550, 551, 552
14	19, 11I, 70, 72
15	19, 7043243, 187-1, 188-1, 189-117T, 72, 72, 70
16	20, 17T, 60, 62
18	20, 17T, 60, 61, 62
20	6, 11T, 50, 51
21	30, 550, 551
22	31, 70, 72, 72
400	1118, 11T, 550, 551
401	1118, 11T, 60, 61, 62
402	1118, 11T, 70, 71, 72, 73
403	1118, 11T, 130, 129, 132
500	3250, 550, 551
501	3251, 60, 61, 62
502	3252, 70, 71, 72
504	3253, 130, 129, 132
505	3250, 50, 51
506	3250, 53, 56
510	3251, 63, 64, 67
511	3252, 66, 64, 63, 67
512	3253, 127, 128, 125, 67
690	3235, 171, 173
691	3235, 171, 173 Illuminated Cars
700	3241, 184-3, 186-3
701	3241, 184-3, 185-3, 186-3
703	3242, 187-3, 188-3, 189-3

704	3243, 187-3, 188-3, 189-3
705	1132, 40T, 184-3, 185-3, 186-3
705R	same as 705, with reverse
7101	132, 40T, 191, 192, 195
710R	same as 710, with reverse
7113	241, 196, 195
7123	241, 196, 191, 192, 195
7133	242, 196, 196, 191, 192, 193, 195

1925

1	1, 11T, 52
2	1, 11T, 50, 51
3	6, 11T, 50, 51, 52
4	1, 11T, 50, 51
8	17, 11T, 564, 569, 567
10	19, 17T, 63, 64, 67
11	17, 11T, 550, 551
12	17, 11T, 550, 551, 552
15	19, 17T, 70, 72, 72
18	20, 17T, 60, 61, 62
20	6, 11T, 50, 51
21	30, 550, 551
22	31, 70, 72, 73
401	1118, 11T, 60, 68
402	1118, 11T, 60, 61, 68
500	3251, 60, 62
501	3252, 60, 68
502	3254, 60, 61, 68
503R	3255-R, 129, 132
504R	3255-R, 130, 129, 132
505	3250, 50, 51
506	3250, 53, 56
510	3251, 64, 63, 67
511	3252, 64, 63, 67
516	3253, 127, 128, 125, 67
610	3251, 550, 552, 201, 107-S, 103
620	1, 11T, 50, 51, 107-S, 89, 201
621	6, 11T, 50, 51, 52, 107-S, 201, 215, 103
691R	3235-R, 184, 186
691	3235, 184, 186 hand reverse
692R	3236-R, 184, 185, 186
692	3236, 184, 185, 186 hand reverse
703R	3242, 187, 188, 189
703	3242, 187, 188, 189 hand reverse
704R	3243-R, 180, 181, 182
704	3243, 180, 181, 182 hand reverse
701R	3241-R, 184, 185, 186
701	3241, 184, 185, 186 hand reverse
706R	3243-R, 180, 182
706	3243, 180, 182 hand reverse
711	3241, 196, 195
712	3241, 196, 192, 191, 195
713	3242, 191, 196, 196, 192, 193, 195

1926

0	5, 11T, 51
1	1, 11T, 52
2	1, 11T, 50, 51

3	6, 11T, 50, 51, 52
4	1, 11T, 50, 51
5	1, 11T, 54, 56
6	6, 11T, 53, 55, 56
8	17, 11T, 564, 569, 567
10	19, 17T, 63, 64, 67
11	17, 11T, 550, 551
12	17, 11T, 550, 551, 552
15	19, 17T, 60, 62, 62
21	30, 550, 551
22	32, 60, 62, 68
500	3258, 551, 552 "Number Five Hundred"
501	3251, 61, 68 "Red Arrow"
502	3252, 60, 62-3, 68-3 "Managers' Special"
503	3254, 135, 135, 136 "Ives Limited"
504R	3255-R, 130, 129, 132 "Fort Orange"
507	3257, 140, 140, 141 "Greyhound"
507-R	same as 507 but with reverse
508	3255, 130, 132 "Green Mountain Express"
510	3251, 64, 63, 67 "Merchants' Despatch"
516	3255, 127, 128, 125, 67 "Ives Fast Freight"
610	3251, 550, 552, 201, 107-S, 103 "Joy Town"
611	3252, 60, 62, 68, 201, 107-D, 215, 111, 103, (6) 86 "Wonderville"
612	3255, 130, 129, 132, 114, 600, 111, 310, 103, (6) 86 "Electric City"
691	3235, 184, 186 "Fifth Avenue Special"
691-R	same as 691 but with reverse
692	3236, 184, 185, 186 "Night Hawk"
701	3242, 184, 185, 186 "New Yorker"
701-R	same as 701 but with reverse
703	3237, 187, 188, 189 "Transcontinental Limited"
703-R	same as 703 but with reverse
704	3243, 180, 181, 182 "Deluxe Special"
704-R	same as 704 but with reverse
705	1132, 40T, 191, 192, 195 "Ives Night Freight"
705-R	same as 705 but with reverse
706	3243, 187, 189 "Bankers' Special"
706-R	same as 706 but with reverse
710	1132, 40T, 184, 185, 186 "Cannonball Express"
710-R	same as 71, but with reverse
711	3242, 196, 195 "Seven Eleven"

1927

0	5, 11T, 51
2	5, 11T, 50, 51
3	6, 11T, 50, 51, 52
4	1, 11T, 50, 51
5	5, 11T, 54, 56
6	6, 11T, 53, 55, 56
8	17, 11T, 564, 569, 567
10	19, 17T, 63, 64, 67
11	17, 11T, 550, 551
12	17, 11T, 550, 551, 552
15	19, 17T, 60, 62, 62

21	30, 550, 551
22	32, 60, 62, 68
500	3258, 551, 552 "Green Mountain Express"
502	3259, 551, 552, 568 "White Owl"
503	3255, 135, 135, 136 "Ives Limited"
503R	same as 503 but with reverse
504	3254, 130, 129, 132 "Fort Orange"
507	3257, 141, 141, 142 "Greyhound"
507R	same as 507 but with reverse
510	3252, 63, 64, 67 "Merchants' Despatch"
516	3255, 127, 128, 125, 67 "Ives Fast Freight"
610	3251, 550, 551, 201, 107-s, 103 "Joy Town"
611	3252, 60, 62, 68, 201, 107-D, 215, 111, 103, (6) 86 "Wonderville"
620	1, 11T, 50, 51, 107-S, 89, 201 "Pleasureville"
621	6, 11T, 50, 51, 52, 215, 103, 107-2, 201 "Happy Town"
691	3235, 184, 186 "Red Arrow"
692	3236, 184, 185, 186 "Nighthawk"
701	3242, 184, 185, 186 "New Yorker"
701R	same as 701 but with reverse
703	3237, 187, 188, 189 "Transcontinental Limited"
703R	same as 703 but with reverse
704	3243, 180, 181, 182 "Deluxe Special"
704R	same as 704 but with reverse
705	1134, 40t, 184, 185, 186 "Capitol Limited"
705R	same as 705 but with reverse
706	3243, 187, 189 "Bankers Special"
706R	same as 706 but with reverse
707	1134, 40T, 187, 188, 188, 189 "Capitol City Special"
707R	same as 707 but with reverse
710	1134, 40T, 191, 192, 195 "Ives Night Fright"
711	3242, 196, 197 "Number Seven Eleven"
712	1134, 40T, 190, 191, 192, 193, 194, 195, 196 "Universal Fast Freight"
712R	same as 712 but with reverse
714R	1134-R, 40T, 190, 191, 192, 193, 194, 195, 196, 115, 116-3, 106, (2) 301, 332, 99-2-3, (3) 307

1928

0	5, 11T, 51
2	0, 11T, 51, 50
3	1, 11T, 50, 51, 52
4	1, 11T, 50, 51
5	0, 11T, 54, 56
8	17, 11T, 564, 569, 567
10	19, 17T, 63, 64, 67
11	6, 11T, 550, 551
12	17, 11T, 550, 551, 552
15	19, 17T, 60, 62, 62
21	30, 550, 551
22	32, 60, 62, 68
415	3258, 563, 56 "Suburban Freight"
418	3258, 551, 552 "Mountain Express"
420	3260, 133, 134 "Blue Racer"

425	3260, 63, 69, 67 "Construction Freight"
428	3254, 137, 137, 138 "Interstate Limited"
431	3254, 63, 64, 69, 67-E "Overnight Freight"
436	3255, 135, 135, 136 "Fort Orange"
436R	same as 436 but with reverse
442	3255, 141, 141, 142 "Greenway Special"
442R	same as 442 but with reverse
445	11 20, 25T, 128, 125, 123, 67-E "Allstate Freight"
445R	same as 445 but with reverse
452	1120, 25T, 135, 135, 136 "Sunbeam Limited"
452R	same as 452 but with reverse
456	3257, 142, 142, 143 "Oriole Special"
456R	same as 456 but with reverse
462	1120, 25T, 142, 142, 143 "Black Diamond Jr."
462R	same as 462 but with reverse
468	3257, 142, 142, 143
468R	same as 468 but with reverse
474	1120, 25T, 142, 142, 143, cars gray with black mottled effect simulating an alkali dust covered train being passed through the Mohave desert.
474R	same as 474, but with reverse
476	3257, 142, 142, 143, gray outfit with the black mottled weathering
476R	same as 476, but with reverse
610	3258, 551, 552, 201, 107-S, 103, 92-3, "Joy Town"
614	3260, 133, 134, 201, 107-D, 215, 111, 103, 87, (6) 86, 308 "Wonderville"
620	0, 11T, 50, 51, 107-S, 89, 201, 87, 111 "Pleasureville"
621	1, 11T, 50, 51, 52, 215, 103, 107-D, 201 "Happy Town"
622	0, 11T, 50, 51, 90
1001	3236, 196, 195 "Short Hauler"
1001R	same as 1001, but with reverse
1010	3236, 185, 186 "Red Arrow"
1010R	same as 1010, but with reverse 1016 3242, 184, 185, 186 "Nighthawk"
1016-R	same as 1016, but with reverse
1034	1134, 40T, 185, 186 "Capitol Limited"
1034R	same as 1034, but with reverse
1035	1134, 40T, 191, 192, 195 "Ives Night Freight"
1035R	same as 1035 but with reverse
1036	3237, 187, 188, 189 "Transcontinental Limited"
1036R	same as 1036 but with reverse
1040	1134, 40T, 187, 188, 189
1040R	same as 1040 but with reverse
1044	3243, 180, 181, 182 "Deluxe Special"
1044R	same as 1044 but with reverse
1050	3245, 241, 242, 243 "Interstate Limited"
1050R	same as 1050 but with reverse
1052	3243, 241, 242, 243
1052R	same as 1052 but with reverse
1054	1134, 40T, 241, 242, 243

1054R	same as 1054 but with reverse
1057	1134, 40T, 190, 191, 192, 193, 194, 195, 196 "Universal Fast Freight"
1057R	same as 1057 but with reverse
1062	1134, 40T, 242, 242, 243
1062R	same as 1062 but with reverse
1070	11 34, 40T, 196, 196, 196, 193, plus Pullman car, tent, (4) wild animal wagons, (2) tent pole wagons, (18) lithographed pieces, (12) wild animals "Ives Railway Circus"
1070R	same as 1070 but with reverse

1929

40	1, 11T, 51
41	1, 11T, 50, 51
42	6, 12T, 50, 51, 52
43	6, 12T, 53, 54, 56
44	17, 12T, 550, 551
45	6, 12T, 50, 51
46	17, 12T, 563, 564, 567
47	17, 12T, 550, 551, 552
48	19, 12T, 62, 62, 68
400-R	1122, 25T, 141, 141, 142, copper and nickel-plated "H.O.D. Seagrave Deluxe"
416	3260, 62, 68, 103, 221, 107-D, 11 1, 215, 87, 308, (6) 86 "Ives Village"
479	3260, 63, 70 "Suburban Freight"
480	3260, 62, 68, "Blue Comet"
481	3260, 133, 134 "Oriole Limited"
482	3261, 133, 133, 134 "Southern Special"
483	3255, 63, 64, 69, 70 "Commerce Freight"
483R	same as 483 but with reverse
484	3255, 135, 135, 136 "Red Hawk Special"
484R	same as 484 but with reverse
485	1122, 25T, 63, 64, 70 "Midwest Fast Freight"
485R	same as 485, but with reverse
486	1122, 25T, 135, 135, 136 "Major H.O.D. Seagrave Special"
486R	same as 486 but with reverse
487	3257, 141, 141, 142 "Dixie Flyer"
487R	same as 487 but with reverse
488	1122, 25T, 141, 141, 142 "Cascade Limited"
488R	same as 488, but with reverse
489	1122, 25T, 141, 141, 142 "Black Diamond, Jr."
489R	same as 489 but with reverse
490	1122, 25T, 123, 124, 125, 127, 128, 121, 122 "Universal Fast Freight, Jr."
490-R	same as 490 but with reverse
623	1, 12T, 50, 51, 52, 221, 103, 215, 107-D, 111
624	1, 12T, 50, 51, 90
1000	1134, 40T, 242, 241, 243, copper and nickel plated "Prosperity Special"
1070	1134, 40T, 196, 196, 196, 193, plus Pullman car, tent, (4) wild animal cages, (2) tent pole wagons, (18) lithographed pieces, (12) wild animals "Ives Railway Circus"
1080	3236, 185, 186 "Cadet Express"

1080R	same as 1080 but with reverse
1081	3236, 198, 195 "Local Freight"
1081R	same as 1081 but with reverse
1082	3236, 184, 185, 186 "Interstate Limited"
1082R	same as 1082 but without reverse
1083	3242, 198, 192, 197, 195 "Lumberjack"
1083R	same as 1083 but with reverse
1084	3242, 184, 185, 185, 186 "Cardinal Special"
1084R	same as 1084 but with reverse
1085	1134, 40T, 192, 198, 195 "Merchants' Fast Freight"
1085R	same as 1085 but with reverse
1086	1134, 40T, 184, 185, 186 "Westerner"
1086R	same as 1086 but with reverse
1087	3237, 244, 245, 246 "Northern Limited"
1087R	same as 1087 but with reverse
1088	3245, 241, 242, 243 "Olymplan"
1088R	same as 1088 but with reverse
1089	1134, 40T, 241, 242, 243 "Black Diamond Senior"
1089R	same as 1089 but with reverse
1090	1134, 40T, 190, 192, 193, 195, 197, 198, 196 "Universal Fast Freight, Senior"
1090R	same as 1090 but with reverse

1930

30	00, 9T, 51, 5 1 "Mohican"
31	00, 11T, 50, 51, 51 "Seneca"
32	10, 11T, 551, 551 "Pequot"
33	176, 12T, 551, 558 "Apache"
34	66, 12T, 53, 54, 56 "Sioux"
35	176, 12T, 550, 551, 558 "Iroquois"
36	176, 12T, 564, 563, 567, "Mohawk"
37	176, 12T, 551, 558 "Pueblo"
38	176, 12T, 551, 558 "Blackfoot"
39	26, 550, 551, 558 "Oswego"
570	3258, 552, 558 "Yankee Clipper"
570X	3258, 552, 558, packed in tunnel box
571	3258, 564, 563, 567 "County Freight"
572	1125, 17T, 550, 552, 558 "Blue Vagabond"
572F	1125, 17T, 564, 563, 567 "Traders Fast Freight"
572FX	1125, 17T, 564, 563, 567 packed in tunnel box
572X	"Blue Vagabond" packed in tunnel box
573	3261, 133, 133, 134 "Knickerbocker"
573F	3261, 63, 64, 69, 562, "Interstate Fast Freight"
574	3255, 135, 135, 136 "Patriot"
574R	same as 574 but with reverse
575	1122, 25T, 125, 128, 121, "MIDWEST FAST FREIGHT"
575R	same as 575 but with reverse
576	1122, 25T, 135, 135, 136 "Commodore Vanderbilt"
576R	same as 576 but with reverse
577	3257, 141, 141, 142 "Columbian"
577R	same as 577 but with reverse

579	1122, 25T, 141, 141, 142 "Black Diamond"
579R	same as 579 but with reverse
590	1122, 25T, 123, 124, 125, 127, 128, 122, 121 "Universal Fast Freight"
590R	same as 590, but with reverse
639	176, 12T, 551, 551, 221, 103, 107-D, 215, 111, (5) 86 "Tribe Village"
1070	1134, 40T, 196, 196, 193, plus Pullman car, tent, (4) wild animal cages, (2) tent pole wagons, (18) lithographed pieces, (12) wild animals "Ives Railway Circus"
1070R	same as 1070 but with reverse
1071	323 6, 185, 186 "Tiger"
1071R	same as 1071 but with reverse
1072	3236, 198, 195 "Local Freight"
1072R	same as 1072 but with reverse
1073	3242, 184, 185, 186 "Skyliner"
1073R	same as 1073 but with reverse
1075	1134, 40T, 192, 198, 195 "Merchants' Fast Freight"
1075R	same as 1075 but with reverse
1076	1134, 40T, 184, 185, 186 "Westerner"
1076R	same as 1976 but with reverse
1077	1134, 40T, 247, 248, 249 "The Chief"
1077R	same as 1077 but with reverse
1078	3245, 247, 248, 249 "Olympian"
1078R	same as 1078 but with reverse
1079	1134, 40T, 246, 247, 248, 249 "National Limited"
1079R	same as 1079 but with reverse
1091	1134, 40T, 198, 190, 192, 197, 195 "Domestic Freight"
1091R	same as 1091 but with reverse

The Ives Treasure Chest

A Railroad & City Built Into A Box Built for O-gauge and Standard gauge.
O-gauge: 89, 103, 334-0, 87, 300, 332, 253, 225, 250, (6) 86, and loop of track
Standard gauge: 89, 106, 334, 87, 301, 332, 253, 225, 250, (6) 86, and loop of track

1931

1580	1501, 1502, 1504, 1504
1581	1501, 1502T, 1504, 1504, 1504
1582	1503, 1502T, 1512, 1517
1583	1503, 1502T, 1811, 1812
1584	1506, 1507T, 1512, 1514, 1517
1585	1506, 1507T, 1811, 1813, 1812
1586	1506, 1507T, 1811, 1813, 1812
1587	1506, 1507T, 1811, 1813, 1812
1588	1506, 1507T, 1811, 1813, 1812, 1560, 1563, 1566, 1567, 1559, 1568, 1561
1601	1651, 1690, 1691
1602	1651, 1690, 1691, 1012
1603	1651, 1677, 1682
1604	1651, 1677, 1682, 1012
1605	257, 257T, 1690, 1691

1606	257, 257T, 1677, 1682
1607	258, 258T, 1677, 1682
1608	258, 258T, 1690, 1691, 1679
1609	1663, 1663T, 610, 610, 612
1609E	same as 1609 but with auto-reverse
1610	1663, 1663T, 1677, 1679, 1678, 1682
1610E	same as 1610 but with auto-reverse
1726	10, 339, 341
1726E	same as 1726 but with auto-reverse
1727	10, 1772, 1771, 1777
1727-E	same as 1727 but with auto-reverse
1728	1760, 1760T, 332, 339, 341
1728E	same as 1728 but with auto-reverse
1729	1760, 1760T, 1772, 1771, 1777
1729E	same as 1729 but with auto-reverse
1730	1760, 1760T, 419, 418, 490
1730E	same as 1730 but with auto-reverse
1800	1810, 1811, 1811, 1012 "Yankee Flyer"
1801	1810, 1512, 1517, 1012 "Yankee Freight"
1802	1815, 1507T, 1811, 1811, 1012 "Yankee Clipper"
1803	1815, 1570T, 1512, 1517, 1012 "Yankee Fast Freight"

1932

1590	1501, 1502T, 1504, 1504, 1504
1591	1501, 1502T, 1512, 1517
1592	1501, 1502T, 1504, 1504

1593	1501, 1502T, 1504, 1504, 1504, 1573, 1574, 1560, (4) 1571
1594	1506, 1507T, 1811, 1813, 1812
1595	1506, 1507, 1514, 1515, 1517
1596	1506, 1507T, 1811, 1813, 1812, 1572, 1574, 1573, 1562, 1561, 1560, (6) 1571
1611	1651, 1690, 1691
1612	1661, 1661T, 1679, 1680, 1682
1613	1661, 1661T, 1690, 1690, 1691
1614	258, 1663T, 610, 610, 612
1615	258, 1663T, 1708, 1707, 1709, 1712
1616	1694, 1696, 1695, 1697
1800	1810, 1811, 1811
1801	1810, 1512, 1517
1802	1815, 1507T, 1811, 1811
1803	1815, 1507T, 1512, 1517
1726	10, 339, 341
1727	10, 1771, 1772, 1777
1731E	10-E, 332, 339, 341
1732	1770, 1760T, 1771, 1772, 1777
1732E	same as 1770 but with auto-reverse
1733	1764-E, 1766, 1767, 1768,
1735-E	1770-E, 1760T, 1767, 1766, 1768
1736-E	1770-E, 1760T, 1771, 1772, 1774, 1775, 1776, 1777

Lionel Trains

Lionel is unquestionably the greatest name in the history of toy trains. Founded in 1902 by Joshua Lionel Cowen (born August 25, 1877), it was incorporated as the Lionel Manufacturing Company on March 13.

In his teens Cowen had worked for New York's Acme Electric Lamp Company as a battery-lamp assembler, and he enjoyed experimenting in his spare time. In 1901, Cowen developed what was to become the first Lionel train—a battery-powered "Electric Express." It was originally designed to be used as a showpiece in a shop window. Customers were curious about the Electric Express, and eventually twelve of the showpieces eventually were sold. Cowen was on his way.

In 1902, Cowen added a trolley car to the display, manufactured for him by Massachusetts' Morton E. Converse. At the same time, six barrels were added to the Electric Express. Other accessories in the first 1902 Lionel catalog included a suspension bridge, a track with a switch, a crossover track that allowed a figure-eight layout and a bumper for the end of a track. The Electric Express, like the trolley, could now be powered by batteries or electricity.

By 1909, Lionel was advertising its trains as "The Standard of the World." Cowen had a knack for advertising, and much of Lionel's early success can be attributed to the companies colorful and punchy ad campaigns and catalogs.

The next twenty years saw tremendous growth for Lionel. In 1915, O-gauge cars were introduced, and they eventually became the most popular scale of train. By the 1920s electricity was found in more homes, and no toy benefited more from electricity than the train. In 1927, Lionel's profits were almost a half-million dollars.

In 1930, the first full year of the Depression, Lionel's profits were down to $82,000, and in 1931 they lost $207,000. The firm temporarily went into receivership in 1934.

That same year the Streamlined Union Pacific diesel M10000 was released. Lionel orchestrated a major publicity campaign timed to coincide with the M10000's release. Sales soared. It was in the fall of this year that Lionel developed the Mickey and Minnie Mouse hand car. It sold more than a quarter million units, and it is very likely the thing that saved the company from bankruptcy. By the next year his company was in the black by $154,000.

Standard gauge was discontinued in 1940, and with the interruption of World War II, Lionel's only war years toy was a cardboard train set as the company fulfilled government contracts.

Lionel's postwar line, known by many as the golden years of Lionel train, was introduced by a sixteen-page catalog contained in the November 23, 1946 issue of *Liberty* magazine. Though competition with American Flyer soon became fierce, Lionel was able to stay ahead. Bakelite and other plastics became prominent, along with such innovations as knuckle couplers, smoke units, a battery-operated diesel horn (1948) and "Mangnetraction" (Magnetized wheels and axles, which gave stronger pulling power) in the 1950s.

However, by the mid 1950s Lionel began to teeter. In 1957, Lionel introduced HO-scale trains, but that year was the last profitable one for the company. Ever sagacious, Cowen retired the next year and sold all of his Lionel stock the following year.

Cowen died at the age of 85 on September 8, 1965.

Contributor: Walter Smith, 2504 Pioneer Ct., Davenport, IA 52804. Smith, retired from G.I. Case, has been collecting postwar Lionel for over 20 years. He welcomes an correspondence from other Lionel collectors.

	C5	C7	C9
90 degrees Crossing, O ga., 1962	4	6	8
Bulb, 1939, 8 volt, clear	—	—	1
Caboose, O72 ga., 1940	165	275	550
Dealer Display, 1928, large cardboard background showing power station, roundhouses, etc.	210	350	700
Electronic Control, 1946, instruction booklet	5	10	15
Electronic Control Unit, 1946	40	60	80
Ewing Merkle Catalog, 1903	21	35	70
Fiber Pins, O ga., 1962, dozen	—	—	1
Half Section Curved Track, O ga., 1966	1	1	1
Half Section Straight Track, O ga., 1966	—	—	1
Lionel Apology Folder, 1919	13	23	45
Lionel Catalog, 1903	21	35	70
Lionel Catalog, 1904	21	35	70
Lionel Catalog, 1905	21	35	70
Lionel Catalog, 1906	21	35	70
Lionel Catalog, 1907	21	35	70
Lionel Catalog, 1908	21	35	70
Lionel Catalog, 1909	21	35	70
Lionel Catalog, 1910	21	35	70
Lionel Catalog, 1911	21	35	70
Lionel Catalog, 1912	21	35	70
Lionel Catalog, 1913	21	35	70
Lionel Catalog, 1913, small	15	25	50
Lionel Catalog, 1914	21	35	70
Lionel Catalog, 1914, small	15	25	50
Lionel Catalog, 1915	21	35	70
Lionel Catalog, 1916	21	35	70
Lionel Catalog, 1917	21	35	70
Lionel Catalog, 1920	21	35	70
Lionel Catalog, 1922	21	35	70
Lionel Catalog, 1923	15	25	50
Lionel Catalog, 1924	21	35	70

	C5	C7	C9
Lionel Catalog, 1925	21	35	70
Lionel Catalog, 1926	18	30	60
Lionel Catalog, 1927	22	38	75
Lionel Catalog, 1928	22	38	75
Lionel Catalog, 1929	21	35	70
Lionel Catalog, 1930	21	35	70
Lionel Catalog, 1931	21	35	70
Lionel Catalog, 1932	22	38	75
Lionel Catalog, 1933	16	28	55
Lionel Catalog, 1934	15	24	48
Lionel Catalog, 1935	17	28	55
Lionel Catalog, 1936	15	24	48
Lionel Catalog, 1937	11	18	35
Lionel Catalog, 1938	14	23	45
Lionel Catalog, 1939	11	18	35
Lionel Catalog, 1940	12	20	40
Lionel Catalog, 1941	14	23	45
Lionel Catalog, 1942	14	23	45
Lionel Catalog, 1945	5	8	16
Lionel Catalog, 1947	20	25	35
Lionel Catalog, 1948	9	15	30
Lionel Catalog, 1949	50	80	110
Lionel Catalog, 1950	25	40	55
Lionel Catalog, 1951	15	25	35
Lionel Catalog, 1952	9	15	30
Lionel Catalog, 1953	7	12	24
Lionel Catalog, 1954	5	9	17
Lionel Catalog, 1955	10	15	20
Lionel Catalog, 1956	5	8	16
Lionel Catalog, 1957	3	6	11
Lionel Catalog, 1958	4	6	12
Lionel Catalog, 1959	4	7	13
Lionel Catalog, 1960	3	5	10
Lionel Catalog, 1961	4	6	12
Lionel Catalog, 1962	3	6	11
Lionel Catalog, 1963	2	3	5
Lionel Catalog, 1964	2	3	5

Cover of the 1961 Lionel catalog.

Cover of the 1962 Lionel catalog.

Cover of the 1968 Lionel Catalog.

	C5	C7	C9
Lionel Catalog, 1965	1	2	4
Lionel Catalog, 1966	1	2	4
Lionel Catalog, 1968	1	2	4
Lionel Catalog, 1969	1	2	4
Lionel Folder, 1917	8	13	25
Lionel Folder, 1918	8	13	25
Lionel Folder, 1919	8	13	25
Lionel Folder, 1920	8	13	25
Lionel Folder, 1921	8	13	25
Lionel Folder, 1946	12	20	40
Lockton, O ga., 1921	—	—	1
Lockton, standard ga., 1921	—	—	1
Lockton, 1937, universal	—	—	1
Lockton, O ga., 1947	—	—	1
Lockton, O27 ga., 1950, w/light	10	15	20
Mechanical Key, 1934, square	3	5	10
Steel Pins, O/standard ga., 1937, dozen	1	2	2
Steel Pins, O ga., 1962, dozen	—	—	1
Straight Track, O ga., 1962	—	—	1
Switches, O ga., 1962, remote control	35	53	70
Track, standard ga., 1906, curved	—	1	2
Track, standard ga., 1906, straight half section	—	1	2
Track, standard ga., 1906, straight	—	1	2
Track, standard ga., 1906, curved half section	—	1	2
Track, standard ga., 1912, curved racing car-type, 30" dia.	25	38	50
Track, standard ga., 1912, curved racing car-type 36" diameter	28	42	55
Track, standard ga., 1915, curved, racing car-type, 36" dia.	28	42	55
Track, O ga., 1915, straight	—	—	1
Track, O ga., 1915, straight, w/battery connections	1	2	3
Track, O ga., 1915, curved, w/battery connections	1	2	3
Track, O ga., 1915, curved	—	—	1
Track, standard ga., 1915, curved, w/battery connections	1	2	3
Track, standard ga., 1915, straight w/battery connections	1	2	3
Track, O ga., 1926, curved w/insulated rails	—	—	1
Track, O ga., 1926, straight w/insulated rails	—	—	1
Track, standard ga., 1926, straight w/insulated rails	1	2	3
Track, 1933, straight, mechanical	—	—	1
Track, 1933, curved, mechanical	—	—	1
Track, 1933, curved, mechanical	—	—	1
Track, 1935, curved, insulated, mechanical	—	—	1
Track, 1935, curved, mechanical	—	—	1
Track, O ga., 1938, remote control	3	4	5
Track, O ga., 1962, curved	—	—	1
Track Clip, standard ga., 1937	—	—	1
Track Clip, O ga., 1937	—	—	1
Transformer, 1914, 150 watt	40	60	80
Transformer, 1914, 75 watt	10	15	20
Transformer, 1915, 50 watt	10	15	20
Transformer, 1915, 50 watt	10	15	20
Transformer, 1915, 75 watt	10	15	20
Transformer, 1916, 40 watt	20	30	40
Transformer, 1917, 50 watt	13	23	45
Transformer, 1922, 75 watt	15	25	50
Transformer, 1923, 75 watt	13	23	45
Transformer, 1930, 60 watt	10	15	20
Transformer, 1933, 75 watt	5	8	10
Transformer, 1933, 50 watt	10	15	20
Transformer, 1938, 75 watt	10	15	20
Transformer, 1939, 75 watt	7	11	14
Transformer, 1939, 150 watt	55	83	110
Transformer, 1939, 75 watt	7	11	14
Transformer, 1939, 250 watt	80	120	160
Transformer, 1939, 100 watt	25	38	50
Transformer, 1942, 50 watt	10	15	20
Transformer, 1947, 90 watt	40	55	75

	C5	C7	C9
Transformer, 1948, 150 watt	98	125	150
Transformer, 1948, 250 watt	140	200	275
Transformer, 1948, 110 watt	48	66	85
Transformer, 1950, 190 watt	115	155	195
Transformer, 1953, 275 watt	177	225	295
Transformer, 1953, 115 watt	77	100	145
Transformer, 1956, 125 watt	105	125	140
Transformer, 1961, 135 watt	55	82	120
Uncoupling Track, O ga., 1949, remote control	8	10	145
Winner Folder, 1930	11	21	35
Winner Folder, 1931	11	21	35
Winner Folder, 1932	11	21	35
1 Bild-A-Motor, 1928, small	75	113	150
1 Bild-A-Motor, O ga., 1928	150	225	300
00-1 Locomotive, OO ga., 1938-42, steam, 4-6-4 Hudson full scale three-rail w/either 001T tender without whistle or 001W w/whistle	120	200	400
1 Trolley, standard ga., 1906-1910, motor car, four wheel, powered, blue body w/blue roof, marked "No. 1 Electric-Rapid Transit No. 1"	1050	1750	3500
1 Trolley, standard ga., 1906-1910, motor car, powered, four wheel, white body w/blue roof, marked "No. 1 Electric-Rapid Transit No. 1"	1110	1850	3700
1 Trolley, standard ga., 1906-1910, motor car, four wheel, powered, cream body w/blue roof, "No. 1 Electric-Rapid Transit No. 1"	750	1250	2500
1 Trolley, standard ga., 1906-1910, motor car, four wheel, powered, cream body w/blue roof, marked "No. 1 Electric-Rapid Transit No. 1"	1260	2100	4200
1 Trolley, standard ga., 1907, trailer, non-powered, white body w/blue roof	1050	1750	3500
1 Trolley, standard ga., 1907, trailer, non-powered, cream body w/blue roof	1050	1750	3500

	C5	C7	C9
2 Bild-A-Motor, O ga., 1928, large..	200	300	400
00-2 Locomotive, OO ga., 1938-42, steam, 4-6-4 Hudson, semi-scale three-rail w/either 002T tender without whistle or OO2W w/whistle	105	175	350
002W Tender, w/whistle	120	200	400
2 Trolley, standard ga., 1906-1915, trailer, non-powered, cream body w/red windows and doors	750	1250	2500
2 Trolley, standard ga., 1906-1915, trailer, non-powered, red body, cream windows and doors	750	1250	2500
2 Trolley, standard ga., 1906-1915, motor car, four-wheel, powered, No. 2 Electric-Rapid Transit No. 2 cream body, red windows and doors	1050	1750	3500
2 Trolley, standard ga., 1906-1915, motor car, four-wheel, powered, No. 2 Electric-Rapid Transit No. 2 red body, cream windows and doors	1050	1750	3500
00-3 Locomotive, OO ga., 1938-1942, steam, 4-6-4 Hudson semi-scale three-rail w/either 002T Tender without whistle or 002W w/whistle	120	200	400
3 Trolley, standard ga., 1906-1909, eight wheel, motor car, powered, No. 3 Electric-Rapid Transit No. 3, dark green body and roof	1350	2250	4500
3 Trolley, standard ga., 1906-1909, eight wheel, motor car, powered, No. 3 Electric-Rapid Transit No. 3, cream body, orange roof	1200	2000	4000
3 Trolley, standard ga., 1906-1909, eight wheel, motor car, powered, No. 3 Electric-Rapid Transit No. 3, light orange body, dark orange roof	1200	2000	4000
3 Trolley, standard ga., 1906-1909, eight-wheel, trailer, non-powered, light orange body, dark orange roof	1200	2000	4000

	C5	C7	C9
4U Locomotive, O ga., 1928, 0-4-0, electric, orange only, marked "You build it," unassembled and complete w/instructions in original box	850	1275	1700
4 Locomotive, O ga., 1928-1932, 0-4-0, electric, gray	300	500	1000
4 Locomotive, O ga., 1928-1932, 0-4-0, electric, orange	270	450	900
00-4 Locomotive, OO ga., 1938-1942, steam, 4-6-4 Hudson semi-scale two-rail w/either 004T Tender without whistle or 004W w/whistle	120	200	400
4 Trolley, standard ga., 1908-1910, eight-wheel, motor car, green body and roof, powered, double motor, "No. 4 Electric-Rapid Transit No. 4"	2700	4500	9000
4 Trolley, standard ga., 1908-1910, eight-wheel, motor car, cream body and green roof, powered, double motor, "No. 4 Electric-Rapid Transit No. 4"	2700	4500	9000
5 Locomotive, standard ga., 1906-1926, 0-4-0, steam, no tender, black cab and boiler, red window trim, marked "NYC&HRRR"	780	1300	2600
5 Locomotive, standard ga., 1906-1926, 0-4-0, steam, no tender, black cab and boiler, red window trim, marked "B&ORR"	360	600	1200
5 Locomotive, standard ga., 1906-1926, 0-4-0, steam, no tender, black cab and boiler, red window trim, "Pennsylvania"	900	1500	3000
5D Repair Station	800	1400	1900
5 Special Locomotive, standard ga., 1910-1911, 0-4-0, steam, no tender, black cab and boiler, red window trim w/tender	450	750	1500
5C Test Set	1500	2500	4000
5 Trolley, standard ga., 1906-1910, motor car, powered, four wheel, No. 1 Electric-Rapid Transit No. 1, cream body, orange roof	1200	2000	4000

	C5	C7	C9
6 Locomotive, standard ga., 1906-1923, 4-4-0, steam w/tender, black cab and boiler, red window trim, marked "B&ORR"	630	1050	2100
6 Locomotive, standard ga., 1906-1923, 4-4-0, steam w/tender, black cab and boiler, red window trim, marked "NYC&HRRR"	300	500	1000
6 Locomotive, standard ga., 1906-1923, 4-4-0, steam, w/tender, black cab and boiler, red window trim, marked "Pennsylvania"	705	1175	2350
6 Locomotive, standard ga., 1908-1909, 4-4-0, special, steam, w/tender, black cab and boiler, red window trim, non-lettered	450	750	1500

No. 6 Locomotive, 4-4-0, $1,500.

No. 7 Locomotive, 4-4-0, $3,500.

	C5	C7	C9
7 Locomotive, standard ga., 1910-1923, 4-4-0, steam, brass boiler, nickel cab and tender	1050	1750	3500
8 Locomotive, standard ga., 1925-1932, 0-4-0, electric, maroon	30	50	100
8 Locomotive, standard ga., 1925-1932, 0-4-0, electric, peacock	75	125	250
8 Locomotive, standard ga., 1925-1932, 0-4-0, electric, olive	45	75	150
8 Locomotive, standard ga., 1925-1932, 0-4-0, electric, red	45	75	150

	C5	C7	C9
8 Locomotive, standard ga., 1925-1932, 0-4-0, electric, mojave	60	100	200
8E Locomotive, standard ga., 1926-1932, 0-4-0, electric, red	80	135	270
8E Locomotive, standard ga., 1926-1932, 0-4-0, electric, mojave	95	162	325
8E Locomotive, standard ga., 1926-1932, 0-4-0, electric, peacock	110	180	360
8E Locomotive, standard ga., 1926-1932, 0-4-0, electric, olive	60	100	200
8E Locomotive, standard ga., 1926-1932, 0-4-0, Macy, electric, pea green, cream stripe	150	250	500
8 Trolley, standard ga., 1908-1909, eight wheel, motor car, powered, cream or dark green, marked "Pay as you enter No. 8,"	1170	1950	3900

	C5	C7	C9
9U Locomotive, standard ga., 1928, electric, orange, assembled	450	750	1500
9E Locomotive, standard ga., 1928, 0-4-0, electric, 242, two-tone green	472	785	1575
9 Locomotive, standard ga., 1929, electric, dark green	600	1000	2000
9E Locomotive, standard ga., 1931, 2-4-2, electric, gray	420	700	1400

No. 9E Locomotive, 0-4-0, $1,575.

Part of an early ad for the No. 9 Trolley.

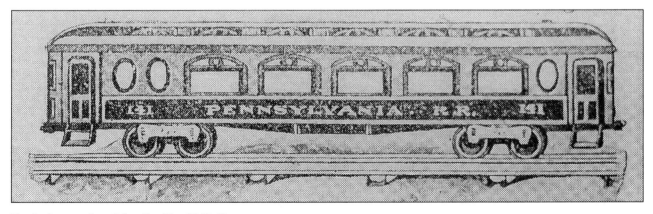

No. 9U Locomotive, $1,500.

	C5	C7	C9
9U Special Locomotive, standard ga., 1929, kit form w/original box, orange, unassembled.........	1200	1800	2400
9 Trolley, standardl ga., 1909, eight wheel, motor car, powered, cream or dark green, marked "Pay as you enter No. 9"..............................	2100	3500	7000
10 Interurban, standard ga., 1910, motor car, powered, maroon or dark green, "Interurban" and "New York Central Lines".......	600	1000	2000
10 Interurban, standard ga., 1910, motor car, powered, marked "Interurban," "New York Central Lines," "10 WB&B&A 10"..	1500	2500	5000
10 Locomotive, standard ga., 1925-1929, 0-4-0, electric, peacock blue, mojave, gray	85	140	280

	C5	C7	C9
10E Locomotive, standard ga., 1926-1930, 0-4-0, electric, peacock or red, w/Bild-a-Loco Motor...	158	260	525
10E Locomotive, standard ga., 1926-1930, 0-4-0, electric, brown, green frame	90	135	275
10E Locomotive, standard ga., 1926-1930, 0-4-0, electric, peacock or gray	74	122	245
10E Macy Locomotive, standard ga., 1930, 0-4-0, electric, peacock w/orange stripe, uncataloged	85	140	280
10 Macy Locomotive, standard ga., 1930, 0-4-0, electric, red	180	300	600
0-11-11 Fiber Pins, O ga., 1937.....	—	—	1
11 Flatcar, standard ga., 1906-1926..	33	55	110
0-11 Switches, O ga., 1933, electric, nonderailing, pair	50	75	100
12 Gondola, standard ga., 1906	30	50	100
0-12 Switches, O ga., 1927, electric.......................................	30	50	100
13 Cattle Car, standard ga., 1906...	45	75	150
0-13 Switches, O ga., 1929, panel board set	25	38	50
14 Boxcar, standard ga., 1906-1926..	60	100	200
00-14 Boxcar, OO ga., 1938, yellow and Tuscan	24	40	80

Part of an early ad for the No. 18 Pullman.

	C5	C7	C9
14 Harmony Boxcar Car Creamery Special, standard ga., 1920, uncataloged	120	200	400
15 Oil, standard ga., 1906-1926	48	80	160
00-15 Tank Car, OO ga., 1938	27	45	90
16 Ballast, standard ga., 1906-1926, dark green	65	108	215
00-16 Hopper, OO ga., 1938	66	110	220
17 Caboose, standard ga., 1906-1926	105	175	350
00-17 Caboose, OO ga., 1938	25	41	82
18 Pullman, standard ga., 1906-1910, dark olive, marked "New York Central Lines," 18"	360	600	1200
18 Pullman, standard ga., 1916-1917, light orange, marked "New York Central Lines, " 18"	360	600	1200
18 Pullman, standard ga., 1918-1923, dark olive, marked "Parlor Car" and "New York Central Lines"	210	350	700
19 Combine, standard ga., 1906-1927	180	300	600
19 Combine, standard ga., 1906-1927	300	500	1000
19 Combine, standard ga., 1906-1927	300	500	1000
0-20X 45 Degrees Crossing, O ga., 1915	10	15	20
20 90 Degrees Crossing, standard ga., 1909	6	9	12
0-20 90 Degrees Crossing, O ga., 1915	6	9	12
20 Direct, 1906, current shunt resistor	2	4	6
21 Crossing, standard ga., 1906	4	6	8
0-21 Switch, O ga., 1915, w/light	12	18	25
21 Switch, standard ga., 1915, w/light	12	18	25
0-22 Switches, O ga., 1946-1949, electric	26	39	125
23 Bumper, standard ga., 1906, red or black	9	13	18
0-23 Bumper, O ga., 1915	4	6	8

	C5	C7	C9
00-24 Boxcar, OO ga., 1939	20	32	65
24 Bulb, 1915, eight volt	—	—	1
24 Station, standard ga., 1906	350	525	700
25 Bulb, 1911, 3-1/2 volt, DC	—	—	1
25 Bulb, 1924, pear shaped	—	—	5
25 Bumper, standard ga., 1928, cream or black	20	30	40
0-25 Bumper, O ga., 1928	17	25	35
25 Station, standard ga., 1906	375	562	750
00-25 Tank Car, OO ga., 1939	30	50	100
26 Bulb, 1911, 14 volt AC	—	—	1
26 Bumper, O ga., 1948, red	32	48	65
26 Bumper, O ga., 1948, gray	65	98	130
26 Passenger Foot Bridge, standard ga., 1906	100	150	200
27 Bulb, 1927, 12 volt, red, green or clear	—	—	1
27-6 Bulb, 1940, 12 volt, clear	—	—	1
27-3 Bulb, 1950, 14 volt, clear	—	—	1
00-27 Caboose, OO ga., 1939	21	35	70
27 Lighting, standard ga., 1911, set for cars	37	52	75
27 Station, standard ga., 1909	250	375	500
0-27-C1 Track Clip, O27 ga., 1949	—	2	3
28 Bulb, 1927, 18 volt, red, green, amber or clear	—	—	1
28-3 Bulb, 1939, 18 volt, clear	—	—	1
28-6 Bulb, 1939, 18 volt, red	—	—	1
29 Bulb, 1915, 3-1/2 volt	—	—	1
29-3 Bulb, 1932, 18 volt, yellow	—	—	1
29 Day Coach, standard ga., 1909, maroon	180	300	375
29 Day Coach, standard ga., 1909, dark olive	112	188	375
30 Bulb, 1915, 14 volt	—	—	1
30 Curved Rubber Roadbed, standard ga., 1931	3	4	5
0-30 Roadbed, 1931, curved, rubber	3	4	5
30 Water Tank Car, 1947-1950, gray support structure	70	150	250

	C5	C7	C9
30 Water Tank Car, 1947-1950, black support structure	125	250	500
31 Combine, standard ga., 1921, orange, green and maroon	48	80	160
0-31 Roadbed, O ga., 1931, straight, rubber	3	4	5
31 Straight Rubber Roadbed, standard ga., 1931	3	4	5
00-31 Track, OO ga., 1939, curved, two-rail	3	5	6
31 Track, Super O ga., 1957, curved	—	2	4
32 Baggage Car, standard ga., 1921, maroon, dark olive, brown, orange	67	112	225
32 Miniature Figures, standard ga., 1910, set of twelve	150	225	300
0-32 Roadbed, O ga., 1931, 90-degree crossing, rubber	3	4	5
32 Rubber Roadbed, standard ga., 1931, 90-degree crossing	3	4	5
32 Track, Super O ga., 1931, straight	5	10	15
00-32 Track, OO ga., 1939, straight, two-rail	5	10	15
33 Half Curve Track, Super O ga., 1957	—	2	4
33 Locomotive, 1913, 0-6-0, electric, engine only, dark green	240	400	800
33 Locomotive, standard ga., 1913-1924, 0-4-0, electric, maroon	120	200	400
33 Locomotive, standard ga., 1913-1924, 0-4-0, electric, red	150	250	500
33 Locomotive, standard ga., 1913-1924, 0-4-0, electric, peacock	75	125	250
33 Locomotive, standard ga., 1913-1924, electric 0-4-0, gray	60	100	200
33 Locomotive, standard ga., 1913-1924, 0-4-0, electric, dark olive or black	50	82	165
0-33 Roadbed, standard O ga., 1931, 45-degree crossing, rubber	3	4	5

	C5	C7	C9
0-33 Roadbed, standard O ga., 1931, 45-degree crossing, rubber	3	4	5
33 Rubber Roadbed, standard O ga., 1931, 45-degree crossing	3	4	5
34 Locomotive, standard ga., 1912, 0-6-0, electric, dark green	150	250	500
34 Locomotive, standard ga., 1913, 0-4-0, electric, dark green, uncataloged	120	200	400
0-34 Roadbed Switch, O ga., 1931, rubber	3	4	5
34 Rubber Roadbed Switch, standard ga., 1913	3	4	5
34 Track, Super O ga., 1957, half, straight	—	2	4
00-34 Track Connection, OO ga., 1939, for curved track	3	4	5
35 Lamp Post, 1940, gray or silver	15	25	50
35 Pullman, standard ga., 1915, dark olive, maroon or brown	21	34	68
35 Pullman, standard ga., 1915, orange	49	65	130
36RM Controller, standard ga., 1937	—	2	3
36 Observation Car, standard ga., 1912, dark olive, maroon or brown	21	35	70
36 Observation Car, standard ga., 1912, orange	60	100	200
37 Uncoupling Track, Super O ga., 1957	8	15	20
38 Accessory Adapter, Super O ga., 1957	—	1	2
38 Locomotive, standard ga., 1913-1924, 0-4-0, electric, black or gray	75	125	250
38 Locomotive, standard ga., 1913-1924, 0-4-0, electric, pea green	96	160	320
38 Locomotive, standard ga., 1913-1924, 0-4-0, electric, red	150	250	500
38 Locomotive, standard ga., 1913-1924, 0-4-0 electric, brown	120	200	400

Top row, left to right: No. 44 US Army Missile Launcher Locomotive, $240; No. 6844 flatcar. Middle row: No. 3419 Helicopter Launching car, $110. Bottom row, left to right: No. 6823 IRBM Missile car, $75; No. 6814 First Aid Caboose, $125.

	C5	C7	C9
38 Water Tower, 1946-1947, red roof	225	338	430
38 Water Tower, 1946-1947, brown roof	175	255	450
39 Bulb, 1927, 12 volt, frosted	—	—	1
39-3 Bulb, 1939, 12 volt, frosted	—	—	1
39-25 Operating and Upcoupling Set, Super O ga., 1960	3	4	5
39-5 Operating Unit Set, Super O ga., 1957	3	4	5
HO-039 Track Cleaning Car, HO ga., 1961	36	60	120
40 Bulb, 1927, 13 volt	—	—	1
40-3 Bulb, 1939, 8 volt	—	—	1
40-25 Four Conductor Cable and Reel, 1950	—	1	2
40-50 Three Conductor Cable and Reel, 1960	—	1	2
41 Accessory Contactor, 1936	—	1	2
41 Locomotive, O27 ga., 1955, army switcher, black shell small motorized unit	130	150	200

	C5	C7	C9
42 Locomotive, standard ga., 1912, 0-4-4-0, electric, square body, dark green	450	750	1500
42 Locomotive, standard ga., 1913-1923, electric, peacock	825	1375	2750
42 Locomotive, standard ga., 1913-1923, electric, maroon	240	400	800
42 Locomotive, standard ga., 1913-1923, electric, mojave	173	288	575
42 Locomotive, standard ga., 1913-1923, electric, dark green, gray and black	142	237	475

No. 42 Locomotive, electric, $475.

	C5	C7	C9
42 Locomotive, O27 ga., 1957, Picatinny Arsenal switcher, olive shell, small motorized unit	135	225	450
0-42 Switch, O ga., 1938, manual, single	12	18	25
43 Bild-A-Motor, standard ga., 1929, gear set	75	108	150
0-43 Bild-A-Motor Gear Set, O ga., 1929	32	48	64
43 Pleasure Boat, 1933-1936, 1939-1941, cream, red and white	400	600	800
43 Power Track, Super O ga., 1957	—	1	2
00-44 Boxcar, OO ga., 1939	25	42	85
00-44K Kit, OO ga., 1939, original box	110	165	220
44 Locomotive, Super O ga., 1959, US Army Missile Launcher	72	120	240
44-80 Missiles, Super O ga., 1959-1962, four	2	3	4
44 Race Boat, 1935-1936, green, white and dark brown	450	675	900
45/45N/045 Automatic Gateman, 1935-1936, 1937-1942, green base cream/e house, red roof w/cream chimney	16	27	55
45 Locomotive, O ga., 1960-1962, U.S. Marine Missile Launcher, olive shell w/white missiles	190	225	340
00-45 Tank Car, OO ga., 1939	21	85	70
00-45K Tank Kit, OO ga., 1939	100	150	200
46 Bulb, 1936, 8 volt	—	—	1
00-46 Hopper, OO ga., 1939	25	41	82
00-46K Hopper Kit, OO ga., 1939	100	150	200
46 Single Arm Crossing, 1939-1942, cream and green base, lantern on tip of gate	45	75	150
47 Bulb, 1916, 6 volt	—	—	1

	C5	C7	C9
47-40 Bulb, 1937, 18 volt, red	—	—	1
47-73 Bulb, 1942, 12 volt	—	—	1
00-47 Caboose, OO ga., 1939	24	40	80
00-47K Caboose Kit, OO ga., 1939	100	150	200
47 Double Arm Crossing Gates, 1937-1942, w/two crossing gates on each side	70	105	140
48 Bulb, 1936, 21 volt	—	—	1
48 Track, Super O ga., 1958, straight, insulated	4	8	12
48W Whistle Station, 1937-1942, lithographed building, red base housing whistle	10	18	36
49 Lionel Airport, 1937-1939, printed cardboard base w/airplane and controls	1000	1250	1500
49 Track, Super O ga., 1958, curved, insulated	4	8	12
50 Airplane, 1936	400	600	800
50 Gang Car, O27 ga., 1954	45	55	70
HO-050 Gang Car, HO ga., 1959	30	50	100
50 Locomotive, standard ga., 1924, electric, maroon	105	175	350
50 Locomotive, standard ga., 1924, electric, dark green	105	175	350
50 Locomotive, standard ga., 1924, electric, mojave	105	175	350
50 Locomotive, standard ga., 1924, 0-4-0, electric gray	90	150	300
50 Paper Train Set, 1943, uncataloged	90	157	315
51 Airport, 1936-1939, printed cardboard base for center control and airplane	300	450	600
51 Locomotive, standard ga., 1912-1923, 0-4-0, steam, "5 Special"	380	650	1300

Top to bottom: No. 45 U.S. Marine Missile Launcher Locomotive, $340; No. 2037 Locomotive, $125. Photo courtesy 1961 Lionel catalog.

	C5	C7	C9
51 Locomotive, O27 ga., 1956-1957, Navy switcher, blue shell small motorized unit	150	190	250
00-51 Track, OO ga., 1939, curved, three-rail	—	1	2

No. 52 Fire Fighting car, $300.

	C5	C7	C9
52 Fire Fighting Car, O27 ga., 1958-1961, red shell w/man	165	225	300
52 Lamp Post, 1933, aluminum	35	52	70
00-52 Track, OO ga., 1939, straight, three-rail	6	8	10
53-8 Bulb, 1932, 18 volt	—	—	1
53 Lamp Post, 1931, gray, aluminum, mojave	37	56	75
53 Locomotive, standard ga., 1912-1914, 0-4-0, electric, mojave, maroon, dark olive	360	600	1200
53 Locomotive, standard ga., 1920, 0-4-0, electric, mojave, maroon, dark olive	150	250	500
53 Snow Plow, O27 ga., 1957, DRG, Rio Grande, black and yellow, "a" in Grande backwards	180	250	330
53 Snow Plow, O27 ga., 1957, DRG, Rio Grande, black and yellow	520	680	900
54 Ballast Tamper, O27 ga., 1957, yellow shell, small motorized unit, w/track trips	100	160	225
54 Lamp Post, 1929, double light, dark green	35	52	70
54 Locomotive, standard ga., 1912, 0-4-4-0, electric, square body, brass	1050	1750	3500

	C5	C7	C9
54 Locomotive, standard ga., 1913-1923, 0-4-4-0, electric, brass, single or double motor	750	1250	2500
00-54 Track Connection, OO ga., 1939, for curved track	—	1	2
55 Airplane, 1937-1939, red and silver w/control	250	375	500
55 Bulb, 1924, 14 volt	—	—	1
HO-055 Locomotive, HO ga., 1961, M&StL switcher	30	50	100
55 Tie Ejector, O27 ga., 1957-1961, red shell w/wooden track ties, small motorized unit and track trips	72	122	245
55-150 Ties, O27 ga., 1957, set of twenty-four	4	6	8
56 Lamp Post, 1925-1949, gray, green, mojave	32	48	65
56 Locomotive, O27 ga., 1958, M&StL Mining, red shell, small motorized unit	250	480	580
HO-056 Locomotive, HO ga., 1959, A.E.C. Switcher	45	75	150
57 Lamp Post, 1924-1942, orange, "Broadway & Main"	25	42	85
57 Lamp Post, 1924-1942, orange, "Broadway & Fifth Ave."	24	40	80
57 Lamp Post, 1924-1942, orange, "Broadway & 42nd Street"	30	50	100

Left to right: No. 57 Boulevard Lamp post with silver lettering, $100; No. 56 Lamp post, $65; No. 53 Lamp post, $75; No. 61 Lamp post, $50; No. 57 Lamp post, $100.

NEW, EXCITING 1962 HO OUTFITS...

HO

Set No. 14003 — 4 Unit Minneapolis & St. Louis Husky Freight includes:

No. 0055 Minneapolis & St. Louis Husky Switcher
　　　with Headlight
No. 0821 Pipe Transport Car
No. 0865-250 Gondola with Crates
No. 0837 Minneapolis & St. Louis Caboose
　　　to match loco
5 sections No. 0988 18" Radius Curved Track—
　　　18" long
1 section No. 0976 Curved Terminal Track—
　　　18" long
No. 0103 800 milliamp Power Pack
Wires and Instruction Sheet

HO

Set No. 14013 — 4 Unit Erie & Lackawanna Diesel Switcher Freight includes:

No. 0545 Erie & Lackawanna GE-44 Diesel Switcher
　　　with Headlight
No. 0850 Missile Launching Car
No. 0847 Exploding Target Car
No. 0838 Caboose to match loco
5 sections No. 0988 18" Radius Curved Track—
　　　18" long
1 section No. 0976 Curved Terminal Track—
　　　18" long
No. 0103 800 milliamp Power Pack
Wires and Instruction Sheet

HO

Set No. 14023 — 6 Unit 2-4-2 "Heavy Cargo" Steam Freight includes:

No. 0642LT 2-4-2 Steam Loco and Slope Back
　　　Tender with Headlight
No. 0357 New Hobo and Cop Car
No. 0861 Timber Transport Car
No. 0865-225 Gondola with Scrap Iron
No. 0841 Caboose
5 sections No. 0988 18" Radius Curved Track—
　　　18" long
1 section No. 0976 Curved Terminal Track—
　　　18" long
No. 0103 800 milliamp Power Pack
Wires and Instruction Sheet

HO

Set No. 14033 — 5 Unit Union Pacific Military Diesel Freight includes:

No. 0568 New Union Pacific Diesel with Headlight
No. 0365 New Minuteman Missile Launching Car
No. 0813 New Mercury Capsule Carrying Car
No. 0809 Helium Tank Transport Car
No. 0841-50 Union Pacific Caboose to match loco
5 sections No. 0988 18" Radius Curved Track—
　　　18" long
1 section No. 0976 Curved Terminal Track—
　　　18" long
No. 0103 800 milliamp Power Pack
Wires and Instruction Sheet

42

Lionel's 1962 catalog illustrates several of the HO-scale locomotives available that year.

	C5	C7	C9
57 Lamp Post, 1924-1942, yellow, "Broadway & Main"	30	50	100
HO-057 Locomotive, HO ga., 1959, U.P. Switcher	30	50	100
57 Locomotive, O27 ga., 1959-1960, A.E.C. Switcher, cream-red shell, small motorized unit	325	500	750
58 Lamp Post, 1922-1950, green, maroon, cream	14	24	48

Three versions of No. 58 Lamp post, $48, each.

	C5	C7	C9
58 Locomotive, O27 ga., 1959-1961, rotary snow plow, green shell	325	450	650
HO-058 Locomotive, 1960, R.I. Switcher	24	40	80
59 Lamp Post, 1920-1936, olive	22	37	75
59 Lamp Post, 1920-1936, green	15	25	50
59 Locomotive, U.S. Air Force switcher, white cab	300	425	600
HO-59 Locomotive, HO ga., 1960, U.S. Air Force Switcher	30	50	100
59 Locomotive, O27 ga., 1963, U.S. Air Force Switcher, Minute Man, white shell	172	288	575
60 Automatic Trip Reverse, standard ga., 1906	3	5	6

	C5	C7	C9
60 Locomotive, standard ga., 1913, 0-4-0, electric, F.A.O. Schwarz Special, uncataloged	360	600	1200
60 Telegraph Pole, standard ga., 1920, set of six	66	110	220
0-60 Telegraph Pole, O ga., 1929, set of six	24	40	80
60 Trolley, O27 ga., 1955-1958, yellow w/red roof, blue lettering	100	150	195
60 Trolley, O27 ga., 1955-1958, black lettering	150	220	300
60 Trolley, O27 ga., 1955-1958, moving silhouettes, motor man in front w/direction of movement	135	225	450
60 Trolley, O27 ga., 1955-1958, red lettering, rare	900	1500	3000
61 Ground Lockon, Super O ga., 1957	—	2	4
61 Lamp Post, 1914-1936, dark green, maroon, mojave, olive	15	25	50
61 Locomotive, standard ga., 1913, 0-4-4-0, electric, F.A.O. Schwarz Special, uncataloged	450	750	1500
00-61 Track, OO ga., 1938, curved, three-rail	3	5	6
62 Automatic Reversing Trip, standard ga., 1914	3	4	5
62 Locomotive, standard ga., 1913, 0-4-0, electric, F.A.O. Schwarz Special, uncataloged	360	600	1200
62 Semaphore, 1920-1932	12	20	40
00-62 Track, OO ga., 1939, straight, three-rail	3	5	6
63-11 Bulb, 1935, 18 volt, opal	—	—	1
63 Lamp Post, 1933-1942, double globe, silver	81	135	270
63-10 Opal Globe, 1933	3	4	5
63 Semaphore, 1915-1921	30	45	60
00-63 Track, OO ga., 1939, half-curve, three-rail	3	5	6
64-15 Bulb, 1940, 12 volt, clear	—	—	5
64-26 Bulb, 1941, 12 volt, opal	—	—	5
64 Lamp Post, 1940-1942, green	14	24	48

	C5	C7	C9
64 Semaphore, 1915-1921	21	35	70
00-64 Track Connection, 1939, curved, three-rail	5	8	10
65 Motorized Hand Car, O27 ga., 1962, yellow, two rubber men, small motorized unit, yellow or dark yellow	135	225	450
65 Semaphore, 1915-1926	30	45	60
65 Semaphore, 1915-1926	35	52	70
00-65 Track, OO ga., 1939, half-straight, three-rail	—	1	2
65 Whistle Controller, 1935	6	9	12
00-66 Straight, OO ga., 1939, straight, three-rail	—	1	2
66 Whistle and Reversing Controller, 1936	3	5	6
67 Lamp Post, 1915-1926	30	50	100
67 Whistle and Reversing Controller, 1936	4	5	7
68 Executive Inspection Car, 1958-1961, red DeSoto, small motorized unit	200	250	350
HO-068 Inspection Car, HO ga., 1961	30	50	100
68 Warning Signal, standard ga., 1926-1939, non-operative	7	11	14
0-68 Warning Signal, O ga., 1926-1942	7	11	14
69-7 Fiber Track Pins, 1933	—	—	1
69 Motorized Maintenance Car, O27 ga., 1960-1962, gray platform, black frame, w/blue man and red danger sign	175	240	310
69 Warning Bell, standard ga., 1921-1935	20	34	68
0-69 Warning Bell, O ga., 1921-1935	25	38	50
69N Warning Bell, standard/O ga., 1936-1942	25	38	50
00-70 90 Degree Crossing, OO ga., 1939, three-rail	8	11	15
70 Accessory Set, 1921, consists of two No. 62, one No. 68 and one No. 59	75	112	150

	C5	C7	C9
70 Lamp Post, 1949-1950, yard light	17	29	58
71 Lamp Post, 1949-1959, crackle gray	12	15	22
71 Telegraph Pole Set, 1921, set of six	54	90	180
071 Telegraph Poles, O ga., 1929, set of six	63	105	210
00-72-70 Bulb, O ga., 1939, 12 volt, yellow	—	—	1
00-72 Switches, OO ga., 1939, electric, three rail, pair	150	225	300
072 T-Rail, curved track, per section	—	2	3
00-74 Boxcar, OO ga., 1939, two-rail	22	38	75
75 Bulb, 1924, 12 volt	—	—	1
75 Lamp Set, 1961-1969, black plastic, set of two	17	26	35
75 Low Bridge Sign, 1921	35	52	70
00-75 Tank Car, OO ga., 1939, two-rail	21	35	70
76 Block Signal, standard ga., 1923	25	42	85
76 Boulevard Lights, 1959-1969, green plastic, set of three	9	12	24
76 Warning Bell and Shant, 1939-1942, red base, orange roof, black bell fastened to cross gate sign post, similar in appearance to forty-five gateman, no watch man bell inside shanty	95	143	190
0-77 Automatic Crossing Gate, O ga., 1923-1939	20	30	40
00-77 Caboose, OO ga., 1939, two-rail	28	48	95
77 Crossing Gate, standard ga., 1923-1939, automatic	35	52	70
77N Crossing Gate, standard/O ga., 1936-1939, automatic	25	38	50
78 Train Control Block Signal, standard ga., 1924, red base, orange base	40	60	80
0-78 Train Control Block Signal, O ga., 1924, red or orange base	45	68	90

	C5	C7	C9
79-23 Bulb, Bulb ga., 1939, 12 volt, red	—	—	1
79 Flashing Signal, 1928-1942, cream or aluminum	60	90	120
80/81 Race Car Set, 1912-1916, includes car, driver, eight sections of curve track	750	1125	1500
80N Semaphore	62	93	125
0-80 Semaphore, O ga., 1926-1935	50	75	100
80 Semaphore, standard ga., 1926-1935	75	112	150
00-81 KW Kit, OO ga., 1938, locomotive and tender, three-rail	600	900	1200
81 Rheostat, 1927	7	11	15
82 Train Control Semaphore, standard ga., 1927-1935, yellow and green	55	82	110
0-82 Train Control Semaphore, O ga., 1927-1935	60	90	120
82N Train Control Semaphore, standard/O ga., 1936-1942	92	138	185
83 Traffic Crossing Signal, red base 35-42	155	225	310
83 Traffic Crossing Signal, tan base 27-34	155	225	310
00-83 W Locomotive and Tender, OO ga., 1939-1942, three-rail	180	300	600
84 Racing Cars, 1912	2000	3000	4000
84 Semaphore, standard ga., 1927-1932	60	90	120
0-84 Semaphore, O ga., 1928-1932	60	90	120
85 Racing Cars, 1912	2000	3000	4000
85 Telegraph Pole, standard ga., 1929-1942, orange	15	22	30
86 Telegraph Poles, standard ga., 1932, set of six, including original box	82	138	185
87 Crossing Signal, 1927, orange or green base	105	158	210
88 Direction Controller, 1933	3	4	5
88 Rheostat, 1915, battery	7	11	15

	C5	C7	C9
89 Flag Pole, 1956-1958	22	33	45
89 Flagstaff and Flag, 1923-1934	50	75	100
90 Flagstaff and Flag, 1927-1942, w/round grass plot	25	38	50
91 Circuit, 1930-1942, automatic, breaker, brown w/red light bulb	38	56	75
91 Circuit Breaker, 1957-1960, brown w/red light	8	11	12
00-91 W Locomotive nad Tender, OO ga., 1939, two-rail	180	300	600
92 Circuit Breaker, 1959, w/controller	11	16	23
92 Floodlight Tower, 1931, red, silver	92	138	185
92 Floodlight Tower, 1931, terra-cotta, green	90	135	180
90-93 W Locomotive, OO ga., 1939, tender, two rail	180	300	600
93 Water Tower, O ga., 1932, silver	47	71	95
93 Water Tower, O ga., 1932, green	20	30	40
94 High Tension Tower, 1932, gray, terra-cotta, silver and red	200	300	400
95 Rheostat, 1934	12	18	25
96 Coal Elevator, 1938-1940, manual control	95	132	190
97 Coal Elevator, 1938-1942, 1946-1950, electric	125	188	250
97C Contactor, 1938	5	8	10
0-97 Telegraph Pole Set, O ga., 1934	25	38	50
0-99 Train Control Block, O ga., 1930	75	112	150
99 Train Control Block Signal, standard ga., 1932, red or black base	85	128	170
99N Train Control Block Signal, standard/O ga., 1936, red or black base	85	128	170

VERSATILE LIONEL HO POWER PACKS

No. 0103 800 milliamp Power Pack—Operates any Lionel HO train. One lever speed and direction control. Listed by UL. $7.95

No. 0104 "Multi-Volt" 2 Train Control 2½ Amp. D.C.-A.C. Power Pack — Supplies power for two separate train circuits. Each train is protected by it's own individual circuit breaker. A.C. power 16 volts with separate circuit breaker. D.C. circuits may be used with common ground. Listed by UL. $29.95

No. 0101 1¼ Amp. D.C., A.C. Power Pack — Has the best "regulation" characteristics of any power pack in its price range. Center-off sweep handle controls train speed and direction. D.C. voltage up to 12 volts under load. Maximum D.C. output of 1¼ amps. adequate for two motors. Has 16 volt A.C. output for operation of switches and accessories. Listed by UL. $10.95

No. 0100 "Multi-Volt" 2½ Amp. D.C., A.C. Power Pack — D.C. circuit has reversing switch, supplies 2½ amps, at 0-14 volts. A.C. circuit has self-resetting circuit breaker, supplies 2½ amps. at 16 volts. Listed by UL. $17.95

Top row, left to right: No. 103-800 Power Pack, $20; No. 104 Power pack, $20. Bottom row, left to right: No. 101 Power Pack, $20; No. 100 Power Pack, $20. Photo courtesy 1962 Lionel catalog.

	C5	C7	C9
100 Bridge Approaches, standard ga., 1920	20	30	40
100 Locomotive, 2-7/8" ga., 1901	100	2000	4200
HO-100 Power Pack, HO ga., 1961	10	15	20
100 Trolley, standard ga., 1910, motor car, blue or red, marked "100 Electric Rapid Transit 100"	600	1000	2000
HO-101 Power Pack, HO ga., 1961	10	15	20
101 Summer Trolley, standard ga., 1910, motor car, blue or red, manual, "101 Electric Rapid Transit 101"	600	1000	2000
101 Three Section Bridge, standard ga., 1920, cream and green	55	82	110
102 Bridge, standard ga., 1920, four section	35	52	70
103 Bridge, standard ga., 1913, five section	90	135	180
HO-103 Power Pack, HO ga., 1959	10	15	20
HO-103-800 Power Pack, HO ga., 1961	10	15	20

	C5	C7	C9
104 Bridge, standard ga., 1920, center span	15	22	30
HO-104 Power Pack, HO ga., 1961	10	15	20
104 Tunnel, standard ga., 1909-1914	50	75	100
105 Bridge, standard ga., 1911, five section	40	60	80
105 Bridge, standard ga., 1913, three section	25	38	50
105 Bridge Approaches, O ga., 1920	7	11	15
106 AC Current Reducer, 1911, 110 or 120 volts	3	4	5
106 Bridge, O ga., 1920, three section	25	38	50
107 DC Current Reducer, 1911, 220 volts	10	15	20
107 DC Current Reducer, 1911, 110 volts	10	15	20
108 Battery Rheostat, 1912	3	4	5
108 Bridge, O ga., 1920, four section	48	72	95
109 Bridge, O ga., 1920, five section	40	60	80
109 Tunnel, standard ga., 1913	50	75	100

	C5	C7	C9
110 Bridge, O ga., 1920, center span	15	22	30
110 Trestle Set, O ga., 1955-1969, twenty-four pieces	10	15	20
HO-110 Trestle Set, HO ga., 1958	10	15	20
111-100 2 Piers, O ga., 1960-1963, two pieces	10	15	20
111 Light Bulb Set, 1920	10	15	20
111 Trestle Set, O ga., 1956-1969, ten pieces	13	17	22
HO-111 Trestle Set, HO ga., 1959	10	15	20
111 Trolley, standard ga., 1910, trailer	600	1000	2000
112 Gondola, standard ga., 1910	135	225	450
112 Gondola, standard ga., 1913	24	40	80
112 Station, standard ga., 1931-1935, cream	162	243	325
112 Switch, Super O ga., 1957-1960, w/controls, pair	42	63	95
113 Cattle Car, standard ga., 1912-1926	33	55	110
113 Station, standard ga., 1931-1934, cream	275	362	550
114 Boxcar, standard ga., 1912	36	60	120
HO-114 Engine House, HO ga., 1958, w/horn	50	75	100
114 Newstand, O ga., 1957-1959, w/horn	52	78	120
114 Station, standard ga., 1931-1934, cream	750	1125	1500
HO-115 Kit, HO ga., 1961, engine house	35	52	70
115 Station, 1935, cream, red or green trim	215	322	450
115 Station, 1949, cream, red or green trim	155	200	310
116 Ballast, standard ga., 1910	54	90	180
116 Station, 1935, cream, double station	600	900	1200
117 Caboose, standard ga., 1912-1926	27	45	90
HO-117 Engine House, HO ga., 1959	45	68	90

No. 115 Station, $450.

	C5	C7	C9
117 Station, 1936-1942	175	262	350
117 Station, 1936-1942, no outside lights	175	262	350
HO-118 Engine House, HO ga., 1958, w/whistle	50	75	100
118 Newstand, O ga., 1958, w/whistle	42	63	90
118 Tunnel, O ga., 1915-1920	45	68	90
118L Tunnel, O ga., 1927, lighted	40	60	80
119 Tunnel, standard/O ga., 1915	40	60	80
119L Tunnel, standard/O ga., 1927, lighted	50	75	100
119 Tunnel, O ga., 1957	40	60	80
HO-119 Tunnel, HO ga., 1959	7	11	15
120 90 Degree Crossing, Super O ga., 1957	8	12	16
120 Tunnel, standard/O ga., 1915	62	93	125
120L Tunnel, standard/O ga., 1927, lighted	67	100	135
121 Special Station, standard ga., 1909	300	450	600
121x Station, standard ga., 1917, w/lights	300	450	600
121 Tunnel, O ga., 1959-1966	20	30	40
122 Station, standard ga., 1920	62	93	125
123 Station, standard ga., 1920	125	188	250

	C5	C7	C9
123 Tunnel, O ga., 1933, curved ...	90	135	180
124 Station, standard ga., 1920	250	375	500
124 Station, standard ga., 1933	137	207	275
125 Station, standard ga., 1923	30	45	60
125 Track Template, 1938..............	5	8	10
125 Whistle Station, 1950-1955, gray or green base....................	22	33	45
126 Station, standard ga., 1923-1936	135	202	270
127 Station, 1923-1936	117	175	235
128 Newsstand, 1957-1960, animated....................	85	127	220
128 Tunnel, O ga., 1920, lighted...	55	83	110
129 Station and Terrace, standard ga., 1929-1940	800	1200	1600
129 Terrace, standard ga., 1928	900	1350	1800
129 Tunnel, standard/O ga., 1920, lighted	70	105	140
130 60 Degrees Crossing, O ga., 1957	10	15	20
130 Tunnel, O ga., 1920	150	225	300
130L Tunnel, O ga., 1927, lighted	125	188	250
131 Corner Elevation, 1924-1928....	350	525	700
131 Tunnel, O ga., 1959-1966, curved	35	53	70
132 Grass Plot, 1924-1928, corner	200	300	400
132 Station, O ga., 1949-1955.......	45	55	105
133 Grass Plot, 1924-1928, heart shaped	200	300	400
133 Station, O ga., 1957-1966......	30	45	85
134 Grass Plot, 1924-1928, oval ...	200	300	400
134 Stop Station, 1937-1942, brown w/red roof	175	263	350
135 Grass Plot, 1924-1928, oval, small........................	200	300	400
136 Stop Station, 1937-1942, lighted	150	225	300
137 Stop Station, 1937-1942, lighted	112	168	225
138 Water Tank, 1953-1957, operating	75	80	145

	C5	C7	C9
140 Banjo Signal, O ga., 1954-1966....................................	25	38	50
HO-140 Banjo Signal, HO ga., 1962....................................	22	33	45
140L Tunnel, standard ga., 1927-1932, lighted	400	600	800
142 Switches, Super O ga., 1957, manual, price per pair	15	23	30
145 Automatic Gateman, O ga., 1950-1966	26	32	49
145C Contactor, O ga., 1950	6	9	12
HO-145 Gateman, HO ga., 1959, automatic........................	30	45	60
147 Whistle Controller, O ga., 1961........................	3	4	5
148-100 Double Pole Switch, 1957........................	4	6	8
148 Dwarf Signal, O ga., 1957	30	45	60
150 Locomotive, O ga., 1918-1925, electric, 0-4-0, dark green	60	100	200
HO-150 Rectifier, HO ga., 1958....	2	3	4
150 Telegraph Poles, O ga., 1947-1950, set of six	19	29	45
151-51 Bulb, 1950, 14 volt, clear........................	—	—	1
151 Semaphore, O ga., 1947-1969	22	35	46
152-33 Bulb, O ga., 1940, 12 volt, red	—	—	1
152 Crossing Gate, O ga., 1945-1948........................	21	32	42
152 Locomotive, O ga., 1917-1927, light gray	113	187	375
152 Locomotive, O ga., 1917-1927, peacock or mojave	135	225	450
152 Locomotive, O ga., 1917-1927, electric, dark gray or dark green........................	75	125	250
153 Block Signal, O ga., 1945-1969........................	22	34	45
153-23 Bulb, 1940, 6 volt, red.......	—	—	1
153-24 Bulb, 1940, 6 volt, green ...	—	—	1
153-48 Bulb, 1940, 14 volt green ..	—	—	1

	C5	C7	C9
153-50 Bulb, 1940, 14 volt, red.....	—	—	1
153C Contactor, O ga., 1940.........	5	8	10
153 Locomotive, O ga., 1924, electric, mojave........................	75	125	250
153 Locomotive, O ga., 1924, dark green	60	100	200
153 Locomotive, O ga., 1924, gray	60	100	200
154-18 Bulb, 1942, 12 volt, red.....	—	—	1
154C Contactor, O ga., 1940........	4	5	7
154 Highway Signal, O ga., 1940-1942	19	27	38
154 Locomotive, O ga., 1917-1923, 0-4-0, electric, dark green	75	125	250
155 Freight Shed, 1930-1939, 1940-1942, yellow base w/maroon roof	220	330	440
155 Freight Shed, 1930-1942, ivory base w/gray roof..............	175	263	350
155 Signal Light, 1955-1957, W.M. Bell	50	75	100
156-13 Bulb, 1939, 18 volt, clear..	—	—	1
156 Locomotive, O ga., 1917-1923, 4-4-4, electric, gray, olive and maroon	225	425	850
156X Locomotive, O ga., 1923-1924, without pilot trucks.........	300	500	1000
156 Station Platform, O ga., 1939-1940, 1946-1951	52	78	105
157 Hand Truck, standard ga., 1930-1932, red........................	15	25	50
157 Station Platform, O ga., 1952-1959	37	56	75
158 Locomotive, O ga., 1919-1923, 0-4-0, electric, black.......	135	225	450
158 Locomotive, O ga., 1919-1923, 0-4-0, electric, gray.........	120	200	400
158 Platform Set, 1940-1942, lighted, two 156 platforms and one 136 station, w/original box	165	275	550
159C Block Signal contractor, 1940	4	5	7
160 Unloading Bin, 1938	—	1	2
161 Baggage Truck, standard ga., 1930-1932, green	30	50	100

	C5	C7	C9
161 Mail Pickup Set, O ga., 1961-1963...........................	35	52	70
162 Dump Truck, standard ga., 1930-1932, red or gray..............	28	48	95
163 Block Signal, O ga., 1961-1963, single target....................	20	25	38
163 Freight Accessory, 1930, includes two 157 hand track, one 161 baggage car and one dump bin, w/original box	145	217	290
164-64 Logs, 1952, set of five	—	—	5
164 Lumber Loader, 1940-1942, 1946-1950	102	170	340
165-53 Bulb, 1940, 18 volt, red.....	—	—	1
165C Controller, 1940	32	48	65
165 Magnetic Crane, 1940-1942 ...	75	125	250
166 Controller, 1938, three button	3	4	5
167 Whistle and Reverse Controller, O ga., 1945	5	8	10
167X Whistle Controller, OO ga., 1940..........................	3	4	5
168 Controller, 1940	3	4	5
169 Uncoupling and Reversing Controller, 1940	—	2	3
170 DC Current Reducer, 1914, 220 volts....................	5	8	10
171 Inverter, 1936, DC to AC	5	8	10
172 Inverter, 1937, DC to AC, 220 volts..........................	5	8	10
175-50 Extra Rockets, O ga., 1958............................	10	15	20
175 Rocket Launcher, O ga., 1958-1960	105	150	300
180 Pullman, standard ga., 1911, maroon, brown and orange	50	85	170
180 Trailer Truck, standard ga., 1915..........................	600	1000	2000
HO-181 Cab Control, HO ga., 1958..........................	7	13	25
181 Combine, standard ga., 1911, maroon, brown and orange	60	100	200
182 Magnet Crane, 1946-1949, w/165C controller	110	150	255

	C5	C7	C9
182 Observation Car, standard ga., 1911, maroon, brown and orange	66	110	220
184 Bungalow, 1923, lighted	45	68	90
185 Bungalow, 1923, no lights	40	60	80
186 Bungalow Set, 1923, set of five	300	450	600
186 Log Loading Outfit, 1940, log loader, car, bin and uncoupler	120	200	400
187 Bungalow Set, 1923, set of five	300	450	600
188 Coal Elevator Outfit, 1938	120	200	400
189 Villa, 1923, lighted	162	243	325
190 Observation Car, standard ga., 1907-1927	180	300	600
190 Observation Car, standard ga., 1907-1927	300	500	1000
190 Observation Car, standard ga., 1907-1927	300	500	1000
191 Villa, 1923, lighted	145	217	290
192 Railroad Control Tower, 1959-1960	90	135	200

	C5	C7	C9
193 Automatic Accessory Set, O ga., 1927-1929, includes one #69, one #76, one #78, one #77, one #80	175	263	350
193 Water Tower, 1953-1955	62	93	125
194 Automatic Accessory Set, standard ga., 1927-1929, includes one #69, one #76, one #78, one #77, one #80	175	263	350
195 Floodlight Tower, 1957-1969.	30	45	60
195-75 Spare Tower Head, 1957, add lights and holder for #195 floodlight tower	10	15	25
195 Terrace, standard ga., 1927, includes one #191 villa, one #189 villa, one #184 bungalow, one #90 flagpole, two #56 lamp posts	600	900	1200
196 Accessory Set, standard/O ga., 1927, Includes #127 station, six #60 telegraph poles, #62 semaphore, #68 warning signal, two #58 lamp posts, w/original box	150	225	300
196 Smoke Pellets, 1946, 100 pellets in bottle/package, price for complete package	15	25	38

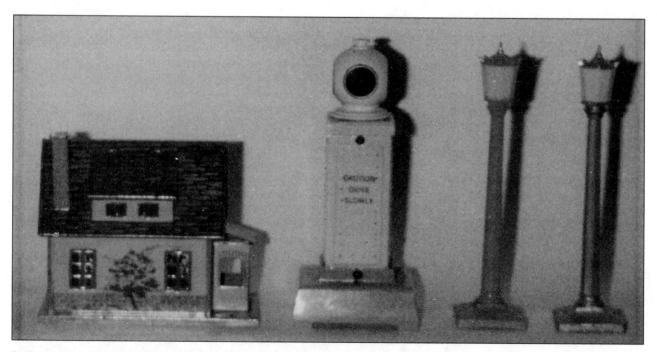

Left to right: No. 184 Bungalow, $90; No. 78 Train Control Block Signal, $80; Two versions of the No. 35 Lamp post, $80, each.

No. 203 Locomotive, $2,300.

	C5	C7	C9
197 Radar Antenna, O ga., 1957-1959, gray w/gray base	30	53	105
HO-197 Radar Antenna, HO ga., 1958	20	30	40
197-75 Replacement Radar Head, 1958	9	15	30
199 Microwave Tower, 1958-1959	37	56	75
199 Scenic Railway Set, standard ga., 1924	120	200	400
200 Gondola, 2-7/8" ga., motorized, auctioned in 1994 in Good to Very Good condition	1000	1500	300
200 Trolley, standard ga., 1910, trailer, non-powered	1200	2000	4000
200 Turntable, standard ga., 1928, green and tan	175	263	350
201 Locomotive, O ga., 1940, 0-6-0, steam, switcher, w/2201 Tender, no bell	210	350	700
201 Locomotive, O ga., 1940, 0-6-0, steam, switcher, w/2201 B bell tender	280	475	950
202 Locomotive, O27 ga., 1957, UP Alco A diesel, orange w/black lettering	30	50	100
202 Summer Trolley, standard ga., 1910, motor car, marked "202 Electric Rapid Transit 202"	900	1500	3000
203 Locomotive, O ga., 1917, 0-4-0, armored, cannon, prewar, oriented locomotive	690	1150	2300
203 Locomotive, O ga., 1940, steam, switcher, 0-6-0, no bell, similar to 201	225	375	750

	C5	C7	C9
204 Locomotive, O ga., 1940-1941, 2-4-2, steam, black, uncataloged	43	72	145
204 Locomotive, O ga., 1940-1941, 2-4-2, steam, gunmetal gray, uncataloged	67	113	225
204 Locomotive, O27 ga., 1957, A.T.S.F., Alco AA, diesel	75	109	150
205 L.C.L. Merchandise Containers, standard ga., 1930-1938, dark green, each	75	112	150
205 Locomotive, O27 ga., 1957, M.P., Alco AA, diesel	75	120	170
208 Locomotive, O27 ga., 1958, A.T.S.F., Alco diesel AA	78	100	165
208 Tool Set, 1934-1942, gray box, includes tools, sledge hammer, pick, rake, shovel and ax	60	90	120
208 Tool Set, 1934-1942, silver box, includes tools, sledge hammer, pick, rake, shovel and ax	50	75	100
0-209 Barrels, O ga., 1934-1942, wooden, set of six	17	26	35
209 Barrels, standard ga., 1934-1942, wooden, set of four	10	15	20
209 Locomotive, O27 ga., 1958, N.H., Alco AA, diesel, two units	270	450	900
210 Locomotive, O27 ga., 1958, Texas Spec. Alco diesel AA	110	160	210
210 Switch, standard ga., 1926, automatic, pair	15	22	30

No. 217 Caboose, $230.

	C5	C7	C9
211 Flatcar, standard ga., 1926-1940, w/wooden load...............	34	57	115
211 Locomotive, O27 ga., 1962, Texas Spec. Alco AA, diesel....	80	130	180
212 Gondola, standard ga., 1926-1940, green and maroon	45	75	150
212 Gondola, standard ga., 1926-1940, gray	60	100	200
212 Locomotive, O27 ga., 1958, Alco diesel A, Marine..............	90	150	300
212 Locomotive, O27 ga., 1964, A.T.S.F. Alco diesel AA..........	78	100	150
213 Cattle Car, standard ga., 1926-1940, cream body w/maroon roof.............................	300	450	600
213 Cattle Car, standard ga., 1926-1940, mojave body w/maroon roof.............................	200	300	400
213 Cattle Car, standard ga., 1926-1940, terra-cotta, orange body w/pea green roof	100	200	300
213 Locomotive, O27 ga., 1964, M&StL Alco AA, diesel..........	75	125	175
214 Boxcar, standard ga., 1926-1940, terra-cotta, orange body w/green roof............................	200	300	400
214 Boxcar, standard ga., 1926-1940, cream body w/orange roof...............................	100	200	300

	C5	C7	C9
214 Boxcar, standard ga., 1926-1940, yellow body w/brown roof...............................	300	400	500
214 Girder Bridge, HO ga., 1953-1969, light or dark gray............	10	20	30
HO-214 Girder Bridge, HO ga., 1958.................................	5	10	15
214R Refrigerator Car, standard ga., 1929-1940, ivory body w/peacock roof.........................	300	400	500
214R Refrigerator Car, standard ga., 1929-1940, white body w/light blue roof......................	500	750	1000
215 Tank Car, standard ga., 1926-1940, pea green	75	125	150
215 Tank Car, standard ga., 1926-1940, ivory, Sunoco decal.........	100	200	300
215 Tank Car, standard ga., 1926-1940, silver, Sunoco decal	200	350	500
216 Hopper Car, standard ga., 1926-1940, dark green	100	200	300
216 Locomotive, O27 ga., Minneapolis & St. Louis, Alco diesel A	75	100	140
216 Locomotive, O27 ga., 1958, Burlington Alco A, diesel	100	200	310
217 Caboose, standard ga., 1926-1940, red and peacock..............	69	115	230
217 Caboose, standard ga., 1926-1940, orange and maroon	90	150	300

LIONEL'S EXCITING ARRAY OF TOP-ACTION

No. 220

SANTA FE

No. 68

44 U. S. ARMY

No. 44

No. 50

50

No. 58

No. 69 Motorized Maintenance Car — A delight to watch! When bumper or other object is struck car reverses direction and flag rotates to read "Danger". Upon striking opposite bumper, car again reverses direction and flag rotates 180° to read "Safety First". Action is continuous. Car 6" long. **$9.95**

No. 50 Section Gang Car — Entertaining and self propelling! When car strikes a bumper or other object, it reverses direction and one of the gangmen moves to the other side of car. Car 6" long. **$7.95**

No. 58 Great Northern Rotary Snow Plow — On the job when snow drifts pile up! Snow plow on the front of the loco actually rotates. This mighty diesel has a rear coupler for adding extra rolling stock. Accurate detailing. Loco 8⅞" long. **$12.95**

No. 52 Fire Fighting Car — Self-propelled with illuminated red "warning" light on top. When car hits bumper, fireman swivels and direction is reversed. Hoses with sprinklers can be extended. Car 7" long. **$12.95**

No. 44 U.S. Army Mobile Missile Launcher with Magne-Traction — As launcher passes over remote control track, missiles can be fired one by one. Missiles can "explode" Exploding Target Range Car and Exploding Ammo Dump. Complete with U.S. Army markings and rear coupler. Launcher 12½" long. **$19.95**

LIONEL STEAM AND DIESEL LOCOMOTIVES

NEW! No. 229 Minneapolis and St. Louis Diesel with Headlight, Magne-Traction and Real Sounding Horn — Loco measures 10¾" long. Appears with outfit No. 1645, page 26-27 **$25.00**

NEW! No. 233 LTS Steam Loco and Tender with Headlight, Magne-Traction, Real Smoke and Authentic Sounding Whistle — Loco and tender measure 17½" long. Appears with outfit No. 1646, page 26-27 **$29.95**

NEW! No. 231 Rock Island Diesel with Headlight and Exclusive Magne-Traction — Diesel unit measures 10¾" long. Appears with outfit No. 1810 "Space Age" Gift Pack, page 32. **$19.95**

No. 218 Santa Fe "AA" Diesel with Headlight, Magne-Traction and Real Sounding Diesel Horn — Units measure 22" long. Appears with outfit No. 1651 page 32-33. **$32.50**

NEW! No. 616 Santa Fe Diesel Switcher with Headlight, Magne-Traction and Authentic Sounding Diesel Horn — Loco measures 12¼" long. Appears with outfit No. 2570, page 36-37. **$27.50**

No. 1872 LT "General" Loco and Tender with Real Smoke, Headlight and Magne-Traction — Loco and tender measure 15¼" long. Appears with outfit No. 2528 WS, page 36-37. **$27.50**

48

Lionel's 1961 catalog shows a wide array of locomotives and motorized cars.

	C5	C7	C9
217 Lighting Set, standard ga., 1914, for cars, eight volts	30	50	100
217 Locomotive, O27 ga., 1959, B&M Alco AB, diesel	75	100	185
218 Dump Car, standard ga., 1926-1940, mojave	78	130	260
218 Locomotive, O27 ga., 1959, A.T.S.F. Alco AA, diesel..........	70	100	185
218C Locomotive, O27 ga., 1961, A.T.S.F. Alco B, diesel............	40	50	80
218 Locomotive, O27 ga., 1961, A.T.S.F. Alco AB, diesel..........	70	100	170
219 Crane, standard ga., 1926, peacock cab..............................	72	120	240
219 Crane, standard ga., 1926, yellow cab................................	115	192	385
219 Crane, standard ga., 1926, white, ivory cab	135	225	450
220 Floodlight, standard ga., 1931, terra-cotta base.........................	75	125	250
220 Floodlight, standard ga., 1931, green base	120	200	400
220 Locomotive, O27 ga., 1961, A.T.S.F. Alco A, diesel	75	100	135
221 Locomotive, O27 ga., 1946, steam, gray..............................	48	80	160
221 Locomotive, 1946, steam, black..	60	100	200
221 Locomotive, O27 ga., 1963, D&RGW Alco A, diesel...........	36	60	120
221 Locomotive, O27 ga., 1963, A.T.S.F. Alco A, diesel, uncataloged.............................	175	250	420
221 Locomotive, O27 ga., 1963, Alco A, diesel, Marine, uncataloged.............................	124	207	415
HO-222 Deck Bridge, HO ga., 1961	10	15	20
222 Switches, standard ga., 1926, price per pair............................	30	45	60
223-50 Locomotive, O27 ga., 1963, A.B.A.T.S.F. Alco, diesel.......................................	85	125	185
223 Switches, standard ga., 1932, non-derailing, price per pair	46	78	155

	C5	C7	C9
HO-224 Girder Bridge, HO ga., 1961..	7	11	14
224/224E Locomotive, 1938-1942, 2-6-2, steam, gunmetal gray, w/2689 sheetmetal tender	66	110	220
224/224E Locomotive, 1938-1942, 2-6-2, steam, black w/2224 die-cast tender	54	90	180
224/224E Locomotive, 1938-1942, 2-6-2, steam, black w/plastic tender	43	72	145
224/224E Locomotive, 1938-1942, 2-6-2, steam, gunmetal gray w/2224 die-cast tender	110	183	365
224 Locomotive, 1943, steam, paper train, w/original box, uncataloged	100	150	200
224 Locomotive, O27 ga., 1960, Alco AB, diesel, Navy	100	150	200
224 Paper Train Set, includes: #224 locomotive, #2224 tender, #2812 red gondola, #61100 yellow boxcar w/brown roof, #47618 red caboose, crossing signal, crossing gate, three figures, baggage car, paper track..	300	450	600
225/225 E Locomotive, O ga., 1939-1940, 2-6-2, steam, black, w/2235, 2265, 2225 or 2245 tenders	114	190	380
225/225 E Locomotive, O ga., 1939-1940, 2-6-2, steam, gunmetal gray...........................	105	175	350
225 Locomotive, O27 ga., 1960, C&O Alco A, diesel.................	65	100	120
226E Locomotive, O ga., 1938-1941, 2-6-4, steam, w/2226 tender......................................	150	250	500
HO-226 Truss Bridge, HO ga., 1961..	7	11	14
227 Locomotive, O ga., 1939, 0-6-0, steam, switcher scale, w/tender 2227T, marked "8976" under cab window, no bell..	375	625	1250
227 Locomotive, O ga., 1939, w/tender 2227B bell..................	378	630	1260

Top row, left to right: No. 217 Caboose, $230; No. 219 Crane, $240. Middle row, left to right: No. 212 Gondola, $200; No. 220 Floodlight, $400. Bottom row, left to right: No. 400E Locomotive with tender, $2,250.

Top of page: No. 218 Locomotive, $170. Bottom of page: Space Age Gift Page, includes a No. 231 Locomotive, $2,000; No. 3665 Minuteman Missile car, $115; No. 3820 Submarine car, $400; No. 3665 Minuteman Missile car, $115; No. 6017 Caboose, $60. Photo courtesy 1961 Lionel catalog.

	C5	C7	C9
227 Locomotive, O27 ga., 1960, C.N. Alco A, diesel, Canadian market distribution, uncataloged	78	100	160
228 Locomotive, O ga., 1939, 0-6-0, steam, switcher scale, similar to 227, w/228T tender, no bell	318	530	1060
228 Locomotive, O ga., 1939, 0-6-0, steam, w/2228B tender, w/bell	480	800	1600
228 Locomotive, O27 ga., 1961, C.N. Alco A, diesel, Canadian market distribution, uncataloged	70	100	150
229/229E Locomotive, O ga., 1939, 2-4-2, steam, black	48	80	160
229/229E Locomotive, O ga., 1939, steam, gunmetal gray	30	50	100
229 Locomotive, O27 ga., 1961, M&StL Alco A, diesel	60	90	120
229P Locomotive, O27 ga., 1962, M&StL Alco A, diesel	90	90	120
229C Locomotive, O27 ga., 1962, M&StL Alco B, diesel	27	45	90
230 Locomotive, 1939, 0-6-0, steam, switcher scale	600	1000	2000
230 Locomotive, O27 ga., 1961, C&O Alco A, diesel	55	80	105
231 Locomotive, O ga., 1939, 0-6-0, steam, switcher scale	600	1000	2000
231 Locomotive, O27 ga., 1961, R.I. Alco A, diesel	50	75	100
232 Locomotive, O ga., 1940, 0-6-0, steam, switcher scale	465	775	1550
232 Locomotive, O27 ga., 1962, N.H. Alco A, diesel	65	109	130
233 Locomotive, O ga., 1940, 0-6-0, steam, switcher scale	600	1000	2000
233 Locomotive, O27 ga., 1961, 2-4-2, steam, w/233W tender	50	85	105
235 Locomotive, O27 ga., 1962, 2-4-2, steam, uncataloged	80	125	160
236 Locomotive, O27 ga., 1961, 2-4-2, steam	18	30	60
237 Locomotive, O27 ga., 1963, steam	25	35	60

	C5	C7	C9
238 or E Locomotive, O ga., 1936-1940, P.R.R., steam, black or gunmetal gray, torpedo-type, w/222T, 2225W or 265W tender	113	188	375
238 Locomotive, O27 ga., 1963, steam 2-4-2	75	125	150
239 Locomotive, O27 ga., 1965, steam, 2-4-2	65	90	140
241 Locomotive, O27 ga., 1963, 2-4-2, steam, uncataloged	75	125	165
242 Locomotive, O27 ga., 1962, steam, 2-4-2	20	40	60
243 Locomotive, O27 ga., 1960, 2-4-2, steam	70	100	150
244 Locomotive, O27 ga., 1960, 2-4-2, steam	25	30	40
HO-245-200 Contactor, HO ga., 1960	4	5	7
245 Locomotive, O27 ga., 1959, 2-4-2, steam	125	175	300
246 Locomotive, O27 ga., 1959, 2-4-2, steam	25	35	45
247 Locomotive, O27 ga., 1959, 2-4-2, B&O, steam	30	35	65
248 Locomotive, O ga., 1926-1932, electric, red, orange, dark green and olive	49	83	165

No. 248 Locomotive, $165.

	C5	C7	C9
249 or E Locomotive, O ga., 1936, steam, gunmetal gray	80	133	265
249 or E Locomotive, O ga., 1936, steam, black	120	200	400
249 Locomotive, O27 ga., 1958, 2-4-2, P.R.R., steam	20	30	50

Top to bottom: No. 229 Locomotive, $120; No. 233LTS, $105. Photo courtesy 1961 Lionel catalog.

Top to bottom: No. 230 Locomotive, $105; No. 1862LT Locomotive, $225. Photo courtesy 1961 Lionel catalog.

Top to bottom: No. 246 Locomotive, $40; No. 244 Locomotive, $40. Photo courtesy 1961 Lionel catalog.

	C5	C7	C9
250 Locomotive, O ga., 1926, 0-4-0, N.Y.C., electric, dark green, peacock and orange	90	150	300
250 Locomotive, O ga., 1934, electric, 0-4-0, orange and terra-cotta, uncataloged	60	100	200
250E Locomotive, O ga., 1935, Hiawatha, steam, w/250W, 250WX or 2250W tenders	450	750	1500
250 Locomotive, O27 ga., 1957, 2-4-2, P.R.R., steam	21	35	70
251 Locomotive, O ga., 1925, 0-4-0, NYC, electric, box cab, gray or red cabs	100	168	335

No. 250E Locomotive, Hiawatha, $1,500.

	C5	C7	C9
251E Locomotive, O ga., 1927, 0-4-0, NYC, electric, box cab, gray or red cabs	100	168	335
252 Crossing Gate, O ga., 1950-1962	20	30	40
HO-252 Crossing Gate, HO ga., 1959	20	30	40

No. 252 Locomotive, 0-4-0, $200.

	C5	C7	C9
252 Locomotive, O ga., 1926, 0-4-0, NYC, electric, maroon, Macy's Special	120	200	400
252 Locomotive, O ga., 1926, 0-4-0, NYC, electric, peacock, olive and dark green	60	100	200

	C5	C7	C9
252 Locomotive, O ga., 1926, 0-4-0, NYC, electric, terra-cotta and orange	75	125	250
252E Locomotive, O ga., 1933-1935, 0-4-0, electric, terra-cotta or orange	84	140	280
253 Automatic Block Sign Signal, O ga., 1956	30	45	60
253 Locomotive, O ga., 1924, 0-4-0, electric, terra-cotta	120	200	400
253 Locomotive, O ga., 1924, 0-4-0, electric, maroon	150	250	500
253 Locomotive, O ga., 1924, 0-4-0, electric, peacock, mojave and dark green	60	100	200
253 Locomotive, O ga., 1924, 0-4-0, electric, red	135	225	450
253E Locomotive, O ga., 1931, 0-4-0, electric, green	125	213	425
253E Locomotive, O ga., 1931, 0-4-0, electric, terra-cotta	120	200	400
254 Locomotive, O ga., 1924, 0-4-0, electric, mojave, olive, dark and pea green	83	138	275
254 Locomotive, O ga., 1924, 0-4-0, electric, apple green	120	200	400
254 Locomotive, O ga., 1924, 0-4-0, electric, red	150	250	500
254E Locomotive, O ga., 1927, 0-4-0, electric, apple green	90	150	300
254E Locomotive, O ga., 1927, 0-4-0, electric, olive green	60	100	200
255E Locomotive, O ga., 1935, 2-4-2, steam, gunmetal gray w/263W tender	300	525	1050
256 Freight Shed, 1950-1953	27	41	55
256 Locomotive, O ga., 1924-1930, electric, orange, rubber-stamped "Lionel"	150	250	500

No. 256 Locomotive, $500.

	C5	C7	C9
256 Locomotive, O ga., 1924-1930, electric, orange, marked "Lionel"	210	350	700
257 Freight Station, 1956-1957, w/horn	32	45	82
257 Locomotive, O ga., 1930, 0-4-0, steam, w/257T or 259T tender	90	150	300
258 Locomotive, O ga., 1930, 2-4-0, steam	75	125	250
258 Locomotive, O ga., 1941, 2-4-2, steam, w/1689T tender, uncataloged	48	80	160
259 Locomotive, O ga., 1932, 2-4-2, steam	54	90	180
259E Locomotive, O ga., 1933, steam, gunmetal gray	48	80	160
259E Locomotive, O ga., 1933, steam, black	34	73	115
260 Bumper, O ga., 1952	10	15	20
260E Locomotive, O ga., 1930, steam, black, w/260T tender	150	250	500
260E Locomotive, O ga., 1930, steam, gunmetal gray, w/263 tender	180	300	600
261 Locomotive, O ga., 1931, 2-4-2, steam, w/257T tender	75	125	250
261E Locomotive, O ga., 1935, steam, w/261T tender	84	140	280
262 Crossing Gate, O ga., 1962	21	32	42
262 Locomotive, O ga., 1931, 2-4-2, steam, w/262T tender	90	150	300
262E Locomotive, O ga., 1933, 2-4-2, steam, w/262T or 265T tender	84	140	280
263E Locomotive, O ga., 1936, 2-4-2, steam, gunmetal gray	255	425	850

	C5	C7	C9
263E Locomotive, O ga., 1936, 2-4-2, steam, Blue Comet, blue	240	400	800
264-150 Boards, 1957, set of twelve	6	8	10
264E Locomotive, O ga., 1935, 2-4-2, Red Comet, steam, streamlined, red	225	375	750
264E Locomotive, O ga., 1935, 2-4-2, steam, streamlined, black	120	200	400
264 Operating Forklift Platform Assembly	85	142	285
265E Locomotive, O ga., 1935, 2-4-2, steam, streamlined, black	87	145	290
265E Locomotive, O ga., 1935, steam 2-4-2, streamlined, gunmetal gray	105	175	350
265E Locomotive, O ga., 1935, 2-4-2, steam, Blue Streak, streamlined, blue	180	300	600
270 Bridge, O ga., 1931, maroon or red	52	78	105
270 Lighting Set, standard ga., 1915, for two cars, 3-1/2 volt	40	60	80
271 Bridge, O ga., 1931, two span	30	45	60
272 Bridge, O ga., 1931, three span	60	90	120
280 Bridge, standard ga., 1931	45	68	90
281 Bridge, standard ga., 1931, two span	45	68	90
282 Bridge, standard ga., 1931, three span	50	75	100
282 Gantry Crane, O ga., 1954	72	120	240
289E Locomotive, O ga., 1937, 2-4-2, steam, streamlined, black, 1689 tender	52	88	175
289E Locomotive, O ga., 1937, 2-4-2, steam, streamlined, 1689 tender, gunmetal gray	45	75	150
299 Code Transmitter Set, 1961-1963	65	80	145
300 Bridge, standard/O ga., 1928, ivory, green, orange base, marked "Hellgate"	925	1390	1850

Front: No. 264E Locomotive, 2-4-2, Red Comet, $750. Back: No. 263E Locomotive, 2-4-2, Blue Comet, $800.

	C5	C7	C9
300 Bridge, standard/O ga., 1928, white, silver and red base, marked "Hellgate," largest single span bridge Lionel ever made	810	1350	2700
HO-300 Lumber Car, HO ga., 1960, operating	8	14	28
300 Trolley, standard ga., 1901, marked "City Hall Park 175"	2100	3500	7000
300 Trolley, standard ga., 1910, trailer, powered	1080	1800	3600
HO-301-16 Cargo Bin, HO ga., 1960	4	5	7
HO-301 Dump Car, HO ga., 1960, operating	12	20	40
303 Summer Trolley, standard ga., 1910, motorcar, marked "303 Electric Rapid Transit 303"	1230	2050	4100
308 Metal Sign Set, O ga., 1945-1949, five piece	13	20	28
309 Plastic Sign Set, 1950-1959, nine piece	12	19	28
309 Pullman, standard ga., 1926, blue, apple green, pea green, maroon, light brown, mojave	43	73	145
309 Trolley, standard ga., 1901	1500	2000	4250
310 Baggage Car, standard ga., 1924-1929, blue, apple green, pea green, maroon, light brown, mojave	40	68	135
310 Baggage Car, standard ga., 1926, blue, apple green, pea green, maroon, light brown, mojave	54	70	140
310R Billboard, O ga., 1963, racing	15	22	30
310 Billboard Set, O ga., 1950-1968, billboard and five different inserts	15	22	30
310 Track, standard ga., 1903	5	8	10
312 Observation Car, standard ga., 1926, blue, apple green, pea green, maroon, light brown, mojave	54	70	140
313 Bascule Bridge, O ga., 1940-1942, gray	312	468	625
313 Bascule Bridge, 1946-1949, silver	240	375	550

	C5	C7	C9
314 Girder Bridge, O ga., 1946-1950, gray	23	34	45
315-20 Bulb, 1940, 12 volt, clear	—	—	1
315 Trestle, O ga., 1946-1947, bridge, illuminated silver	100	175	250
317 Trestle Bridge, gray	35	52	70
318 Locomotive, standard ga., 1924, 0-4-0, electric, mojave, pea green, gray	110	185	370
318 Locomotive, standard ga., 1924, 0-4-0, electric, state brown	140	238	475
318E Locomotive, standard ga., 1926, 0-4-0, electric, pea green, mojave, gray	100	170	340
318E Locomotive, standard ga., 1926, 0-4-0, electric, state brown	180	300	600
318E Locomotive, standard ga., 1926, 0-4-0, electric, black	240	400	800
HO-319 Helicopter Car, HO ga., 1960, operating	16	27	55
319 Pullman, standard ga., 1924	54	85	170
320 Baggage Car, standard ga., 1925	60	100	200
320 Switch, standard ga., 1903	20	30	40
321 Trestle Bridge, O ga., 1958	15	22	30

No. 322 Observation Car, $190.

	C5	C7	C9
322 Observation Car, standard ga., 1924	57	95	190
330 90 Degrees Crossing, standard ga., 1903	10	15	20
332 Arch Bridge, O ga., 1959-1966, gray	20	30	46

Top row, left to right: No 341 Observation car, $90; No. 339 Pullman car, $90. Bottom row, left to right: No. 10E Locomotive, $275; No. 332 Baggage car, $95.

	C5	C7	C9
332 Baggage Car, standard ga., 1926, gray, red, peacock, olive	28	48	95
332 Baggage Car, standard ga., 1926, beige body w/maroon roof	90	150	300
332 Macy Baggage Car, standard ga., 1930, uncataloged	60	100	200
334 Operating Dispatching Board, O ga., 1957-1960	100	150	250
HO-337 Giraffe Car, HO ga., 1961, operating	15	25	50
337 Macy Pullman, standard ga., 1930, red, uncataloged	60	100	200
337 Pullman, standard ga., 1925, pea green, olive, red, mojave	40	65	130
338 Macy Observation Car, standard ga., 1930, uncataloged	60	100	200
338 Observation Car, standard ga., 1925, pea green, olive, red, mojave	33	55	110

	C5	C7	C9
339 Macy Pullman, standard ga., 1930, red, uncataloged	60	100	200
339 Pullman, standard ga., 1925, peacock, brown, gray	27	45	90
339 Pullman, standard ga., 1925, beige body, maroon roof	90	150	300
340 Bridge, standard ga., 1903	175	262	350
341 Macy Observation Car, standard ga., 1930, red, uncataloged	60	100	200
341 Observation Car, standard ga., 1925, peacock, brown, gray	27	45	90
341 Observation Car, standard ga., 1925, beige body, maroon roof	90	150	300
342 Culvert Loader, O ga., 1956-1958	115	150	285
345 Automatic Culvert Unloader, O ga., 1957	165	190	365
348 Manual Culvert Unloader, O ga., 1966	70	100	185

	C5	C7	C9
HO-349 Turbo Missile Firing Car, HO ga.	30	50	100
350 Bumper, standard ga., 1903	25	38	50
350 Transfer Table, O ga., 1957-1960	155	200	350
350-50 Transfer Table Extension, O ga., 1957-1960	53	88	175
352-55 Ice Blocks, O ga., 1955, set of seven	10	15	20
352 Ice Depot, O ga., 1955-1957, red or brown base	120	160	260
353 Trackside Signal, O ga., 1960-1961	14	25	40
356-25 Baggage Truck, O ga., 1952, set of two	9	14	18
356 Freight Station, O ga., 1952-1957, w/green and orange carts	50	75	110
HO-357 Cop and Hobo Car, HO ga., 1962	12	20	40
362 Barrel Loader, O ga., 1952-1957	39	65	130
362-78 Barrels, O ga., 1952, set of six	7	11	15
364 Lumber Loader, O ga., 1948-1967, smooth or crackle gray	85	100	125
364C On-Off Switch, 1959	—	—	15
365 Dispatching Station, O ga., 1958-1959	70	105	140
HO-365 Missile Launching Car, HO ga., 1962	12	20	40
HO-366 Milk Car, HO ga., 1961, operating	18	30	60
HO-370 Sheriff and Outlaw Car, HO ga., 1962	12	20	40
375 Turntable, O ga., 1962-1964, motorized	120	185	245
380 Elevated Pillars, standard ga., 1903, each	30	45	60
380 Locomotive, standard ga., 1923, 0-4-0, electric, maroon	192	320	640
380 Locomotive, standard ga., 1923, 0-4-0, electric, mojave, dark green	180	300	600
380E Locomotive, standard ga., 1926, 0-4-0, electric, maroon	180	300	600

No 380E Locomotive 0-4-0, electric, $600.

	C5	C7	C9
380E Locomotive, standard ga., 1926, 0-4-0, electric, mojave or dark green	180	300	600
381 Locomotive, standard ga., 1928, 4-4-4, electric, green body	1200	2000	4000
381E Locomotive, standard ga., 1928, 4-4-4, electric, green body and frame	1260	2100	4200

No. 381E Locomotive, 4-4-4, electric, $4,200.

	C5	C7	C9
381U Locomotive, standard ga., 1928, electric, kit includes tools, track and original box	2300	3450	4600
384E Locomotive, standard ga., 1930, 2-4-0, steam, w/384T tender	175	293	585
384 Locomotive, standard ga., 1930, 2-4-0, steam, w/384T tender	180	300	600

No. 384 Locomotive, $600.

	C5	C7	C9
385E Locomotive, standard ga., 1933, 2-4-2, steam, gunmetal gray w/384T, 385T, 385TW or 385W tender	295	490	980
390C Control Switch, O ga., 1960	3	6	9
390E Locomotive, two-tone green	540	900	1800
390E Locomotive, standard ga., 1929, steam, black, w/tender 390T	300	500	1000
390 Locomotive, standard ga., 1929, 2-4-2, steam, w/390T, black	250	420	840
390E Locomotive, standard ga., 1930, two-tone blue, w/tender	420	700	1400
392E Locomotive, standard ga., 1932, 4-4-2, steam, gunmetal gray	495	825	1650
392E Locomotive, standard ga., 1932, 4-4-2, steam, black	380	630	1260
394-37 Beacon Cap, 1953	5	10	15
394-10 Bulb, 1951, 14 volt, clear	—	—	1
394 Rotary Beacon, 1949-1953, aluminum, red or green tower frame	22	33	45
395 Floodlight Tower, 1949-1956, four lights, silver tower	25	35	55
395 Floodlight Tower, 1949-1956, four lights, green tower	32	48	65
395 Floodlight Tower, 1949-1956, four lights, yellow tower	48	80	160
395 Floodlight Tower, 1949-1956, four lights, red tower	50	75	85
397 Diesel Type Coal Loader, 1948-1957, later model, blue diesel motor cover	90	100	165
397 Diesel Type Coal Loader, 1948-1957, yellow diesel motor cover	120	200	400
400 Budd RDC Car, O ga., 1956-1958, powered	125	150	270
400 Gondola, 2-7/8" ga., 1901, trailer	720	1200	2400
400E Locomotive, standard ga., 4-4-4 , steam, w/400T tender, black	675	1125	2250

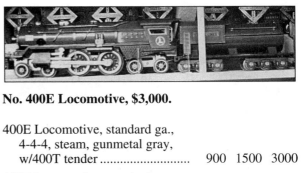

No. 400E Locomotive, $3,000.

	C5	C7	C9
400E Locomotive, standard ga., 4-4-4, steam, gunmetal gray, w/400T tender	900	1500	3000
400E Locomotive, standard ga., 4-4-4, steam, w/400T tender, blue	855	1425	2850
402 Locomotive, standard ga., 1923, 0-4-4-0, electric, mojave	200	330	660
402E Locomotive, standard ga., 1926, 0-4-4-0, electric, mojave	180	300	600

No. 402E Locomotive 0-4-4-0, $600.

	C5	C7	C9
404 Budd RDC Baggage Car, O ga., 1957-1958, powered	165	200	370
404 Summer Trolley, standard ga., 1910, motor car	1500	2500	5000
408E Locomotive, standard ga., 1927, 0-4-4-0, electric, apple green or mojave	385	640	1280
408E Locomotive, standard ga., 1927, 0-4-4-0, electric, state brown	660	1100	2200

No. 408E Locomotive, 0-4-4-0, $2,200.

	C5	C7	C9
408E Locomotive, standard ga., 1927, 0-4-4-0, electric, green....	1080	1800	3600
410 Billboard Blinker, 1956-1958	22	35	44
HO-410 Suburban Ranch House, HO ga., 1959	10	15	20
HO-411 Figure Set, HO ga., 1959	10	15	20
HO-412 Farm Set, HO ga., 1959...	10	15	20
412 Pullman, standard ga., 1929, California State Car, light green	600	1000	2000
412 Pullman, standard ga., 1929, California State Car, light brown	660	1100	2200
413 Countdown Control Panel, 1962	38	50	72
413 Pullman, standard ga., 1929, Colorado State Car, light green	600	1000	2000

	C5	C7	C9
413 Pullman, standard ga., 1929, Colorado State Car, light brown	660	1100	2200
HO-413 Railroad Structure Set, HO ga., 1959	10	15	20
414 State Car, 1930, Illinois, light green	600	1000	2000
414 State Car, 1930, light brown ...	660	1100	2200

No. 414 State Car, $2,000.

	C5	C7	C9
HO-414 Village Set, HO ga., 1959	10	15	20
415 Diesel Fueling Station, 1955-1967	100	150	200

Top row: No. 408E Locomotive, $1,280. Middle row, left to right: No. 419 Combine, $360; No. 431 Dinning car, $635. Bottom row, left to right: No. 418 Pullman, $345; No. 490 Observation car, $360.

Top row: No. 422 Observation car, $820. Middle row, left to right: No. 421 Observation car, $820; No. 420 Observation car, $820. Bottom row, No. 400E Locomotive with tender, $2,850.

	C5	C7	C9
416 Observation Car, standard ga., 1929, New York State Car, light green	320	533	1065
416 Observation Car, standard ga., 1929, light brown	310	515	1030
418 Pullman, standard ga., 1923, apple green	105	173	345
418 Pullman, standard ga., 1923, mojave	63	105	210
419 Combine, standard ga., 1923, mojave	60	100	200
419 Combine, standard ga., 1928-1932, apple green	130	250	360
419 Heliport, 1962, control tower	125	188	250

	C5	C7	C9
420 Pullman, standard ga., 1930, Blue Comet car, light blue body, dark blue roof, marked "Faye"	245	410	820
421 Pullman, standard ga., 1930, Blue Comet car, light blue body, dark blue roof, "Westphal"	245	410	820
422 Observation Car, standard ga., 1930, Blue Comet car, light blue body, dark blue roof, marked "Tempel"	245	410	820
424 Pullman, standard ga., 1931, Stephen Girard set, light green, marked "Liberty Bell"	155	258	515
HO-425 Figure Set, HO ga., 1962	7	11	14

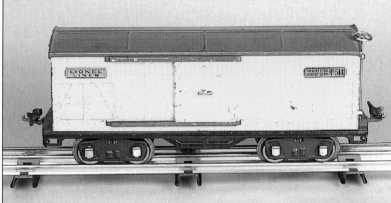

No. 514 Refrigerator car,
Lionel, $175.

No. 515 Tank Car,
Lionel, $100.

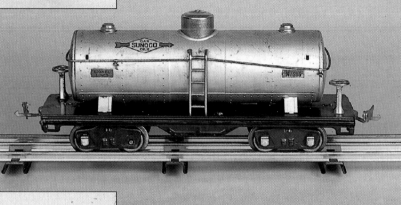

No. 517 Caboose,
Lionel, $100.

No. 116 Station,
Lionel, $1,200.

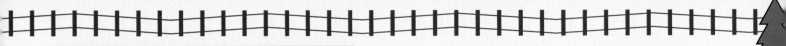

Membership to The Lionel Railroader Club (LRRC) has its benefits. The Gold Member Kit for 1999 is a Lionel collector's dream. With all LRRC memorabilia going up in value, this first Gold Member Kit will be no exception. Photo courtesy Gordon Wong.

The carrying case for the 1999 Gold Member Kit available only through The Lionel Railroader Club. Photo courtesy Gordon Wong.

Lionel Blue Comet.
Top row: No. 400E Locomotive, $2,200.
Middle row, left to right:
No. 400T tender; No. 421 Pullman, $820.
Bottom row, left to right:
No. 420 Pullman, $820;
No. 422 Observation car, $820.

No. 217 Caboose, Lionel, $230.

No. 408E Locomotive, Lionel, $2,200.

No. 385E Locomotive, Lionel, $980.

No. 731 Pike Planning kit; No. 26 Service kit, American Flyer S gauge, $18.

No. 919 Coal Dump car, American Flyer S gauge, $100.

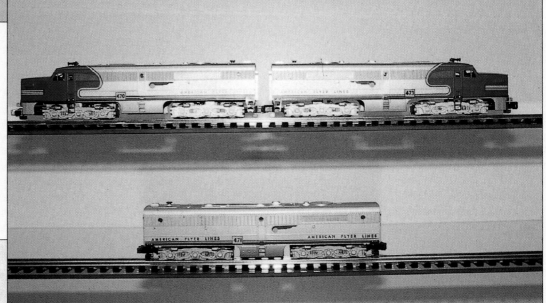

Nos. 470-471-473, American Flyer S gauge, priced as set, $490.

No. 23743 Track Maintenance car, American Flyer S gauge, $90.

Northern Pacific Passenger, American Flyer HO. Back row: left to right: No. 543 Observation car, $53; No. 542 Vista Dome, $55. Middle row, left to right: No. 541 Coach car, $53; No. 540 Combine car, $50; Front row, left to right: No. 424 Locomotive, $125; No. 423 Locomotive. Photo courtesy Larry Shick.

Late 1950s American Flyer HO Gilbert Boxcars. Back row, left to right: No. 522 B&M Boxcar, $45; No. 33513 B&O Boxcar, $75; Front row, left to right: No. 33002 NYC Boxcar, $45; No. 33012 SF Boxcar, $180. Photo courtesy Larry Shick.

American Flyer HO. No. 426 F-3 B-unit GMD dummy diesel,. Photo courtesy Larry Shick.

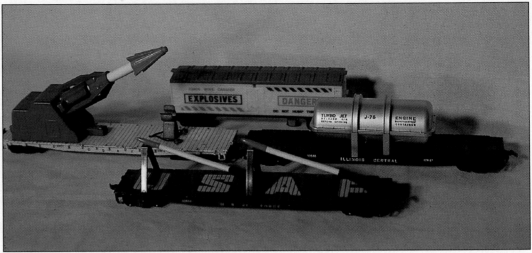

American Flyer HO. Back row: No. 33806 Mine Boxcar, $70. Middle row, left to right: No. 33812 USAF Rocket Launcher car, $80; No. IC Flat car, $70. Front row: No. 33538 USAF Flat car, $135. Photo courtesy Larry Shick.

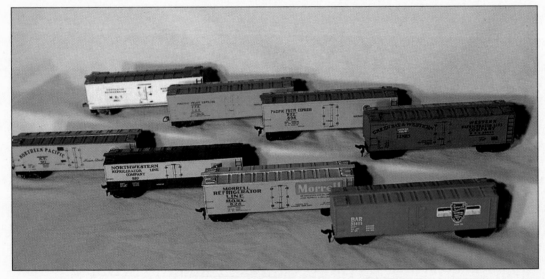

American Flyer HO. Back row, left to right: No. 124 MDT Refrigerator car, $25; No. 123 PFE Refrigerator car, $180; No. 504 PFE Refrigerator car, $36; No. 33526 GB&W Refrigerator car, $55. Front row, left to right: No. 521 NP Refrigerator car, $30; No. 520 CNW Refrigerator car. Photo courtesy Larry Shick.

American Flyer HO-scale tank car kit from 1939. Photo courtesy Larry Shick.

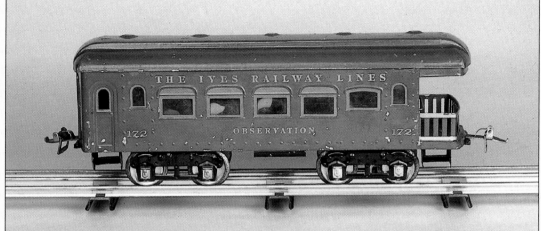

No. 172 Observation Car, Ives, $65.

Box for Ives' Elevated Railway, c. 1906.

No. 190 Tank Car, Ives, $190-200.

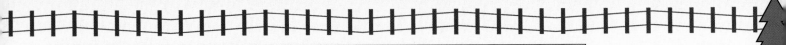

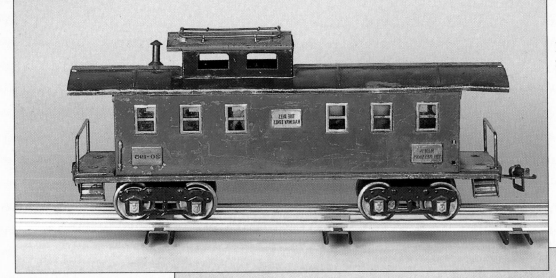

No. 195 Caboose, Ives, $250-265.

In addition to the Industrial Train roundhouse, Buddy "L" also made an Outdoor Railroad Three Stall Roundhouse.

No. 1002 Boxcar, Buddy "L," $1,000.

No. 11 Tootsietoy Passenger Train set. Top row, left to right: No. 4621 Tender, No. 4620 Engine; Middle row and bottom rows: three No. 4623 Pullman cars. This boxed set, with the station, is valued at $450.

No. 186 Fast Freight set. Top row, left to right: No. T186 Locomotive, NY Central Tender; middle row, left to right: Cracker Jack Boxcar, Texaco Tank car; Bottom row: NYCRR Caboose; $275 for the set.

Three floor trains by Marx, inluding the Army Floor Train, valued at $600. Photo courtesy Richard Mac-Nary.

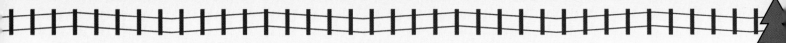

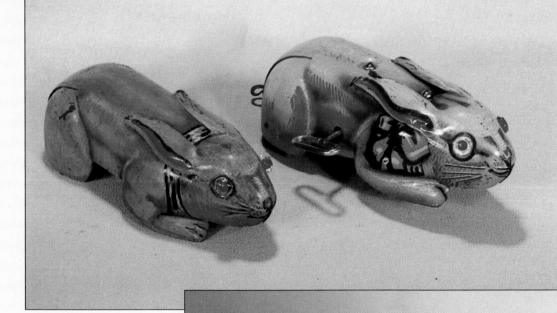

Left to right: No. 107
Rabbit locomotive, Marx,
$1,400; original hand-
painted rabbit.
Photo courtesy
Richard MacNary.

The Bunny Express,
Marx. Left to right: No.
107 Rabbit locomotive;
two No. 352 (c) Gondolas,
$100. Photo courtesy
Richard MacNary.

Pennsylvannia Set, Marx.
Top row, left to right: No.
401 Locomotive, $80;
Tender. Bottom row, left to
right: No. 09528c Erie
Flat car; No. 18326 P.C.
Caboose, $30. Photo
courtesy Richard Mac-
Nary.

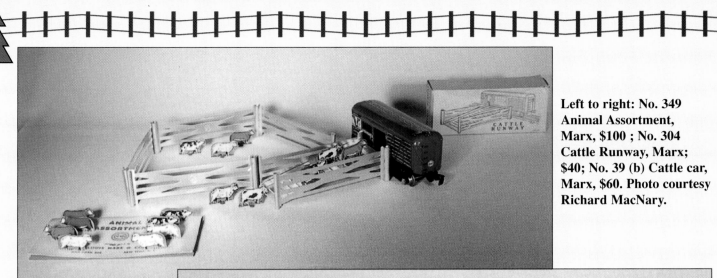

Left to right: No. 349 Animal Assortment, Marx, $100 ; No. 304 Cattle Runway, Marx; $40; No. 39 (b) Cattle car, Marx, $60. Photo courtesy Richard MacNary.

The Joy Line, Marx. Top row, left to right: No. 105 Locomotive; No. 351 Tender, $45. Bottom row, left to right: two Nos. 357 Passenger cars, $150; No. 458 (a) Observation car, 60. Photo courtesy Richard MacNary.

Mickey Mouse Meteor, Marx. Top row, left to right: No. 734 Locomotive, $150; No. 941 Tender, $200. Bottom row, left to right: No. 1476 Boacar, $150; Gondola, $100; No. 691521 Caboose, $100. Photo courtesy Richard MacNary.

Left to right: No. 200 (b) Trolley, Marx, $500; No. 200 (a) Trolley, Marx, $400. Photo courtesy Richard MacNary.

No. 44572 Gondola, Marx, $15.

No. 254000 Gondola, Marx, $30.

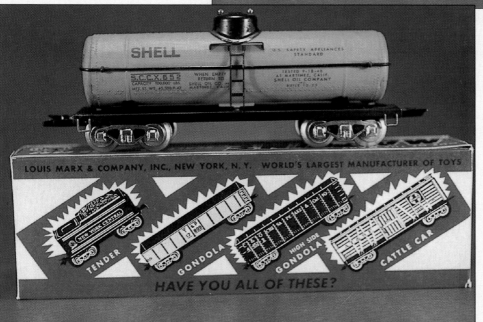

No. 652 Tank Car, Marx, $30.

No. 309B Tunnel,
Marx, $20.

No. 065 Water Tower,
Marx, $1.

No. 3880 Railroad Station,
Marx, $20.

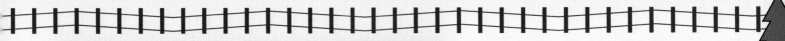

No. 436 Searchlight Tower, Marx, $6.

Box for Marx's Searchlight Tower.

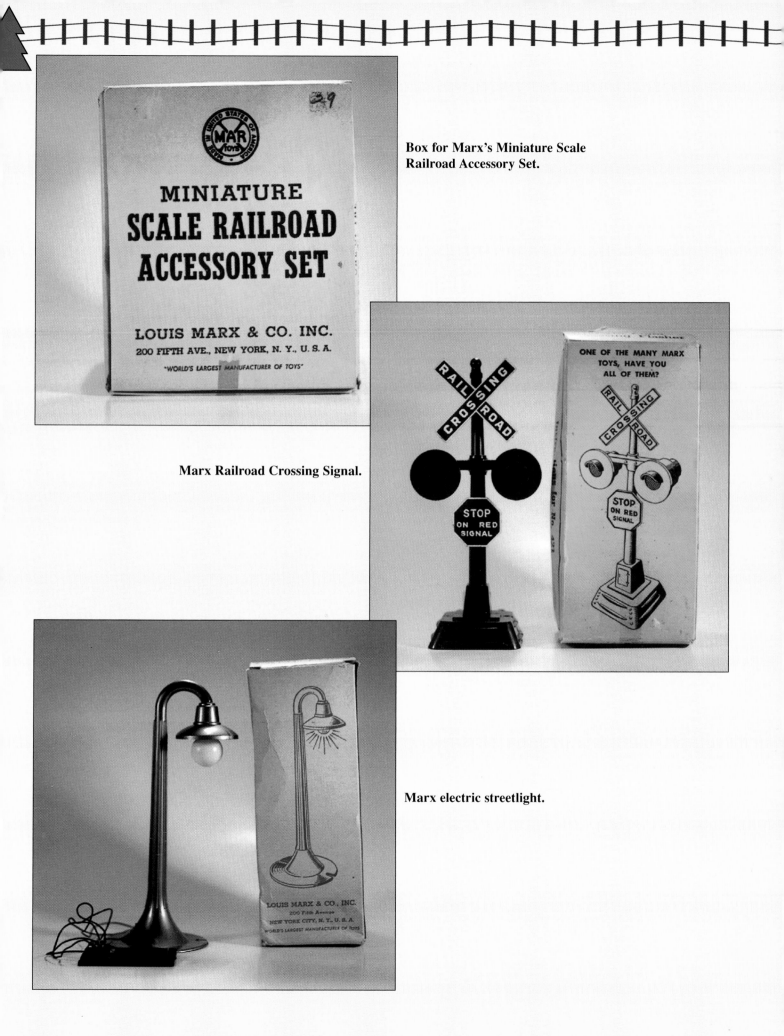

Box for Marx's Miniature Scale Railroad Accessory Set.

Marx Railroad Crossing Signal.

Marx electric streetlight.

Train set. No. 999 Locomoitve with tender and two cars, Pratt & Letchworth (Miscellaneous), $5,500.

Wells-Brimtoy Mickey Mouse & Donald Duck Handcar. McNary Collection. Photo: RLM.

Pratt & Letchworth cast-iron loco #999 c. 1900, "NYC&HR RR" and pressed steel cars ("Wagner Buffet" and "Vanderbilt"). Courtesy Christie's East.

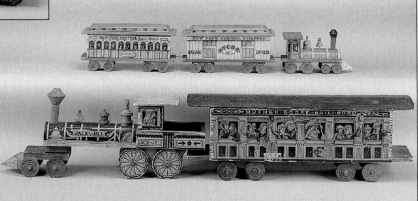

Top: Bliss "New York Central Rail Road" litho on wood. Bottom: Reed "Mother Goose Rail Road," circa 1895. Paper litho on wood. Courtesy Christie's East.

	C5	C7	C9
425 Pullman, standard ga., 1932, Stephen Girard set, light green	150	272	515
426 Observation Car, standard ga., 1931, Stephen Girard set, light green, "Coral Isle"	150	272	515
428 Pullman, standard ga., 1926, dark green	90	150	300
428 Pullman, standard ga., 1926, orange	150	250	500
429 Combine, standard ga., 1926, dark green	135	225	450
429 Combine, standard ga., 1926, orange	105	175	350
430 Observation Car, standard ga., 1926, dark green	90	150	300
430 Observation Car, standard ga., 1926, orange	105	175	350
HO-430 Tree Assortment, HO ga., 1959	6	9	12
431 Diner, standard ga., 1927, mojave	180	300	600

	C5	C7	C9
431 Diner, 1928-1929, apple green, orange, dark green	190	317	635
HO-431 Landscape Set, HO ga., 1959	10	15	20
HO-432 Tree Assortment, HO ga., 1961	7	11	14
435 Power Station, 1926	83	138	275
436 Power Station, 1926	95	155	310
437 Signal Tower, 1926, orange roof	180	300	600
437 Signal Tower, 1926, green roof	150	255	510
437 Signal Tower, 1926, peacock roof	125	212	425
438 Signal Tower, 1927, orange, red	200	300	400
438 Signal Tower, 1927, white, red	235	350	470
439 Panel Board, 1928, silver, rare	150	225	300
439 Panel Board, 1928, maroon	90	135	180

No. 444 Roundhouse Section, $3,400.

	C5	C7	C9
439 Panel Board, 1928, red	100	150	200
440C Panel Board.........................	62	93	125
0440 Signal Bridge, standard ga., 1932	235	350	470
440N Signal Bridge, O/standard ga., 1936	175	262	350
441 Weighing Scale Platform, standard ga., 1932-1936, green base, cream building	300	500	1000
442 Diner, 1938........................	120	180	240
443 Missile Launching Platform, 1960-1962..............................	30	45	60
444 Roundhouse Section, standard ga., 1932-1935	1700	2550	3400
445 Switch Tower, 1952-1957, operating	42	63	85
448 Missile Firing Range Set, 1961-1963..............................	70	75	140
450 Macy Special Locomotive, O ga., 1930, electric, 0-4-0 red w/black frame, uncataloged......	300	500	1000

	C5	C7	C9
450 Signal Bridge, 1952-1958, gray or tan base	35	52	70
450L Signal Light Head, 1952.......	20	25	35
452 Gantry Signal, 1961-1963.......	65	80	120
455 Electric Range, 1932-1933	700	1100	1500
455 Oil Derrick, 1950-1954, red base	110	165	220
455 Oil Derrick, 1950-1954, green base	90	135	180
456 Coal Ramp and Hopper Car, 1950-1955	75	125	250
460 Piggyback Terminal, 1955-1957...................................	75	112	150
460-150 Two Trailers, 1956	80	90	100
461 Piggyback, 1957, w/truck and trailers, most include, "Midge Toy Tractor," red	300	450	600
462 Derrick Platform Set, 1961-1962..	135	165	290
464-150 Boards, 1956, set of six ...	5	10	15
464 Lumber Mill, 1956-1960	87	130	175

Top row, left to right: No. 490 Observation car, $250; No. 431 Dining car, $600. Bottom row, left to right: No. 419 Combine, $200; No. 418 Pullman, $200.

"ADD-ON" ACTION ACCESSORIES

No. 140 Banjo Signal—A real railroading accessory! As train approaches, red light flashes and banjo "Stop" arm begins to swing to and fro. Action stops when train has passed. Signal measures 7½" high.   **$5.95**

New! No. 163 Single Target Block Signal—Serves as a guide to oncoming traffic! As train approaches, signal light changes from green to red automatically. Signal can be wired to control a second train in a two-train operation. Signal measures 9" high.   **$5.95**

New! No. 161 Mail Pickup Set—By remote control, dispatching arm is pivoted in the direction of the oncoming train. Magnetic force pulls the mail bag from the arm and transfers pouch to the train. Any Lionel freight or passenger car can be used for this operation. Tower 5½" high.   **$5.95**

No. 145 Automatic Gateman—When train nears, door opens and gateman comes out swinging lantern. When train passes, man goes back into shack and door closes. Shack is illuminated. **$6.95**
145C Contactor (not illus.)—Single pole, single throw for 145, 252, 151, 140 and 1047.   **$1.50**

New! No. 448 Missile Firing Range Set With Camouflage and Exploding Target Range Car—By rotating the "firing wheel" missiles are fired in sequence. Missiles will "explode" the Target Range Car on contact. Unit 9" by 5½".   **$10.95**

New! No. 452 Overhead Gantry Signal—As train approaches, overhead signals change from green to red to warn approaching traffic. Can be used to control second train in a two-train operation. Bridge 7¾" high.   **$7.95**

No. 494 Rotary Beacon—Beacon has a red and green light which revolves in a circular motion. Tower is 11¾" high, base 5" x 5".   **$6.95**
No. 394-37 (not illus.)—Beacon Cap for 394.   **$1.50**

No. 353 Trackside Control Signal—Signals change from green to red. Signal can be wired to control 2 trains. Signal 9" high.   **$5.95**
153C Contactor (not illus.)—1 pole, 2 throw for 353, 163, 452.   **$1.50**

No. 195 Eight-Bulb Tower—Tower has eight powerful bulbs set in silver reflectors to give greater illumination. Tower 12½" high.   **$5.95**

Top of page, left to right: No. 494 Rotary Beacon, $50; No. 443 Missile Launching Platform, $60; No. 353 Trackside Signal, $40; No. 195 Floodlight Tower, $60. Middle of page: No. 448 Missile Firing Range set, $140. Bottom of page, left to right: No. 161 Mail Pickup set, $70; No. 140 Banjo Signal $50; No. 145 Automatic Gateman, $49. Photo courtesy 1961 Lionel catalog.

	C5	C7	C9
465 Sound Dispatching Station, 1956-1957	75	112	150
470 IRBM Missile Launch, 1959-1962	105	125	155
HO-470 Missile Launching Platform, HO ga., 1960	34	51	68
479-1 Lionel Trucks, 1955, accompanies 6362	5	10	15
480-25 Conversion Coupler, 1950	—	—	4
HO-480 Missile Firing Range Set, HO ga., 1961	7	11	14
490 Observation Car, standard ga., 1923, mojave	75	125	250

	C5	C7	C9
490 Observation Car, standard ga., 1923, apple green	109	180	360
494 Rotary Beacon, 1954, silver, red	25	38	50
497 Coaling Station, 1953-1958	100	150	200
500 Motorized Derrick, standard ga., 1903	4000	5000	7000
511 Flatcar, standard ga., 1927, dark green	34	58	115
511 Flatcar, standard ga., 1927, medium green	30	50	100
512 Gondola, standard ga., 1927, bright green	36	60	120

Top row, left to right: No. 512 Gondola, $120; No. 517 Caboose, $100. Middle row: two No. 511 flatcars, $115, each. Bottom row, left row: No. 385E Locomotive with 384T, 385T, 385TW or 385W tender, $980.

	C5	C7	C9
512 Gondola, standard ga., 1927, peacock	22	38	75
513 Cattle Car, standard ga., 1927	39	65	130
513 Cattle Car, standard ga., 1927, nickel trim................................	150	250	500
514 Boxcar, standard ga., 1929, ivory and brown........................	57	95	190
514 Boxcar, standard ga., 1929, yellow/brown...........................	50	85	170
514 Refrigerator, standard ga., 1927, Lionel ventilated refrigerator...............................	52	88	175
514R Refrigerator, standard ga., 1929, ivory body, peacock roof	60	100	200

	C5	C7	C9
514R Refrigerator, standard ga., 1929, nickel trim	123	208	415
515 Tank Car, standard ga., 1927, Shell, orange	240	400	800
515 Tank Car, standard ga., 1927, Sunoco logo, terra-cotta, ivory and silver	54	90	180
516 Hopper, standard ga., 1928	72	120	240
517 Caboose, standard ga., 1927, red, nickel trim.........................	30	50	100
517 Caboose, standard ga., 1927, red and black, coal train, nickel trim..	90	150	300
517 Caboose, standard ga., 1927, pea green	24	40	80

Top row, left to right: No. 514 Refrigerator car, $175; No 517 Caboose, $300. Middle row, left to right: No. 512 Gondola, $75; No. 515 Tank car, $180; No. 516 Hopper, $240. Bottom row, left to right: No. 390E Locomotive, $1,000.

	C5	C7	C9
520 Locomotive, O27 ga., 1956, diesel, eighty ton, original pantograph must not be broken	60	100	200
520 Search Light, standard ga., 1931, terra-cotta platform	50	85	170
520 Search Light, standard ga., 1931, green platform	75	128	255
529 Pullman, O ga., 1926, olive green or terra-cotta	13	21	42
HO-530 Locomotive, HO ga., 1958, DRGW, diesel F-3 powered A	20	32	65
530 Observation Car, O ga., 1926, olive green or terra-cotta	10	17	35
HO-531 Locomotive, HO ga., 1958, C.M. St. P&P, diesel F-3 powered A	20	32	65
HO-532 Locomotive, HO ga., 1958, diesel F-3 powered A, B&O	20	32	65
HO-533 Locomotive, HO ga., 1958, New Haven, diesel F-3 powered A,	20	32	65
HO-535 Locomotive, HO ga., 1962, Santa Fe, diesel Alco, AB	20	32	65
HO-536 Locomotive, HO ga., 1963, Sante Fe, diesel Alco	20	32	65
HO-537 Locomotive, HO ga., 1966, diesel Alco, AB Santa Fe	20	32	65
HO-540 Locomotive, HO ga., 1958, DRGW, diesel F-3, Dummy B	15	25	50
HO-541 Locomotive, HO ga., 1958, CMST P&P, diesel F-3, Dummy B	15	25	50
HO-550 Locomotive, HO ga., 1958, DRGW, diesel F-3, Dummy A	15	25	50
550 Miniature Figures, 1932, set of six, includes original box	125	188	250
551 Miniature Figure, 1932, engineer	15	22	30
552 Miniature Figure, 1932, conductor	15	22	30

	C5	C7	C9
553 Miniature Figure, 1932, porter	15	22	30
554 Miniature Figure, 1932, male passenger	15	22	30
HO-555 Locomotive, HO ga., 1963, Santa Fe, diesel F-3 powered A	19	32	64
555 Miniature Figure, 1932, female passenger	15	22	30
556 Miniature Figure, 1932, red cap	15	22	30
HO-561 Rotary Snowplow, HO ga., 1959, MSTL	60	100	200
HO-564 Locomotive, HO ga., 1960, C&O, diesel Alco, powered A	19	32	64
HO-565 Locomotive, HO ga., 1959, Santa Fe, diesel Alco, powered A	19	32	64
HO-566 Locomotive, HO ga., 1959, Texas special, diesel Alco, powered A	19	32	64
HO-567 Locomotive, HO ga., 1959, Alaska, diesel Alco, powered A	19	32	64
HO-568 Locomotive, HO ga., 1962, Union Pacific, diesel Alco, powered A	19	32	64
HO-569 Locomotive, HO ga., 1963, Union Pacific, diesel Alco, powered A	19	32	64
HO-571 Locomotive, HO ga., 1963, PRR, diesel Alco, powered A	19	32	64
HO-576 Locomotive, HO ga., 1959, Texas special, diesel F-3, Dummy B	19	32	64
HO-577 Locomotive, HO ga., 1959, Alaska, diesel F-3, Dummy B	19	32	64
HO-581 Locomotive, HO ga., 1960, PRR, rectifier	19	32	64
HO-586 Locomotive, HO ga., 1959, Texas special, diesel F-3, Dummy A	15	25	50

	C5	C7	C9
HO-587 Locomotive, HO ga., 1959, Alaska, diesel F-3, Dummy A	15	25	50
HO-591 Locomotive, HO ga., 1959, New Haven, rectifier	19	32	64
HO-592 Locomotive, HO ga., 1966, Santa Fe, diesel GP9	19	32	64
HO-593 Locomotive, HO ga., 1963, Northern Pacific, diesel GP9	19	32	64
HO-594 Locomotive, HO ga., 1963, Santa Fe, diesel GP9	19	32	64
HO-595 Locomotive, HO ga., 1959, Santa Fe, diesel F-3, Dummy A	15	25	50
HO-596 Locomotive, HO ga., 1959, NYC, diesel GP9	19	32	64
HO-597 Locomotive, HO ga., 1961, Northern Pacific, diesel GP9	19	32	64
HO-598 Locomotive, HO ga., 1961, NYC, diesel GP7	19	32	64
600 Derrick Trailer, standard ga., 1903	2000	4500	9000
600 Locomotive, O27 ga., 1955, diesel SW2, MKT	54	90	180
600 Pullman, O ga., 1915, four wheel, maroon, dark green, brown	18	30	60
600 Pullman, O ga., 1933, gray w/red roof	45	75	150
600 Pullman, O ga., 1933, eight wheel, red w/red roof	54	90	180
600 Pullman, O ga., 1933, light blue w/silver roof	18	30	60
601 Locomotive, O27 ga., 1956, diesel, Seaboard	60	100	200
601 Observation Car, O ga., 1933, red w/red roof	45	75	150
601 Observation Car, O ga., 1933, light blue w/silver roof	18	30	60
601 Observation Car, O ga., 1933, gray w/red roof	40	65	130
601 Pullman, O ga., 1915, seven, dark green	25	42	85

	C5	C7	C9
602 Baggage Car, O ga., 1915, dark green	21	35	70
602 Baggage Car, 1933, gray w/red roof	37	63	125
602 Baggage Car, 1933, light blue w/silver roof	54	90	180
602 Baggage Car, 1933, red w/red roof	63	108	215
602 Locomotive, O27 ga., 1957, diesel SW2, Seaboard	62	105	210
HO-602 Locomotive, HO ga., 1960, steam	15	25	50
603 Pullman, O ga., 1920, later, orange	19	32	64
603 Pullman, O ga., 1921, orange, uncataloged	21	35	70
603 Pullman, O ga., 1931, late, red, green, orange, maroon	30	50	100
604 Observation Car, O ga., 1920, orange	24	40	80
604 Observation Car, O ga., 1931, red, green, orange, maroon	25	43	85
HO-605 Locomotive, HO ga., 1959, steam	20	32	64
605 Pullman, O ga., 1925, gray	30	50	100
605 Pullman, O ga., 1925, olive	48	80	160
605 Pullman, O ga., 1925, red	48	80	160
605 Pullman, O ga., 1925, orange	48	80	160
606 Observation Car, O ga., 1925, gray	48	80	160
606 Observation Car, O ga., 1925, orange	48	80	160
606 Observation Car, O ga., 1925, red	48	80	160
606 Observation Car, O ga., 1925, olive	48	80	160
606 Observation Car, O ga., 1930, Macy, uncataloged	48	80	160
607 Pullman, O ga., 1926	25	43	85
607 Pullman, O ga., 1931, Macy, uncataloged	80	135	270
608 Observation Car, O ga., 1926	25	44	88

A HEAVY-DUTY SUPER "O" WORK TRAIN...WITH A BRAND NEW SANTA FE DIESEL SWITCHER

No. 2570 SUPER "O" 5-CAR "HUSKY" DIESEL FREIGHT $49.95

★ New Diesel Switcher

★ Horn

★ Headlight

★ Magne-Traction

★ New Night Crew Searchlight Car

When repair or construction work is needed . . . this "jack-of-all-trades" is called on to do the job! In the event there should be a nighttime emergency . . . the freighter has as part of its standard equipment . . . a searchlight car. In addition there is a Crane Car for construction, a Maintenance Car for overhead repairs and a Hopper Car for carrying loads. The new No. 616 Diesel Switcher adds the muscle to pull the heavy cargo and is equipped with headlight, Magne-Traction and horn. Train measures 5 ft., 6½" long.

Lionel's No. 2570 Train Set includes:

No. 616	New Santa Fe Diesel Switcher
No. 6822	New Night Crew Searchlight Car
No. 6828	Harnischfeger Mobile Construction Crane Car
No. 6812	Track Maintenance Car
No. 6736	Mackinac Mac Hopper
No. 6130	Santa Fe Work Caboose
12 Sections	No. 31 Super "O" Curved Track
2 Sections	No. 32 Super "O" Straight Track
No. 39-25	Complete Operating Set for uncoupling and operating cars.

Lubricant, Oil, Wires and Instruction Sheet.

Left to right: No. 616 Locomotive, $220; No. 6822 Searchlight car, $220. Photo courtesy 1961 Lionel catalog.

	C5	C7	C9		C5	C7	C9
608 Observation Car, O ga., 1931, Macy, uncataloged	90	150	300	612 Observation Car, O ga., 1915, early	40	68	135
609 Pullman, O ga., 1937, uncataloged	27	45	90	612 Observation Car, O ga., 1926, Macy	21	35	70
610 Locomotive, O27 ga., 1955, diesel SW2, Erie	85	120	160	612 Observation Car, O ga., 1926, late	21	35	70
610 Pullman, O ga., 1915, early	45	78	155	613 Locomotive, O27 ga., 1958, U.P., diesel, SW2	125	200	415
610 Pullman, O ga., 1926, late	21	35	70	613 Pullman, O ga., 1931, blue, Blue Comet set	180	338	675
610 Pullman, O ga., 1926, Macy, uncataloged	24	40	80	613 Pullman, O ga., 1931, red, aluminum roof	60	100	200
611 Locomotive, O27 ga., 1957, diesel SW2, CNJ	66	110	220	613 Pullman, O ga., 1931, terra-cotta	85	140	280
611 Observation Car, O ga., 1937, uncataloged	18	30	60				

	C5	C7	C9
614 Locomotive, O27 ga., 1959-1960, Alaska, diesel, SW2, blue, yellow structure on roof...	65	110	220
614 Observation Car, O ga., 1931, Blue Comet set, blue	66	112	225
614 Observation Car, O ga., 1931, red, aluminum roof	60	100	200
614 Observation Car, O ga., 1931, terra-cotta	63	105	210
615 Baggage Car, O ga., 1933, terra-cotta	75	125	250
615 Baggage Car, O ga., 1933, Blue Comet set, blue	60	100	200
615 Baggage Car, O ga., 1933, red, aluminum roof	75	125	250
616-13 Bulb, 1935, 12 volt, clear	—	—	1
616 E or W Diesel Type Power Car, O ga., 1935, Streamliner, Flying Yankee, black cast frame, chrome shells	60	105	210
616 Locomotive, O27 ga., 1961, diesel, SW2, ATSF	66	110	220
616T Vestibule, O ga., 1935	12	20	40
617 Coach, O ga., 1935, Streamliner, black and chrome	24	39	78
617 Coach, O ga., 1935, blue and white, Blue Streak	36	60	120
617 Locomotive, O ga., 1963, ATSF, diesel, SW2, black	90	150	300
618 Observation Car, O ga., 1935, Streamliner, black and chrome	25	43	85
618 Observation Car, O ga., 1935, Blue Streak, blue and white	45	75	150
619 Combine, O ga., 1935, Blue Streak, Streamliner, blue and white	90	150	300
620 Floodlight, O ga., 1937	30	45	60
621 Locomotive, O27 ga., 1956, diesel, SW2, CNJ	60	75	145
622 Locomotive, 1949, diesel, SW2, Santa Fe, black	150	175	325
623 Locomotive, O ga., 1952, diesel, SW2, ATSF, black	73	123	245
624 Locomotive, O ga., 1952, diesel, SW2, C&O, blue, yellow stripe	110	150	270
625 Locomotive, O27 ga., 1957, diesel, forty-four ton, LV	75	120	150
HO-625 Locomotive, HO ga., 1959, steam	27	45	90
626 Locomotive, O27 ga., 1957, B&O, diesel, forty-four ton	135	225	450
HO-626 Locomotive, HO ga., 1963, steam	19	33	65
627 Locomotive, O27 ga., 1956, diesel, 45 ton, LV, red body, white stripe	80	110	145
628 Locomotive, O27 ga., 1956, diesel, 45 ton, NP, black w/yellow stripe	50	83	165
629 Locomotive, O27 ga., 1956, Burlington, diesel, forty-four ton, silver, red stripe	105	175	350
629 Pullman, O ga., 1924, four wheel	20	32	65
629 Pullman, O ga., 1934, eight wheel, uncataloged	39	65	130
630 Macy Observation Car, O ga., 1931, four wheel, uncataloged	24	40	80
630 Observation Car, O ga., 1924, four wheel	16	28	55
630 Observation Car, O ga., 1934, eight wheel, uncataloged	27	45	90
633 Locomotive, O ga., 1962, diesel, SW2, Santa Fe	100	150	215
634 Locomotive, O ga., 1962, diesel, SW2, Santa Fe, blue body	18	30	60
HO-635 Locomotive, HO ga., 1961, steam	19	32	65
636-13 Bulb, 1936, 8 volt, clear	—	—	1
636W Diesel Type Power Car, O ga., 1936, U.P., Streamliner, yellow and brown, marked "City of Denver"	42	70	140
HO-636 Locomotive, HO ga., 1963, steam	19	33	65

Set No. 14043 — 6 Unit "Weapons Carrier" Steam Freight includes:

No. 0635LT Pacific Steam Loco and Tender with Headlight and Smoke
No. 0349 New Turbo Missile Firing Car
No. 0847 Exploding Target Car
No. 0805 Illuminated Radioactive Waste Disposal Car
No. 0841 Caboose
5 sections No. 0988 18" Radius Curved Track—18" long
1 section No. 0909 Straight Track—9" long
1 section No. 0976 Curved Terminal Track—18" long
1 section No. 0919 Uncoupler Re-Railer 9" long
No. 0103 800 milliamp Power Pack
Wires and Instruction Sheet

Set No. 14054 — 5 Unit Diesel Passenger includes:

No. 0566 Texas Special Diesel with Headlight
No. 0704 Texas Special Baggage Car
No. 0706 Texas Special Vista-Dome
No. 0706 Texas Special Vista-Dome
No. 0707 Texas Special Observation Car
5 sections No. 0988 18" Radius Curved Track—18" long
1 section No. 0909 Straight Track—9" long
1 section No. 0976 Curved Terminal Track—18" long
1 section No. 0919 Uncoupler Re-Railer 9" long
No. 0101 1¼ Amp. D.C.,A.C. Power Pack
No. 950 U.S. Railroad Map
Wires and Instruction Sheet

Set No. 14064 — Northern Pacific GP-9 Diesel Freight includes:

No. 0597 Northern Pacific GP-9 Diesel with Headlight
No. 0365 New Minuteman Missile Launching Car
No. 0366 Operating Milk Can Unloading Car
No. 0319 Helicopter Launching Car
No. 0301 Operating Dump Car
No. 0841 Caboose
5 sections No. 0988 18" Radius Curved Track—18" long
1 section No. 0976 Curved Terminal Track—18" long
1 section No. 0919 Uncoupler Re-Railer 9" long
No. 0900 Remote Control Operating Platform
No. 0101 1¼ Amp. D.C.,A.C. Power Pack
Wires and Instruction Sheet

Set No. 14108 — 6 Unit Santa Fe Passenger with Horn includes:

No. 0535 New Santa Fe "AB" Diesel with Headlight, Horn & Horn Controller
No. 0712 Illum. Santa Fe Baggage Car
No. 0713 Illum. Santa Fe Pullman Car
No. 0714 Illum. Santa Fe Vista-Dome
No. 0715 Illum. Santa Fe Observation
5 sections No. 0988 18" Radius Curved Track—18" long
1 section No. 0909 Straight Track—9" long
1 section No. 0976 Curved Terminal Track—18" long
1 section No. 0919 Uncoupler Re-Railer 9" long
No. 0100 2½ Amp. D.C.,A.C. Power Pack
Wires and Instruction Sheet

HO

HO

HO

HO

Diesel has real sounding horn

Top to bottom: No. HO-635 Locomotive, $65; No. HO-566 Locomotive, $64; No. HO-597 Locomotive, $64; No. HO-535 Locomotive, $65. Photo courtesy 1962 Lionel catalog.

	C5	C7	C9
637 Coach, O ga., 1936, Streamliner, marked "City of Denver"	30	50	100
637 Locomotive, Super O ga., 1959, 2-6-4, steam, 2046W tender or 2040W tender	52	88	175
638 Observation Car, O ga., 1936, Streamliner, yellow and brown, marked "City of Denver"	30	50	100
HO-642 Locomotive, HO ga., 1961, steam	19	33	65
HO-643 Locomotive, HO ga., 1963, steam	19	33	65
HO-645 Locomotive, HO ga., 1962, steam	19	33	65
645 Locomotive, O27 ga., 1963, diesel, SW2, Union Pacific, yellow body	41	68	135
646 Locomotive, O ga., 1954, 4-6-4, steam, 2046W tender	88	148	295
HO-646 Locomotive, HO ga., 1963, steam	19	33	65
HO-647 Locomotive, HO ga., 1966	19	33	65
651 Flatcar, O ga., 1935	15	25	50
652 Gondola, O ga., 1935	16	28	55
653 Hopper, O ga., 1934	19	33	65
654 Tank Car, O ga., 1934, silver, orange	15	25	50
655 Boxcar, O ga., 1934	16	28	55
656 Cattle Car, O ga., 1935	30	50	100
657 Caboose, O ga., 1934	10	18	35
659 Dump Car, O ga., 1935	24	40	80
665 Locomotive, O ga., 1954, 4-6-4, steam, w/6026W or 2046W tender	100	160	235
671 Locomotive, O ga., 1946, steam, 6-8-6, 671W tender	70	115	230
671 Locomotive, O ga., 1946, steam, 6-8-6, w/2671 tender	90	150	300
671 R&R Locomotive, O ga., 1952, steam, 671W tender	75	125	250
671-75 Smoke Bulb, 1946, 14 volt	5	10	15

	C5	C7	C9
675 Locomotive, O ga., 1947, 2-6-2, steam, w/2466W, 2466WX or 6466WX tender	70	115	230
681 Locomotive, O ga., 1950, 6-8-6, steam, 2671W tender	78	130	260
682 Locomotive, O ga., 1954, 6-8-6, steam, w/2046W tender	140	233	465
685 Locomotive, O ga., 1953, 4-6-4, steam, w/6026W tender	85	142	285
700E250 Display Stand and Track, 1938, w/Lionel ID plate	810	1350	2700
700 Locomotive, O ga., 1913-1916, 0-4-0, electric, dark green NYC Lines	225	375	750
700E Locomotive, O72 ga., 1937, 4-6-4, steam, black, w/700/700W twelve-wheel cast tender	750	1250	2500
700EWX Locomotive, O72 ga., 1937, steam, black, w/700/700W twelve-wheel cast whistle tender	1200	2000	4000
700K Locomotive, O72 ga., 1939, 4-6-4, steam kit, gray, six kits all original boxes	2800	4200	5600
700 Window Display Set, standard ga., 1904	—	—	—
701 Locomotive, 1913-1916, 0-4-0, electric, dark green	270	450	900
703 Locomotive, O ga., 1913-1916, 4-4-4, electric, dark green	660	1100	2200
703-10 Smoke Bulb, O ga., 1946	15	25	30
HO-704 Baggage Car, HO ga., 1959, Texas Special	18	30	60
HO-705 Pullman, HO ga., 1959, Texas Special	18	30	60
706 Locomotive, O ga., 1913-1916, 0-4-0, electric, dark green	420	700	1400
HO-706 Vista Dome, HO ga., 1959, Texas Special	18	30	60
HO-707 Observation Car, HO ga., 1959, Texas Special	18	30	60
HO-708 Baggage Car, HO ga., 1960, Pennsylvania	5	10	20

Top to bottom: No. 637 Locomotive, $175; No. 2359 Locomotive, $300. Photo courtesy 1961 Lionel catalog.

	C5	C7	C9
708 Locomotive, O72 ga., 1939, 0-6-0, steam, scale switcher, "8976" cast in boiler front	900	1500	3000
HO-709 Vista Dome, HO ga., 1960, Pennsylvania	8	13	26
HO-710 Observation Car, HO ga., 1960, Pennsylvania	6	10	20
710 Pullman, O ga., 1924, green, orange	75	125	250
710 Pullman, O ga., 1924, red	60	100	200
710 Pullman, O ga., 1924, two-tone blue	67	112	225
HO-711 Baggage Car, HO ga., 1960, Pennsylvania	6	10	20
711 Switches, O72 ga., 1935, electric, pair	75	112	150
HO-712 Baggage Car, HO ga., 1961, Santa Fe	14	22	45
712 Observation Car, O ga., 1924, green, orange	72	120	240
712 Observation Car, O ga., 1924, red	60	100	200
712 Observation Car, O ga., 1924, two-tone blue	66	110	220
HO-713 Pullman, HO ga., 1961, Santa Fe	14	22	45
714 Boxcar, O72 ga., 1940............	120	200	400
714K Boxcarcar, O72 ga., 1940, kit, new only	—	—	1000
HO-714 Vista Dome, HO ga., 1961, Santa Fe	8	13	26
HO-715 Observation Car, HO ga., 1961, Santa Fe	6	10	20
715K Tank Car, O72 ga., 1940, kit, new only	—	—	1000
715 Tank Car, O72 ga., 1940	120	200	400
716K Hopper, O72 ga., 1940, kit, new only	—	—	1000
716 Hopper, O72 ga., 1940	97	163	325
717-54 Bulb, 1940, 18 volt, clear	—	1	—
717K Caboose, O72 ga., 1940, kit, new only	—	—	500

	C5	C7	C9
720 90 Degrees Crossing, O72 ga., 1935..	2	5	8
721 Switches, O72 ga., 1935, non-electric, pair..............................	42	70	140
HO-723 Pullman, HO ga., 1963, Pennsylvania	6	10	20
HO-725 Observation Car, HO ga., 1963, Pennsylvania	6	10	20
726 Locomotive, O ga., 1946, 2-8-4, steam, w/2426W tender...	200	330	660
726 Locomotive, O ga., 1946, 2-8-4, steam, w/2046W tender...	210	330	385
730 90 Degrees Crossing T-Rail, O72 ga., 1935...........................	15	22	30
731 Switches, O72 ga., 1935, electric, T-rail, pair	175	263	350
HO-733 Pullman, HO ga., 1964, Santa Fe...................................	6	10	20
HO-735 Observation Car, HO ga., 1964, Santa Fe........................	6	10	20
736 Locomotive, O ga., 1950, 2-8-4, steam, w/2046W tender...	250	300	400
746 Locomotive, O ga., 1957, 4-8-4, steam, w/long stripe........	580	900	1500
746 Locomotive, O ga., 1957, 4-8-4, steam, w/746W tender w/short stripe, marked "Norfolk & Western"	500	850	1195
752-9 Bulb, 1934, 18 volt, clear	—	—	1
752E or W Streamliner Power Car, O ga., 1934...............................	140	235	470
753 Coach, O ga., 1934, streamliner................................	42	70	140
754 Observation Car, O ga., 1934, streamliner................................	42	70	140
760 Pack of Curved Track, 1935, sixteen sections	16	24	32
761 Track, O72 ga., 1934, curved.....................................	—	1	2
762 Track, O72 ga., 1934, straight...................................	—	1	2

THE MIGHTIEST OF STEAMERS
FREIGHT CARS...ALL

★ Die-Cast Steam Loco
★ Whistle and Smoke
★ Headlight and Magne-Traction
★ New Operating TV Monitor Car
★ New Four Boat Transport Car
★ New Piggyback Van Transport Car

THE CRACK SANTA FE SUPER CHIEF...

No. 2574 SUPER "O"

★ Headlight
★ Twin Units and Two Motors
★ Magne-Traction and Horn
★ New Fighting Equipment
★ Trestle Set and Missile Firing Range

The Santa Fe that packs a wallop! All may look serene from the outside...but should there be a call for action...this Santa Fe will be ready to serve. Hidden in a box car is a mighty Minuteman Missile that will fire at the press of a button. In addition to its land punch there is a Launching Helicopter and an Operating Submarine. With the sleek two motor Santa Fe diesel out in front ...top speed is assured. Train measures 6 ft., 6½" long.

Top to bottom: No. 736 Locomotive, $400; No. 2383 Locomotive, $650. Photo courtesy 1961 Lionel catalog.

No. 763E Locomotive, 4-6-4, $1,850.

	C5	C7	C9
762S Track, O72 ga., 1934, straight, insulated, w/lock-on....	—	2	3
763E Locomotive, O ga., 1937, 4-6-4, steam, gunmetal gray, w/2226W or 2226WX tender ...	720	1200	2400
763E Locomotive, O ga., 1937, 4-6-4, steam, semi-scale Hudson, black, w/2226WX tender or gunmetal gray 263 or 2263W tender	555	925	1850
771 Track, O72 ga., 1935, curved, T-rail	—	2	3
772 Track, O72 ga., 1935, straight, T-rail	—	2	3
772S Track, O72 ga., 1940, straight, insulated, T-rail	3	4	5
773 Fish Plate Set, O72 ga., 1936, 100 bolts, 100 nuts, fifty fishplates and wrench	25	38	50
773 Locomotive, O ga., 1950, 4-6-4 steam, Hudson, w/2426W tender	700	650	1530
773 Locomotive, 1964, 4-6-4, Hudson, w/2046W tender	455	650	900
782 Streamliner Front Coach, O72 ga., 1935, part of articulated Hiawatha set, gray roof, orange sides and maroon underframe, marked "The Milwaukee Road"	150	250	500

	C5	C7	C9
783 Coach, O72 ga., 1935, streamliner, part of articulated Hiawatha set, gray roof orange sides and maroon underframe, marked "The Milwaukee Road"	150	250	500
784 Observation Car, O72 ga., 1935, streamliner, part of articulated Hiawatha set, gray roof, orange sides and maroon underframe, marked "The Milwaukee Road"	150	250	500
792 Front Coach, O72 ga., 1937, streamliner, part of Rail Chief set, w/700E Loco, maroon roof, red sides, red underframe, marked "792 Lionel Lines 792"	150	250	500
793 Coach, O72 ga., 1937, streamliner, part of Rail Chief set, marked "793 Lionel Lines 793"	150	250	500
794 Observation Car, O72 ga., 1937, streamliner, part of Rail Chief set, maroon roof, red sides, red underframe, marked "794 Lionel Lines 794"	150	250	500
800 Boxcar, O ga., 1915	33	55	110
800 Express Motor Car, standard ga., 1904	1000	2000	4000
HO-800 Flatcar, HO ga., 1958, w/airplane	18	30	60
801 Caboose, O ga., 1915	19	33	65

	C5	C7	C9
HO-801 Flatcar, HO ga., 1958, w/boat	9	15	30
802 Stock, O ga., 1915	21	35	70
803 Hopper, O ga., 1923, dark green	15	25	50
803 Hopper, O ga., 1923, peacock	25	43	85
803 Hopper, O ga., 1929	15	25	50
804 Tank Car, O ga., 1923, Sunoco, silver	21	35	70
804 Tank Car, O ga., 1923, terra-cotta	20	33	65
804 Tank Car, O ga., 1923, early, dark gray	20	33	65
804 Tank Car, O ga., 1929	21	35	70
HO-805 AEC Car, HO ga., 1959, w/light	12	20	40
805 Boxcar, O ga., 1927, orange, maroon	15	25	50
805 Boxcar, O ga., 1927, pea green, orange	23	38	75
806 Cattle Car, O ga., 1927	30	50	100
HO-806 Flatcar, HO ga., 1959, w/helicopter	15	25	50
807 Caboose, O ga., 1927	14	23	45
HO-807 Flatcar, HO ga., 1959, w/bulldozer	14	23	45
HO-808 Flatcar, w/tractor	14	23	45
809 Dump Car, O ga., 1931	18	30	60
HO-809 Helium Transport Car, HO ga., 1961	11	19	38
810 Crane, O ga., 1930-1940	60	100	200
HO-810 Generator Transport Car, HO ga., 1961	8	13	26

	C5	C7	C9
HO-811-25 Flat, HO ga., 1958, w/stakes	6	10	20
811 Flatcar, O ga., 1926, silver	40	68	135
811 Flatcar, O ga., 1926, maroon	13	21	42
812 Gondola, O ga., 1926	24	40	80
812T Tool Set, O ga., 1937	16	24	32
813 Cattle Car, O ga., 1926	36	60	120
HO-813 Mercury Capsule Car, HO ga., 1962	10	16	32
HO-814 Auto Transport Car, HO ga., 1958	15	25	50
814 Boxcar, O ga., 1926, orange body, brown roof	30	50	100
814 Boxcar, O ga., 1926, nickel plate	66	110	220
814R Refrigerator, O ga., 1929, white body, brown roof	85	143	285
814R Refrigerator, O ga., 1929, w/rubber-stamped lettering	360	600	1200
815 Tank Car, O ga., 1926, aluminum, silver	57	95	190
815 Tank Car, O ga., 1926, Shell, orange	40	68	135
HO-815 Tank Car, HO ga., 1958	11	18	35
HO-815-75 Tank Car, HO ga., 1963	8	13	25
HO-815-50 Tank Car, HO ga., 1964	8	13	25
HO-815-85 Tank Car, HO ga., 1964	8	13	25
816 Hopper, O ga., 1927, red, olive green	37	63	125
816 Hopper, O ga., 1927, black	75	125	250

Left to right: No. 806 Cattle car, $100; No. 805 Boxcar, $75; No. 807 Caboose, $45.

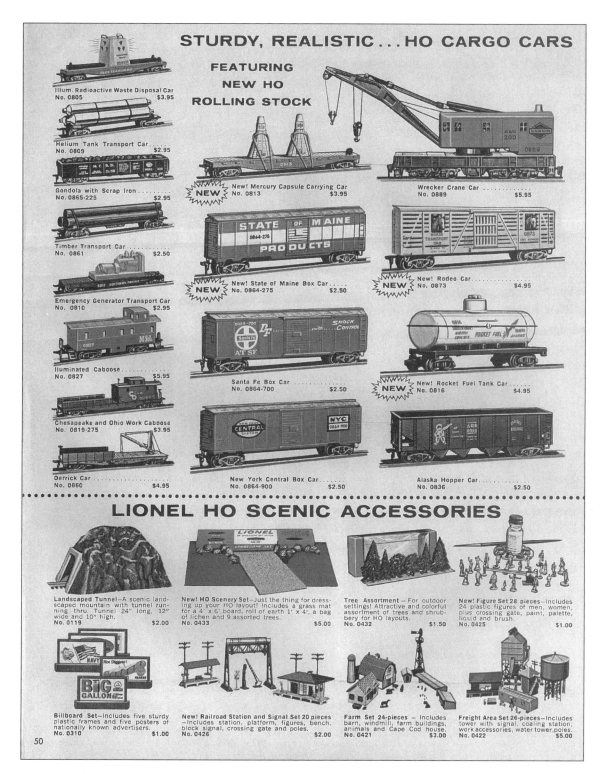

A variety of HO-scale rolling stock. Left row, top to bottom: No. HO-805 AEC car, $40; No. HO-809 Helium Transport car, $38; No. HO-865-225 Gondola, $25; No. HO-861 Timber Transport car, $20; No. HO-Generator Transport car, $26; No. HO-827 Caboose, $20; No. 819-275 Work Caboose, $25; No. 860 Derrick, $32. Middle row, top to bottom: No. HO-813 Mercury Capsule car, $32; No. 864-700 Boxcar, $20; No. HO-873 Rodeo car, $20; No. HO-816 Rocket Fuel Tank car, $25; No. HO-836 Hopper, $20. Also shown are a variety of HO-scale accessories. Top row, left to right: No. HO-119 Tunnel, $15; No. HO-432 Tree assortment, $14; No. HO-425 Figure set, $14. Photo courtesy 1962 Lionel catalog.

	C5	C7	C9
HO-816-50 Rock Fuel Tank Car, HO ga., 1962	8	13	25
HO-816 Rocket Fuel Tank Car, HO ga., 1962	8	13	25
817 Caboose, O ga., 1926, flat red, brown roof, rubber-stamped lettering	60	100	200
817 Caboose, O ga., 1926	28	48	95
HO-817 Caboose, HO ga., 1958	7	12	24
HO-817-250K Caboose, HO ga., 1959, Texas Special	6	10	20
HO-817-300 Caboose, HO ga., 1959, Southern Pacific	6	10	20
HO-817-275 Caboose, HO ga., 1959, New Haven	6	10	20
HO-817-200 Caboose, HO ga., 1959, AEC	6	10	20
HO-817-225 Caboose, HO ga., 1959, Alaska	6	10	20
HO-817-150 Caboose, HO ga., 1960, Santa Fe	6	10	20
HO-817-350 Caboose, HO ga., 1960, Rock Island	6	10	20
HO-819-1 Work Caboose, HO ga., 1958, P.R.R.	8	13	25
HO-819-100 Work Caboose, HO ga., 1958, B&M	8	13	25
HO-819-200 Work Caboose, HO ga., 1959, B&M	8	13	25
HO-819-225 Work Caboose, HO ga., 1960, Santa Fe	8	13	25
HO-819-250 Work Caboose, HO ga., 1960, NP	8	13	25
HO-819-275 Work Caboose, HO ga., 1960, C&O	8	13	25
HO-819-285 Work Caboose, HO ga., 1963, C&O	8	13	25
820 Boxcar, O ga., 1915, orange or maroon	27	45	90
820 Boxcar, O ga., 1915, dark olive, rubber stamped "ATSF" and "48522"	60	100	200
820 Floodlight, O ga., 1931, green base	68	113	225
820 Floodlight, O ga., 1931, terra-cotta base	45	75	150

	C5	C7	C9
821 Cattle Car, O ga., 1915	27	45	90
HO-821 Pipe Car, HO ga., 1960	8	13	25
HO-821-100 Pipe Car, HO ga., 1963	10	16	32
HO-821-50 Pipe Car, HO ga., 1964	8	13	25
822 Caboose, O ga., 1915	22	38	75
HO-823 Twin Missile Car, HO ga., 1960	21	35	70
HO-824 Flatcar, HO ga., 1958, w/two cars	14	22	45
HO-827 Caboose, HO ga., 1961, Lionel	6	10	20
HO-827-50 Caboose, HO ga., 1963, AEC	6	10	20
HO-827-75 Caboose, HO ga., 1963, Lionel	6	10	20
HO-830 Flatcar, HO ga., 1958, w/two vans	12	20	40
831 Flatcar, O ga., 1927	18	30	60
HO-834 Poultry Car, HO ga., 1959	13	21	42
HO-836 Hopper, HO ga., 1961	6	10	20
HO-836-100 Hopper, HO ga., 1964, Lionel	6	10	20
HO-836-60 Hopper, HO ga., 1966, Alaska	6	10	20
HO-837 Caboose, HO ga., 1961, M&StL	5	8	15
HO-837-100 Caboose, HO ga., 1963, M&StL	6	10	20
HO-838 Caboose, HO ga., 1961, Lackawanna	6	10	20
HO-840 Caboose, HO ga., 1961, NYC	6	10	20
HO-841 Caboose, HO ga., 1961	6	10	20
HO-841-50 Caboose, HO ga., 1962, Union Pacific	6	10	20
HO-841-175 Caboose, HO ga., 1962, Santa Fe	6	10	20
HO-842 Culvert Pipe Car, HO ga., 1960	8	12	25
HO-845 Gold Bullion Car, HO ga., 1962	10	16	32

	C5	C7	C9
HO-847-100 Exploding Target Car, HO ga., 1960	17	29	58
HO-847 Exploding Target Car, HO ga., 1960	6	9	18
HO-850-100 Missile Launching Car, HO ga.	11	19	38
HO-850 Missile Launching Car, HO ga., 1960	11	18	35
HO-860 Derrick, HO ga., 1958	10	16	32
HO-861 Timber Transport Car, HO ga., 1960	6	10	20
HO-861-100 Timber Transport Car, HO ga., 1961	8	13	26
HO-862-25 Gondola, HO ga., 1958	3	5	10
HO-863 Rail Truck Car, HO ga., 1960	8	13	26
HO-864-175 Boxcar, HO ga., 1958, Timken	6	10	20
HO-864-225 Boxcar, HO ga., 1958, Central of Georgia	6	10	20
HO-864-25 Boxcar, HO ga., 1958, NYC	6	10	20
HO-864-200 Boxcar, HO ga., 1958, Monon	6	10	20
HO-864-250 Boxcar, HO ga., 1958, Wabash	6	10	20
HO-864-125 Boxcar, HO ga., 1958, Rutland	6	10	20
HO-864-50 Boxcar, HO ga., 1958, State of Maine	6	10	20
HO-864-1 Boxcar, HO ga., 1958, Seaboard	6	10	20
HO-864-100 Boxcar, HO ga., 1958, New Haven	6	10	20
HO-864-150 Boxcar, HO ga., 1958, M&StL	6	10	20
HO-864-900 Boxcar, HO ga., 1959, NYC	6	10	20
HO-864-300 Boxcar, HO ga., 1959, Alaska	6	10	20
HO-864-325 Boxcar, HO ga., 1959, D.S.S.A.	6	10	20
HO-864-350 Boxcar, HO ga., 1959, State of Maine	9	15	30

	C5	C7	C9
HO-864-400 Boxcar, HO ga., 1960, B&M	6	10	20
HO-864-700 Boxcar, HO ga., 1961, Santa Fe	6	10	20
HO-864-275 Boxcar, HO ga., 1962, State of Maine	6	10	20
HO-864-935 Boxcar, HO ga., 1963, NYC	6	10	20
HO-864-925 Boxcar, HO ga., 1964, NYC	6	10	20
HO-865 Gondola, HO ga., 1958, w/canisters	10	16	32
HO-865-225 Gondola, HO ga., 1960, w/scrap iron	8	13	25
HO-865-250 Gondola, HO ga., 1960, w/crates	8	13	25
HO-865-300 Gondola, HO ga., 1963, w/crates	8	13	25
HO-865-350 Gondola, HO ga., 1963, NYC	6	10	20
HO-865-375 Gondola, HO ga., 1963, NYC	6	10	20
HO-865-400 Gondola, HO ga., 1963, NYC w/crates	6	10	20
HO-865-435 Gondola, HO ga., 1964	6	10	20
HO-866-1 Cattle Car, HO ga., 1958, M.K.T.	6	10	20
HO-866-25 Cattle Car, HO ga., 1958, Santa Fe	6	10	20
HO-866-200 Circus Car, HO ga., 1959	10	16	32
HO-870 Maintenance Car, HO ga., 1959, w/generator	9	15	30
HO-872-50 Reefer, HO ga., 1958, El Capitan	6	10	20
HO-872-25 Reefer, HO ga., 1958, Illinois Central	6	10	20
HO-872-1 Reefer, HO ga., 1958, Fruit Growers	6	10	20
HO-872-200 Reefer, HO ga., 1959, Railway Express	6	10	20
HO-873 Rodeo Car, HO ga., 1962	6	10	20
HO-874 Boxcar, HO ga., 1964, NYC	15	25	50

	C5	C7	C9
HO-874-60 Boxcar, HO ga., 1964, B&M	6	10	20
HO-874-25 Boxcar, HO ga., 1965, NYC	6	10	20
HO-875 Flatcar, HO ga., 1959, w/missile	10	17	34
876 Helios 21 Spaceship, 1965	12	20	40
HO-877 Miscellaneous Car, HO ga., 1958	6	10	20
HO-879 Derrick, HO ga., 1958	8	13	26
HO-880 Maintenance Car, HO ga., 1959, w/light	18	30	60
900 Boxcar, O ga., 1917, ammunition, part of armored train set	150	250	500
900 Express Trail Car, 2-7/8" ga., 1904	1000	2000	4500
900 or B Locomotive, O ga., 1939, catalog number for 230 and tender, 0-6-0, similar to loco 227	450	750	1500
HO-900 Operating Platform, HO ga., 1960	11	18	36
901 Gondola, O ga., 1919, gray or maroon	20	33	65
902 Gondola, O ga., 1927, peacock	8	13	25
902 Gondola, O ga., 1927, apple green	8	13	25
902-5 Rocks, 1958	—	—	3
HO-903 Track, HO ga., 1958, straight, 3"	—	—	1
HO-905 Track, HO ga., 1958, straight, 1-1/2"	—	—	1
HO-906 Track, HO ga., 1968, straight, 6"	—	—	1
909 Smoke Fluid, 1957, full bottle	—	—	5
HO-909 Track, HO ga., 1958, straight, 9"	—	—	1
910 Grove, 1932, eleven trees	150	225	300
911 Country Estate, 1932, 191 villa, shrubbery and trees	450	675	900
912 Suburban Home, 1932, 189 villa, shrubbery and trees	375	525	750

	C5	C7	C9
913 Bungalow, 1932, w/garden, flowers and trees	250	375	500
914 Formal Garden Park, 1932, two grass plots, centerpiece, flowering bushes, cream base	175	268	350
915 Curved Tunnel Mountain, O ga., 1932, large	200	300	400
916 Tunnel, O ga., 1932, curved	175	263	350
917 Mountain, 1932, medium	200	300	400
918 Mountain, 1932, small	175	263	350
919 Park Grass, 1932, 8 ounces	9	14	18
920-8 Lichen, 1958	—	—	3
920 Scenic Display Set, 1957	57	76	95
920 Scenic Park, 1932, small	2000	3000	4000
920-2 Tunnel Portals, 1958	15	23	30
921 Scenic Park, 1932, large	1400	2100	2800
921C Scenic Park, 1932, center section	400	600	800
922 Lamp Terrace, 1932	175	263	350
HO-922 Remote Control Switch, HO ga., 1958, right	—	2	3
HO-923 Remote Control Switch, HO ga., 1958, left	—	2	3
923 Tunnel, standard ga., 1933	200	300	400
924 Tunnel, O72 ga., 1935, curved	150	225	300
HO-925-10 Insulating Clip, HO ga., 1960	—	—	1
HO-925 Terminal Track, HO ga., 1958, straight	—	1	2
926 Tube of Lubrication, 1955, full	—	—	3
927 Flag Plot, 1937-1942	40	60	80
927-3 Liquid Track Cleaner, 1955, full can	—	—	5
927 Lubrication and Maintenance, 1950-1953, kit	10	17	33
928 Maintenance Kit, 1960-1963	31	36	40
HO-929 Upcoupling Track, HO ga., 1958, 9"	2	3	4
HO-930 30 Degrees Crossing, HO ga., 1960	2	3	4

	C5	C7	C9
HO-939 Uncoupler, HO ga., 1958	—	2	3
HO-942 Manual Switch, HO ga., 1958, right	—	2	3
943 Exploding Ammo Dump Car, 1959	20	30	40
HO-943 Manual Switch, HO ga., 1958, left	—	2	3
950 Railroad Map, 1958-1966	25	38	50
HO-950 Re-railer, HO ga., 1958	—	2	3
951 Farm Set, 1958, plastic, thirteen pieces	8	15	38
952 Figure Set, 1958, plastic, thirty pieces	8	15	34
953 Figure Set, 1959, plastic, thirty-two pieces	8	15	35
954 Swimming Pool and Playground Set, 1959, plastic, thirty pieces	10	15	35
955 Highway Set, 1958, plastic, twenty-two pieces	10	15	30
956 Stockyard, 1959, plastic, eighteen pieces	10	15	30
957 Farm Building and Animal Set, 1958, plastic, thirty-five pieces	10	15	30
958 Vehicles, 1958, plastic, twenty-four pieces	10	20	31
959 Barn Set, 1958, plastic, twenty-three pieces	6	15	33
960 Barn Yard Set, 1959, plastic, twenty-nine pieces	6	15	33
HO-960 Bumper Track, HO ga., 1960	—	—	1
HO-961 Bumper Track, HO ga., 1961, illuminated	—	—	1
961 School Set, 1959, plastic, thirty-six pieces	10	15	32
962 Turnpike Set, 1958, plastic, twenty-four pieces	10	15	38
963 Frontier Set, 1959, plastic, eighteen pieces	10	15	40
964 Factory, 1959, plastic, twenty-two pieces	10	15	50

	C5	C7	C9
965 Farm Set, 1959, plastic, thirty-six pieces	13	15	35
966 Firehouse, 1958, plastic, forty-five pieces	13	15	35
967 Post Office, 1958, plastic, twenty-five pieces	10	15	35
968 TV Transmitter, 1958, plastic, twenty-eight pieces	10	15	34
969 Construction Set, 1960, plastic, twenty-three pieces	10	15	30
970 Ticket Booth, 1958-1960, cardboard	65	98	130
971 Box of Lichen, 1959	2	5	10
972 Trees, 1959	2	5	10
973 Landscaping Set, 1959	7	11	15
974 Scenery Set, 1962	11	17	22
HO-975 Terminal Track, HO ga., 1958, curved	1	1	1
980 Ranch Set, 1960, plastic, fourteen pieces	10	15	36
981 Freight Yard Set, 1960, plastic, ten pieces	10	15	34
982 Surburban House, 1960, plastic, eighteen pieces	10	15	34
HO-983 Curved Track, HO ga., 1958, curved, 3", 18" radius	—	—	1
983 Farm Set, 1960, plastic, seven pieces	10	15	34
HO-984 Curved Track, HO ga., 1958, 4-1/2", 18" radius	—	—	1
984 Railroad Set, 1961, plastic, twenty-two pieces	10	15	30
HO-985 Curved Track, HO ga., 1958, 9", 15" radius	—	—	1
985 Freight Area Set, 1961, plastic, thirty-two pieces	13	15	32
986 Farm Set, 1962, plastic, twenty pieces	10	15	33
HO-986 Track, HO ga., 1958, curved, 4-1/2", 15" radius	—	—	1
987 Town Set, 1962, plastic, twenty-four pieces	10	25	33
988 Railroad Structure, 1962, sixteen pieces	10	25	33

	C5	C7	C9
HO-989 Track, HO ga., 1958, curved, 9", 18" radius	—	—	1
HO-990 90 Degrees Crossing, HO ga., 1958	3	5	7
1000 Passenger Car, 2-7/8" ga., 1904, motorized	1000	2000	4000
1000 Trailer Truck, standard ga., 1910, 100 series	840	1400	2800
1000 Trolley, standard ga., 1910, trailer	840	1400	2800
1001 Locomotive, O27 ga., 1948, 2-4-2, steam, w/1001T tender	15	25	50
1002 Gondola, O27 ga., 1948	4	7	14
1004 Boxcar, O27 ga., 1948	7	11	22
1005 Tank Car, O27 ga., 1948	4	7	13
1007 Caboose, O27 ga., 1948	3	4	8
1007 Platform and Background, O27 ga., 1936	30	45	60
1008-50 Automatic Uncoupling Track, O27 ga., 1961, each	—	—	2
1008 Uncoupling Track, O27 ga., 1957, each	—	—	2
1009 Manumatic Uncoupling Track Set, O27 ga., 1948	5	7	9
1010 Interurban Trolley, standard ga., 1910	1750	2625	3500
1010 Transformer, 1961, 35 watt	8	12	20
1010 Winner Locomotive, O27 ga., 1931, 0-4-0, electric	30	50	100
1011 Interurban Trolley, standard ga., 1910, motor car	1050	1750	3500
1011 Transformer, 1961, 15 watt	8	12	20
1011 Winner Pullman, O27 ga., 1931	9	15	30
1012 Interurban Trolley, standard ga., 1910	1050	1750	3500
1012 Transformer, 1950, 35 watt	7	9	19
1012 Winner Station Transformer, 1931	22	33	45
1013 Track, O27 ga., 1934, curved	—	—	1
1013 Track, O27 ga., 1968, curved, half-section	—	—	1
1013-17 Track Pins, O27 ga., 1938, steel, price per dozen	—	1	2

	C5	C7	C9
1014 Lockton, O27 ga., 1931	—	1	2
1014 Transformer, 1955, 40 watt	10	15	20
1015 Transformer, 1956, 45 watt	8	12	32
1015 Winner Locomotive, O27 ga., 1931, 0-4-0, steam, w/1016 tender, black	30	50	100
1016 Transformer, 1959, 35 watt	6	12	30
1016 Winner Locomotive, w/tender, black	30	50	100
1017 Lionel-Ives Transformer Station, 1933	22	34	45
1017 Winner Transformer Station, 1931	22	34	45
1018 Track, O27 ga., 1934, straight	—	—	1
1018 Track, O27 ga., 1968, straight, half section	—	—	1
1019 Track Set, O27 ga., 1938, remote control	5	8	10
1019 Winner Observation Car, O27 ga., 1931	7	13	25
1020 90 Degrees Crossing, O27 ga., 1955	1	2	6
1020 Winner Baggage Car, O27 ga., 1931	7	13	25
1021 90 Degrees Crossing, O27 ga., 1933	1	2	6
1022 Curved Tunnel, O27 ga., 1935	20	30	40
1022 Switch, O27 ga., 1955, manual, price per pair	8	12	25
1023 45 Degree Crossing, O27 ga., 1955, each	1	2	3
1023 Tunnel, O27 ga., 1934, straight	18	27	35
1024 Switches, O27 ga., 1935, manual, price per pair	5	8	11
1025 Bumper, O27 ga., 1946	6	10	15
1025 Transformer, 1961, 45 watt	12	18	30
1026 Transformer, 1963, 25 watt	5	7	12
1027 Transformer Station, 1934	20	30	40
1028 Transformer, 1935, 25 watt	3	4	5
1029 Transformer, 1936, 25 watt	3	4	5
1030 Transformer, 1936, 40 watt	4	6	12

Top row, left to right: No. 1107 Donald Duck hand car, $1,200; No. 1103 Peter Rabbit hand car, $1,000. Bottom row, left to right: No. 110 Mickey Mouse hand car, $1,000; No. 1005 Santa Claus hand car, $1,800.

Donald Duck Rail Car with original box.

	C5	C7	C9
1030 Winner Locomotive, O27 ga., 1932, 0-4-0, electric, orange w/green roof	30	50	100
1032 Transformer, 1948, 90 watt	30	40	60
1033 Transformer, 1948, 90 watt	40	55	75
1034 Transformer, 1948, 75 watt	28	35	55
1035 Transformer, 1947, 60 watt	12	18	25

	C5	C7	C9
1035 Winner Locomotive, O27 ga., 1932, 0-4-0, steam, w/1016 tender	30	50	100
1037 Transformer, 1941, 40 watt	10	15	20
1039 Transformer, 1938, 35 watt	10	15	20
1040 Transformer and Whistle Controller, 1938, 60 watt	12	18	25
1041 Transformer, 1940, 60 watt	12	18	25

	C5	C7	C9
1042 Transformer, 1942, 75 watt ..	12	18	25
1043-500FX Girls Train Transformer, 1957, 60 watt, ivory case	55	75	115
1043 Transformer, 50 watt	12	20	35
1043 Transformer, 1953, 60 watt ..	10	15	20
1044 Transformer, 1957, 90 watt ..	30	40	65
1045C Contactor, 1938	—	—	1
1045 Operating Watchman, 1938, nickel or brass sign	25	38	50
1046 Mechanical Gateman and Crossing, 1936	45	68	90
1047 Switchman, 1959-1961, w/flat	50	80	150
1050 Passenger Car, 2-7/8" ga., 1905, trailer	2000	3500	7500
1053 Transformer, 1956, 60 watt ..	30	45	60
1055 Locomotive, O ga., 1960, Alco A diesel, Texas Special, uncataloged	20	32	65
1060 Locomotive, O27 ga., 1960, Scout team, 2-4-2, w/1050T tender, uncataloged	12	20	30
1061 Locomotive, O27 ga., 1969, 2-4-2, steam, w/1061T tender...	12	20	30
1062 Locomotive, O27 ga., 1963, 2-4-2, w/1062T tender	12	19	38
1063 Transformer, 1961, 75 watt ..	18	25	55
1065 Locomotive, O ga., Alco A unit only, diesel, Union Pacific, uncataloged	35	55	90
1066 Locomotive, O ga., Alco A unit only, diesel, Union Pacific, uncataloged	50	75	105
1073 Transformer, 1961, 60 watt ..	20	25	55
1100 Mickey Mouse Handcar, 1935, mechanical, wind-up, orange base	600	900	1200
1100 Mickey Mouse Handcar, 1935, green base	500	750	1000
1100 Mickey Mouse Handcar, 1935, red base	500	700	900
1100 Summer Trolley, standard ga., 1911	1050	1750	3500

	C5	C7	C9
1100 Trailer Trucks, standard ga., 1924, thirty-five series	3	5	10
1101 Locomotive, 2-4-2	15	25	50
1101 Trailer Trucks, standard ga., 1924, w/lights, thirty-five series	3	5	10
1103 Peter Rabbit Handcar, 1935, mechanical, wind-up, track operation	500	700	1000
1103 Peter Rabbit Handcar, 1935, floor operation	500	700	900

Santa Claus Handcar with original box.

	C5	C7	C9
1105 Santa Claus Handcar, 1935, mechanical, wind-up, green base	900	1400	1800
1105 Santa Claus Handcar, 1935, mechanical, red base	800	1200	1600

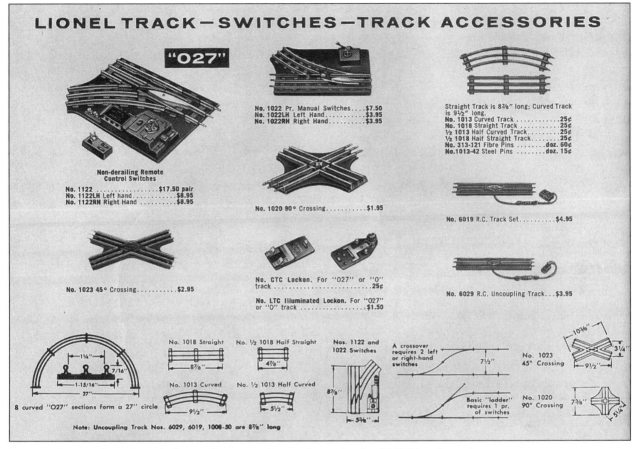

Various forms of track, switches and accessories as shown in the 1961 Lionel catalog.

	C5	C7	C9
1107 Donald Duck Rail Car, 1936, mechanical, wind-up, green roof	600	900	1200
1107 Donald Duck Rail Car, 1936, red roof	600	900	1200
1110 Locomotive, O27 ga., 1949, 2-4-2, scout steam	14	23	45
1120 Locomotive, O27 ga., 1950, 2-4-2, scout steam	15	25	50
1121 Switches, O27 ga., 1937, electric, remote control, pair	12	18	25
1122-520 Adapter Kit, O27 ga., 1957	5	8	10
1122-234 Insulating Pins, O27 ga., 1957	—	—	1
1122-100 Switch Control, O27 ga., 1957	3	4	5
1122 Switches, O27 ga., 1952, remote control	17	26	35

	C5	C7	C9
1130 Locomotive, O27 ga., 1953, 2-4-2, steam, w/1130T tender	16	13	35
1144 Transformer, 1968, 75 watt	22	33	45
1200 Trailer Truck, standard ga., 1923, ten series	4	6	12
1201 Trailer Truck, standard ga., 1923, ten series w/lights	4	6	12
1229 Transformer, 1938, 220 volts	50	75	100
1230 Transformer, 1938, 220 volts	50	75	100
1239 Transformer, 1941, 220 volts	50	75	100
1241 Transformer, 1941, 220 volts	50	75	100
1300 Trailer Truck, standard ga., 1925, 200 series	4	6	12
1301 Trailer Truck, standard ga., 1925, 200 series w/lights	4	6	12

	C5	C7	C9
1400 Trailer Truck, standard ga., 1925, 418 series	5	8	16
1401 Trailer Truck, standard ga., 1925, 418 series w/lights	5	8	16
1506-8 Bulb, 1935, 1-1/2 volt, clear	—	—	1
1506 L.I. Locomotive, 1933, steam, mechanical....................	36	60	120
1506L Locomotive Outfit, 1933, mechanical, w/1502T tender.....	36	60	120
1506 Locomotive Outfit, 1935, mechanical, w/1509T Tender, 1515 tank and 1517 caboose.....	75	125	250
1508 Locomotive Outfit, 1935, 0-4-0, mechanical, Vanderbilt-type, w/1509T tender................	81	135	270
1511 Locomotive Outfit, 1936-1937, 0-4-0, mechanical, Commodore Vanderbilt-type, black, w/1516 tender.................	45	75	150
1511 Locomotive Outfit, 1936-1937, 0-4-0, mechanical, red, w/1516 tender	54	90	180
1512 Gondola, O27 ga., 1936........	18	30	60
1512 L.I. Gondola, O27 ga., 1933	18	30	60
1512 Winner Gondola, O27 ga., 1931	18	30	60
1514 Boxcar, O27 ga., 1934..........	12	21	42
1514 L.I. Boxcar, O27 ga., 1933 ...	7	11	22
1514 Winner Boxcar, O27 ga., 1932..................................	9	15	30
1515 L.I. Tank Car, O27 ga., 1933..................................	11	19	38
1515 Tank Car, O27 ga., 1934.......	19	32	64
1516T Tender, O27 ga., 1936........	12	21	42
1517 Caboose, O27 ga., 1931-1937..................................	11	18	36
1517 L.I. Caboose, O27 ga., 1933..................................	9	15	30
1517 Winner Caboose, O27 ga., 1931..................................	7	11	22
1520 Animal, 1935	60	100	200
1521 Locomotive Outfit, 1937, mechanical, w/1516T tender	180	300	600
1536 Mickey Mouse Circus Train Outfit, includes cardboard figures, circus facade, tickets and Mickey as barker; train loco 1508, 1509 red, 1536 dinner, 1536 band and 1536 animal car, w/original box	1500	2500	3500
1550 Switches-mechanical, 1933, remote control, price per pair....	20	30	40
1551 90 Degrees Crossing, 1936, mechanical	2	3	4
1555 90 Degrees Crossing, 1933, mechanical	3	5	5

No. 1536 Mickey Mouse Circus Train Outfit, $3,500.

	C5	C7	C9
1560 Station, 1933, mechanical	15	22	30
1572 Lionel Jr. Telegraph Posts, 1934, mechanical	11	18	36
1573 Lionel Jr. Warning Signal, 1934, mechanical	8	12	16
1574 Lionel Jr. Clock, 1934, mechanical	5	8	16
1588 Locomotive Outfit, 1936, 0-4-0, mechanical, torpedo type, w/1588 or 1516 tender	66	110	220
1615E L.I. Locomotive, O27 ga., 1933, 0-4-0, electric, red cab, brown roof	75	125	250
1615 Locomotive, O27 ga., 1955, 0-4-0, w/1615T tender, switcher....................................	85	145	200
1625 Locomotive, O27 ga., 1958, 0-4-0, steam, switcher, w/1625 tender	90	150	250
1630 Pullman, O27 ga., 1938, blue sides w/aluminum roof	20	33	65
1630 Pullman, O27 ga., 1938, blue sides w/gray roof	20	33	65
1631 Observation Car, O27 ga., 1938, blue sides w/aluminum roof..	23	39	78
1640-100 Presidential Kit, 1960....	80	90	100

	C5	C7	C9
1654 Locomotive, O27 ga., 1946, 2-4-2, steam, w/1654W tender...	30	50	100
1655 Locomotive, O27 ga., 1945, 2-4-2, steam, w/6654W tender...	45	75	150
1656 Locomotive, O27 ga., 1948, 0-4-0, steam, switcher, w/6403 tender...	110	185	370
1661E L.I. Locomotive, O27 ga., 1933, 2-4-0, steam, glossy black, w/1661 Tender...............	39	65	130
1662 Locomotive, O27 ga., 1940, 0-4-0, steam, switcher, w/2203 tender...	125	205	410
1663 Locomotive, O27 ga., 1940, 0-4-0, steam, switcher, 2201 tender...	138	230	460
1664 or E Locomotive Outfit, O27 ga., 1938, 2-4-2, black or gunmetal gray, w/1689T, 1689W, 2666T or 2666W tender...	60	103	205
1665 Locomotive, O27 ga., 1946, 0-4-0, steam, switcher w/2403B tender...	125	210	420
1666 or E Locomotive Outfit, O27 ga., 1938, 2-4-2, black, w/2666T, 2666W, 2689T, 2689W or 1689W tender...........	39	65	130
1666 or E Locomotive Outfit, O27 ga., 1938, 2-4-2, gunmetal gray, w/tender....................................	36	60	120

No. 1666 Locomotive Outfit 2-4-2, black, with 2666T, 2666W, 2689T, 2689W or 1689W tender, $130.

	C5	C7	C9
1668 or E Locomotive, O27 ga., 1937, steam, black, 2-6-2, w/1689T or 1689W tender	40	68	135
1668 or E Locomotive, O27 ga., 1937, 2-6-2, steam, gunmetal gray	42	70	140
1673 Coach, 1936, streamliner, mechanical, red	14	23	45
1674 Pullman, 1936, streamliner, mechanical	14	23	45
1675 Observation Car, 1936, streamliner, mechanical	14	23	45
1677 Gondola, O27 ga., 1934	12	20	40
1677 L.I. Gondola, O27 ga., 1933	12	20	40
1679 Boxcar, O27 ga., 1934	8	13	25
1679 L.I. Boxcar, O27 ga., 1933 ...	12	20	40
1680 L.I. Tank Car, O27 ga., 1933	12	20	40
1680 Tank Car, O27 ga., 1934	13	21	42
1681 or E Lionel Jr. Locomotive, O27 ga., 1934, 2-4-0, steam, red	48	80	160
1681 or E Lionel Jr. Locomotive, O27 ga., 1934, 2-4-0, steam, black	42	70	140
1682 Caboose, O27 ga., 1934	6	10	20
1682 L.I. Caboose, O27 ga., 1933	9	15	30
1684 Locomotive, O27 ga., 1942, 2-4-2, steam, black, w/1689T, 1688T, 2689T or 2689W tender	45	78	155
1684 Locomotive, O27 ga., 1942, 2-4-2, steam, gunmetal gray	29	48	95
1685 Pullman, O ga., 1933, Ives transitional car, blue body w/silver roof, four-wheel trucks, uncataloged	120	200	400
1685 Pullman, O ga., 1933, red body w/maroon roof, four-wheel trucks, uncataloged	90	150	300
1685 Pullman, O ga., 1933, gray body w/maroon roof, six-wheel trucks, uncataloged	135	225	450

	C5	C7	C9
1686 Baggage Car, O ga., 1933, Ives transitional car, blue body w/silver roof, four-wheel trucks, uncataloged	120	200	400
1686 Baggage Car, O ga., 1933, red body w/maroon roof, four-wheel trucks, uncataloged	90	150	300
1686 Baggage Car, O ga., 1933, gray body w/maroon roof, six-wheel trucks, uncataloged	135	225	450
1687 Observation Car, O ga., 1933, Ives transitional car, blue body w/silver roof, four-wheel trucks, uncataloged	120	200	400
1687 Observation Car, O ga., 1933, red body w/maroon roof, four-wheel trucks, uncataloged .	90	150	300
1687 Observation Car, O ga., 1933, gray body w/maroon roof, six-wheel trucks, uncataloged	135	225	450
1688 or E Locomotive, O27 ga., 1936, 2-4-2, steam, black, w/1689T tender	36	90	120
1688 or E Locomotive, O27 ga., 1936, 2-4-2, steam, gunmetal gray	60	100	200
1689E Locomotive, O27 ga., 1936, 2-4-2, steam, black, w/1689T tender	35	55	110
1689E Locomotive, O27 ga., 1936, 2-4-2, steam, gunmetal gray	39	65	130
1690 L.I. Pullman, O27 ga., 1933, red w/red or brown roof	15	25	50
1690 Pullman, O27 ga., 1934, red, w/red or brown roof	12	20	40
1691 L.I. Observation Car, O27 ga., 1933, red w/red or brown roof	12	20	40
1691 Observation Car, O27 ga., 1934, red w/red or brown roof	12	20	40
1692 Pullman, O27 ga., 1937, peacock body and roof, uncataloged	12	20	40
1693 Observation Car, O27 ga., 1937, peacock body and roof, uncataloged	12	20	40

	C5	C7	C9
1697 Locomotive, Tender and Transformer Outfit, O27 ga., 1937	45	75	150
1698E Locomotive, Tender and Transformer Outfit, O27 ga., 1936	60	100	200
1699E Locomotive, Tender and Transformer Outfit, O27 ga., 1936	60	100	200
1700 or E Power Car, O27 ga., 1935, diesel, streamliner, aluminum, red, marked "Lionel Jr."	66	110	220
1701 Coach, O27 ga., 1935, streamliner, aluminum, red or chrome	36	60	120
1702 Observation Car, O27 ga., 1935, streamliner, aluminum, red or chrome	36	60	120
1703 Front Coach, O27 ga., 1935, w/drawbar, streamliner	12	20	40
1717 Gondola, O ga., 1933, orange and tan or yellow and green, uncataloged	15	25	50
1719 Boxcar, O ga., 1933, peacock w/blue roof, orange doors, yellow and brown, uncataloged	13	23	45
1722 Caboose, O ga., 1933, orange or red body, uncataloged	18	30	60
1766 Pullman, standard ga., 1934	85	142	285
1767 Baggage Car, standard ga., 1934	90	150	300
1768 Observation Car, standard ga., 1934	105	175	350
1811 L.I. Pullman, O27 ga., 1933	22	36	72
1811 Pullman, O27 ga., 1934	22	36	72
1812 L.I. Observation Car, O27 ga., 1933	22	36	72
1812 Observation Car, O27 ga., 1934	22	36	72
1813 Baggage Car, O27 ga., 1934	18	30	60
1813 L.I. Baggage Car, O27 ga., 1933	18	30	60

	C5	C7	C9
1816 or W Power Car, 1935, diesel, streamliner, wind-up mechanical, marked "Silver Streak"	42	70	140
1817 Coach, 1935, streamliner, mechanical, chrome and orange	10	16	32
1818 Observation Car, 1935, streamliner, mechanical, chrome and orange	10	16	32
1835E Locomotive, standard ga., 1934, 2-4-2, steam, w/1835T, 1835TW or 1835W tender	230	380	760
1862LT Locomotive, O27 ga., 1959, 4-4-0, steam, Civil War, w/1862T tender, marked "General"	100	160	225
1865 Coach, O27 ga., 1959, Western & Atlantic	20	34	68
1866 Baggage Car, O27 ga., 1959, Western & Atlantic	30	50	100
1872 Locomotive, Super O ga., 1959, 4-4-0, steam, w/1872W tender, Civil War, marked "General"	100	200	300
1875 Coach, Super O ga., 1959, Western & Atlantic	125	150	250
1875W Coach, Super O ga., 1959, Western & Atlantic, w/whistle	85	125	200
1876 Baggage Car, Super O ga., 1959, Western & Atlantic	36	60	120
1877 Flatcar, O27 ga., 1959, part of general set, w/six horses	30	50	80
1882 Locomotive, Super O ga., 1959, steam, Sears production, Civil War General, 4-4-0, also called Halloween General, uncataloged	200	300	500
1885 Coach, Super O ga., 1959, Sears production, Western & Atlantic, uncataloged	95	150	275
1887 Flatcar, O27 ga., 1959, Sears production, w/six horses, uncataloged	80	130	180

	C5	C7	C9
1910 Locomotive, standard ga., 1910, 0-6-0, electric, dark olive green, marked "New York, New Haven and Hartford"	600	1000	2000
1910 Pullman, standard ga., 1910, dark olive green w/maroon doors, "1910 Pullman 1910," uncataloged	540	900	1800
1911 Locomotive, standard ga., 1910, 0-4-0, electric, dark olive	330	550	1100
1911 Locomotive, standard ga., 1910, 0-4-0, electric, maroon	300	500	1000
1911 Special Locomotive, standard ga., 1911, 0-4-4-0, electric, maroon, marked "New York, New Haven and Hartford" or "New York Central Lines"	420	700	1400
1912 Locomotive, standard ga., 1910, 0-4-4-0, electric, dark olive green	660	1100	2200
1912 Locomotive, standard ga., 1910, 0-4-4-0, electric, marked "New York, New Haven and Hartford"	720	1200	2400
1912 Special Locomotive, standard ga., 1911, 0-4-4-0, electric, all brass engine	1500	2500	5000
1926-3 Lionel-Ives Bulb, 1933, 6 volt	—	—	1
2016 Locomotive, O27 ga., 1955, 2-6-4, steam, w/6026W tender	60	100	200
2018 Locomotive, O27 ga., 1956, 2-6-4, steam, w/6026W tender	60	85	120
2020 Locomotive, O27 ga., 1946, 6-8-6, steam, w/2020W, 2466WX or 6020W tender	100	140	210
2023 Color Variation, yellow body w/gray roof and gray nose	900	1500	3000
2023 Locomotive, O27 ga., 1950, UP Alco AA, diesel, yellow body w/gray roof or silver body w/gray roof	90	155	310
2024 Locomotive, O27 ga., 1969, Alco A, diesel, C&O	30	45	80

	C5	C7	C9
2025 Locomotive, O27 ga., 1947, 2-6-2, steam, w/6466WX or 6466W tender	70	100	175
2026-58 Bulb, 1950, 18 volt, clear	—	—	1
2026 Locomotive, O27 ga., 1948, 2-6-2, steam, w/6466WX or 6466W tender	60	80	135
2028 Locomotive, O27 ga., 1955, diesel, GP-7 PRR, Tuscan brown	140	375	500
2029 Locomotive, O ga., 1964, 2-6-4, steam, w/243W tender	70	90	125
2031 Locomotive, O27 ga., 1952, R.I. Alco AA, diesel, black body w/red middle stripe	150	275	410
2032 Locomotive, O27 ga., 1952, Erie Alco AA, diesel, black body w/yellow middle stripe	125	150	275
2033 Locomotive, O27 ga., 1952, U.P. Alco AA, diesel, silver body	155	200	350
2034 Locomotive, O27 ga., 1952, 2-4-2, steam	36	60	120
2035 Locomotive, O27 ga., 1950, 2-6-4, steam, w/2466W tender	65	95	190
2036 Locomotive, O27 ga., 1950, 2-6-4, steam, w/6466W tender	65	90	150
2037-500 Girlís Locomotive, O27 ga., 1957, 2-6-4, steam, pink	360	600	1200
2037 Locomotive, O27 ga., 1953, 2-6-4, steam, w/6026W or 6026T tender	60	90	125
2041 Locomotive, O27 ga., 1969, R.I., Alco AA, diesel, black body w/white stripe	60	85	120
2046 Locomotive, O27 ga., 1950, 4-6-4, steam, w/2046W tender	135	185	270
2055 Locomotive, O27 ga., 1953, 4-6-4, steam, w/1025W or 2046W tender	75	130	220
2056 Locomotive, O27 ga., 1952, 4-6-4, steam, w/2046W tender	105	175	250

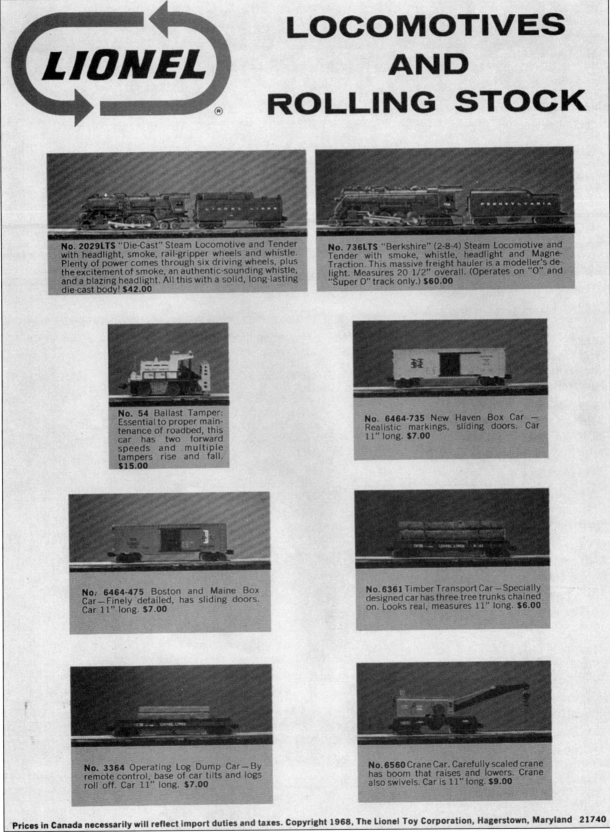

LIONEL

LOCOMOTIVES AND ROLLING STOCK

No. 2029LTS "Die-Cast" Steam Locomotive and Tender with headlight, smoke, rail-gripper wheels and whistle. Plenty of power comes through six driving wheels, plus the excitement of smoke, an authentic-sounding whistle, and a blazing headlight. All this with a solid, long-lasting die-cast body! **$42.00**

No. 736LTS "Berkshire" (2-8-4) Steam Locomotive and Tender with smoke, whistle, headlight and Magne-Traction. This massive freight hauler is a modeller's delight. Measures 20 1/2" overall. (Operates on "O" and "Super O" track only.) **$60.00**

No. 54 Ballast Tamper: Essential to proper maintenance of roadbed, this car has two forward speeds and multiple tampers rise and fall. **$15.00**

No. 6464-735 New Haven Box Car — Realistic markings, sliding doors. Car 11" long. **$7.00**

No. 6464-475 Boston and Maine Box Car — Finely detailed, has sliding doors. Car 11" long. **$7.00**

No. 6361 Timber Transport Car — Specially designed car has three tree trunks chained on. Looks real, measures 11" long. **$6.00**

No. 3364 Operating Log Dump Car — By remote control, base of car tilts and logs roll off. Car 11" long. **$7.00**

No. 6560 Crane Car. Carefully scaled crane has boom that raises and lowers. Crane also swivels. Car is 11" long. **$9.00**

No. 2029 Locomotive 2-6-4, $125. Photo courtesy 1968 Lionel catalog.

No. 2333 Locomotive, $1,000.

	C5	C7	C9
2065 Locomotive, O27 ga., 1954, 4-6-4, steam, 2046W or 6026W tender	100	150	225
2200 Summer Trolley, standard ga., 1910, trailer, non-powered, marked "2200 Rapid Transit 2200"	1050	1750	3500
2240 Locomotive, O27 ga., 1956, Wabash F-3 AB, diesel, gray and blue shell, single motor	400	600	800
2242 Locomotive, O27 ga., 1958, New Haven F-3 AB, diesel, checkerboard scheme, silver and black, single motor	500	800	1200
2243 Locomotive, O27 ga., 1955, Santa Fe F-3 AB, diesel, silver shell, red nose, single motor	300	400	495
2245 Locomotive, O27 ga., 1954, Texas Special F-3 AB, diesel red shell, single motor	300	400	700
2257 Caboose, non-illuminated, w/red plastic smokestack	175	300	400
2321 Locomotive, O ga., 1954, Lackawanna, diesel, double motor, gray	300	390	550
2321 Locomotive, O ga., 1954, Lackawanna, diesel, gray w/maroon roof	400	600	800
2322 Locomotive, O ga., 1965, Virginian, diesel, double motor, yellow w/blue roof	300	495	635
2328 Locomotive, O27 ga., 1955, Burlington, diesel, silver shell	200	300	435
2329 Locomotive, O ga., 1958, Virginian, electric, blue shell w/yellow striping	315	540	750
2330 Locomotive, O ga., 1950, New Brunswick Green, GG-I, electric, double motor, green w/five gold stripes	625	900	1550
2331 Locomotive, O ga., 1955, Virginian, diesel, double motor, yellow shell w/black stripe and gold lettering	720	1150	1400
2331 Locomotive, 1955, Virginian, diesel, yellow shell w/blue stripe and yellow lettering	600	900	1200
2331 Locomotive, 1955, Virginian, diesel, yellow w/black roof	720	1150	1500
2332 Locomotive, 1947, GG-I, electric, five silver stripes	900	1400	2000
2332 Locomotive, 1947, New Brunswick GG-I, electric, single motor, green w/five gold stripes	320	450	880
2332 Locomotive, 1947, GG-I, electric, satin black w/five gold or silver stripes	510	850	1700
2333 Locomotive, O ga., 1948, Santa Fe or NYC F-3 AA, diesel, silver w/red nose	425	750	1000
2333 Locomotive, O ga., 1948, NYC F-3 AA, diesel, gray	425	750	1000
2333 Locomotive, O ga., 1948, NYC F-3 AA, diesel	300	500	1000
2337 Locomotive, O27 ga., 1958, Wabash, GP-7, diesel, blue and gray body w/white striping	110	200	315
2338 Locomotive, O27 ga., 1955, Milwaukee Rd. GP-7, diesel, black and orange	150	200	260
2339 Locomotive, O ga., 1957, Wabash GP-7, diesel, blue and gray w/white striping	165	210	325
2340-1 Locomotive, O ga., 1955, GG-1, electric, maroon, double motor, Tuscan brown, w/five stripes	700	1000	1800

	C5	C7	C9
2340-25 Locomotive, O ga., 1955, New Brunswick, GG-1, electric, double motor, green w/five stripes	650	950	1700
2341 Locomotive, O ga., 1956, Jersey Central, diesel, double motor, orange body w/blue stripe	950	1300	2000
2343C Locomotive, O ga., 1950, Santa Fe, diesel	100	200	295
2343 Locomotive, O ga., 1950, Santa Fe AA, F-3, diesel, double motor, silver w/red nose	350	400	675
2344 Locomotive, O ga., 1950, NYC F-3 AA, diesel, double motor, gray	290	400	625
2344C Locomotive, O ga., 1950, NYC F-3 B, diesel	120	225	310
2345 Locomotive, O ga., 1952, Western Pacific F-3 AA, diesel, double motor, silver and orange, screen roof	1100	1400	2075
2345 Locomotive, O ga., 1952, Western Pacific F-3 AA, diesel, louvered roof	1100	1400	2075
2346 Locomotive, O27 ga., 1965, Boston and Maine GP-7, diesel, blue shell, black cab w/white trim	145	225	320
2347 Locomotive, O27 ga., 1962, C&O GP-7, diesel, Sears, blue shell w/yellow lettering, uncataloged	1350	2250	4500
2348 Locomotive, 1958, diesel, GP-9, M.St.L., O27 red shell w/blue roof	175	275	425
2349 Locomotive, O ga., 1959, diesel, GP-O, Northern Pacific, black shell, red striping w/gold lettering	200	295	415
2350 Locomotive, O ga., 1956, New Haven, electric, black shell w/orange and white striping	220	370	515
2351 Locomotive, O ga., 1957, electric, Milwaukee Rd., yellow shell w/black roof and red stripe	200	350	575

	C5	C7	C9
2352 Locomotive, O ga., 1958, diesel, PRR, Tuscan brown	225	375	615

No. 2352 Locomotive, $615.

	C5	C7	C9
2353 Locomotive, O ga., 1953, diesel AA, F-3, Santa Fe, double motor, silver w/red nose	270	400	640
2353C Locomotive, O ga., 1954, diesel, F-3, Santa Fe	120	200	400
2354 Locomotive, O ga., 1953, diesel, AA, F-3, NYC, double motor, gray	270	425	720
2354C Locomotive, O ga., 1954, diesel, B, F-3, NYC	80	133	265
2355 Locomotive, O ga., 1953, diesel, AA, F-3, Western Pacific, double motor, silver and orange	800	1300	1900
2356 Locomotive, O ga., 1954, diesel, AA, F-3, Southern RY, double motor, green	500	1100	1400
2356C Locomotive, O ga., 1954, diesel, B, F-3, Southern Ry,	150	250	500
2357 Caboose, O ga., 1948	12	20	40
2358 Locomotive, O ga., 1959, Great Northern, electric, orange and green shell, yellow stripes	360	750	1200
2359 Locomotive, O27 ga., 1961, B&M GP-9, diesel, blue shell w/black cab and white trim	185	200	300
2360-25 Locomotive, O ga., 1956, New Brunswick GG-1, electric, double motor, green, heat stamped letters and numbers, five rubber stamped stripes	575	1000	1300

A LEGEND IN MODEL RAILROADING ... THE

SAFETY

PENNSYLVANIA 2360
2360

★ Two Motors
★ Horn and Headlight
★ Magne-Traction
★ Twin Pantographs
★ Authentic Work Cars

THE ULTIMATE IN PASSENGER

2383   SANTA FE   SANTA FE

★ Headlight
★ Two Motors
★ Magne-Traction
★ Horn
★ Illuminated Passenger Cars

Top to bottom: No. 2360 Locomotive, $1,800; No. 2383 Locomotive, $1,650. Photo courtesy 1961 Lionel catalog.

	C5	C7	C9

2360-10 Locomotive, O ga., 1956, GG-1, electric, double motor, five stripes, Tuscan brown, heat-stamped letter and number, five rubber stamped stripes.. 750 1250 2500

2360-1 Locomotive, 1961, GG-1, electric, double motor, single stripe, Tuscan brown, decal letters and numbers rubber stamped stripe........................... 600 1050 1800

No. 2360 locomotive, GG-1, $1,800.

No. 2360-1 Locomotive, GG-1, $745.

2360-1 Locomotive, 1961, GG-1, electric, heavy heat stamped letters and numbers.................. 225 373 745

2360-1 Locomotive, 1961, GG-1, electric, light pressed letters and numbers, rubber stamped stripe 600 1000 2000

2363 Locomotive, O ga., 1955, Illinois Central F-3 AB, diesel, double motor, brown shell w/orange stripe and yellow trim.. 450 900 1350

2365 Locomotive, O27 ga., 1962, C&O GP-7, diesel, blue shell ... 135 250 400

	C5	C7	C9

2367 Locomotive, O ga., 1955, Wabash F-3 AB, diesel, double motor, gray and blue shell w/white stripe and trim 400 800 1200

2368 Locomotive, O ga., 1956, B&O F-3 AB, diesel, double motor, blue shell w/black, white and yellow trim 800 1750 2500

2373 Locomotive, Super O ga., 1957, Canadian Pacific AA F-3, diesel, double motor, gray and maroon w/yellow trim 950 1500 2100

2378 Locomotive, O ga., 1956, Milwaukee Rd. F-3 AB, diesel, double motor, gray w/orange stripe.. 1000 1700 2400

2379 Locomotive, Super O ga., 1957, Rio Grande AB F-3, diesel, double motor, yellow body w/silver roof and stripe 600 800 1100

2383 Locomotive, Super O ga., 1958, Santa Fe AA, F-3, diesel, double motor, silver w/red nose 300 500 650

2400 Pullman, O27 ga., 1948, Maplewood, green shell w/gray roof and yellow trim.................. 60 85 150

2401 Observation Car, O27 ga., 1948, Hillside............................ 60 85 150

2402 Pullman, O27 ga., 1948, Chatham 60 85 150

2404 Vista Dome, O27 ga., 1964, Santa Fe, aluminum, blue lettering 30 50 70

2405 Pullman, O27 ga., 1964, Santa Fe, aluminum, blue lettering 30 50 70

2406 Observation Car, 1964, Santa Fe, aluminum, blue lettering 30 50 70

2408 Vista Dome, O27 ga., 1964, Santa Fe, aluminum, blue lettering 35 60 75

2409 Pullman, O27 ga., 1964, Santa Fe, aluminum, blue lettering 35 60 75

2410 Observation Car, Santa Fe ga., 1964, aluminum, blue lettering 35 60 75

	C5	C7	C9
2411 Flatcar, O27 ga., 1946, w/load of pipes, gray metal frame	50	70	90
2412 Vista Dome, O27 ga., 1959, silver, blue stripe through windows, illuminated	35	58	115
2414 Pullman, O27 ga., 1959, silver, blue stripe through windows, illuminated	35	58	115
2416 Observation Car, O27 ga., 1959, silver, blue stripe through windows, illuminated	27	45	90
2419 Wrecker Caboose, O27 ga., 1946, DL&W, gray metal frame w/gray cab	27	45	90
2420-20 Bulb, 1946, 14 volt-clear	—	—	1
2420 Wrecker Caboose, O ga., 1946, DL&W, w/light, gray metal frame w/gray cab	40	70	100
2421 Pullman, O27 ga., 1950, silver roof, no stripe	40	50	75
2421 Pullman, O27 ga., 1950, aluminum, gray roof w/black stripe	40	60	95
2422 Pullman, O27 ga., 1950, aluminum, gray roof w/black stripe	40	60	85
2422 Pullman, O27 ga., 1950, silver roof, no stripe	18	30	60
2423 Observation Car, O27 ga., 1950, aluminum, gray roof w/black stripe	40	60	100
2423 Observation Car, O27 ga., 1950, silver roof, no stripe	40	50	75
2426 WX Tender, O ga., 1946	87	145	290
2429 Pullman, O27 ga., 1952, aluminum, gray roof w/black stripe	50	85	120
2429 Pullman, O27 ga., 1952, silver roof, no stripe	50	85	120
2430 Pullman, O27 ga., 1946, sheet metal, blue w/silver roof	20	45	65
2431 Observation Car, O27 ga., 1946, sheet metal, blue w/silver roof	20	45	90

	C5	C7	C9
2432 Vista Dome, O27 ga., 1954, silver, red lettering reads "Clifton"	24	40	80
2434 Pullman, O27 ga., 1954, silver, red lettering reads "Newark"	24	40	80
2435 Pullman, O27 ga., 1954, silver, red lettering reads "Elizabeth"	30	40	75
2436 Observation Car, O27 ga., 1954, silver, red lettering "Summit"	25	42	85
2436 Observation Car, O27 ga., 1954, "Mooseheart"	25	42	85
2440 Pullman, O27 ga., 1946, blue w/silver roof	21	35	70
2440 Pullman, O27 ga., 1946, green w/dark green roof	21	35	70
2441 Observation Car, O27 ga., 1946, blue w/silver roof	21	35	70
2441 Observation Car, O27 ga., 1946, green w/dark green roof	21	35	70
2442 Pullman, O27 ga., 1946, sheet metal, brown	36	60	120
2442 Vista Dome, O27 ga., 1956, aluminum, red window stripe, marked "Clifton"	45	75	100
2443 Observation Car, O ga., 1956, sheet metal, brown	27	45	90
2444 Pullman, O ga., 1956, aluminum, red window stripe	45	75	140
2452 Gondola, O27 ga., 1945, "Pennsylvania"	8	12	25
2452X Gondola, O27 ga., 1946, "Pennsylvania"	11	19	38
2454 Boxcar, O27 ga., 1946, "Baby Ruth"	9	15	30
2454 Boxcar, O27 ga., 1946, "Pennsylvania"	60	100	160
2456 Hopper, O ga., 1948, Lehigh Valley	8	14	27
2457 Caboose, O ga., 1945, N5 type, "Pennsylvania"	15	25	50
2458 Boxcar, O ga., 1945, automatic, double door, "Pennsylvania"	20	33	65

	C5	C7	C9
2460 Operating Crane, O ga., 1946, Bucyrus Erie	35	50	85
2461 Transformer Car, O27 ga., 1947, metal, gray frame	36	60	120
2465 Tank Car, O27 ga., 1946, double dome, Sunoco logo	5	10	17
2472 Caboose, O27 ga., 1946, N5 type, "Pennsylvania"	10	18	35
2481 Pullman, O27 ga., 1950, illuminated, yellow w/red stripes and gray roof, Anniversary Set	105	150	275
2482 Pullman, O27 ga., 1950, illuminated, yellow w/red stripes and gray roof, Anniversary Set	105	150	275
2483 Observation Car, O27 ga., 1950, illuminated, yellow w/red stripes and gray roof, Anniversary Set	85	125	230
2521 Observation Car, Super O ga., 1962, "Pres. McKinley," illuminated, extruded aluminum shell, gold stripe	80	125	180
2522 Vista Dome, Super O ga., 1962, "Pres. Harrison," extruded aluminum shell, illuminated, gold stripe	80	125	180
2523 Pullman, Super O ga., 1962, "Pres. Garfield," illuminated, extruded aluminum shell, gold stripe	80	125	185
2530 Baggage Car, O ga., 1956, small doors	125	175	225
2530 Baggage Car, O ga., 1956, Railway Express Agency, extruded aluminum shell, large door	250	400	550
2531 Observation Car, O ga., 1952, extruded aluminum shell, illuminated, marked "Silver Dawn"	65	85	110
2532 Vista Dome, O ga., 1952, marked "Silver Range"	65	85	115
2533 Pullman, O ga., 1952, marked "Silver Cloud"	65	85	110
2534 Pullman, O ga., 1952, marked "Silver Bluff"	75	100	140
2541 Observation Car, O ga., 1955, Penn., illuminated, extruded aluminum, brown stripes, marked "Alexander Hamilton"	75	123	245
2542 Vista Dome, O ga., 1955, Penn., marked "Betsy Ross"	75	123	245
2543 Pullman, O ga., 1955, Penn., marked "William Penn"	120	200	400
2544 Pullman, O ga., 1955, Penn., marked "Molly Pitcher"	120	200	400
2550 Budd R.D.C. Mail Baggage Trailer, O ga., 1957, Baltimore and Ohio dummy to match motorized Budd 404, silver shell w/blue lettering	200	350	575
2551 Observation Car, Super O ga., 1957, extruded aluminum shell, illuminated, two brown stripes, top Canadian Pacific, bottom, name of car, "Banff Park"	100	150	265
2552 Vista Dome, Super O ga., 1957, "Skyline 500"	100	150	375
2553 Pullman, Super O ga., 1957, "Blair Manor"	175	250	500
2554 Pullman, Super O ga., 1957, "Graig Manor"	150	225	350
2555 Tank-One-Dome, O ga., 1945	17	28	55
2559 Budd Car Coach, O ga., 1957, Baltimore & Ohio, silver shell, blue lettering, dummy to match motorized 400 Budd	150	200	350
2560 Crane, O27 ga., 1946, marked "Lionel Lines"	30	50	100
2561 Observation Car, O ga., 1959, extruded aluminum shell, marked "Santa Fe Set, Vista Valley"	100	150	260
2562 Vista Dome, O ga., 1959, marked "Royal Pass"	125	200	310
2563 Pullman, O ga., 1959, marked "Indian Falls"	125	200	310
2600 Pullman, O ga., 1938, red body and roof	60	100	200
2601 Observation Car, O ga., 1938, red body and roof	60	100	200
2602 Baggage Car, O ga., 1938, red body and roof	60	100	200

	C5	C7	C9
2613 Pullman, O ga., 1938, green	84	140	280
2613 Pullman, O ga., 1938, Blue Comet, two-tone blue	81	135	270
2614 Observation Car, O ga., 1938, green	84	140	280
2614 Observation Car, O ga., 1938, Blue Comet, two-tone blue	81	135	270
2615 Baggage Car, O ga., 1938, Blue Comet, two-tone blue	81	135	270
2615 Baggage Car, O ga., 1938, green	120	200	400
2620 Floodlight, O ga., 1938, red frame on searchlight	23	38	75
2623 Pullman, O ga., 1941, Irvington, Bakelite, Tuscan brown	150	250	500
2623 Pullman, O ga., 1941, Manhattan, Bakelite, Tuscan brown, uncataloged	80	133	265
2624 Pullman, O ga., 1941, Manhattan, Bakelite, Tuscan brown, uncataloged	240	400	800
2625 Pullman, O ga., 1946, Irvington, Bakelite, Tuscan brown	95	150	220
2625 Pullman, O ga., 1946, Manhattan	112	188	375
2625 Pullman, O ga., 1946, Madison	95	175	250
2627 Pullman, O ga., 1946, Madison, Bakelite, Tuscan brown	95	150	220
2628 Pullman, O ga., 1946, Manhattan, Bakelite, Tuscan brown	95	150	245

No. 2628 Pullman, Manhattan, $245.

	C5	C7	C9
2630 Pullman, O ga., 1938, light blue and silver or gray roof	30	50	100

	C5	C7	C9
2631 Observation Car, O ga., 1938, light blue and silver or gray roof	30	50	100
2640 Pullman, O ga., 1938, light blue w/silver roof	20	33	65
2640 Pullman, O ga., 1938, green w/dark green roof	20	33	65
2641 Observation Car, O ga., 1938, light blue w/silver roof	24	40	80
2641 Observation Car, O ga., 1938, green w/dark green roof	21	35	70
2642 Pullman, O ga., 1941, light blue w/silver or gray roof	24	40	80
2643 Observation Car, O ga., 1941, light blue w/silver or gray roof	15	25	50
2651 Flatcar, O ga., 1938, bright green w/lumber load	15	25	50
2652 Gondola, O ga., 1938, yellow	18	30	60
2652 Gondola, O ga., 1938, brown	18	30	60
2653 Hopper, O ga., 1938, black	38	62	125
2653 Hopper, O ga., 1938, light green	15	25	50
2654 Tank Car, O ga., 1938, light gray, marked "Sunoco"	18	30	60
2654 Tank Car, O ga., 1938, marked "Shell"	21	35	70
2654 Tank Car, O ga., 1938, aluminum, marked "Sunoco"	20	33	65
2655 Boxcar, O ga., 1938, cream body w/maroon roof	18	30	60
2655 Boxcar, O ga., 1938, cream body w/Tuscan brown roof	20	34	68
2656 Cattle Car, O ga., 1938, light gray body w/red roof	38	63	125
2657 Caboose, O ga., 1938, red body w/red roof	12	20	40
2657 Caboose, O ga., 1938, red body w/brown roof	9	15	30
2659 Dump Car, O ga., 1938, green, black frame	12	23	45
2660 Crane, O ga., 1938, red roof, green boom	27	45	90

	C5	C7	C9
2672 Caboose, O27 ga., 1942, Pennsylvania N5 type, Tuscan brown	12	20	40
2677 Gondola, O27 ga., 1940, red w/black frame	11	18	36
2679 Boxcar, O27 ga., 1938, yellow w/blue roof	9	15	30
2679 Boxcar, O27 ga., 1938, yellow w/maroon roof	9	15	30
2680 Tank Car, O27 ga., 1938, orange, marked "Shell"	8	12	25
2680 Tank Car, O27 ga., 1938, gray, marked "Sunoco"	8	12	25
2680 Tank Car, O27 ga., 1938, aluminum, marked "Sunoco"	8	12	25
2682 Caboose, O27 ga., 1938, red w/red roof	7	12	23
2682 Caboose, O27 ga., 1938, brown w/brown roof	7	12	23
2717 Gondola, O ga., 1938, orange and tan, uncataloged	37	63	125
2719 Boxcar, O ga., 1938, peacock and blue roof, uncataloged	37	63	125
2722 Caboose, O ga., 1938, red w/maroon roof, uncataloged	37	63	125
2755 Tank Car, O ga., 1941, gray, marked "Sunoco"	45	75	150
2757 Caboose, O ga., 1941, PRR-N5 type, Tuscan brown	12	20	40
2758 Boxcar, O ga., 1941, automobile, Tuscan body, marked "Pennsylvania"	21	35	70
2810 Crane, O ga., 1938, yellow cab and red roof	74	123	245
2811 Flatcar, O ga., 1938, aluminum w/eight logs	36	60	120
2812 Gondola, O ga., 1938, dark green	21	35	70
2812 Gondola, O ga., 1938, bright green	21	35	70
2813 Cattle Car, O ga., 1938, cream body w/maroon roof	60	100	200
2814 Boxcar, O ga., 1938, light yellow body w/maroon roof	50	83	165
2814 Boxcar, O ga., 1938, orange body w/brown roof	120	200	400

	C5	C7	C9
2814R Refrigerator, O ga., 1938, white body w/brown roof	185	325	650
2815 Tank Car, O ga., 1938, silver, Sunoco	54	90	180
2815 Tank Car, O ga., 193 8, orange, Shell	75	125	250
2816 Hopper, O ga., 1938, red	60	100	200
2816 Hopper, O ga., 1938, black, white rubber-stamped lettering	54	90	180
2817 Caboose, O ga., 1938, red, Tuscan roof, white rubber-stamped lettering	29	48	95
2817 Caboose, O ga., 1938, light red body and roof	31	53	105
2820 Floodlight, O ga., 1938, two searchlights, green base, plate-stamped lights	54	88	175
2820 Floodlight, O ga., 1938, green base, cast lights	90	150	300
2855 Tank Car, O ga., 1946, one-dome, black, S.U.N.X.	62	103	205
2855 Tank Car, O ga., 1946, gray	59	98	195
2954 Boxcar, O47 ga., 1940, Tuscan brown, marked "Pennsylvania"	105	175	350
2955 Tank Car, O72 ga., 1940, black, marked "S.U.N.X."	78	130	260
2956 Hopper, O72 ga., 1940, B&O, black	83	138	275
2957 Caboose, O72 ga., 1940, NYC, Tuscan brown	93	155	310
3300 Summer Trolley, standard ga., 1910, trailer, gold rubber-stamped, 3300 Electric Rapid Transit, 3300, non-powered	1200	2000	4000
3330 Flatcar, O ga., 1960, w/submarine	24	40	80
3330-100 Operating Submarine Kit, O27 ga., 1960	100	150	200
3349 Turbo Missile Firing Car, O ga., 1960	17	28	55
3356-150 Horse Corral, O ga., 1956, white fencing, corral only	52	60	80
3356 Operating Horse Car, O ga., 1956, w/horses and corral	40	68	135

	C5	C7	C9
3356-2 Operating Horse Car, O ga., 1956, green, car alone	40	70	100
3356-100 Set of Nine Horses, O ga., 1956, black horses..............	6	10	20
3357 Operating Cop and Hobo Car, O ga., 1962, blue boxcar w/hydraulic lift and figures.......	30	50	100
3359 Operating Dump Car, O ga., 1955, two gray dump bins	18	35	55
3360 Operating Burro Crane, O ga., 1956, yellow cab and boom, motorized, including track trips	150	265	340
3361 Lumber Car, O ga., 1955, operating	20	30	55
3362 Helium Tank Car, O ga., 1961, operating, green frame....	20	32	64
3364 Log Dump Car, O ga., 1966, operating, green frame..............	18	33	65
3366 Circus Car, O ga., 1959, operating, white stock car, nine horses, white, and corral	125	150	250
3366-100 White Horses, O ga., 1959, set of nine.......................	9	15	30
3370 Sheriff and Outlaw Car, O ga., 1961, operating, green stock car..................................	25	43	85
3376 Giraffe Car, O ga., 1960, operating, blue stock car, including track trips, w/teletails and poles	20	30	55
3376 Giraffe Car, O ga., 1960, operating, green stock car	36	75	125
3410 Helicopter Launching Car, O ga., 1961, operating, blue flat w/helicopter	45	80	150
3413-150 Mercury Capsule Launching Car, O ga., 1961, red flat, gray platform...............	65	110	175
3419 Helicopter Launching Car, O ga., 1959, operating, blue flat w/helicopter	40	75	110
3424 Brakeman Car Set, O ga., 1956, operating, blue boxcar, set of track trips and teletails w/poles....................................	30	50	80

	C5	C7	C9
3424-100 Low Bridge Warning Poles, O ga., 1956, w/track clips, set of two	15	25	30
3428 Mail Car, O ga., 1959, operating, red white and blue boxcar, man dumps mail bag	48	80	160

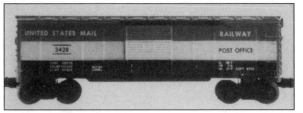

No. 3428 Mail Car, $160.

	C5	C7	C9
3429 U.S.M.C. Helicopter Car, O ga., 1960, olive frame	200	325	465
3434 Chicken Sweeper Car, O ga., 1959, brown stock car, man at door sweeps back and forth.......	50	75	105
3435 Aquarium Car, O ga., 1959, operating, green box w/four clear windows, fish move around on two spindles	100	175	250
3435 Aquarium Car, O ga., 1959, operating, green boxcar, gold letters marked "Tank 1" and "Tank 2"	400	600	1000
3444 Animated Hobo Gondola, O ga., 1957, red gondola, cop chases hobo around freight load, marked "Erie"	30	45	80
3451 Operating Lumber Car, O ga., 1946, operating, black die-cast base, black platform w/log stacks....................................	14	23	45
3454 Merchandise Car, O ga., 1946, operating, silver boxcar, discharges five brown cubes	65	100	130
3456 Hopper Car, O ga., 1950, operating, black, "N&W," drops ore....................................	17	28	55
3459 Dump Car, O ga., 1946, operating, die-cast frame, black	24	40	80
3459 Dump Car, O ga., 1946, operating, silver........................	93	155	310
3459 Dump Car, O ga., 1946, operating, green........................	25	43	85

	C5	C7	C9
3460 Piggyback Flatcar, O ga., 1955, red flat w/two trailer containers	22	45	65
3461 Lumber Car, O ga., 1949, operating, black die-cast frame	11	25	35
3461 Lumber Car, O ga., 1949, operating, green frame	17	30	55
3462-70 Milk Cans, 1952, set of five	6	8	10
3462P Milk Car Platform, O ga., 1952	8	15	75
3462 Milk Car Set, O ga., 1947, white boxcar, platform, green base, five cans, man discharges cans onto platform	20	40	55
3464 Boxcar, O ga., 1949, operating, Santa Fe, orange shell, black doors, plunger mechanism opens door w/man	12	20	40
3464 Boxcar, O ga., 1952, operating, NYC, brown shell, black doors, plunger mechanism opens door w/man	11	18	35
3469 Dump Car, O ga., 1949, operating, black die-cast frame	18	30	60
3470 Aerial Target Launching Car, O ga., 1962, blue flatcar, white top shell, blue balloon carriage, batter operation inflates balloons	30	50	75
3472 Milk Car Set, O27 ga., 1949, operating, white boxcar, five cans, man discharges cans onto platform, green base	20	35	60
3474 Boxcar, O27 ga., 1952, operating, W.P., silver box, yellow feather, plunger mechanism	27	45	90
3482 Milk Car Set, O ga., 1954, operating, white boxcar, man discharges cans onto platform, green base, five cans	24	40	80
3484 Boxcar, O ga., 1953, operating, Pennsylvania, Tuscan brown, plunger mechanism	18	35	60
3484-25 Boxcar, O ga., 1954, operating, Santa Fe, orange shell, orange doors, plunger mechanism	33	60	110
3494 Boxcar, O ga., 1955, operating, NYC Pacemaker, red and gray, red doors, plunger mechanism	40	75	110
3494-150 Boxcar, O ga., 1956, operating, MP, blue and gray, plunger mechanism	55	90	120
3494-275 Boxcar, O ga., 1956, operating, B.A.R., State of Maine, red, white and blue, plunger mechanism	55	90	130
3494-550 Boxcar, O ga., 1957, operating, Monon, maroon shell w/white stripe, plunger mechanism	125	225	400
3494-625 Boxcar, O ga., 1957, Operating, Soo Line, Tuscan brown, plunger mechanism	120	210	400
3509 Satellite Car, O ga., 1959, operating, green flat, black and silver satellite, yellow radar scope, manually operated	22	45	60
3510 Satellite Car, O ga., 1959, operating, red flat	45	90	155
3512 Fireman and Ladder Car, O ga., 1959, red frame and structure, black ladders	40	65	130
3512 Fireman and Ladder Car, O ga., 1959, silver ladders	83	138	275
3519 Automatic Satellite Car, O ga., 1961, remote track operated	20	30	55
3520 Searchlight, O ga., 1952, gray die-cast frame, orange generator	30	40	58
3530 G.M. Generator Car, O ga., 1956, blue boxcar w/white markings, transformer pole, remote searchlight	66	110	220
3535 AEC Security Car, O ga., 1960, red shell, white lettering, gray gun and gray rotating searchlight, one man	35	80	125

	C5	C7	C9
3540 Radar Scanning Car, O ga., 1959, operating, red flat, gray structure, yellow radar scope and silver radar antenna, revolving	39	85	135
3545 TV Monitor Car, O ga., 1961, operating, black base, blue structure, yellow camera and screen, two men	53	110	175
3559 Ore Dump Car, O ga., 1946, operating, black die-cast frame	15	28	45
3562-25 Barrel Car, O ga., 1954, operating, red lettering	150	250	500
3562 Barrel Car, O ga., 1954, operating, black, six wood barrels	75	100	180
3562-25 Barrel Car, O ga., 1954, operating, gray, blue lettering	25	40	55
3562-50 Barrel Car, O ga., 1955, operating, yellow	35	50	85
3562-75 Barrel Car, O ga., 1958, operating, orange	35	50	92
3619 Reconnaissance Helicopter Car, O ga., 1962, yellow shell, black double door, w/helicopter	38	63	125
3620 Searchlight, O ga., 1954, gray die-cast frame, orange generator	25	35	45
3650 Searchlight Extension Car, O ga., 1956, gray die-cast frame, gray generator, remote searchlight w/wire	40	50	80
3651 Operating Lumber Car, O ga., 1939, operating, black frame, nickel stakes, w/logs and bin	13	20	40
3652 Operating Gondola, O ga., 1939, operating, yellow	25	42	85
3656 Cattle Car, O ga., 1950, operating, orange stock car, set includes car, cattle and corral, white lettering reads "Armour"	35	50	85
3656 Cattle Car, O ga., 1950, operating, black lettering	120	200	400
3656-150 Cattle Car Platform, O ga., 1952, green base, ivory fencing	45	55	75
3656-34 Cattle Set, O ga., 1952, black, set of nine	10	15	20
3657 Dump Car, 1939, silver w/brown bin	120	200	400
3659 Dump Car, O ga., 1939, operating, black frame, red hopper	20	33	65
3662-79 Milk Cans, O ga., 1955, set of five	6	9	12
3662 Operating, O ga., 1955, operating, white shell, brown roof, includes five cans and platform	30	50	70
3665 Minuteman Missile Car, O ga., 1961, operating, white shell, blue double door roof, w/missile	50	80	115
3666 Marine Missile Car, O ga., 1960, operating, Sears, white shell, blue double door roof, w/missile	170	350	535
3672 Bosco Boxcar, O ga., 1959, operating, yellow shell and brown roof, set includes seven Bosco cans and brown and yellow platform	120	265	430
3672-79 Bosco Cans, O ga., 1959, brown and yellow, set of seven	35	75	125
3811 Operating Flatcar, O ga., 1939, black frame w/lumber	18	30	60
3814 Merchandise Car, O ga., 1939, operating, Tuscan body and roof, discharges five cubes	48	80	160
3820 Submarine Car, O ga., 1960, operating, olive, "U.S.M.C.," gray	120	200	400
3830 Submarine Car, O ga., 1960, operating, blue, marked "Lionel," w/gray submarine	29	48	95
3854 Merchandise Car, O ga., 1946, operating, Tuscan brown, doors open and eject five merchandise cubes	200	400	600

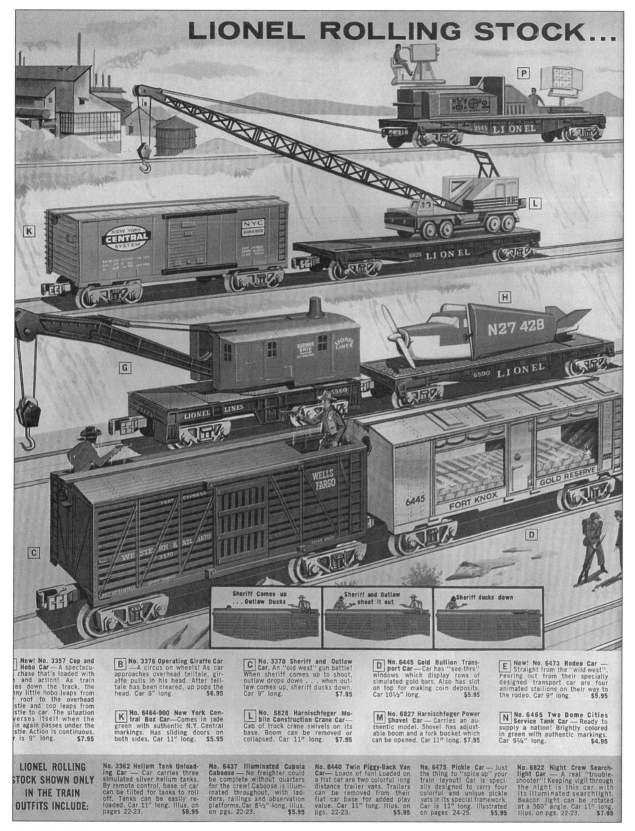

LIONEL ROLLING STOCK...

New! No. 3357 Cop and Hobo Car—A spectacular chase that's loaded with and action! As train es down the track, the ny little hobo leaps from roof to the overhead stle and cop leaps from stle to car. The situation verses itself when the in again passes under the stle. Action is continuous. r is 9" long. **$7.95**

B **No. 3376 Operating Giraffe Car**—A circus on wheels! As car approaches overhead telltale, giraffe pulls in his head. After telltale has been cleared, up pops the head. Car 9" long. **$6.95**

C **No. 3370 Sheriff and Outlaw Car.** An "old west" gun battle! When sheriff comes up to shoot, outlaw drops down . . . when outlaw comes up, sheriff ducks down. Car 9" long. **$7.95**

D **No. 6445 Gold Bullion Transport Car**—Car has "see-thru" windows which display rows of simulated gold bars. Also has slot on top for making coin deposits. Car 10½" long. **$5.95**

E **New! No. 6473 Rodeo Car**—Straight from the "wild west". Peering out from their specially designed transport car are four animated stallions on their way to the rodeo. Car 9" long. **$5.95**

K **No. 6464-900 New York Central Box Car**—Comes in jade green with authentic N.Y. Central markings. Has sliding doors on both sides. Car 11" long. **$5.95**

L **No. 6828 Harnischfeger Mobile Construction Crane Car**—Cab of truck crane swivels on its base. Boom can be removed or collapsed. Car 11" long. **$7.95**

M **No. 6827 Harnischfeger Power Shovel Car**—Carries an authentic model. Shovel has adjustable boom and a fork bucket which can be opened. Car 11" long. **$7.95**

N **No. 6465 Two Dome Cities Service Tank Car**—Ready to supply a nation! Brightly colored in green with authentic markings. Car 9¼" long. **$4.95**

LIONEL ROLLING STOCK SHOWN ONLY IN THE TRAIN OUTFITS INCLUDE:

No. 3362 Helium Tank Unloading Car — Car carries three simulated silver helium tanks. By remote control, base of car can be tilted for tanks to roll off. Tanks can be easily reloaded. Car 11" long. Illus. on pages 22-23. **$6.95**

No. 6437 Illuminated Cupola Caboose — No freighter could be complete without quarters for the crew! Caboose is illuminated throughout, with ladders, railings and observation platforms. Car 8½"-long. Illus. on pgs. 22-23. **$5.95**

No. 6440 Twin Piggy-Back Van Car — Loads of fun! Loaded on a flat car are two colorful long distance trailer vans. Trailers can be removed from their flat car base for added play value. Car 11" long. Illus. on pgs. 22-23. **$5.95**

No. 6475 Pickle Car — Just the thing to "spice up" your train layout! Car is specially designed to carry four colorful and unique pickle vats in its special framework. Car is 11" long. Illustrated on pages 24-25. **$5.95**

No. 6822 Night Crew Searchlight Car — A real troubleshooter'! Keeping vigil through the night is this car with its illuminated searchlight. Beacon light can be rotated at a 360° angle. Car 11" long. Illus. on pgs. 22-23. **$7.95**

Top: No. 3545 TV Monitor car, $175. **Second row, left to right:** No 6464-900 Boxcar, $120; No. 6828 Flatcar, $140. **Third row, left to right:** No. 6560 Crane, $55; No. 6500 Beechcraft Bonanza Transport car, $850. **Fourth row, left to right:** No. 3370 Sheriff and Outlaw car, $85; No. 6445 Fort Knox Gold car, $140. Photo courtesy 1962 Lionel catalog.

	C5	C7	C9
3859 Dump Car, O ga., 1938, operating, black	25	41	82
3927-75 Can of Liquid Track Cleaner, 1956, full	—	—	35
3927 Track Cleaner Car, O ga., 1956, orange shell, motor-operated cleaning disk, includes two gray washol containers	60	80	120
3927-50 Track Cleaner Pads, O ga., 1956, package of twenty-five	5	10	25
4357 Caboose, O ga., 1948, Pennsylvania N5 type, electronic, metal, green and white, "Electronic Control" decal, red	68	112	225
4400 Summer Trolley, standard ga., 1910, trailer	1200	2000	4000
4452 Gondola, O ga., 1946, electronic, black, Pennsylvania	42	75	140
4454 Boxcar, 1946, electronic, Baby Ruth, P.R.R., orange w/brown doors	90	150	300
4457 Caboose, O ga., 1946, electronic	45	80	165
4671 Locomotive, O ga., 1946, 6-8-0, steam, electronic, 4671W tender	130	220	315
5100 Roadway, O ga., 1963, straight	—	—	1
5101 Roadway, O ga., 1963, straight	—	—	1
5102 Railroad and Roadway Crossway, O ga., 1963	—	—	1
5103 Roadway, O ga., 1963, straight, w/power connection	—	—	1
5104 Lane Change Over, O ga., 1963	—	—	1
5105 Roadway Intersection, O ga., 1963	—	—	1
5106 Inner Roadway, O ga., 1963, curved	—	—	1
5107 Inner Roadway, O ga., 1963, curved	—	—	1
5108 Outer Roadway, O ga., 1963, curved	—	—	1

	C5	C7	C9
5109 Outer Roadway, O ga., 1963, curved	—	—	1
5150 Banking Set, 1963	5	8	15
5151 Trestle Set, O ga., 1963	5	8	15
5152 Guard Rail and Flag Set, O ga., 1963	5	8	15
5154 Electric Lap Counter, O ga., 1963	5	8	15
5155 Pacesetter Timer, O ga., 1963	5	8	15
5156-24 Rail Clips, O ga., 1963	2	3	4
5157-34 Roadway Clips, o ga., 1963	2	3	4
5158 Barrels, 1963	2	3	4
5159 Lubrication Kit, 1963	3	4	5
5159-50 Lubrication Kit, 1968	3	4	5
5160 Official Viewing Stand, 1963	10	15	20
5163 Maintenance Kit, 1965	3	4	6
5200 Ferrari Racing Car, O ga., 1963	6	9	12
5201 ìDî Jaguar Racing Car, O ga., 1963	6	9	12
5202 Corvette Racing Car, O ga., 1963	6	9	12
5210 Cooper Racing Car, O ga., 1963	6	9	12
5211 B.R.M. Racing Car, O ga., 1963	6	9	12
5222 Cooper Racing Car, O ga., 1964	6	9	12
5223 Corvette Racing Car, O ga., 1964	6	9	12
5230 Ferrari Racing Car, O ga., 1964	6	9	12
5231 B.R.M. Racing Car, O ga., 1964	6	9	12
5232 ìDî Jaguar Racing Car, O ga., 1964	6	9	12
5233 Ford Racing Car, O ga., 1964	6	9	12
5234 Buick Racing Car, O ga., 1964	6	9	12

	C5	C7	C9
5235 Jaguar XKE Racing Car, O ga., 1964	6	9	12
5236 Buick Riviera Racing Car, O ga., 1964	6	9	12
5237 Buick Riviera Racing Car, O ga., 1964	6	9	12
5238 Ford Racing Car, O ga., 1964	6	9	12
5239 Ford Convertible Racing Car, O ga., 1964	7	11	15
5240 Ford Police Racing Car, O ga., 1964	7	11	15
5242 Conversion Kit, 1966	5	9	18
5300 Racemaster Power Pack, 1963	7	11	15
5302 Racemaster Power Pack, 1965	7	11	15
5304 HO Control Transformer, 1965	5	9	18
5310 Touch-A-Matic Speed Control, 1963	3	6	9
5320 Touch-A-Matic Speed Control, 1963	3	6	9
5321 Touch-A-Matic Speed Control, 1965	3	6	9
5322 Touch-A-Matic Speed Control, 1965	3	6	9
5400 Straight Roadway, HO ga., 1963	—	—	1
5401 Straight Roadway, HO ga., 1963, w/power connector	—	—	1
5402 Railroad and Roadway Crossing, HO ga., 1963	—	1	2
5403 Roadway Intersection, HO ga., 1963	—	1	2
5404 Lane Change Over, HO ga., 1963	—	1	2
5405 Roadway, HO ga., 1963, curved	—	—	1
5406 Roadway, HO ga., 1963, curved, 45 degree	—	—	1
5407 Inner Roadway, HO ga., 1963, curved, 90 degree	—	—	1
5408 Outer Roadway, HO ga., 1963, curved, 45 degree	—	—	1

	C5	C7	C9
5409 Inner Roadway, HO ga., 1963, curved, 45 degree	—	—	1
5410 Roadway, HO ga., 1963, straight	—	—	1
5411 Roadway, HO ga., 1963, straight	—	—	1
5412 Roadway, HO ga., 1963, straight	—	—	1
5415 Roadway, HO ga., 1963, straight, w/power connection	—	—	1
5421 Touch-A-Matic Speed Controller, HO ga., 1965	5	8	10
5422 Touch-A-Matic Speed Controller, HO ga., 1965	5	8	10
5425 Loop-the-Loop Kit, HO ga., 1960	10	15	20
5430 Universal Roadway Kit, HO ga., 1966	9	14	18
5431 Mystery Route Selector, HO ga., 1966	5	10	15
5433 Car Lane Controller, HO ga., 1965	6	9	13
5434 Car Lane Controller, HO ga., 1965	6	9	13
5450 Trestle Set, HO ga., 1963	4	6	8
5455 Car Lane Controller, HO ga., 1966	6	9	13
5457 Relay Kit, HO ga., 1966	10	15	20
5459 Dump Car, O ga., 1948, operating, electronic, black, "Lionel Lines"	55	115	175
5478 Guard Rail and Flag Set, HO ga., 1966	10	15	20
5511 Tie-Jector, O ga., 1958-1961	51	85	170
5531 Buick Riviera Racing Car, HO ga., 1965	3	5	10
5532 Buick Patrol Racing Car, HO ga., 1965	3	5	10
5533 Ford Hardtop Racing Car, HO ga., 1965	3	5	10
5534 Ford Convertible Racing Car, HO ga., 1965	3	5	10
5535 Ford Police Racing Car, HO ga., 1965	3	5	10

	C5	C7	C9
5537 Rolls Royce Racing Car, HO ga., 1965	3	5	10
5538 Bentley Racing Car, HO ga., 1965	3	5	10
5539 Jaguar XKE Racing Car, HO ga., 1965	3	5	10
5540 Car Lane Control Car, HO ga., 1965, Thunderbird	4	6	12
5541 Car Lane Control Car, HO ga., 1965, Jaguar XKE	4	6	12
5542 Car Lane Control Car, HO ga., 1965, Thunderbird	4	6	12
5767-15 Valise Carrying Pack, HO ga., 1961	8	13	25
6002 Gondola, O27 ga., 1949, NYC	5	9	18
6004 Boxcar, O27 ga., 1950, Baby Ruth, P.R.R.	4	7	13
6007 Caboose, O27 ga., 1950, Lionel Lines, SP type	3	5	10
6009 Remote Control Track, O27 ga., 1953	3	5	6
6012 Gondola, O27 ga., 1955, black, Lionel	3	4	8
6014 Boxcar, O27 ga., 1951, Air Ex., red	25	45	75
6014 Boxcar, O27 ga., 1951, Air Ex., blue	15	25	50
6014 Boxcar, O27 ga., 1955, Baby Ruth, P.R.R.	5	8	10
6014 Boxcar, O27 ga., 1957, Frisco	4	6	8
6014 Boxcar, O27 ga., 1958, Bosco, P.R.R., red or orange body	5	8	11
6014 Boxcar, O27 ga., 1958, white body	35	50	70
6014-325 Boxcar, O27 ga., 1964, Frisco	7	11	22
6014-335 Boxcar, O27 ga., 1965, Frisco	7	11	22
6014-85 Boxcar, O27 ga., 1969, Frisco	7	11	22
6014-410 Boxcar, O27 ga., 1969, Frisco	7	11	22
6014-325 Frisco Savings Bank Car, O27 ga., 1963	7	11	22
6014 WIX, cream/white	80	120	175
6015 Tank Car, O27 ga., 1954, Sunoco, silver, one dome	5	8	15
6017 Caboose, O27 ga., 1951, Lionel, brown	3	5	10
6017-50 Caboose, O27 ga., 1958, Marine, dark blue	20	30	55
6017-100 Caboose, 1959, B&M, light blue	15	25	50
6017-100 Caboose, 1959, B&M, dark blue	250	450	800
6017-185 Caboose, O27 ga., 1959, ATSF, gray	10	20	35
6017-200 Caboose, O27 ga., 1960, Navy, dark blue	35	50	85
6017-225 Caboose, O27 ga., 1961, ATSF	25	35	60
6019 Remote Control Track, 1948	3	5	10
6024 Boxcar, O27 ga., 1957, Nabisco	12	20	28
6024 Boxcar, O27 ga., 1957, RCA-Whirlpool, red, uncataloged	30	50	70
6025 Tank Car, O27 ga., 1956, gray	11	18	36
6025 Tank Car, O27 ga., 1956, Gulf, orange	9	15	29
6025 Tank Car, O27 ga., 1956, black	5	8	15
6027 Caboose, O27 ga., 1959, Alaska, blue	25	45	80
6029 Uncoupling Track Set, 1955	3	5	6
6032 Gondola, O27 ga., 1952, black, "Lionel"	2	4	6
6034 Boxcar, O27 ga., 1953, Baby Ruth, P.R.R.	8	14	28
6035 Tank Car, O27 ga., 1950, gray, single dome	4	6	8
6037 Caboose, O27 ga., 1952, brown, marked "Lionel Lines"	12	20	40

	C5	C7	C9
6042 Gondola, marked "Lionel," uncataloged..............................	2	4	7
6044 Boxcar, O27 ga., Airex, light blue, uncataloged.....................	12	20	40
6045 Tank Car, green, Cities Service...................................	12	20	35
6047 Caboose, O27 ga., 1962, marked "Lionel Lines".............	2	4	7
6050 Savings Bank Car, O27 ga., 1961, Libby Tomato Juice, Libby promotional car, uncataloged..............................	18	30	50
6050 Savings Bank Car, O27 ga., 1961, white and green..............	12	25	35
6050-110 Savings Bank Car, O27 ga., 1962, Swift's, red..............	22	38	75
6050-100 Savings Bank Car, O27 ga., 1963, Swift's, red..............	22	38	75
6057 Caboose, O27 ga., 1959, Lionel Lines, red......................	3	4	10
6057-50 Caboose, O27 ga., 1962, H.H., orange...........................	12	15	25
6058 Caboose, O27 ga., 1961, C&O, yellow............................	15	25	45
6059-50 Caboose, O27 ga., 1961, M&StL, maroon.......................	8	13	25
6059-60 Caboose, O27 ga., 1969, M&StL, shiny or flat red..........	5	8	15
6062 Gondola, O27 ga., 1959, glossy black.............................	7	12	18
6076 Hopper, O27 ga., 1959, A.T.S.F., gray.........................	10	15	22
6076-75 Hopper, O27 ga., 1963, LV, gray or black or red...........	6	10	20
6076-100 Hopper, O27 ga., 1963, Lionel.....................................	6	10	20
6110 Locomotive, O27 ga., 1951, 2-4-2, steam.............................	15	25	50
6111 Flatcar, O27 ga., 1955, w/logs or pipes......................	8	13	25
6112-25 Canisters, O27 ga., 1956, white or red, set of four............	5	10	15
6112 Gondola, O27 ga., 1956, w/canisters, white..................	15	25	50

	C5	C7	C9
6112 Gondola, O27 ga., 1956, w/canisters, blue, marked "Lionel"................................	3	5	9
6119 Work Caboose, O27 ga., 1955................................	14	23	45
6119-25 Work Caboose, O27 ga., 1957, DL&W..........................	10	15	30
6119-100 Work Caboose, O27 ga., 1963, DL&W...........................	12	24	28
6119-110 Work Caboose, O27 ga., 1964, DL&W...........................	12	24	28
6121 Flatcar, O27 ga., 1956, w/pipes.....................................	5	8	16
6130 Work Caboose, O27 ga., 1965, Santa Fe........................	10	20	34
6139 Uncoupling Track, O27 ga., 1963, remote control.................	4	6	8
6142 Gondola, O27 ga., 1963, w/canisters..............................	3	5	7
6142-75 Gondola, O27 ga., 1963, w/canisters..............................	3	5	10
6142-100 Gondola, O27 ga., 1964, w/canisters..............................	3	5	10
6142-125 Gondola, O27 ga., 1964....................................	3	5	10
6142-150 Gondola, O27 ga., 1964....................................	3	5	10
6149 Uncoupling Track, O27 ga., 1964, remote control.................	3	5	10
6151 Range Patrol.........................	40	80	120
6157 Caboose, O27 ga., brown, uncataloged..............................	3	5	10
6162-50 Gondola, O27 ga., 1959, w/canisters, Alaska, yellow.......	30	50	100
6162-25 Gondola, O27 ga., 1959, w/canisters, blue......................	5	9	12
6162 Gondola, O27 ga., 1963, w/canisters, NYC, red..............	17	28	55
6162-100 Gondola, O27 ga., 1964, w/canisters, NYC....................	9	16	25
6162-110 Gondola, O27 ga., 1965, w/canisters, NYC....................	9	16	25
6167-50 Caboose, O27 ga., 1963, D.R.W.	3	4	5
6167 Caboose, O27 ga., 1963, Lionel.....................................	4	6	12

	C5	C7	C9
6167-100 Caboose, O27 ga., 1964, Lionel.........................	3	6	10
6167-125 Caboose, O27 ga., 1964, unlettered	3	6	10
6167-85 Caboose, O27 ga., 1969, U.P.	10	15	30
6175 Rocket Car, O27 ga., 1958, red and white rocket, red or black frame	25	50	70
6176 Hopper, O27 ga., 1964, yellow	4	6	12
6176-50 Hopper, O27 ga., 1964, L.V., yellow	3	7	10
6176-75 Hopper, O27 ga., 1964, L.V., gray	3	7	10
6219 Work Caboose, O27 ga., 1960, C&O, blue cab	25	35	75
6220 Locomotive, O27 ga., 1949, diesel, SW2, NYC or Santa Fe, black, similar to 622, w/bell	150	180	360
6250 Locomotive, O27 ga., 1954, diesel, SW2, Seaboard, blue and orange...............................	125	175	315
6257-25 Caboose, O27 ga., uncataloged.............................	4	7	13
6257-50 Caboose, O27 ga., uncataloged.............................	3	5	9
6257 Caboose, O27 ga., 1948........	4	6	12
6257-100 Caboose, O27 ga., 1964	7	10	18
6262 Wheel Car, O ga., 1956, black or red frame w/eight set of wheels....................................	30	50	65
6264 Forklift Accessory Flatcar, red frame, brown lumber rack ..	20	40	55
6311 Flatcar, O ga., 1955, brown, no load	23	38	75
6315-60 Chemical Car, O ga., 1963, orange, single dome tank, marked "Lionel Lines"	11	19	37
6315 Tank Car, O ga., 1956, orange, three dome, marked "Gulf"	22	36	72
6342 Culvert Car, O ga., 1957, red gondola, w/inclined rake for culvert pipes............................	11	18	36
6343 Barrel Ramp Car, O ga., 1961, red, gray ramp	15	25	47
6346 Covered Hopper, O ga., 1956, Alcoa, silver	17	28	55
6352 Refrigerator Car, O ga., 1955, for ice depot, Pacific Fruit Express, orange shell, door on roof for deposit of ice blocks, side door discharges	45	80	110
6356 Stock, O ga., 1954, NYC, yellow......................................	16	27	53
6357 Caboose, O27 ga., 1948, maroon, red, Tuscan brown	7	11	23
6361 Timber Flatcar, O ga., 1960, green frame w/three lumber branches	25	50	83
6362 Rail Truck Car, O ga., 1955, orange frame w/three sets of trucks	20	40	60
6376 Circus Car, O ga., 1956, white stock car	30	50	80
6401 Flatcar, O ga., 1965, w/two vans	15	25	50
6402-50 Flatcar, O ga., 1964, w/cable reels, gray frame w/orange reels	22	38	75
6405 Flatcar, O ga., 1961, w/piggyback van, brown frame w/two trailer vans.....................	12	25	40
6407 Flatcar, O ga., 1963, w/rocket, red frame, gray supports w/red and white rocket, blue nose, actually a pencil sharpener	125	300	425
6408 Flatcar, O ga., 1963, w/pipes	10	20	30
6409-25 Flatcar, O ga., 1963, w/pipes	10	20	30
6411 Flatcar, O27 ga., 1948, w/logs, gray die-cast frame, five logs....................................	11	20	35
6413 Mercury Capsule Car, O ga., 1962, blue frame w/two gray Mercury capsules	70	110	140
6414-25 Autos, O ga., 1955, set of four...	55	64	75

EXCITING LIONEL LAND,

A "Minuteman" Missile Launching Car – A real headline maker complete with Strategic Air Command markings! By remote control, roof of car separates and launching mechanism elevates to firing position . . . at this point missile blasts off automatically toward target. Missile will "shoot down" the Aerial Target Balloon and "explode" the Target Range Car. No. 3665 — $9.95

B New! Solid Fuel Motorboat Car – A twofold operation! Boat has a specially designed tank into which a pill is inserted. When placed in water, boat will accelerate at top speed as though it were jet-propelled. Boat is secured in its own cradle on the railroad flat car. Car is 11" long. No. 6501 — $6.95

C Operating Helicopter Launching Car – A favorite with everyone! After spring in the launching mechanism is wound, the "whirlybird" can be sent high into the air by remote control. A real delight to watch. Car 11" long. No. 3419 — $7.95

D New! Rocket Fuel Tank Car–No missile could be launched without its supply of essential rocket fuel! Brightly colored in white with red markings. A real "missile age" railroad accessory with minute detailing. Car is 9¼" long. No. 6463 — $4.95

Top row, left to right: No. 6413 Mercury Capsule car, $140; No. 3830 Submarine car, $95. Bottom: No. 6501 Flatcar with motorboat, $120. Photo courtesy 1962 Lionel catalog.

	C5	C7	C9
6414 Evans Loader Car, O ga., 1961, red frame, black metal car rack w/four cars	40	70	100
6415 Tank Car, O ga., 1953, Sunoco, silver, three dome	9	15	30
6415-60 Tank Car, O ga., 1969, Sunoco	9	15	30
6416 Four Boat Loader, O ga., 1961, red frame, black metal boat rack	80	150	200
6417 Caboose, O ga., 1953, P.R.R., 536417, N5C type, Tuscan brown	12	20	40
6417 Caboose, O ga., 1953, P.R.R., Lehigh Valley, gray	50	65	140
6417 Caboose, O ga., 1953, P.R.R., Tuscan	600	1000	2000
6418 Girder Flatcar, O ga., 1955, depressed center, gray die-cast frame w/two orange girder sections, four sets of trucks	45	75	100
6419 Wrecker Caboose, O27 ga., 1948, DL&W, gray cab	15	25	45
6419-100 Wrecker Caboose, O27 ga., 1954, N&W, light gray cab, 576419	45	75	135
6420 Wrecker Caboose, O ga., 1949, DL&W, dark gray, die-cast frame w/searchlight	35	65	105
6424 Twin Auto Car, O ga., 1956, black frame, two autos	16	30	45
6425 Tank Car, O ga., 1956, Gulf, silver, three dome	15	25	50
6427 Caboose, O ga., 1954, 64273, Tuscan brown, N5C type	14	23	45
6427-500 Caboose, O ga., 1957, Girl's train, 57, 6427, blue shell, white lettering	125	200	350
6427-60 Caboose, O ga., 1958, Virginian, 6427, blue shell, yellow lettering, N5C type	120	200	400
6428 Boxcar, O ga., 1960, U.S. Mail, red, white and blue	15	25	45
6429 Wrecker Caboose, O ga., 1963, gray die-cast frame, gray cab	125	200	310

	C5	C7	C9
6430 Flatcar, O ga., 1956, w/piggyback van, red frame w/two trailer vans	20	40	60
6434 Poultry Car, O ga., 1958, red stock car, gray doors, illuminated	40	60	80
6436 Hopper, O ga., 1955, N&W, red	12	20	40
6436-25 Hopper, O ga., 1956, L.V., maroon	15	25	50
6436-1 Hopper, O ga., 1956, L.V., black	15	25	50
6436-57 Hopper, O ga., 1957, L.V., girl's set, lilac, maroon lettering,	75	150	225
6436-100 Hopper, O ga., 1957, L.V.	14	24	48
6436-110 Hopper, O ga., 1963, L.V.	23	38	75
6437 Caboose, O ga., 1961, Pennsylvania, N5C, Tuscan brown	13	23	45
6440 Pullman, O27 ga., 1948, green sheetmetal body, dark green roof	20	30	45
6441 Observation Car, O27 ga., 1948, green sheetmetal body, dark green roof	20	30	45
6442 Pullman, O27 ga., 1949, brown sheetmetal body and roof	20	33	65
6443 Observation Car, O27 ga., 1949, brown sheetmetal body and roof	24	40	80
6445 Fort Knox Gold Car, O ga., 1961, silver w/four clear windows, showing gold bullion	60	100	140
6446-54 Covered Cement, O ga., 1954, N&W, black	17	28	55
6446-54 Covered Cement, O ga., 1954, N&W, gray	30	50	100
6446-25 Covered Hopper, O ga., 1956, N&W, gray	23	38	75
6447 Caboose, O ga., 1963, N5C type, Tuscan brown	125	200	350

	C5	C7	C9
6448 Expolding Target Range Car, O ga., 1961, red shell, white lettering	11	20	35
6454 Boxcar, O27 ga., 1948, P.R.R., Tuscan brown	60	130	200
6454 Boxcar, O27 ga., 1949, NYC, brown	15	35	50
6454 Boxcar, O27 ga., 1950, Erie, brown	20	35	55
6454 Boxcar, O27 ga., 1950, Erie, SP	20	35	55
6456 Hopper, O ga., 1948, maroon, black, gray	6	10	20
6456 Hopper, O ga., 1948, shiny red, yellow letters	48	80	160
6456 Hopper, O ga., 1948, white letters	200	350	500
6457 Caboose, O ga., 1949, brown or maroon, SP type	12	15	28
6460 Crane, O ga., 1952, black cab	23	40	75
6460 Crane, O ga., 1952, gray cab	25	40	75
6461 Transformer Car, O27 ga., 1949, gray die-cast frame, black transformer	32	53	105
6462C Gondola, O ga., 1949, NYC	4	6	12
6462-25 Gondola, O ga., 1954, NYC, black, bright red, green	5	8	15
6462-500 Gondola, O ga., 1957, Girl's train, pink, marked "NYC"	65	110	170
6463 Rocket Fuel Tank Car, O ga., 1962, white shell, two dome, red lettering	23	38	75
6464-1 Boxcar, O ga., 1953, W.P., silver	35	60	88
6464-25 Boxcar, O ga., 1953, G.N., orange	35	65	90
6464-50 Boxcar, O ga., 1953, M&StL, maroon	35	65	90
6464-75 Boxcar, O ga., 1953, R.I., green	40	65	85
6464-200 Boxcar, O ga., 1954, P.R.R., Tuscan brown	70	100	140

	C5	C7	C9
6464-225 Boxcar, O ga., 1954, S.P., black	50	75	135
6464-150 Boxcar, O ga., 1954, M.P., blue and gray	39	80	130
6464-175 Boxcar, O ga., 1954, R.I., silver	50	85	125
6464-100 Boxcar, 1954, W.P., silver w/yellow feather	60	90	125
6464-100 Boxcar, 1954, W.P., orange w/blue feather	350	600	1000
6464-125 Boxcar, O ga., 1954, red and gray, marked "Pacemaker"	40	80	130
6464-275 Boxcar, O ga., 1955, red, white and blue, marked "State of Maine"	50	75	100
6464-300 Boxcar, O ga., 1955, Rutland, green and yellow	40	70	125
6464-425 Boxcar, O ga., 1956, N.H., black	30	50	75
6464-325 Boxcar, O ga., 1956, B&O, silver and aqua, "Sentinel"	280	450	605
6464-350 Boxcar, O ga., 1956, M.K.T., maroon	115	205	290
6464-400 Boxcar, O ga., 1956, B&O, blue and orange, "timesaver"	42	70	140
6464-450 Boxcar, O ga., 1956, G.N., olive and orange	60	100	135
6464-375 Boxcar, O ga., 1956, C.G., maroon and silver	45	85	120
6464-475 Boxcar, O ga., 1957, B&M, blue	30	45	60
6464-500 Boxcar, O ga., 1957, Timken, yellow and white	60	100	130
6464-510 Boxcar, O ga., 1957, Girl's train, NYC, lilac	300	460	620
6464-515 Boxcar, O ga., 1957, Girl's train, M.K.T., yellow	260	430	600
6464-525 Boxcar, O ga., 1957, M&StL, red	30	50	77
6464-650 Boxcar, O ga., 1957, D.R.G.W., yellow and silver	50	90	130
6464-825 Boxcar, O ga., 1959, Alaska, blue and yellow	111	185	370

	C5	C7	C9
6464-900 Boxcar, O ga., 1960, NYC, light green	50	85	120
6464-700 Boxcar, O ga., 1961, Santa Fe, red	50	90	130
6464-725 Boxcar, O ga., 1962, New Haven, black	30	50	65
6464-250 Boxcar, O ga., 1966, W.P., orange w/blue feather	90	150	225
6465 Tank Car, O27 ga., 1948, silver, two dome, marked "Sunoco"	12	20	40
6465 Tank Car, O27 ga., 1958, Gulf, black, two dome	25	50	75
6465 Tank Car, O27 ga., 1958, black, Lionel Lines, two dome	10	20	30
6465 Tank Car, O27 ga., 1958, orange, Lionel Lines, two dome	5	10	15
6465 Tank Car, O27 ga., 1960, Cities Service, green, two dome	12	15	30
6466T W or WX Tender, O27 ga., 1948	30	50	100
6467 Bulkhead Car, O ga., 1956, red frame, two black bulkheads	18	35	50
6468 Automobile, O ga., 1953, B&O, brown	140	215	320
6468 Automobile, O ga., 1953, B&O, blue, double door	20	40	60
6468-25 Automobile, O ga., 1956, N.H., orange, double door	25	45	72
6469 Liquefied Gas Tank Car, O ga., 1963, red frame, white cylinder	75	125	150
6470 Exploding Boxcar, O ga., 1959, red w/white lettering, spring mechanism	12	28	40
6472 Refrigerator, O ga., 1950, white boxcar	18	28	38
6473 Horse Transport Car, 1963, yellow, two horse heads bob in and out	10	20	30
6475 Pickle Car, O ga., 1960, Heinz 57	—	—	—
6475 Pineapple Car, O ga., 1960, Libby, uncataloged	36	63	125

	C5	C7	C9
6476 Hopper, O ga., 1957, red, white letters	4	10	15
6476-25 Hopper, O ga., 1963, L.V., gray, black letters	3	5	10
6476-75 Hopper, O ga., 1963, L.V., red, white letters	4	7	10
6477 Pipe Car, O ga., 1957, red frame, two black bulkheads, w/sidestakes	24	40	80
6500 Beechcraft Bonanza Transport Car, O ga., 1962, black frame w/red and white plane	245	425	850
6501 Flatcar, O ga., 1962, w/motor boat, red frame w/white and brown boat	55	85	120
6502 Flatcar, O ga., 1962, w/girder, blue flat w/orange bridge	20	40	50
6511 Pipe Car, O ga., 1953, brown or red flat w/three aluminum colored pipes	15	25	50
6512 Cherry Picker Car, O ga., 1962, black or blue frame, gray ladder support, black ladder w/man	35	70	105
6517 Caboose, O ga., Erie, bay window, red, uncataloged	180	250	465
6517 Caboose, O ga., 1955, bay window, red, marked "Lionel Lines"	30	50	70
6518 Transformer Car, O ga., 1956, gray die-cast frame, four sets of trucks, black transformer	45	80	120
6519 Allis Chalmers Car, O ga., 1958, orange car, gray reactor	27	45	90
6520 Operating Searchlight, O ga., 1949, gray die-cast base, green	132	225	450
6520 Operating Searchlight, O ga., 1949, orange or maroon generator	25	40	65
6520 Operating Searchlight, O ga., 1949, tan generator	200	350	500
6530 Fire Prevention Car, O ga., 1960, red shell, white lettering	40	60	75

..."SPACE AGE" ACTION CARS

New! Mercury Capsule Launching Car —Ready to conquer "new horizons"! Mounted on a railroad car is a high powered missile ready to "boost" a Mercury Capsule by remote control. At a specific height after launching, missile falls back to earth and Mercury Capsule continues to soar. At its peak height Mercury Capsule turns upside down and descends back to earth slow and gracefully through the use of a parachute. Car 11" long.
No. 3413 $9.95

New! Cherry Picker Car — An essential part of any space launching! Ladder which can be raised and extended holds a compartment that houses an Astronaut. By turning a knob, Astronaut swivels out into full view. Cherry Picker can be used with the Mercury Capsule Launching Car to give the effect that an Astronaut is being loaded into the capsule. Car 11" long.
No. 6512 $6.95

NEW! Cherry Picker Car

CHERRY PICKER RISES TO MERCURY CAPSULE

ASTRONAUT PREPARES TO ENTER CAPSULE

ASTRONAUT DISAPPEARS FROM VIEW

New! Aerial Target Launching Car — A thrilling sight to behold! When train starts up . . . Target Balloon is launched by a jet of compressed air. Specially designed air compressor on the car keeps balloon aloft as train goes around the track. Car 11" long.
No. 3470 $9.95

2 "D" Batteries Required (Not included)

Top to bottom: No. 6512 Cherry Picker, $105; No. 3470 No. 3470 Aerial Target Launching car, $75. Photo courtesy 1962 Lionel catalog.

	C5	C7	C9
6536 Hopper, O ga., 1958, M&StL, red w/white lettering	20	30	55
6544 Missile Firing Car, O ga., 1960, blue frame, gray launch platform, red firing control w/four white rockets, white console	45	80	110
6555 Tank Car, O ga., 1949, silver, single dome, metal tank, "Sunoco"	18	30	60
6556 Stock, O ga., 1958, M.K.T., Katy, red shell, white lettering and doors	70	150	240
6557 Smoking Caboose, O ga., 1958, SP-type, Tuscan brown w/smoke unit, liquid type, marked "Lionel"	85	150	250
6560 Crane, O ga., 1955, black frame, gray cab, marked "Bucyrus Erie"	40	50	90
6560 Crane, O ga., 1955, red cab, "Bucyrus Erie"	20	30	55
6560-25 Crane, O ga., 1961, black frame, red cab 6560-25, "Bucyrus Erie"	45	65	110
6561 Cable Car, O ga., 1953, gray die-cast frame w/two orange or gray spools wrapped w/aluminum wire	20	65	110
6562 Gondola, O ga., 1956, NYC, black	12	25	35
6562 Gondola, O ga., 1956, NYC, gray	14	23	45
6562 Gondola, O ga., 1956, NYC, red	12	25	35
6572 Railway Express Reefer, O ga., 1958, green	45	70	90
6572 Railway Express Reefer, O ga., 1958, light green	45	70	90
6630 IRBM Missile Launcher Car, O ga., 1960, black frame, blue ramp, w/red and white missile	30	70	105
6636 Hopper, O ga., 1959, Alaska, black w/orange lettering	21	35	70
6640 U.S.M.C. Missile Launcher, 1960, olive frame, black ramp, w/white missile	85	150	225

	C5	C7	C9
6646 Stock, O ga., 1957, orange shell, black lettering, "Lionel Lines"	17	29	58
6650 IRBM Missile Car, O ga., 1959, red frame, blue support, black ramp w/red and white missile	28	48	95
6650-80 Missile for 6650-0, 1959, five white missiles	5	8	16
6651 Marine Cannon Car, O ga., 1960, olive frame and cannon w/four cannon loads, uncataloged	63	110	210
6656 Stock, O ga., 1950, yellow shell, black lettering	8	13	26
6657 Caboose, O ga., 1957, D.R.G.W., SP type, yellow cab w/silver lower stripe, black lettering	50	83	165
6660 Flatcar, O ga., 1958, car w/boom, red flat, yellow crane, turn control	30	55	80
6670 Flatcar, O ga., 1959, car w/derrick, red flat, yellow crane, no turn control	20	50	70
6672 Refrigerator, O ga., 1954, "Santa Fe," white shell, brown roof, black lettering	25	50	80
6672 Refrigerator, O ga., 1954, blue lettering	25	50	70
6736 Hopper, O ga., 1960, Detroit & Mackinac, red shell, white lettering	17	30	70
6800 Flatcar, O ga., 1957, w/airplane, red frame w/black and yellow plane	75	125	175
6801 Flatcar, O ga., 1957, w/white boat, red flat	45	75	110
6801-50 Flatcar, O ga., 1957, w/yellow boat, red flat	45	75	110
6801-75 Flatcar, O ga., 1957, w/blue boat, red flat	48	80	160
6802 Flatcar, O ga., 1958, w/bridge, red flat w/black bridge	14	24	48

AIR ACTION CARS

No. 6650

New! No. 6448

No. 6544

No. 3419

New! No. 3519

STRATEGIC AIR COMMAND

U.S. AIR FORCE   3665   MINUTEMAN

Roof separates . . . launcher rises . . . missile blasts off!

New! No. 3665

No. 3376 Operating Giraffe Car — Always entertaining! As the car approaches the overhead telltale, giraffe pulls in his head. After the telltale has been cleared, up pops the giraffe's head. Car 11″ long.   **$6.95**

No. 3830 Operating Submarine Car — A double treat! Just wind sub's mechanism, set in water and watch it cruise, dive and return to surface. When not in water sub can be set on flat car base. Car 11″ long.   **$8.95**

No. 6650 Missile Launching Car — When firing button is pressed, launching unit rises to firing position and missile blasts off automatically. Missile can explode No. 6448 Target Range Car and No. 943 Exploding Ammo Dump. Car 11″ long.   **$7.95**

New! No. 6448 Exploding Target Range Car — Just hit the bullseye and see the action! Projectile from any of Lionel's cars and accessories will explode this target car. Reassembles easily. Car 10½″ long.   **$5.95**

No. 6544 Missile Firing Car — By rotating wheel on side, missiles can be fired in sequence. Missiles will explode No. 6448 Target Range Car and No. 943 Exploding Ammo Dump. Car 11″ long.   **$7.95**

51

Top row, left to right: No. 6650 IRBM Missile car, $95; No. 6448 Exploding Target Range car, $35; No. 6544 Missile Firing car, $110. Middle row: two No. 3419 Helicopter Launching car, $110, each. No. 3519 Automatic Satellite car, $55. Photo courtesy 1961 Lionel catalog.

Top row, left to right: No. 6804 Flatcar, $205; No. 6803 Flatcar, $205. Middle row: No. 6806 Flatcar, $175. Bottom row: No. 212 Locomotive, $300.

	C5	C7	C9
6803 Flatcar, O ga., 1958, w/tank and sound truck, red frame, two gray vehicles	70	140	205
6804 Flatcar, O ga., 1958, w/sound truck, red frame, two gray trucks	70	140	205

No. 6804 Flatcar with two gray trucks, $205.

	C5	C7	C9
6805 Atomic Energy Car, O ga., 1958, red frame, two gray radioactivity containers, lights under containers.......................	48	80	160
6806 Flatcar, O ga., 1958, w/radar and medical truck, red frame, two gray vehicles	70	125	175

	C5	C7	C9
6807 Flatcar, O ga., 1958, w/duck, amphibian boat, red frame, one gray boat..................................	60	100	150
6808 Flatcar, O ga., 1958, w/tank and searchlight, red flat w/two gray vehicles	100	175	250
6809 Flatcar, O ga., 1958, w/medical trucks, red frame, two gray vehicles	85	155	210
6810 Flatcar, O ga., 1958, w/piggyback van, red frame, one trailer container, "Cooper Jarretting".................................	18	35	50
6812 Track Maintenance Car, O ga., 1959, red frame, gray, blue or yellow platform, w/two blue men...	33	55	110
6814 First Aid Caboose, O ga., 1959, white frame, cab and tool boxes, two stretchers, oxygen tank and man, marked "Rescue Unit"...	37	63	125
6816-100 Bulldozer, O ga., 1959...	75	125	250

ACTION BY THE CARLOAD...

No. 6828

No. 6827

NEW! No. 6416

BOAT-LOADER

LIONEL

No. 6414

AUTO-LOADER

LIONEL

NEW! No. 6445

6445

FT. KNOX   GOLD RESERVE

NEW! No. 3362

3362

New! No. 3545 Operating TV Monitor Car—A newsworthy car! As car moves along the track, TV cameraman rotates at a 360° angle photographing everything in sight. Includes a bank of simulated floodlights. Car 11″ long. $7.95

New! No. 6822 Night Crew Searchlight Car—A real troubleshooter! Keeping vigil through the night is this car with its illuminated searchlight. Beacon light is adjustable and can be rotated at a 360° angle. Car 11″ long. $7.95

New! No. 6445 Ft. Knox Gold Bullion Transport Car—Has "see-thru" windows which display rows of simulated gold bars on their way to Ft. Knox for safekeeping. Slot on top is used for making deposits. Car 10½″ long. $5.95

No. 3535 Operating Security Car with Rotating Searchlight—As train moves, searchlight revolves in a complete circle. Guns on top of car revolve manually in any direction. Car 11″ long. $7.95

New! No. 3362 Helium Tank Unloading Car—Car carries three simulated silver helium tanks. By remote control, base of car can be tilted and tanks roll off. Tanks can be easily reloaded to use again and again. Car 11″ long. $5.95

No. 6465 Two Dome Cities Service Oil Car—Keeping the nation on the go by supplying vital oil for our industries! Brightly colored with authentic Cities Service markings. Just like the real thing. Car 9¼″ long. $3.95

52

Top row: No. 6828 Flatcar, $140. No. 6827 Flatcar, $175. Middle row, left to right: No. 6416 Four Boat loader, $200; No. 6414 Evans Loader car, $100. Bottom Row: No. 6445 Fort Knox Gold car, $140; No. 3362 $64. Photo courtesy 1961 Lionel catalog.

	C5	C7	C9
6816 Flatcar, O ga., 1959, w/bulldozer, orange bulldozer, red flat, marked "Allis-Chalmers"	200	320	450
6817 Flatcar, O ga., 1959, w/scraper, same as 6816, except bulldozer replaced by scraper	200	320	425
6817-100 Scraper, O ga., 1959	27	45	90
6818 Flatcar, O ga., 1958, w/transformer, red frame, black transformer	25	45	60
6819 Flatcar, O ga., 1959, w/helicopter, red frame w/gray helicopter	30	50	100
6820 Aerial Missile Car, O ga., 1960, blue frame, navy helicopter	90	150	300
6821 Flatcar, O ga., 1959, w/crates, red frame, tan crates	20	28	40
6822 Searchlight Car, O ga., 1961, red frame, gray searchlight, black housing w/blue man	20	30	45
6823 IRBM Missile Car, O ga., 1959, red frame, gray supports, two white missiles	25	45	75

	C5	C7	C9
6824 First Aid Caboose, O ga., 1960, olive frame, cab, tool boxes, w/two stretchers, oxygen tank and man, "Rescue Unit"	63	105	210
6825 Flatcar, O ga., 1959, w/arch bridge, red frame, black bridge, or gray bridge	20	32	65
6826 Flatcar, O ga., 1959, w/trees, red frame w/bundles of life-like Christmas trees	50	90	145
6827 Flatcar, O ga., 1960, w/power shovel, black frame, yellow and black steam shovel	65	100	175
6828-100 Construction Crane, O ga., 1960	80	130	180
6828 Flatcar, O ga., 1960, w/construction crane, black frame, yellow and black crane	45	70	140
6830 Submarine Car, O ga., 1960, blue frame, gray sub, marked "U.S. Navy"	50	90	120
47618 Caboose, 1943, paper train, uncataloged	25	38	50
61100 Boxcar, 1943, paper train, uncataloged	25	38	50

Lionel, Modern Era

Lionel's modern era was born in 1969 when the original Lionel Corporation closed it doors. General Mills stepped in to rescue the dying company, and their first catalog in 1970 signaled the new beginning of a new, colorful Lionel.

The first few years were a struggle for General Mills. Many of the collectors were skeptical of the new Lionel located in Mt. Clemens, Michigan. As luck would have it, General Mills would not only be a protective and proud owner of one of the most popular names in trains, they also nursed Lionel with the funds for new tooling and decorating techniques that were vivid and some would say even superior to postwar Lionel.

In the early 1980s, the manufacturing arm of Lionel moved to Mexico, and some collector's feel the production quality from the years 1982 and 1983 were not up the standards of previous Lionel items.

Kenner Toys took control of Lionel in 1985, when they began offering trains through direct mail. This arrangement took many collectors by surprise and ultimately failed.

Real estate developer and train collector, Richard Kughn, purchased Lionel Trains, Inc. (LTI) in 1986. It was during his time that Lionel reached their peak in sales. Not only did Kughn invest in new tooling like the Reading T-1 and Rock Island Northern type engines, but everything from customer and employee relations to product changed under his management. With locomotives like the Texas & Pacific, it's easy to see why the trains and scarce Side Track items of the LTI era are on the must-have list of the discriminating Lionel collector.

In 1995, Lionel Trains, Inc. was sold to an investment group based in new York City. Today, under the ownership of Wellspring Associates LLC and musician Neil Young, the Lionel Corporation LLC is meeting all manner of challenges in this very competitive market, and in many ways exceeding them.

As with anything you do, information is power. There are several regional Lionel clubs that collector's may consider joining, but it is the two national clubs—the Lionel Collectors Club of America (LCCA) and the Lionel Railroader Club—that collectors will find the most helpful. The first is the Lionel Collectors Club of America.

Pricing

Because there isn't a market for Modern-era Lionel trains not in the box, prices are only listed for items in Mint in Box condition.

Contributor: Dennis Leon Clad, P.O. Box 647, Amelia, VA 23002. Clad has been an avid Lionel train collector since the 1970s. As a contributing editor for the flagship publication of the Lionel Collector's Club of America, *The Lion Roars*, Clad shares his excitement and extensive knowledge of these toys, while keeping fellow club members up-to-date on current special offerings through his column, "The Main Line."

Years of research in all areas of Modern-era Lionel trains have only served to increase his enthusiasm. He is a charter member of the Lionel Ambassador Society. Most recently, Clad was the recipient of the coveted Joshua Lionel Cowen Award given by Lionel to those Ambassadors who best exemplify the joy and spirit of collecting Lionel trains and have actively sought to bring others to the hobby.

A few tips to get started
- Lionel advertising and complete, ready-to-run promotional sets are a smart area to start collecting as are novelty, LCCA and LRRC club cars.
- If you can, buy the top of the line locomotives, diesels and standard O cars.
- Save all of your Lionel paper and memorabilia.
- Always buy the first and last of a series.

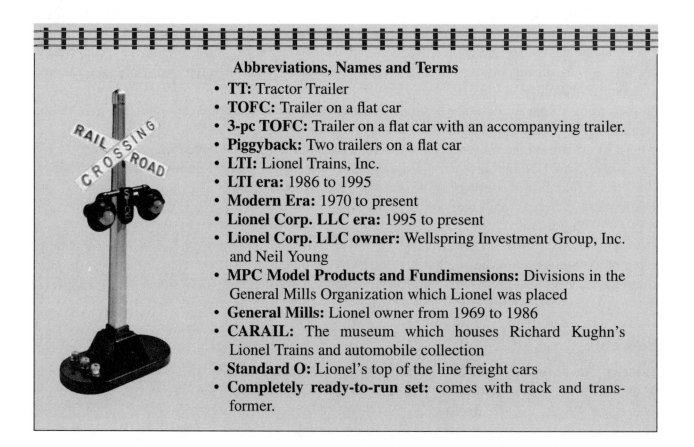

Abbreviations, Names and Terms
- **TT:** Tractor Trailer
- **TOFC:** Trailer on a flat car
- **3-pc TOFC:** Trailer on a flat car with an accompanying trailer.
- **Piggyback:** Two trailers on a flat car
- **LTI:** Lionel Trains, Inc.
- **LTI era:** 1986 to 1995
- **Modern Era:** 1970 to present
- **Lionel Corp. LLC era:** 1995 to present
- **Lionel Corp. LLC owner:** Wellspring Investment Group, Inc. and Neil Young
- **MPC Model Products and Fundimensions:** Divisions in the General Mills Organization which Lionel was placed
- **General Mills:** Lionel owner from 1969 to 1986
- **CARAIL:** The museum which houses Richard Kughn's Lionel Trains and automobile collection
- **Standard O:** Lionel's top of the line freight cars
- **Completely ready-to-run set:** comes with track and transformer.

Accessories

	C10
6-1076 Lionel Service Station Clock, 1976, extremely rare	1000
6-2110 Graduated Trestle Set, 1971	15
6-2111 Elevated Trestle Set, 1971	15
6-2126 Whistling Freight Shed, 1982	50
6-2127 Diesel Horn Shed, 1982	45
6-2133 Lighted Freight Shed, 1982	50
6-2140 Banjo Signal, 1982	15
6-2145 Automatic Gateman, 1982	75
6-2151 Automatic Operating Semaphore, 1982	15
6-2152 Automatic Grossing Gate, 1982	20
6-2154 Automatic Highway Flasher, 1982	25
6-2162 Automatic Crossing Gate/Signal, 1982	15
6-2170 Street Lamps, 1982	20
6-2175 Sandy Andy Gravel Loader, 1979	45
6-2214 Girder Set, 1971	15
6-2290 Lighted Bumpers, 1982	20
6-2305 Getty Oil Derrick, 1983	250
6-2306 Icing Station w/Pacific Fruit Express Ice Car, 1983	325
6-2307 Lighted Billboard, 1982	25
6-2308 Animated Newsstand, 1983	250
6-2309 Mechanical Crossing Gate, 1982	15
6-2313 Floodlight Tower, 1982	25
6-2314 Searchlight Tower, 1982	25
6-2315 Operating Coaling Station, 1983	315
6-2316 Norfolk Western Operating Gantry Crane, 1983	225

	C10
6-2317 Remote Control Drawbridge, 1979	45
6-2318 Operating Control Tower, 1983	125
6-2323 Operating Switch Tower, 1987	100
6-2710 Billboard Set, 1971	20
6-2785 Engine House Kit, 1975	45
6-8459 Rio Grande Rotary Snow Plow, 1984	225
6-8578 NYC Track Ballast Tamper, 1987	275
6-12700 Operating Fueling Station, 1987	125
6-12701 Operating Control Tower, 1987	75
6-12703 Icing Station, 1988	75

No. 6-12703 Icing Station, $75. Courtesy 1988 Lionel catalog.

No. 6-12707 Billboard Set, $20. Courtesy 1988 Lionel catalog.

TRADITIONAL SERIES

OPERATING ACCESSORIES

Bring your layout to life with these exciting operating accessories. Add sound, lights and action to your railroad. All necessary lockons, wires, pressure contactors and control buttons are included.

Floodlight Tower. Eight bright lights illuminate your railyard from 12" high tower.

Searchlight Tower. Spotlight your layout with two adjustable searchlights on a 12" tower.

Street Lamps. Set of three 6" tall lamps to add realism and light.

Automatic Crossing Gate and Signal. Gate swings down and red lights blink until train passes.

Banjo Signal. Stop sign swings while red light flashes. 7½" high and rugged die-cast construction.

Automatic Operating Semaphore. Red light turns to green as arm raises for approaching train, lowers when train passes.

Automatic Crossing Gate. Gate lowers and red lights turn on when train nears, raises when it passes.

Automatic Highway Flasher. Red lights flash alternately when train approaches, stop when train passes.

Mechanical Crossing Gate. Gate lowers when train reaches crossing, raises when past, snaps together easily.

Mechanical Semaphore. Snaps together in minutes, operates from weight of train.

Billboard Light. Illumination for Lionel billboards. Light blinks on and off. Billboard included.

Lighted Bumpers. Used to stop and hold train at the end of a spur. Two illuminated bumpers per pack.

Lighted Freight Station. A detailed, colorful illuminated and realistic building. 12" x 8" x 6½" high.

Whistling Freight Shed. Railyard building with remote-controlled steam whistle sound.

Diesel Horn Shed. Remote controlled sound of a diesel horn from the off-track shed.

Automatic Gateman. Gateman moves out waving his lantern at passing train, returns to his shed when it is passed.

6-2314 Searchlight Tower

6-2313 Floodlight Tower

6-2170 Street Lamps

6-2290 Lighted Bumpers

6-2162 Automatic Crossing Gate & Signal

6-2140 Banjo Signal

6-2151 Automatic Operating Semephore

6-2152 Automatic Crossing Gate

6-2154 Automatic Highway Flasher

6-2309 Mechanical Crossing Gate

6-2307 Billboard Light

First row, top to bottom: No. 2314 Searchlight Tower, $25; No. 6-2170 Street Lamps, $20; No. 2162 Automatic Crossing Gate/Signal, $15; No. 6-2151 Automatic Operating Semephore, $15; No. 6-2154 Automatic Highway Flasher, $25; No. 6-2307 Lighted Billboard, $25. **Second row, top to bottom:** No. 6-2133 Lighted Freight Shed, $50; No. 2290 Lighted Bumpers, $20; 6-2140 Banjo Signal, $15; No. 6-2152 Automatic Crossing Gate, $20; No. 6-2309 Mechanical Crossing Gate, $15. Courtesy 1982 Lionel catalog.

Sandy Andy Automatic Gravel Loader, 6-2175 Dump cart moves up and down ramp with continuous, gravity operated, load, dump and reload action. No batteries needed. Just position the hopper and turn the loader on and off. Easy assembly, multi-color parts, no painting necessary.

No. 6-2175 Sandy Andy Gravel Loader, $45. Courtesy 1980 Lionel catalog.

OPERATING ACCESSORIES

6-2315 Operating Coaling Station

6-2301 Saw Mill

6-2306 Icing Station

6-2318 Operating Control Tower

6-2308 Animated Newsstand

6-2305 Oil Derrick

6-2316 Remote Control Operating Gantry Crane

Operating Coaling Station
For continuing action, this remote controlled station works with an operating coal dump car (not included). Activated car dumps load into station's bin. Bin rises and dumps coal into overhead hopper. When activated, hopper opens and reloads coal dump car. (Controller included, operating track section not included.)

Remote Control Operating Gantry Crane
Cab swivels and hook raises and lowers all by remote control. Sturdy enough to lift heavy loads.

Operating Control Tower
Dispatchers move around inside the illuminated control room in continuous action. Tower is 12" high, detailed and authentic.

Operating Saw Mill
Logs travel on concealed conveyor or belt into mill and are apparently sawed into planks. Saw mill is remotely controlled, 16 1/2" x 6" x 6" high. Logs, lumber and controller included.

Icing Station and Pacific Fruit Express Ice Car
Remotely controlled. Blocks of ice slide down ramp from ice house and ice man shoves them into special hatch in the top of the car.

Animated Newsstand
Newsboy moves around waving his paper while vendor moves inside newsstand and neighborhood dog inspects fireplug. Remotely controlled.

Oil Derrick
Walking beam rocks up and down apparently pumping oil into stand pipe which bubbles to simulate oil flow. Realistic derrick includes a hand operating winch, ladder and oil drums. Base is of sturdy sheet metal.

LC-13

Various operating accessories by Lionel. Top row, left to right: No. 6-2315 Operating Coaling Station, $315; No. 6-2316 Norfolk Western Operating Gantry Crane, $225. Second row, left to right: No. 6-2306 Icing Station, $325; No. 6-2318 Operating Control Tower, $125. Bottom row, left to right: No. 6-2308 Animated Newsstand, $250; No. 6-2305 Getty Oil Derrick, $250. Courtesy 1983 Lionel catalog.

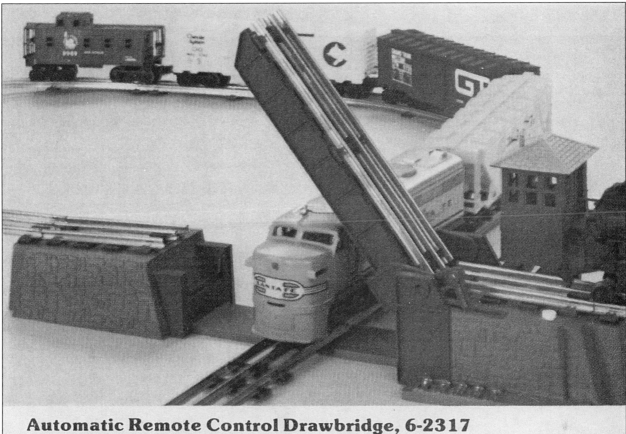

Automatic Remote Control Drawbridge, 6-2317
Train stops automatically at blocked crossing. Bridge is moved by remote control to ringing bell. Train proceeds automatically. 19¾" bridge fully assembled. Includes 6 pier graduated trestle set.

No. 6-2317 Remote Control Drawbridge, $45. Courtesy 1980 Lionel catalog.

Top row, left to right: No. 6-2133 Lighted Freight Shed, $50; No. 6-2126 Whistling Freight Shed, $50; No. 6-2127 Diesel Horn Shed, $5. Bottom row: No. 6-1245 Automatic Gateman, $75. Courtesy 1982 Lionel catalog.

No. 6-12713 Automatic Gateman, $60. Courtesy 1988 Lionel catalog.

No. 6-12719 Animated Refreshment Stand, $175. Courtesy 1988 Lionel catalog.

No. 6-12720 Rotary Beacon, $75. Courtesy 1988 Lionel catalog.

6-12707 Billboard Set, 1988	20
6-12713 Automatic Gateman, 1988	60
6-12719 Animated Refreshment Stand, 1988	175
6-12720 Rotary Beacon, 1988	75
6-12722 Roadside Diner w/Smoke, 1988	65
6-12725 Lionel TT, 1988	45
6-12729 Mail Pick-up Set, 1988	15
6-12731 LOTS Convention Souvenir Station Platform, 1995	100
6-12749 Rotary Radar Antenna, 1990	45
6-12761 Animated Billboard, 1990	45
6-12767 Steam Clean & Wheel Grind Shop, 1993	300
6-12771 Mom's Roadside Diner, 1990	135
6-12777 Chevron TT, 1990	20
6-12778 ConRail TT, 1990	25
6-12779 Lionel Tractor & Grain Rig, 1990	35
6-12781 Norfolk Western Intermodal Crane, 1990	225
6-12782 Lift Bridge, 1992	525
6-12785 Lionel Tractor & Gravel Truck, 1991	25
6-12786 Burning Switch Tower, 1990	275

C10

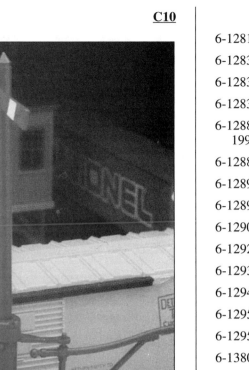

No. 6-12729 Mail Pick-up Set, $15. Courtesy 1988 Lionel catalog.

	C10
6-12786 Lionel Steel TT, 1991	30
6-12791 Animated Passenger Station, 1991	175
6-12794 Die-Cast Lionel Tractor, 1991	60
6-12798 Forklift Loader Station, 1992	35
6-12802 Chat 'n Chew Diner w/Smoke and Lights, 1993	125
6-12806 Lionel Caesar's TT, 1992	55
6-12808 Mobil TT Tanker, 1992	45
6-12809 Animated Billboard, 1993	40
6-12811 Alka Selzer TT, 1992	35

	C10
6-12818 Animated Freight Station, 1992	150
6-12831 Rotary Beacon, 1993	55
6-12836 Santa Fe Quantum TT, 1993	30
6-12837 Humble Oil TT Tanker, 1993	20
6-12882 Visitor's Center Lighted Billboard, 1995	35
6-12889 Windmill, 1995	40
6-12891 Lionel Lines Refrigerator TT, 1995	25
6-12892 Automated Flagman, 1995	45
6-12902 Marathon Oil Derrick, 1995	250
6-12929 Rail Truck Loading Dock, 1996	20
6-12932 Laimbeer Packaging TT, 1996	20
6-12948 Bascule Bridge, 1997	250
6-12952 Big L Diner Kit, 1997	20
6-12958 Industrial Water Tower, 1997	35
6-13804 437 Tower, 1991	600
6-16660 Fire Car w/Ladders, 1993, operating	65
6-18400 Santa Fe Rotary Snow Plow, 1987	275
6-18401 Lionel Hand Car, 1988	50
6-18402 Lionel Lines Burro Crane, 1988	295
6-18404 San Francisco Trolley, 1988	295
6-18407 Snoopy/Woodstock Hand Car, 1990	75
6-18410 Penn Burro Crane, 1990	175
6-18411 Canadian Pacific Fire Car, 1990	150
6-18413 Charlie Brown/Lucy Hand Car, 1991	75
6-18416 Bugs Bunny/Daffy Duck Hand Car, 1993	225
6-18423 On Track Step Van, 1995	25
6-18424 On Track Pickup, 1995	25
6-18425 Goofy/Pluto Hand Car, 1995	45
6-18427 Penn RR Tie-Jector Motorized Unit, 1997	35
6-18430 NYC Crew Car, 1996	25
6-18431 Lionel Transit Trolley Car, 1996	30
6-18433 Mickey/Minnie Hand Car, 1996	55
6-18434 Porky/Petunia Hand Car, 1996	45
6-18436 NYC Dodge Ram Truck Inspection Vehicle, 1997	30
6-19405 Southern Six Wheel Crane, 1991	75

	C10
6-19412 Frisco Six Wheel Crane Car, 1992	75
6-52100 LCCA Convention Souvenir Station Platform, 1996	125
6-52131 LCCA Airplane, 1997, orange	75
6-52135 LCCA Four-pack Cars, 1998	75
6-52138 LCCA Airplane, 1997, blue	75
401001478 United Delco Lionel TT, available only through Merchandising Incentives Corporation	75

Chicago Lionel Railroaders Club

	C10
52148-558 Santa Fe REA Express Operating Boxcar, 1998	60
64287 Burlington Northern Maxi-stack	65
999556 Santa Fe Extended Vision Caboose, 1996, black roof	100
999758 Santa Fe Extended Vision Caboose, 1996, red roof	75

Engines and Cabooses

	C10
6-6256 Dept. 56 Caboose, 1998	65
6-6421 Joshua L. Cowan Lighted Bay Window Caboose, 1982	100
6-6425 Erie Lackawanna Bay Window Caboose, 1983	125
6-6426 Reading Maintenance Caboose, 1982	25

	C10
6-6493 LNC Bay Window Caboose, 1987	35
6-6903 Santa Fe Extended Vision Caboose, 1983	200
6-6910 NYC Extended Vision Caboose, 1984	150
6-8030 Illinois Central GP-9 Diesel, 1971	110
6-8056 Chicago Northwestern FairBanks Morse Diesel Engine, 1980	225
6-8065 Florida East Coast Bay Window Caboose, 1980	90
6-8154 Alaska SW1 Switcher, 1982	135
6-8155 Monon U36-B Powered Engine, 1982	125
6-8156 Monon Dummy, 1982	100
6-8158 Duluth Missabe GP-9 Powered Engine, 1982	125
6-8159 Duluth Dummy, 1982	100
6-8210 Joshua L. Cowan 4-6-4 Hudson, 1982, American Express Credit Card Edition, w/display case, track and brass name plate	600
6-8210 Joshua L. Cowan 4-6-4 Hudson, 1982	475
6-8214 Penn 2-4-2 Steam Engine w/Tender, 1982	175
6-8263 Santa Fe GP-7 Engine, 1982	150
6-8307 Southern Pacific Daylight 4-8-4 Steam Engine, 1983	650
6-8353 Grand Trunk GP-7 Diesel, 1975	125
6-8362 Western Pacific Alco B Dummy, 1975	75

No. 6-8056 Chicago Northwestern FairBanks Morse Diesel Engine, $225. Courtesy 1980 Lionel catalog.

TRADITIONAL SERIES

LOCOMOTIVES

Powerful locomotives for your expanding railroad empire. Authentic, detailed and engineered for dependable service.

Pennsylvania 2-4-2 Steam Engine and Tender Features: • Die-cast cab • Metal chassis, wheels and drive rods • Operating headlight • Puffing smoke • New solid state reversing mechanism for silent, smooth forward-neutral-reverse functions controlled from the transformer • Mechanical sound of steam • Gold Pennsylvania markings.

Santa Fe GP-7 Features: Operating headlight • Operating knuckle coupler • Metal wheels and chassis • New solid state reversing mechanism for silent, smooth forward-neutral-reverse functions controlled from the transformer.

Monon U36B Features: Working headlight • Illuminated running lights • Operating, self-centering knuckle couplers front and rear • Metal trucks, wheels and chassis. **Powered Unit Also Features:** Transformer controlled forward-neutral-reverse.

Duluth Missabe, GP-9 Diesel Features: Working headlight • Illuminated number plates • Operating, self-centering knuckle couplers front and rear • Metal trucks, wheels, handrails and chassis. **Powered Unit Also Features:** Transformer controlled forward-neutral-reverse.

Alaska SW1 Switcher Features: Working headlight • Illuminated running lights • Transformer controlled forward-neutral-reverse • Operating, self-centering knuckle couplers front and rear • Metal trucks, wheels and chassis • Lionel Pullmor™ motor.

Conrail Rectifier Features: Working headlight • illuminated number plates • Transformer controlled forward-neutral-reverse • Operating, self-centering knuckle couplers front and rear • Metal trucks, wheels, handrails and chassis • Lionel Pullmor™ motor • Pantograph raises and lowers. Can be wired to take overhead current.

Santa Fe GP-7 6-8263

Monon U36B Powered 6-8155, Dummy 6-8156

Duluth Missabe GP-9 Powered 6-8158, Dummy 6-8159

Alaska SW1 Switcher 6-8154

Conrail Rectifier 6-8859

Pennsylvania 2-4-2 Steam Engine and Tender 6-8214

LT-12

Top to bottom: No. 6-8263 Santa Fe GP-7 engine, $150; No. 6-8156 Monon dummy, $100; No. 6-8159 Duluth dummy, $100; No. 6-8154 Alaska SW1 switcher, $135; No. 6-8859 ConRail rectifier, $150; No. 6-8214 Penn 2-4-2 Steam engine with tender, $175. Courtesy 1982 Lionel catalog.

Top: No. 6-8369 Erie Lackawanna GP-20 Diesel, $125; No. 6-8374 Burlington Northern Switcher, $110. Courtesy 1983 Lionel catalog.

	C10
6-8363 B&O E A Unit Diesel, 1975	250
6-8364 B&O Dummy, 1975	175
6-8369 Erie Lackawanna GP-20 Diesel, 1983	125
6-8374 Burlington Northern Switcher, 1983	110
6-8406 NYC 4-6-4 Locomotive, 1984	900
6-8412 C&O 4-4-2 Steam Locomotive, 1971	225
6-8466 Amtrak F-3 Diesel, 1976	175
6-8467 Amtrak Dummy, 1976	125
6-8471 Penn Switcher, 1976	125
6-8477 NYC GP-9 Diesel, 1984	350
6-8503 C&N 4-6-4 Steam Engine, 1976	200
6-8550 Jersey Central Dummy, 1976	125
6-8551 Penn Electric, 1976	225
6-8552 Western Pacific Alco A, 1975	100
6-8556 Chessie Diesel Switcher, 1975	100
6-8558 Milwaukee Electric, 1976	175
6-8562 Missouri Pacific Dummy, 1976	150
6-8566 Southern F-3 A Diesel, 1976	250
6-8567 Southern Dummy, 1976	175

	C10
6-8571 Frisco U36 B Diesel Powered, 1975, dummy	75
6-8571 Frisco U36 B Diesel Powered, 1975	100
6-8576 Penn Central GP-7, 1976	115
6-8652 Santa Fe F-3 A Unit Powered, 1976	250
6-8653 Santa Fe Dummy, 1976	200
6-8654 Boston & Maine GP-9 Powered, 1976	125
6-8655 Boston & Maine Dummy	100
6-8850 Penn Central GG-1 Electric Engine, 1979	275
6-8859 ConRail Rectifier, 1982	150
6-8950 Southern Pacific FairBanks Morse Diesel Engine, 1979	250
6-8951 Virginian FairBanks Morse Diesel Engine, 1979	250
6-9173 Jersey Central Lighted Caboose, 1977	20
6-9175 Virginian Lighted Caboose, 1977	45
6-9180 The Rock Lighted Caboose, 1977	25
6-9182 Norfolk Western Lighted Caboose, 1977	55
6-9185 Grand Trunk Lighted Caboose, 1977	25
6-9186 ConRail Lighted Caboose, 1977	55

No. 6-8950 Southern Pacific FairBanks Morse Diesel Engine, $250. Courtesy 1980 Lionel catalog.

No. 6-8951 Virginian FairBanks Morse Diesel Engine, $250. Courtesy 1980 Lionel catalog.

	C10
6-9271 Minneapolis/St. Louis Bay Window Caboose, 1979	65
6-9272 New Haven Bay Window Caboose, 1979	55
6-9317 Santa Fe Bay Window Caboose, 1979	65

	C10
6-9326 Burlington Northern Bay Window Caboose, 1979	60
6-9326 Burlington Northern Bay Window Caboose, 1979	55
6-9382 Florida East Coast Bay Window Caboose, 1980	90

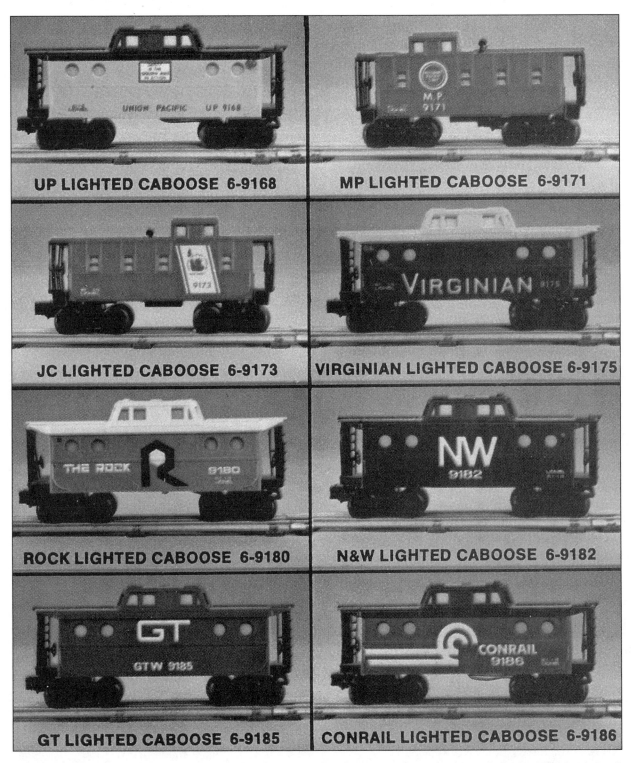

UP LIGHTED CABOOSE 6-9168   MP LIGHTED CABOOSE 6-9171

JC LIGHTED CABOOSE 6-9173   VIRGINIAN LIGHTED CABOOSE 6-9175

ROCK LIGHTED CABOOSE 6-9180   N&W LIGHTED CABOOSE 6-9182

GT LIGHTED CABOOSE 6-9185   CONRAIL LIGHTED CABOOSE 6-9186

First row, top to bottom: No. 6-9173 Jersey Central Lighted caboose, $20; No. No. 6-9180 The Rock Lighted caboose, $25; No. 6-9185 GT Lighted caboose, $45. Second row, top to bottom: No. 6-9175 Virginian Lighted caboose, $45; No. 6-9182 Norfolk Western Lighted caboose, $55; No. 6-9186 ConRail Lighted caboose, $55. Courtesy 1977 Lionel catalog.

	C10
6-11713 Santa Fe Dash 8-40 B Set, 1990	475
6-11718 Norfolk Western Dash 8-40 C Set, 1992, Standard O	675
6-16517 Atlantic Coastline Bay Window Caboose, 1990	35
6-16547 Square Window Lighted Caboose, 1993	40
7-17600 NYC Woodside Caboose, 1987	100
6-17601 Southern Woodside Caboose, 1988	75
6-17603 Rock Island Woodside Caboose, 1988....	75
6-17604 Delaware. Lackawanna, Western Woodside Caboose, 1988	75
6-17606 NYC Steelside Caboose w/Smoke, 1990	75
6-17608 Chessie Steelside Caboose w/Smoke, 1991	75
6-17613 Southern Steelside Caboose, 1992	75
6-17615 Northern Pacific Woodside Caboose w/Smoke, 1992	60
6-17617 Denver Rio Grande Steelside Caboose, 1995	125
6-18001 Rock Island 4-8-4 Locomotive, 1987 ..	475
6-18002 NYC 4-6-4 Steam Locomotive, 1987	800
6-18003 Delaware, Lackawanna, Western 4-8-4 Locomotive, 1988	575
6-18005 700E Scale NYC Hudson, 1990	1000
6-18007 Southern Pacific GS-2 Daylight 4-8-4 Locomotive, 1991	350
6-18008 Disneyland 35th Anniversary 0-4-0 American Locomot, 1990	235
6-18010 Penn S2 6-8-6 Steam Turbine, 1992	1500

	C10
6-18011 Chessie Steam Special 4-8-4 Locomotive, 1991	350
6-18016 Northern Pacific 4-8-4 Locomotive, 1992	675
6-18018 Southern Mikado 2-8-2 Locomotive, 1992	800
6-18021 Frisco 2-8-2 Mikado Locomotive, 1995	650
6-18022 Pre Marquette 2-8-4 Locomotive, 1993	400
6-18023 Western Maryland Shay Locomotive, 1992	1800
6-18040 Norfolk & Western J 4-8-4 Locomotive, 1995	650
6-18042 B&A 4-6-4 Hudson Locomotive, 1995	650
6-18043 C&O Streamline Hudson, 1995, semi-scale	1000
6-18052 Penn Torpedo 4-6-2 Pacific Locomotive, 490	490
6-18054 NYC 0-4-0 Steam Locomotive, 1997	150
6-18056 NYC J 1-E Hudson Locomotive, 1997	490
6-18072 Lionel Lines 4-6-2 Torpedo Steam Locomotive, 1998	375
6-18107 Denver Rio Grande PA-1 A-B-A Set, 1992	1000
6-18226 GE-9 Diesel Engine, 1996	500
6-18300 Penn GG-1 Electric Engine, 1987	425
6-18301 Southern Fairbanks Morse Diesel, 1988	275
6-18303 Penn N8 Caboose, 1992	500

No. 6-18301 Southern Fairbanks Morse Diesel, $275. Courtesy 1988 Lionel catalog.

6-18803 SANTA FE RS-3 DIESEL

6-18804 SOO LINE RS-3 DIESEL

6-18601 GREAT NORTHERN 4-4-2 STEAM LOCOMOTIVE AND TENDER
• Die cast metal body • Stamped metal chassis and drive rods • Wire handrails on cab • Metal wheels • Operating headlight • Operating smoke unit for smoke emissions from the stack • Authentic, two color paint scheme • Smooth forward-neutral-reverse remote operation • Dependable long-life motor that runs on either AC or DC power • Famous Great Northern markings.
18″ long. Pack: 3 Wt: 11 Cube: 1.0

Top to bottom: No. 6-18803 Santa Fe RS-3 Diesel, $150; No. 6-18804 SOO Line RS-3 Diesel, $115; No. 18601 Great Northern 4-4-2 Locomotive, $125. Courtesy 1988 Lionel catalog.

	C10
6-18503 Southern Pacific Diesel Switcher, 1990	175
6-18601 Great Northern 4-4-2 Locomotive, 1988	125
6-18609 Northern Pacific 2-6-4 Locomotive, 1990	100
6-18610 Rock Island 0-4-0 Locomotive, 1990	75
6-18615 Grand Trunk Western 4-4-2 Locomotive, 1988	75
6-18653 Boston & Albany 4-6-2 Pacific Locomotive, 1997	100
6-18803 Santa Fe RS-3 Diesel, 1988	150
6-18804 Soo Line RS-3 Diesel, 1988	115
6-18807 Lehigh Valley RS-3 Diesel, 1990	125
6-18808 Atlantic Coastline SD-18 Diesel, 1990	115
6-18827 Christmas RS-3 Diesel Engine, 1993	150
6-18901 Penn RR Double A Alco, 1988	75
6-19702 Penn Porthole Caboose, 1987	50
6-19714 NYC Searchlight Caboose w/Smoke, 1992	150
6-19726 NYC Bay Window Caboose, 1995, add-on to 1994 Service Station Set	100
6-19807 Penn Extended Vision Caboose w/Smoke, 1988	45
6-33002 Railscope Locomotive w/TV, 1988	275
6-51701 NYC Caboose, 1991, semi-scale	175
6-51702 Penn N8 Caboose, 1992	450
6-71715 Lionel 90th Anniversary Set, 1990	250

Lionel Ambassador Society

6-19957 Lionel Ambassador Woodside Caboose, 1997, w/special Ambassador box	800

Lionel Century Club

An exclusive Lionel club, The only way a new collector can join the Century Club is to purchase a membership from an original member. Members can only have one of each club offering. For these reason, all Century Club items have built-in value.

671 Berkshire Boxcar, 1997	200
726 Berkshire Engine, w/display case	900
2332 Penn GG1 Electric Engine	900

	C10
6-18068 Penn 671 Turbine Tender	425
6-29204 First Century Club Boxcar	1000
6-29226 Berkshire Boxcar, 1998	200
6-29228 Penn Turbine Boxcar, 1999	175

Lionel Collectors Club of America

The following information is from the Lionel Collectors Club of America and its president, Albert F. Otten.

6-2601 Detroit & Toledo Shoreline Two Bay ACF Hopper, 1993	75
6-6112 Commonwealth Edison Quadhopper, 1983, w/coal load	175
6-6323 Virginia Chemicals Tank Car, 1986	95
6-6567 Illinois Chemicals Gulf Crane Car, 1985	110
6-7403 Louisville, New Albany & Crydon Boxcar, 1984	35
6-8068 Rock Island GP-20 Engine, 1980	125
6-9118 Corning Glass Covered Quadhopper, 1974	90
6-9155 Monsanto Tank Car, 1975	125
6-9212 Tuscan Seaboard Piggyback, 1976	75
6-9259 Southern Bay Window Caboose, 1977	70
6-9358 Sand's of Iowa Covered Hopper, 1980	90
6-9460 Detroit & Toledo Shoreline Double Door Boxcar, 1982	35
6-9701 B&O Double Door Boxcar, 1972	150
6-9727 Tennessee Alabama Georgia Boxcar, 1973	260
6-9728 Union Pacific Stock Car, 1978	45
6-9733 Airco Boxcar, 1979, w/tank body inside car	90
6-9739 D&RG Western Boxcar, 1978, banquet size, rare	600
6-9771 N&W Boxcar, 1977, banquet size, rare	600
6-17870 East Camden & Highland Boxcar, 1987, Standard O	90
6-17873 Ashland Oil Three Dome Tanker, 1988	80
6-17876 CN&L Boxcar, 1989, standard O	85
6-17880 D&RGW Steam Locomotive, 1990	500

C10

6-17887 Flat w/Armstrong Trailer, 1991,
standard O 150

6-17888 Flat w/Ford Trailer, 1991,
standard O 150

6-17889 NASA Tanker, 1992, standard O 100

6-360794 Southern Railway Three Bay Hopper,
1994, w/coal load, standard O 95

Lionel Employee Christmas Cards

These cards were given to personnel as gifts along with a Lionel Employee Calendar or Christmas Card.

6-16246 Boxcar, 1996 400

6-16273 Boxcar, 1997 400

6-19913 Boxcar, 1991, signed by owner
Richard Kughn, w/thank you to employee 450

6-19916 Boxcar, 1992, signed by owner
Richard Kughn, marked "Employee"
on box 550

6-19921 Boxcar, 1993, signed by owner
Richard Kughn 550

6-19928 Boxcar, 1994, signed by owner
Richard Kughn 475

6-19939 Boxcar, 1995, marked "Employee" on
box 400

6-52054 CARAIL Commemorative Boxcar,
given only to friends of Richard Kugh,
signed by Kughn w/CARAIL logo to the
right of door, blue and red circle "L" logo to
the left of door, extremely rare 5000

Lionel Promotional sets

These uncataloged sets are very collectible.

Lionel Celebrate the Century Boxcar
w/Postcard, 1998 110

6-11810 Budweiser Modern Era Set, last beer
set.. 350

6-11819 Georgia Power Employee Set, limited
to run of 2500 800

6-11821 Sears Brand Central/Zenith Set,
customer promotion.. 500

6-11827 Zenith Nationwide Independent Dealer
Set 500

6-11827 Zenith Limited Employee Set 400

6-11846 KalKan Express Promotional Set,
contest set, limited to run of 1,000 1000

C10

6-11935 Little Zenith, 1997, Official Sponsor
Set 250

6-11957 Mobile Steam Special Set, only
available from Mobile Oil Distributors,
limited to production run of 1,200 400

6-11985 Quaker State Express Set, employee
set, limited to run of 1,100 400

Lionel Visitor Center

These cars are uncatalogued and for sale only at Lionel's headquarters.

6-19920 Boxcar 175

6-19927 Boxcar 100

6-19932 Boxcar 75

6-19934 Boxcar 65

6-19944 Tank Car.. 125

6-19948 Piggyback.. 75

Nassau Operating Engineers

Information courtesy of NLOE members Richard Williams and Alan Schwartz.

6-5019 Long Island RR Bay Window Caboose,
1993, limited to 425 300

8389 Long Island RR Boxcar, 1989, limited to
51 295

8390 Long Island RR Quadhopper, 1990,
limited to 45 325

8390 Long Island RR Quadhopper, 1990,
w/gray roof, limited to 3 2500

8391A Long Island RR Bunk Car, 1991, limited
to 51 375

8391B Long Island RR Tool Car, 1991, limited
to 51 375

6-17839 Long Island RR One Dome Tank Car,
1992, limited to 55 350

6-52007 Long Island RR RS-3 Diesel Engine,
1993, limited to 65 575

6-52026 Long Island three-piece TOFC Set,
1994, w/Grumman TT, limited to 144 1000

6-52061 Long Island RR Vat Car, 1995, limited
to 114 400

6-52076 Long Island RR Montauk Observation
Car, 1996, limited to 89 750

6-52112 Long Island RR Ronkonkoma Vista
Dome, 1997, limited to 102 650

COLLECTOR SERIES

WOODSIDE REEFERS

Crisp authentic markings distinguish the highly detailed woodsided bodies and roofs of this series.

Featuring: • Authentic opening reefer doors • Realistic period trucks • Metal wheels • Operating knuckle couplers at both ends.

6-5713 SSW Woodside Reefer

6-5714 Michigan Central Woodside Reefer

6-5715 Santa Fe Woodside Reefer

6-5716 Central Vermont Woodside Reefer

6-5709 Railway Express Woodside Reefer

6-5710 Canadian Pacific Woodside Reefer

6-5711 Commercial Express Woodside Reefer

6-5708 Armour Woodside Reefer

SANTA FE BUNK CAR

Santa Fe Bunk Car: • A sleeper car for track gangs. New design first time offered by Lionel **Features:** • Interior illumination • Operating knuckle couplers front and rear • Realistic trucks • Metal wheels.

6-5717 Santa Fe Bunk Car

Lionel Rolling Stock. Top of page: No. 6-5713 Cotton Belt Woodside reefer, $35. First row, top to bottom: No. 6-7514 Michigan Central Woodside reefer, $55; No. 6-7515 Santa Fe Woddside reefer, $35; No. 6-5710 Canadian Pacific Woodside reefer, $35. Second row: No. 6-5716 Central Vermont Woodside reefer, $55. Third row: No. 6-7509 Railway Express Woodside reefer, $55. Bottom of page: No. 5717 Santa Fe Bunk car, $20. Courtesy 1983 Lionel catalog.

	C10
6-52123 Long Island RR Hicksville Dining Car, 1998, limited to 100	700
6-52123 Meenan Oil Tank Car, 1997, limited to 884	650
6-52144 Long Island RR three-piece TOFC 15th Anniversary S, 1998, w/Grumman TT, limited to 1,115	125
6-52145 Long Island RR Jamaica Coach, 1999, limited to 96	790
6-52145 Long Island RR Penn Station Coach, 1999, limited to 97	750
6-52166 Long Island RR three-piece TOFC Set, 1999, w/Northrop TT	100
6-52174 Long Island RR Baggage Car, 2000, limited to 102	800
6-57173 Long Island RR F-3 AA Body Shells, 2000, limited to 108	700

Rolling Stock

	C10
Amtrak Tool Car, 1990	20
Pinto Valley Mine Ore Car, 1994, Gasden Pacific Division TTOM	55
6-5700 Oppenheimer Casing Company Weathered Reefer, 1981	20
6-5701 Dairyman's League Weathered Reefer, 1981	20
6-5702 National American Dispatch Weathered Reefer, 1981	20

	C10
6-5704 Budweiser Weathered Reefer, 1981	75
6-5705 Ball Glass Jar Weathered Reefer, 1981	35
6-5706 Lindsay Brothers Weathered Reefer, 1981	35
6-5707 American Refrigerator Transit Company Weathered Re, 1981	35
6-5709 Railway Express Woodside Reefer, 1983	55
6-5710 Canadian Pacific Woodside Reefer, 1983	35
6-5713 Cotton Belt Woodside Reefer, 1983	35
6-5714 Michigan Central Woodside Reefer, 1983	25
6-5715 Santa Fe Woodside Reefer, 1983	35
6-5716 Central Vermont Woodside Reefer, 1983	55
6-5717 Santa Fe Bunk Car, 1983	20
6-5726 Southern Bunk Car, 1984	55
6-6101 Burlington Voered Hopper, 1982	35
6-6107 Shell Covered Hopper, 1982	75
6-6109 C&O Hopper, 1983, operating	50
6-6110 Missouri Pacific Hopper, 1983	75
6-6111 L&N Hopper, 1983	75
6-6156 Dept. 56 Holly Brothers Petroleum Three Dome Tank	75
6-6201 UP Animated Gondola, 1982	50

No. 7517 Philadelphia Mint car, $100. Courtesy 1982 Lionel catalog.

TRADITIONAL SERIES

ROLLING STOCK

As your train grows longer the fun of railroading grows with Lionel's wide selection of rolling stock. All have knuckle couplers that can be operated manually or by remote control.

6-6107 Shell Covered Hopper

6-6441 Alaska Bay Window Caboose

6-6101 Burlington Covered Hopper

6-6100 Ontario Northland Covered Hopper

6-9282 Great Northern Piggyback

6-6308 Alaska Single Dome Tank Car

Some of the examples of rolling stock available in 1982 include the No. 6-6101 Burlington Covered hopper, $35; the No. 6-6107 Shell Covered hopper, $75; the No. Alaska Single Dome tank car, $55. Courtesy 1982 Lionel catalog.

OPERATING CARS

Lionel operating cars make your railroad really come alive. Here is a selection of realistic and exciting cars to keep the action going on and on.

Cop and Hobo Car. Here is non-stop action as the cop attempts to capture the hobo. They continually change places on the car and overhead trestle in a never-ending chase.

Animated Gondola. As this car moves, the security guard chases the hobo around the load of crates, but the nimble hobo always manages to stay ahead.

Outlaw Car. Train robbers with guns drawn move in and out of the windows in an imaginary Wild West shootout as the car moves.

Santa Fe Log Dump. Log cradle on car tilts and logs roll into bin next to track. Operates manually or with remote control track section, available separately.

Union Pacific Coal Dump. Coal carrier tilts and side drops open unloading coal into bin. Operates manually or with remote control track section, available separately.

Conrail Searchlight Car. Bright searchlight can be swiveled and tilted, great for nighttime running.

Post Office Car. Door slides open, mailman swings forward and throws out the mailbag. Operates with remote control track section, available separately.

6-6201 Animated Gondola

6-7900 Outlaw Car

6-9312 Conrail Searchlight Car

6-9301 Post Office Car

6-9311 Union Pacific Coal Dump

6-9310 Santa Fe Log Dump

6-7901 Cop and Hobo Car

Lionel offered a variety of Operating Rolling Stock in 1982, including, No. 6-6201 UP Animated Gondola, $50; No. 6-7900 Outlaw car, $35; No. 6-7901 Cop/Hobo Lionel Lines car, $45. Courtesy 1982 Lionel catalog.

	C10
6-6205 Canadian Pacific Gondola, 1983	35
6-6209 NYC Gondola w/Coal, 1984	100
6-6214 Lionel Lines Gondola, 1984	25
6-6308 Alaska Single Dome Tank Car, 1982	55
6-6310 Shell Tanker, 1983	20
6-6313 Lionel Lines Tank Car, 1984	25
6-6521 NYC Flat Car w/Stakes, 1984, standard O	100
6-7302 Texas Pacific Stock Car, 1983, O27	20
6-7515 Denver Mint Car, 1981	100
6-7517 Philadelphia Mint Car, 1982	110
6-7518 Carson Pacific Gondola, 1983	35
6-7522 New Orleans Mint Car, 1984	55
6-7701 Camel Woodside Reefer, 1976	40
6-7702 Prince Albert Woodside Reefer, 1976	40
6-7703 Beechnut Woodside Reefer, 1976	40
6-7706 Sir Walter Raleigh Plug Door Reefer, 1977	45
6-7707 White Owl Plug Door Reefer, 1977	55
6-7708 Winston Plug Door Reefer, 1977	50
6-7800 Pepsi Cola Boxcar, 1977	75
6-7801 A&W Rootbeer, 1977	80
6-7802 Canada Dry Boxcar, 1977	45
6-7900 Outlaw Car, 1982, operating	35
6-7901 Cop/Hobo Lionel Lines Car, 1982, operating	45
6-7902 Santa Fe Boxcar, 1982, O27	25
6-7903 The Rock Boxcar, 1983, O27	20
6-7904 San Diego Z Giraffe Car, 1983, operating	75

No. 6-7902 Santa Fe Boxcar, $25. Courtesy 1982 Lionel catalog.

	C10
6-9040 Wheaties Boxcar, 1971, O27	15
6-9064 Hershey Boxcar, 1971, O27	15
6-9095 Rolling Stock Assortment, 1982	55
6-9107 Dr. Pepper Vat Car, 1987	75
6-9114 Morton's Salt Covered Hopper, 1976	55
6-9115 Planter's Peanuts Covered Hopper, 1976	65
6-9116 Domino Sugar Covered Hopper, 1976	65
6-9117 Alaska Covered Hopper, 1975	25
6-9117 Alaska RR Hopper, 1976	45
6-9121 L&N Flat w/Scraper & Dozer Kits, 1975	45
6-9122 NP Piggyback, 1974	20
6-9128 Heinz Pickle Vat Car, 1975	18
6-9133 Burlington Northern Piggyback, 1977	35
6-9145 ICG Auto Carrier, 1977	25
6-9146 Mogen David Wine Vat Car, 1979	25
6-9147 Texaco Tank Car, 1977	80
6-9148 Dupont Tank Car, 1977	50
6-9149 CP Rail Piggyback, 1977	45
6-9152 Shell Tank Car, 1975	25
6-9153 Chevron Tank Car, 1975	20
6-9153 Chevron Tank Car, 1976	35
6-9154 Borden Tank Car, 1976	65
6-9156 Mobil Gas Tank Car, 1977	80
6-9156 Mobil Tank Car, 1976	55
6-9193 Budweiser Vat Car, 1983	250
6-9200 Illinois Central Boxcar, 1971	20
6-9201 Lancaster & Chester Boxcar, 1987	65
6-9203 Penn Central HiCube, 1976	35
6-9206 Great Northern Boxcar, 1971	20
6-9207 SooLine Boxcar, 1971	15
6-9208 Canadian Pacific Boxcar, 1971	20
6-9209 Burlington Northern Boxcar, 1971	20
6-9211 Penn Central Boxcar, 1971	15
6-9214 Northern Pacific Boxcar, 1971	15
6-9215 Norfolk Western Boxcar, 1971	15
6-9217 SooLine Boxcar, 1983, operating	35

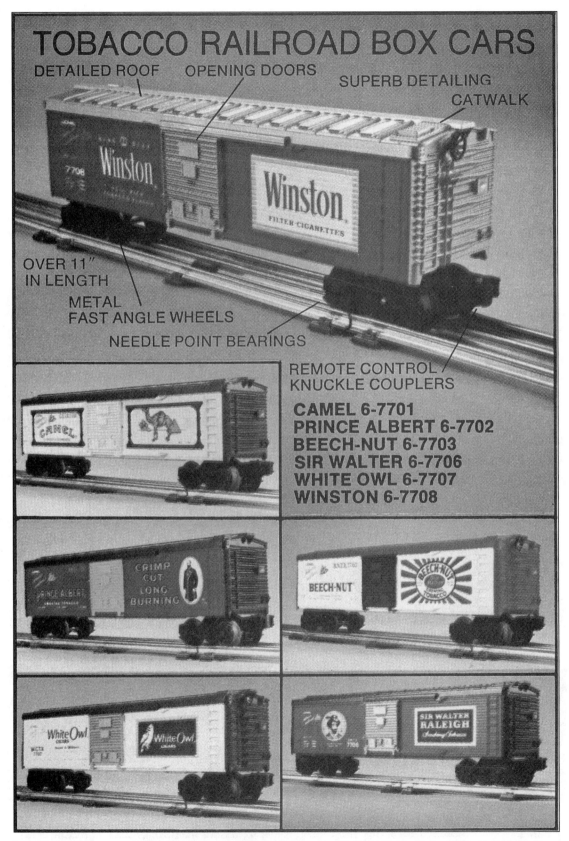

Lionel offered several different tobacco railroad boxcars in 1977, including a Winston Plug Door reefer, $45; White Owl Plug Door reefer, $55; Sir Walter Raleigh Plug Door reefer, $45. Courtesy 1977 Lionel catalog.

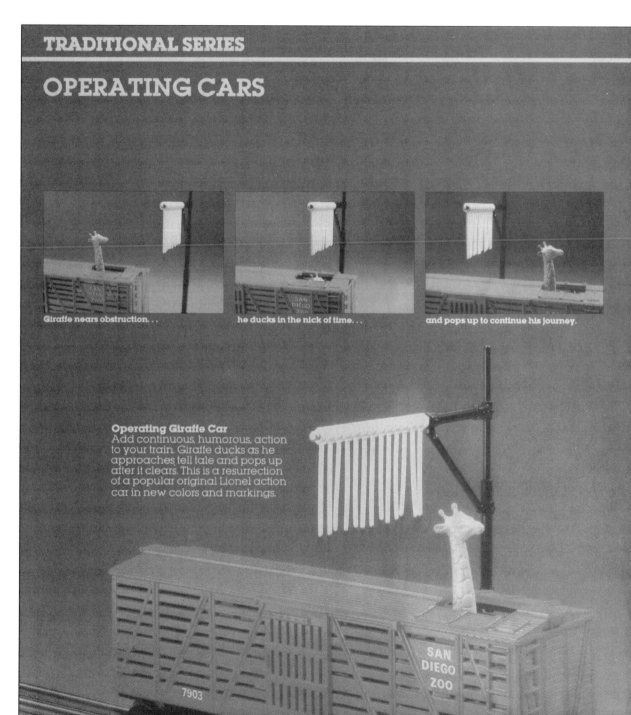

TRADITIONAL SERIES

OPERATING CARS

Giraffe nears obstruction. . .

he ducks in the nick of time. . .

and pops up to continue his journey.

Operating Giraffe Car
Add continuous, humorous, action to your train. Giraffe ducks as he approaches tell tale and pops up after it clears. This is a resurrection of a popular original Lionel action car in new colors and markings.

6-7904 Operating Giraffe Car

No. 6-7904 San Diego Z Giraffe Car, $75. Courtesy 1983 Lionel catalog.

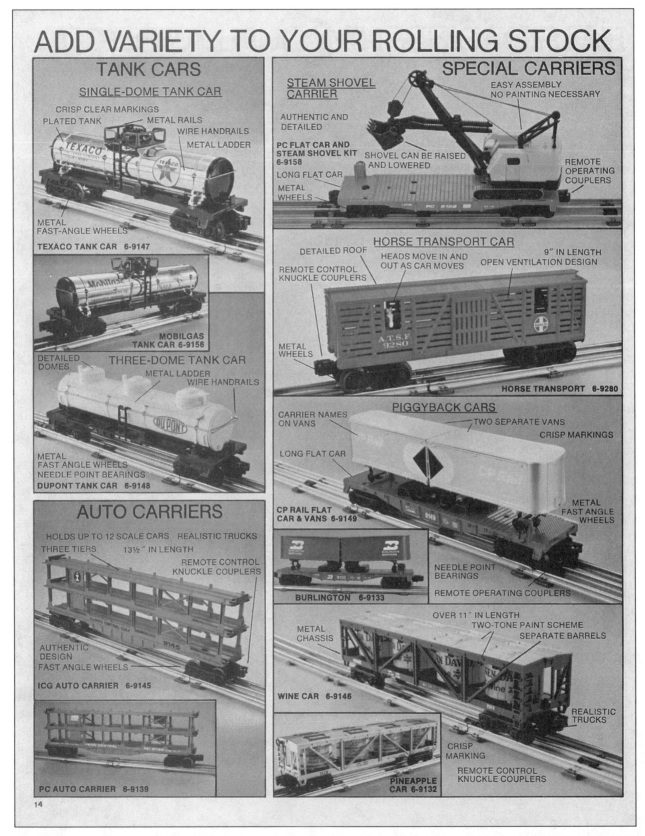

First row, top to bottom: No. 6-9147 Texaco Tank car, $80; No. 6-9148 Dupont Tank car, $80; No. 6-1-9145 ICG Auto carrier, $25. Second row: No. 6-9149 CP Rail Piggyback, $45. Courtesy 1977 Lionel catalog.

	C10
6-9219 Missouri Pacific Boxcar, 1983, operating	40
6-9220 Borden milk Car, 1983, operating	175
6-9221 Poultry Dispatch Car, 1983, operating	75
6-9222 L&N Piggyback, 1983	75
6-9260 Ralston Purina Covered Hopper, 1976	75
6-9260 Reynolds Aluminum Covered Hopper, 1976	60
6-9261 Sun Maid Raisins Covered Hopper, 1976	75
6-9263 Penn Hopper, 1976	35
6-9265 Chessie Hopper, 1976	25
6-9278 Lifesaver Tank Car, 1979	275
6-9281 Santa Fe Auto Carrier, 1979	25
6-9282 Great Northern Piggyback, 1979	40
6-9301 US Mail Post Office Car, 1982, operating	45
6-9302 L&N Searchlight Car, 1975	20
6-9303 UP Log Dump Car, 1975	18
6-9304 C&O Coal Dump Car, 1975	18

	C10
6-9307 Erie Animated Gondola, 1983	150
6-9308 Aquarium Car, 1983	375
6-9310 Santa Fe Log Dump Car, 1982, operating	25
6-9311 UP Coal Dump Car, 1982, operating	35
6-9312 ConRail Searchlight Car, 1982, operating	55
6-9324 Tootsie Roll Tank Car, 1980	175
6-9327 Bakelite Tank Car, 1980	65
6-9333 Southern Pacific Piggyback, 1979	40
6-9334 Humble Tank Car, 1979	40
6-9349 San Francisco Mint Car, 1980	150
6-9353 Crystal Tank Car, 1980	55
6-9354 Pennzoil Tank Car, 1980	100
6-9398 Penn Coal Dump, 1983	25
6-9406 ConRail Boxcar, 1976	20
6-9412 RF&P Boxcar, 1979	90
6-9413 Napierville Junction Boxcar, 1979	20
6-9415 Providence Worchester RR Boxcar, 1979	30

Mogen David Wine Car, 6-9146

TANK CARS
Detailed latticework, metal wheels and operating knuckle couplers are featured on these brightly decorated cars.

Dupont 3-Dome, 6-9148

Tootsie Roll, 6-9324

Bakelite, 6-9327

Crystal 3-Dome, 6-9353

Pennzoil, 6-9354

First row, top to bottom: No. 6-9327 Bakelite Tank car, $175; No. 6-9354 Pennzoil Tank car, $100. Second row, top to bottom: No. 6-9324 Tootsie Roll Tank car, $175; No. 6-9353 Crystal Tank car, $55. Courtesy 1980 Lionel catalog.

Top: No. 6-9415 Providence Worchester RR boxcar, $20. First row, left to right: No. 6-9412 RF&P boxcar, $90; No. 6-9413 Napierville Junction boxcar, $90. Third row: No. 6-9416 MD&W boxcar, $20; Third row, left to right: No. 6-9786 C&NW boxcar, $20; No. 6-9787 Jersey Central boxcar, $25. Courtesy 1979 Lionel catalog.

FAMOUS NAME BOX CARS

Detailed cars with authentic markings representing famous North American rail lines. Each features:
• Realistic trucks • Sliding doors • Operating knuckle couplers • Metal wheels

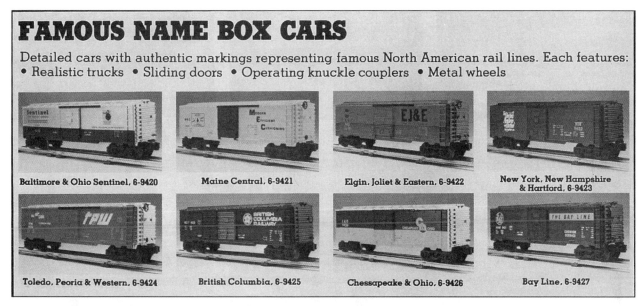

Baltimore & Ohio Sentinel, 6-9420   Maine Central, 6-9421   Elgin, Joliet & Eastern, 6-9422   New York, New Hampshire & Hartford, 6-9423

Toledo, Peoria & Western, 6-9424   British Columbia, 6-9425   Chessapeake & Ohio, 6-9426   Bay Line, 6-9427

Lionel issued several Famous Name Boxcars in 1980, including: No. 6-9422 EJ&E Boxcar, $25; No. 6-92424 TP&W Boxcar; No. 6-9425 British Columbia Boxcar, $20; No. 6-9426 C&O Boxcar, $25; No. 6-9427 Bay Line Boxcar, $20. Courtesy 1980 Lionel catalog.

	C10		C10
6-9416 MD & W Boxcar, 1979	20	6-9626 Santa Fe HiCube, 1982	20
6-9420 B&O Sentinel Boxcar, 1980	35	6-9627 UP HiCube, 1982	20
6-9422 EJ&E Boxcar, 1980	25	6-9628 Burlington Northern HiCube, 1982	25
6-9424 TP&W Boxcar, 1980	20	6-9629 Chessie HiCube, 1983	20
6-9425 British Columbia Boxcar, 1980	20	6-9709 State of Maine Boxcar, 1974	20
6-9426 C&O Boxcar, 1980	25	6-9710 Rutland Boxcar, 1974	20
6-9427 Bay Line Boxcar, 1980	20	6-9713 CP Rail Boxcar, 1974	20
6-9429 The Early Years Boxcar, 1980	125	6-9717 UP Boxcar, 1974	20
6-9430 Prewar Years Boxcar, 1980	100	6-9718 Canadian National Boxcar, 1974	15
6-9432 Postwar Years Boxcar, 1980	175	6-9723 Western Pacific Boxcar, 1974	15
6-9433 Golden Years Boxcar, 1980	175	6-9724 Missouri Pacific Boxcar, 1974	20
6-9453 MPA Railroad Boxcar, 1983	15	6-9725 MKT Cattle Car, 1974	15
6-9454 New Hope/Ivyland RR Boxcar, 1983	20	6-9730 CP Rail Boxcar, 1974	25
6-9455 Milwaukee Road Boxcar, 1983	20	6-9731 Milwaukee Road Boxcar, 1974	15
6-9462 Southern Pacific Boxcar, 1983	20	6-9737 Central Vermont Boxcar, 1974	15
6-9463 Texas Pacific Boxcar, 1983	30	6-9740 Chessie Boxcar, 1974	20
6-9464 North Carolina/St. Louis Boxcar, 1983	15	6-9747 Chessie Double Door Boxcar, 1976	15
6-9465 Santa Fe Boxcar, 1983	35	6-9748 Canadian Pacific Rail Boxcar, 1976	25
6-9469 NYC Boxcar, 1984, standard O	100	6-9749 Penn Central Boxcar, 1976	20
6-9475 Delaware & Hudson NY Boxcar, 1984	75	6-9750 DT&I Double Door Boxcar, 1976	15
6-9604 Norfolk Western HiCube, 1976	35	6-9751 Frisco Boxcar, 1976	20
6-9605 New Haven HiCube, 1976	25	6-9752 L&N Boxcar, 1976	20

FAMOUS NAME BOX CARS

Box cars authentically modeled from famous North American rail lines.

Each Car Features: • Authentic markings • Detailed bodies • Realistic trucks • Metal wheels • Operating knuckle couplers front and rear • Sliding doors.

6-9462 Southern Pacific Box Car

6-9463 Texas & Pacific Box Car

6-9464 North Carolina & St. Louis Box Car

6-9465 ATSF Box Car

6-9452 Western Pacific Box Car

6-9453 MPA Railroad Box Car

6-9454 New Hope & Ivyland Railroad Box Car

6-9455 Milwaukee Road Box Car

FAVORITE SPIRITS

Bright markings, representing favorite spirit brands, decorate these highly detailed reefers.

Each Features: • Realistic trucks • Operating knuckle couplers at both ends • Opening doors • Metal wheels

6-9835 Jim Beam® Billboard Reefer

6-9837 Wild Turkey® Billboard Reefer

6-9834 Southern Comfort® Billboard Reefer

6-9836 Old Grand-dad® Billboard Reefer

LC-11

Famous Name Boxcars. First row, left to right: No. 6-9462 Southern Pacific boxcar, $20; No. 6-9463 Texas Pacific boxcar, $30. Second row, left to right: No. 6-9464 North Carolina/St. Louis boxcar, $15; No. 6-9465 Santa Fe boxcar, $35. Favorite Spirits. Top row: No. 9835 Jim Beam Plug Door reefer, $35. Bottom row, left to right: No. 6-9837 Wild Turkey Plug Door reefer, $55; No. 6-9834 Southern Comfort Plug Door reefer, $55; No. 6-9836 Old Granddad Plug Door reefer, $55. Courtesy 1983 Lionel catalog.

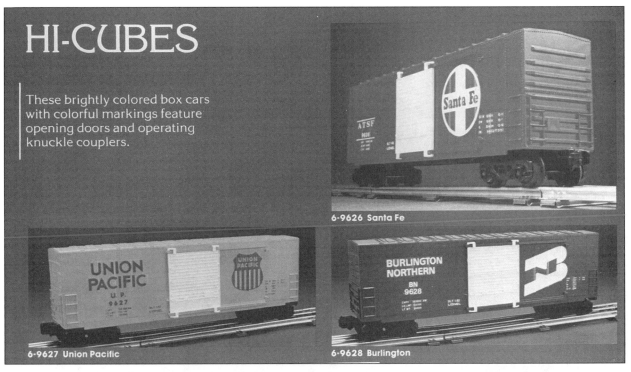

Top row: No. 6-9626 Sante Fe HiCube, $20. Bottom row, left to right:. Courtesy 1982 Lionel catalog.

Top row: No. 9629 Chessie Hi-Cube, $20. Second row, left to right: 6-9627 UP HiCube, $20; No. 6-9626 Santa Fe HiCube, $20; No. 6-9628 Burlington Northern HiCube, $25. Third row, left to right: No. 6-6310 Shell Tanker, $20; No. 6-9193 Budweiser Vat car, $250; No. 6-9222 L&N Piggyback, $75. Courtesy 1983 Lionel catalog.

FAMOUS NAME COLLECTOR SERIES

The most famous names in railroading are here in authentic colors and crisp, clear markings. The cars feature sliding doors, remote control knuckle couplers, metal fast angle wheels and needlepoint bearings. All are 10½ inches in length.

STATE OF MAINE BOX CAR
No. 6-9709

PENN CENTRAL BOX CAR
No. 6-9716

MKT CATTLE CAR
No. 6-9725

RUTLAND BOX CAR
No. 6-9710

UP BOX CAR
No. 6-9717

CP RAIL BOX CAR
No. 6-9730

B & O AUTO BOX CAR
No. 6-9712

CN BOX CAR
No. 6-9718

MILWAUKEE BOX CAR
No. 6-9731

CP RAIL BOX CAR
No. 6-9713

SOUTHERN BOX CAR
No. 6-9711

GRAND TRUNK BOX CAR
No. 6-9735

D&RGW BOX CAR
No. 6-9714

WESTERN PACIFIC BOX
CAR No. 6-9723

CENTRAL VERMONT BOX
CAR No. 6-9737

C & O BOX CAR
No. 6-9715

MISSOURI PACIFIC
No. 6-9724

CHESSIE BOX CAR
No. 6-9740

First row, top to bottom: No. 6-9709 State of Maine boxcar, $15; No. 6-9710 Rutland boxcar, $20; No. 6-9713 CP Rail boxcar, $20. Middle row, top to bottom: No. 6-9717 UP boxcar, $20; No. 6-9718 Canadian National boxcar, $15; No. 6-9273 Western Pacific boxcar, $15; No. 6-9724 Missouri Pacific boxcar. Last row, top to bottom: No. 6-9725 MKT Cattle car, $15; No. 6-9730 CP Rail boxcar, $25; No. 6-9731 Milwaukee Road boxcar, $15; No. 6-9737 Central Vermont boxcar, $15; No. 6-9740 Chessie boxcar, $20. Courtesy 1977 Lionel catalog.

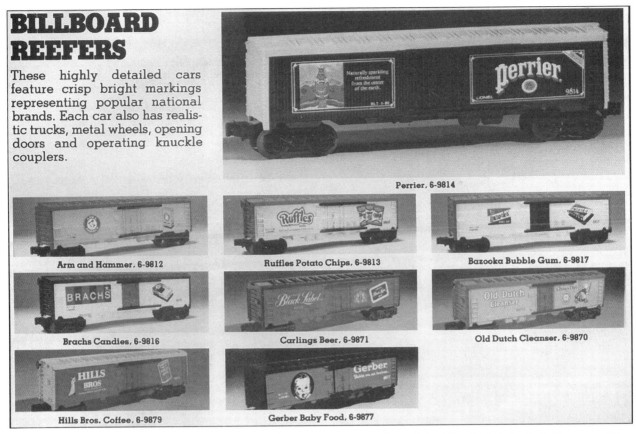

BILLBOARD REEFERS

These highly detailed cars feature crisp bright markings representing popular national brands. Each car also has realistic trucks, metal wheels, opening doors and operating knuckle couplers.

Perrier, 6-9814

Arm and Hammer, 6-9812

Ruffles Potato Chips, 6-9813

Bazooka Bubble Gum, 6-9817

Brachs Candies, 6-9816

Carlings Beer, 6-9871

Old Dutch Cleanser, 6-9870

Hills Bros. Coffee, 6-9879

Gerber Baby Food, 6-9877

Top row: No. 6-9814 Perrier Plug Door reefer, $80. Second row, left to right: No. 6-9812 Arm & Hammer Plug Door reefer, $110; No. 6-9813 Ruffles Plug Door reefer, $60; No. 6-9817 Bazooka Plug Door reefer, $55. Second row: No. 6-9816 Brachs Plug Door reefer, $55; Third row: 6-9877 Gerber Baby Plug Door reefer, $110. Courtesy 1980 Lionel catalog.

	C10
6-9753 Maine Central Boxcar, 1976	25
6-9754 NYC Boxcar, 1976	35
6-9755 Union Pacific Boxcar, 1976	20
6-9756 Dept. 56 Snow Village Boxcar, blue	100
6-9758 Alaska RR Boxcar, 1976	45
6-9763 DRGW Cattle Car, 1976	20
6-9764 Grand Trunk Double Door Boxcar, 1976	20
6-9767 RailBox Boxcar, 1976	35
6-9768 Boston Maine Boxcar, 1976	25
6-9769 B&LE Boxcar, 1976	20
6-9770 Northern Pacific Boxcar, 1976	35
6-9771 Norfolk Western Boxcar, 1976	35
6-9777 Virginian Hopper, 1976	35
6-9786 C&NW Boxcar, 1979	20
6-9787 Jersey Central Boxcar, 1979	25

	C10
6-9796 Dept. 56 Heritage Village Single Door Boxcar, green	75
6-9801 B&O Boxcar, 1975, Standard O	45
6-9803 Johnson Boxcar, 1975, standard O	45
6-9805 Grand Trunk Reefer, 1975, standard O	45
6-9806 Rock Island Boxcar, 1975, standard O	100
6-9807 Stroh's Reefer, 1976, standard O	175
6-9808 UP Boxcar, 1976, standard O	100
6-9809 Clark Reefer, 1976, standard O	150
6-9812 Arm & Hammer Plug Door Reefer, 1980	60
6-9813 Ruffles Plug Door Reefer, 1980	60
6-9814 Perrier Plug Door Reefer, 1980	80
6-9815 NYC Reefer, 1984, standard O	125
6-9816 Brach's Plug Door Reefer, 1980	55
6-9817 Bazooka Plug Door Reefer, 1980	55

	C10
6-9821 Southern Pacific Gondola, 1975	45
6-9823 Santa Fe Slat w/Load, 1976, standard O	150
6-9824 NYC Gondola, 1976	125
6-9825 NYC Boxcar, 1976, standard O	125
6-9825 Shaefer Reefer, 1976, standard O	75
6-9832 Cheerios Plug Door Reefer, 1982	175
6-9833 Vlasic Pickles Plug Door Reefer, 1982	75
6-9834 Southern Comfort Plug Door Reefer, 1983	55
6-9835 Jim Beam Plug Door Reefer, 1983	35
6-9836 Old Granddad Plug Door Reefer, 1983	50
6-9837 Wild Turkey Plug Door Reefer, 1983	55
6-9850 Budweiser Pull Door Reefer, 1975	35
6-9851 Schlitz Plug Door Reefer, 1975	45
6-9852 Miller High Life Plug Door Reefer, 1976	40
6-9853 Cracker Jacks Plug Door Reefer, 1975, caramel	45
6-9853 Cracker Jacks Plug Door Reefer, 1975, white	25
6-9854 Baby Ruth Plug Door Reefer, 1975	25
6-9855 Swift's Premium Plug Door Reefer, 1976	35
6-9856 Old Milwaukee Plug Door Reefer, 1976	45
6-9858 Butterfinger Plug Door Reefer, 1976	40
6-9860 Gold Medal Plug Door Reefer, 1976	40
6-9861 Tropicana Plug Door Reefer, 1977	40

	C10
6-9862 Hamm's Beer Plug Door Reefer, 1976	40
6-9866 Coors Plug Door Reefer, 1976	55
6-9867 Hershey Plug Door Reefer, 1976	50
6-9870 Dutch Cleanser Plug Door Reefer, 1977	35
6-9871 Carling Black Label Plug Boor Reefer, 1977	35
6-9872 Pacific Fruit Express Reefer, 1979	45
6-9874 Miller Light Reefer, 1979	45
6-9875 A&P Reefer, 1979	50
6-9877 Gerber Baby Plug Door Reefer, 1980	110
6-9878 Good 'n Plenty Reefer Plug Door Reefer, 1979	65
6-9879 Hills Brothers Plug Door Reefer, 1980	110
6-9884 Frit Brand Plug Door Reefer, 1981	90
6-9886 Mounds Plug Door Reefer, 1981	70
6-12819 Inland Steel Flatbed Truck w/Stakes, 1992	25
6-15000 D&RG Waffleside Boxcar, 1995	15
6-15001 Seaboard Waffleside Boxcar, 1995	15
6-15002 Chesapeake & Ohio Waffleside Boxcar, 1996	15
6-15003 Green Bay & Western Waffleside Boxcar, 1996	25
6-16031 Penn Dining Car, 1990	75
6-16033 Amtrak Baggage Car, 1990	75
6-16103 Lehigh Valley Two Dome Tank Car, 1988	20
6-16107 Sunoco Two Done Tank Car, 1990	30

Lionel offered several different reefers in 1980, including the No. 9872 Pacific Fruit Express reefer, $45; No. 6-9874 Miller Light reefer, $45; No. 6-9875, $50; No. 6-9878 Good 'n Plenty Plug Door reefer, $65. Courtesy 1980 Lionel catalog.

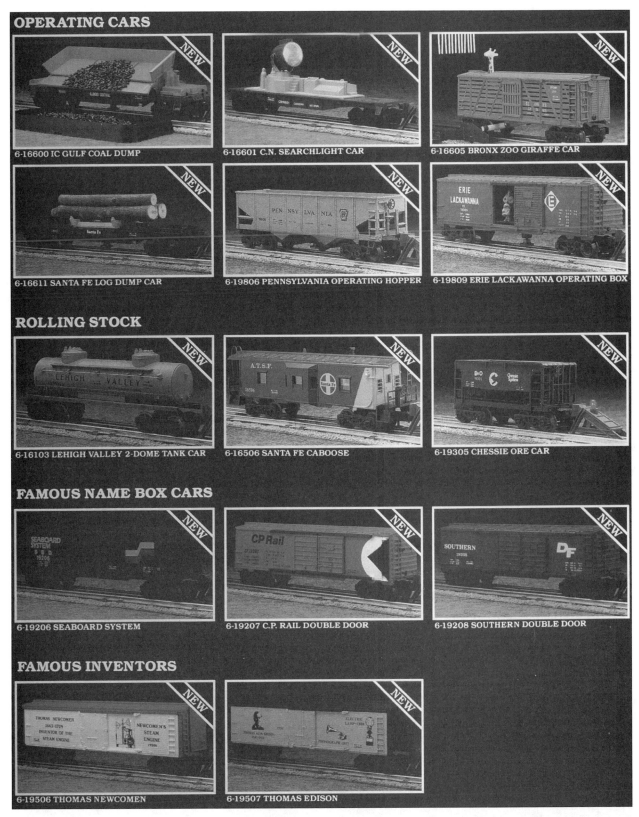

OPERATING CARS

6-16600 IC GULF COAL DUMP

6-16601 C.N. SEARCHLIGHT CAR

6-16605 BRONX ZOO GIRAFFE CAR

6-16611 SANTA FE LOG DUMP CAR

6-19806 PENNSYLVANIA OPERATING HOPPER

6-19809 ERIE LACKAWANNA OPERATING BOX

ROLLING STOCK

6-16103 LEHIGH VALLEY 2-DOME TANK CAR

6-16506 SANTA FE CABOOSE

6-19305 CHESSIE ORE CAR

FAMOUS NAME BOX CARS

6-19206 SEABOARD SYSTEM

6-19207 C.P. RAIL DOUBLE DOOR

6-19208 SOUTHERN DOUBLE DOOR

FAMOUS INVENTORS

6-19506 THOMAS NEWCOMEN

6-19507 THOMAS EDISON

Operating Cars—First row, left to right: 6-16600 ICG Coal Dump car, $25; No. 16601 Canadian National Searchlight car, $20; No. 16605 Bronx Zoo Giraffe car, $50. Second row: No. 6-16611 Santa Fe Barrel Ramp car, $25. Rolling Stock—No. 6-16103 NO. Lehigh Valley Two Dome Tank car, $20. Famous Name Boxcars—No. 6-19206 Seaboard boxcar, $20; No. 6-19207 CP Rail Double Door boxcar; No. 6-19208 Southern Double Door boxcar, $20. No. 6-19506 Thomas Newcomen reefer, $15; No. 6-19507 Thomas Edison reefer, $15. Courtesy 1988 Lionel catalog.

	C10
6-16115 MKT Three Dome Tank Car, 1992	20
6-16125 Viginian Stock Car, 1993	30
6-16127 Mobil Single Dome Tank Car, 1993	25
6-16138 Goodyear Single Dome Tank Car, 1995	25
6-16140 Domino Sugar Tank Car, 1995	20
6-16144 San Angelo Three Dome Tank Car, 1995	25
6-16146 Dairy Dispatch Plug Door Reefer, 1995	15
6-16153 AEC Reactor Tank Car, 1997, Biohazard Blue	175
6-16154 AEC Reactor Tank Car, 1997, Plutonium Purple	100
6-16155 AEC Reactor Tank Car, 1997, Geiger Green	110
6-16214 D&RG Two Tier Auto Carrier, 1990	35
6-16215 ConRail Two Tier Auto Carrier, 1990	35
6-16217 Burlington Northern Auto Carrier, 1992	45
6-16228 Southern Express TTUX Set, 1992	90
6-16232 Lionel Lines Piggyback, 1990	30
6-16245 Contadina Boxcar, 1993	20
6-16255 Wabash Double Door Boxcar, 1995	15
6-16258 Lehigh Valley Boxcar, 1995	20
6-16301 Lionel Barrel Ramp Car, 1987	20
6-16303 Penn Piggyback, 1987	50
6-16307 Nickel-plate Piggyback, 1988	40
6-16320 Great Northern Barrel Ramp Car, 1990	20
6-16322 Sealand TTUX Set, 1990	35

	C10
6-16324 Penn Depressed Flatcar w/Cable Reels, 1990	20
6-16334 Chicago Northwestern TTUX Set, 1991	90
6-16342 CSX Gondola w/Coil Cover, 1992	20
6-16343 Burlington Gondola w/Coil Cover, 1992	20
6-16348 Lionel Liquefied Petroleum Car, 1992	35
6-16352 Cruise Missile Car w/Decals, 1992	20
6-16360 N&W Maxistack Set, 1993	65
6-16363 Southern TTUX Set, 1993	100
6-16379 Northern Pacific Flatcar w/Wood Load, 1993	25
6-16380 UP Center I-Beam Flatcar, 1993	25
6-16381 CSX Center I-Beam Flatcar, 1993	25
6-16416 D&RG Covered QuadHopper, 1995	25
6-16417 Wabash Quad Hopper w/Coal, 1995	30
6-16418 C&NW Two Bay Hopper w/Coal, 1995	35
6-16419 Tennessee Central Hopper, 1996	20
6-16424 GT & Western Auto Carrier, 1993	35
6-16600 ICG Coal Dump, 1988	25
6-16601 Canadian National Searchlight Car, 1988	20
6-16602 Erie Coal Dump Car, 1987	30
9-16603 Detroit Zoo Giraffe Car, 1987	65
6-16605 Bronx Zoo Giraffe Car, 1988, operating	50
6-16606 Southern Searchlight Car, 1987	40
6-16610 Track Maintenance Car, 1988	20
6-16611 Santa Fe Barrel Ramp Car, 1988	25

Left to right: No. 6-9107 Dr. Pepper Vat car, $75; No. 6-16301 Lionel Barrel Ramp car, $20. Courtesy 1987 Lionel catalog.

	C10
6-16619 Wabash Coal Dump Car, 1990	25
6-16621 Alaskan Log Dump, 1990	25
6-16622 CSX Boxcar w/ETD, 1990	35
6-16625 NYC Searchlight Car, 1990	40
6-16631 Rock Island Boxcar w/Diesel Sounds, 1990	125
6-16632 Burlington Boxcar w/Diesel Sounds, 1990	125
1-16634 Western Maryland Coal Dump, 1991	30
6-16664 L&N Coal Dump Car, 1993	30
6-16666 Toxic Waste Car, 1993	35
6-16670 Lionel TV Car, 1993	30
6-16681 Animated Aquarium Car, 1995	75
6-16706 Bobbing Giraffe Boxcar, 1995	35
6-16711 Penn Searchlight Car, 1995	30
6-16712 Pinkerton Animated Gondola, 1995	35
6-16714 CB&Q Coal Dump, 1995	25
6-16724 Mickey & Friends Submarine Car, 1996	25
6-16725 Rhino Transport Car, 1996	25
6-16750 Lionel City Aquarium, 1997	55
6-16922 C&O Piggyback, 1995	35
6-16923 Lionel Lines Flatcar w/chocs, 1995	20
6-16926 Frisco Piggyback, 1995	35
6-16927 NYC Flatcar w/Gondola, 1995	45
6-16934 Penn Flatcar w/Road Grader, 1995	25
6-16935 UP Flatcar w/Bulldozer, 1995	30
6-16936 Sealand MaxiStack Set, 1995	60
6-16946 C&O F9 Well Car, 1997	55
6-17004 MKT Two Bay ACF Hopper, 1991, standard O	35
6-17005 Cargill Two Bay ACF Hopper, 1992, standard O	30
6-17008 D&RG Two bay ACF Hopper, 1995, standard O	35
6-17009 NYC Two Bay Hopper, 1996, standard O	55
6-17105 C&O Three Bay Hopper, 1995, standard O	35
6-17109 N&W Three Bay ACF Hopper, 1991, standard O	45

	C10
6-17110 UP Three Bay Hopper w/Coal Load, 1991, standard O	50
6-17111 Reading Three Bay ACF Hopper w/Coal, 1991, standard O	35
6-17112 Erie Lackawanna Three Bay ACF Hopper, 1992, standard O	35
6-17113 Lehigh Valley Three Bay Hopper w/Coal, 1992, standard O	55
6-17114 Peabody Three Bay Hopper w/Coal, 1992, standard O	55
6-17123 Cargill Three Bay Hopper, 1995, standard O	35
6-17124 ADM Three Bay Hopper, 1995, standard O	35
6-17128 C&N Three Bay Hopper w/Coal Load, 1996, standard O	45
6-17203 Cotton Belt Double Door Boxcar, 1991, standard O	45
6-17204 Missouri Pacific Double Door Boxcar, 1991, standard O	50
6-17207 Chicago Illinois Midland Double Door Boxcar, 1992, standard O	35
6-17208 UP Double Door Boxcar, 1992, standard O	40
6-17217 State of Maine New Haven Boxcar, 1995, standard O	60
6-17218 State of Maine Bangor Aroostock Boxcar, 1995, standard O	60
6-17223 Milwaukee Road Double Door Boxcar, 1996, standard O	40
6-17224 Central of Georgia boxcar, 1997, standard O	35
6-17225 Penn Central Boxcar, 1997, standard O	35
6-17226 Milwaukee Road Boxcar, 1997, standard O	35
6-17307 Tropicana Reefer, 1995, standard O	35
6-17308 Tropicana Reefer, 1995, standard O	35
6-17403 Chessie Gondola w/Coal Covers, 1993, standard O	30
6-17404 Illinois Central Gulf Gondola w/Coil Covers, 1993	50
6-17406 Penn Gondola w/Steel Covers, 1995, standard O	35
6-17407 Nickel Plate Road Gondola w/Scrap Load, 1996, standard O	35

	C10
6-17508 Burlington I Beam flatcar w/Wood Load, 1992	30
6-17509 Southern I Beam Flatcar w/Wood Load, 1992	30
6-17511 Western Maryland Flatcar w/Logs, 1995, standard O, set of three	175
6-17515 N&W Flatcar w/Tractors, 1995, standard O	125
6-17516 Texas & Pacific Flatcar w/two Airplanes, 1997, standard O	30
6-17517 Western Pacific Flatcar w/Caterpillar Frontloader, 1997, standard O	30
6-17901 Chevron Tank Car, 1990, standard O	40
6-17902 New Jersey Zinc Tank Car, 1991, standard O	45
6-17904 Texaco Tank Car, 1992, standard O	45
6-17905 Archer Daniels Midland Tank Car, 1992, standard O	45
6-17908 Marathon Oil Tank Car, 1995, standard O	125
6-17910 Sunoco Tank Car, 1997, standard O	55
6-18900 Cattle Car, 1988, operating	175
6-19200 Tidewater Southern Boxcar, 1987	20

No. 6-19200 Tidewater Southern Boxcar, $20. Courtesy 1988 Lionel catalog.

No. 6-19202 Penn RR Boxcar, $65. Courtesy 1988 Lionel catalog.

	C10
6-19202 Penn RR Boxcar, 1987	65
6-19203 Detroit & Toledo Shoreline Boxcar, 1987	15
6-19206 Seaboard Boxcar, 1988	20
6-19207 CP Rail Double Door Boxcar, 1988	20
6-19208 Southern Double Door Boxcar, 1988	20
6-19209 Florida East Coast Boxcar, 1988	20
6-19215 UP Double Door Boxcar, 1990	20
6-19216 Santa Fe Boxcar, 1990	20
6-19217 Burlington Boxcar, 1990	20
6-19218 New Haven Boxcar, 1990	20
6-19228 Cotton Belt Boxcar, 1991	90
6-19231 Tennessee Alabama Georgia Double Door Boxcar, 1991	20
6-19232 Rock Island Double Door Boxcar, 1991	20
6-19233 Southern Pacific Boxcar, 1991	20
6-19237 Chicago & Illinois Midland Boxcar, 1992	20
6-19238 Kansas City Southern Boxcar, 1992	20
6-19239 Toronto Hamilton & Buffalo Double Door Boxcar, 1992	20
6-19240 Great Northern Double Door Boxcar, 1992	20
6-19245 Mickey's World Tour HiCube, 1992	25
6-19246 Disney World 20th Anniversary HiCube, 1992	25
6-19251 Montana Rail Link Double Door Boxcar, 1993	25
6-19289 Hoosier Line 6464 Boxcar, 1997	40

No. 6-19300 Penn Ore Car, $35. Courtesy 1988 Lionel catalog.

	C10
6-19290 Silver Meteor 6464 Boxcar, 1997	50
6-19291 Great Northern 6464 Boxcar, 1997	50
6-19292 6464 Boxcar series No. 6, 1997	99
6-19300 Penn Ore Car, 1987	35
6-19305 Chessie Ore Car, 1988	30
6-19311 Southern Pacific Covered Hopper, 1990	30
6-19312 Reading Hopper w/Coal Load, 1990	30
6-19313 B&O Ore Car, 1990	25
6-19313 B&O Ore Car w/Load, 1991	30
6-19315 Amtrak Ore Car w/Load, 1991	45
6-19320 Penn Ore Car w/Load, 1992	20
6-19321 Besseme & Lake Erie, 1992	20
6-19413 Frisco Flatcar w/Stakes, 1992	30
6-19419 Charlotte Mint Car, 1993	75
6-19421 Hirsch Brothers Vat Car, 1995	20
6-19502 Northwestern Woodside Reefer, 1987	25
6-19504 Northern Pacific Woodside Reefer, 1987	25

No. 6-19502 Northwestern Woodside Reefer, $25. Courtesy 1988 Lionel catalog.

No. 6-19504 Northern Pacific Woodside Reefer, $25. Courtesy 1988 Lionel catalog.

	C10
6-19506 Thomas Newcomen Reefer, 1988	15
6-19507 Thomas Edison Reefer, 1988	15
6-19512 Wright Brothers Reefer, 1990	15
6-19513 Ben Franklin Reefer, 6-19513	15
1-19522 Guglielmo Marconi Woodside Reefer, 1991	15
1-19523 Robert Goddard Woodside Reefer, 1991	15
6-19528 AC Gilbert Woodside Reefer, 1992	15
6-19530 Rock Island Stock Car, 1992	45
6-19599 Old Glory Set, 1989, Woodside Reefer Set, three pieces	75
6-19651 Santa Fe Tool Car, 1987	30
6-19655 Amtrak Tool Car, 1991	30
6-19656 Milwaukee Road Bunk Car, 1990	40
6-19657 Wabash Bunk Car w/Smoke, 1992	30
6-19658 N&W Tool Car, 1991	50
6-19801 Poultry Dispatch, 1987	65
6-19802 Carnation Milk Car, 1987	225
6-19803 Reading Ice Car, 1987	225
6-19804 Wabash Hopper, 1987, operating	50
6-19805 Santa Fe Boxcar, 1987, operating	50
6-19806 Penn Hopper, 1988, operating	50
6-19808 NYC Ice Car, 1988	60
6-19809 Erie Lackawanna Boxcar, 1988, operating	50
6-19810 Bosco Milk Car, 1988	250
6-19811 Monon Brakeman Car, 1990	55
6-19815 Delaware Hudson Brakeman Car, 1992	75
6-19821 UP Boxcar, 1995, operating	55
6-19822 Pork Dispatch Car, 1995	65
6-19823 Burlington Northern Ice Car, 1995	35
6-19827 NYC Boxcar, 1996, operating	45
6-19901 I Love Virginia Boxcar, 1987	75
6-19905 I Love California Boxcar, 1988	30
6-19909 I Love New Jersey Boxcar, 1990	25
6-19915 I Love Texas Boxcar, 1992	20
6-19919 I Love Ohio Boxcar, 1991	20
6-19933 I Love Illinois Boxcar, 1995	20

	C10
6-19943 I Love Arizona Boxcar, 1996.............	25
6-19945 Holiday Boxcar, 1996	35
6-51300 Shell Tank Car, 1991, semi-scale	125
6-51301 Lackawanna Reefer, 1992, semi-scale	300
6-51401 Penn Boxcar, 1991, semi-scale	135
6-51402 C&N Stock Car, 1992, semi-scale	200
6-51501 B&O Hopper, 1991, semi-scale...........	125
52154 Southern Pacific Ore Car.......................	50
6-69195 Rolling Stock Assortment, 1988..........	45
6-92112 D&RGW Covered Hopper, 1974.........	15
617127 Delaware & Hudson Three Bay Hopper, 1996, standard O..	45

Sets

	C10
6-1070 Mid-Atlantic Limited Set, 1980.............	475
6-1070 Royal Limited Set, 1980	450
6-1072 Cross Country Express Set, 1980...........	295
6-1150 L.A.S.E.R. Train Set, 1982	325
6-1151 Thunder Freight Set, 1982	125
6-1154 Yard King Set, 1982	175
6-1183 Silver Star Set, 1971	125
6-1184 Allegheny Set, 1971..............................	150
6-1252 Heavy Iron Set, 1982	250
6-1253 Quicksilver Express Set, 1982	300
6-1351 Baltimore Ohio Set, 1983	135
6-1352 Rocky Mountain Freight Set, 1983........	110
6-1354 Northern Freight Flying Set, 1983.........	120
6-1355 Commando Assault Train Set, 1983	250
6-1355 Southern Streak Set, 1983.....................	115
6-1361 Gold Coast Limited Set, 1983, includes 6-8376 Union Pacific SD-40 Diesel Engine, 6-9290 UP Operating barrel Car, UP Double Door boxcar, Frisco Single Dome Tank Car, Green Bay/Western Plug Door Reefer, Northwestern Covered Hopper, UP Extended Vision Caboose..	625
6-1451 Erie Lackawanna Limited SD40, 1984.....	575
6-1489 Santa Fe Double Diesel Set, 1976..........	125
6-1503 James Gang Set, 1982...........................	125
6-1581 Cannonball Freight Set, 1976	120

	C10
6-1582 Yard Chief Set, 1976............................	110
6-1585 Lionel 75th Anniversary Set, 1976	250
6-1586 Chesapeake Flyer Set, 1976	100
6-1660 Yard Boss Set, 1976.............................	110
6-1662 Black River Freight Set, 1976	100
6-1665 NYC Empire State Express Set, 1976....	350
6-1764 Heartland Express Set, 1977	125
6-1765 Rocky Mountain Special Set, 1977	100
6-1766 Service Station Set, 1977	225
6-1866 Great Plains Express Set, 1979	110
6-1868 Service Station Set, 1978	350
6-1965 Smoky Mountain Line Set, 1979...........	100
6-1970 Southern Pacific Limited Set, 1979........	400
6-1971 Quaker City Limited Set, 1979	375
6-8635 Service Station Set, 1986	225
6-11700 ConRail Limited Set, 1987, Standard O	525
6-11701 Rail Blazer Set, 1988..........................	100
6-11702 Black Diamond Set, 1987.....................	575
6-11703 Iron Horse Freight Set, 1988	110
6-11704 Service Station Set, 1987	250
6-11705 Chessie System Unit Train, 1988.........	500
6-11706 Service Station Set, 1988	175
6-11707 Silver Spike Set, 1988	100
6-11712 Service Station Set, 1990	250
6-11714 Badlands Express Set, 1990	100
6-11716 Lionelville Circus Special Set, 1990	175
6-11717 CSX Freight Set, 1990	250
6-11723 Amtrak Maintenance Set, 1991	250
6-11729 Louisville & Nashville Express Set, 1992	300
6-11735 NYC Flyer Set, 1996...........................	100
6-11738 Service Station Set, 1993	275
6-11740 ConRail Consolidated Set, 1993	400
6-11744 Service Station Set, 1994	250
6-11745 UP Express Set, 1995	175
6-11745 US Navy Train Set, 1995	175
6-11747 Lionel Lines Steam Set, 1995	275
6-11748 Amtrak Passenger Set, 1995................	120

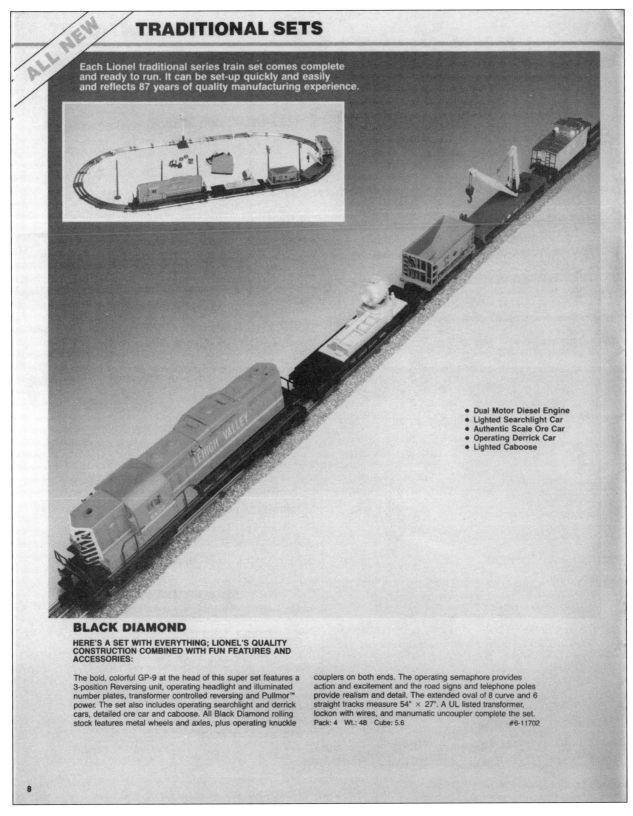

TRADITIONAL SETS

ALL NEW

Each Lionel traditional series train set comes complete and ready to run. It can be set-up quickly and easily and reflects 87 years of quality manufacturing experience.

- Dual Motor Diesel Engine
- Lighted Searchlight Car
- Authentic Scale Ore Car
- Operating Derrick Car
- Lighted Caboose

BLACK DIAMOND

HERE'S A SET WITH EVERYTHING; LIONEL'S QUALITY CONSTRUCTION COMBINED WITH FUN FEATURES AND ACCESSORIES:

The bold, colorful GP-9 at the head of this super set features a 3-position Reversing unit, operating headlight and illuminated number plates, transformer controlled reversing and Pullmor™ power. The set also includes operating searchlight and derrick cars, detailed ore car and caboose. All Black Diamond rolling stock features metal wheels and axles, plus operating knuckle couplers on both ends. The operating semaphore provides action and excitement and the road signs and telephone poles provide realism and detail. The extended oval of 8 curve and 6 straight tracks measure 54" × 27". A UL listed transformer, lockon with wires, and manumatic uncoupler complete the set.

Pack: 4   Wt.: 48   Cube: 5.6   #6-11702

8

No. 6-11702 Black Diamond Set, $575. Courtesy 1987 Lionel catalog.

No. 6-61602 Nickel-plate Special Set, $150. Courtesy 1988 Lionel catalog.

	C10
6-11749 Western Maryland Service Station Set, 1995	400
6-11758 Service Station Set, 1989	250
6-11809 Village Trolley Company Set, 1996	45
6-11813 Crayola Activity Train Set, 1995	75
6-11828 New Jersey Transit Set, 1996	175
6-11833 New Jersey Transit Set, 1997	175
6-11900 Santa Fe Special Set, 1996	100
6-11905 US Coast Guard Set, 1996	100
6-11920 Port of Lionel City Set, 1997	190
6-11982 New Jersey Transit Set, 1998	500
6-12544 Black Cave Flyer Set, 1982	350
6-19154 Atlantic Coastline Passenger Set, 1996	390
6-21029 Little ChooChoo Set, 1995	55
6-21753 Service Station Set, 1998	500
6-61602 Nickel-plate Special Set, 1988	150
6-61615 Cannonball Express Set, 1988	110

	C10
6-197095 Iowa Beef Packers Reefer, 1995, Standard O	50
408001477 Chevrolet Bow Tie Express Collector Train Set, available only through Merchandising Incentives Corporation	175
408612319 Dodge MotorSports Collector Train Set, available only through Chrysler Corporation, w/four pack of racing trucks and matching 6279 boxcar	300

B&A Hudson Direct Mail Offer Set

	C10
6-6134 Burlington Northern Two Bay ACF Hopper, Standard O	250
6-6135 Northwestern Two Bay ACF Hopper, Standard O	250
6-6230 Erie Reefer, Standard	200
6-6231 Railgon Gondola, Standard O	200
6-6232 Illinois Central Boxcar, Standard O	200
6-6233 CP Rail Flatcar w/stakes, Standard O	200
6-6907 NYC Woodside Caboose	400
6-6920 B&A Woodside Caboose	300
6-8606 B&A Hudson Locomotive	1500

neutral-reverse remote control operation on either AC or DC power. Completing this five unit train set is a square back coal tender, gondola with removable canisters, box car and caboose. All the cars come with two operating knuckle couplers and metal wheels and axles. Included with the train is enough track to make a 45" x 27" oval layout, a mechanically operating semaphore, manumatic uncoupler, lockon with wires and a U.L. approved transformer.

Pack: 4 Wt.: 40 Cube: 4.1   #6-11703

Top to bottom: No. 6-61615 Cannonball Express Set, $110; No. 6-11703 Iron Horse Freight Set, $110. Courtesy 1988 Lionel catalog.

	C10

Blue Comet Set

6-8801 Blue Comet 4-6-4 Locomotive, 1979	400
6-9536 Baggage Car, 1979	75
6-9537 Combo Car, 1979	100
6-9538 Passenger Car, 1979	75
6-9539 Passenger Car, 1979	75
6-9540 Observation Car, 1979	100

Burger King Fast Food Set

6-6449 Wendy's Lighted Porthole Caboose, 1982	95
6-7509 Kentucky Fried Chicken Plug Door Reefer, 1982	90
6-7510 Red Lobster Plug Door Reefer, 1982	100
6-7511 Pizza Hut Plug Door Reefer, 1982	125
6-7513 Arthur Treacher Plug Door Reefer, 1982	80
6-7514 Taco Bell Plug Door Reefer, 1982	125
6-8160 Burger King GP-20 Diesel Engine, 1982	175

Chessie Set

6-8003 Chessie 2-8-4 Steam Locomotive, 1980	250
6-9581 Baggage Car, 1980	75
6-9582 Combo Car, 1980	75
6-9583 Passenger Car, 1980	75
6-9584 Passenger Car, 1980	75
6-9585 Observation Car, 1980	75

F.A.R. Set #1
(Famous American Railroads)

6-7712 Santa Fe Boxcar, 1979	35
6-8900 Santa Fe 4-6-4 Locomotive, 1979	225
6-9321 Santa Fe Tank Car, 1979	29
6-9322 Santa Fe Covered Hopper, 1979	40
6-9323 Santa Fe Bay Window Caboose, 1979	40
6-9366 UP Covered Hopper, 1980	45
6-9880 Santa Fe Plug Door Reefer, 1979	30

	C10

F.A.R. Set #2
(Famous American Railroads)

6-8002 UP 2-8-2 Steam Engine, 1980	250
6-9367 UP Tank Car, 1980	50
6-9368 UP Bay Window Caboose, 1980	65
6-9419 UP Boxcar, 1980	45
6-9811 UP Plug Door Reefer, 1980	50

F.A.R. Set #4
(Famous American Railroads)

6-6104 Covered Hopper, 1983	50
6-6306 Tank Car, 1983	45
6-6431 Bay Window Caboose, 1983	55
6-8309 Southern 2-8-2 Steam Locomotive, 1983	275
6-9451 Boxcar, 1983	45

F.A.R. Set #5
(Famous American Railroads)

6-6123 Penn Covered Hopper, 1984	50
6-6307 Penn Tank Car, 1984	45
6-8404 Penn S2 6-8-6 SteM Turbine, 1984	300
6-9456 Penn Double Door Boxcar, 1984	45
6-9476 Penn Boxcar, 1984	40
6-9608 Penn Lighted Porthole Caboose, 1984 ...	65

Frisco Set

6-18504 Frisco GP-7 engine, 1991	150
6-19229 Frisco Boxcar w/sound, 1991	125
6-19230 Frisco Double Door Boxcar, 1991	50
6-19408 Frisco Coal Gondola, 1991	40
6-19519 Frisco Stock Car, 1991	45
6-19602 Johnson Single Dome Tank Car, 1991	55
6-19710 Frisco Extended Vision Caboose w/smoke, 1991	75

Gold Coast Limited Set

6-6357 Frisco Single Dome Tankcar, 1983	100
6-6904 UP Extended Vision Caboose, 1983	125
6-8376 Union Pacific SD-40 Diesel Engine, 1983	275

COLLECTOR SERIES

FAMOUS AMERICAN RAILROAD

In 1830, the first regularly scheduled steam-powered railroad service in America was run by "The South Carolina Canal and Railroad Company", the predecessor of the Southern Railroad.

"Southern Serves the South" is the slogan of the modern Southern Railway System; however, they now have over 10,000 miles of line ranging far to the north and west in thirteen states.

This beautiful set, the fourth in our limited edition Famous American Railroad Series, features the prima donna of Southern Railway excursion locomotives, the No. 4501, the first of a roster of Mikados on the Famous Southern line.

Southern, Mikado, 2-8-2 Steam Engine Features: • Electronic whistle • Magne traction TM • Puffing smoke • Working headlight • Forward-neutral-reverse controlled from the transformer • Pullmor TM motor • Detailed die-cast body.

Tender Features: • Die-cast body • Electronic whistle • Electronic Mighty Sound of Steam TM • Six-wheel die-cast trucks.

Famous American Railroad No. 4. Courtesy 1983 Lionel catalog.

COLLECTOR SERIES

GOLD COAST LIMITED

The Union Pacific Railroad, created to serve the west, helped to complete the transcontinental railline. To this day the U.P. provides a vital link between the mines, forests and agricultural areas in the west and the eastern markets. This seven-unit limited edition set is headed by a big, 16 inch long, "O" gauge, SD-40 diesel and features an operating barrel car, resurrected from the 50's.

Gold Coast Limited. Courtesy 1983 Lionel catalog.

	C10
6-9290 UP Operating Barrel Car, 1983	125
6-9468 UP Double Door Boxcar, 1983	75
6-9888 Green Bay/Western Plug Door Reefer, 1983	100

Great Northern Set

	C10
6-11724 Great Northern F-3 Diesel A-B-A Set, 1992	520
6-18302 GN Electric Engine, 1987	250
6-19116 Baggage Car, 1992	100
6-19117 Combo Car, 1992	100
6-19118 Passenger Car, 1992	90
6-19119 Vista Dome, 1992	120
6-19120 Observation Car, 1992	125
6-19205 GN Double Door Boxcar, 1987	30
6-19304 GN Covered Hopper, 1987	35
6-19401 GN Gondola, 1987	30
6-19402 GN Crane Car, 1987	75
6-19505 GN Plug Door Reefer, 1987	55
6-19703 GN Extended Vision Caboose, 1987	60

Madison Cars

	C10
6-19015 Irvington Madison Car, 1991	75
6-19016 Madison, 1991	75
6-19017 Manhattan, 1991	75
6-19018 Sager Place, 1991	75

Mickey Mouse Express

	C10
6-8773 U-36 B Diesel Engine, 1977	225
6-9183 Mickey Mouse Express Caboose, 1977	75
6-9660 Mickey Mouse Hi-Cube Boxcar, 1977	100
6-9661 Goofy Hi-Cube Boxcar, 1977	100
6-9662 Donald Duck Hi-Cube Boxcar, 1977	100

Milwaukee Road Set

	C10
6-18500 Milwaukee Road GP-9 Diesel Engine, 1987	225
6-19204 MR Boxcar, 1987	75
6-19302 MR Coal Hopper, 1987	100
6-19400 MR Gondola, 1987	75
6-19500 MR Reefer, 1987	75

	C10
6-19600 MR Tank Car, 1987	75
6-19701 MR Illuminated Caboose, 1987	100

Missouri Pacific Passenger Cars

	C10
6-16075 Baggage, 1995	40
6-16076 Combo, 1995	40
6-16077 Passenger, 1995	40
6-16078 Passenger, 1995	40
6-16079 Observation, 1995	50

New York Central Set

	C10
6-8370 NYC F-3 A Diesel Engine, 1983	300
6-8371 NYC F-3 B Dummy Unit, 1983	200
6-8372 NYC F-3 A Dummy Unit, 1983	150
6-9594 Baggage Car, 1983	100
6-9595 Combo Car, 1983	100
6-9596 Passenger Car, 1983	125
6-9597 Passenger Car, 1983	100
6-9598 Observation Car, 1983	125

Nickle Plate Set

	C10
6-17612 NP Steelside Caboose, 1992	60
6-18505 Nickel Plate Double Headed GP-7 Diesel Engine, 1992	300
6-19236 NP Double Door Boxcar, 1992	40
6-19318 NP Quadhopper w/coal, 1992	35
6-19411 NP Piggyback, 1992	100
6-19527 NP Plug Door Reefer, 1992	40
6-19603 NP GATX Single Dome Tank Car, 1992	35

Santa Fe Set

	C10
6-11711 Santa Fe F3 Diesels A-B-A, 1991	700
6-19109 SF Baggage Car, 1991	100
6-19110 SF Combo Car, 1991	100
6-19111 SF Dining Car, 1991	100
6-19112 SF Passenger Car, 1991	125
6-19113 SF Observation, 1991	150

Southern Pacific Car Set

	C10
6-1384 Southern Express Set, 1976	100
6-19023 Passenger Car, 1992	125

	C10
6-19024 Passenger Car, 1992	125
6-19025 Passenger Car, 1992	125
6-19026 Observation Car, 1992	150

Spirit of '76 Commemorative Series

6-1776 U-36 B Diesel Engine, 1976	175
6-7505 Connecticut Boxcar, 1976	75
6-7600 Spirit of ë76 Caboose, 1976	75
6-7601 Delaware Boxcar, 1976	90
6-7602 Penn Boxcar, 1976	95
6-7603 New Jersey Boxcar, 1976	100
6-7604 Georgia Boxcar, 1976	75
6-7606 Massachusetts Boxcar, 1976	75
6-7607 Maryland Boxcar, 1976	50
6-7608 South Carolina Boxcar, 1976	75
6-7609 New Hampshire Boxcar, 1976	75
6-7610 Virginia Boxcar, 1976	190
6-7611 New York Boxcar, 1976	150
6-7613 Rhode Island Boxcar, 1976	125
6-76112 North Carolina Boxcar, 1976	100

Union Pacific Set

6-7210 Dining Car, 1984	150
6-8480 UP F-3 Powered A Diesel Unit, 1984	275
6-8481 UP F-3 Dummy B, 1984	200
6-9545 Baggage Car, 1984	125
6-9546 Combo Car, 1984	125
6-9547 Observation Car, 1984	150
6-9549 Passenger Car, 1984	125

Wabash Passenger Set

6-7227 Dining Car, 1987	75
6-7228 Baggage Car, 1987	75
6-7229 Combo Car, 1987	50
6-7230 Coach, 1987	75
6-7231 Coach, 1987	75
6-7232 Observation Car, 1987	75
6-8610 Wabash 4-6-2 Locomotive, 1987	400

St. Louis Lionel Railroader Club

Frisco three-piece TOFC set, 1998	150

	C10
Missouri Pacific TOFC set, 1996, first of series	125
Santa Fe three-piece TOFC set, 1999	125
Wabash Three-piece TOFC set, 1997	125
6-52136A Christmas Tractor Trailer, 1997, available to club members only, low production run	150
6-52136B Frisco Pigs Are Beautiful Tractor Trailer, 1998, available to club members only, low production run	125

Toy Train Operating Society

6464 Santa Fe Boxcar, 1995, Central California Division	100
6464 Western Pacific Feather River Boxcar, 1995, convention car	75
ConRail Flatcar w/Blum Coal of Carrolton Ohio Shov, 1998, convention car	60
Cotton Belt Woodside Caboose w/smoke, 1993, Cal Stewart Convention Center	75
Grand Trunck three-piece TOFC, 1994, Wolverine Division	60
Pacific Fruit Express Standard O Reefer, 1995, Cal Stewart	35
Southern Pacific Piggyback, 1991, TTOS silver Anniversary car	75
Southern Pacific Three Bay Hopper, 1992, Cal Stewart convention car	25
Union Equity Three Bay ACF Hopper, 1992, convention car	45
Western Pacific Boxcar, 1993, Sacramento Valley Division	100

Vapor Records

Recording company owned by recording artist and part owner of Lionel, Neil Young.

6-26208 , second public-sale car, only cataloged Vapor car to date	30
6-26228 , third not-for-public-sale car	375
6-29218 6464 Boxcar, first public-sale car, uncataloged	125
6-29229 9700 Series-type Boxcar, second not-for-public-sale car	300
6-29606 6464 Boxcar, first not-for-public-sale car	500

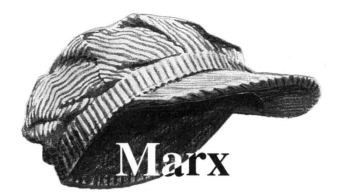

Marx

Although the exact year is disputable, Louis Marx began working with toy-king Ferdinand Strauss in the early 1900s and quickly moved up the ranks before joining the Army in 1917. After attaining the rank of sergeant, Marx returned from the military to join his brother in the manufacturing of toys from molds bought from Strauss. The first Marx trains to hit the market, The Joy Line, were actually produced by the Girard Model Works under a commission sales agreement.

The early, fragile No. 350 Joy Line locomotive and matching cars were first produced in 1927 or 1928. By 1930, a heavier stamped-steel frame and both clockwork and electric cast-iron engines were used by Girard. The third major Joy Line engine appeared in 1932. Made of red and black stamped steel, they were produced into 1935 after the complete take over of Girard by Marx.

The first trains produced following the 1935 acquisition were the Commodore Vanderbilt and the widely-recognized six-inch cars that would be produced in a wide array of colors until the 1970s. These cars, all four wheel, have somewhat unusual colors and numbers and are mounted on black frames lithographed in silver to look like eight-wheel cars and utilized the left-over Joy Line couplers. The Commodore Vanderbilt engine with a swinging coupler peg extending down through its cab floor is quite difficult to find, but it is the proper engine for these first Marx cars. It makes sense that these early cars were sold for a short period later on, as they also accept the stan-

How to Use These Listings

- Numbers listed, i.e., 552, appear on the engine or car.
- Numbers in parenthesis, i.e., (551), are generally accepted catalog numbers even though they don't appear on the engine or car.
- Major variations are shown by small letters (a), (b), etc.
- No divisions have been attempted by truck style, frame type, or coupler variation as these permutations are too numerous for this volume.
- AR transformers and track sections are so common they aren't listed separately. At the most, working Marx transformers are worth $1 each and track worth 10- to 25-cents each.
- Prices for complete sets may be obtained by adding together each car and engine; for sets with original boxes, add forty percent.
- Remember, there are very few Mint (C10) Marx trains even though hundreds and hundreds of thousands have been made.

dard Marx hook coupler; their general availability seems much too high to have been limited only to the swinging-peg Commodores.

The golden age of Marx trains runs from the late 1930s to World War II. Trains from this period were produced in a wide variety of colors, with four and eight wheels, with simple hook couplers as well as complex automatic couplers, in both articulated cheap and fancy passenger trains, and, of course, six-inch passenger cars. The most popular Marx train—the Army Train—was introduced during this period.

Prior to World War II, Marx produced a line of 3:16-scale freight cars. The die-cast No. 999 made its first appearance prior to the stopping of all non-war essential production in May 1942. While there may not have been many produced, Spiegel's Holiday Greetings catalog from 1942 offers an excellent view of this prewar set. The 3:16-scale line may have been produced to give American Flyer a good run as it follows closely behind the Gilbert's (American Flyer) introduction of trains in this scale in 1939. Marx continued production of 3:16-scale line well into the 1950s.

By the early 1950s, a corresponding set of 3:16-scale passenger cars were manufactured in two-tone gray coupled with a nicely-proportioned, die-cast Pacific No. 333 engine and tender. These passenger cars went through several color and marking changes over the next several years before ending up with Western Pacific markings pulled by a plastic E3 three-unit diesel which was longer than the normal three car set. Continuing a practice started in the late 1930s, Marx sometimes included both freight cars and passenger cars in a single set to enhance the "play value" of the train set while at the same time quietly capitalizing on the suspected higher profit margin for cars without the expenses of more track, transformer, engine, packaging and sales overheads.

By 1950, Marx was producing a line of seven-inch tin trains, including the Mickey Mouse Meteor set, a jewel for both Disney and Marx collectors. These trains may have been a successful attempt to run Unique trains out of business, if not the whole Unique operation. The majority of Unique Manufacturing Company toys seem to have been made with left over or leased Marx dies with new lithography. One can speculate that as long as Marx was finished with the dies, it was a good situation; as soon as Unique introduced a brand new line of their own toy trains in 1949, that all changed. Not long after Unique disappeared in 1952, the Marx line of seven-inch cars started its conversion to plastic. The basic seven-inch tin cars lasted to 1962 with the Wm. Crooks (General type) old-time passenger cars.

The period from the early 1950s until the demise of the original Marx company in 1975, saw a wide variety of trains produced, including an assortment of attractive, dependable cars and loco-

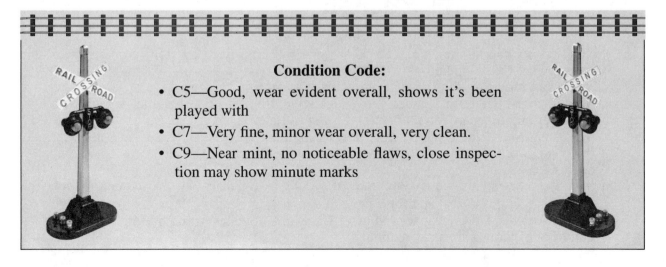

Condition Code:
- C5—Good, wear evident overall, shows it's been played with
- C7—Very fine, minor wear overall, very clean.
- C9—Near mint, no noticeable flaws, close inspection may show minute marks

motives. The die-cast No. 666 engine, sold with the deluxe eight-wheel plastic is a reliable smoking unit.

Marx sold his company to Quaker Oats in 1972 for a sum close to $50 million. Quaker Oats tried to run it the same way as one of their other rather successful divisions but it just didn't work out. After losing a noticeable amount of money in 1975, Marx was sold to the English combine of Dunbee Combex-Marx.

Louis Marx passed away in 1982. He left behind a legacy of wonderful toys, and particularly toy trains that "ran better than they should for the price."

Jay Horowitz, president of the current Marx Toy Company, has licensed Jim and Debby Flynn of Chicago to produce new Marx tin-litho trains.

Contributor: Richard MacNary, 4727 Alpine Dr., Lilburn, GA 30247. MacNary was born in Hammond, Indiana (Chicago area) prior to World War II. The Monon RR was close—just an alley away—which has permanently unbalanced him. Those "toy-less" war years have also pushed him into a rather large collection of Barclay and Manoil lead soldiers (not produced 1942-45) as well as thousands of paper-wood-cardboard war-time substitute toys.

His first train was a Hafner 1010 wind-up in red and cream with three matching passenger cars. The motor has survived and still works well! The first Marx was a 1939 Commodore Vanderbilt electric four-wheel set. Woolworth's added a 1942 Christmas car, the eight-wheel Army Ordnance gondola, which was fought over with his much older sister because it was "so real looking."

MacNary is the Atlanta Manager for Hubbell Power Systems, manufacturer of premium high voltage electric equipment. He and his wife Marilyn have taken a tax write-off on their two boneless chicken ranches (lack of reproduction) and are now owners of "Fuzzy Balls," a high tech firm specializing in the retrofit of fuzz to used tennis balls.

MacNary is still looking for a couple of tin-lithographed Marx train items, and he has often exclaimed, "[T]here is no such thing as a complete Marx train collection. Just when you think you hav

Army Floor Train, four pieces, $600 for the set. Photo Courtesy of Richard L. MacNary.

	C5	C7	C9
— Army Floor Train Set, loco and tender, gondola w/shells, flat w/large dummy searchlight, flat w/AA gun; olive drab, set of four...	300	450	600
— Caboose, plastic, four wheel, red, white/silver lettering reads "Marlines"	20	30	40
— Floor Train...............................	25	35	50

	C5	C7	C9
— Floor Train, lithographed tin, no. 999, clockwork....................	50	75	100
— Floor Train Locomotive, w/two Gondolas	20	30	40
— Gondola, 7" tin, four wheel, blue w/blue frame, Mickey Mouse characters	50	75	100
— Green Giant Valley Express, promotional set..........................	50	75	100

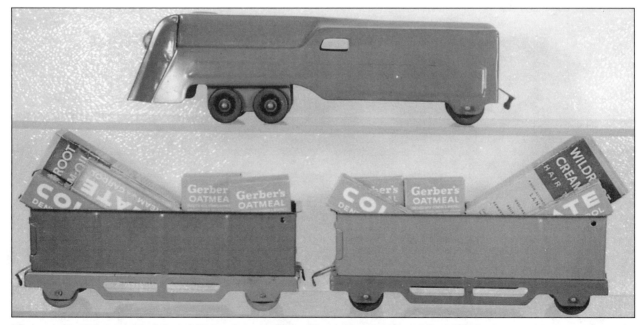

Floor train with two gondolas, $40 for the set. Photo Courtesy of Richard L. MacNary.

Top row: Two versions of the Mickey Mouse & Donald Duck Hand car, $300, each. Bottom row: No. 2002 Hand car, $80; No. 2028 Flintstones Hand car, $200. Photo Courtesy of Richard L. MacNary.

	C5	C7	C9		C5	C7	C9
— Honeymoon Express, early.......	75	125	150	— Locomotive, 0-4-0, stamped steel, black, clockwork..............	30	45	60
— Honeymoon Express, late.........	35	45	55	— Locomotive, 0-4-0, stamped steel, red frame, black top, electric.......................................	30	45	60
— Locomotive, 0-4-0, cast iron, black, no markings, clockwork	100	150	200				

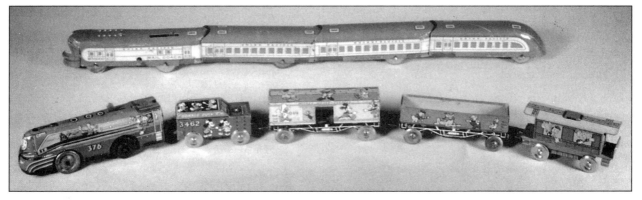

Top: M10,000 four unit set: M10,000 Locomotive, two Pullman cars and one Coach buffet. Bottom: Donald Duck Railroad Set: No. 376 Locomotive, No. 3462 Tender, No 1914 Gondola, No. 9049 Boxcar, and Caboose, $400 for the set. Photo Courtesy of Richard L. MacNary.

Zig-Zag trains. Top to bottom: Dodge City Express, $50; Flintstones Bedrock Express, $100; Jetson Express, $100. Photo Courtesy of Richard L. MacNary.

	C5	C7	C9
— Locomotive, 0-4-0, stamped steel, red frame, black top or black frame, red top, clockwork	30	45	60
— Locomotive, 0-4-0, cast iron, black, no markings, electric	125	175	250
— Loco Riding Floor Train, stamped steel, black w/red plastic trim, marked "Pioneer Express"	50	75	100
— Marx-Tronic Set, no. 2893	10	20	30
— Mickey Mouse & Donald Handcar, tin board or track	100	200	300
— Miniature Donald Duck Railroad, inlcudes 376 Loco, 3462 Tender, 1914 Gondola, 9049 Box Car, and Caboose; multi-colored, five pieces	200	300	400
— Miniature M10,000 UP, includes M10,000 Loco, two Pullmans, and Coach Buffet; tan and cream, four pieces	100	150	200
— Moon Mullins & Kayo Handcar, simple spring wound	125	175	250
— Moon Mullins & Kayo Hnadcar, deluxe	150	200	300
— Musical Choo Choo, Linemar	10	15	20

Casey Jr. Disneyland with three different locomotives, $50, each. Photo Courtesy of Richard L. MacNary.

	C5	C7	C9
— Plastimarx Mexican Marx, set no. 5063	50	75	100
— Rail Car, 6" x 6" tin, 4 x 4 wheels, two flat cars coupled together, carries ten to twelve individual rails	50	75	100
— Shuttle Choo-Choo, w/Marx logo	20	30	40
— Tender, die-cast, for 333 engine only, black, marked "New York Central"	20	30	40
— Wheel Car, 6" tin, four wheel w/second car riveted on top w/extra wheels, top frame is red	40	60	80

	C5	C7	C9
— Zig Zag Type, Marlines, passenger	20	40	60
— Zig Zag Type, Casey Jr. Disneyland	30	40	50
— Zig Zag Type, Jetsons Express	50	75	100
— Zig Zag Type, Flintstones Bedrock Express	50	75	100
— Zig Zag Type, Dodge City Express	30	40	50
— Zig Zag Type, Crazy Express	20	30	40
— Zig Zag Type, Cocoa Puffs	50	75	100
— Zig Zag Type, Scenic Express, w/tin board	20	30	40

Top to bottom: Crazy Express, $40; Choo Choo Train, $20. Photo Courtesy of Richard L. MacNary.

Zig-Zag trains. Top to bottom: Disneyland, $80; Cocoa Puffs, $100. Photo Courtesy of Richard L. MacNary.

Top row, left to right: No. 1 (c) Locomotive, $50; No. 3651 tender. Bottom row, left to right: No. 56 Flat car w/lumber, $56; No. 45 Caboose, $30. Photo Courtesy of Richard L. MacNary.

	C5	C7	C9
— Zig Zag Type, Super Heroes	75	100	125
— Zig Zag Type, Choo Choo Train..	10	15	20
— Zig Zag Type, Disneyland Express, w/tin board	40	60	80
(M) Locomotive, diesel switcher, plastic, four wheel, blue and white lettering reads "Missouri Pacific"	20	40	60
1 Baggage Car, 7" tin, both four and eight wheel, yellow body, black frame, black and yellow lettering reads "St. Paul and Pacific"	20	30	40
1 (a) Locomotive, 4-4-0, plastic, black, marked "Wm. Crooks" and "1," electric drive, w/smoke..................................	50	75	100
1 (b) Locomotive, 4-4-0, clockwork, no smoke...............	80	120	160
1 (c) Locomotive, 0-4-0, short stack, no smoke, electric drive..	25	37	50
(I) Locomotive, diesel switcher, plastic, four wheel, orange w/black lettering reads "Illinois Central"....................................	20	30	40

	C5	C7	C9
(U1) Locomotive, diesel "A" unit, plastic, eight wheel, orange w/black lettering reads "Union Pacific"....................................	25	37	50
(U2) Locomotive, dummy "A" unit	50	75	100
(U3) Locomotive, dummy "B" unit	40	60	80
3 Passenger Car, 7" tin, four wheel and eight wheel, yellow body and black frame, yellow lettering reads "St. Paul and Pacific"....................................	20	30	40
(9) The Cannon Ball Express, pedal-operated ride-on train, engine, metal, red and yellow ...	60	90	120
10 (a) Locomotive, diesel switcher, blue w/yellow stripe..................	10	15	20
10 (b) Locomotive, diesel switcher, green w/yellow stripe................	10	15	20
20 (a) Locomotive, 0-4-0, plastic, black, orange lettering reads "NH"	12	18	25
20 (b) Locomotive, 0-4-0, white, "AT&SF"	12	18	25

	C5	C7	C9
20 (c) Locomotive, 0-4-0, white, "Rock Island"	12	18	25
20 (d) Locomotive, 0-4-0, white, "NYC"	12	18	25
21 (a) Locomotive, diesel "A" unit, large lithographed tin, red and silver w/black lettering reads "Santa Fe," powered "A" unit	20	30	40
21 (b) Locomotive, diesel "A" unit, non-powered "A" unit	20	30	40
21 (c) Locomotive, diesel GP7/9, plastic, red and gray w/black lettering reads "Monon,"	15	23	30
24 Drop Center Searchlight, plastic, deluxe eight wheel, black w/gray searchlight, yellow generator	20	30	40
41 Locomotive, 4-4-0, plastic floor toy, flashlight, green, gold, red	40	60	80

	C5	C7	C9
44 (a) Locomotive, streamlined steam, lithographed tin, engine and tender one piece, gray-red-white w/"Super Chief," clockwork	20	40	60
44 (b) Locomotive, streamlined steam, lithographed tin, engine and tender one piece, light gray-red-white w/"Super Chief," friction	20	40	60
45 Caboose, plastic, eight wheel, brown w/white lettering "45"	15	23	30
47 Hopper, plastic, red w/white lettering reads "Huron Portland Cement"	2	4	6
49 Old Time Western Set, plastic, all marked "Marlines," battery-operated train w/plastic 0-27 two-rail track, black locomotive and black tender, yellow gondola, red caboose	50	75	100

First row, left to right: No. 20 (b) AT &SF Locomotive, $25; Sante Fe Tender. Second row, left to right: No. 20 (a) Rock Island Locomotive, $25; Rock Island Tender; 1961 (a) Rock Island Caboose, $3. Third row, left to right: No. 20 (d) NYC Locomotive, $25; NYC Tender; No. 20295 Caboose, $10 Photo Courtesy of Richard L. MacNary.

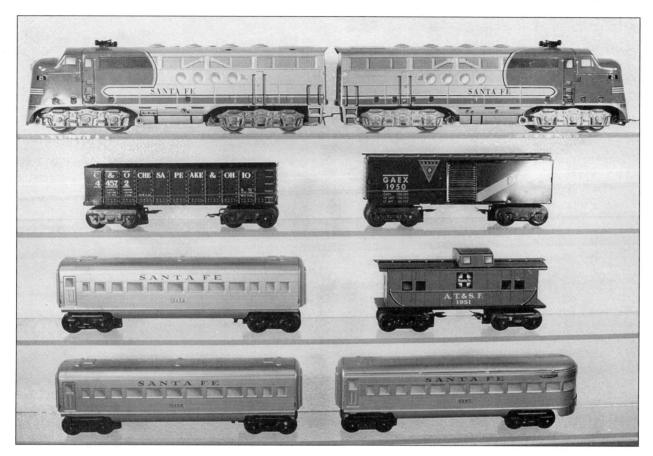

First row, left to right: No. 21 (a) Locomotive, $40; No 21 (b) Locomotive, $40. Second row, left to right: No. 44572 Gondola, $15; No. 1950 Boxcar, $40. Third row, left to right: No. 3152 (b) AT&SF Passenger car, $40; No. 1951 Caboose, $20. Fourth row, left to right: No. 3152 (b) Santa Fe Passenger car, $40; No. 3197 (b) Passenger car, $40. Photo Courtesy of Richard L. MacNary.

Left to right: No. 21 (c) Locomotive, $30; No. 320 Work Caboose, $10. Photo Courtesy of Richard L. MacNary.

No. 49 Old Time Western Set, $100. Photo Courtesy of Richard L. MacNary.

	C5	C7	C9
49 (a) Locomotive, 2-4-0, riding floor toy, plastic, black, marked "Pioneer" on cab and "49" on tender	25	50	75
49 (b) Locomotive, 2-4-0, riding floor toy, plastic, red, marked "Pioneer" on cab and "49" on red tender	30	60	90
(51) Locomotive, diesel "A" unit, plastic, eight wheel, orange w/black lettering reads "Allstate"	60	90	120
(52) Locomotive, dummy "A" unit	60	90	120
(53) Locomotive, dummy "B" unit	60	90	120
54 (a) Locomotive, diesel "A" unit , small lithographed tin, red-yellow-black w/yellow and white lettering reads "Kansas City Southern," powered "A" unit 20	40	60	50

	C5	C7	C9
54 (b) Locomotive, dummy "A" unit , small lithographed tin, red-yellow-black w/yellow and white lettering reads "Kansas City Southern," powered "A" unit 20	60	75	90
(55) (a) Locomotive, dummy "B" unit, four wheel	50	75	100
(55) (b) Locomotive, dummy "B" unit, eight wheel	60	75	90
56 Flat Car, plastic, eight wheel, maroon w/yellow side rails, white lettering reads "56"	5	10	15
59 (a) Cattle Car, 6" tin, four wheel and eight wheel brown w/red lettering reads "Union Pacific"	15	23	30
59 (b) Cattle Car, 6" tin, four wheel and eight wheel brown w/red lettering reads "Union Pacific," w/punched out slotted sides	30	45	60
(061) Telephone Pole, 7", plastic	—	—	1

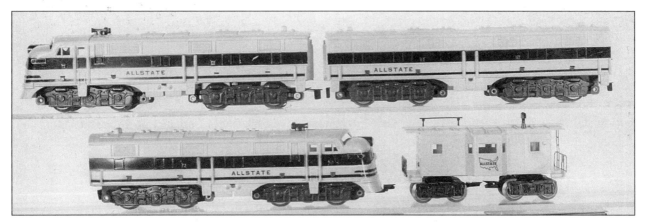

Top row, left to right: No. 51 Allstate Locomotive, $120; No. 53 Allstate Locomotive, $120. Bottom row, left to right: No. 52 Allstate Locomotive, $120; No. 2225 (b) Caboose, $100. Photo Courtesy of Richard L. MacNary.

Top row: No. 52 Locomotive, $120. Middle row, left to right: No. 5594 Flat car, $20; No. 9553 (a) Tank car, $20. Bottom row, left to right: No. 347100 Gondola, $3; No. 3900 (a) Caboose, $20. Photo Courtesy of Richard L. MacNary.

Left to right: No. 62 (a) Locomotive, $50; No. 62 (b) Locomotive, $60. Photo Courtesy of Richard L. MacNary.

	C5	C7	C9
(062) Lamp Post, 6", plastic, dummy	—	—	1
62 (a) Locomotive, diesel, lithographed tin, silver and blue w/black and white lettering reads "Baltimore & Ohio," powered, "A" unit	30	45	60
62 (b) Locomotive, dummy "A" unit, lithographed tin, silver and blue w/black and white lettering reads "Baltimore & Ohio," powered, "A" unit	25	37	50
(063) Semaphore, 6-1/8", plastic, mech.	—	—	1
(064) Crossing Gate, 8-1/4", plastic	—	—	1
(065) Water Tower, 8-1/4", plastic	—	—	1
(067) Twin Crossing Light, 6", plastic dummy	—	—	1
(073/3) Lamp Post Set, w/light, Boulevard	5	7	9

	C5	C7	C9
81F (a) Locomotive, diesel, lithographed tin, red and gray w/yellow and white lettering reads "Monon," powered "A" unit	60	75	90
81F (b) Locomotive, dummy "A" unit, lithographed tin, red and gray w/yellow and white lettering reads "Monon"	60	80	100
81F (c) Locomotive, lithographed tin, red and gray w/yellow and white lettering reads "Monon," clockwork w/wind-up motor	55	85	110
(82) (a) Locomotive, dummy "B" unit, four wheel	35	55	75
(82) (b) Locomotive, dummy "B" unit, eight wheel	40	60	80
93 (a) Locomotive, streamlined steam, lithographed tin, engine and one-piece tender, black and blue, yellow lettering reads "Lumar Lines," clockwork	20	40	60

Top row, left to right: No. 81F (a) Locomotive, $90; No. 82 Locomotive, $75; No. 31055 Caboose, $40. Bottom row, left to right: No. 81F (c) Locomotive, $110; No. C-350 Caboose, 4 wheel, $25; No. C-350 Caboose, 8 wheel, $25. Photo Courtesy of Richard L. MacNary.

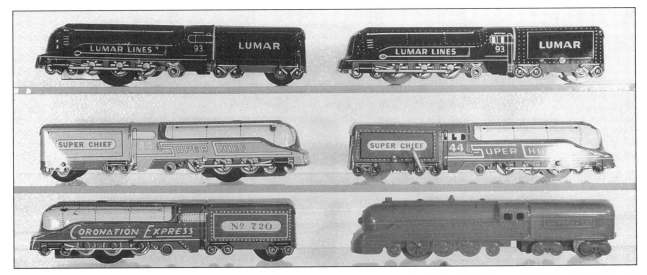

Top row, left to right: No. 93 (b) Locomotive, $60; No. 93 (a) Locomotive, $60. Middle row, left to right: No. 44 (b) Locomotive, $60; No. 44 (a) Locomotive, $60. Bottom row, left to right: No. 720 Locomotive, $50; No. 93 (c) Locomotive, plastic, $100. Photo Courtesy of Richard L. MacNary.

	C5	C7	C9
93 (b) Locomotive, streamlined steam, lithographed tin, engine and one-piece tender, black and blue, yellow lettering reads "Lumar Lines," friction	20	40	60
93 (c) Locomotive, streamlined steam, plastic, engine and one-piece tender, red, yellow lettering reads "Lumar Lines"	50	75	100
99 (a) Locomotive, diesel "A" unit, plastic, black, white lettering reads "Rock Island," powered	30	45	60
99 (b) Locomotive, dummy "A" unit	30	45	60
99 (c) Locomotive, 2-4-2T, riding floor train, plastic, red, marked "The Chief" under cab window, "Marx RR" embossed on tender and marked "99" on headlight	40	60	90
(107) Bunny, Rabbit Locomotive, lithographed tin, pink w/glass eyes, clockwork	700	1050	1400
109 (a) Hopper, plastic, blue, white lettering reads "Lehight Portland Cement"	5	7	10
109 (b) Hopper, plastic, gray, black lettering reads "Lehight Portland Cement"	5	7	10

	C5	C7	C9
112 Locomotive, diesel switcher, plastic, red, white lettering reads "Lehigh Valley"	20	30	40
128 Weck Generator, black	10	15	20
161 Drop Center Searchlite, plastic, black, white lettering reads "GEX"	10	15	20
198 Locomotive, 0-4-0, plastic, red or black, w/"Marline" cast on side, clockwork	50	75	100
200 (a) Trolley, lithographed tin, green and red, white lettering "Rapid Transit"	200	300	400
200 (b) Trolley, lithographed tin, green and red, white lettering "Rapid Transit," w/front bumper and battery headlight	200	350	500
201 Observation, 6" tin, four wheel, red w/black lettering, black and silver or all black frame	20	30	40
(0211) Signal Set, plastic, three pieces	1	2	3
(232) Locomotive, See 597, "Commodore Vanderbilt"	—	—	—
(233) Locomotive, See 635, "Mercury"	—	—	—

Left to right: No. 242 Locomotive, gray and No. 242 Locomotive, black, $30. Photo Courtesy of Richard L. MacNary.

	C5	C7	C9
234 Caboose, plastic, eight wheel, Army olive drab, white lettering reads "USA"	20	30	40
234 (a) Passenger Car, 3:16-scale, lithographed tin, eight wheel, two-tone gray, white lettering reads "New York Central"	20	30	40
234 (b) Passenger Car, 3:16-scale, lithographed tin, eight wheel, two-tone gray, white lettering reads "New York Central," w/Vista Dome	20	30	40
(235) Locomotive, See 396, 397, "Canadian Pacific"	—	—	—
(236) Passenger Car, 3:16-scale, lithographed tin, eight wheel observation, two tone gray, white letterng reads "New York Central" and "Meteor"	20	30	40
242 Locomotive, 4-4-2, floor toy, plastic, marked "Sparkling Friction RR"	15	25	30
245 Coach, 6" tin, four wheel, red, black lettering reads "Bogota," w/either black and silver or all black frame	20	30	40
246 Coach, 6" tin, four wheel, red, black lettering w/"Montreal," either black and silver or all black frame	20	30	40
246 Passenger Car, 6" tin, four and eight wheel, Canadian Pacific, maroon, gold lettering reads "Montreal"	75	125	150
X-246 Tank Car, plastic, four wheel, white and cream, red lettering reads "Chemical Rocket Fuel"	10	15	20

	C5	C7	C9
246 Tank Car, plastic, eight wheel, white, cream, red lettering reads "Chemical Rocket Fuel" and "Danger"	10	15	20
247 Passenger Car, 6" tin, four and eight wheel, Canadian Pacific, maroon, gold lettering reads "Toronto"	75	125	150
248 Passenger Car, 6" Tin, four and eight wheel, Canadian Pacific, maroon, gold lettering reads "Quebec"	75	125	150
249 Passenger Car, 6" tin, four and eight wheel, Canadian Pacific, maroon, gold lettering reads "Ottawa"	75	125	150
250 Passenger Car, 6" tin, four and eight wheel, Canadian Pacific, maroon, gold lettering reads "Winnipeg"	75	125	150
251 Passenger Car, 6" tin, four and eight wheel, Canadian Pacific, maroon, gold lettering reads "Vancouver"	75	125	150
252 Passenger Car, 6" tin, four and eight wheel, Canadian Pacific, maroon, gold lettering reads "Calgary"	75	125	150
253 Passenger Car, 6" tin, four and eight wheel, Canadian Pacific, maroon, gold lettering reads "Hamilton"	75	125	150
256 Tank Car, 3:16-scale, lithographed tin, eight wheel, silver, red lettering reads "N.I.A.X." and "Niagara Falls, NY"	5	7	10

Top row, left to right: No. 333 (a) Locomotive, $40; No. 3991 NYC Tender. Middle row, left to right: No. 234 (a) Passenger car, $40; No. 234 (b) Passenger car, $40. Bottom row: No. 236 Passenger car, $40. Photo Courtesy of Richard L. MacNary.

	C5	C7	C9
284 Tank Car, plastic, deluxe, eight wheel, gray, red lettering reads "UTLX"	10	15	20
304 Cattle Runway, silver ramp	20	30	40
(309B) Tunnel, Tin litho	10	15	20
320 Work Caboose, Tuscan red, white lettering reads "Monon," boom	5	7	10
(321) Railroad Signal Set, steel	5	7	10
333 Locomotive, 4-4-4, floor toy, plastic, w/whistle and bell	10	15	20
333 (a) Locomotive, 4-6-2, die-cast, black	40	60	80
333 (b) Locomotive, 4-6-2, die-cast, black, w/smoke	45	65	90
349 Animal Assortment, eight small lithographed tin animals, on card	50	75	100
C-350 Caboose, plastic, eight wheel, red, white lettering reads "Monon"	10	18	25

	C5	C7	C9
350 Locomotive, 0-4-0, tin, Joy Line, red and gold body, blue frame, clockwork	400	600	800
351 (a) Tender, tin, Joy Line, yellow w/blue frame, marked "Koal Kar"	40	60	80
351 (b) Tender, tin, unmarked black top, black frame	20	30	40
351 (c) Tender, tin, unmarked, black or red	25	35	45
352 (a) Gondola, tin, Joy Line, blue body w/blue frame, marked "Venice Gondola"	40	60	80
352 (b) Gondola, tin, Joy Line, blue body w/black frame, marked, "Venice Gondola"	30	45	60
352 (c) Gondola, tin, Joy Line, either baby chicks or ducklings w/red or blue backgrounds, marked "Bunny Express"	50	75	100
352 (d) Gondola, tin, Joy Line, either baby chicks or ducklings w/red or orange backgrounds, w/wood lithographed stakes, marked "Bunny Express"	40	60	80

Joy line Electric Passenger Kit. Top row, left to right: Locomotive with two rubber drive wheels, $250; No. 351 (b) Tender, $40; No. 357 (b) Coach, $60. Bottom row, left to right: Two No. 357 (b) Coach cars; No. 458 (b) Observation with light, $150. Photo Courtesy of Richard L. MacNary.

Joy Line Clockwork Cast-iron Passenger Set. Top row, left to right: Locomotive, $200; No. 351 (b) Tender, $40. Bottom row: three No 357 (b) Passenger cars. Photo Courtesy of Richard L. MacNary.

	C5	C7	C9		C5	C7	C9
353 (a) Tank Car, tin, Joy Line, gold body w/blue frame, marked "Everful Tank Car"......	40	60	80	354 (b) Side Dump, tin, Joy Line, yellow body w/black frame, marked "Contractor Dump Car"...	30	45	60
353 (b) Tank Car, tin, Joy Line, gold body w/black frame, marked "Everful Tank Car"......	30	45	60	355 (a) Boxcar, tin, Joy Line, red body w/blue frame, marked "Hobo Rest".............................	40	60	80
354 (a) Side Dump, tin, Joy Line, yellow body w/blue frame, marked "Contractor Dump Car"...	40	60	80	355 (b) Boxcar, tin, Joy Line, red body w/black frame, marked "Hobo Rest".............................	30	45	60

Joy Line Cast-iron Electric Freight Set. Top row, left to right: No. 355 (b) Hobo Rest Boxcar, $60; No. 354 (b) Dump car; No. 353 (b) Tank car. Bottom row, left to right: transformer with square case; No. 356 (b) Caboose, $60. Photo Courtesy of Richard L. MacNary.

Joy Line Blue Frame Set. Top row, left to right: No. 357 (a) Coach, $150; No. 351 (a) Tender, $80; No. 350 Locomotive, $800. Middle row, left to right: No. 350 Locomotive; No. 351 (a) Tender; No. 352 (a) Gondola, $80; No. 353 (a) Tank car, $80. Bottom row, left to right: No. 354 (a) Dump car, $80; No. 355 (a) Boxcar, $80; No. 356 (a) Caboose, $80. Photo Courtesy of Richard L. MacNary.

	C5	C7	C9
356 (a) Caboose, tin, Joy Line, red body w/blue frame, marked "Eagle Eye Caboose"................	40	60	80
356 (b) Caboose, tin, Joy Line, red body w/black frame, marked "Eagle Eye Caboose"................	30	45	60
357 (a) Coach, tin, green body and yellow round roof w/blue frame, marked "The Joy Line Coach"	75	100	150
357 (b) Coach, tin, orange or red roof and green body w/black frame, marked "The Joy Line Coach"	30	45	60
391 Locomotive, 0-4-0 and 2-4-2, Canadian Pacific, various boiler colors and side boards..............	40	60	80
396 Locomotive, 0-4-0 and 2-4-2, Canadian Pacific-style, various boiler colors and side boards	40	60	88
397 Locomotive, 2-4-2, Canadian Pacific-style, varous boiler colors and side boards..............	40	60	80

	C5	C7	C9
400 (a) Locomotive, 0-4-0, plastic, black, clockwork and electric ...	20	30	40
400 (b) Locomotive, 0-4-0, plastic, black, clockwork and electric, w/rubber bulb and powder smoke	30	45	60
400 (c) Locomotive, 0-4-0, plastic, Army olive drab, clockwork and electric, w/rubber bulb and powder smoke	30	45	60
400 (d) Locomotive, 0-4-0, plastic, dark gray, clockwork and electric, w/rubber bulb and powder smoke	30	40	50
(401) Locomotive, 0-4-0, plastic, black, "Mar" cast on side, clockwork................................	40	60	80
(404) Block Signal, stamped steel, 6-5/8" high	5	7	10
(405) Block Signal, stamped steel, two lights w/separate controller	10	15	20
(408) Twin Light Lamp Post, stamped steel, 7-1/4" high.........	5	7	10

Top row, left to right: No. 396 Locomotive, $88; Canadian Pacific tender. Middle row, left to right: No. 552 (b) Gondola, $10; No. 553 (b) Tank car, $10; No. 554 (b) Hopper, $9. Bottom row, left to right: No. 562D Flat car with dump truck, $100; No. 555 (b) Refer, $20; No. 556 (a) Caboose, $3. Photo Courtesy of Richard L. MacNary.

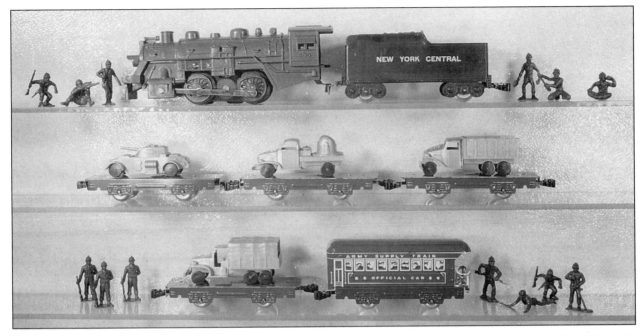

Top row, left to right: No. 400 (c) Locomotive, $60; No. 1951 Tender. Middle row, left to right: No. 572M (d) Flat car with armored car, $40; No. 572M (e) Flat car with searchlight, $40; No. 572M (b) Flat car with 2-1/2-ton truck, $40. Bottom row, left to right: 572 M (b) Flat with 2-1/2-ton truck; No 558 (a) Observation car, $60. Photo Courtesy of Richard L. MacNary.

Top row, left to right: No. 401 Locomotive, $80; No. 1951 Tender. Bottom row: No. 467110 Boxcar, $20. Photo Courtesy of Richard L. MacNary.

Left to right: No. 405 Block signal, two light, $40; No. 1404 Block signal, five position, $30; No. 404 Block signal three light, $10; No. 1405 Block signal, two light, $40; No. 405 Block signal. Photo Courtesy of Richard L. MacNary.

	C5	C7	C9
(409) Twin Light Blinking Caution Signal, stamped steel, 7-1/4" high	6	9	12
(412) RR Derrick Loader, boom on top, straddles track, winch	20	30	40
(413) Switchman Tower, stamped steel, w/light, 9-1/4"	8	12	15
(414) RR Crossing Warning Bell	5	7	10
X415 (a) Tank Car, plastic, white and blue or black, red lettering reads "Hydrocarbon Rocket Fuel"	5	8	10
X415 (b) Tank Car, plastic, white and blue, or black, red tank w/yellow frame, red lettering reads "Hydrocarbon Rocket Fuel"	10	15	20
(416) Floodlight, black, plastic, four bulbs	5	7	10
(416A) Floodlight Tower, stamped steel, two bulbs, red, black or silver	5	10	15
(418) Automatic Bell Ringing Signal, stamped steel, 7-1/2" tall	5	10	15

	C5	C7	C9
(419) Lamp Post, stamped steel, single bulb	5	7	10
(423) Automatic Twin Light Highway Crossing Signal, flashing, two bulbs, 7-1/2" high	5	7	10
(424) Radio Control Tower, stamped steel and pin, operated by voice, 9-1/2" x 2-3/4" x 2-3/4"	5	10	15
(429) Lamp Post, stamped steel, twin bulbs	5	7	10
(434) Block Signal, stamped steel, 7"	5	7	10
(436) Searchlight Tower, plastic	2	4	6
(438) Automatic Crossing Gate, stamped steel, 9" gate arm	6	9	12
(439) Semaphore, w/light, stamped steel, 9"	6	9	12
(451) Tender, 6" tin, four wheel, C.P.-style, black w/white or cream lettering reads "Pennsylvania"	20	30	40

Left to right: No. 418 Crossing signal with ringing bell, $15; No. 405 Block signal, two light; No. 408 Street light, $10; No. 404 Block signal, three light; No. 409 Caution signal, $12. Photo Courtesy of Richard L. MacNary.

No. 424 Radio Control Tower in three different heights, left to right: 13-1/2", 11-1/2", 9-1/2", $15, each. Photo Courtesy of Richard L. MacNary.

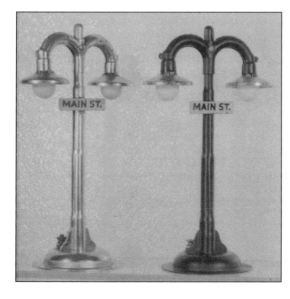

Two twin lamp posts, $10, each. Photo Courtesy of Richard L. MacNary.

	C5	C7	C9
458 (a) Observation, tin, Joy Line, orange or red roof, green body w/black frame, marked "Observation"	30	45	60
458 (b) Observation, tin, Joy Line, orange or red roof, green body w/black frame, marked "Observation," w/light	50	100	150
X467 Caboose, plastic, four wheel and eight wheel, red, white lettering reads "Rocket Computing Center"	10	20	30
490 (a) Locomotive, 0-4-0, plastic, black	10	15	20
490 (b) Locomotive, 0-4-0, plastic, black w/white stripe	10	15	20
490 (c) Locomotive, 0-4-0, plastic, gray w/white stripe	10	15	20
500 Locomotive, 0-4-0 and 2-4-2, Canadian Pacific-style, Army olive drab	50	75	180
500 Tender, 6" tin, four and eight wheel, Army olive drab, white lettering reads "Army Supply Train"	20	30	40

	C5	C7	C9
504 Caboose, plastic, four wheel, blue, yellow lettering "B&O"	100	150	200
504/518 Caboose, tin, four wheel, blue and black, yellow and white lettering reads "B&O," 7" (some exist as eight wheel versions)	25	37	50
547 (a) Baggage Car, 6" tin, four wheel, red, black lettering reads "Express Baggage"	20	30	40
547 (b) Baggage Car, 6" tin, four wheel, red, silver lettering reads "Express Baggage"	20	30	40
547 (c) Baggage Car, 6" tin, four and eight wheel, red, yellow lettering reads "Express Baggage"	20	30	40
548 Gondola, 6" tin, four wheel and eight wheel, light blue, blue and white lettering reads "Guernsey Milk" and "CRI&P"	20	35	50

Penny's Special NYC Set with miscellaneous cardboard buildings and plastic signals. Top row, left to right: No. 490 Locomotive, $20; No. 1951 Tender. Middle row, left to right: NYC Wrecker; No. 347100 Gondola. Bottom row: NYC Pacemaker Caboose. Photo Courtesy of Richard L. MacNary.

Top row, left to right: No. 500 Locomotive, $180; No. 500 Tender (not legitimate), $50; No. 557 (b) Passenger car (not legitimate), $80. Middle row, left to right: No. 557ST (b) Flat car with tank, $200; No. 561 (c) Searchlight car, $40; No. 572AA Flat car with AA gun, $100. Bottom row, No. 572G Flat car, $100; No. 552 (e) Gondola, $80; 572MG Flat car, $100. Photo Courtesy of Richard L. MacNary.

Top row, left to right: No. 555 (a) Refer, $60; No. 384299 (a) Boxcar, $60; No. 554 (a) Hopper, $7. Middle row, left to right: No. 553 Tank car with round ends; No. 553 Tank car with flat ends; No. 554 Hopper. Bottom row, left to right: No. 412 Derrick, $40; No 552 Gondola, $20; No. 556 Caboose, $3. Photo Courtesy of Richard L. MacNary.

	C5	C7	C9
(550) (a) Wrecker/Crane, 6" tin, four wheel orange cab, red boom and either black and silver or all black frame, black lettering reads "Wrecker," w/rail clips	10	20	30
(550) (b) Wrecker/Crane, 6" tin, four and eight wheel orange cab, red boom and either black and silver or all black frame, black lettering reads "Wrecker"	10	15	20
(551) (a) Tender, 6" tin, four wheel, black w/black and silver frame, silver lettering reads "New York Central"	5	7	10
(551) (b) Tender, 6" tin, four and eight wheel, black w/black, red or nickel frame, silver lettering reads "New York Central"	5	10	15
(551) (c) Tender, 6" tin, four wheel, red, silver lettering reads "New York Central"	20	30	40
(551) (d) Tender, 6" tin, four wheel, blue w/gray band, silver lettering reads "New York Central"	30	45	60
(551) (e) Tender, 6" tin, four wheel, copper or brass frame, silver lettering reads "New York Central"	20	30	40
(551) (f) Tender, 6" tin, four wheel, black w/gray band, silver lettering reads "New York Central"	20	30	40
(551) (g) Tender, 6" tin, four wheel, black, silver lettering reads "Union Pacific," late	5	7	10
(551) (h) Tender, 6" tin, four wheel, black, silver lettering reads w/"1st DIV", St.P & P.R.R., late	15	22	30
552 (a) Gondola, 6" tin, four wheel, red w/black and silver or all black frame, black lettering reads "CRI&P"	10	15	20
552 (b) Gondola, 6" tin, four and eight wheel, red w/black and silver or all black frame, green w/red and white lettering reads "CRI&P"	5	7	10

	C5	C7	C9
552 (c) Gondola, 6" tin, four and eight wheel, red w/black and silver or all black frame, light blue w/blue and white lettering reads "CRI&P"	5	10	15
552 (d) Gondola, 6" tin, four wheel, yellow and brown, brown and white lettering reads "CRI&P," car marked "552G"	20	30	40
552 (e) Gondola, 6" tin, four wheel, Army olive drab, black and white lettering reads "Ordinance Department," w/original shells add $40.00	40	60	80
552 (f) Gondola, 6" tin, eight wheel, dark blue w/black and silver or all black frame, black lettering reads "CRI&P"	5	10	15
553 (a) Tank Car, 6" tin, four wheel, silver, red lettering reads "UTLX"	5	7	10
553 (b) Tank Car, 6" tin, four wheel, yellow w/black and silver or all black frame, black lettering reads "Middle States Oil" and "Santa Fe"	9	12	15
553 (c) Tank Car, 6" tin, four and eight wheel, silver w/black and silver or all black frame, black lettering reads "Middle States Oil" and "Santa Fe"	3	4	5
554 High Side Gondola, 6" tin, four wheel red, yellow lettering reads "General Coal Co.," and "N.P."	5	7	10
554 (a) Hopper, 6" tin, four wheel and eight wheel red, yellow lettering reads "General Coal Co.," and "N.P."	3	5	7
554 (b) Hopper, 6" tin, four wheel red, blue and white lettering reads "General Coal Co.," and "N.P."	3	6	9
555 (a) Refrigerator Car, 6" tin, both four wheel and eight wheel, cream w/red roof, red lettering reads "C&S," sliding doors	30	45	60

	C5	C7	C9
555 (b) Refrigerator Car, 6" tin, both four wheel and eight wheel, cream w/blue roof, blue lettering reads "C&S," sliding doors	10	15	20
555 (c) Refrigerator Car, 6" tin, both four wheel, cream w/red roof, red lettering reads "C&S," solid lithographed doors	50	75	100
555 (d) Refrigerator Car, 6" tin, four wheel and eight wheel, cream w/blue roof, blue lettering reads "C&S," solid lithographed doors	10	15	20
556 (a) Caboose, 6" tin, four wheel and eight wheel, red, white lettering reads "NYC"	1	2	3
556 (b) Caboose, 6" tin, four wheel and eight wheel, red, white lettering reads "NYC," w/light	40	60	80
557 (a) Passenger Car, 6" tin, four wheel, Army olive drab, lettering reads "Radio Car" and "Army Supply Train," w/rooftop antenna	30	45	60
557 (b) Passenger Car, 6" tin, four wheel, Army olive drab, lettering reads "Radio Car" and "Army Supply Train," without rooftop antenna, no holes	40	60	80

	C5	C7	C9
557 (c) Passenger Car, 6" tin, four or eight wheel, red, black or white lettering reads "Bogota" and "Montclair," w/rooftop antenna	10	15	20
557 (d) Passenger Car, 6" tin, four wheel, green, yellow lettering reads "Bogota" and "Montclair," w/rooftop antenna	20	30	40
557 (e) Passenger Car, 6" tin, four wheel, blue, ivory lettering reads "Bogota" and "Montclair," w/rooftop antenna	30	40	60
(558) (a) Observation Car, 6" tin, four wheel, Army olive drab, white lettering, w/ and without light	30	45	60
(558) (b) Observation Car, 6" tin, four or eight wheel, red, white lettering reads "Observation," w/ and without light	15	22	30
(558) (c) Observation Car, 6" tin, four wheel, green, yellow lettering reads "Observation," w/ and without light	20	30	40
(558) (d) Observation Car, 6" tin, four wheel, blue, ivory lettering reads "Observation," w/ and without light	30	40	60
(559) Floodlight, 6" tin, four wheel, two lights	20	30	40
(561) (a) Searchlight Car, 6" tin, four wheel, one light	20	30	40

Top row, left to right: No. 558 (b) Observation car, $30; No. 557 (c) Refrigerator car, $100; No. 557 (c) Passenger car, $20. Bottom row, left to right: No. 555 (c) Refrigerator car, $100; Commodore Vanderbilt Locomotive and tender, $400. Photo Courtesy of Richard L. MacNary.

Left to right: Three versions of the No. 562D Dump car, $100, each. Photo Courtesy of Richard L. MacNary.

	C5	C7	C9
(561) (b) Searchlight Car, 6" tin, eight wheel, one light	100	150	200
(561) (c) Searchlight Car, 6" tin, four wheel, one light, Army olive drab	20	30	40
(562D) Flat Car, 6" tin, four wheel and eight wheel, w/different colored stamped steel dump trucks	50	75	100
(563A) Lumber Car, 6" tin, four wheel and eight wheel, w/four pieces of lumber and clamp	20	30	40
564 Caboose, plastic, eight wheel, brown, white lettering reads "All State"	5	7	10

	C5	C7	C9
566 Cable Car, 6" tin, four wheel and eight wheel, large wooden cable reel mounted through base w/string	30	45	60
567 Dump Car, 6" tin, four wheel and eight wheel, yellow, red lettering reads "Side Dumping Car" and "New York Central," both copper and brass based	10	20	30
(572A) Flat Car, 6" tin, four wheel, Army olive drab w/olive drab airplane..............................	100	150	200
(572AA) Flat Car, 6" tin, four wheel and eight wheel, Army olive drab w/attached AA gun.............	50	75	100
(572FG) Flat Car, 6" tin, four wheel and eight wheel, ARMY olive drab w/attached field gun	20	30	40

Top row: Rail car, $100. Middle row, left to right: No. 566 Cable reel car, $60; No. 572A Flat car, $200; No. 563A Lumber car, $40. Bottom row, left to right: No. 562D Flat, $100; Wheel car, $80; No. 574 Barrel car, $40. Photo Courtesy of Richard L. MacNary.

Left to right: No. 588 (a) Locomotive, $40; No. 347100 Gondola, $3; NYC Caboose. Photo Courtesy of Richard L. MacNary.

	C5	C7	C9
(572G) Flat Car, 6" tin, four wheel and eight wheel, Army olive drab w/attached large bore siege gun	50	75	100
(572M) (a) Flat Car, 6" tin, four wheel, Army olive drab w/stamped steel olive drab dump truck	100	150	200
(572M) (b) Flat Car, 6" tin, four wheel, Army olive drab w/gray plastic two-ton truck	20	30	40
(572M) (c) Flat Car, 6" tin, four wheel, Army olive drab w/w/gray plastic "Duck"	20	30	40
(572M) (d) Flat Car, 6" tin, four wheel, Army olive drab w/gray plastic armored car	20	30	40
(572M) (e) Flat Car, 6" tin, four wheel, Army olive drab w/gray search-lite truck	20	30	40
(572M) (f) Flat Car, 6" tin, four wheel, Army olive drab w/gray plastic tank	20	30	40
(572M) (g) Flat Car, 6" tin, four wheel, Army olive drab w/gray plastic staff car	20	30	40
(572MG) Flat Car, 6" tin, four wheel and eight wheel, Army olive drab w/attached machine gun	50	75	100
(572ST) (a) Flat Car, 6" tin, four wheel, Army olive drab w/no. 5 lithographed tin tank	100	200	300
(572ST) (b) Flat Car, 6" tin, four and eight wheel, Army olive drab w/no. 5 lithographed tin tank w/midget sparkling tank	100	150	200
(574) Barrel Car, 6" tin, four wheel and eight wheel w/seven wooden barrels	20	30	40

	C5	C7	C9
586 Caboose, plastic, wrecker-type, eight wheel, brown, white lettering reads "Rock Island"	5	7	10
(586) (a) Flat Car, plastic, eight wheel, red, white lettering reads "Rock Island"	2	4	6
(586) (b) Flat Car, plastic, eight wheel, maroon w/yellow lettering reads "Erie"	1	2	3
(586) (c) Flat Car, plastic, eight wheel, Army olive drab, white lettering reads "USA," w/silver plastic tank and truck	20	30	40
588 (a) Locomotive, diesel switcher, four wheel, black, white lettering reads "New York Central"	20	30	40
588 (b) Locomotive, diesel switcher, four wheel, maroon, yellow lettering reads "New York Central"	20	30	40
588 (c) Locomotive, diesel switcher, four wheel, gray w/black lettering reads "New York Central"	25	37	50
(591) Locomotive, 0-4-0 tin, black, no markings	5	8	10
(592) Locomotive, 0-4-0 tin, black, no markings	5	8	10
(593) Locomotive, 0-4-0, tin, black, no markings	5	8	10
(595) Locomotive, 0-4-0, tin, black, no marking, electric	5	8	10
(597) (a) Locomotive, 0-4-0, stamped steel, green, "Commodore Vanderbilt," clockwork	200	300	400

Top row, left to right: No. 597 (b) Locomotive, $80; No. 551 (b) Tender, $15; No. 550 (a) Wrecker, $30. Bottom row, left to right: No 553 (a) Tank car, $10; No. 552 (a) Gondola, $20. Photo Courtesy of Richard L. MacNary.

Top row, left to right: No. 597 (c) Locomotive, $100; No. 952 Tender, $60; No. 557 (a) Passenger car, $60. Middle row, left to right: No. 572FG Flat car, $40; No. 572A Flat car, $200; No. 572M Flat car, $200. Bottom row, left to right: 572ST (a) Flat car, $300; No. 2572 Ramp car, $200. Photo Courtesy of Richard L. MacNary.

	C5	C7	C9		C5	C7	C9
(597) (b) Locomotive, 0-4-0, stamped steel, black, "Commodore Vanderbilt," clockwork or electric	40	60	80	(597) (c) Locomotive, 0-4-0, stamped steel, red or gray, "Commodore Vanderbilt," clockwork or electric	50	75	100

	C5	C7	C9
(597) (d) Locomotive, 0-4-0, stamped steel, Army olive drab, "Commodore Vanderbilt," clockwork or electric	100	150	200
C-630 Caboose, plastic, red, white lettering reads "NH"	2	4	6
C-635 Caboose, plastic, eight wheel, red, white lettering reads "New Haven"	8	12	16
(635) (a) Locomotive, 0-4-0, tin, black, no marking	5	8	10
(635) (b) Locomotive, 0-4-0, stamped steel, articulated, gray, red or black, Mercury-style, electric or clockwork	30	45	60
(635) (c) Locomotive, 0-4-0, stamped steel, regular book coupler, blue, Mercury-style, electric or clockwork	50	75	100
643 (a) Caboose, plastic, four wheel, green w/yellow, or gold, lettering reads "Western Pacific"	5	10	15

	C5	C7	C9
643 (b) Caboose, plastic, eight wheel, bay window, green w/yellow, or gold, lettering reads "Western Pacific"	20	30	40
645 (a) Caboose, plastic, work type, red, white lettering reads "NH"	2	4	6
645 (b) Caboose, plastic, bay window, green, yellow lettering reads "Western Pacific"	5	7	10
652 Tank Car, 3:16-scale, lithographed tin, eight wheel, orange, red lettering reads "SCCX" and "SHELL"	10	20	30
(657) (a) Passenger Car, lithographed tin, streamline, four-wheel trailing truck for M10,000 train, tan and cream, red lettering reads "Union Pacific" and "Coach"	10	15	20
(657) (b) Passenger Car, lithographed tin, streamline, four-wheel trailing truck for M10,000 train, maroon and silver, black lettering reads "Union Pacific" and "Coach" ...	15	22	30

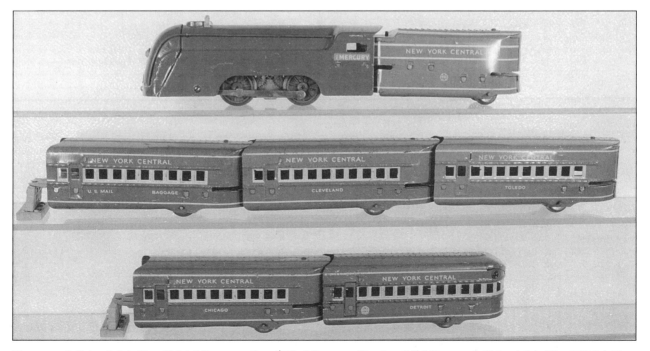

Top row, left to right: No. 635 (a) Locomotive, $60; Mercury Tender. Middle row, left to right: No. 657 (p) Passenger car, $20; No. 657 (s) Passenger car, $20; No. 657 (r), $20. Bottom row, left to right: No. 657 (q) Passenger car, $20; No. 658 Passenger car, $15. Photo Courtesy of Richard L. MacNary.

	C5	C7	C9
(657) (c) Passenger Car, lithographed tin, streamline, four-wheel trailing truck for M10,000 train, green and cream, red lettering reads "Union Pacific" and "Coach" ...	8	12	16
(657) (d) Passenger Car, lithographed tin, streamline, two-wheel for M10,005 train, green and cream, white, red lettering reads "REA/ROP" and "Union Pacific"	5	10	15
(657) (e) Passenger Car, lithographed tin, streamline, two-wheel for M10,005 train, green and cream, white, red lettering reads "Los Angeles"...	5	10	15
(657) (f) Passenger Car, lithographed tin, streamline, two-wheel for M10,005 train, green and cream, white, red lettering reads "Omaha"	5	10	15
(657) (g) Passenger Car, lithographed tin, streamline, two-wheel for M10,005 train, green and cream, white, red lettering reads "Denver"	5	10	15
(657) (h) Passenger Car, lithographed tin, streamline, two-wheel for M10,005 train, red and silver, blue lettering reads "REA/RPO" and "Union Pacific"	6	9	12
(657) (i) Passenger Car, lithographed tin, streamline, two-wheel for M10,005 train, red and silver, blue lettering reads "Los Angeles"	6	9	12
(657) (j) Passenger Car, lithographed tin, streamline, two-wheel for M10,005 train, red and silver, blue lettering reads "Omaha"	6	9	12
(657) (k) Passenger Car, lithographed tin, streamline, two-wheel for M10,005 train, red and silver, blue lettering reads "Denver"	6	9	12

	C5	C7	C9
(657) (l) Passenger Car, lithographed tin, streamline, two-wheel for M10,005 train, yellow and brown, orange lettering reads "REA/RPO" and "Union Pacific"	10	15	20
(657) (m) Passenger Car, lithographed tin, streamline, two-wheel for M10,005 train, yellow and brown, orange lettering reads "Los Angeles" ...	10	15	20
(657) (n) Passenger Car, lithographed tin, streamline, two-wheel for M10,005 train, yellow and brown, orange lettering reads "Omaha"	10	15	20
(657) (o) Passenger Car, lithographed tin, streamline, two-wheel for M10,005 train, yellow and brown, orange lettering reads "Denver"	10	15	20
(657) (p) Passenger Car, lithographed tin, streamline, two-wheel for NYC Mercury train, gray, white lettering reads "US Mail-Baggage"	10	15	20
(657) (q) Passenger Car, lithographed tin, streamline, two-wheel for NYC Mercury train, gray, white lettering reads "Chicago"	10	15	20
(657) (r) Passenger Car, lithographed tin, streamline, two-wheel for NYC Mercury train, gray, white lettering reads "Toledo"	10	15	20
(657) (s) Passenger Car, lithographed tin, streamline, two-wheel for NYC Mercury train, gray, white lettering reads "Cleveland"	10	15	20
(657) (t) Passenger Car, lithographed tin, streamline, two-wheel for NYC Mercury train, copper and brass, black lettering reads "US Mail-Baggage"	15	20	25
(657) (u) Passenger Car, lithographed tin, streamline, two-wheel for NYC Mercury train, copper and brass, black lettering reads "Chicago"	15	20	25

	C5	C7	C9
(657) (v) Passenger Car, lithographed tin, streamline, two-wheel for NYC Mercury train, copper and brass, black lettering reads "Toledo"	15	20	25
(657) (w) Passenger Car, lithographed tin, streamline, two-wheel for NYC Mercury train, copper and brass, black lettering reads "Cleveland"	15	20	25
(657) (x) Passenger Car, lithographed tin, streamline, two-wheel, for NYC Mercury train, red, white lettering reads "Chicago"	10	15	20
(657) (y) Passenger Car, lithographed tin, streamline, two-wheel, for NYC Mercury train, red, white lettering reads "Toledo"	10	15	20
(657) (z) Passenger Car, lithographed tin, streamline, two-wheel, for NYC Mercury train, red, white lettering reads "Cleveland"	10	15	20

	C5	C7	C9
(658) (a) Passenger Car, lithographed tin, observation, streamline, four-wheel trailing truck for M10,000 train, tan and cream, red lettering reads "Union Pacific" and "Coach Buffet"	10	15	20
(658) (b) Passenger Car, lithographed tin, observation, streamline, four-wheel trailing truck for M10,000 train, maroon and silver, black lettering reads "Union Pacific" and "Coach Buffet"	15	22	30
(658) (c) Passenger Car, lithographed tin, observation, streamline, four-wheel trailing truck for M10,000 train, green and cream, red lettering reads "Union Pacific" and "Coach Buffet"	8	12	16
(658) (d) Passenger Car, lithographed tin, observation, streamline, two-wheel for M10,005 train, green and cream, red lettering reads "Squaw Bonnet"	5	10	15

Top row, left to right: No. 666 Locomotive, $60; No. 951A Tender, $10. Middle row, left to right: No. 3557 (a) Passenger car, $200; No. 3558 (a) Passenger car, $200. Bottom row, left to right: No. 1950 (b) Boxcar, $40; No. 254000 Gondola, $30; No. 20102 (c) Caboose, $10. Photo Courtesy of Richard L. MacNary.

Top row, left to right: No. 666 Locomotive, $80; No. 1951 Tender. Middle row, left to right: No. 2236 Gondola, $20; No. 2246 Flat car, $60. Bottom row, left to right: No. 2824 Flat car, $60; No. 234 Caboose, $40. Photo Courtesy of Richard L. MacNary.

	C5	C7	C9
(658) (e) Passenger Car, lithographed tin, observation, streamline, two-wheel for M10,005 train, red and silver, blue lettering reads "Squaw Bonnet"	6	9	12
(658) (f) Passenger Car, lithographed tin, observation, streamline, two-wheel for M10,005 train, yellow and brown, orange lettering reads "Squaw Bonnet"	10	15	20
(658) (g) Passenger Car, lithographed tin, observation, streamline, two-wheel for NYC Mercury train, gray, white lettering reads "Detroit"	10	15	20

	C5	C7	C9
(658) (h) Passenger Car, lithographed tin, observation, streamline, two-wheel for NYC Mercury train, copper, black lettering reads "Detroit"	15	20	25
(658) (i) Passenger Car, lithographed tin, observation, streamline, two-wheel for NYC Mercury train, red, white lettering reads "Detroit"	10	15	20
(663) Pole Car, 6" tin, four wheel and eight wheel w/thirteen poles and clamp, black	20	30	40
666 (a) Locomotive, 2-4-2, die-cast, black, w/ and without white stripe, w/ and without smoke	30	45	60
666 (b) Locomotive, 2-4-2, die-cast, Army olive drab, w/ and without white stripe, w/smoke	40	60	80

Top row: Two versions of No. 702 Locomotive, $40, each. Middle row, left to right: No. 588 (a) Locomotive, $40; No. 799 Locomotive, $40. Photo Courtesy of Richard L. MacNary.

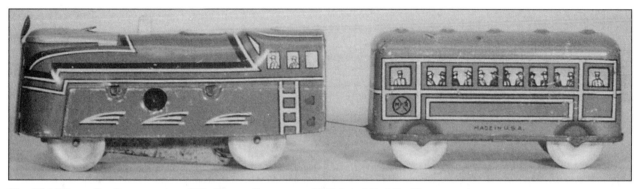

No. 896 Hiawatha Locomotive, $20. Photo Courtesy of Richard L. MacNary.

	C5	C7	C9
694 Caboose, 6" tin, four wheel, red w/black and silver or all black frame, black lettering reads "New York Central"	10	15	20
702 Locomotive, diesel switcher, plastic, four wheel, green, yellow or gold lettering reads "Western Pacific"	10	20	30
720 Locomotive, streamline steam, lithographed tin, one piece engine and tender, red-white-blue, marked "Coronation Express," made in Great Britain, friction powered	30	40	50
(734) Locomotive, See 994/995, "Mickey Mouse" type	—	—	—
(735) Locomotive, See 994/995, "Nickel Plate" style	—	—	—
799 Locomotive, diesel switcher, plastic, four wheel, black, white lettering reads "Rock Island"	20	30	40
799 Locomotive, diesel switcher, plastic, four wheel, green, yellow lettering reads "Western Pacific"	25	35	50

	C5	C7	C9
817 Boxcar/Refrigerator, 6" tin, four wheel, yellow w/black and silver or all black frame, black lettering reads "Colorado & Southern"	10	15	20
(834) Locomotive, See 400 Locomotive	—	—	—
(896) Locomotive, Hiawatha-type, lithographed tin, red and white, 4-1/2" long, w/3-3/4" passenger car	10	15	20
897 (a) Locomotive, 0-4-0, lithographed tin, black w/gray and white details	30	45	60
897 (b) Locomotive, 0-4-0, lithographed tin, Army olive drab	60	90	120
898 Locomotive, 0-4-0, tin, black enamel, electric	5	7	10
901 (a) Locomotive, diesel, plastic, eight wheel, green, yellow lettering reads "Western Pacific," powered "A" unit	25	37	50

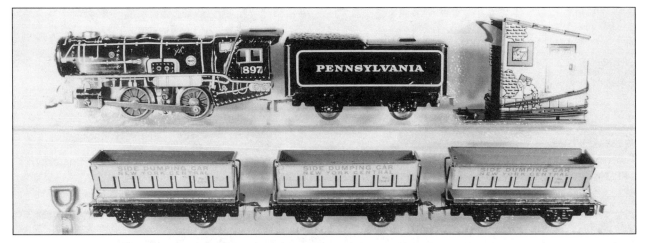

Top row, left to right: No. 897 (a) Locomotive, $60; No 451 Tender, $40; No. 1614 Automatic Dump Unit, $80. Bottom row: Three No. 567 Dump cars, $30, each. Photo Courtesy of Richard L. MacNary.

Left to right: No. 897 (b) Locomotive, $120; No. 952 Tender, $60; No. 561 (c) Searchlight car, $40. Photo Courtesy of Richard L. MacNary.

Top row, left to right: No. 898 Locomotive, $10; No. 951A Tender, $10. Middle row: No. 2124Rail diesel car, $200. Bottom row, left to right: No. 504 Caboose, $200; No. C350 Caboose, $25. Photo Courtesy of Richard L. MacNary.

First row, left to right: No. 901 (b) Locomotive, $80; No. 901 (d) Locomotive, $80. Second row: No. 902 (b) Locomotive. Third Row, left to right: No. 1217 (b) Passenger car, $40; N0. 1217 (a) Passenger car, Passenger car, $80. Fourth row, left to right: No. 1217 (a) Passenger car; No. 1007 Observation car, $40. Photo Courtesy of Richard L. MacNary.

	C5	C7	C9		C5	C7	C9
901 (b) Locomotive, diesel, plastic, eight wheel, gray, black lettering reads "Western Pacific," powered "A" unit	40	60	80	(951A) Tender, 6" tin, four wheel and eight wheel, wedge-style, black, white lettering reads "New York Central"	5	7	10
901 (c) Locomotive, diesel, plastic, eight wheel, green, yellow lettering reads "Western Pacific," dummy "A" unit	25	37	50	952 Tender, 6" tin, four wheel, wedge-style, Army olive drab, marked "Army Supply Train"	30	45	60
901 (d) Locomotive, diesel, plastic, eight wheel, gray, yellow lettering reads "Western Pacific," dummy "A" unit	40	60	80	956 (a) Caboose, 7" tin, four wheel, red and gray, black and white lettering reads "Nickel Plate Road"	5	8	10
(902) (a) Locomotive, similar to 901, dummy "B" unit, green	25	37	50	956 (b) Caboose, 6" tin, four wheel, green and yellow, black lettering reads "Seaboard Air Lines"	20	30	40
(902) (b) Locomotive, similar to 901 dummy "B" unit, gray	40	60	80	(961A) Tender, 6" tin, four wheel and eight wheel, wedge-style, black, white lettering reads "New York Central," w/light on top	40	60	80
941 Tender, 7" tin, four wheel, "Mickey Mouse Meteor"	100	150	200				

Top row, left to right: No. 994 (a) Locomotive, $40; No. 941 Tender. Photo Courtesy of Richard L. MacNary.

No. 994 (b) Locomotive, $200. Photo Courtesy of Richard L. MacNary.

Mickey Mouse Meteor. Top row, left to right: No. 994 (c) Locomotive, $150; No. 941 Tender, $200. Bottom row, left to right: No 1476 Boxcar, $150; Gondola, $100; No. 691521 Caboose, $100. Photo Courtesy of Richard L. MacNary.

No. 999 (e) Locomotive, Plastimarx, $100. Photo Courtesy of Richard L. MacNary.

	C5	C7	C9
967 (a) Dump Car, plastic, four wheel, black, white lettering reads "New York Central"........	50	75	100
967 (b) Dump Car, plastic, four wheel, blue, white lettering reads "New York Central"........	50	75	100
969/980 Caboose, 7" tin, four wheel, red, yellow and black, black and yellow lettering reads "Kansas City Southern"............	75	125	150
969 Caboose, plastic, four wheel and eight wheel, red, white lettering reads "Kansas City Southern".................................	5	8	10
994 (a) Locomotive, 0-4-0, lithographed tin, nickel plate-style, black, white lettering reads "994," electric or clockwork	20	30	40
994 (b) Locomotive, 0-4-0, lithographed tin, nickel plate-style, red, white lettering reads "994," electric or clockwork.....	100	150	200
994 (c) Locomotive, 0-4-0, lithographed tin, Mickey Mouse Meteor, clockwork........	75	110	150
999 (a) Locomotive, 2-4-2, die-cast, black, early w/spoked pilot, three-piece slider pick-up	40	60	80

	C5	C7	C9
999 (b) Locomotive, 2-4-2, die-cast, black, early w/solid pilot, three-piece slider pick-up	20	30	40
999 (c) Locomotive, 2-4-2, die-cast, black, early w/solid pilot, three-piece slider pick-up, disk drivers	10	20	30
999 (d) Locomotive, lithographed tin, floor-type, red and black, clockwork...................................	100	150	200
999 (e) Locomotive, 0-4-0, plastic, black Plastimarx, made in Mexico, set	50	75	100
1007 Passenger Car, 3:16-scale, lithographed tin, observation, eight wheel, silver, red lettering reads "Western Pacific"	20	30	40
1015 Caboose, work, plastic, eight wheel, black and orange, white lettering reads "Illinois Central Gulf"	10	15	20
(1020) Railroad Trestle Bridge, steel	10	15	20
1020 Wrecker, plastic, eight wheel, black, white lettering reads "IC"..................................	10	15	20
1024 Flat Car, plastic, eight wheel, black, white lettering reads "IC"..	10	15	20

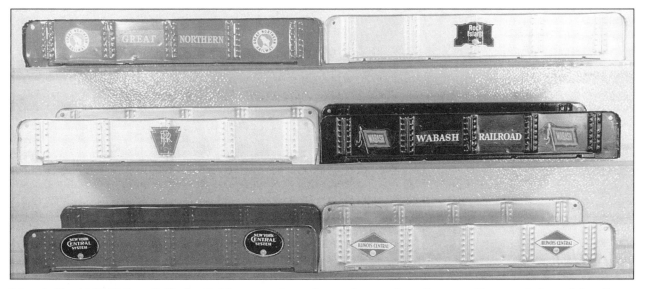

Marx's No. 1305 Railroad Girder Bridge came in various colors and road names. Top row, left to right: Great Northern, blue; Rock Island, silver. Middle row, left to right: PRR, silver; Wabash, black. Bottom row, left to right: NYC, red; Illinois Central, silver. Each is valued at $30 Photo Courtesy of Richard L. MacNary.

	C5	C7	C9
1095 (a) Locomotive, diesel, plastic, eight wheel, red and gray or silver, black lettering reads "Santa Fe," powered "A" unit	20	30	40
1095 (b) Locomotive, diesel, plastic, eight wheel, red and gray or silver, black lettering reads "Santa Fe," dummy "A" unit	20	30	40
(1096) Locomotive, diesel, plastic, eight wheel, red and gray or silver, black lettering reads "Santa Fe," dummy "B" unit	20	30	40
1182 Rite-O-Way Signs, plastic	1	2	3
1217 (a) Passenger Car, full length Vista Dome, 3:16-scale, lithographed tin, eight wheel, silver, red lettering reads "Western Pacific"	20	30	40
1217 (b) Passenger Car, 3:16-scale, coach, lithographed tin, eight wheel, silver, red lettering reads "Western Pacific"	40	60	80
1231 (a) Caboose, plastic, four wheel, blue, white lettering reads "Missouri Pacific"	10	15	20
1231 (a) Caboose, plastic, four wheel, white, black lettering reads "Missouri Pacific"	8	12	16
1235 Caboose, 7" tin, four wheel, red and silver, white lettering reads "Southern Pacific"	2	4	6
1281 Rite-O-Way Signs, plastic	1	2	3
(1305) Railroad Girder Bridge, stamped steel, various RR names	15	22	30
(1404) Block Signal, stamped steel, five lights	10	20	30
(1405) Block Signal, stamped steel, "Trainmaster" w/four-button controller, three lights	20	30	40
(1430) Station, lithographed tin, "Union Station," 12" x 6-3/4" x 3-1/2"	10	15	20
(1440) Grade Crossing Signal Man, tin and plastic, automatic	10	20	30

No. 1440 Grade Crossing Signal Man, $30. Photo Courtesy of Richard L. MacNary.

	C5	C7	C9
1476 Boxcar, 7" tin, four wheel, yellow w/blue frame, Mickey Mouse characters	75	110	150
1500 Caboose, plastic, eight wheel, orange, black lettering reads "Rio Grande"	10	15	20
(1614) Automatic Dumping Unit, lithographed tin, arms swing out to dump car no. 567, 3-3/4" x 2-3/4"	40	60	80
1621 Locomotive, 2-4-2, plastic, "New Haven"	10	15	20
1654 Caboose, plastic, orange and red, marked, "Union Pacific"	5	7	10
1666 (a) Locomotive, 2-4-2, plastic, gray, w/smoke	20	30	40
1666 (b) Locomotive, 2-4-2, plastic, black, w/smoke	10	12	15
1678 Hopper, 6" tin, four wheel, olive w/black and silver frame or all black frame, black lettering reads "General Coal Co."	10	15	20

	C5	C7	C9
1796 (a) Flat Car, w/missile launcher, plastic, four wheel, white, blue lettering	20	30	40
1796 (b) Flat Car, w/missile launcher, deluxe eight wheel, plastic, four wheel, white, blue lettering	30	45	60
1798 Locomotive, diesel switcher, plastic, four wheel, red-white-blue, white lettering reads "Cape Canaveral Express"	50	75	100
1799 (a) Gondola, plastic, four wheel, blue, white lettering reads "USAX Danger"	15	22	30
1799 (b) Gondola, plastic, eight wheel, red, white lettering reads "USAX Danger"	20	30	40
1829 (a) Locomotive, 4-6-4, plastic, black	25	37	50
1829 (b) Locomotive, 4-6-4, plastic, black, w/smoke	30	45	60

	C5	C7	C9
1935 (a) US Mail Car, 6" tin, four wheel, green w/black and silver frame, yellow lettering reads "NYC" and "US Mail Car 1935"	25	37	50
1935 (b) US Mail Car, 6" tin, four and eight wheel, red w/black and silver frame, yellow lettering reads "NYC" and "US Mail Car 1935"	15	22	30
1950 (a) Boxcar, 3:16-scale, lithographed tin, eight wheel, green, yellow lettering reads "GAEX-DF" on yellow diagonal stripe	20	30	40
1950 (b) Boxcar, 3:16-scale, lithographed tin, eight wheel, green, yellow lettering reads "DF" on yellow diagonal stripe	20	30	40
1951 Caboose, 7" tin, eight wheel, red, black lettering reads "AT&SF"	10	15	20

Top row, left to right: No. 1798 Locomotive, $100; No. 1796 (b) Flat car ""Rocket Launch,"" $60. Middle row, left to right: No. 1799 (a) USAX Gondola, $30; Automatic Light Generator. Bottom row, left to right: Missile Launcher & Generator; No. 1963 Caboose, $200. Photo Courtesy of Richard L. MacNary.

	C5	C7	C9
1958 AT&SF Work Caboose, plastic	1	2	3
1961 Caboose, plastic, red and black, white lettering reads "Rock Island"	1	2	3
1961 (b) Caboose, plastic, yellow and gray, marked "Santa Fe"	5	7	10
1963 Work Caboose, plastic, eight wheel, blue frame, red shed, white tank; white lettering reads "USAX Missile Express," red lettering on tank reads "Rocket Fuel"	100	150	200
(1972) (a) Caboose, plastic, red, marked "Santa Fe"	1	2	3
(1972) (b) Caboose, plastic, brown, marked "Santa Fe"	1	2	3
1977 (a) Caboose, plastic, four and eight wheel, red, white lettering reads "Santa Fe"	5	10	15

	C5	C7	C9
1977 (b) Caboose, plastic, eight wheel, red, yellow and gray, white lettering reads "Santa Fe"	10	15	20
1988 Caboose, plastic, four wheel, orange, black lettering reads "Bessemer & Lake Erie"	10	15	20
1998 (a) Locomotive, diesel switcher, plastic, eight wheel, maroon, yellow lettering reads "AT&SF"	20	30	40
1998 (b) Locomotive, diesel switcher, plastic, eight wheel, black, white lettering reads "AT&SF"	40	60	80
1998 (c) Locomotive, diesel switcher, plastic, eight wheel, blue, white lettering reads "All State"	50	75	100
1998 (d) Locomotive, diesel switcher, plastic, eight wheel, yellow and gray, red lettering reads "Union Pacific"	30	45	60

First row, left to right: No. 1829 (a) Locomotive, $50; No. 2731 Tender, $20. Second row, left to right: No. 284 Tank car, $20; No. 147815 Boxcar, $30. Third row, left to right: No. 3152 (a) Passenger car, $40; No. 4427 Caboose, $10. Fourth row, left to right: No. 3152 (c) Vista Dome, $40; No. 3197 (a) Observation car, $40. Photo Courtesy of Richard L. MacNary.

Top row, left to right: No. 1998 Locomotive, powered; No. 1998 Locomotive, dummy; $40, each. Middle row, left to right: No. 51170 (a) Gondola, $30; No. 4528 (b) Flat car w/two red tractors, $40. Bottom row, left to right: No. 54099 (a) Stock car, $40; No. 3824 Caboose, $40. Photo Courtesy of Richard L. MacNary.

Top row, left to right: No. 1998 (e) Locomotive, powered; No. 1998 Locomotive, dummy; $40, each. Middle row, left to right: No. 4528 (c) Flat car w/two silver tractors, $60; No. 4528 (b) Flat car w/two red tractors, $40; No 4528 (d) Flat car w/ two green tractors, $150. Bottom row, left to right: No. 28236 (a) Hopper, $40; No. 28236 (c) Hopper, $60; No. 17858 Caboose, $30. Photo Courtesy of Richard L. MacNary.

Top row, left to right: No. 2002(a) Locomotive, $60; No. 2003 Caboose, $60. Middle row, left to right: No. C-635 Caboose, $16; No. 18326 (a) Caboose, $$30. Bottom row, left to right: No. 4000 (a) Locomotive, $100; No. 4000 (b) Locomotive, $100. Photo Courtesy of Richard L. MacNary.

	C5	C7	C9
1998 (e) Locomotive, diesel switcher, plastic, eight wheel, gray and red, white lettering reads "Rock Island"	20	30	40
(2002) (a) Hand Car, plastic, brown base, w/two men	40	60	80
(2002) (b) Hand Car, plastic, red base, w/two men	50	75	100
2002 (a) Locomotive, diesel, plastic, eight wheel, black, red and white lettering reads "New Haven," powered "A" unit	30	45	60
2002 (b) Locomotive, diesel, plastic, eight wheel, black, red and white lettering reads "New Haven," powered "A" unit	30	45	60
(2003) Locomotive, diesel, plastic, eight wheel, black, red and white lettering reads "New Haven," powered "A" unit, dummy "B" unit	30	45	60
2028 Flintstones Bedrock Handcar	100	150	200
2071 Passenger Car, 6" tin, four wheel, silver, blue lettering reads "New York Central"	20	30	40

	C5	C7	C9
2072 Passenger Car, 6" tin, observation, four wheel, silver, blue lettering reads "New York Central"	20	30	40
2124 Rail Diesel Car, plastic, eight wheel, passenger, gray, silver, black lettering reads "Boston & Maine"	100	150	200
2130 Caboose/Work, plastic, eight wheel, olive drab, white lettering reads "USA" and star	30	45	60
2225 (a) Caboose, plastic, eight wheel, bay window, dark red, white lettering reads "Santa Fe"	20	30	40
2225 (b) Caboose, plastic, eight wheel, bay window, orange, black lettering reads "All State"	50	75	100
2225 (c) Caboose, plastic, eight wheel, bay window, blue, white lettering reads "All State"	50	75	100
2226 Caboose, plastic, bay window, red, white lettering reads "Santa Fe"	1	2	3

No. 2260 Guide-A-Train, $40. Photo Courtesy of Richard L. MacNary.

Top row, left to right: No. 2532 (b) Tank car, $40; No. 588 (c) Locomotive, $50. Bottom row, left to right: No. 467110 (a) Boxcar, $20; No. 21913 Hopper, $10. Photo Courtesy of Richard L. MacNary.

	C5	C7	C9
2236 Caboose, plastic, eight wheel, dark red, white lettering reads "Canadian Pacific"	20	30	40
2236 Gondola, plastic, eight wheel, Army, olive drab, white lettering reads "USA"	10	15	20
(2246) Flat Car, plastic, deluxe eight wheel, Army olive drab w/plastic jeep, truck, etc.	30	45	60
2260 Guide-A-Train, plastic, set	20	30	40
2532 (a) Tank Car, 3:16-scale, lithographed tin, eight wheel, green, white lettering reads "Cities Service"	20	30	40
2532 (b) Tank Car, plastic, four and eight wheel, green, white lettering reads "Cities Service"	5	10	15

	C5	C7	C9
2552 Locomotive, 2-8-2 kit, plastic snap-together 5:16-scale	60	90	120

No. 2552 Locomotive, Fix-All, $120. Photo Courtesy of Richard L. MacNary.

	C5	C7	C9
(2572) Ramp Car, 6" tin, 3:16-scale, eight wheel trucks, ARMY olive drab w/end unloading ramp and OD truck	100	150	200
(2572) Ramp Car, 6" tin, 3:16-scale, eight wheel, Army olive drab, w/end unloading ramp and OD truck	100	150	200
2700 (a) Flat Car, 3:16-scale, lithographed tin, eight wheel, black, white lettering reads "NKP," w/three sets of stakes	20	30	40
2700 (b) Flat Car, 3:16-scale, lithographed tin, eight wheel, black, white lettering reads "NKP," no stakes	50	75	100
2731 Tender, plastic, deluxe eight wheel, black, white lettering reads "Santa Fe" and "2731"	10	15	20
2824 Flat Car, plastic, deluxe eight wheel, Army olive drab, white lettering, missile launcher	30	45	60
2824 Gondola, plastic, eight wheel, missile launcher, yellow, red lettering reads "USAF"	50	75	100
2858 Boxcar, plastic, deluxe eight wheel, Army olive drab, white lettering reads "Bureau of Ordinance"	100	150	200
(2889) Station, whistling, lithographed tin, battery operated, 9" x 5-1/2" x 2-5/8"	10	15	20
2900 Station, lithographed tin, lamp post, mechanical gate, "Glendale Freight Depot," 13-5/8" x 10" x 5"	100	150	200

No. 2900 Glendale Freight Depot, $200. Photo Courtesy of Richard L. MacNary.

No. 2940 Grand Central Station, $120. Photo Courtesy of Richard L. MacNary.

	C5	C7	C9
(2940) Station, lithographed tin, illuminated, "Grand Central Station," 17" x 11" x 4-3/4"	60	90	120
(2959/2970) Station, whistling, lithographed tin, "Girard," 9" x 5-1/2" x 5"	20	30	40
(2980) Station, diesel horn, lithographed tin, "Oak Park," 9" x 5-1/2" x 5"	30	45	60
3000 Locomotive, 0-4-0 and 2-4-2, Canadian Pacific-style, various boiler colors and side boards	40	60	80
3000 Locomotive, riding floor toy, stamped steel, red or gray front wheel controlled by handle in boiler top	50	100	150

No. 3000 Locomotive, riding floor toy, $150. Photo Courtesy of Richard L. MacNary.

	C5	C7	C9
3152 (a) Passenger Car, 3:16-scale, lithographed tin, eight wheel, silver, red lettering reads "Santa Fe"	20	30	40
3152 (b) Passenger Car, 3:16-scale, lithographed tin, eight wheel, silver, red lettering reads "Santa Fe," solid window	20	30	40

Left to right: No. 2980 Oak Park station, $60; No. 2889 Whistling station, $20. Photo Courtesy of Richard L. MacNary.

Top row, left to right: No. 3000 Locomotive, $80; Canadian Pacific Tender; No. 248 Passenger car, $150. Front, left to right: No. 249 Passenger car, $150; No. 251 Passenger car, $150; No. 252 Passenger car, $150; No. 253 Passenger car, $150. Photo Courtesy of Richard L. MacNary.

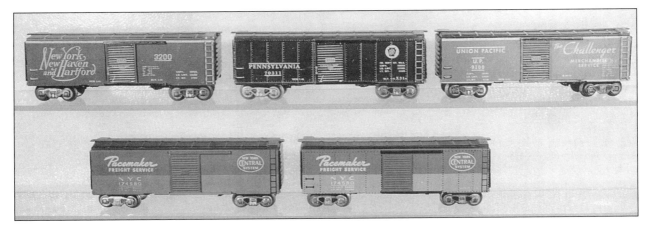

Top row, left to right: No. 3200 (a) Boxcar, $40; No. 70311 Boxcar, $60; No. 9100 Boxcar, $40. Bottom row, left to right: No. 174580 Boxcar, $40; No. 174580 Boxcar, $40. Photo Courtesy of Richard L. MacNary.

Top row, left to right: No. 4000 (a) Locomotive, $1,000; No. 3557 (b) Passenger car, $400. Bottom row, left to right: No. 3557 (b); No. 3558 (b) Passenger car, $400. Photo Courtesy of Richard L. MacNary.

	C5	C7	C9
3152 (c) Passenger Car, 3:16-scale, lithographed tin, eight wheel, silver, red lettering reads "Santa Fe," vista dome	20	30	40
3152 (d) Passenger Car, 3:16-scale, lithographed tin, eight wheel, silver, red lettering reads "Santa Fe," vista dome w/solid windows	10	15	20
3197 (a) Passenger Car, 3:16-scale, lithographed tin, observation, eight wheel, silver, red lettering reads "Santa Fe"	20	30	40
3197 (b) Passenger Car, 3:16-scale, lithographed tin, observation, eight wheel, silver, red lettering reads "Santa Fe," w/solid windows	20	30	40
3200 (a) Boxcar, 3:16-scale, lithographed tin, eight wheel, brown, white lettering reads "NY, NH & H"	20	30	40
3280 (b) Boxcar, plastic, eight wheel, orange, black lettering reads "Santa Fe"	2	4	6
3280 (c) Boxcar, plastic, four wheel, white, black or red lettering reads "Santa Fe"	2	4	6
3281 (a) Boxcar, plastic, green, white lettering reads "SFRD" and "Santa Fe"	4	6	8
3281 (b) Boxcar, plastic, orange, black lettering reads "SFRD" and "Santa Fe"	3	4	5

	C5	C7	C9
3550 Wrecker, 3:16-scale, lithographed tin, eight wheel, silver w/red crane, blue lettering "New York Central"	50	75	100
(3550) Wrecker, 3:16-scale, lithographed tin, eight wheel, gray and black w/plastic top	30	45	60
3557 (a) Passenger Car, 3:16-scale, lithographed tin, eight wheel, all silver, blue lettering reads "New York Central"	100	150	200
3557 (b) Passenger Car, 3:16-scale, lithographed tin, eight wheel, all silver, blue lettering reads "New York Central," solid windows	200	300	400
3557 (c) Passenger Car, 3:16-scale, lithographed tin, eight wheel, all silver, blue lettering reads "New York Central," vista dome	100	150	200
3557 (d) Passenger Car, 3:16-scale, lithographed tin, eight wheel, all silver, blue lettering reads "New York Central," vista dome, solid windows	200	300	400
3558 (a) Passenger Car, 3:16-scale, lithographed tin, eight wheel, observation, silver, blue lettering reads "NYC"	100	150	200
3558 (b) Passenger Car, 3:16-scale, lithographed tin, eight wheel, observation, silver, blue lettering reads "NYC," solid windows	200	300	400

Top row, left to right: No. 4000 (f) Locomotive, $80; No. 4000 (g) Locomotive, $20. Bottom row, left to right: No. 557 (d) Montclair, $40; No. 557 (d) Bogata, $40; No. 558 Observation car, $40. Photo Courtesy of Richard L. MacNary.

	C5	C7	C9
(3561) Flat Car, 3:16-scale, lithographed tin, base, eight wheel, red and black, w/plastic searchlight................................	50	75	100
(3563) Lumber Car, 3:16-scale lithographed tin base, eight wheel, black, w/lumber load.....	20	30	40
(3591A) Searchlight, 3:16-scale, eight wheel, black frame w/large red plastic light	50	75	100
3824 (a) Caboose, 6" tin, four wheel, yellow, orange and brown w/black frame, orange lettering reads "Union Pacific"	1	2	3
3824 (b) Caboose, 6" tin, four wheel, yellow, orange and brown w/brown frame, orange lettering reads "Union Pacific"	10	15	20
3824 (c) Caboose, plastic, eight wheel, dark red w/bay window, white lettering reads "Union Pacific"	20	30	40
3824 (d) Caboose, work, plastic, eight wheel, dark red w/bay window, white lettering reads "Union Pacific".........................	15	22	30
3827 Tank Car, plastic, green, white lettering reads "Sinclair"	1	2	3
3855 Caboose, 7" tin, four wheel, red, gray and white, white lettering reads "Monon"	20	30	40
3880 Railroad Station, plastic, 11-3/4" x 6-1/4" x 4-5/8"	10	15	20

	C5	C7	C9
3900 (a) Caboose, plastic, eight wheel, orange or yellow, black lettering reads "Union Pacific" ..	10	15	20
3900 (b) Caboose, plastic, eight wheel, brown, white lettering reads "Union Pacific"	10	15	20
3900 (c) Caboose, plastic, four wheel, yellow, black lettering reads "Union Pacific"	20	30	40
3903 Caboose, plastic, bay window, red, white lettering reads "Union Pacific"	1	2	3
4000 (a) Locomotive, diesel, plastic, eight wheel, black, white lettering reads "New York Central," powered "A" unit	50	75	100
4000 (b) Locomotive, diesel, plastic, eight wheel, black, white lettering reads "New York Central," dummy "A" unit	50	75	100
4000 (c) Locomotive, diesel, plastic, eight wheel, green, white lettering reads "New York Central," powered "A" unit	75	110	150
4000 (d) Locomotive, diesel, plastic, eight wheel, green, white lettering reads "New York Central," dummy "A" unit	75	100	150

Top row, left to right: No. 4588 Caboose, $40; No. 4589 Caboose, $60. Middle row, left to right: No. 4590 Caboose, $40; No. 586 Caboose, $10. Bottom row, left to right: No 4427 Caboose with black lettering, $10; No. 4427 Caboose with white lettering, $10. Photo Courtesy of Richard L. MacNary.

	C5	C7	C9
4000 (e) Locomotive, diesel, small lithographed tin, four wheel, green, yellow lettering reads "Seaboard," powered "A" unit	40	60	80
4000 (f) Locomotive, diesel, small lithographed tin, four wheel, green, yellow lettering reads "Seaboard," dummy "A" unit	40	60	80
4000 (g) Locomotive, diesel "A" unit, plastic, black, marked "NYC"	10	15	20
4015 Reefer, plastic, white, marked, "NYC"	6	8	10
(4414, 16, 18) Station, lithographed tin, "Glendale," 20-5/8" x 10" x 6"	15	22	30
4427 Caboose, plastic, eight wheel, red , white or black lettering reads "Santa Fe"	5	7	10
4484 Boxcar, 7" tin, four wheel, blue, white and red, white and blue lettering reads "BAR" and "State of Maine"	20	30	40
4485/4500 Boxcar, 6" tin, four wheel, blue, white and red, white and blue lettering reads "BAR" and "State of Maine"	30	45	60

	C5	C7	C9
4528 (a) Flat Car, plastic, deluxe eight wheel, maroon, yellow lettering reads "Erie," w/searchlight	20	30	40
4528 (b) Flat Car, w/two red tractors	20	30	40
4528 (c) Flat Car, w/two silver tractors	30	45	60
4528 (d) Flat Car, Orange, w/two green tractors	75	110	150
4546 (a) Caboose, plastic, deluxe eight wheel, red, black lettering reads "New York Central"	10	15	20
(4556) (b) Caboose, plastic, four wheel and eight wheel, red white lettering reads "Southern Pacific"	1	2	3
(4556) (c) Caboose, plastic, four wheel, green white lettering reads "Southern Pacific"	2	4	6
(4564) Caboose, plastic, eight wheel, red, white or black lettering reads "New York Central"	5	8	10

Top row: Two versions of No. 5545 Flat car, $30, each. **Middle row, left to right:** No. 4583 Flat car, $60; No. 4566 Flat car, $40. **Bottom row, left to right:** Two versions of No. 5545 Flat car. Photo Courtesy of Richard L. MacNary.

	C5	C7	C9
4566 Flat Car, plastic, deluxe, eight wheel, drop center, w/two cable reels, blue, white lettering reads "C.W.E.X."	20	30	40
4571 (a) Flat Car, plastic, deluxe eight wheel, red, white lettering reads "W.E.C.X.," w/searchlight.....	20	30	40
4571 (b) Flat Car, plastic, deluxe eight wheel, white, lettering reads "U.S.A.F.," w/searchlight.....	50	75	100
4571 (c) Flat Car, plastic, deluxe eight wheel, maroon, white lettering reads "A.T.&S.F.," w/searchlight.....	15	22	20
4581 Flat Car, plastic, deluxe eight wheel, red w/white lettering reads "B.K.X.," w/searchlight.....	10	15	20
4583 Flat Car, plastic, deluxe eight wheel, black w/white lettering reads "G.E.X.," w/searchlight.....	10	15	20
4586 Caboose, plastic, work type, eight wheel, red w/white lettering reads "Union Pacific," w/light.....	20	30	40

	C5	C7	C9
(4587) Caboose, plastic, work type, eight wheel, red w/white lettering reads "A.T.&S.F." w/light.....	20	30	40
(4588) Caboose, plastic, work type, eight wheel, red w/white lettering reads "All State," w/light.....	20	30	40
(4589) Caboose, plastic, work type, eight wheel, red w/white lettering reads "New York Central," no light, w/tank.....	30	45	60
4590 Caboose, plastic, work type, eight wheel, red w/white lettering reads "A.T.&S.F.," w/light.....	20	30	40
5011/5026 Baggage Car, 6" tin, four wheel, blue and gray, white lettering reads "New York Central" and "US Mail"...	50	75	100
(5424) RR Freight Terminal, lithographed tin, some come w/plastic trucks and accessories, 28" x 11" x 8"........	50	75	100
5532 (a) Gondola, plastic, eight wheel, blue, white lettering reads "All State"	5	10	15

Top row: Two versions of No. 5553 (b) tank car, $40, each. Middle row: No. 284 Tank car, $20; No. 5553 (a) Tank Car, $100; No. 5553 (c) Tank car, $400. Bottom row, left to right: No. 5543 (a) Flat car, $$15; No. 5543 (c) Flat car, $60; No. 5543 (b) $40. Photo Courtesy of Richard L. MacNary.

	C5	C7	C9
5532 (b) Gondola, plastic, four wheel, blue, white lettering reads "All State"	20	30	40
(5543) (a) Tank Car, plastic, deluxe eight wheel, two maroon tanks, white lettering reads "All State"	30	45	60
(5543) (b) Tank Car, plastic, deluxe eight wheel, blue and orange, black lettering reads "Gulf"	50	75	100
(5543) (c) Tank Car, plastic, deluxe eight wheel, maroon, green and white lettering reads "Cities Service"	20	30	40
5545 (a) Flat Car, plastic, deluxe eight wheel, maroon, white lettering reads "C.B.&Q" and orange "All State" trailers	40	60	80
5545 (b) Flat Car, plastic, deluxe eight wheel, silver or white, white lettering reads "C.B.&Q" and orange "Burlington" trailers	30	45	60
5545 (c) Flat Car, plastic, deluxe eight wheel, maroon, white lettering reads "C.B.&Q" and "Erie" girders	15	22	30

	C5	C7	C9
(5553) (a) Tank Car, plastic, deluxe eight wheel, three domes, blue and white, red lettering reads "Exxon"	50	75	100
(5553) (b) Tank Car, plastic, deluxe eight wheel, three domes, black and blue, white lettering reads "All State"	20	30	40
(5553) (c) Tank Car, plastic, deluxe eight wheel, three domes, cream or white, red lettering reads "Milk"	200	300	400
5563 Caboose, 6" tin, four wheel, black, yellow and red, red and yellow lettering reads "Kansas City Southern"	20	30	40
5586 Caboose, work-type, plastic, eight wheel, red-brown, yellow lettering reads "Western Pacific"	20	30	40
5590 (a) Wrecker, plastic, deluxe eight wheel, black, white lettering reads "New York Central"	30	45	60
5590 (b) Wrecker, plastic, deluxe eight wheel, black, white lettering reads "New York Central," w/roof searchlight	40	60	80

Left to right: No. 5553 (c) Tank car, $400; No. 54099 (d) Stock car, $150. Photo Courtesy of Richard L. MacNary.

Top row, left to right: No. 5590 (a) Wrecker without light, $60; No. 5590 (b) Wrecker with light, $80. Bottom row, left to right: No. 21429 Hopper, $15; No. 20309 Gondola, $40. Photo Courtesy of Richard L. MacNary.

Top row, left to right: No. 5595 Boxcar, $30; No 249319(b) Boxcar, $30; No. 249319 (a) Boxcar, $30. Middle row, left to right: No. 259199 Boxcar, $60; No. 186028 Boxcar, $30; No. 43461 Boxcar, $30. Bottom row, left to right: No. 176893, Boxcar, $30; No. 18918 Boxcar, $30; No. 77003 Boxcar, $30. Photo Courtesy of Richard L. MacNary.

	C5	C7	C9
5594 Flat Car, plastic, eight wheel, operating, maroon, yellow lettering reads "Erie"	10	15	20
5595 Boxcar, plastic, deluxe eight wheel, operating, cream, red lettering reads "Farm Master Brand"	15	22	30
(5772) Locomotive, Diesel F3, plastic, black, white lettering reads "New York Central"	10	15	20
6000 Locomotive, diesel, lithographed tin, eight wheel powered "A" unit	10	15	20
6000 Locomotive, diesel, lithographed tin, eight wheel, dummy "A" unit	10	15	20
6028 Erie Flat Car, w/side racks	1	2	3
6096 Locomotive, 4-6-4, plastic, black, white lettering and stripe, w/NYC tender	30	45	60
(6150) Wrecker, plastic, black, white "NYC" emblem	5	7	10
6420 (a) Roof, whistle	20	30	40

	C5	C7	C9
(6420) Trestle Bridge	—	—	1
6938 Locomotive, GP-7, plastic, black and gold, gold lettering reads "Northern Pacific"	20	30	40
7210 Boxcar, plastic, green, white and yellow lettering reads "Railway Express Agency"	5	8	10
8330 Western Loco, floor toy, lithographed tin w/plastic cow catcher, Hong Kong	30	45	60
9100 Boxcar, 3:16-scale, lithographed tin, eight wheel, red and black, white lettering reads "Union Pacific"	20	30	40
(9553) (a) Tank Car, plastic, eight wheel, blue, white lettering reads "All State"	10	15	20
(9553) (b) Tank Car, plastic, eight wheel, white, red lettering reads "All State Rocket Fuel"	20	30	40
(9553) (c) Tank Car, plastic, four and eight wheel, orange, black lettering reads "Gulf"	20	30	40

Top row, left to right: No. 6096 Locomotive, $60; Sante Fe Tender. Middle Row: X415 (a) Tank car, $10. Bottom row, left to right: No. 3281 (b) Boxcar, $5; No. 1961 Caboose, $10. Photo Courtesy of Richard L. MacNary.

	C5	C7	C9

No. 8330 Western Loco, $60. Photo Courtesy of Richard L. MacNary.

	C5	C7	C9
M10,000 (a) Locomotive, streamliner, lithographed tin, four drivers, four trailing wheels, tan and cream, red lettering reads "Union Pacific," electric	40	60	80
M10,000 (b) Locomotive, streamliner, lithographed tin, four drivers, four trailing wheels, maroon and silver, black lettering reads "Union Pacific," electric	50	75	100
M10,000 (c) Locomotive, streamliner, lithographed tin, four drivers, four trailing wheels, green and cream, red lettering reads "Union Pacific," electric	40	60	80
M10,000 (d) Locomotive, streamliner, lithographed tin, four drivers, four trailing wheels, brown and yellow, red lettering reads "Union Pacific," electric	50	75	100
M10,003 Locomotive, streamliner, lithographed tin, one unit, tan and cream, black lettering reads "Union Pacific," clockwork	100	150	200
M10,005 (a) Locomotive, streamliner, lithographed tin, four drivers, silver and red, blue lettering reads "Union Pacific," electric and clockwork	25	37	50
M10,005 (b) Locomotive, streamliner, lithographed tin, four drivers, yellow and brown, orange lettering reads "Union Pacific," electric and clockwork	25	37	50
M10,005 (c) Locomotive, streamliner, lithographed tin, four drivers, white/cream and green, grean and orange lettering reads "Union Pacific," electric and clockwork	25	37	50

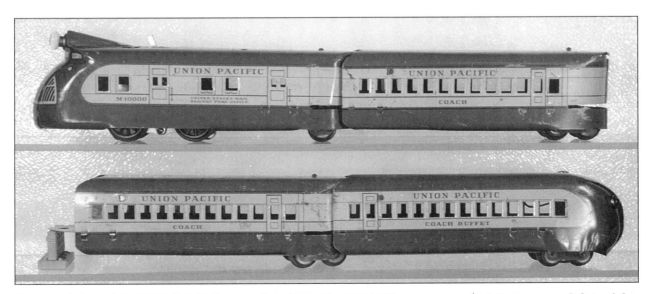

Top row, left to right: M10,000 (b) Locomotive, $100; No. 657 (c) Passenger car, $16. Bottom row, left to right: No. 657 (c) Passenger car; No. 658 (c) Passenger car, $16. Photo Courtesy of Richard L. MacNary.

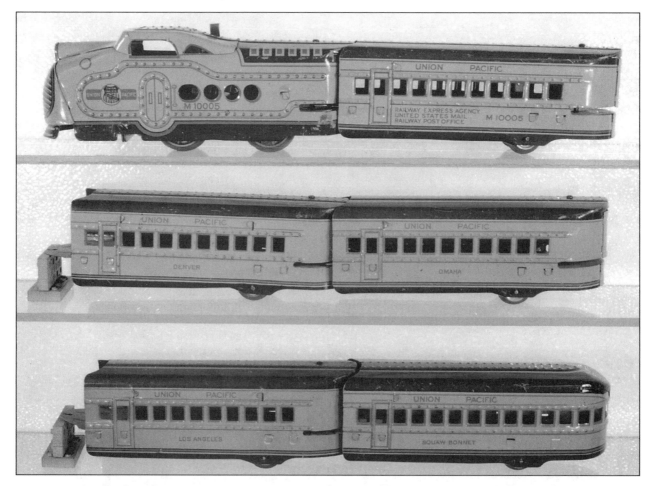

Top row, left to right: No. M10,005 (b) Passenger car, $50; No. 657 (l) Passenger car, $20. Middle row, left to right: No. 657 (o) Passenger car, $20; No. 657 (n) Passenger car, $20. Bottom car, left to right: No. 657 (m) Passenger car, $20; No. 657 (f) Passenger car, $20. Photo Courtesy of Richard L. MacNary.

	C5	C7	C9
10049 Flat Car, w/lumber load, plastic, black, white lettering reads "LV"	2	4	6
10961/10976 Refrigerator Car, 6" tin, four wheel, yellow w/gray roof, black lettering reads "Fruit Growers Express"	60	90	120
11874 Boxcar, plastic, green or red, white lettering reads "Great Northern"	5	8	10
13079 Hopper, 3:16-scale, lithographed tin, eight wheel, black, white lettering reads "LNE"	30	45	60
13549 Stock Car, 3:16-scale, lithographed tin, four wheel, orange and yellow, brown lettering reads "A.T.&S.F."	30	45	60

	C5	C7	C9
13795 Stock Car, plastic, eight wheel, yellow, black lettering reads "A.T.&S.F."	5	8	10
13795 (a) Stock Car, plastic, four and eight wheel, brown, white lettering reads "A.T.&S.F."	2	4	6
13795 (b) Stock Car, plastic, eight wheel, maroon/red, white lettering reads "A.T.&S.F."	2	4	6
17858 (a) Caboose, plastic, eight wheel, bay window, red, white lettering reads "Rock Island"	15	22	30
17858 (b) Caboose, plastic, four and eight wheel, bay window, red, white lettering reads "Rock Island"	5	10	15

Top row, left to right: No. 13079 LNE Hopper, $60; two No. 17899 T&P Gondola, $40, each. Middle row, left to right: No. 254000 B&O Gondola, $30; No. 71499 NYC&S+L Gondola, $40; No. 347000 PRR Gondola, $40. Bottom row, left to right: No. 44572 (b) C&O Gondola, $15; No. 44572 (a) Gondola, $15. Photo Courtesy of Richard L. MacNary.

	C5	C7	C9
17899 Gondola, 3:16-scale, lithographed tin, eight wheel, gray w/white lettering reads "T&P"	20	30	40
18326 (a) Caboose, plastic, four wheel and eight wheel, red, white lettering reads "New York Central" some read "Pacemaker"	15	22	30
18326 (b) Caboose, plastic, four wheel and eight wheel, brown, white lettering reads "New York Central" some read "Pacemaker"	10	15	20
18326 (c) Caboose, plastic, four wheel and eight wheel, yellow, black lettering reads "New York Central" some read "Pacemaker"	15	22	30
18326 (d) Caboose, plastic, four wheel and eight wheel, white/cream, black lettering reads "New York Central" some read "Pacemaker"	10	15	20
18326 (e) Caboose, plastic, eight wheel, white, black and green, red lettering reads "New York Central" some read "Pacemaker"	15	22	30

	C5	C7	C9
(18326) (f) Caboose, plastic, four wheel and eight wheel, orange, black lettering reads "New York Central" some read "Pacemaker"	5	8	10
18326 (g) Caboose, plastic, four wheel and eight wheel, green, white lettering reads "New York Central" some read "Pacemaker"	5	8	10
18326 (h) Caboose, plastic, four wheel and eight wheel, white, black lettering reads "New York Central" some read "Pacemaker"	10	15	20
18326 (i) Caboose, plastic, four wheel, yellow, black lettering reads "New York Central" some read "Pacemaker"	5	8	10
18918 Boxcar, plastic, deluxe eight wheel, brown, white lettering reads "Great Northern"	15	22	30
19847 (a) Tank Car, 6" tin, four wheel, black, white lettering reads "Sinclair"	30	45	60
19847 (b) Tank Car, 6" tin, four wheel, green, white lettering reads "Sinclair"	20	30	40

Left to right: No. 19847 (a) Tank car, $60; No. 10966 FGEX Reefer; No. 5563 Caboose, $40. Photo Courtesy of Richard L. MacNary.

Left to right: No. 20053 Boxcar red, No 20053 Boxcar, brown, $60, each; No. 225 (c) Caboose, $100. Photo Courtesy of Richard L. MacNary.

	C5	C7	C9
20053 Boxcar, plastic, deluxe eight wheel, dark red or brown, white lettering reads "Seaboard"	30	45	60
20102 (a) Caboose, 6" tin, four wheel, red and gray body, white lettering reads "NYC"	5	8	10
20102 (b) Caboose, 6" tin, four wheel, red and gray body, white lettering reads "NYC," w/light	30	45	60
20102 (c) Caboose, 3:16-scale, lithographed tin, eight wheel red and gray, white lettering reads "NYC"	5	8	10
20110/20124 Caboose, 7" tin, four and eight wheel, red and gray, white "NYC" and "Pacemaker"	20	30	40
20295 Caboose, plastic, black and red, white lettering reads "NYC"	5	8	10
20298 Caboose, plastic, bay window, red, white lettering reads "NYC"	5	8	10
20309 (a) Gondola, plastic deluxe eight wheel, brown, "L&N"	20	30	40

	C5	C7	C9
20309 (b) Gondola, plastic deluxe eight wheel, yellow, "L&N"	15	22	30
21429 Hopper, plastic, deluxe, eight wheel, black w/yellow, orange lettering reads "Lehigh Valley"	8	12	15
21913 (a) Hopper, plastic, four and eight wheel, black, yellow lettering reads "Lehigh Valley"	5	8	10
21913 (b) Hopper, plastic, four and eight wheel, blue, white lettering reads "Lehigh Valley"	5	8	10
21913 (c) Hopper, plastic, four and eight wheel, orange, black lettering reads "Lehigh Valley"	5	8	10
21913 (d) Hopper, plastic, four and eight wheel, red, white lettering reads "Lehigh Valley"	5	8	10
21913 (e) Hopper, plastic, four wheel, green, white lettering reads "Lehigh Valley"	5	8	10

	C5	C7	C9
25000 Hopper, plastic, black w/orange lettering reads "LV" (Lionel's Number).....................	1	2	3
28233 Hopper, plastic, brown, white lettering reads "Virginian"	1	3	5
28236 (a) Hopper, plastic, deluxe eight wheel, brown, white lettering reads "Virginian"........	20	30	40
28236 (b) Hopper, plastic, deluxe eight wheel, maroon, white lettering reads "Virginian"........	25	37	50
28236 (c) Hopper, plastic, deluxe eight wheel, red, white lettering reads "Virginian"......................	30	45	60
28500 High Side Gondola, 6" tin, four wheel, green, silver lettering reads "Lehigh Valley"........................	5	8	10
31055 Caboose, 6" tin, four wheel, red and gray, white lettering reads "Monon"...........................	20	30	40
33618 Caboose, plastic, bay window, red and white, marked "Erie"	5	8	10
33773 Flat Car, 3:16-scale, lithographed tin, eight wheel, black, white lettering reads "B&M"	20	30	40
34178 Boxcar, plastic, eight wheel, green, white lettering reads "Great Northern"	10	15	20
35461 Refrigerator, 3:16-scale, lithographed tin, eight wheel, yellow sides w/brown roof, black lettering reads "PFE"	30	45	60
36000 (a) Gondola, 7" tin, four wheel, brown, white lettering reads "C&O"...........................	5	7	10

	C5	C7	C9
36000 (c) Gondola, plastic, blue, white lettering reads "C&O".....	1	2	3
36000 (c) Gondola, plastic, black, white lettering reads "C&O".....	1	2	3
36000 (d) Gondola, plastic, red, white lettering reads "C&O".....	1	2	3
37950/37959 Boxcar, 7" tin, four wheel, red and gray w/gray roof, black lettering reads "Pennsylvania" and "Merchandise Service"	30	45	60
37960/37975 Boxcar, 6" tin, four wheel, red and gray w/gray roof, black lettering reads "Merchandise Service" and "Pennsylvania," also one without number	40	60	80
39520 (a) Flat Car, plastic, deluxe eight wheel, tool box generator, winch, maroon, yellow lettering reads "S.P."	30	45	60
39520 (b) Flat Car, plastic, deluxe eight wheel, tool box generator, winch, black, white lettering reads "S.P."	30	45	60
40397 Boxcar, plastic, black, white and red lettering reads "New Haven"	5	8	10
43461 Boxcar, plastic, deluxe eight wheel, white/cream, red lettering reads "Pacific Fruit Express"	15	22	30
44534 Flat Car, plastic, deluxe eight wheel, gray w/black or gray pipe, blue lettering reads "S.A.L."	40	60	80
44572 (a) High Side Gondola, 3:16-scale, lithographed tin, eight wheel, black, white lettering reads "C&O"..............	5	10	15

Left to right: No. 36000 Gondola, $10; No. 4484 Boxcar, $40. Photo Courtesy of Richard L. MacNary.

	C5	C7	C9
44572 (b) High Side Gondola, 3:16-scale, lithographed tin, eight wheel, black, white lettering reads "C&O," no rivet detail	5	10	15
46010 (a) Boxcar, 6" tin, four and eight wheel, sliding door, brown, yellow lettering reads "SSW Cotton Belt Route"	40	60	80
46010 (b) Boxcar, 6" tin, four and eight wheel, sliding door, red, yellow lettering reads "SSW Cotton Belt Route"	40	60	80
46010 (c) Boxcar, 6" tin, four wheel, sliding door, red, yellow lettering reads "SSW Cotton Belt Route"	30	45	60
46010 (d) Boxcar, 6" tin, four and eight wheel, sliding door, blue, white lettering reads "SSW Cotton Belt Route"	30	45	60

	C5	C7	C9
46010 (c) Boxcar, 6" tin, four and eight wheel, sliding door, yellow, white lettering reads "SSW Cotton Belt Route"	50	75	100
46010 (d) Boxcar, 6" tin, four and eight wheel, sliding door, orange, white lettering reads "SSW Cotton Belt Route"	50	75	100
51100 (a) Flat Car, double auto carrier, plastic, deluxe eight wheel, maroon, yellow lettering reads "Southern," w/four vehicles	20	30	40
51100 (b) Flat Car, double auto carrier, plastic, deluxe eight wheel, blue, white lettering reads "Southern," w/four vehicles	30	45	60
51170 (a) Gondola, plastic, deluxe eight wheel, black, white lettering reads "Erie"	15	22	30

Top row, left to right: No. 51100 (b) Flat car, white letters, $60; No. 51100 Flat car with yellow letters, $60. Middle row, left to right: No. 39520: Flat car, $60; Eries Dump car. Bottom row, left to right: No. 51100 (a) Flat car with white letters, $40; No. 51100 (a) Flat car with yellow letters, $40. Photo Courtesy of Richard L. MacNary.

Top row: No. 4000 (c) Locomotive, $150. Middle row, left to right: No. 553 (a) Tank car, $100; No. 54099 (b) Cattle car, $100. Bottom row, left to right: No. 51170 Gondola, $60; No. 18326 Caboose, $10. Photo Courtesy of Richard L. MacNary.

Top row, left to right: No. 51998 (c) Boxcar, $80; No. 51998 (a) Boxcar, $60; No. 51998 (d), $60. Bottom row, left to right: No. 51998 (f) Boxcar, $100; No. 51998 (e) Boxcar, $100; No. 51998 (b) Boxcar, $80. Photo Courtesy of Richard L. MacNary.

	C5	C7	C9
51170 (b) Gondola, plastic, deluxe eight wheel, orange, black lettering reads "Erie"	30	45	60
51170 (c) Gondola, plastic, deluxe eight wheel, blue, white lettering reads "Erie"	15	22	30
51170 (d) Gondola, plastic, deluxe eight wheel, gray, white lettering reads "Erie"	30	45	60
51998 (a) Boxcar, 6" tin, four and eight wheel, sliding door, blue, white lettering reads "Chicago and North Western" and "400 Stream Liners"	30	45	60
51998 (b) Boxcar, 6" tin, four and eight wheel, sliding door, brown, yellow lettering reads "Chicago and North Western" and "400 Stream Liners"	40	60	80

	C5	C7	C9
51998 (c) Boxcar, 6" tin, four and eight wheel, sliding door, red, yellow lettering reads "Chicago and North Western" and "400 Stream Liners"	40	60	80
51998 (d) Boxcar, 6" tin, four wheel, sliding door, red, silver lettering reads "Chicago and North Western" and "400 Stream Liners"	30	45	60
51998 (e) Boxcar, 6" tin, four and eight wheel, sliding door, orange, white lettering reads "Chicago and North Western" and "400 Stream Liners"	50	75	100
51998 (f) Boxcar, 6" tin, four and eight wheel, sliding door, yellow, white lettering reads "Chicago and North Western" and "400 Stream Liners"	50	75	100

Left to right: No. 53941 Stock Car, $150; No. 1354 Stock car, $60; No. 35461 Refrigerator car, $60. Photo Courtesy of Richard L. MacNary.

	C5	C7	C9
53941 Stock Car, 3:16-scale, lithographed tin, eight wheel, brown, white lettering reads "Pennsylvania"	75	110	150
54099 (a) Stock Car, plastic, deluxe eight wheel, red, white lettering reads "Missouri Pacific" and "I-GN"	20	30	40
54099 (b) Stock Car, plastic, deluxe eight wheel, yellow, black lettering reads "Missouri Pacific" and "I-GN"	50	75	100
54099 (c) Stock Car, plastic, deluxe eight wheel, green, white lettering reads "Missouri Pacific" and "I-GN"	25	37	50
54099 (d) Stock Car, plastic, deluxe eight wheel, orange, black lettering reads "Missouri Pacific" and "I-GN"	75	100	150
54201 Gondola, plastic, red, white lettering reads "Western Maryland"	5	8	10
61962 Work Caboose, plastic, Tuscan red w/gray tank, marked "N.P."	10	15	20
70018 Hopper, plastic, red, white lettering reads "Western Maryland"	5	8	10
70311 Boxcar, 3:16-scale, lithographed tin, eight wheel, brown, white lettering reads "Pennsylvania"	30	40	60
71499 Gondola, 3:16-scale, lithographed tin, eight wheel, black, white lettering reads "NKP" and "NYC" and "STL"	20	30	40
74005 Boxcar, plastic, blue, white lettering reads "B&M"	5	8	10

	C5	C7	C9
74563 Flat Car, plastic, deluxe w/lumber, red, white or black lettering reads "A.C.L."	20	30	40
77000 Boxcar, plastic, blue, white lettering reads "Boston & Maine"	5	8	10
77003 Boxcar, plastic, deluxe eight wheel, blue, white lettering reads "B&M"	20	30	40
78450 Tank Car, plastic, gray, black "GATX" and "Hooker"	5	10	15
80410 Flat Car, 3:16-scale, lithographed tin, eight wheel black, white lettering reads "C&O"	15	22	30
80982 Gondola, 7" lithographed tin, four wheel, yellow lettering reads "Wabash"	6	8	10
86000 (a) High Side Gondola, 6" tin, four wheel, bright blue, red lettering reads "Lackawanna"	10	20	30
86000 (b) Hopper, 6" tin, four wheel, bright blue, red lettering reads "Lackawanna"	6	8	10
90171 (a) Boxcar, 6" tin, four and eight wheel, yellow, white lettering reads "B&LE" and "Bessemer"	50	75	100
90171 (b) Boxcar, 6" tin, four and eight wheel, orange, white lettering reads "B&LE" and "Bessemer"	50	75	100
90171 (c) Boxcar, 6" tin, four and eight wheel, brown, yellow lettering reads "B&LE" and "Bessemer"	40	60	80
90171 (d) Boxcar, 6" tin, four and eight wheel, blue, white lettering reads "B&LE" and "Bessemer"	30	45	60

Top row, left to right: No. 4000 (f) Locomotive, $80; No. 956 (b) Caboose, $40. Bottom row, left to right: No. 91257 (c) Gondola, $20; No. 91257 (b) Gondola, $40; No. 91257 (a) $50. Photo Courtesy of Richard L. MacNary.

	C5	C7	C9
90171 (e) Boxcar, 6" tin, four wheel, red, silver lettering reads "B&LE" and "Bessemer"	30	45	60
90171 (f) Boxcar, 6" tin, four and eight wheel, red, yellow lettering reads "B&LE" and "Bessemer"	40	60	80
90171 (g) Boxcar, 6" tin, four wheel, brown, white lettering reads "B&LE" and "Bessemer"	20	30	40
90798 Caboose, plastic, red, marked "CRI&D"	5	8	10
91257 (a) Gondola, 6" tin, four wheel, light brown, white lettering reads "Seaboard"	25	38	50
91257 (b) Gondola, 6" tin, four wheel, blue, white lettering reads "Seaboard"	20	30	40
91257 (c) Gondola, 6" tin, four wheel, red, white lettering reads "Seaboard"	10	15	20
91453 Refrigerator Car, 6" tin, four wheel, yellow w/black and silver or all black frame, black lettering reads "Colorado & Southern RR"	25	38	50
92812 Caboose, 3:16-scale, lithographed tin, eight wheel, red, white lettering reads "Reading"	5	8	10

	C5	C7	C9
95050 Caboose, plastic, four wheel, red, white lettering reads "Lehigh Valley"	5	8	10
104436 Boxcar, plastic, red, lettering reads "Union Pacific"	6	8	10
131000 (a) Gondola, plastic, four wheel, yellow, black lettering reads "SCL"	6	8	10
131000 (b) Gondola, plastic, four wheel, blue, white lettering reads "SCL"	15	22	30
144479 Boxcar, plastic, red and gray, marked "NYC"	6	8	10
147815 (a) Boxcar, plastic, deluxe eight wheel, red, white lettering reads "Rock Island"	10	20	30
147815 (b) Boxcar, plastic, deluxe eight wheel, orange, black lettering reads "Rock Island"	20	40	60
160149 Gondola, plastic, gray, black lettering reads "Southern Pacific"	1	2	3
161755 Boxcar, plastic, four wheel, yellow, black lettering reads "NYC"	6	8	10
174479 Boxcar, plastic, four wheel, green, white lettering reads "NYC"	6	8	10

Top row, left to right: No. 339234 (a) Gondola, $50; No. 339234 (b) Gondola (b), $50. Bottom row, left to right: No. 259199 Boxcar, $60; No 2366 Caboose. Photo Courtesy of Richard L. MacNary.

	C5	C7	C9
174580/174595 Boxcar, 6" tin, four wheel, red and gray w/black roof, white lettering reads "NYC Pacemaker"	50	75	100
174580 (a) Boxcar, 3:16-scale, lithographed tin, eight wheel, red and gray w/black roof, white lettering reads "NYC"	20	30	40
174580 (b) Boxcar, 3:16-scale, lithographed tin, eight wheel, red and gray w/black roof, white lettering reads "NYC," no rivet detail	20	30	40
174853 Boxcar, plastic, red w/white lettering reads "NYC".	6	8	10
176893 Boxcar, plastic, deluxe eight wheel, green, white lettering reads "New York Central"	10	20	30
186028 Boxcar, plastic, deluxe eight wheel, red, white lettering reads "Union Pacific"	10	20	30
200309 (a) Gondola, plastic, eight wheel, brown w/sewer tiles, white lettering reads "L&N"	20	40	60
200309 (b) Gondola, plastic, eight wheel, yellow w/sewer tiles, black lettering reads "L&N"	20	40	60
241708 Gondola, 6" tin, four wheel, yellow, black lettering reads "B&O"	2	4	6
249319 (a) Boxcar, plastic, deluxe eight wheel, operating, red, white lettering reads "Marlines"	10	20	30

	C5	C7	C9
249319 (b) Boxcar, plastic, deluxe eight wheel, operating, white, red lettering reads "Marlines"	10	20	30
254000 Gondola, 3:16-scale, lithographed tin, eight wheel, gray, white lettering reads "B&O" and "Baltimore and Ohio"	15	22	30
259199 Boxcar, plastic, deluxe eight wheel, Tuscan red, white lettering reads "Canadian Pacific"	20	40	60
339234 (a) Gondola, plastic, deluxe eight wheel, brown, white lettering reads "Canadian Pacific"	25	37	50
339234 (b) Gondola, plastic, deluxe eight wheel, black, white lettering reads "Canadian Pacific"	25	37	50
339234 (c) Gondola, plastic, deluxe eight wheel, red, white lettering reads "Canadian Pacific"	25	37	50
347000 Gondola, 3:16-scale, lithographed tin, eight wheel, black, white lettering reads "Pennsylvania"	20	30	40
347100 Gondola, plastic, four and eight wheel, several colors, marked "Pennsylvania"	1	2	3
384299 (a) Boxcar, 6" tin, four and eight wheel, sliding door, blue, white lettering reads "B&O" and "Baltimore and Ohio"	30	40	60

Top row, left to right: No. 738701 Gondola, $30; No. 28500 Gondola, $10. Bottom row, left to right: Loads sample boxes; No. 20102 (a) Caboose, $10. Photo Courtesy of Richard L. MacNary.

	C5	C7	C9
384299 (b) Boxcar, 6" tin, four and eight wheel, sliding door, orange, white lettering reads "B&O" and "Baltimore and Ohio"	50	75	100
384299 (c) Boxcar, 6" tin, four and eight wheel, sliding door, yellow, white lettering reads "B&O" and "Baltimore and Ohio"	50	75	100
384299 (d) Boxcar, 6" tin, four and eight wheel, sliding door, red, silver lettering reads "B&O" and "Baltimore and Ohio"	20	30	40
384299 (e) Boxcar, 6" tin, four and eight wheel, sliding door, brown, yellow lettering reads "B&O" and "Baltimore and Ohio"	40	60	80
384299 (f) Boxcar, 6" tin, four and eight wheel, sliding door, red, yellow lettering reads "B&O" and "Baltimore and Ohio"	40	60	80
384299 (g) Boxcar, 6" tin, four wheel, solid door, blue, white lettering reads "B&O" and "Baltimore and Ohio"..............	20	30	40
467110 (a) Boxcar, plastic, four and eight wheel, red, white lettering reads "B&O"	10	15	20
467110 (b) Boxcar, plastic, four and eight wheel, blue, white lettering reads "B&O"...............	5	8	10
467110 (c) Boxcar, plastic, four and eight wheel, orange, black lettering reads "B&O"...............	10	15	20
467110 (d) Boxcar, plastic, four wheel, yellow, black lettering reads "B&O"............................	10	15	20
499898 Work Caboose, plastic, red, marked "NYC"	6	8	10
691521 Caboose, 7" tin, four wheel, orange Mickey Mouse characters	50	75	100
715100 (a) Gondola, plastic, four and eight wheel, blue, white lettering reads "NYC"...............	5	8	10
715100 (b) Gondola, plastic, four wheel and eight wheel, green, black lettering reads "B&O".....	5	10	15
715100 (c) Gondola, plastic, four wheel and eight wheel, red, black or white lettering reads "B&O"	5	8	10
738701 High Side Gondola, 6" tin, four wheel, red, silver lettering reads "Pennsylvania"	15	22	30
738701 Hopper, 6" tin, four wheel, tuscan, red-brown, white lettering reads "Pennsylvania".........................	30	45	60

Tootsietoy

Tootsietoy trains, products of a Chicago concern that now has a century of manufacturing behind it, have long appealed to parents because of their cheap price, and to kids because of their high play value. The Tootsietoy line through the years has included toy cars, trucks, trains, dollhouse furniture, airplanes, and toy soldiers. During the company's heyday, roughly from the 1930s through 1960s, a person would have had to search long and hard to find a child with no knowledge of the trademark.

Dowst and Company started in 1876 in the publishing trade, and moved into manufacturing after the 1893 Columbian World Exposition in Chicago, where the new die-casting technology was introduced to the public. By then named Dowst Brothers, the company released its first toy in 1911. In 1921 the company issued its first train. The name Tootsietoy was adopted in the early 1920s and was registered in 1924 as the company's trademark. Theodore Dowst, who joined the firm in 1906, is generally seen as the guiding force behind the growth of toy production at Dowst Brothers. He remained with the company even after its purchase by Nathan Shure in 1926, until 1945. For most collectors, the toys of the Ted Dowst period are the most noteworthy.

Tootsietoys are still being produced by Strombecker Corporation of Chicago, Illinois.

Contributor: John Gibson. Gibson has always been a collector of sorts, from Winchester Firearms to the Arts and Crafts Movement, art glass, art deco, art nouveau, vintage posters, pin up art, tobacco tin advertising and stained glass. While antique hunting in 1989, he discovered a mint, boxed set of Deluxe Tootsietoy Grahams and has been actively involved with collecting and writing about them ever since. He currently serves as the Corporate Historian for the Strombecker Corporation in Chicago, Illinois, home of Tootsietoy. Gibson is currently employed in the Washington, D.C. area in the specialized field of decorative painting. After years of research, he is now writing a definitive book on pre-war Tootsietoys and has branched into Civil War collecting.

No. 0117, Zephyr Railcar, 1935, $95. Photo By John Gibson.

No. 188, Pennsylvania RR Broadway Limited, 1937, $150. Photo By John Gibson.

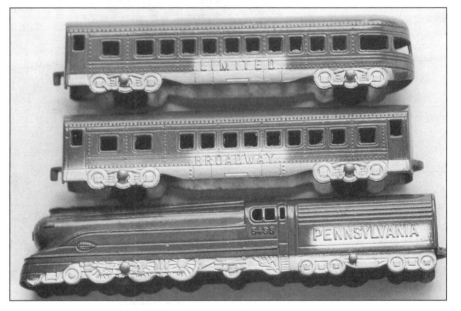

	C5	C7	C9
0117 Zephyr Railcar, 1935	45	70	95
188 Pennsylvania RR Broadway Limited, 1937	75	100	150
195 Tootsietoy Flyer Streamline Train, 1935	75	100	150
0196 Tootsietoy Flyer Deluxe Streamline Train, 1935	85	125	170
1076 Santa Fe RR Locomotive, 1904	17	25	35
1086 Pennsylvania RR Locomotive, 1939....................	12	18	25
1087 Wrecking Crane, 1939..........	17	25	35
1088 Armour Refrigerator Car, 1939	12	18	25

	C5	C7	C9
1089 Southern Boxcar, 1939	12	18	25
1090 Coal Car, 1939	12	18	25
1091 Pioneer Stock Car, 1939	12	18	25
1092 Log Car, 1939	12	18	25
1093 Borden's Milk Tank Car, 1939..	17	25	35

No. 1091, Pioneer Stock car, 1939, $25. Photo By John Gibson.

No. 0196, Tootsietoy Flyer Deluxe Streamline Train, 1935, $170. Photo By John Gibson.

No. 1086, Pennsylvania RR Locomotive, 1939, $25. Photo By John Gibson.

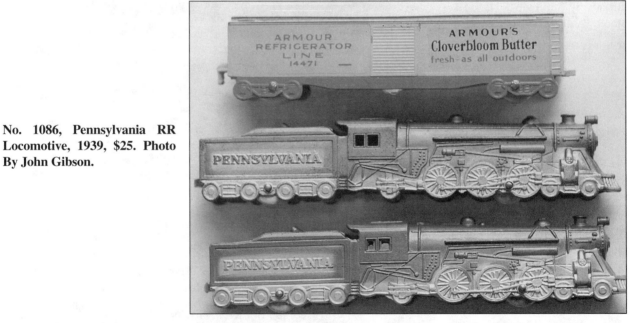

No. 1088, Armour Refrigerator car, 1939, $25.

No. 1756, Locomotive, 1930s, lithographed tin, Cracker Jack, $35. Photo By John Gibson.

	C5	C7	C9
1094 Sinclair Oil Tank Car, 1939	12	18	25
1095 Caboose, 1939	12	18	25
1654 American Flyer Car, 1922, Cosmo Toy Co.	25	35	50
1660 Coach, 1922, Cosmo Toy Co.	6	8	12
1692 Zephyr Railcar	6	8	12

	C5	C7	C9
1756 Locomotive, 1930s, lithographed tin, Cracker Jack	17	25	35
1757 Coach, 1930s, lithographed tin, Cracker Jack	17	25	35
4469 Trolley, 1913 or earlier	6	8	12
4551 Locomotive Charm, 1921	2	3	4
4620 Locomotive, 1921, 2-6-0	12	18	25

No. 4620, Locomotive, 1921, Two examples of Tootsietoy's No. 4620 2-6-0 Locomotive; The example on the left is from 1921 and the one on the right is dated 1924, $25. Photo By John Gibson.

No. 186, Fast Freight, 1940, boxed set includes: T186 Locomotive, NY Central tender, Cracker Jack Boxcar, Texaco Oil tanker, NYCRR caboose, $275. Photo By John Gibson.

	C5	C7	C9
4621 Tender, 1921, D.B. Co.	15	22	30
4621 Tender, 1924, No. 221	10	15	20
4622 Baggage Car, 1921, marked "Baggage & Express"	15	22	30
4623 Pullman Coach, 1921, marked "D.B. Co."	17	26	35
4623 Pullman Coach, 1924	10	15	20
4624 Gondola Flat Car, 1921, marked "D.B. Co".	17	26	35
4625 Boxcar, 1921, marked "D.B. Co. 711"	17	26	35
4628 Trolley, 1913 or earlier........	6	8	12
4690 Baggage Car, 1929	15	20	30
4691 Pullman Car, 1929	15	20	30
4692 Observation Car, 1929.........	15	20	30
4695 Boxcar, 1929	10	15	20
4696 Gondola Car, 1929	10	15	20
4697 Caboose, 1929	10	15	20

Sets

	C5	C7	C9
11 Tootsietoy Train and Station, 1924, boxed set includes: 4620 locomotive, 4621 tender, three 4623 pullman coaches, folding cardboard station	200	325	450
186 Fast Freight, 1940, boxed set includes: T186 locomotive, NY Central tender, Cracker Jack box car, Texaco Oil tanker, NYCRR caboose	135	210	275
193 Passenger Train, 1933, boxed set includes: 4620 locomotive, 4621 tender, 4690 baggage car, 4691 pullman car, 4692 observation car	135	210	275
194 Freight Train, 1933, boxed set includes: 4620 locomotive, 4621 tender, 4695 box car, 4696 gondola, 4697 caboose	135	210	275
4397 Train Set, 1913 or earlier, set includes: 53 locomotive, 54 tender, two 55 coaches	25	35	50

	C5	C7	C9

No. 11, Tootsietoy Train and Station, 1924, boxed set includes: No. 4620 Locomotive, No. 4621 tender, three No. 4623 Pullman coaches, folding cardboard station, $450. Photo By John Gibson.

	C5	C7	C9
4626 Passenger Train, 1924, TT Limited; boxed set includes: 4620 locomotive, 4621 tender, 4623 pullman coach	125	185	250
4627 Freight Train, 1924, boxed set includes: 4620 locomotive, 4621 tender, 4624 gondola	125	185	250
5015 Akana Midnight Flyer, 1929, boxed set includes: 4620 locomotive, 4621 tender, 4690 baggage car, 4691 pullman car, 4692 observation car	250	375	500
5020 Akana Fast Freight, 1929, boxed set includes: 4620 locomotive, 4621 tender, 4695 box car, 4696 gondola, 4697 caboose	250	375	500
5550 Freight Train, 1939, boxed set includes: 1086 Pennsylvania RR locomotive, 1087 wrecking crane, 1093 Borden's Milk tank car, 1092 log car, 1091 pioneer stock car	150	225	300
5600 Freight Train, 1939, boxed set includes: 1085 Pennsylvania RR locomotive, 1087 wrecking crane, 1088 Armour refrigerator car, 1089 southern box car, 1090 coal car, 1091 Pioneer stock car, 1092 log car, 1093 Borden's Milk tank car, 1094 Sinclair Oil tank car, 1095 caboose	250	375	500

No. 194, Freight Train, 1933, boxed set includes: No. 4620 Locomotive, No. 4621 Tender, No. 4695 Boxcar, No. 4696 gondola, No. 4697 caboose, $275. Photo By Richard L. MacNary.

	C5	C7	C9
5610 Diesel Freight Train, 1955, boxed set includes: Union Pacific Diesel locomotive, box car, tank car, stock car, coal car, caboose	300	450	600
5850 Pennsylvania RR Passenger Train, 1940, boxed set includes: 1086 Pennsylvania RR locomotive, 1101 baggage car, 1102 pullman car, 1103 observation car	135	210	275

	C5	C7	C9
5851 Santa Fe RR Passenger Train, 1940, boxed set includes: 1076 Santa Fe RR locomotive, 1101 baggage car, 1102 pullman car, 1103 observation car	145	215	285
7001 Midnight Flyer, 1931, boxed set includes: 4620 locomotive, 4621 tender, 4690 baggage car, 4691 pullman car, 4692 observation car	135	210	275
7002 Fast Freight, 1931, boxed set includes: 4620 locomotive, 4621 tender, 4695 box car, 4696 gondola, 4697 caboose	135	210	275

No. 4626 Passenger Train, 1924, TT Limited; boxed set includes: No. 4620 Locomotive, No. 4621 tender, No. 4623 Pullman Coach, $250. Photo By John Gibson.

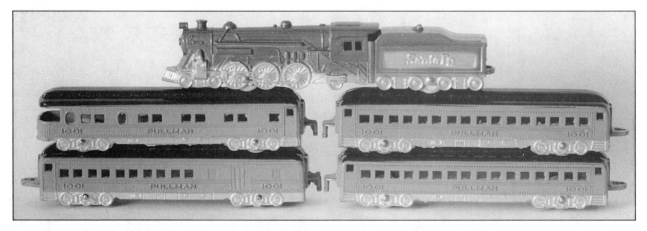

No. 5851, Santa Fe RR Passenger Train, 1940, boxed set includes: No. 1076 Santa Fe RR Locomotive, No. 1101 Baggage car, No. 1102 Pullman car, No. 1103 Observation car, $285. Photo By John Gibson.

Unique

Unique trains were manufactured by Unique Art Manufacturing Company of Newark, New Jersey. According to their World War II-era ads, they had been making toys since 1916. Their first mechanical (clockwork) trains were introduced in 1949; electric trains soon followed. Due to pressure from both the Louis Marx Company and Korean War material shortages, the complete Unique operation ceased in 1951. Most of their train items carried no numbers but the pieces are easy to identify. All items are somewhat rare but most are not too desirable.

	C5	C7	C9

Control Tower, $60. Photo courtesy Richard L. MacNary.

	C5	C7	C9
Control Tower, lithographed tin, two-story, cream w/green roof, some have reverse button, 3" x 2" x 4"	15	30	60
High Side Gondola, tin, orange w/red inside, without punched out sides, black lettering reads "Unique Lines," 7-1/2"	30	45	60
Hobo Boxcar, lithographed tin, clockwork, rolls along floor w/dog biting hobo	500	750	1000

	C5	C7	C9

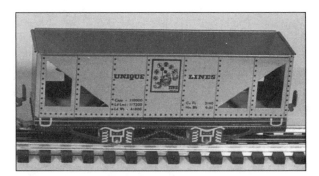

High Side Gondola, $60

Hobo Boxcar, $1000

	C5	C7	C9
100 Boxcar, tin, silver w/red lettering reads "Unique Lines" and "3509," 7-1/2"	40	60	80
101 Hopper Car, tin, orange w/red inside, black lettering reads "Unique Lines," 7-1/2"	25	38	50

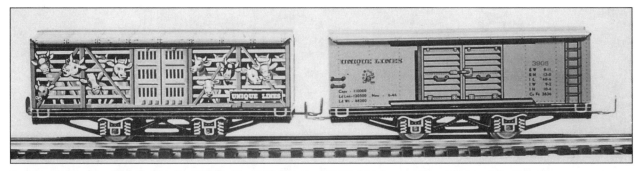

Left to right: No. 107 Cattle Car, $100; No. 100 Boxcar, $80". Photo courtesy Richard L. MacNary.

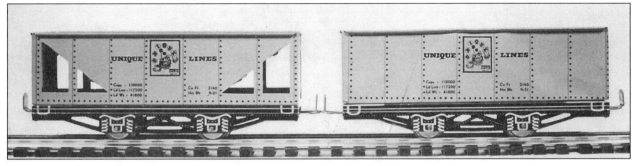

Left to right: No. 101 Hopper Car, $50; High Side Gondola, $60. Photo courtesy Richard L. MacNary.

Front row, left to right: "City of Joplin" Boxcar, $200; "Garden City" Boxcar, $200. Back row: No. 742 Locomotive w/tender, $80

	C5	C7	C9
102 Passenger Car, 9" tin, blue body w/silver roof, white and black lettering reads "Pullman" and "City of Joplin"	100	150	200
102 Passenger Car, tin, blue body w/silver roof, white and black lettering reads "Pullman" and "Garden City," 9"	100	150	200
105 Caboose, tin, red w/yellow lettering reads "Unique Lines," Alfred E. Neuman-type looking out window, 7-1/2"	30	45	60
105 Caboose, tin, red w/yellow w/swing-out, lettering read "Unique Lines" and "Benny the Brakeman" on the rear platform, Alfred E. Neuman-type looking out window, 7-1/2"	40	60	80

	C5	C7	C9
107 Cattle Car, tin, red w/yellow roof, marked "Unique Lines," 7-1/2"	50	75	100

No. 107, Cattle Car, $100

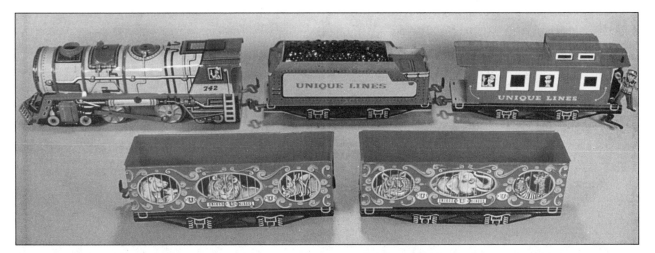

Front to back: No. 109 Circus Car with lion in center, open top, $200; No. 109 Circus Car with elephant in center, open tope, $200. Back row, left to Right: No. 742 Locomotive w/tender; No. 105 Caboose with Benny the Brakeman. Photo courtesy Richard L. MacNary.

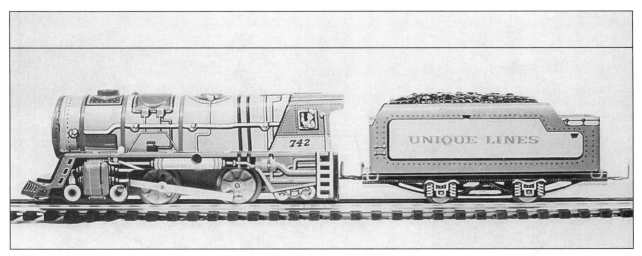

Left to right: Circus Car with lion in center, closed roof, $100; Circus Car with elephant in center, closed roof, $100; No. 105 Caboose without Benny the Brakeman

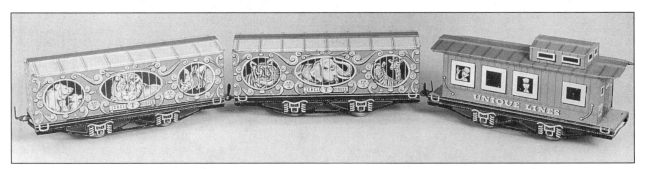

No. 742, Engine, $80. Photo courtesy Richard L. MacNary.

	C5	C7	C9
109 Circus Car, tin, mostly red w/open roof, marked "Jewel T Circus," elephant in center panel, 7-1/2", rare	100	150	200
109 Circus Car, tin, mostly red w/yellow roof, marked "Jewel T Circus," lion in center panel, 7-1/2"	50	75	100
109 Circus Car, tin, mostly red w/open roof, marked "Jewel T Circus," lion in center panel, 7-1/2", rare	100	150	200
109 Circus Car, tin, mostly red w/yellow roof, marked "Jewel T Circus," elephant in center panel, 7-1/2"	50	75	100
515 Hillbilly Express, lithographed tin, clockwork, runs back and forth along inclined track	100	150	200
702 Finnegan the Baggage Man, lithographed tin, clockwork, package has cut-out cardboard luggage.....................................	50	75	100
742 Engine, tin, clockwork, multicolored and gray w/tender, marked "Unique Lines," 7-1/2" tender, 10" engine.....................	40	60	80

	C5	C7	C9
1950 Engine, tin, electric w/reverse and headlight, multicolored and blue, w/tender, marked "Unique Lines," 7-1/2" tender, 10" engine..	30	45	60
1950 Engine, tin, multicolored and blue, w/tender, marked "Unique Lines," 7-1/2" tender, 10"...	30	45	60
2000 Engine, tin, diesel, powered A and dummy A, multicolored and maroon, marked "Rock Island," 14"	30	45	60

No. 2000, Engine, $60. Photo courtesy Richard L. MacNary.

No. 1950, Engine, electric w/reverse and headlight, $60, Photo courtesy Richard L. MacNary.

Miscellaneous

Auburn Rubber (Also Aub-Rub'r and Arcor)

Founded in 1913, in Auburn, Indiana as the Double Fabric Tire Corporation, making auto tubes and tires for Model T Fords, Auburn's first toys were produced in 1935. Within a few years it also made train sets, with at least two sold sets before World War II. After the end of the War, toy production, including trains, had resumed. While rubber was initially used, vinyl was employed in the 1950s and was eventually used exclusively. In 1960, Auburn's toy production was transferred to Deming, New Mexico, where it remained until it went out of business in 1969.

Doepke

Located in Rossmoyne, Ohio, Doepke was in business from the end of World War II until the late 1950s. Most of its toys were highly detailed, authorized replicas of vehicles. Its Yardbirds set of rideable trains was produced as early as 1956.

Hafner

William Hafner originally sold wind-up cars and truck and eventually began producing trains. When Hafner realized he needed more capital to continue his endeavor, he entered into a partnership with Chicago hardware store owner William Coleman. By 1910, train production had come to dominate the business and the company's name was changed to American Flyer. In 1914, Hafner formed his own rival company, calling his trains Overland Flyer

All Hafner trains were O Gauge wind-ups. In 1951, John Hafner sold the company to All Metal, manufacturer of Wyandotte toys. Wyandotte kept the name Hafner on most of its trains until bankruptcy was declared in 1956. The Louis Marx Company bought the Hafner-Wyandotte dies and produced the same trains south of the border in Mexico with new lithography.

Kansas Toy & Novelty

Arthur L. Haynes, an auto mechanic, began molding toys in a shed in Clifton, Kansas in 1923. With clever hands and an artist's eye, he charmed his friends and local townspeople with his bright-colored toys. His patterns were made from advertising pictures, from local vehicles, and probably from other toys. He made his own production tools. His range was diverse.

Haynes believed that he invented hollow-casting of metal toys. The process of making the slush or hollow-cast toys was a very simple one. The metal was melted down to a molten state and poured into a mold. After a few seconds, the liquid metal was poured off leaving a thin shell of metal solidified against the walls of the mold. The thickness of the shell varied depending on mold temperature, the alloy used and the length of time the molten metal was allowed to remain in the mold.

During its good years, Kansas Toy & Novelty produced more toys than any in the industry, except Barclay, yet the company was in financial trouble by 1930. The company reorganized and changed locations, but it was too late. Kansas Toy & Novelty continued until 1935, when Best Toy & Novelty Company acquired the Kansas Toy molds in 1933.

Collectors should note that not all slush molds with numbers are Kansas Toy & Novelty Company and many were not numbered. Because these were unlabeled, unboxed bin-toys, the number may have been a convenience to certain wholesale buyers.

Manoil

Manoil began production of slush lead toys in 1934, and was located in New York City until 1940, when it moved to Waverly, New York, where it remained until it went out of business about 1954. Manoil mostly produced toy soldiers and vehicles, but in the early 1940s designed a military train that never reached production due to the Second World War.

Auburn Rubber

	C5	C7	C9
Army Train Set, No. 945, set includes: Locomotive, two flat cars, two jeeps, two cannon, two soldiers; shown in 1958 catalog	75	100	150
Caboose, No. 1576, pre-WWII, 4-1/2" l.	5	8	11
Dump Car, No. 1574, pre-WWII, 5-1/2" l.	8	12	15
Engine and Tender, No. 1570, pre-WWII, 11" l.	10	15	20
Gondola, No. 1572, pre-WWII, 5-1/2" l.	6	9	12
Locomotive, No. 599, vinyl, diesel, not sold w/other cars; shown in 1958 catalog	8	12	15

Locomotive, No. 599, Auburn Rubber, $15

	C5	C7	C9
Locomotive, No. 649, part of 529 train set	20	30	40
Locomotive and Tender, No. 999, part of 577 set	30	45	60
Train Set, No. 325, pre-WWII, contents of set unknown	50	75	100

Train Set, No. 525, Auburn Rubber, in original box, $80

	C5	C7	C9
Train Set, No. 525, vinyl, set includes: Locomotive-tender, coal car, gondola, caboose, three trainmen; shown in 1958 catalog	40	60	80
Train Set, No. 529, set includes: red and silver or black and silver 9-1/2" l. Locomotive; green and black or red and black 6" l. dump car; red or black 6" l. gondola; red 5" l. caboose; Marked "Arcor Safe Play Toys"; shown in 1953 catalog	45	68	90
Train Set, No. 575, pre-WWII, set includes: engine, tender, crane flat car, caboose	45	68	90

Train Set, No. 529, Auburn Rubber, $90

Train Set, No. 577, Auburn Rubber, $100

Western Train Set, No. 922, Auburn Rubber, late 1950s, $80

	C5	C7	C9
Train Set, No. 577, set includes: 10-1/2" l. Locomotive, gray and tender, tender marked "999"; 5" l. dump car, black and orange; 4-3/8" l. caboose, red	50	75	100
Union Station Set, No. 965, vinyl, set includes: Locomotive-tender, coal car, gondola, caboose, three trainmen; shown in 1958 catalog.........................	40	60	80
Western Train Set, No. 922, late 1950s, vinyl, 8" l. Locomotive, black w/red wheels; 5-1/2" l. tender, green; passenger car 6-1/2" l., pink and gold	40	60	80

Barclay Mfg. Co.

	C5	C7	C9
Boxcar, No. 62, shown in 1931 catalog......................................	12	18	25
Caboose, No. 65, shown in 1931 catalog......................................	12	18	25
Coal Car, No. 63, shown in 1931 catalog......................................	12	18	25

Freight Train Set, with electric light, Barclay Mfg. Co.

	C5	C7	C9
Freight Train Set, electric lighted, set includes: Locomotive, coal car, freight car, oil car and caboose; sold in 1935................	12	18	25
Locomotive, No. 335, 0-4-0	17	26	35
Locomotive and Tender, No. 59, 0-6-0, shown in 1931 catalog....	20	30	40
Mail and Baggage Car, No. 60, shown in 1931 catalog	12	18	25
Oil Tank Car, No. 64, shown in 1931 catalog	12	18	25
Passenger Car, No. 337.................	12	18	25

Left to right: Barclay Mfg. Co.: No. 335 Locomotive, $35; No. 336 Tender, $25; No. 337 Passenger Car, $25

Train Set, post-WWII, No. 335, Barclay Mfg. Co., $80

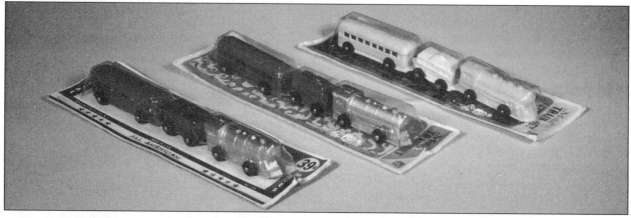

Three No. 335 Barclay Train Sets in original packages.

Another variation of Barclay's three-piece train set; this example, with metal wheels, is probably pre-WWII.

Train Set, No. 550, Barclay Mfg. Co., in original box, $100

	C5	C7	C9
Passenger Coach, No. 61, shown in 1931 catalog...........................	12	18	25
Tender, No. 336.............................	12	18	25
Train, No. 365, sold in 1935, marked "Streamline Train".......	12	18	25
Train Set, set includes: Locomotive and tender, passenger coach, mail and baggage car, marked "Passenger Train Set," shown in 1931 catalog...........................	25	38	50
Train Set, No. 335, post-WWII, marked "3-Piece Train Set"......	40	60	80
Train Set, No. 550, marked "5-Car Freight Train Set," shown in 1931 catalog.............................	50	75	100
Train Set, No. 566, marked "5 Car Freight Train Set".....................	35	53	70
Train Set, No. 577, marked "5 Car Freight Train Set".....................	30	45	60

Beggs

	C5	C7	C9
Locomotive, No. 1, brass and painted tin, lead wheels, together w/lithographed paper/cardboard coach w/tin roof and ends and lead wheels...................................	900	1350	1800
Locomotive, No. 3, live steam.......	375	562	750

Bliss

	C5	C7	C9
Locomotive, lithographed on wood, marked "New York Central Railroad," 28" l.............	550	875	1100
Train Set, No. 295, set includes: 7" l. Locomotive, tender, two lithographed-paper coaches, marked "Nickel Plate Line Railroad No. 295"	300	450	600

Converse

	C5	C7	C9
Train Set, lithographed tin, set includes: Locomotive, tender and box car	500	750	1000
Trolley, c. 1900, marked "City Hall Park-Union Depot," 16" l.	600	900	1200

Corcor

	C5	C7	C9
Engine and Pullman, 48" l.	400	600	800
Train Set, 1940, set includes: engine, tender, box car and caboose, 5" l.	375	562	750

Dayton

	C5	C7	C9
Engine, 2-4-2, marked "Hillclimber," 17" l.	150	225	300
Engine, 2-4-0, marked "Hillclimber," 20" l.	125	188	250
Engine and Tender, 2-4-0, marked "Hillclimber," 27" l.	150	225	300
Locomotive and Tender, painted wood and pressed steel, friction, marked "Hillclimber" and "150," 19" l.	550	820	1100
Locomotive and Tender, painted pressed steel and wood, friction, marked "Hillclimber," 20" l.	275	402	550
Streetcar, steel, yellow w/red roof	225	338	450

Dent

	C5	C7	C9
Passenger Train Set, cast iron, includes: Locomotive, tender and four cars	550	825	1100
Train Set, cast iron, includes: Locomotive and two passenger Cars, 38" l.	700	1050	1400

	C5	C7	C9
Train Set, c. 1890s, pressed steel and cast iron, set includes: Locomotive, tender marked "999," 4-4-0, flat car, woody	450	675	900
Train Set, nickel-plated cast iron, set includes: Locomotive, tender marked "999," three passenger cars, 13" l.	550	825	1100

Doepke

	C5	C7	C9
Engine, electric, red and blue, streamliner	550	825	1100
Flat Car	100	150	200
Handcar	200	300	400
Rail, per foot	1	2	3

George Brown

Locomotive, 1875, tin, George Brown

	C5	C7	C9
Locomotive, 1875, painted tin, marked "Union"	1250	1875	2500
Locomotive, 1875, tin, keywind, 10" l.	1200	1500	1700
Train Set, 1875, tin, marked "NY Elevated RR," 22" l.	2500	3750	5000

Train Set, No. 295, Bliss, $600

Train Set, Hafner, $140

	C5	C7	C9
Hafner			
Caboose, No. 3057	8	12	16
Caboose, No. 41021	10	14	18
Caboose, No. 81932	8	12	16
Gondola, No. 91746	4	8	12
Hopper, No. 91876	12	18	25
Locomotive, No. 109....................	20	40	60
Locomotive, No. 112....................	40	75	100
Locomotive and Tender, No. 1010, black and silver or red and silver..................................	15	30	45
Locomotive and Tender, No. 115041	15	30	45
Locomotive and Tender, No. 2000	15	40	60
Overland Flyer Set, green..............	90	125	175
Overland Flyer Set, red and cream..........................	75	100	125
Santa Fe Boxcar............................	10	15	25
Santa Fe Refrigerator Car..............	10	15	25

	C5	C7	C9
Tanker, No. 1010	10	14	20
Tender, No. 78100	4	8	12
Tender, No. 90131	4	8	12
Train Set, Freight, w/No. 2000 Locomotive	60	120	140
Union Pacific Streamliner Train Set, No. M10000	75	100	150
Hoge Mfg. Co.			
Burlington Zephr Streamline Coach, five rail, automatic bell..	300	450	600
Circus Train, No. 750, 1932	400	600	800
Observation Car, No. 881	15	22	30
Pullman, No. 881	15	22	30
Streamliner, No. 900.....................	90	135	180
Tom Thumb Boxcar, No. 1902......	45	68	90
Tom Thumb Flat Car	35	53	70
Tom Thumb Locomotive, No. 881, electric..............................	20	30	40
Union Pacific Streamline Coach, sheet brass, three-piece unit	300	450	600

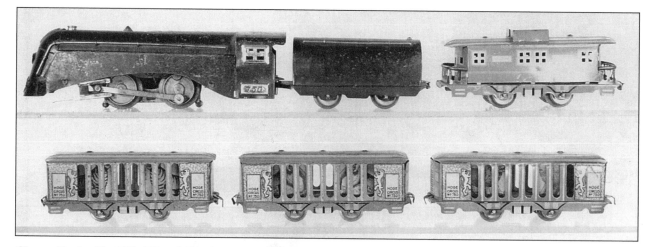

Circus Train, No. 750, Hoge Mfg. Co., 1932, $800

	C5	C7	C9
Hubley			
Elevated Railway, No. 3, 1893, marked "Single Track Elevated Railway", 31" dia., 15" h.	1500	3100	6300
Floor Train Set, includes: PRR Locomotive, two No. 44 Washington coaches and a Narcissus observation car	200	300	400

	C5	C7	C9
Hopper, cast iron	40	60	80
Narcissus Coach, No. 44	200	300	400
Train Set, 1915, includes: Locomotive, tender and two skiddoo passenger cars	250	375	500
Train Set, c. 1906, cast iron, clockwork, includes: Locomotive and two "Whist" passenger cars	700	1050	1400

Single Track Elevated Railway, No. 3, Hubley, $6,300

Train Set, 1915, Hubley, $500

Front row, left to right: Kansas Toy & Novelty trains: No. 36 Locomotive, $40; three No. 37 Pullman cars, $25 each. Back row, left to right: No. 36 Locomotive, No. 41 Stock Car, $25; No. 39 Tank Car, $25; No. 38 Boxcar, $25; No. 40 Caboose, $40

	C5	C7	C9
Kansas Toy & Novelty			
Boxcar, No. 38, marked "KT&NRR," 3-1/4" l.	12	18	25
Caboose, No. 40, marked "KT&NRR," 2-3/4" l.	12	18	25
Locomotive, No. 36, marked "KT &NRR," 4-1/2" l.	17	26	35
Pullman, No. 37, marked "KT&NRR", 4" l.	15	18	25
Stock Car or Boxcar, No. 41, marked "KT&NRR," 3-1/4" l.	12	18	25
Tank Car, No. 39, marked "KT&NRR," 3-1/4" l.	12	18	25

	C5	C7	C9
Kenton			
Passenger Train Set, electroplated cast iron, includes: "70" Locomotive and tender, "705 Blackwater" passenger car, "704 Overbrook" baggage and passenger car, 15-1/2" l.	350	575	700
Train Set, cast iron, includes Locomotive, tender and three cars	250	375	500
Train Set, cast iron, 9" l. Locomotive, and two 9-1/4" l. Cattle Cars, no tender	250	375	500
Train Set, No. 999	900	1350	1800

Train Set, No. 999, Kenton, $1,800

	C5	C7	C9
Keystone			
Backyard Train Set, 1930, 8" l., four pieces	425	675	850
Locomotive, riding toy, 26" l.	225	338	450

Keystone, Locomotive, No. 6400, $140

	C5	C7	C9
Locomotive, No. 6400, 27" l.	70	105	140
Train Set, includes Locomotive, coal car and pullman	900	1350	1800
Trolley, green and yellow, 20" l.	175	262	350
Kingsburg			
Locomotive and Tender, friction floor runner, 17" l.	200	300	400
Trolley, 14" l.	425	638	850
Kingsbury			
Locomotive, floor pull toy, two wheels w/ringing bell	100	150	200
Locomotive and Tender, tin, friction, red and gold, 17" l.	200	300	400
Nosco Plastics			
Train Set, four-piece set, 21" l.	22	33	45
Train Set, marked "City of Los Angeles," three-piece set, 16" l.	25	38	50

	C5	C7	C9
Ranger Fast Freight-Ranger Steel Products			
Locomotive, tin plate, wind-up	10	15	20
Train Set, c. 1940, tin plate, wind-up, includes: engine w/ tender, flat car, caboose key and freight station	100	150	200
Reed			
Drawing Room Car, c. 1877, lithographed wood, marked "Princess," 19" l.	250	375	500
Train Set, c. 1895, lithographed wood, includes engine, tender and passenger car, marked "Mother Goose Rail Road" 38" l.	1200	1800	2400
Trolley, c. 1895, lithographed wood, marked "Bowery and Central Park," 28" l.	200	300	400
Remco			
Gondola, No. 7503, red, B & O Railroad	20	30	40
Locomotive, No. 7501, 1969, diesel, battery powered, yellow w/black seat and handle, marked "Mighty Casey Ride'm Railroad"	50	75	100
Locomotive, No. 7501, 1969, diesel, floor/push toy, white, marked "Mighty Casey Ride'm Railroad"	20	30	40
Locomotive, No. 7501, 1969, yellow with red seat and handle	30	45	60

Train Set, Reed, c. 1895, $2,400

Locomotive, No. 7501, yellow with black seat and handle, Remco, 1969, $100

Locomotive, No. 7501, yellow with red seat and handle, Remco, 1969, $60

	C5	C7	C9
Revell			
Great Northern Boxcar, No. 4041	8	12	16
Norfolk & Western Hopper Car, No. 4042, w/load, HO scale	8	12	16
NYC Gondola, No. 4050, low side w/load, HO scale	8	12	16
Pacific Fruit Express Boxcar, No. 4011, HO gauge	8	12	16
Union Pacific Caboose, No. 4060, HO gauge	8	12	16

	C5	C7	C9
Union Pacific Stock Car, No. 4020, HO gauge	8	12	16
Union Pacific Switcher, No. 3550, 1956, HO gauge	14	21	28
Schiebel			
Engine, 2-4-0 friction motor, iron driving wheels, w/tender, marked "Hillclimber," 25" l.	150	225	300
Trolley, friction motor, navy blue with red roof, marked "Hillclimber" and "Rapid Transit," 21" l.	132	200	265

Locomotive and Tender, No. 2100, Voltamp, $4,500

	C5	C7	C9
Voltamp			
Interurban, No. 2115	3000	5000	8000
Locomotive and Tender, No. 2100, 2 gauge	2250	3375	4500
Weeden			
Locomotive, alcohol-burning, marked "1887" and "Dart"	700	1050	1400
Train Set, live steam, includes: Locomotive marked "Dart 1887," tender marked "I.&A.R.R.," coach marked "City of New Bedford"	850	1275	1700
Wilkins			
Coal Car, 9" l.	100	150	200
Engine and Tender	500	750	1000
NYC & Hudson River Baggage and Smoking car	100	150	200

	C5	C7	C9
NYC & Hudson River Passenger Car	100	150	200
NYC & Hudson River Pullman Car	75	113	150
Oil Tank Car, 13-1/2" l.	75	113	150
Train Set, cast iron, includes: Locomotive, tender and two cars	500	750	1000
Train Set, includes, Locomotive, coal car and passenger car, 36" l.	500	750	1000
Train Set, cast iron, includes: Locomotive, tender, passenger car and baggage car, 30" l.	500	750	1000
Train Set, includes: Locomotive, tender and two cars, 36-1/2" l.	600	900	1200
Trolley, c. 1900, cast-iron, horse-drawn, 14" l.	1250	1875	2500
Trolley, c. 1895, marked "Broadway Car Line," 18" l.	1400	2300	3200

NYC & Hudson River Baggage and Smoking car, Wilkins, $200

NYC & Hudson River Passenger Car, Wilkins, $200

NYC & Hudson River Pullman Car, Wilkins, $150

Train Set, Wilkins, $1,000

Train Set, cast iron, includes Locomotive, tender, passenger car and baggage car, Wilkins, $1,000

Trolley, Wilkins, c. 1900, $2,500

Various Manufacturers

	C5	C7	C9
90-degree Cross Over, No. 7508, black..	2	4	6
Atomic Train, tin, 4" l.	6	9	12
Atomic Train Set, plastic, w/missile, Eldon	40	60	80
Big 6 Train Set, c. 1885, includes: Locomotive, tender, gondola, 18" l., Stevens	250	375	500
Boxcar, w/moving doors, marked "Merchants Dispatch"..............	45	68	90
Boxcar, No. 7502, blue, B & M Railroad	30	45	60
Caboose, No. 22-14, Playland Railroad, 3" l., Criterion Products	5	8	10

Circus Car, $250

	C5	C7	C9
Circus Car, tin and wood w/lithographed paper animals, N.D. Cass	125	188	250
Coal Car, No. 976, cast iron	37	56	75
Curved Track, No. 7517, black......	1	2	3
Dump Car, cast iron, 6-1/2" l.........	17	25	35

Erector Hudson Engine and Tender, A.C. Gilbert, $2,000

	C5	C7	C9
Elevated Railway, c. 1890, wood, trolley, platform depot, 27" dia., Shepard Hardware	1400	2100	2800
Engine, cast iron, 8" l.	20	30	40
Engine, pulltoy	50	75	100
Engine, tin and wood, friction, 12" l.	150	225	300
Engine, cast iron, four wheel w/tall stack	75	113	150
Engine, cast iron, eight wheel, w/cow catcher and bell	100	150	200
Engine, cast iron steam, 8-3/4" l.	30	45	60
Engine, iron and tin, decorated, 12" l.	100	150	200
Engine, gas	750	1125	1500
Engine, c. 1885, w/two flatbed cars, 17" l., Carpenter	262	393	525
Engine, cast iron, steam, 9-1/4" l.	38	53	75
Engine and Coal Car, cast iron, PRR & Co., 14" l.	75	113	150
Engine and Tender, tin, clockwork	2000	3000	4000
Engine and Tender, c. 1900, lithographed tin, 25" l.	225	338	450
Engine and Tender, friction, coal tender, 15" l.	110	165	220
Engine and Tender, tin, steam, marked "NRA"	125	188	250
Erector Hudson Engine and Tender, A.C. Gilbert	1000	1500	2000
Flat Car, tin plate, small w/steel wheels and axle	5	8	10
Flyer Train, Overland	125	188	250

	C5	C7	C9
Freight Set, No. 7500, includes: Locomotive, box car, gondola, two straight and eight curved tracks, and battery charger	100	150	200
Gondola, low side, Wyandotte	15	23	30
Hand Car, lithographed tin and composition, clockwork, Mickey Mouse and Donald Duck, clockwork, English, Wells-Brimtoy	600	900	1200

Mickey Mouse and Donald Duck Handcar, Wells-Brimtoy, $1,200

	C5	C7	C9
Locomotive, diesel, Mitch Toy	11	16	22
Locomotive, plastic, wind-up, marked "Casey Jr. Disneyland Express," 12" l.	75	113	150
Locomotive, c. 1880, cast iron, keywind, 11-1/2" l., Welker & Crosby	1100	1650	2200
Locomotive, wood and metal, friction, w/cow catcher	75	113	150
Locomotive, wood, ride'm type, 21" l.	55	82	110

<u>C5</u> <u>C7</u> <u>C9</u>   <u>C5</u> <u>C7</u> <u>C9</u>

Locomotive, c.1870, Hull & Stafford, $600

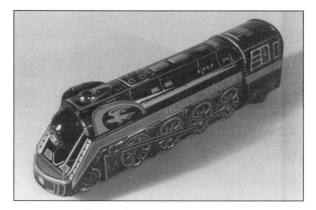

Locomotive, No. 6682, Modern Toys, $80

Locomotive, c. 1880, marked "American," $2,100

Locomotive and Tender, c. 1880, Stevens & Brown, $350

Locomotive, c. 1880, possibly Brown and Stevens, $350

	C5	C7	C9
Locomotive, c.1870, tin, marked "Active," 7" l., Hull & Stafford	300	450	600
Locomotive, c. 1880, tin keywind, marked "American," 12" l.	1050	1575	2100

	C5	C7	C9
Locomotive, c. 1880, tin, w/passenger car, marked "Skip," possibly Stevens & Brown	175	262	350
Locomotive, No. 6682, battery-operated, marked "Silver Streak," Modern Toys	40	60	80
Locomotive and Coal Car, tin, friction, iron wheels, 24" l.	150	225	300
Locomotive and Tender, c. 1880, tin, keywind, Stevens & Brown	175	250	350
Locomotive and Tender, wind-up, marked "369" and "Penn R.R.," 10" l., Mohawk Toy Co	500	750	1000
Locomotive and Tender, pressed steel, hillclimber, friction	120	180	240
Locomotive and Tender, cast iron, Pennsylvania Railroad, 13"	50	75	100

	C5	C7	C9
Locomotive and Tender, marked "Eagle Train," Japan, 11" l.	37	56	75
Locomotive and Tender, No. 1085, cast iron, 8-1/2" l.	150	225	300
Passenger Car, tin, 6" l.	20	30	40
Passenger Car, cast iron, w/stencils and numbers, 13" l.	38	57	75
Passenger Car, cast iron, w/stenciling and numbers, 14-3/4" l.	45	68	90
Passenger Car, No. 7504, yellow	40	60	80
Passenger Coach, cast iron, 13" l.	150	225	300
Passenger Coach, cast iron, marked "America," 7" l.	10	15	20
Passenger Set, No. 7515, includes: Locomotive, two passenger cars, two straight and eight curved tracks, and battery charger (set)	150	225	300
Pedal Train, sheet metal, marked "Casey Jones, The Cannonball Express," 33-1/2" l.	150	225	300

Pedal Train, marked "Casey Jones, The Cannonball Express," $300

	C5	C7	C9
Pedal Train, No. 67, c. 1880, "Velo-King"	500	750	1000
Pull Locomotive and Car, wood, Tinkertoy	12	18	25

Pedal Train, c. 1880, marked "Velo-King," $1,000

	C5	C7	C9
Pull Toy, lithographed tin, Streamline Railway, 17" l., Wolverine	40	60	80
Pull Train, lithographed tin	30	45	60
Pullman Car, "Sleep-Dolly-Sleep," Playskool	200	400	600
Pullman Railplane, 1934, cast iron, No. 3800 X, 9" l., Arcade	100	150	200

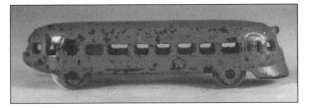

Pullman Railplane, Arcade, 1934, $200

Another variation of Arcade's Pullman Railplane

	C5	C7	C9
Railroad Caboose, No. 22-14, die-cast body and wheels, Playland	5	7	10
Railroad Gun, No. 108, lead alloy, w/slightly modified Kansas Toy No. 23 cannon on flat car, Ralstoy	12	18	25
Railroad Station, w/ticket and telegraph office, Schoenhut	188	282	375

	C5	C7	C9
Railroad Station, No. 19, cardboard, w/box, Built-Rite	50	75	100
Station, painted tin, w/awnings and accessories, marked "Central Station"	1000	1500	2000
Station, tin, marked "Central Station"	350	525	700
Stock Car, cast iron, 11" l.	60	90	120
Straight Track, No. 7510, black	10	15	20
Street Car, c. 1926, steel, yellow w/green trim and red roof, 16" l., Republic	220	330	440
Toonerville Trolley, 1920s, lithographed tin, clockwork, many actions, Germany, Nifty	600	900	1200

Toonerville Trolley, Nifty, 1920s, $1,200

	C5	C7	C9
Traction Engine, 4-1/2" l., Avery	150	225	300
Train, Pennsylvania Railroad, carved wood and lithographed paper	22	33	45
Train, lithographed tin, 17" l.	30	45	60

	C5	C7	C9
Train Cars, cast iron, cars w/elephant marked "Elephant Car," other marked "Greatest Show on earth"	1500	2250	3000
Train Set, cast iron, includes: engine, tender and two flat cars, 20" l.	250	375	500
Train Set, tin, pull toy, includes: engine, coal car and two passenger cars, engine stenciled "Apollo," 22-1/2" l.	600	900	1200
Train Set, tin, includes: Locomotive, coal car and passenger car, 23" l.	250	375	500
Train Set, steam, includes: Locomotive, tender and one passenger car, marked "Victor," 11" l.	50	75	100
Train Set, wood, includes: engine, tender, open freight car, tanker car and caboose	140	210	280
Train Set, c. 1895, lithographed wood, engine marked "Inter Ocean," cars marked "Chicago Limited," 46" l.	1150	1725	2300
Train Set, wood, set includes: Locomotive, tank car, flat car and caboose, Cass Limited	60	90	120
Train Set, cast iron, includes: Locomotive, tender and three flat cars, 23" l.	100	150	200
Train Set, post-WWII, zinc alloy, marked "New York Flyer," copy of Barclay No. 566 set without six-wheel Locomotive, M&L	25	38	50
Train Set, cast iron, three pieces, 14" l.	55	82	110
Train Set, c. 1930s, wood, six pieces, Strombecker	65	98	130
Train Set, plastic, set includes: engine, tender, box car, tanker, cattle car, gondola and caboose, Banner	15	22	30
Train Set, painted tin, includes: engine, tender and two cars, Rocket	1300	1900	2600

Train Set, Harco, $50

Close-up of Harco's Metal Streamline Train Set

	C5	C7	C9		C5	C7	C9
Train Set, lithographed tin and pressed steel, mechanical, set includes, Locomotive, tender and car, marked "NYC," 18" l.,	25	38	50	Train Set, cast iron, Locomotive w/engineer in cab waving, coal car and two passenger cars	100	150	200
Train Set, wood, paper and lithographed tin, includes: 14" l. Locomotive, tender and two 13" l. gondolas, w/rubber-stamped lettering	1500	2250	3000	Train Set, cast iron, includes: Locomotive, coal car and passenger car, 17-1/2" l.	50	75	100
Train Set, cast iron, Pennsylvania Railroad, includes: Locomotive, coal car and two passenger cars, 28-1/2" l.	438	658	875	Train Set, cast iron, includes Locomotive and two cars marked "Michigan Central Railroad"	125	188	250
				Train Set, 1930, tin, wind-up, 20" l., wooden wheels, three piece set	125	188	250
				Train Set, tin, includes: engine, coal car and passenger car	300	450	600

Train Set, Marilyn Products, c. 1950, No. 1249, $200

Advertisement for Metal Cast's No. 68 Train Set

	C5	C7	C9		C5	C7	C9
Train Set, Streamliner in three sections, 11" l., Futurematic	15	22	30	Train Set, No. 122, paper, streamline flyer, set includes: engine, station, crossing signal, baggage truck, baggage and people, Concord Toy Co.	27	41	55
Train Set, alloy, marked "Metal Streamline Train," Harco..........	25	38	50				
Train Set, cast iron, Pennsylvania Railroad, includes: Locomotive, coal car and open car	63	88	125	Train Set, No. 1249, c. 1950, battery-operated, includes track w/cardboard base and tin rail, train marked "The 49er," Marilyn Products......................	100	150	200

	C5	C7	C9
Train Set, No. 1858, tin, includes Locomotive, and three passenger cars	125	188	250
Train Set, No. 68, Metal Cast	22	33	45
Train Set, No. 700, c. 1950, electric passenger train, Shilling Co., J.L.	50	75	100
Train Set, No. 999, cast iron and pressed steel, includes Locomotive and cars, marked "NYL & HR RR," 60" l., Pratt & Letchworth	2600	4100	5500
Trolley, spring lever action, marked "City Trolley," Cragstan	60	90	120
Trolley, tin friction, painted	75	113	150
Trolley, tin, marked "Broadway 270"	250	375	500

	C5	C7	C9
Trolley, tin, marked "Pay As You Enter," 22" l.	162	243	325
Trolley, c. 1905-10, cast iron, horse-drawn, small	100	150	200
Trolley, marked "Consolidated Street R.R.," Harris	1750	2625	3500
Trolley, tin, marked "Public Service 365"	250	375	500
Trolley, tin, hillclimber	200	300	400
Trolley, pressed steel, hillclimber, early, 15" l.	250	375	500
Trolley, tin friction, 13" l.	85	128	170
Trolley, tin, marked "City Hall Park," 15" x 5"	600	900	1200
Universal Choo Choo, No. 206, 1930, wood Locomotive, natural finish w/red painted wheels and stenciling of engineer and name	60	90	120

Auction Houses

Bill Bertoia Auctions
2413 Madison Ave.
Vineland, NJ 08360

Brooks
81 Westside
London SWA 9AY Great Britain
0171-288-8000

Butterfield & Butterfield
220 San Bruno Ave.
San Francisco, CA 90046

Christie's
502 Park Ave.
New York, NY 10022
(212) 548-1119

Continental Hobby House
P.O. Box 193
Sheboygan, WI 53082
(920) 693-3371
Trains of all types and replacement parts.

Garth's Auctions
2690 Stratford Rd.
Delaware, OH 43015
(616) 362-4771

James Julia
P.O. Box 830
Fairfield, ME 04937
(207) 453-7125

Lloyd Ralston Toys
400 Long Beach Rd.
Norwalk, CT 06615
(203) 386-9399

Mapes Auctioneers & Appraisers
1729 Vestal Parkway West
Vestal, NY 13850
(607) 754-9193

Noel Barrett Antiques and Auctions
P.O. Box 300
Carversville, PA 18913
(215) 297-5109

Phillips
406 East 79th St.
New York, NY 10021
(212) 570-4830

Skinner
357 Main St.
Bolton, MA 01740
(508) 779-6241

Sotheby's
1334 York Ave.
New York, NY 10021
(212) 606-7424

Ted Maurer Auctioneer
1003 Brookwood Dr.
Pottstown, PA 19646
(215) 323-1573

Clubs

American Flyer Collectors Club (AFCC)
P.O. Box 13269
Pittsburgh, PA 15243

LGB Model Railroad Club
1854 Erin Dr.
Altoona, PA 16602-7612

Lionel Collectors Club of America (LCCA)
P.O. Box 479
La Salle, IL 61301

Lionel Operating Train Society (LOTS)
P.O. Box 66240
Cincinnati, OH 4562-0240

Lionel Railroader Club
26570 Twenty-three Mile Rd
Chesterfield, MI 48051-1956

Marklin Club of North America
P.O. Box 51559
New Berlin, WI 53151

National Model Railroad Association (NMRA)
4121 Cromwell Rd
Chattanooga, TN 37421

Toy Train Operating Society (TCA)
P.O. Box 248
Strasburg, PA 17579

Collectors and Dealers

Barry's Train Shop
188 Dogwood Dr.
Elizabethtown, PA 17022
(717) 367-4745

Dennis Leon Clad
P.O. Box 647
Amelia, VA 23002
Collector of Modern-era Lionel

John Gibson
9857 Dockside Terrace
Gaithersburg, MD 20879
Tootsietoy restoration and service

Marx Trains
209 Butterfield Rd. No. 228
Elmhurst, IL 60126
(630) 941-3843
(630) 941-3829
marxusa@aol.com
Currently producing new tin lithographed Marx trains.

Old Toy Trading Co.
665 Virginia Ave.
North Bend, OR 97459
(503) 756-4594

Richard MacNary
4727 Alpine Dr.
Lilburn, GA 30247
Collector of Marx trains

The Red Caboose
23 West 45th St.
New York, NY 10036
(212) 575-0155

Toy Train Depot
681 4th St.
Oakland, CA 94607
(510) 444-8724

Train Collectors Warehouse, Inc.
1521 Route 46 East
Parsippany, NJ 07054
(973) 339-3399
Lionel trains

Walt Smith
2504 Pioneer Ct.
Davenport, IA 52804
Collector of postwar Lionel

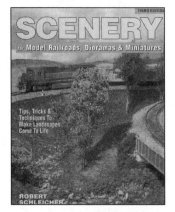

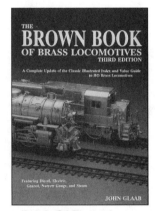